The Political Philosophy of

MONTAIGNE

The Political Philosophy of
MONTAIGNE

David Lewis Schaefer

Cornell University Press

ITHACA AND LONDON

This book has been published with the aid of a grant from The Lynde and Harry Bradley Foundation.

First published 1990 by Cornell University Press.

International Standard Book Number (cloth) 0-8014-2179-9
International Standard Book Number (paper) 0-8014-9741-8
Library of Congress Catalog Card Number 90-1586
Printed in the United States of America
Librarians: Library of Congress cataloging information appears on the last page of the book.

⊗ The paper used in this publication meets the minimum requirements of the American National Standard for Permanence of Paper for Printed Library Materials Z39.48–1984.

For Roberta, Naomi, and Rebecca

Contents

Preface

This book offers a new interpretation of Montaigne's *Essays*. In it I argue that Montaigne was a more consistent and systematic thinker than most scholars have thought him to be. I contend that political matters, broadly understood, lay at the core of his authorial intention. And I represent Montaigne as one of the earliest philosophic architects of the modern liberal regime, helping to lay the theoretical foundations on which such subsequent liberal political philosophers as Locke and Montesquieu erected their edifices, while also preparing the public mind for the moral transformation that such edifices required if they were to be accepted.

The scope and intention of this volume are both greater and smaller than its title might suggest. They are greater in that by treating Montaigne as a political philosopher, I have not aimed merely to describe one "aspect" of his thought, as has been done by other scholars who have produced studies of Montaigne's views on such matters as education, medicine, and religion. Rather, I hold, for reasons to be elaborated in Chapter One, that Montaigne conceived and intended the *Essays* to be, *fundamentally*, a work of political philosophy in the broadest sense of that term; and that it is from that perspective, therefore, that his book is best understood. In its broadest and, I believe, most accurate sense, political philosophy is not simply one discipline among many, concerned with a particular aspect of human life (that is, governmental institutions). It is rather, as Aristotle suggests, the "architectonic" science, supervening over other sciences, inasmuch as its guiding concern is with the nature of the good society, and consequently of the good life.[1] Political philosophy, properly understood, is thus inseparable from

[1] *Nicomachean Ethics*, I.2. On the ambiguity of the term *political philosophy*, which may denote a particular *mode* of philosophizing as distinguished from a branch of the subject

ix

.eration of such subjects as religion, ethics, psychology, natural epistemology, education, and economics—all of which bear more directly on the question of the best way of life and the means of its a. .iment. But a focus on the political problem gives a particular sort of unity to these studies, rather than viewing them (as the typical contemporary college curriculum might suggest) as a set of essentially separate but equal disciplines. Montaigne dealt with all of these subjects, and in pursuit of an understanding of his teaching, I survey and attempt to explain in some measure his thought about each of them. In so doing, however, I try to demonstrate how his thought about each particular topic reflects his more fundamental and unifying political intention.

While thus being broader, in one way, than its title might suggest, my book is narrower in another respect. I must acknowledge at the outset—with far greater sincerity than Montaigne practiced when he deprecated the significance of the *Essays* in his preface—that this book is far from being a complete or definitive interpretation of Montaigne's political philosophy. There can be no truly comprehensive interpretation of the *Essays* without a thorough understanding of every chapter and, indeed, every passage in it. Despite many years of study, I cannot claim to approach such an understanding, for some chapters remain almost complete enigmas to me. Nonetheless—and possibly in violation of Montaigne's prudent warning to authors against premature publication in his essay "Of Vanity"—I have chosen to bring my findings before the public at this time. It is my hope thereby to stimulate and assist others to advance further in the direction I have pointed.

Aside from the emphasis I put on the systematic character of Montaigne's reflections and on the political character of his intention, this book is distinct from most other studies of the *Essays* in its method, in that it includes detailed, page-by-page analyses of a sizable number of chapters. I have been compelled to adopt this approach by the character of Montaigne's rhetoric. As is well known, Montaigne, by his own profession, speaks diversely and often inconsistently about almost every major subject he discusses. In Chapter One I argue that this superficially inconsistent and rambling rhetorical manner conceals a thoroughly consistent and precise chain of reasoning and a coherent political project. But I can demonstrate that claim only by surveying the argument of a number of critical chapters in detail. It would have been easy enough to support a variety of my claims—that Montaigne was an atheist; that his thought did not evolve as

---

matter of philosophy, see Leo Strauss, *What Is Political Philosophy?* (Glencoe, Ill., 1959), pp. 93–4; and E. L. Fortin, *Dissidence et philosophie au moyen âge* (Paris, 1981), pp. 19ff. In this alternative but related sense, political philosophy, as understood by its historical practitioners, denotes a kind of philosophizing about any subject that is "deliberately accommodated to the opinions of the society in the midst of which the philosopher lives" (Fortin, p. 19).

he wrote; that his political intention was revolutionary rather than conservative; that he was favorably disposed toward rather than distrustful of scientific progress—simply by extracting passages from various chapters that appear to confirm them. But such an approach would have made it equally easy for other interpreters to contradict my assertions by citing other passages from those same chapters (or other ones) that have an apparently opposed sense. Montaigne emphasizes that his thought cannot be understood if his book is read cursorily or in snatches. In an effort, therefore, to conform to the rules of reading that he suggests, and to provide sufficient support for my interpretation to defend it against easy refutation or charges of one-sidedness, I have endeavored to explain the particular passages I discuss in the overall context in which they occur. Hence I try to show how remarks that seem on the surface to belie my interpretation do not really do so, either because a careful reading shows their true meaning to be different from the surface one or because Montaigne directly or indirectly indicates that these remarks are not to be taken seriously. Though my method inevitably entails some repetition of themes, such as Montaigne's opposition to Stoicism—since these themes do recur in more than one chapter that I analyze—some such redundancy is the necessary price of thoroughness.

By analyzing entire chapters when it is feasible to do so and by seeking to explain how my interpretation of Montaigne's thought harmonizes with the overall rhetorical movement of the *Essays,* I also seek to respond to the criticism that Gérard Defaux and Jean-Yves Pouilloux have leveled against such scholars as Hugo Friedrich for arbitrarily rearranging Montaigne's thoughts into categories of their own devising, in disregard of the actual textual structure of his book. I wholly agree with Defaux's rejection of the notion "that literary analysis consists in isolating fragments of the text in order to make them say, if not everything, then at least something entirely different from what they would say if they were interpreted *in vivo,* in their original context." But unlike Defaux, I am not persuaded that a confrontation with the authentic character of Montaigne's text is incompatible with "a thematic reading" of it—one that would aspire, "by bringing to the surface systems and structures, intentions and reasons concealed in the profundity of the text," to elaborate the author's thought about particular themes in a more systematic fashion than that in which the author himself presented it. And unlike Pouilloux, I am not convinced that it is impossible to find objective grounds for identifying one of the essayist's contradictory statements on a given subject as a more authentic expression of his belief than its converse.[2]

[2]See Gérard Defaux, "Editor's Preface" to *Montaigne: Essays in Reading,* Yale French Studies, 64 (1983), pp. vi–vii; Jean-Yves Pouilloux, *Lire les "Essais" de Montaigne* (Paris, 1970), pp. 19–38.

Viewing Montaigne's thought, as I do, as the result of a deep and comprehensive process of reflection, I have endeavored not merely to summarize what he believes but to trace as fully as I can the often recondite reasoning that leads him to that belief. And because I view that reasoning as the product of a systematic, lifelong meditation on and intellectual confrontation with the writings of the ancient philosophers and poets whom Montaigne cites so extensively, I have undertaken to juxtapose his reasoning at numerous points with the classical philosophic teachings that constitute, in his own view, the most serious alternative to his position.

After nearly three decades of study of political philosophy, which began in my undergraduate years at Cornell University and continued during my graduate work at the University of Chicago, I remain deeply indebted to four great teachers: Allan Bloom, Joseph Cropsey, and the late Leo Strauss and Herbert Storing. Although none of these men should be held responsible for any defects this book may contain, whatever merits it has are due to a great extent to the introduction my mentors gave me to the fundamental issues of political philosophy and the instruction they provided in how to read serious books with the care they deserve.

I am also grateful to several other persons and institutions whose support and assistance—intellectual, moral, economic, and/or clerical—made this book possible. Richard Flathman made several valuable criticisms and suggestions regarding my original manuscript. I am indebted to Robert Eden, Timothy Paterson, and Patrick Henry for their thoughtful and painstaking comments on subsequent versions of the manuscript and for their encouragement, and to Ernest Fortin and Daniel Martin for the illumination they provided on particular points.

Several institutions generously provided research support, without which this book would never have been completed. I have been the beneficiary of a Ford Foundation–sponsored fellowship awarded by the University of Chicago, a Richard M. Weaver Fellowship from the Intercollegiate Studies Institute, and fellowships granted by the National Endowment for the Humanities, the Earhart Foundation, and Holy Cross College. I am also grateful to the Centre Universitaire International, which furnished research facilities during my stay in Paris; and to the Rockefeller Foundation, which provided a residency at its Cultural Center in Bellagio, Italy, during a critical stage in my writing.

For assistance in procuring research materials, I am indebted to the interlibrary loan staff of Holy Cross College and to my colleague Maurizio Vannicelli. I thank Jean Evanowski for her patient and thorough clerical assistance, Ellen Keohane for help in using the college's word processing system, and Joseph Busher for help in composing the index. I am grateful to the editors of the journals that published portions of some of my chapters for permission to reprint these materials: Chapter One is a revised and expanded version of "Montaigne's Intention and His Rhetoric," published in *Interpretation: A Journal of Political Philosophy* 5, no. 1 (Summer 1975): 57–90. Portions of Chapters Two, Three, and Four appeared in "Montaigne's Political Skepticism," *Polity* 11, no. 4 (Summer 1979): 512–41. Chapter Five is a revised and expanded version of "Montaigne's Political Reformation," *Journal of Politics* (published by the University of Texas Press) 42, no. 3 (August 1980): 766–91. Chapter Six is a revised version of "Of Cannibals and Kings: Montaigne's Egalitarianism," *Review of Politics* 43, no. 1 (January 1981): 43–74. Portions of Chapters Seven and Eight appeared in "The Good, the Beautiful, and the Useful: Montaigne's Transvaluation of Values," *American Political Science Review* 73, no. 1 (March 1979): 139–53. Chapter Ten is a revised and expanded version of " 'To Philosophize Is to Learn How to Die': Montaigne vs. Socrates," *Independent Journal of Philosophy* 5–6 (1988): 23–30.

My debt to my wife for her unwavering encouragement and support, and to my daughters for the inspiration they provided simply by being themselves, is of a kind that I can signify only inadequately in print by dedicating this book to them.

DAVID LEWIS SCHAEFER

Worcester, Massachusetts

Note on Citations
and Translations

Citations of Montaigne's works, unless I have noted otherwise, are to the Pléiade edition of Montaigne's *Oeuvres complètes,* edited by Albert Thibaudet and Maurice Rat and published by Gallimard (Paris, 1962); the first three numbers in each reference to the *Essais* respectively denote book, chapter, and page in uppercase roman, lowercase roman, and arabic numerals. The fourth, bracketed number refers to the page in Donald Frame's English translation of *The Complete Works of Montaigne* (Stanford University Press, 1957), which I have followed with some modifications. (Pagination of the *Essays* in that edition is the same as in the separately published volume containing Frame's translation of the *Essays* alone [1958].) Book and chapter numbers have been omitted in the case of a series of references to the same chapter, or where the chapter being cited is otherwise evident, as in most references to the "Apology for Raymond Sebond" in Chapters Two through Four. Italics in quotations from the *Essays* are my own. I have placed quotation marks around passages from other authors that Montaigne quotes in Latin.

Unless I have noted otherwise, all other translations of French works are mine. In the case of references to Machiavelli's *Discourses on the First Ten Books of Livy,* I have cited Sergio Bertelli's edition of *Il Principe e Discorsi* (Milan, 1960) but have generally followed the literal translations provided by Harvey C. Mansfield, Jr., in his commentary on the *Discourses* titled *Machiavelli's New Modes and Orders* (Cornell University Press, 1979).

The abbreviation *BSAM* in footnotes refers to the *Bulletin de la Société des Amis de Montaigne.*

The Political Philosophy of

MONTAIGNE

Montaigne's Intention
and His Rhetoric

After more than four centuries, Montaigne's *Essays* remains one of the most widely read, enjoyed, and admired works of the French literary canon. Yet, paradoxically, the chief reasons for which it is esteemed today are not those for which the author wanted it to be remembered. Even more than La Rochefoucauld, Montaigne is widely reputed and quoted on account of his witty maxims about life. But Montaigne suggests that to understand his book requires careful study; an undiligent audience that reads merely for amusement will miss his point (III, viii, 916–17 [716]; III, ix, 973–4 [761–2]). Montaigne enjoys his greatest academic readership nowadays, at least outside his homeland, among literary scholars, who acclaim the *Essays* as a stylistic masterpiece. Yet the author disdains such praise, remarking, "when I hear someone dwell on the language of these Essays, I would rather he said nothing. This [praise of his style] is not so much to extol the style as to depreciate the sense; the more galling for being more oblique" (I, xl, 245 [184–5]). The *Essays* is also esteemed by contemporary scholars as one of the first examples (perhaps the first) of the modern genre of "authentic" literary self-portrayal, in which an author openly confesses faults as well as virtues and freely expresses personal emotions as well as opinions. Yet Montaigne, while sometimes purporting to present such a self-revelation, elsewhere denies that this is his intention and even mocks the very notion of such an enterprise. He asks whether it is plausible that a man who is so private in his habits as he claims to be should reasonably be expected to give the public such knowledge of himself as he pretends to provide (III, ii, 783 [611]). "Amusing fancy," he remarks: "many things that I would not want to tell anyone, I tell the public; and for my most secret knowledge and thoughts I send my most faithful friends to the bookseller's shop" (III, ix,

959 [750]). In other passages he suggests that his true audience is not the public at large, but a discerning few (I, xxvi, 146 [108]; II, xvi, 607 [472–3]; II, xviii, 646–7 [503]; III, viii, 916–17 [716]).

On the one hand, then, the *Essays* is praised by contemporary readers for qualities that, according to the author, are either nonexistent or unimportant in it. On the other hand, the real value that Montaigne attributed to his book—the profound and revolutionary character of the thought it embodies—is rendered doubtful, or even denied, by much recent scholarship. Because the *Essays* is commonly viewed as a disconnected series of more or less random reflections, most scholars deny (explicitly or implicitly) that it can be understood as a coherent or comprehensive philosophic work. While applauding Montaigne's insights into particular aspects of human affairs, scholars are wont, at the same time, to accuse him of such intellectual weaknesses as an extreme credulity with regard to popular stories and superstitions, a foolish disregard for the value of science, and a naive understanding of politics. More generally, the *Essays* is thought to record a sweeping fluctuation or evolution of its author's thought, rather than a serious intellectual consistency. Yet, contrary to these interpretations, Montaigne insists that his thought has remained consistent (III, ii, 790 [616]; III, ix, 941 [736]). In opposition to those who accuse him of writing carelessly, he denies ever "erring" unknowingly (II, xvii, 637 [496]).[1] He disclaims any credulity with regard to other men's reports, insisting that he will follow only his own reason and experience (III, xi, 1005–10 [786–90]). Far from being politically naive, he describes himself as an eminently successful negotiator, and as qualified to have served as an adviser to kings (III, i, 768–9 [600–01]; III, xiii, 1055 [825–6]). He expresses the hope of an infinite progress in natural science and endeavors to explain how it might be achieved (II, xii, 543 [421]; II, xxxvii, 762–3 [594–5]; III, xiii, 1045 [817–18]). And he speaks in the most comprehensive terms of the importance of his reflections, suggesting that even amidst seeming trivialities, the careful reader will discover a profound and serious point (I, xl, 245 [185]; II, vi, 358 [273]; III, xii, 1016 [795]).

The present study is premised on the belief that there are indeed important lessons to be learned from Montaigne about human nature and our place in the universe; and, more specifically, about the philosophic foundations of modern politics and morality. If those lessons are to be recovered, however, it will be necessary to strive anew to recapture Montaigne's intention as an author, by taking most seriously such remarks as I have cited. It remains possible, of course, that Montaigne's understanding of his

---

[1]Admittedly, Montaigne appears to contradict this denial by professing to be full of "accidental" errors at III, v, 853 [667]; but a few lines later he suggests that the "faults" others discover in his work may be the products of deceit or playfulness rather than "inadvertence." And though professing a readiness in that passage to correct "accidental" mistakes, Montaigne later denies correcting anything (III, ix, 941 [736]; see n. 77 below).

book and himself was deficient in the manner suggested by many scholars, and that the most painstaking analysis will reveal the *Essays* to embody naïveté, credulity, carelessness, and inconsistency, as well as the wit, insight, and beauty that almost all readers have recognized in it. Yet there is good reason to suspend such patronizing assumptions. When an author of generally acknowledged erudition and insight asserts that his thought is consistent, profound, and comprehensive, the reader is well advised to take him at his word, until and unless thorough examination of his work reveals irrefutable evidence to the contrary. A further reason for taking Montaigne seriously in this manner is the fact that the *Essays* was regarded as worthy of close study by a number of the most profound thinkers of centuries before our own. Pascal's debt to Montaigne, despite their differences, is well known.[2] Such a systematic thinker as Descartes drew extensively on the *Essays* in composing his *Discourse on Method.*[3] Montaigne's apparent influence on the thought of Locke and Rousseau is well documented,[4] and the essayist has been called the "common teacher" of both philosophers.[5] The scope and depth once recognized in Montaigne's thought are indicated by a nineteenth-century scholar's remark that the essayist had endeavored "before the great Bacon, to reform human understanding" and that he was, with Bacon and Descartes, "the restorer or the founder of philosophy in Europe."[6]

The neglect of the *Essays* by contemporary students of philosophy and politics is due, I believe, to a lack of understanding of the mode of rhetoric by which Montaigne aimed both to convey and to conceal his deepest teachings. In the remainder of this chapter, I seek to explain that rhetoric.

Montaigne's Irony

The most obvious evidence for interpreting the *Essays* as an artless personal narrative is provided by the author's foreword, "To the Reader."

[2]See especially Article II of Pascal's *Pensées*, ed. Léon Brunschvicg, particularly nos. 64, 72–3, 82–4, 89, 127, 139, 143, 148, 156, 172; Léon Brunschvicg, *Descartes et Pascal: Lecteurs de Montaigne* (Neuchâtel, 1945), pp. 135–210; Alan M. Boase, *The Fortunes of Montaigne: A History of the "Essays" in France, 1580–1669* (London, 1935), ch. 25.
[3]See the references in Etienne Gilson's edition of the *Discours de la méthode* (Paris, 1947); Brunschvicg, *Descartes et Pascal*, pp. 95–134; Boase, *Fortunes of Montaigne*, ch. 16; also, Michael G. Paulson, *The Possible Influence of Montaigne's "Essais" on Descartes' "Treatise on the Passions"* (Lanham, Md., 1988).
[4]See Pierre Villey, *L'Influence de Montaigne sur les idées pédagogiques de Locke et Rousseau* (Paris, 1908); Colette Fleuret, *Rousseau et Montaigne* (Paris, 1980); Gustave Lanson, *Les Essais de Montaigne* (Paris, n.d.), p. 348.
[5]Charles Dédéyan, *Montaigne chez ses amis Anglo-Saxons* (Paris: Boivin, n.d.), pp. 32–3. See also Ernest Seillère, *Le Naturisme de Montaigne* (Paris, 1938), pp. 64–81; and, on Nietzsche's esteem for Montaigne, Brendan Donnellan, *Nietzsche and the French Moralists* (Bonn, 1982), passim.
[6]Pierre-François Tissot, *Leçons et modèles de littérature française*, 2 vols. (Paris, 1835–6), 1:117; cited in Donald Frame, *Montaigne in France, 1812–52* (New York, 1940), p. 108.

4 | The Political Philosophy of Montaigne

In the very first sentence Montaigne describes his book as one of "good faith." As evidence, he seems to discourage the public from reading it. He claims to have set himself only a "domestic and private goal," aiming to provide his "relatives and friends" with a record through which, after his death, "they may recover . . . some features of my habits and temperament, and by this means keep the knowledge they have had of me more complete and alive." Disclaiming any thought either of serving the reader or of advancing his own glory, to which his "powers are inadequate," Montaigne proposes to make himself the "matter" of the book, presenting himself in his "simple, natural, ordinary fashion, without straining or artifice." There is no reason, he advises the reader, "to spend your leisure on so frivolous and vain a subject" ("A.L.," 9 [2]).[7]

To judge from the popularity of the *Essays* ever since it was first published, not many readers who once opened the book accepted this advice. Those who paused to think about such matters apparently did not take the author's statement of his intention at its face value. In other words, they were led to doubt Montaigne's "good faith" from the outset.

At the risk of belaboring the obvious, we note that the foreword itself provides ground for such distrust. Had Montaigne wished only to leave a record for a few friends and relatives, it would not seem necessary to have had it published and sold to the public.[8] Moreover, if the author indeed wished his friends and relatives to keep his memory alive, one must doubt the sincerity of his disclaiming any concern for glory (small as the glory to be achieved thereby might be). If this disclaimer is suspect, must we not also question Montaigne's good faith in denying that his book is meant to serve others as well? Any author not exclusively concerned with personal profit and reputation must think, in publishing a book, that it will be of some benefit to at least a few readers. In any event, the author would derive neither earnings nor fame from discouraging potential readers at the outset.

Thus we are driven, as many other readers have been, to suspect that Montaigne's preface is in some sense ironic. This inference may be supported by citing a couple of the numerous passages in the *Essays* in which the author attests to the value and utility of his work. By imparting what he has learned from studying himself, Montaigne claims to contribute to a knowledge that is incomparably more useful than any other science (II, vi, 358 [273]). Few other writers, if any, he asserts, offer more substance (I, xl, 245 [185]). As for his supposed goal of being remembered by his friends after his death, Montaigne later dismisses it as of no real benefit to himself (II, xvi, 610 [474–5]).

---

[7]The abbreviation "A.L." refers to the French title of the preface, "Au lecteur."
[8]As noted by Richard A. Sayce in *The Essays of Montaigne: A Critical Exploration* (London, 1972), p. 51. Cf. also Nicolas Malebranche, *La Recherche de la vérité* (Paris, 1897 [1674–75]), ch. 5, p. 158.

Contrary to the implication of his prefatory remarks, Montaigne thus seems to intend the *Essays* to be of value to readers other than his "relatives and friends." But even if this be the case, it would be wrong to dismiss the foreword as merely a humorous expression of mock modesty. "To the Reader," rather, encapsulates the fundamental rhetorical problem of the *Essays*. From the outset Montaigne compels the thinking reader to choose between two alternatives: either the book is not simply one of good faith, in that its author dissimulates; or else—if he is wholly honest—the book can have no serious value. The reader who fails to take the foreword as seriously as it deserves will be unable to appreciate the seriousness of the *Essays* as a whole.

Surveying that whole, we are indeed confronted with a strange picture, apparently justifying the author's claim that his work is "pieced together of diverse members, without definite shape, having no order, sequence, or proportion other than accidental" (I, xxviii, 181 [135]). Its 107 chapters, divided into three books, treat a seemingly infinite variety of subjects in no evident order. Three successive chapter titles, for instance (I, lv–lvii), refer respectively to "smells," "prayers," and "age." Montaigne admits, moreover, that his chapter titles "do not always embrace their matter; often they denote it only by some sign" (III, ix, 973 [761]). Even when the relation between a chapter's title and overall theme seems evident, the argument of practically every chapter appears to jump abruptly from one topic to another. To further confuse matters, Montaigne made voluminous additions to and alterations in the original text of the *Essays*, which was first published in 1580. The bulk of these modifications fall into two groups: those included in the fifth edition (in which Book III appeared for the first time), in 1588, which practically doubled the previous size of the volume; and those made by Montaigne between 1588 and the time of his death in 1592, constituting some one-fourth of the final version, which were incorporated in posthumous editions of the *Essays*.[9] These alterations raise the problem of whether the "early" and the "late" Montaigne are consistent; moreover, the new material is sometimes inserted in such a way as apparently to disrupt or render incoherent the train of thought of the original passage.

The content as well as the form of the *Essays* has a puzzling character. Considerable portions consist of quotations and paraphrases of other authors, usually ancient ones. More often than not, Montaigne gives no explicit indication of their "borrowed" character. Although the publication

---

[9]A much smaller and less significant group of additions was inserted in the edition of 1582. Estimates of the proportion of the additions to the original text are from Donald M. Frame, *Montaigne: A Biography* (New York, 1965), pp. 250, 289. Although the 1588 edition is labeled the "fifth," only three previous editions (including the edition of 1587, which reprinted the 1582 version) are known to exist (ibid., p. 145).

of compendia of wise men's sayings, or the silent insertion of secondhand materials into a new book, was not an uncommon practice in Montaigne's era,[10] we need to know Montaigne's own purpose in adopting this practice. Less striking to a twentieth-century audience, but perhaps unique in literature up to Montaigne's time, is another aspect of the *Essays:* Montaigne's extensive description of himself, as promised in the foreword, including the relation of many apparently trivial feelings and experiences, and explicit details of his bodily states and functions. While rambling discourse about oneself is now a recognized literary genre, its intellectual value is far from self-evident and was severely questioned by critics at the time the book was published.[11] To Montaigne, his practice of describing his common experiences and dispositions in apparently random fashion helped make the *Essays* "the only book in the world of its kind" (II, viii, 364 [278]).

To appreciate the purpose underlying the peculiar structure and content of the *Essays,* we must avoid looking at it from a perspective derived from post-sixteenth-century conceptions of literary form and function. Although the literature of free "self-expression" or self-description (as distinguished from the recording by great men of the great events in which they took part) may have owed its start to Montaigne, it is not clearly evident that Montaigne intended to found a literary tradition, or that his motives in adopting the form he did were the same as those of his imitators. Similarly, we cannot simply place the *Essays*—the title of which Montaigne originated as the name of a literary work—within the contemporary genre denoted by that term. Whereas a book of essays is now understood to contain a number of short prose compositions, each treating a particular subject without any necessary continuity among them, the themes of Montaigne's chapters are not so neatly distinguishable. On the one hand, a single chapter may treat a number of topics, the relation of which is at best obscure; on the other hand, there is an obvious continuity among some chapters (for instance, I, ix–x), and even more frequently a repetition of similar or identical themes in different chapters. Montaigne's title seems to refer not to the chapters as entities, but to the much more numerous succession of particular thoughts or inquiries within the book as a whole.[12] It also remains possible that Montaigne's book has an underlying unity and order that are not typical of the usual book of essays.[13]

---

[10]See I, xxvi, 145–6 [108]; III, xii, 1033 [808]; and Pierre Villey, *Les Sources et l'évolution des "Essais" de Montaigne,* 2 vols. (Paris, 1908; reprinted New York, 1968), 2:7–37.

[11]Pierre Villey, *Montaigne devant la postérité* (Paris, 1935), pp. 70–76.

[12]As suggested by Donald Frame in *Montaigne's "Essais": A Study* (Englewood Cliffs, N.J., 1969), p. 72. Frame remarks that "Montaigne was both the first essay writer and the only one who never thought of himself as one." Montaigne at one point calls a chapter an "article" (I, xxvi, 147 [109]) and elsewhere a "treatise" or "tract" (III, xii, 1033 [808]). Richard Sayce notes two passages in Book III, however, wherein Montaigne seems to call his chapters "essays" (Sayce, *Essays,* pp. 21–2).

[13]Montaigne's periodic intimations that the disorderly surface of his book masks an underlying consistency or "design" (II, viii, 364 [278]) and his reference in the central chapter to the

The term *essai,* as used in Montaigne's time, signified a tentative investigation or a trial or test of something. Montaigne's title thus suggests a series of tentative, uncertain investigations rather than a rigorous or dogmatic argument.[14] He describes the book, more specifically, as an "essay" of his "natural faculties," and especially of his judgment. "Undertaking to speak indiscriminately of everything that comes to my fancy without employing any but my own natural resources," professing to choose his sub-

---

practice of organizing a literary work around a particular pattern (I, liv, 297 [225]) encourage the suspicion that the *Essays,* the exterior form of which resembles Machiavelli's *Discourses on Livy,* embodies a recondite numerical ordering of chapters such as Leo Strauss, in his *Thoughts on Machiavelli* (Glencoe, Ill., 1958), demonstrated to exist in the *Prince* and *Discourses.* (It has been noted, for instance, that two of Montaigne's professions of randomness occur in brief chapters numbered symmetrically, equidistant from the ends of Book I: I, viii, 34 [21]; I, l, 289 [219]. The reference just cited to Montaigne's "design" occurs in the chapter in Book II having the same number as the one containing the claim of randomness cited in Book I, while the symmetrically placed essay toward the end of Book II is "Of a Monstrous Child" (II, xxx), recalling the description of Montaigne's thoughts as "monsters" in the same chapter of Book I and the reference to his book as his "child" in the earlier chapter of Book II—I, viii, 34 [21]; II, viii, 383 [293].) Useful contributions toward the discovery of such an order have been made by Michel Butor in *Essais sur les "Essais"* (Paris, 1968); by Richard Sayce in "L'Ordre des *Essais* de Montaigne," *Bibliothèque d'humanisme et renaissance* 18 (1956): 7–22; and by Daniel Martin in "Démonstration mathématique de l'architecture des *Essais* de Montaigne," *BSAM,* 6th ser., nos. 7–8 (1981): 79–91, and "En comptant les pages de l'édition originale du *Livre Trois* des *Essais* de Montaigne," *BSAM,* 7th ser., nos. 5–6 (1986): 27–9.

Provocative, although incomplete, is Michael Gillespie's attempt to demonstrate that the *Essays* follows a plan based on the years of its author's life ("The Structure of the *Essays,*" presented at the 1983 meeting of the American Political Science Association). Gillespie points out that the age Montaigne had just reached at the time the first edition of the *Essays* was published (according to the foreword) was exactly half the number of chapters (94) that the book then contained, and that his age at that point was also the mean between the numbers of chapters contained in the first two books. (Montaigne refers to the date of his birth at I, xx, 82 [58].) The date Montaigne affixed to the first edition, as Gillespie notes, also marked the anniversary of the Vassy massacre, which had set off the French religious wars. Gillespie's interpretation is consistent with Montaigne's claim that his book is "consubstantial" with its author (II, xvii, 648 [504]) and with the "evolution" that he appears to undergo as he writes.

The symmetry between Montaigne's age and the number of chapters in the *Essays* would seem to have vanished with the appearance of the fifth edition in 1588, since Montaigne dated the foreword to that edition June 12, after his fifty-fifth birthday: had the foreword been dated before his birthday, his age (fifty-four) would have been the midpoint of the number of chapters in the book (now 107). Note, however, that if we disregard the "leap" of ten days that Pope Gregory XIII had made in 1582 in reforming the calendar—a change to which Montaigne professes to be unable to adapt comfortably (III, x, 988 [773])—June 12 becomes June 2, or 94 days after Montaigne's birthday, the same figure as the number of chapters in the first two books. (As evidence of the attention Montaigne apparently gave to choosing the date he affixed to a book, consider the odd fact of his having dated the dedication to his translation of Raymond Sebond's *Natural Theology*—purportedly undertaken at his father's request—on the day of his father's death, while wishing his father a "very long and very happy life"! [*Oeuvres,* pp. 1360–61 and n. 1 to p. 1360 on p. 1718].)

[14]For reference to discussion by Montaigne's contemporaries about the precise meaning of the title, see Boase, *Fortunes of Montaigne,* pp. 2–3. See also Andréas Blinkenburg, "Quel sens Montaigne a-t-il voulu donner au mot 'Essais' dans le titre de son oeuvre?" *BSAM,* 3d ser., no. 29 (1964): 22–32; Sayce, *Essays,* pp. 20–22; E. V. Telle, "A propos du mot *Essai* chez Montaigne," *Bibliothèque d'humanisme et renaissance* 30 (1968): 225ff.

jects at random, he seeks to determine the capacity of his judgment in each matter he investigates (I, xxvi, 145 [107]; I, l, 289 [219]).

Montaigne explains the apparently rambling and disorganized character of his book as the consequence of his "essaying" method. Because "judgment is a tool to use on all subjects," he employs his everywhere, even on subjects it does not understand, testing their depth. Unable to "see the whole of anything," he chooses only one of "a hundred members and faces that each thing has," giving it "a stab, not as widely, but as deeply as I know how," preferably "from some unusual point of view" (I, l, 289 [219]). He purports to speak "in disconnected parts," without any system (III, xiii, 1054 [824]):

> Sowing one word here, there another, samples separated from the piece to which they belong, scattered, without a design and without a promise, I am not bound to make something good of them or to hold to them myself without varying when it pleases me and giving myself up to doubt and uncertainty, and to my ruling quality, which is ignorance. (I, l, 289–90 [219])

On the surface, Montaigne's method (or lack of it) seems the product of humility, laziness, or both. He describes the book as a place for recording the "chimeras and fantastic monsters" that his mind produces "without order or purpose," in the hope of making it "ashamed of itself" (I, viii, 34 [21]). Such a work may have a therapeutic value for Montaigne and may even hold some interest for his relatives, but other readers would seem well advised to heed the author's prefatory counsel not to waste their time reading it.

Yet Montaigne gives ample evidence in other passages that the very display of his uncertainty and ignorance has a more serious purpose, which could make it of great benefit to others. He decries people's tendency to follow received opinions rather than exercise their own judgment. The "learning" on which they pride themselves is a collection of other people's thoughts, with which they fill their memories while leaving "the understanding and the conscience empty." Such learning makes people "conceited and arrogant" without improving their judgment or character, leaving them inferior to "the peasant and the shoemaker," who "go their way simply and naturally talking about what they know."[15] By being trained to memorize opinions that they have never tested for themselves, leaning "on the arms of others," people "annihilate [their] own powers" (I, xxv, 137–8 [101–2]). In response, Montaigne proposes a system of education in which

---

[15]Montaigne's praise of the common people in this regard mimics the posture of Socrates: see Plato, *Apology of Socrates*, 22a. But cf. ibid., 22e, concerning the presumption of the artisans, and Montaigne's allusion to the confidence that the multitude have in their good sense, which suggests that they lack it: II, xvii, 641 [499]; III, xiii, 1052 [823].

pupils would be induced to use their judgment. Presented with the variety of philosophic opinions, without being constrained to adopt any "by mere authority and on credit," the student "will choose if he can; if not, he will remain in doubt. Only fools are certain and resolute" (I, xxvi, 150 [111]). Montaigne attributes "all the abuses in the world" to "our being taught to fear professing our ignorance and our being bound to accept all that we cannot refute" (III, xi, 1007 [788]).

In this light, Montaigne's written record of his investigations seems intended to encourage his readers to undertake the same sort of liberating self-education. Rather than imposing a body of doctrine on his audience, he teaches by example. The very disorder of his style seems to be motivated by the desire to faithfully represent his thought processes, rather than pretend to have acquired comprehensive knowledge through an impersonal, coldly logical course of reasoning.[16] Like Socrates, he calls into question, by his example, the dogmatism of others: "I wonder at [admire] the assurance and confidence that everyone has about himself, whereas there is almost nothing that I know I know" (II, xvii, 617 [480]).

Montaigne's extensive examination of his character and dispositions, as well as his intellectual capacities, similarly recalls Socrates' endeavor to know himself, and the Athenian philosopher's admonition to others to examine their lives. Like Socrates, Montaigne stresses the greater importance of self-knowledge, as compared with all other studies (I, iii, 18 [8–9]; II, vi, 358 [273]; III, ix, 929 [726]). He encourages his readers to turn their gaze inward and to recognize their own imperfections, rather than hypocritically instructing others in their duties (I, xxiii, 114 [83]; I, liii, 296 [224]; II, viii, 375 [287]; III, ix, 969 [758]). He seems to pursue this goal more prudently than Socrates did by describing his own imperfections: his self-criticism is an indirect means of criticizing the faults of others, who he hopes will recognize themselves in his self-portrait (I, xxvi, 146 [108]; cf. II, viii, 375 [287]).

Montaigne's pedagogy has a further goal than the Socratic pursuit of self-knowledge, however. More so than Socrates, Montaigne links the practice of self-examination with the need to *reveal* oneself to others, as he professes to do, naturally and without "artifice." He is "an enemy of subtle and dissimulated actions" and a hater of the "servitude" of unnecessary ceremony (I, xxi, 99 [71]; I, xiii, 48 [32]). He explains the purpose of his public "confession" as follows:

> I have ordered myself to dare to say all that I dare to do, and even thoughts that are unpublishable displease me. The worst of my actions and conditions does not seem so ugly to me as I find it ugly and cowardly not to dare to avow it.

---

[16]Cf. Friedrich Nietzsche, *Beyond Good and Evil* pt. I, 5.

Everyone is discreet in confession; they ought to be so in action; boldness in sinning is somewhat compensated and bridled by the boldness of confessing it. Whoever would oblige himself to say all, would oblige himself not to do anything about which one is constrained to keep silent. God grant that this excess of my license may draw our men to liberty, rising above these cowardly and affected virtues born of our imperfections; that at the expense of my immoderation I may draw them on to the point of reason! It is necessary to see one's vice and study it in order to tell about it. Those who hide it from others ordinarily hide it from themselves. And they do not consider it covered up enough if they see it; they withdraw and disguise it from their own conscience. (III, v, 822–3 [642])

In accordance with this advice, Montaigne appears to bare himself and his defects freely before the public. He admits to laziness, irresolution, uselessness, forgetfulness, and a lack of fortitude, as well as ignorance of the most commonplace things (II, xvii, 626–7 [487–8], 632–6 [492–5]). His book, "the record of the essays of my life," is exemplary for the health of the soul only if its lesson is taken in reverse, so he confesses (III, xiii, 1056 [826]). Apparently undeterred by the harm such lessons might cause if taken in a positive sense, he urges that all people be permitted to portray themselves freely as he does, not limiting this privilege to the great (II, xvii, 637 [496]).

Montaigne's recommendation that people openly admit and reveal their vices might constitute a sufficient explanation of his self-portrayal if the *Essays* belonged to that genre of literature, such as Augustine's *Confessions*, in which authors bring forth their vices in order to condemn them and hence to encourage both themselves and their readers to mend their ways. The *Essays* is not this sort of book, however. Much as Montaigne may avow his faults, he seldom blames himself for them. In fact, he not only questions the value of repentance but disdains any effort at self-reformation (III, ii, 784, 791–3 [612, 619–20]; III, ix, 924 [722]; III, x, 987 [772]). Nor are the defects he mentions such terribly serious ones that most people would regard them as worthy of severe condemnation. Indeed, the essayist's petty vices seem to increase the charm of his self-portrait; hence Rousseau, who admitted to rather more lurid sins, accused Montaigne of disingenuousness, observing that the only faults he acknowledged were "lovable" ones.[17]

The justness of Rousseau's charge is confirmed by a number of passages in which Montaigne denies that his book embodies a truly frank and public

[17]Jean-Jacques Rousseau, *Confessions,* Book X, in *Oeuvres complètes,* ed. Bernard Gagnebin and Marcel Raymond, 4 vols. (Paris, 1958–69), 1:516–17; *Fragments autobiographiques,* in *Oeuvres,* 1:1150. Cf. Jacob Zeitlin, ed. and tr., *The Essays of Michel de Montaigne,* 3 vols. (New York, 1935), 2:475–6, 564–70; Malebranche, *La Recherche,* pp. 159–60; Paul Ballaguy, "La Sincérité de Montaigne," *Mercure de France* 245 (August 1, 1933): 571.

self-revelation. Far from wishing to uncover himself before the vulgar multitude, whose opinion is "the mother of ignorance, injustice, and in-constancy," he desires only the esteem of "men of understanding," whose praise "alone has any weight" (I, xxvi, 146 [108]; II, xvi, 607 [473]; II, xvii, 640–41 [498]; III, ii, 783 [612]; cf. II, xviii, 646–7 [503]; III, ix, 961 [751]). He claims that he would have preferred to write letters, rather than a book, had he a friend to whom he could address them (I, xl, 246 [185–6]). It is perhaps in this sense that we may understand Montaigne's remark in the foreword that his book is meant for his "friends."[18] He seeks the friendship of "talented gentlemen," "the rarest type"; such friendship has as its aim the sharing of thoughts (III, iii, 802 [625]).[19] But by virtue of the very rarity of such individuals, it is a piece of luck if a perfect friendship should arise even "once in three centuries" (I, xxviii, 182 [136]). In the absence of such friendship, "association with books" offers a more reliable, if less delightful, companionship for the mind (III, viii, 805 [628]).[20] In the study of books one is really associating with the minds of their authors. For Montaigne, writing a book may be the sole available means of finding and communicating with (perhaps only posthumously) the rare companions that he seeks (III, ix, 959 [750]).[21]

Writing books is more difficult than writing letters, Montaigne suggests, because it compels an author to consider the variety of the audience and accommodate their different humors (I, xl, 246 [186]; III, v, 867 [678]).[22] The essayist claims that his style is ill adapted for dealing with the public: success in such dealings commonly requires ceremony, dishonesty, and flattery, all of which go counter to his open and natural manner (I, xl, 246 [186]).[23] In public one is compelled to cover up rulers' vices; to accommo-date popular opinions and religious beliefs, as the ancient writers did; to discuss frivolous subjects and stories in which one entirely disbelieves; and generally to "stoop to the level of those you are with, and sometimes *affect* ignorance" (I, iii, 19 [9]; II, xii, 527 [408]; III, iii, 799–800 [624]; III, vii, 898–9 [702–3]; III, viii, 917, 920 [716, 719]; III, xi, 1004 [785]).

---

[18]Cf. Montaigne's citation of Seneca's remark that others would acquire the "glory of true friends" by preserving his memory (II, xxxv, 726 [566]) with II, xviii, 646–7 [503], where he implies the hope that his own portrait, like those of his "friends and predecessors," will endure.

[19]For a similar account of the essence of friendship, see Aristotle, *Nicomachean Ethics*, 1170a14–19, 1170b11–14; on its rarity, 1156b23–27.

[20]Cf. III, iii, 806–7 [629], with Niccolò Machiavelli to Guicciardini, in Allan Gilbert, ed. and tr., *The Letters of Machiavelli* (New York, 1961), p. 142; the parallel is noted by John Owen, *The Skeptics of the French Renaissance* (London, 1893), p. 473. Cf. also Butor, *Essais*, pp. 213–16.

[21]Cf. Zbigniew Gierczynski, "Le Fidéisme apparent de Montaigne et les artifices des 'Es-sais,'" *Kwartalnik Neofilologiczny* 16 (1969): 147–8.

[22]Cf. Plato, *Phaedrus*, 275e, 277b–c.

[23]But compare III, v, 867 [678]: "I wish to satisfy everyone."

The readiness with which Montaigne seems to describe the most intimate personal details has caused most readers to assume that he was undaunted by such considerations, and that he presented himself as openly and "naturally" before the public in his book as he would in writing to a friend. But in describing his customary practice as a speaker and negotiator, Montaigne provides ground for suspecting such apparent openness. His "plan" in speaking, he writes, is "to display a thorough carelessness and casual and unpremeditated gestures, *as if* they arose from the immediate occasion." He seeks earnestly not to "*show* I have come prepared to speak well, an unbecoming thing, above all for men of my profession, and too binding for one who cannot live up to much" (III, ix, 940 [735]).[24] In the "little negotiating" he has conducted among princes, Montaigne reports having gained their trust to a singular extent by "*carefully* avoiding letting them be mistaken about me," presenting himself as a "tender and inexperienced negotiator." By his "open" manner, he has freed himself from "any suspicion of dissimulation" (III, i, 768–9 [600]). These remarks hardly show Montaigne to have been a "careless" speaker or "inexperienced" negotiator. A planned or studied carelessness is not truly careless. One may well distrust this admittedly successful negotiator's profession of inexperience, just as his success belies his claim that his style is "inept for public negotiations" (I, xl, 246 [186]).[25] What his remarks convey is the need to *appear* casual to others in order to win their trust. It is quite imprudent, he

---

[24]Note how the last clause of this sentence exemplifies the rhetorical practice described earlier in the sentence. Montaigne's reference to his "profession" is somewhat ambiguous: he variously describes his profession as being "to establish and contain myself completely within myself" (III, ii, 793 [618]) and to live "comfortably and rather relaxedly than busily" (III, ix, 926 [724]); he "make[s] no other profession" than to be aware of himself and his ignorance (III, xiii, 1052 [823]). Frame (*The Complete Works of Montaigne*, ed. Donald Frame [Stanford, 1957], p. 11n.) is almost surely wrong in judging that "Montaigne considered his profession to be that of a soldier": Montaigne recommends that military men write about their "business," chiefly the "exploits" at which they were present, whereas he has chosen to describe his thoughts rather than his actions, since his "trade" and "art" are "living" (I, xvii, 72 [50]; II, vi, 359 [274]). Sayce points out, moreover, that Montaigne "had little real experience" as a soldier (Sayce, *Essays*, p. 69). Frame himself cites the mockery that Montaigne's contemporary Pierre Brantôme directed at the essayist's receipt of the Order of Saint-Michel, in view of his pacific inclinations and the paucity of his military accomplishments (*Montaigne*, p. 118). See also Maurice Weiler, *Pour connaître la pensée de Montaigne* (Paris, 1948), p. 15; Ballaguy, "La Sincérité," pp. 566–9; for the contrary view, Marc Citoleux, *Le Vrai Montaigne: Théologien et soldat* (Paris, 1937), chs. 4–5.

After recommending that writers who "have no profession but letters" should be judged by their "style and language"—praise of which, as previously noted, he disdains for the *Essays*—Montaigne lists various particular areas of expertise on which authors respectively experienced in each area have the greatest claim to be believed (medicine, law, theology, manners, war, diplomacy) (I, xvii, 72 [50]). Montaigne himself discusses all these subjects in the *Essays*, thus signifying the comprehensiveness of his claim to knowledge (cf. I, xxxi, 203 [152], where he wishes that people would write only of what they know). Theology, interestingly, is the central one of the seven professions listed.

[25]Cf. III, ix, 970 [758], concerning Montaigne's discovery that the genuinely innocent "opinions and rules" he once tried to employ in public affairs were "inept and dangerous" for such matters, which implies that his success as a negotiator arose from his subsequent use of

observes, to let it be known that one speaks prudently (I, ix, 37 [23]).[26] These considerations may apply with even greater force to Montaigne's writing than to his speech, given the relative permanence of the written word and the potentially unlimited character of the audience for a book.[27] Thus it is not surprising that Montaigne confesses to being less open in writing than in conversation (III, ix, 961 [751]). Although his primary aim is to appeal to a few "men of understanding," as an author he must take account of the humors and prejudices of rulers and the general public so as not to suffer the consequences of their displeasure. Needless to say, those consequences were much more severe, and the range of tolerance more limited, in the France of Montaigne's era than in the liberal regimes of the twentieth century.[28] "In this time," Montaigne writes, "one cannot speak about the world except dangerously or falsely" (III, iii, 798–9 [623]; cf. III, vii, 899 [702–3]).

Montaigne is thus presented with the problem of speaking differently to

---

methods other than purely "innocent" ones. For accounts of Montaigne's extensive participation in "public negotiations" at a high level, see Frame, *Montaigne*, ch. 15; Arthur Armaingaud, "Etude sur Michel de Montaigne," in Armaingaud, ed., *Oeuvres complètes de Michel de Montaigne*, 12 vols. (Paris, 1924–41), 1: ch. 10; M. Dreano, *La Religion de Montaigne* (Paris, 1969), bk. II, ch. 1; Géralde Nakam, *Montaigne et son temps: Les événements et les Essais* (Paris, 1982), chs. 4–5.

[26]Cf. Plato, *Apology*, 17a–c; Aristotle, *Rhetoric*, 1404b17–22. See also I, ix, 35 [22]: Montaigne's apparent forgetfulness should not be interpreted as carelessness.

[27]Cf. Plato, *Phaedrus*, 275d–e; *Second Letter*, 314b–c.

[28]The *Essays* were finally put on the Roman Church's index of prohibited books in 1676, having been included in the Spanish index by 1640 (Sayce, *Essays*, p. 206n). Montaigne's entry in his *Travel Journal* for March 20, 1581, lists several points for which the *Essays* were criticized by church authorities during his visit to Rome (*Oeuvres*, pp. 1228–9 [955–6]). A measure of the spirit of the time is that one of the points deemed contrary to the church's teaching was Montaigne's condemnation of torture. Montaigne reports that he managed to make satisfactory excuses for his "errors," no doubt assisted by the fact that the official before whom he defended himself could not read French and had to rely on the report of "some French friar" (ibid.). Another, more acute reader, Antoine de Laval, the royal geographer of Henry III, described parts of the *Essays* as "heretical" and remarked that he "would not be surprised" if Montaigne's "Apology for Raymond Sebond" were "prohibited on pain of anathema" (Zeitlin, *Essays of Montaigne*, 2:514, n. 2). Montaigne was even criticized shortly after his death for his "heretical" unbelief in witchcraft and for his doubt about the power of spells to cause impotence (Boase, *Fortunes of Montaigne*, pp. 23, 39–43).

Villey (*Les Sources*, 2:357) acknowledges Montaigne's need to practice an "intellectual prudence" in criticizing existing laws and customs, given the political circumstances of the time. In his study *Montaigne fidéiste* (Nijmegen-Utrecht, 1930), p. 137, Herman Janssen lists several books of the era that were condemned by the church for intimations of "rationalism." In 1600 the Italian philosopher Giordano Bruno was burned alive for heresy; the French humanist Etienne Dolet had suffered the same fate in 1546. See also Armaingaud, "Etude," pp. 187, 191, 194, 196–203; Nakam, *Montaigne et son temps*, pp. 20–21, 38–9; Patrick Henry, *Montaigne in Dialogue* (Saratoga, Calif., 1987), ch. 1; Edme Champion, *Introduction aux Essais de Montaigne* (Paris, 1900), p. 163; Carnes Lord and Dain A. Trafton, "Introduction" to *Tasso's Dialogues* (Berkeley, 1982), pp. 3–5.

Armaingaud ("Etude," pp. 196–7) plausibly hypothesizes that the church initially refrained from condemning the *Essays* for heresy only because of Montaigne's apparent opposition to Protestantism, which represented a more immediate danger to ecclesiastical authority, and on account of the author's influential friends.

different audiences: of communicating his thought to sympathetic "men of understanding," present and future, most of whom he does not know, while giving as little offense as possible to the public and particularly the authorities, both secular and religious.[29] His book, he predicts, would not much please either of two classes of good "believers": the simple minds, who would not understand it well enough, and the penetrating ones, who would understand it too well. He hopes it might get by among the "middle" range of people, such as himself—people who question the old ways, without having been led to a deeper confirmation of the Christian faith (I, liv, 299–300 [227]).[30]

The *Essays* is not meant to be understood by "common and vulgar" readers. Montaigne asserts that his "disposition is not suited, any more in speaking than in writing, for beginners." He disdains "to go and preach to the first passerby and play schoolmaster to the ignorance or ineptitude of the first man we have met" (III, viii, 916–17 [716]). The primary means by which he prevents the bulk of readers from discovering the "most secret thoughts" embodied in his book is to cloak those thoughts in an appearance of disorder and aimlessness. Despite the frustratingly diffuse surface aspect of the *Essays*, Montaigne remarks that "it is the undiligent reader who loses my subject, not I; there will always be found in a corner some word about it, which will not fail to be sufficient, although it may be concise" (III, ix, 973 [761]). While admitting to being more reserved in writing than in speech, he advises that "if one looks, one will find that I have said everything or pointed out everything . . . I leave nothing about me to be desired or guessed." What he "cannot express," he has pointed to, but he quotes Lucretius to the effect that these hints will suffice to reveal the rest to a keen mind (III, ix, 961 [751]). Less shrewd or diligent readers will lose the track; but Montaigne remarks, "who is there who would not rather not be read than be read sleepily or fleetingly?" (III, ix, 974 [761]). The very "essayistic," apparently rambling form of the *Essays* serves to weed out careless readers, who will miss Montaigne's deeper meaning because they will read in snatches and merely be amused (ibid.). Though Montaigne may still have a profound influence on such readers, this influence will be the result of his rhetoric rather than his reasoning: they are likely to be unconscious, in other words, of the very fact of his influence.[31]

[29]On the previous history of this mode of writing, see Leo Strauss, *Persecution and the Art of Writing* (Glencoe, Ill., 1952), ch. 2; Fortin, *Dissidence et philosophie;* Abel Lefranc, *Rabelais* (Paris, 1953), pp. 177–219; Gierczynski, "Le Fidéisme apparent de Montaigne," pp. 142–9.
[30]Zeitlin, *Essays of Montaigne,* 1:414, notes the "insinuating subtlety," or irony, of Montaigne's self-description here. Compare Montaigne's tripartite classification of human intellects at II, xvii, 640–41 [498], wherein the third and smallest class consists of "souls regulated and strong in themselves."
[31]Cf. Guillaume Guizot, *Montaigne: Etudes et fragments* (Paris, 1899), pp. 72–4; Weiler, *Pour connaître la pensée de Montaigne,* pp. 2–6.

Of course, it remains possible that some "men of understanding" who grasp Montaigne's meaning will be unsympathetic to his purpose. It is even more likely that the authorities will recognize parts of Montaigne's argument to contradict established doctrine. In such instances, Montaigne's "essayistic" mode of expression, with its appearance of innocent frankness, may still serve to blunt criticism and protect him from punishment, just as his studied "inexperience" enabled him to gain the trust of the princes among whom he negotiated. Such a purpose is indicated in the remark quoted earlier that by scattering his words, renouncing any design, and admitting his ignorance, Montaigne frees himself from being "bound" to what he has written, and from the obligation to "make something good" of it.[32] It is even more evident in the preface to a particularly bold discussion of prayers:

> I put forth formless and unresolved fancies, as do those who publish doubtful questions in the schools, not to establish the truth, but to seek it. And I submit them to the judgment of those whose concern it is to regulate not only my actions and writings, but even my thoughts. Condemnation will be equally as acceptable and useful to me as approval, since I hold it as execrable if anything is said by me, ignorantly or inadvertently, against the holy prescriptions of the Catholic, Apostolic, and Roman Church, in which I die and in which I was born. And therefore, always submitting to the authority of their censure, which has absolute power over me, I meddle rashly with every kind of discourse, as I do here. (I, lvi, 302–3 [229])

Some scrutiny of this passage may be required before the reader realizes how Montaigne has managed to deduce the privilege of a practically unlimited license of speech from the pious profession of submission and humility. (In fact, contrary to his avowal, Montaigne did not remove from the final version of the *Essays* any of the remarks that the papal censors found objectionable in the first edition; his only act of "deference" was to add this profession!)[33]

[32]Cf. Guizot, *Montaigne*, pp. 47–8, 51, 184, 231–2, 236–9; Hugo Friedrich, *Montaigne*, tr. Robert Rovini (Paris, 1968), p. 27; and the discussion of Erasmus' rhetoric in Margaret McGowan, *Montaigne's Deceits* (London, 1974), p. 43.

[33]In the 1588 edition, the first that he revised extensively after his visit to Rome, Montaigne did suppress the doubt he had expressed that Julian the Apostate had died with the words "Thou hast conquered, Nazarene," on his lips; but "he restored these remarks, with very little change from their original form," after 1588 (Frame, ed., *Complete Works*, p. 508n.; *Essais*, II, xix, 654 [509]).
It is significant that nowhere in the passage quoted above does Montaigne apologize for saying things *consciously and intentionally* against the church's "prescriptions." In view of his later denial that he ever errs "fortuitously" (II, xvii, 637 [496]), we must infer that he has no regrets for any of his deviations from church doctrine. Cf. Weiler, *Pour connaître la pensée de Montaigne*, pp. 64–5; Butor, *Essais*, pp. 149–50. See also I, xxvii, 181 [134], where Montaigne recommends that we "either submit completely to the authority of our ecclesiastical government, *or do without it completely*"; Jean Starobinski identifies this passage as "one of

The rhetorical use of the posture of tentativeness, uncertainty, and ignorance that pervades the *Essays* is not limited to the negative function of self-protection. It also serves, like Montaigne's manner as a negotiator, to help win agreement to his positive assertions:

> There is a certain kind of subtle humility born of presumption, like this one: that we acknowledge our ignorance in many things and are so courteous as to avow that there are in the works of nature certain qualities and conditions that are imperceptible to us and of which our capacity cannot discern the means and causes. By this honest and conscientious declaration, we hope to gain credence also about those things that we claim to understand. (II, xxxvii, 741 [578])[34]

To recognize that Montaigne's posture of uncertainty and ignorance serves as a protective and subtly persuasive rhetorical device is not to deny that it has a serious meaning, which will be elaborated most fully in the "Apology for Raymond Sebond." But it is clear at any rate that in describing his "ignorance," Montaigne does not really mean he is less competent than most people. Rather, he suggests that ignorance is a universal human condition, and that to recognize it is a sign of superior wisdom (II, xvii, 617, 640–41 [480, 498–9]). His self-deprecatory way of stating this is "ironic" in the original, Socratic sense of that term.[35]

The irony of many of Montaigne's self-deprecatory remarks is evident to almost every reader. Less obvious is the ironic character of the *Essays* as a whole. Montaigne's customary method of meeting "accusations," he tells us, is to enhance his accusers' charges by an "ironic and mocking confession" (III, xii, 1021 [799]).[36] This suggests that his many admissions of personal defects such as idleness, softness, and uselessness, as well as ignorance, are ironic and are part of a calculated policy, rather than the result of genuine openness. But the same may also be true of the deprecatory remarks Montaigne makes about his book, and of the generally "careless" appearance of the *Essays*. Montaigne is disposed "to promise a little less than I can do and what I hope to attain" (III, x, 1002 [784]). Thus he may

the clearest statements of [Montaigne's] religious conservatism," apparently because he dismisses out of hand the possible seriousness of the second alternative (*Montaigne in Motion*, tr. Arthur Goldhammer [Chicago, 1985], p. 282).

[34]Cf. Armaingaud, "Etude," p. 34; Barbara C. Bowen, *The Age of Bluff* (Urbana, Ill., 1972), ch. 3; and McGowan, *Montaigne's Deceits*, ch. 1, especially the quotations from Plutarch at p. 4 and n. 10, p. 171. For an illuminating discussion of Locke's similar use of the "essay" as a rhetorical device, see Rosalie Colie, "The Essayist in His Essay," in John W. Yolton, ed., *John Locke: Problems and Perspectives* (Cambridge, Eng., 1969), pp. 234–61.

[35]See Leo Strauss, *The City and Man* (Chicago, 1964), pp. 51ff.

[36]Cf. III, xi, 958 [749], and the quotation from Martial, II, xvii, 637 [496]; also the story of how Alcibiades distracted the people, at III, iv, 814 [635].

really "do" and "hope to attain" much more in the *Essays* than he leads the casual reader to suspect.[37]

By pretending to be playful and inconsistent, Montaigne can speak his mind in a way that an obviously serious and calculating author in his time could not have dared.[38] One must read the *Essays* in the light of Montaigne's approbation of mixing serious opinions with "games," and his quotation of Horace's query, "what prevents you from saying the truth while laughing?" (III, v, 855 [669]). He admits to emulating the "useful" practice of the "wisest" authors in scattering "around one good argument" several that are "flimsy" and indeed, to one who scrutinizes them closely, "bodiless" (III, xii, 1016 [795]). By his pretense of disorder and casualness, Montaigne lulls the inattentive reader into dismissing his boldest remarks as the harmless sallies of a frivolous mind.

The essence of Montaigne's irony is to draw hostile readers' ire *toward* the personal defects he "confesses," as well as the apparent triviality of his book, and thereby away from his serious teaching, which might cause far more wrath if it were widely understood. As he observes, mere "uselessness" (unlike heterodoxy) is unlikely to be punished (III, ix, 923 [722]). Pierre Villey has noted that Montaigne apologizes for his self-description rather than for his philosophy.[39] This fact hardly supports Villey's inference, however, that Montaigne thought his self-portraiture, rather than his ideas, to constitute the truly controversial novelty of the *Essays*. By apologizing profusely for the defects of his character and literary style, Montaigne drew attention to them and away from his substantive arguments. His "ironic and mocking confession" was apparently quite successful in his time, despite a few criticisms of his religious attitude. According to Villey, the main criticisms of the *Essays* during the period immediately following its publication concerned Montaigne's colloquial and neologistic language; his licentious attack on ceremony; the obscurity, disorderliness, triviality, and uselessness of his book; his practice of publicly avowing his errors and faults; his tiresome pretense of naturalness; and the endless

---

[37]It is in this light, I believe, that Montaigne's disclaimer of being "a philosopher" must be understood: "I am not a philosopher; evils crush me according to their weight" (III, ix, 927 [725]; cf. 931 [728]). Here the sort of philosopher Montaigne denies being is a caricature: specifically, the model of the Stoic "sage," typified by Posidonius (I, xiv, 55 [37]; II, xii, 469 [361]), whose pretense of being exempt from physical suffering he repeatedly mocks. By indicating that he himself is indifferent to purported evils that are feared only on account of "opinion" (I, xiv, 61 [42]; II, xxxvii, 738 [575]), Montaigne demonstrates that he shares the philosophic aspiration of transcending the horizon of convention to arrive at that of nature. And elsewhere he explicitly describes himself as a "philosopher," albeit an "unpremeditated and fortuitous" one (II, xii, 528 [409]).

[38]Cf. Armaingaud, "Etude," p. 88; Géralde Nakam, *Les Essais de Montaigne: Miroir et procès de leur temps* (Paris, 1984), p. 223.

[39]Villey, *Montaigne devant la postérité*, pp. 10–16.

lamentation of his forgetfulness and similar personal weaknesses.[40] Not until late in the seventeenth century, after the *Essays* had been frequently re-published and widely circulated, was Montaigne's essential Catholicism (as distinguished from his orthodoxy on particular theological issues) openly challenged, culminating in the proscription of his book by the church.[41]

The supreme beauty of Montaigne's irony is that it is double-edged. On the one hand, to the degree that his profession of honesty and ignorance is persuasive to his readers, he gains their confidence: they are not likely to suspect him of concealing any dangerous intentions. On the other hand, to the extent that his self-deprecatory remarks are recognized to be humorous, Montaigne's readers are encouraged not to take anything he says seriously. Thus, even his quite open assertions of the seriousness and care with which he writes are dismissed as idle boasts. The success with which Montaigne scattered bold remarks about his purposes and his tactics throughout the *Essays* without their being comprehended by most readers amply justifies his assertion that "you can more easily dare what no one thinks you will dare" (III, v, 868 [679]).[42] This very assertion exemplifies Montaigne's rhetorical technique: it occurs in a passage ostensibly devoted to the shameless description of the author's practices in love. The frankness of this account might easily distract the reader from recognizing an underlying seriousness in it, unless that reader had well meditated on Montaigne's remark that his "stories . . . often bear, outside of my discourse, the seed of a richer and bolder material, and sound obliquely a subtler note, both for me, who do not wish to express anything more, and for those who get my drift" (I, xl, 245 [185]).

A number of commentators have been aware of the "prudence" that Montaigne exercised, particularly in discussing religious topics. Yet even such perspicacious critics as André Gide, Zbigniew Gierczynski, and Arthur Armaingaud, while recognizing the disingenuousness of Montaigne's professions of piety ("I know of no other quality so easy to counterfeit," he wrote—III, ii, 791 [617]), have preferred to believe in the overall sincerity

[40]Ibid., ch. 4. Interestingly, each of these supposed defects is pointed out to the reader by Montaigne himself. See also Frame, *Montaigne*, pp. 310–12.

[41]Villey, *Montaigne devant la postérité*, p. 107. According to Dreano (*La Religion de Montaigne*, p. 279), the *Essays* went through thirty-seven editions from 1580 to 1669.

[42]Cf. also I, xxvi, 172 [127], regarding the habit of "most readers." Gierczynski, in "Le Fidéisme apparent de Montaigne," pp. 153–9, singles out a number of strikingly bold remarks in Montaigne's "Apology for Raymond Sebond" which contradict the surface thrust of that chapter.

The principle underlying this rhetorical technique was beautifully described by the Islamic philosopher Alfarabi in his introduction to Plato's *Laws* (tr. Muhsin Mahdi, in Ralph Lerner and Muhsin Mahdi, eds., *Medieval Political Philosophy* [Glencoe, Ill., 1963], p. 84). See also Leo Strauss, "How Fārābi Read Plato's *Laws*," in *What Is Political Philosophy?* (Glencoe, Ill., 1959), pp. 135–7; Machiavelli, *Discourses*, II, xxxiii, with Strauss, *Thoughts on Machiavelli*, pp. 106–7; Thomas West, *Plato's "Apology of Socrates"* (Ithaca, N.Y., 1979), p. 215.

and honesty of the *Essays* in matters other than religion.[43] Not only is such a judgment rendered questionable, however, by Montaigne's previously quoted remarks; its grounds are explicitly challenged by his discussion of "honesty."

In a chapter titled "Of Liars" Montaigne asserts that the remarkable weakness of his memory forces him to renounce any ambition for public life, because it makes him unable to dissemble consistently and convincingly (I, ix, 35 [22]). We have already observed, however, that Montaigne did take part in public negotiations, succeeding (according to his testimony) by virtue of the studied *impression* he gave of frankness and casualness. In the same chapter in which he denies his ability to speak "prudently," he counsels that "if the reputation [for prudence] is there, the effect [of prudence] cannot be" (I, ix, 37 [23]). Though Montaigne denounces lying as an "accursed vice" in the next sentence, the denunciation is rendered suspect by what follows as well as what preceded it. The succeeding examples do not demonstrate that lying is vicious, but that *clumsy* lying is dangerous (I, ix, 38–9 [24–5]). The lesson Montaigne draws from them is stated at the beginning of the following chapter: some people have the gift of "facility and promptness" in speech, and hence (he implies) can lie successfully, on the spot; others do not and get caught if they try to lie (I, x, 40 [25]). Montaigne professes to be one of those who must speak without premeditation—that is, *promptly*—a disposition that not only enables but leads him, as he later admits, to lie at least occasionally (I, x, 41 [26]; II, xvii, 631 [491]). Though he elsewhere gives us reason to doubt his lack of premeditation in the *Essays*, he amply confirms his tendency to dissimulate. He admits to not having done everything he says, to lying by exaggerating the good qualities of others, to exaggerating his subject in other respects, to feigning credence in stories which he entirely disbelieves, to having lied about his wealth, and to "erring" on purpose (I, xiv, 65 [44–5]; II, xvii, 637, 642 [496, 500]; III, xi, 1004–5 [785–6]). As for the lack of memory that purportedly prevents Montaigne from lying, one must consider his statement elsewhere that he prefers to write "without the company and remembrance of books" (III, v, 852 [666]). Observing the voluminous number of quotations from other books with which Montaigne fills the *Essays*, one infers that either this last claim or his asserted lack of memory (or, most

---

[43]See Gide's introduction to *Les Pages immortelles de Montaigne* (Paris, n.d.); Gierczynski, "Le 'Que sais-je?' de Montaigne: Interpretation de l'*Apologie de Raimond Sebond*," *Roczniki Humanistyczne* 18 (1970): 71–2. Armaingaud frequently relies on Montaigne's self-description as a literal record of the essayist's life, despite his recognition of Montaigne's "prudence" ("Etude," pp. 5, 8, 11, 22–3, etc.). The most striking challenge to Montaigne's sincerity is Ballaguy's "La Sincérité de Montaigne," which is insightful, though excessively colored by moral indignation. See also Eva Marcu, "Quelques invraisemblances et contradictions dans les *Essais*," in Georges Palassie, ed., *Mémorial du Ier Congrès International des Etudes Montaignistes* (Bordeaux, 1964), pp. 238–46.

likely, both) must be another lie.[44] Montaigne subsequently admits that his avoidance of public life is the result of his choice, not of any deficiency (such as forgetfulness) (III, ix, 966 [756]).

Montaigne warns the attentive reader in even more specific terms that the *Essays* cannot be relied upon to give a frank and honest portrait of its author. He observes that one cannot really see into another person: "others do not see you at all, they guess at you by uncertain conjectures; they see not so much your nature as your art" (III, ii, 785 [613]).[45] Even in the foreword, Montaigne admits that he has revealed his "natural form" only "so far as public respect [*révérence*] has allowed": he has covered himself more than he would have if he "had been placed among those nations that are said to live still in the sweet freedom of nature's first laws" ("A.L.," 9 [2]; II, vi, 358 [273]). In an age of "dissimulation" like Montaigne's, one must be especially cautious about believing anyone when he "speaks of himself"; people customarily "form" and "fashion" themselves to lie. But the age also requires one to dissimulate in speaking of others and uncovering their pretensions, for modern people are particularly sensitive about being contradicted and "given the lie" (II, xviii, 649–50 [505–6]). Montaigne has been saved from suffering harm for his "indiscreet liberty" of speech only by his trustworthy "visage," in which people can easily "read . . . the simplicity of my intentions" (III, xii, 1040 [814]). But "the face is a weak guarantee"; "anyone can put on a good face outside," and especially someone with Montaigne's admitted ability at adapting his "visage," his "voice," and his "gesture" to "the roles I undertook"; thus people "do not see my heart, they see only my countenance" (I, xxvi, 176 [130]; III, xii, 1036 [811]; II, xvi, 609 [474]).[46] By similarly putting on a "good visage," Caesar deceived his antagonists (II, xxxiv, 714 [557]).

Montaigne implies that his own "visage," his pretense of innocent frankness, may be no more reliable than Caesar's. Therefore, no particular statement he makes should be accepted uncritically either as necessarily representing his true thought or as honestly descriptive of his life and

---

[44]Regarding Montaigne's memory, consider the account of his success as a pupil of Latin and as an actor (I, xxvi, 173, 176 [129, 131]), as noted in this connection by Butor, *Essais*, pp. 45–6; also Malebranche, *La Recherche*, pp. 160–61. Montaigne's admission of sometimes "disguising and deforming" his "borrowings" (III, xii, 1034 [809]) reminds us of that class of liars who, he says, "disguise and alter" the truth (I, ix, 36 [23]). He also acknowledges that others find his claim to lack memory incredible (I, ix, 35 [22]).

[45]Cf. Machiavelli, *The Prince*, tr. Harvey C. Mansfield, Jr. (Chicago, 1985), ch. 18, p. 71: "Everyone sees how you appear, few touch what you are." Champion, in his *Introduction aux Essais*, pp. 53–60, complains of how little Montaigne actually tells us about himself, contrary to the promise of the foreword: the essayist leaves us largely in the dark about his family, his loves, his military and political experiences, while filling his book with an "abundance of superfluous details."

[46]At I, ix, 38 [24], Montaigne expresses doubt of his capacity to save himself by means of a "solemn lie"; he does not deny his ability to tell unsolemn lies.

character. Recalling Montaigne's reference to the technique of surrounding a solid argument with others that are insubstantial, the serious reader of the *Essays* must seek to determine whether a particular remark is actually supported by the body of the author's argument.[47] After reading the "Apology for Raymond Sebond," with its far-reaching critique of human beliefs, for instance, one must be sensitive to the irony of Montaigne's apparently uncritical recounting of a series of more or less fantastic stories in another chapter entitled, appropriately, "Of the Power of the Imagination." Incautious indeed was the critic who assumed that Montaigne swallowed these stories whole and attributed his "credulity" to "the ignorance of his age."[48]

Scholars have discovered a multitude of little "mistakes" in the *Essays:* the confusion of two different men having the same name, errors in chronology and arithmetic, attribution of a quotation to the wrong author, and so on. But further examination suggests that at least some of these slips are almost certainly intentional ones. Montaigne "confuses" two different Scipios, for instance, after having mocked the pedants who make a great deal out of an author's having "taken one of the Scipios for the other" (III, xiii, 1089 [851]; II, xvii, 640 [498]). Just prior to his denial of making fortuitous errors, the essayist mistakes Abdera for Athens in retelling a story, thus apparently justifying the claim he made a few lines earlier that his weak memory causes him to forget such "circumstances" (II, xvii, 635–6 [494–5]). He exaggerates the number of troops opposing Caesar at the siege of Alésia, in the same chapter where he notes that Caesar was wont to practice such exaggeration in addressing his soldiers (II, xxxiv, 713, 718 [556, 560]).[49] He refers expressly to the occasional "transposition[s] of chronology" that occur in the *Essays* immediately after emphasizing the care with which one ought to prepare a book for publication and describing his "plan" of displaying "extreme carelessness" (III, ix, 940–41 [735–6]). Surely, too, it is hard to believe that a writer of Montaigne's erudition, who continually worked over and revised his book, could have committed and left standing a simple error in subtraction unawares (II, xxxvii, 743 [579]).[50]

Whatever else these supposed errors may signify, as a whole they suggest

---

[47]Cf. III, viii, 914–16 [715–16], on the need to scrutinize a speaker's reasoning to determine the thought and intent underlying his remarks; and the advice of Armaingaud ("Etude," pp. 32–3), on the care that must be exercised in reading the *Essays.*

[48]Grace Norton, in *The Essays of Michel de Montaigne,* ed. and tr. George B. Ives, with commentary by Grace Norton, 3 vols. (New York, 1946), 1:126. Zeitlin, *Essays of Montaigne,* 1:326–8, falls into the same error.

[49]At p. 721 [562] of the same chapter, Montaigne again exaggerates, this time regarding the number of pieces into which a certain Scaeva's shield was broken. See Zeitlin, *Essays of Montaigne,* 2:600 (note to p. 394).

[50]See Frame, ed., *Complete Works,* p. 579, n. 2. Cf. III, ix, 971 [759], where Montaigne asks whether Socrates' claim to have been incapable of counting and reporting the votes of his tribe (Plato, *Gorgias,* 474a) is "credible"; with reference to that question, cf. I, xxv, 134 [98–9].

even further the unreliability of the *Essays* as a record of Montaigne's life. These errors are matched by a great number of contradictions in the essayist's account of his tastes, habits, upbringing, and temperament.[51] Sometimes, for instance, Montaigne purports to adopt a Stoical posture toward pain and death; yet elsewhere he expresses an extreme sensitivity to physical pain and a wish to die "insensibly" (I, xiv; I, xx; I, xix, 79 [55]; II, xxxvii, 738 [575]). In the same chapter wherein he expresses "hatred and contempt" for the art of medicine of his time, he admits having a doctor call on him when he is sick (II, xxxvii, 742, 760 [579, 593]). His claim that he inherited his hatred for the physicians' art from his father, who (he says) spent his whole life without ever tasting any medicine, is certainly rendered suspect, as Jacob Zeitlin points out, by a subsequent reference to his customarily following a prescription of his father's doctor for drinking wine (II, xxxvii, 742 [575]; III, xiii, 1084 [847]).[52] Nor can one easily square his contiguous statements about his adaptability and his subordination to habit (III, xiii, 1061–2 [830–31]) without further reflection.

Given the likelihood that the "errors" and contradictions in Montaigne's self-portrayal are intentional, it is also naive to assume that one can discern indications of the essayist's true personality in the discrepancies between what he says about himself and the facts of his life as they are known from other sources. Critics have been amused, for instance, to note Montaigne's "vanity" in exaggerating the nobility of his ancestry while mocking others who do so, in underestimating the trouble to which he went (according to his *Travel Journal*) to obtain an honorary certificate of Roman citizenship, and in entailing his estate after mocking that practice. The irony that the first two instances of "vanity" occur in a chapter entitled "Of Vanity," the first sentence of which refers to the "obvious vanity" of Montaigne's writing, has not been sufficiently considered.[53] Their placement certainly suggests that Montaigne was conscious of the vanity, real or apparent, of his remarks. It is highly likely that he expected this "vanity" to be discovered; he could not have expected to keep secret the recent origin of his family title.[54] In any case, it is unwise to assume that Montaigne inserted these "vain" remarks simply to enhance his personal reputation.

To some critics it has seemed that to question the avowed "good faith" of

[51]As noted by Sayce, *Essays*, pp. 67–8; and by Marcu, "Quelques invraisemblances et contradictions."

[52]Zeitlin, *Essays of Montaigne*, 3:452 (note to p. 305).

[53]I, xlvi, 267–8 [202–3]; II, viii, 378 [289]; III, ix, 948, 978 [741, 765], with Frame's notes on the last three pages listed. Armaingaud ("Etude," p. 6) observes that Montaigne dissimulated even in his private family records. One may not, therefore, assume the truthfulness of the *Travel Journal* (which was apparently not intended for publication and was not discovered until the eighteenth century) either. In "La Sincérité," Ballaguy points out some suspect passages in the *Journal*, although he nonetheless cites other passages to contradict claims that Montaigne makes in the *Essays*.

[54]According to one contemporary, Joseph Scaliger, Montaigne's "pretensions to nobility were the object of general raillery in Bordeaux" (cited by Ballaguy, "La Sincérité," p. 564).

the *Essays* is to accuse its author of moral turpitude.[55] But in seeking to elevate Montaigne's moral stature, these apologists lower his intellectual rank: he becomes the author of an amusing but dilettantish and philosophically flawed work, full of errors, inconsistencies, and superstitions, reflecting the backwardness of his time. Despite Villey's adulation of Montaigne, for instance, most of his studies of the *Essays* do not show it to embody a truly original or profound body of thought, but rather an especially felicitous and "original" expression of the "collective thought" of Montaigne's century.[56] Villey even explains the apparent disorder of the *Essays* by saying that "the men of the sixteenth century do not know how to compose," as if Montaigne lacked the capacity to surpass the "compilers" he mocked.[57] Similarly, Montaigne's more recent scholarly admirers often adopt an implicitly patronizing attitude, praising his ability partly to transcend the prejudices of his time while excusing his mistakes or biases as the product of his historical milieu.[58] Even the "insights" for which scholars pay Montaigne the greatest homage, such as his recognition of the diversity of human nature, are hard to distinguish from the banalities that constitute the universal "wisdom" of the present time; while their delight in uncovering the supposed psychological roots of his thought reflects an unstated assumption that they are better equipped to understand and evaluate that thought than he was. In sum, most recent studies of Montaigne's thought make it doubtful that present-day readers might learn anything important from the *Essays* that they do not already know.

[55] See Zeitlin, *Essays of Montaigne*, 2:488–90, on the scholarly reaction to Sainte-Beuve's "accusation of deliberate treachery" in the "Apology for Raymond Sebond." Guizot (*Montaigne*, pp. 132–3) is a striking example. Cf., on the similar disinclination of modern scholars to take seriously Bacon's intimations of his "authorial insincerity," which was motivated by considerations comparable to Montaigne's, Timothy H. Paterson, "Bacon's Myth of Orpheus," *Interpretation* 16 (1989): 428–30.

[56] Villey, *Montaigne devant la postérité*, p. 3; cf. Weiler, *Pour connaître la pensée de Montaigne*, pp. 105–6. Villey does stress the originality of Montaigne's "self-portrait" and his project of "organiz[ing] life in the light of reason alone," and judges him "ahead of his time" in his condemnation of torture and of trials for witchcraft, as well as in his scientific attitude (*Les Sources*, 1:6; 2:352–3; *Montaigne et François Bacon* [Geneva, 1973], esp. pp. 106–9). But even in his "originality" Montaigne remains essentially a child of his time, whose thought "evolved" in conformity with "the Renaissance itself" (*Les Sources*, 2:546). Cf. Henri Busson, *Les Sources et le développement du rationalisme dans la littérature française de la Renaissance, 1533–1601* (Paris, 1922), pp. 434, 439.

[57] Villey, *Les Sources*, 2:282; *Essais*, I, xxvi, 145–6 [108]; III, xii, 1033–4 [808].

[58] According to Frieda S. Brown, "Montaigne's ultimate position was the resultant of irresistible forces, social and intellectual, that determined his political and religious attitudes throughout his life" (*Religious and Political Conservatism in the "Essais" of Montaigne* [Geneva, 1963], p. 95). Jean Starobinski explains Montaigne's supposed unconcern with achieving any long-term project on the ground "that in Montaigne's time the ideas of a 'historical' future and of action directed toward the future were not current among people generally or even among intellectuals" (*Montaigne in Motion*, p. 258). Even Géralde Nakam, who often emphasizes the novelty of Montaigne's insights, nonetheless finds the essayist in important respects to have "remained [the] prisoner of habits of thought and schemas inherited from his milieu and his epoch" (*Les Essais*, p. 169; cf. p. 456).

To save Montaigne's reputation in this manner is hardly to do him honor.[59] Moreover, the critics' simplistic moral horizon fails to take account, as Montaigne's thought does, of the possibility that dissimulation may be *justifiable* as a means to some goals, such as the public good, or one's own preservation from unjust persecution.[60] Distinguishing between "the useful and the honorable" (or "honest"), Montaigne declares that "the public good requires that one betray and lie" (III, i, 768 [600]).[61] Private citizens may seek to remain pure and righteous, but "affairs of state have bolder precepts" (III, ix, 969–70 [758]). Thus the conduct of public affairs is properly a matter for those with stronger, less delicate consciences (III, i, 768 [600]).[62] In his advice to princes regarding honesty, Montaigne clearly indicates the secondary character of this virtue in political affairs. Having warned against the "folly" of "saying everything," he cautions the prince not "to make a *profession* of covering up." One may, the essayist acknowledges, successfully "deceive men once or twice"; indeed, by a single breach of his word, a prince may secure his affairs permanently. Princes commonly lack the prudence, however, to avoid lying so frequently that they are no longer believed (II, xvii, 631–2 [491–2]). Although he expresses himself more reservedly, Montaigne says nothing here about the value of honesty that contradicts the advice given by that notoriously devious counselor of rulers, Machiavelli (to whom Montaigne refers in the same essay), in chapter 18 of *The Prince*. To understand Montaigne may require an openness to the possible truths contained in Machiavellianism.

The Problem of Montaigne's "Evolution"

Apart from the apparently random contradictions on particular points with which the *Essays* abounds, a deeper problem for the interpreter lies in the overall *pattern* of "evolution" that Montaigne's thought, his attitudes, and even his style seem to undergo as the book proceeds. Montaigne

[59]Montaigne, on the contrary, regards it as an "honor" when others claim "that what I call frankness, simplicity, and naïveté in my conduct [*moeurs*] is art and subtlety, and rather prudence than goodness, skill than nature, good sense than good luck" (III, i, 773 [603]).

[60]The apolitical character from which the merely "literary" analysis of the *Essays* has suffered is exemplified by Zeitlin's complaint of Montaigne's lack of "moral courage" in not stating his thinly concealed views on witchcraft more forthrightly (Zeitlin, *Essays of Montaigne*, 3:414). Zeitlin should have considered the lesson Montaigne conveys in chs. v, vi, and xv of Book I (and elsewhere) that the most direct and open mode of attack is likely to be unsuccessful as well as dangerous when one confronts a more powerful "enemy." Cf. *Essais*, II, viii, 375 [287], regarding the error of authors who run "rashly forward to meet the one they are attacking"; Armaingaud, "Etude," pp. 191, 198–203; and Machiavelli, *Discourses*, III, ii.

[61]Cf. III, i, 774 [604], where Montaigne implicitly questions whether any "useful" things may rightly be called "*deshonnêtes*."

[62]Note, in this connection, Montaigne's emphasis in the following chapter (III, ii) on his own lack of susceptibility to remorse.

himself invites the reader to understand this evolution as reflecting a transformation that he experienced as he wrote—both by describing the book as the record of his vacillating mind or self (III, ii, 782 [610–11]) and by referring expressly to contemporary events or stages in his life that seem to indicate the times at which different chapters or passages were composed.

This seeming evolution on Montaigne's part constitutes the basis of the most influential twentieth-century interpretation of the *Essays*, developed most fully by Pierre Villey. Villey claimed to identify three major stages of Montaigne's intellectual development in the book: an initial, "Stoical" phase; a "Skeptical crisis," reflected in the "Apology for Raymond Sebond" (II, xii); and a final stage of "intellectual prudence," stress on the individual, and the working out of a "personal," hedonistic morality. The style of the *Essays* evolved in accordance with the development of Montaigne's thought, Villey observed, from the "impersonality" of the early chapters, stuffed with historical anecdotes and classical quotations, to the more "personal" later essays (and late additions to the earlier chapters), where Montaigne truly makes himself the "matter" of his book and is most original.[63]

Although a surface reading of the *Essays* renders some support to Villey's interpretation, I believe that a more careful examination of individual chapters and passages decisively refutes it. Villey himself was forced to qualify his thesis repeatedly. For instance, his claim that Montaigne decided only at a relatively late stage of his work on the first edition to make himself the essential "matter" of the *Essays* is contradicted by the book's foreword, as well as by a remark Montaigne made to Henry III in 1580 that the *Essays* "contain nothing else than a discourse on my life and on my actions."[64] Villey assumes that this claim, as well as the foreword, was an "anachronism" in which Montaigne ignored the great change that had taken place in

[63]Villey, *Les Sources*, 1:281–5, and 2: passim. The pioneering attempt to interpret the *Essays* as a record of Montaigne's evolution was Champion's *Introduction aux Essais*, which, however, places less emphasis than Villey's interpretation on Montaigne's supposed early Stoicism, and unlike the latter emphasizes the antitheological bearing of the essayist's "skepticism." An evolutionary interpretation closer to Villey's was set forth two years before the publication of *Les Sources* by Fortunat Strowski in *Montaigne* (Paris, 1906; subsequent references to this work will cite the second edition of 1931, reprinted in 1971 in New York). The inspiration for Villey's and Strowski's interpretations is said to have been provided by their common teacher Ferdinand Brunetière, whom Floyd Gray terms "the Darwin of literary criticism" (Gray, "The Unity of Montaigne in the *Essais*," *Modern Language Quarterly* 22 [1961]: 79n; Armaingaud, "Etude," p. 110; Donald M. Frame, "Pierre Villey [1879–1933]: An Assessment," *Oeuvres et Critiques* 8 [1983]: 31). Brunetière expounded his own interpretation of the *Essays* in his *Histoire de la littérature française classique* (Paris, 1904–17), 2:577–638. Armaingaud sets forth a forceful challenge to the Villey-Strowski interpretation in chs. 6–9 of his "Etude." On the influence of Villey's and Strowski's work on subsequent Montaigne scholarship, see Zbigniew Gierczynski, "La Science de l'ignorance de Montaigne," *Roczniki Humanistyczne* 15 (1967): 14; Donald M. Frame, *Montaigne's Discovery of Man* (New York, 1955), p. 6; idem, "Pierre Villey," pp. 39–41.
[64]Villey, *Les Sources*, 2:239–40.

his intentions (according to Villey) shortly before 1580. Montaigne, Villey hypothesizes, had only recently altered his authorial intent but nonetheless published the *Essays* in its original form in 1580, and republished it in 1582 without any further progress in personalness.[65] On other·occasions Villey represents Montaigne as simultaneously maintaining contradictory positions without being aware of those inconsistencies.[66] And the entire "evolution" that he attributes to the essayist from Stoic to skeptic to libertine is supposed to have taken place within a mere six or seven years (although it became fully manifest only in later editions of the *Essays*)—beginning, as Jacob Zeitlin notes, at a time when Montaigne was already "a mature man, thirty-eight years old, with a considerable experience of life and books."[67]

It is not difficult to find a multitude of instances where the text of the *Essays* contradicts Villey's interpretation. On the one hand, many of the chapters that Villey assigns to Montaigne's early period contain thoughts he attributes to the "late" Montaigne. The 1580 text of the third chapter of Book II, which Villey regards as one of the earlier essays, contains a forthright attack on the Stoical view that suicide is an appropriate remedy for the ills of life—a view to which Montaigne had seemed to assent in another "early" chapter (II, iii, 334 [254–5]; cf. II, iii, 332 [253]; I, xiv, 68 [47]). Similarly, I, xlvii, which Villey attributes to the early period, concerns "The Uncertainty of Our Judgment"—a theme presumably connected with the skepticism that Villey identifies as the second stage of Montaigne's development. On the other hand, the "Stoical" attitudes that Villey believes

[65]Ibid., pp. 239, 242. Sayce notes, however, that the texts of two chapters as published in 1580 (II, vi, and II, xvii) carry Montaigne's self-portrait "almost as far as it will ever go," and that "the self-portrait is fully developed, at least in its general lines, by 1580" (Sayce, *Essays*, p. 52). On this point, see also Henry E. Genz, "First Traces of Montaigne's Progression towards Self-Portraiture," *Symposium* 16 (1962): 206–12; Raymond C. La Charité, "Montaigne's Early Personal Essays," *Romanic Review* 62 (1971): 5–15; Jean-Pierre Boön, "Emendations des emprunts dans le texte des essais dits 'stoiciens' de Montaigne," *Studies in Philology* 65 (1968): 147–62.

[66]See, e.g., Villey's *Les Essais de Michel de Montaigne* (Paris, 1967 [1932]), pp. 46–7; and *Les Sources*, 1:284.

[67]Zeitlin, *Essays of Montaigne*, 1:li. Cf. also the critical remarks of Armaingaud, "Etude," pp. 125–7. As Floyd Gray points out, the fact of Montaigne's maturity at the time his book first appeared was emphasized by Villey himself in the preface to his 1930 edition of the *Essais*. There Villey advocated what Gray believes to have been "a completely different approach" from his former one, in which the focus would be on the "evolution" of Montaigne's book, rather than on any alleged evolution of its author. However, Marcel Françon notes that even in the second edition of *Les Sources*, published in 1933, Villey continued his profession of revealing "the evolution of Montaigne's thought." Villey's inconsistency suggests not merely that "late in life" he "tired" of claiming to demonstrate Montaigne's evolution, as Donald Frame puts it, but that he came to doubt whether his central thesis could successfully be defended against its critics (Gray, "The Unity of Montaigne," p. 80; Françon, "La Chronologie des Essais de 1580," *Symposium* 8 [1954]: 245–6; Frame, "What Next in Montaigne Studies?" *French Review* 36 [1962–3]: 580; cf. idem, "Pierre Villey," p. 40). On the "different approach" that Gray develops on the basis of Villey's late remarks, see n. 71 below.

reflect Montaigne's early views were also expressed by the essayist in his last years, as in his additions to II, xxi.[68] Another problem arises when Villey distinguishes three concepts of nature in the *Essays*, which he attempts to relate to the evolution of Montaigne's thought but then must admit cannot be said to have succeeded one another chronologically in the book.[69]

Many further questions may be raised about the evidence on which Villey relies in his dating of individual chapters and passages.[70] Yet it is undeniable that an overall (if far from uniform) shift in form, spirit, and argument does take place in the *Essays*. What is in doubt is not the fact of this development, but Villey's contention that it reflects a change in the author's thought and intention.[71] Neither Villey nor his critics seem to have considered the possibility that the changes of style and emphasis in the *Essays* were *a thoroughly planned rhetorical technique* adopted by Montaigne so as to have a maximal influence on his readers at minimal danger to himself.[72]

The evidence Villey marshals to demonstrate the evolution of Montaigne's thought is given a quite different explanation by the essayist. Whereas Villey attributes the heavy use of quotation and impersonal example in the early chapters to the influence of the literary compilations popular in Montaigne's time,[73] Montaigne denies that his purpose is comparable to that of the compilers. Unlike "the undiscerning writers of our century, who amid their obscure [or "nonexistent"] works scatter whole passages of the ancient authors to do themselves honor," Montaigne explains, "I do not speak the minds of others, except further to speak my own mind" (I, xxvi,

[68]Cf. Zeitlin, *Essays of Montaigne*, 2:556–7; Sayce, *Essays*, pp. 165–6, 172.

[69]Villey, *Les Sources*, 2:231–2.

[70]See Françon, "La Chronologie," pp. 242–8, with the articles by Genz, La Charité, and Gray cited in nn. 65 and 67 above; Gierczynski, "La Science de l'ignorance," pp. 17, 32n.; Jean-Pierre Boön, "La Pensée de Montaigne sur la mort, a-t-elle évolué?" *Modern Language Notes* 80 (1965): 307–17.

[71]As indicated in n. 67, Villey began to modify his position by 1930, sometimes denying that the evolution he had traced in the *Essays* reflected a comparable evolution in Montaigne himself. Floyd Gray, in "Unity of Montaigne," attempts to develop Villey's "late" position by arguing that there is an underlying "unity" to the "multiplicity" of Montaigne's thought (p. 81). But neither Gray nor such other critics of the evolutionary interpretation as Françon and Armaingaud provide an adequate rejoinder to Donald Frame's query as to "why, if Montaigne himself does not change somewhat, he says such radically different things at different times" ("What Next in Montaigne Studies?" p. 580). I attempt to answer Frame's question in the text above.

[72]An exception: Steven Rendall, "Dialectical Structure and Tactics in Montaigne's 'Of Cannibals,'" *Pacific Coast Philology* 12 (1977): 56–62.

[73]Villey, *Les Sources*, 2: Book I, passim. Strowski (*Montaigne*, pp. 38, 176) points out that the greater part of Montaigne's citations were added *after* 1580. At the very conclusion of his study Villey calls attention to the multitudinous borrowings that Montaigne added from 1588 on and interprets them as a sign of his having returned, in his last years, to the "pedantic" and "bookish" manner with which he had begun (*Les Sources*, 2:545–6).

145–6 [108]).[74] Whereas Villey's mode of dating Montaigne's chapters rests largely on an analysis of the apparent chronology of the essayist's reading of the authors he quotes, and the consequent influence they exerted on his thought, Montaigne states that in writing he uses other authors "not at all to form my own opinions; but to assist those I formed long ago, to second and support them" (II, xviii, 648–9 [505]).[75] His quotations are a concession to "public opinion" (III, xii, 1033 [808]). Montaigne explains the increasing boldness and personalness of Book III as the result not of a change in his intentions, but rather of the confidence with which the early public reception of the *Essays* inspired him, and his taking advantage of the greater license of speech that is customarily allowed to older men (III, ii, 783 [611]; III, ix, 942 [736]).[76] He has added to his earlier work, but he has not changed it; rather than altering an already published work, an author should think carefully before publishing (III, ix, 941 [736]).[77] His judgment and his general opinions have remained constant; his book "is always one" (I, xxvi, 165 [122]; III, ii, 790 [616]; III, ix, 941 [736]). The additions Montaigne made to the *Essays* after 1588, one scholar has noted, do not represent a significant change in his thought but simply exemplify an increasing boldness, especially in five areas: "self-revelation, obscenity, his book and his plan, the evils of religion in his time, and his own independent morality."[78] It is possible, therefore, that Montaigne's thought had actually

---

[74]Guizot (*Montaigne*, pp. 165–6) notes how Montaigne distorts the thought of those he quotes to support his own argument, a practice to which Montaigne admits (III, xii, 1034 [809]).

[75]Note that Montaigne does not deny that his readings may have influenced the formation of his opinions *before* he began to write, but only that his thought has changed during the course of his writing. But cf. Champion, *Introduction aux Essais*, pp. 260–72, which emphasizes the freedom of Montaigne's thought from any dependence on the "authorities" he cites.

[76]A similar cause may underlie the typically greater length of the chapters of Book III. The shortness of the earlier chapters, Montaigne observes, tends to "disrupt" and "dissolve" his readers' attention, thus arousing their "disdain" (III, ix, 974 [762]). Perhaps this disruption was intentional, serving to discourage casual readers from expecting to find a serious and continuous stream of thought in the book. By the time Book III was published, Montaigne could more safely dare, for the reasons stated above, to make his purpose somewhat clearer. (Cf. I, xxi, 105 [76], where he relates his avoidance of "extended narration" to his wariness of saying "illegitimate and punishable" things; his claim there to be incapable of such narration was of course belied, in the first edition, by the "Apology for Raymond Sebond.")

[77]Montaigne did in fact change particular words and phrases of his original text in later editions of the *Essays*, but the remark quoted above may signify a denial that these stylistic modifications altered the book's substantive teaching. Cf. III, viii, 902 [705]: Montaigne has often altered his writings "more out of civility than to improve them"; also II, xxxvii, 736–7 [574]: he "correct[s]" an occasional word only "to diversify, not to delete." See also Gierczynski, "Le Fidéisme apparent de Montaigne," p. 152.

Guizot (*Montaigne*, ch. 6), among others, points out the care that Montaigne put into his style and choice of language. In view of the essayist's denial that he wishes his fame to rest on his style, how much more reason there is to expect that he composed his thoughts with care before putting them into print.

[78]Frame, *Montaigne*, p. 290.

remained constant since at least as far back as 1571 (when he "retired" to his château and apparently began writing the *Essays*), but that he masked his thought more cautiously in the early editions with the appearance of conventionality that Villey finds most marked in the first chapters. Villey himself observes that the "Stoical" aspect of the first two books helped win the *Essays* an initial acceptance much warmer than that which was forthcoming after the bolder, more "personal," and less conventional Book III was added.[79] As we shall discover, however, even the first chapters, if read carefully, make it doubtful that Montaigne ever adhered to Stoicism.

To seek for hidden purposes in a book is no doubt an enterprise in which one can easily go astray. It is at least equally dangerous, however, to assume that one has understood the "evolution" of a learned writer's thought, or to explain away difficulties by casual reference to the writer's apparently conflicting moods, such as "moral optimism coupled with an intellectual pessimism,"[80] without having given the most serious consideration to the author's repeated claim that his thought remained consistent. I suggest that Montaige's professions of consistency can be reconciled with the apparent evolution of the *Essays,* once we recognize this evolution as an instrument of the author's rhetoric rather than a literal record of his thought processes. Montaigne's purported account of his life and of his apparently changing thoughts and feelings is less, in reality, a record of his life than a vehicle he employs to convey a teaching about how one *ought* to live. Montaigne suggests at several points that his ostensible self-portrayal is designed to have precisely this effect. Despite the remark quoted earlier from III, xiii, in which he professes to be a bad example, he elsewhere remarks that "it ill befits anyone to make himself known save him who has qualities to be imitated, and whose life and opinions may serve as a model" (II, xviii, 646 [503]). In another previously cited passage he expresses the hope that by publicizing his own "license" and "immoderation" he may draw others toward liberty and reason (III, v, 822 [642]). Montaigne's seeming evolution is a means of encouraging a certain change in the thought and life of his readers. Perhaps the most obvious instance of this technique is his purportedly evolving attitude toward death, to be examined in Chapter Ten, below. Montaigne's treatment of that theme moves from a putatively Stoical emphasis on the need to prepare oneself by forethought to meet death steadfastly (I, xiv, xix, xx), through an account of a personal "experience" that calls his previous attitude into question (II, vi), and culminates, near the end of the *Essays,* in an outright rejection of the Stoical view. But although the overall surface of the text seems to reflect a radical evolution of Mon-

[79]Villey, *Montaigne devant la postérité*, pp. 17–18, 31–35, 286. See also Nakam, *Montaigne et son temps*, p. 18.

[80]Boase, *Fortunes of Montaigne*, p. xxviii; for other examples, see Strowski, *Montaigne*, pp. 33–4; idem, *Montaigne, sa vie publique et privée* (Paris, 1938), pp. 153–4, 157–8.

taigne's attitude in this regard, a careful reader will find that even the original text of the earlier, quasi-Stoical chapters contains remarks contradicting the dominant thrust of the argument, thereby casting doubt on the sincerity of the argument.

Montaigne's treatment of death typifies the overall movement of the *Essays*. Early in the book the author seeks to win his readers' confidence by appealing to a prejudice they are likely to share: the admiration both of classical wisdom and of the classical model of the morally virtuous man.[81] The classical models are questioned even in the early chapters, but the questioning is largely in the form of a subtle irony. As Villey perceived, the dry impersonality of these chapters indicates that they do not simply represent their author's true beliefs. Villey failed to recognize, however, that the very progress of "personalness" in the *Essays,* and the contrast between Montaigne's engaging "frankness" in the later chapters and the dryness of many of the earlier, "Stoical" ones, was a consciously adopted rhetorical device, intended to make the overt teaching of the later chapters more appealing to readers than the conventional wisdom it was intended to supplant—albeit at the cost of offending the traditional-minded.

We thus observe a further element in Montaigne's rhetoric besides the irony already discussed. Whereas Montaigne's irony serves the defensive purpose of concealing the seriousness of his thought from vulgar readers, his purported self-revelation and evolution serve as a vehicle for positively influencing the generality of his audience in a particular direction. By enticing ordinary readers with the charm of the "self" he portrays, he aims to have an effect on their opinions and feelings that accords with the intention of the reasoned philosophic argument that he sets forth at a deeper level of his book—an argument that he expects only a few readers to grasp. To understand the *Essays* as a whole, one must comprehend both its rhetorical surface and the philosophic discourse that underlies the surface, and their interrelation. To treat the *Essays* as a philosophic text is by no means to deny its beauty as a literary work, but ought to increase our appreciation for Montaigne's art by enabling us to recognize that it was not practiced merely "for art's sake."[82]

---

[81] Cf. the appeal to the prejudice in favor of antiquity in the proem to Book I of Machiavelli's *Discourses* with the retraction of that appeal in the proem to Book II; Strauss, *Thoughts on Machiavelli*, p. 136; and Francis Bacon, *The Great Instauration*, in James Spedding et al., eds., *The Works of Francis Bacon*, 7 vols. (London, 1860), 4:22, regarding the need to win a reader's confidence by first "tell[ing] him that which is in his own heart." Montaigne alludes to the same principle in his account of the manner a "doctor" of the soul must employ to "gain credit" with his patients, so as to dispose them to accept his cure (III, iv, 808 [630]). See also Rendall, "Dialectical Structure," pp. 57–9; Harvey C. Mansfield, Jr., "Necessity in the Beginnings of Cities," in Anthony Parel, ed., *The Political Calculus: Essays on Machiavelli's Political Philosophy* (Toronto, 1972), p. 105.

[82] Here I take issue with Pouilloux, *Lire les "Essais" de Montaigne*, pp. 57–8. Cf. Allan Bloom and Harry Jaffa, *Shakespeare's Politics* (New York, 1964), ch. 1.

If this account of the didactic function of Montaigne's self-portrait is correct, it follows that the *Essays* can no more be taken as a historically accurate picture of their author than the dialogues of Plato and Xenophon can be assumed to constitute a literal historical record of the life of Socrates. Rather, the "Montaigne" described in the *Essays* is a literary persona who must be distinguished from the "historical" Montaigne, of whom we have relatively little independent knowledge, but whom it may be unnecessary to know independently in order to understand his book.[83]

It is true that Montaigne on occasion denies the possibility of separating his book from its author, asserting that the two are "consubstantial" (II, xviii, 648 [504]). Such remarks need not—and, in light of the preceding evidence, should not—be interpreted to mean, however, that every particular report concerning one of his alleged attributes or experiences is literally accurate. Rather, they suggest that Montaigne's overall self-portrait represents his "essential" self, just as Plato's dialogues, by "beautifying" Socrates, aim to reveal all the more clearly what was essential to him.[84] And indeed, just before asserting his consubstantiality with his book, Montaigne admits that he has "painted" himself in it with colors "clearer" than his original ones (II, xviii, 648 [504]). It is the hallmark of art to abstract from merely fortuitous circumstances in order to represent the truth of nature

[83]Here I differ with Sayce (*Essays*, p. 70), who denies the possibility of distinguishing Montaigne the author and Montaigne the persona. It should be added that Montaigne himself furnishes occasional hints as to the differences between his real life and his dominant portrayal of it in the *Essays*. Though generally representing himself as "licentious," he at one point admits having been more faithful to his marital duties than he is "thought to be" (III, v, 830 [648]). Though he criticizes teachings that order people "to maintain a good countenance . . . in the endurance of pain" and openly complains of the suffering engendered by his kidney stone—thus rejecting the Stoicism he had previously seemed to preach—he claims to have borne his illness "with a little better countenance" than that which he deems to be generally necessary (II, xxxvii, 739–40 [577]). After recounting the trouble he supposedly once underwent to preserve his wealth, he admits that he "did not do exactly what I say" (II, xiv, 65 [45]). Similarly, he suggests that his account of his passion for travel need not be taken "literally" (III, ix, 966 [755]). Despite frequently denouncing the vanity of the pursuit of glory and claiming to seek no goal beyond tranquility (II, xvi, 605 [471]), Montaigne admits near the end of the book that he may be motivated to benefit others by the hope of achieving glory thereby (III, xiii, 1079 [844]). And though generally professing to have avoided public affairs and the service of others, he at one point suggests that, were he inclined to publicize his actions, he might refute criticisms of his seeming inactivity on others' behalf (I, xxvi, 176 [130–31]).

The sort of distinction that I have suggested may be drawn between Montaigne's persona and his real character on the basis of his own hints in that regard is to be differentiated from the endeavor of some scholars, to which I alluded earlier, to distinguish Montaigne's "real" self on the basis of evidence extrinsic to the *Essays*. Of course such evidence, where it exists, must be taken into account; but I believe that Montaigne provides or points to all the evidence we need to understand his thought within the text of the *Essays;* and it would be unwise, for reasons noted earlier, to rely on his private records or correspondence as a truer guide than his book to his motives or character. The paucity of our biographical knowledge of Montaigne is emphasized by Weiler, *Pour connaître la pensée de Montaigne*, pp. 20–21.

[84]See Plato, *Second Letter*, 314c; cf. Aristotle, *Poetics*, 1454b8–12, with Montaigne's comparison of himself to a painter at I, xxviii, 181 [135].

with the utmost clarity. I suggest that Montaigne's purported evolution is such an artistic tool—"historically" false in some of its details, but intended thereby to present the truth about fundamental things all the more clearly and persuasively. In portraying his essential self in this manner, Montaigne suggests that he is actually describing the common nature of humanity (II, xvii, 617 [481]; III, ii, 782 [610–11]; III, xiii, 1053 [824]).[85] The real criterion of Montaigne's honesty is thus the accuracy with which he succeeds in understanding and representing what he calls "the human condition" (III, ii, 782 [611]). The *Essays* is in truth a work of self-presentation, not in representing Montaigne's life and actions in a factually accurate manner, but rather as a statement of the author's thoughts (II, vi, 339 [274]; II, xviii, 647 [503]).

If Montaigne's proclaimed frankness and openness are a deceptive rhetorical tool, however, they are also something more. Montaigne's substantive purpose in the *Essays,* I shall argue, is to undermine those moral and religious conventions that obstruct freedom of thought and discourse as well as the freedom to indulge in earthly pleasures. Michel Butor rightly attributes to Montaigne the vision "of a state of the world where it would finally be possible to be sincere."[86] But Montaigne clearly recognized, as most of his twentieth-century interpreters (who take these things for granted) do not, the political and moral preconditions and ramifications of the triumph of "sincerity" and toleration. The central thesis of this book is that Montaigne was a *political* philosopher who foresaw that the way of life he advocated could be brought about for the generality of human beings only through a radical transformation of the political and social order. In the following section I bring forth some preliminary evidence to suggest the plausibility of this thesis.

Montaigne's Political Intention

Montaigne's proclamation of his honesty, as noted, is linked through most of the *Essays* to a profession of incapacity for public life that proves, upon examination, to be ironic. Toward the end of the book his pretense of inability to benefit others is gradually replaced by an admission that he has avoided public life out of choice rather than incompetence (III, ix, 929–30, 960 [727, 756]). Montaigne explains that he is "disgusted with mastery, both active and passive" (III, vii, 898 [700]). In public, one must live as others tell one to, rather than as one pleases (III, ix, 970 [758–9]). Montaigne finds it "bad and unnatural" to "abandon healthy and gay living in order to serve others" (III, x, 984 [770]).

As his argument proceeds, Montaigne nonetheless indicates the pos-

---

[85]Cf. Erich Auerbach, *Mimesis,* tr. Willard Trask (New York, 1957), p. 264.
[86]Butor, *Essais,* p. 214.

sibility of a political role that is not incompatible with the satisfactions of private life. He reports "taking part in public office without departing from myself by the width of a fingernail, and giving myself to others without taking myself from myself" (III, x, 985 [770]). Nor is such an attitude on the part of a governor necessarily contrary to the interests of the governed: Montaigne's administration as mayor of Bordeaux was one of "order" and "sweet and mute tranquility," which he suggests was no mean accomplishment, given the strife-torn condition of his country. Montaigne's very lack of ambition saved him from the "iniquitous and quite common disposition" of seeking to "exalt and honor" an administration by "the trouble and sickness of affairs" (III, x, 998–1002 [781–3]). The moderation of Montaigne's commitment to serving others is mirrored by the moderation of his demands on them: his account of himself as one who seeks less than he deserves conforms to Aristotle's description of the equitable human being, and to Plato's portrayal of the "true" ruler as one who does not seek to "get the better" of others.[87]

Montaigne ultimately suggests that he is eminently qualified to benefit the public and has been prevented from doing so only by "fortune." Fortune has placed his position in life too low for his actions to be worthy of record (III, ix, 922 [721]).[88] Fortune, rather than merit, largely determines the distribution of "dignities and offices"; consequently, "the chief places are commonly seized by the least capable men, and . . . greatness of fortune is hardly ever found in common with ability" (I, xxvi, 154–5 [114]; cf. III, viii, 911 [712]). Seeing governments "seized by incapable men," some wise men of the past, competent in action as well as in knowledge, withdrew from public life (I, xxv, 134 [99]). In Montaigne's time persons "rare and remarkable" for their learning who could be of great benefit to others, and whom the latter could support in return, have been overlooked, with the result that both parties are left in "extreme need" (I, xxxv, 220–21 [165–6]). Although Montaigne does not suffer from poverty, his talents, too, have been overlooked: no one thought to use him, at the right age, in the office for which he was suited, as an adviser to kings (III, xiii, 1055 [825]).[89]

[87]III, x, 995 [778]; cf. III, ix, 947 [740]; Aristotle, Nicomachean Ethics, 1137b34–1138a3; Plato, Republic, 350b–c, with 340d–341a; and Butor, Essais, p. 57. On Montaigne's avoidance of contention, see III, ix, 959 [749]; III, x, 992 [776]. Both Donald Frame and Eva Marcu observe, however, that the essayist's claim never to have been involved in a lawsuit (III, xiii, 1049 [820]) is misleading (Frame, Montaigne, p. 117; Marcu, "Quelques invraisemblances et contradictions," pp. 242, 245; cf. Plato, Apology, 17d, with 32a–c).
Montaigne's denial of political ambition similarly conforms to the Platonic and Aristotelian portrayal of the "true" ruler: see Plato, Republic, 347a–d, 540a–b; Aristotle, Politics, 1271a10–17; Sayce, Essays, p. 59.
[88]Note the similarity to the epistle dedicatory of Machiavelli's Prince; and cf. Butor, Essais, pp. 35–7.
[89]But see Armaingaud, "Etude," ch. 10, and the other references cited in n. 25 regarding the extensive services Montaigne did render to Henry of Navarre, later Henry IV. As noted above, Montaigne admits (I, xxvi, 176 [130–31]) that his public service may have been more

The charge of which Montaigne professes himself capable is a most important one. The publicity of a king's actions ought to operate as "a singular incitement to virtue" for him. However, this motive is rendered ineffectual because the conduct of kings is badly judged, both by the people, whose understanding is weak and who are prohibited in any case from expressing a critical judgment of their ruler during his lifetime, and by most royal advisers, who fear to oppose their master's wishes (III, vii, 896 [700]; I, iii, 18–19 [9]; III, xiii, 1054–6 [825–6]). Kings need to be safeguarded by "good education and good advice" against the poisonous effect of flattering speech (I, li, 293 [222]).[90] As things are, whatever good qualities they possess are "dead and wasted," while their "defects and vices" are "authorized" by the flattery of their servants and subjects. Both the king and his subjects are prevented from giving a sincere judgment on most matters by their relations of "superiority and inferiority," which force human beings into a "natural envy and contention" (III, vii, 896–8 [701–2]). Montaigne, however, places himself considerably outside these relations, as one who has no wish to be master over others and does not even demand as much as he deserves. His judgment is not infected by partisanship, nor is he blind to the defects of those he follows (III, x, 989 [774]; I, xxi, 104–5 [76]; cf. III, i, 769 [601]). He further conforms to the requirement that a royal adviser be possessed of, and content with, a middling fortune, thus giving him the advantage of ready "communication with all sorts of people" without being dependent on the king's favor for his maintenance (III, xiii, 1055 [826]; II, xvii, 626 [487]). Montaigne's best qualities, which he has found "useless in this age"—"fidelity and conscience," "frankness and independence"— would serve him well, he suggests, in the office he describes (II, xvii, 629 [490]; III, xiii, 1055–6 [825–6]). While having the courage to speak frankly to the monarch, he would know how to give his advice prudently and hence most effectively (as one may judge from his many remarks about the art of speaking and writing) (III, xiii, 1056 [826]).

The point of Montaigne's recommendation of himself as an adviser to kings emerges in its sequel. From discussing the need that monarchs have for guidance and good counsel, Montaigne turns abruptly to a review of the purpose of his book, which he calls "a register of the essays of my life." But the words with which this new discussion begins, *en fin*—"in sum" or "in conclusion"—suggest that it is linked with, or follows from, the preceding argument. There follows a lengthy account by Montaigne of "the practice that has guided me thus far." No longer pretending that his book is of no concern to others, he invites them to learn from his example. "For bodily

---

extensive than he makes known in his book. He also acknowledges "the access that fortune has given me to the leaders of different parties" (I, xxi, 105 [76]).

[90]Cf. *The Prince*, ch. 23, p. 93.

health," he asserts, "no one can furnish more useful experience than I" (III, xiii, 1056–7 [826]). Montaigne has previously indicated the need for reliable records of "experience" as a foundation for the science of medicine (II, xxxvii, 763 [595]). Although he purports at this point to deny the utility of his book as a guide to the health of the soul, he has already suggested that his remarks about medicine are meant to be applied to the soul as well as the body, to which the soul is so intimately linked (I, xxi, 103 [74]; I, xxx, 198 [148]; II, xii, 547 [424]; III, iv, 808 [630]). In fact, the discussion that follows from here to the end of the book culminates in a treatment not merely of the preservation of life, but of life's goal. Montaigne openly holds up his own way of life at the end as an example for others, contrasting it with the erroneous views of "the people," as well as some leading figures of antiquity, concerning the purpose of human existence (III, xiii, 1090, 1096–7 [852, 856–7]).

We may understand the relation of Montaigne's concluding account of his way of life to the preceding theme of advice to kings in the following manner: perhaps it is not necessary for Montaigne to be appointed a royal adviser in order to succeed in guiding the conduct of rulers and their subjects. He may have a far greater and longer lasting influence in that regard by means of his book.[91] Further evidence that this was Montaigne's intention may be found in his discussion of historians.

Montaigne distinguishes three classes of historians. The "simple" ones, lacking the ability to "mix in anything of their own," merely "register in good faith" everything that "comes to their notice," "without choice or selection." By setting forth "the material of history, naked and unformed," they "leave our judgment intact to discern the truth." At the other extreme, the few most excellent historical writers "have the capacity to choose what is worth knowing" and rightfully "assume the authority to regulate our belief by their own." But the third, middle class of historians "spoil everything for us" by wrongfully usurping "the right to judge." By omitting as "incredible" whatever they do not understand, they prevent their readers from learning the truth (II, x, 396–7 [303–4]).[92]

In claiming to represent his experience uncorrupted by "art" or "opinion," Montaigne appears to place himself among the simple historians (III,

[91]Cf. the epistle dedicatory of *The Prince*, p. 4, where Machiavelli, despite his "low" status, expresses the intention to "give rules for the governments of princes"; also Nakam, *Les Essais*, pp. 226–31.

[92]Montaigne's designation of those who rightfully claim "the authority to regulate our belief" sheds light on his ostensible profession of obedience to the church, quoted earlier, in which he submits "to the judgment of those whose concern it is . . . to regulate my thoughts" (I, lvi, 302 [229]). Political society, he has indicated, ought not possess this authority (I, xxiii, 117 [86]). Elsewhere he assigns to "theologians and philosophers" the task of regulating "common beliefs" (III, viii, 920–21 [720]), but regarding the former, cf. I, lvi, 308 [234], criticizing theologians who "write too humanly."

xiii, 1056 [826]). He is at pains throughout the *Essays* to emphasize the infinite variety of things and events, in opposition to narrow and particular human interpretations of the world. He appears to bend over backward to avoid obscuring the phenomena by interpretation, uncritically repeating anecdotes derived from authors who themselves expressed doubts about their credibility.[93] Near the end of a chapter that began with a number of stories illustrating "the power of the imagination," he claims to "surpass . . . all historical fidelity [*foy*]" to a "superstitious" degree (I, xxi, 104 [75–6]). Since he indirectly indicates in this same chapter his own disbelief in such stories, and elsewhere (notably in III, xi) challenges such reports more overtly, it must nonetheless be doubted that Montaigne is truly the uncritical reporter he professes to be. Indeed, just before avowing his historical fidelity, he explains that his aim is "to speak of what *can* happen" rather than merely what has happened (ibid.).[94] Hence he selects from the histories he reads those stories that are "most rare and memorable." While denying that he falsifies his reports out of "conscience," he leaves open the possibility that he does so out of "knowledge"; elsewhere, we have seen, he admits to "erring" knowingly. He suggests one reason for his filling the *Essays* with anecdotes from the distant past: there is no danger in "an old report" being "this way or that," whereas in writing of present affairs, one must fear saying things that are "illegitimate and punishable." What matters to Montaigne, as it did (he observes) to Plutarch, is the utility, rather than the factual truth, of his examples (I, xxi, 104–5 [75–6]).[95]

Montaigne's remarks about his historical fidelity square with what we learned from his admissions about the deceptive "frankness" of his self-portrait. Contrary to the surface impression conveyed by his rhetoric, Montaigne's "history" is selected and contrived to convey a particular understanding of things. Rather than writing merely as a "simple" historian, Montaigne has taken upon himself the authority he allows to few authors to "regulate our belief." Through the influence of his book, he may guide the understanding that others have of the nature of things, including human nature. This guidance may have important effects on people's conception of the proper way of life and, consequently, on the political arrangements they adopt to secure it.

Montaigne continually denies that he has any public ambitions and that he seeks to change the political order in any way. But he suggests that

[93]For example, see Zeitlin, *Essays of Montaigne*, 2:496–7. Strowski (*Montaigne*, p. 175) marvels that "this so sharp critic of ideas, this so penetrating judge of men, is inconceivably credulous with regard to history; he never debates a fact: he takes it just as it is given to him." But cf. *Essais* III, xi, 1003–10 [785–90].

[94]This remark assimilates Montaigne's aim and technique to the quasi-philosophic work of poets rather than that of historians in the usual sense: see Aristotle, *Poetics*, 1451a35–b10.

[95]Cf. Zeitlin, *Essays of Montaigne*, 1:328; Nakam, *Les Essais*, pp. 229–30.

anyone who exercises his own judgment, as he does, will find much to question and challenge in established customs and institutions (I, xxiii, 114–16 [83–5]). He warns us, moreover, that greater ambition may lurk in the very denial of ambition (I, xli, 248–9 [187]; III, vii, 894 [699]; III, x, 1001 [783]).[96] In explaining that he has chosen to record his thoughts, rather than his actions, because fortune has placed the latter on too low a level to be worthy of note, he implies that his thoughts *are* noteworthy (III, ix, 922 [721]). Contrary to the foreword, Montaigne does not eschew all glory from his book; he merely disdains praise of its style, as noted earlier, for he denies "that the perfection of fine speaking could bring any glory suitable to a great personage" (I, xl, 243–5 [183–5]).[97] In spite of the admitted strength of his self-love and his preference for a private life, he is also prone to devote himself "to the little people [*aux petits*]," perhaps "because there is more glory in it" (III, xiii, 1079 [844]). He is not prevented from obtaining glory by the "lowness" of his actions, because great thoughts, as conveyed through books, may secure their author a glory rivaling or surpassing that of Alexander and Caesar (II, viii, 383 [293]; cf. II, xxxiv, 715 [558]). The greatest philosophers not only "instructed" the world but "regulated" it "with governments and laws" (II, xii, 481 [371]); we have just seen evidence of Montaigne's similarly undertaking to "regulate" his readers' belief. He cites a remark of Plato to indicate that the "immortal children" of men like Lycurgus, Solon, and Minos—that is, the laws they promulgated—"immortalize" and even "deify" their progenitors (II, viii, 381 [291]).[98]

We are led to suspect that while recommending himself as a royal counselor, Montaigne actually seeks an immortality surpassing that won by the most famous rulers and lawgivers by acting as a teacher of legislators, or a legislator-founder. He is not dependent for his success on a royal appointment; the means of his political activity is his book and the teaching it conveys to other "men of understanding," who will extend Montaigne's

[96]Cf. Ballaguy, "La Sincérité," pp. 571–3. Ballaguy rightly emphasizes the strength of Montaigne's ambition, but his interpretation of that ambition as directed primarily at political advancement and at earning the personal admiration of readers of the *Essays* founders on his inability to explain why Montaigne should deprecate his actual political achievements in the book—or why he should make specious boasts of the nobility of his lineage which could easily be found out by his contemporaries.

[97]Again there is a parallel to the epistle dedicatory of *The Prince*, wherein Machiavelli denies having "ornamented" the language of his book as others do, "for I wanted it either not to be honored for anything or to please solely for the variety of the matter and the gravity of the subject" (p. 4). Cf. also Plato, *Apology*, 17b–c.

[98]Montaigne replaces Darius in Plato's list of statesmen (*Phaedrus*, 258b–c) with Minos, thus making it more strictly a list of legislator-founders. Montaigne is somewhat more emphatic than Plato's Socrates in saying that these men *are* deified, not merely that they are thought to be so. (Minos would exemplify deification in an almost literal sense, since he was reputed to have been the son of Zeus.) Cf. Strauss, *Thoughts on Machiavelli*, pp. 287–8.

influence still further.[99] The *Essays* is a "private" project only in having been undertaken by a private citizen; its implications may be of the greatest consequence for the public.

[99]Even Armaingaud and Nakam, who most fully stress the political character of Montaigne's intention (see Armaingaud, "Etude," ch. 10, esp. pp. 205–11; Nakam, *Montaigne et son temps*, p. 222, and *Essais*, ch. 3), underestimate the breadth of that intention by interpreting it primarily with reference to the circumstances of sixteenth-century France. I hope to demonstrate that Montaigne's teaching in the *Essays* (as distinguished from his political actions) aims at a broader transformation.

The "Apology," I: Sebond and His Book; Human Beings and Animals

I have sought in the preceding chapter to provide reasons for suspecting that the *Essays* embodies a system of thought and a unifying political intention that belie its surface appearance of randomness, as well as its author's initial disclaimer of public concern. In beginning my exposition of Montaigne's teaching, however, I—along with every other interpreter—am faced with a considerable problem of organization. Unless one undertakes a chapter-by-chapter commentary—a work that, by virtue of its length and the frequent repetition of themes it would require, might prove more confusing than explanatory—the interpreter is compelled to present Montaigne's thought in a more overtly systematic fashion than Montaigne himself did. There is an obvious risk, however, that such a process will obscure rather than clarify Montaigne's reasoning, subordinating his thought to that of the interpreter. If this risk is to be avoided, it seems vital that the interpreter choose an appropriate starting point: either the point from which Montaigne himself appears to have begun his reflections, or one to which he directs the reader.

As I have indicated, the textual beginning of the *Essays*, "To the Reader," is quite misleading as a statement of Montaigne's intention, and therefore of his starting point. Though it introduces some themes that prove to be of critical importance—self-portrayal; our natural freedom—it provides no guidance as to how one might follow out these themes, the treatment of which is scattered throughout the book. Upon looking immediately beyond the foreword to the first chapter, the reader is even more mystified. This chapter is entitled "By Diverse Means We Arrive at the Same End." Its explicit theme is the relative utility of "audacity and constancy" and "submission" as means of "softening the hearts of those we have offended, when, vengeance in hand, they hold us at their mercy" (I, i, 11 [3]). Montaigne does not seem to arrive at any definite conclusion regarding this question. Moreover, the chief stylistic features of the chapter are those that Villey attributed to the "early" and least original stage of Montaigne's writing: it is brief, largely impersonal, and filled with a series of borrowed historical anecdotes. Although an adequate interpretation of the *Essays* must explain the significance of this chapter and the reasons for its placement, its obscurity makes it even less suitable than the foreword as a means of entrée into Montaigne's thought.

An obvious alternative approach, adopted by many twentieth-century interpreters, is to trace the overall "evolution" of the *Essays,* starting with the "Stoical" appearance of a number of the earlier chapters. Although the character of the text does encourage such an order, the problem here (as noted in Chapter One) is that none of the earlier essays is consistently Stoical in its argument, while even the "Epicurean" chapters of Book III include occasional "Stoical" reflections. Thus, to attempt to follow Montaigne's apparent evolution, even as a provisional interpretative device, quickly enmeshes the reader in a tissue of textual contradictions that are difficult to resolve within the confines of the chapters in which they arise.

I believe that Montaigne suggests a surer route to uncovering the fundamental principles of his thought in the twenty-eighth chapter of Book I, "Of Friendship." Here he reports having thought of imitating a painter who—employing the Mannerist technique then in vogue—"chooses the best spot, the middle of each wall, to put a picture labored over with all his skill," and fills "the empty space all around it . . . with grotesques, which are fantastic paintings the only charm of which lies in their variety and strangeness." Montaigne compares "these things of mine"—that is, the *Essays*—to the painter's "grotesques," since they lack "order, sequence, or proportion" other than a "fortuitous" one. He professes to lack the capacity, however, to produce a "rich, polished picture" for the middle. Thus he has chosen to "borrow" one from his late friend, Etienne de la Boétie, which "will do honor to all the rest of this work." At first Montaigne indicates that the borrowed work is to be La Boétie's antimonarchical treatise *Discourse of Voluntary Servitude* (I, xxviii, 182 [135]). But at the end of the chapter he explains that because that work "has since been brought to light, and with evil intent, by those who seek to disturb and change the state of our government without worrying whether they will improve it" (apparently referring to the publication of the treatise by Protestants in 1574 and 1576), and because these men "have mixed his work up with some of their own concoctions," he has decided against including it in the *Essays.* He substitutes for it a "gayer and more lusty" work by the same author, a set of twenty-nine sonnets, which are incorporated into the central (twenty-ninth) chapter of Book I (I, xxviii, 193 [144]).

For some reason, after having included the sonnets in all editions of the *Essays* published during his lifetime, Montaigne removed them from his final manuscript, adding to his introduction to them (which he left standing) the remark that "[t]hese verses may be seen elsewhere" (I, xxix, 194 [145]). Although this remark seems to imply that someone else published the sonnets between 1588 (the date of the last edition of the *Essays* in which they appeared) and 1592, no such publication has been discovered by scholars.

Even if the sonnets were in fact published elsewhere, this hardly seems a sufficient explanation of Montaigne's decision to omit them from the final edition, while retaining his laudatory introduction. I cannot pursue here the possible reasons for this omission, or the broader and no less intriguing question of the relation of Montaigne's thought to that of La Boétie.[1] My present concern is with Montaigne's indication that the most "polished" part of his book is to be found in its middle. I believe this remark can be taken as a confirmation of the fundamental significance for his project of what readily appears, even to the cursory reader, as the core of the *Essays*, the "Apology for Raymond Sebond" (II, xii). This chapter is not only the longest one by far (over three times the size of the next longest), but is literally the center of the *Essays*, in that it contains the numerically central pages of the book (as well as the central pages of the central volume). In addition, as Michel Butor has pointed out, the "Apology" is closely linked by its theme to the numerically central chapter of the central volume, "Of Freedom of Conscience," which itself sheds important light on the intent of the "Apology."[2]

One hardly risks great controversy by attesting the importance of the "Apology" for Montaigne's thought: the chapter embodies Montaigne's most extended and systematic philosophic argument, entailing a critique of both religion and philosophy, as well as (I shall argue) a fundamental reconstruction of the latter. But I take his remark about putting the most important part of his book in the middle to signify as well the relation

---

[1]In his not yet published article "Montaigne, auteur de *La Servitude Voluntaire*," Daniel Martin of the University of Massachusetts marshals impressive evidence to demonstrate that Montaigne was the real author of *Voluntary Servitude*, as well as the other works that the essayist published under La Boétie's name. He suggests that the omission of the sonnets from the last edition of the *Essays* was meant to invite readers to restore *Voluntary Servitude* to its rightful place at the center of Book I. See also, on this issue, Arthur Armaingaud, *Montaigne pamphlétaire* (Paris, 1910); Michael Platt, "Montaigne on Friendship and Tyranny" (paper presented at the 1980 meeting of the American Political Science Association).

[2]Butor, *Essais*, p. 128. Of course, one might also interpret Montaigne's remark about the importance of the middle as referring to the numerically central chapter of the *Essays* as a whole, I, liv, "Of Vain Subtleties." But although that brief chapter contains some significant remarks regarding Montaigne's intention—notably an admission that he is a doubter both of Christianity and of "the old course" generally (299–300 [227])—and hinting at his book's plan, it seems unlikely that it constitutes the most important part of the whole work.

between the "Apology" and the rest of the *Essays*. That is: although the "Apology" is more systematic and serious in its tone than many of the other chapters, it is integrally related to the rest of the book as the core to the outer surface. On this assumption I shall begin my substantive examination of Montaigne's political philosophy with a study of the "Apology," analyzing each stage of its argument in detail.[3] In the process of interpreting the "Apology," I shall occasionally engage in excurses into other chapters in order to elucidate remarks contained in it. But I shall postpone my treatment of the bulk of the *Essays*—including the specifics of Montaigne's political and moral teaching contained therein—until after the philosophic foundations of his position, as stated in the "Apology," have been uncovered.

A long debate has been carried on over the interpretation of the "Apology" between those who accept and those who deny the sincerity of the author's professions of pious intent; proponents of each view have been inspired to claim final victory.[4] As indicated in Chapter One, I believe that those who understand Montaigne's intent as anti-Christian and, indeed, antireligious, have the stronger case. However, no advocate of either interpretation, to my knowledge, has attempted to provide the kind of page-by-page analysis that I undertake in the next three chapters.[5]

[3]Craig Brush points out that from the mid–seventeenth century until the end of the nineteenth, the "Apology" was generally regarded "as the focal point" of Montaigne's thought (*Montaigne and Bayle* [The Hague, 1966], p. 109). The more recent shift of scholarly attention, noted by Brush, to other chapters may reflect a remoteness from the religious and philosophical issues that Montaigne regarded as most important; I suspect that there is a connection between this shift and the tendency of recent interpreters to soften the antireligious character of Montaigne's position, as expressed in the "Apology."

[4]See the references at pp. 297–8 of Donald Frame, "Did Montaigne Betray Sebond?" *Romanic Review* 38 (1947), and see Frame's subsequent claim that "the debate is over—at least for the time—and that the burden of proof rests heavily on those who . . . think that Montaigne was a perfidious unbeliever" ("What Next in Montaigne Studies?" p. 583). A useful summary history of interpretations of Montaigne's religious thought and an account of the recent state of the dispute are provided by Zbigniew Gierczynski in "La Science de l'ignorance," pp. 5–18. See also Andréas Blinkenburg, "La Religion de Montaigne," in Palassie, ed., *Mémorial*, pp. 163–5.

[5]Commenting on the debate in 1967, Gierczynski observed that despite the strength of the arguments that a number of twentieth-century interpreters (such as Armaingaud and Gide) had set forth to demonstrate the essayist's "rationalism," their studies were "insufficient," since "they presented [only] partial analyses, supported by isolated and rather scanty citations, of the text of the *Essais*, in place of an exact analysis of the entire work." Hence their interpretations were vulnerable to being "eclipsed by the partisans of Montaigne's orthodoxy," who could cite numerous passages in which Montaigne professes his piety, as well as biographical details demonstrating that the essayist continued to practice the Catholic religion until his death (Gierczynski, "La Science de l'ignorance," pp. 12–15).

Armaingaud, who provided the most systematic development of the rationalistic interpretation of Montaigne's thought before Gierczynski, rightly noted the deficiencies of the sort of evidence relied on by believers in Montaigne's orthodoxy. When an author living in an age when people are persecuted for heterodoxy expresses contradictory sentiments regarding religion, the burden of proof, Armaingaud pointed out, lies with those who would uphold the author's piety ("Etude," pp. 190–91; cf. Strauss, *Persecution*, ch. 2). It is similarly unwise, as

As an aid to the reader in following my interpretation, I provide here an outline of the "Apology," with page numbers for each section included in parentheses.

 I. Prologue: the value of knowledge (415 [319])
 II. Sebond and his book (415–17 [319–21])
III. "Defense" of Sebond (417–542 [321–420])
   A. Reply to the first objection: the all-too-human roots of faith; the value of Sebond's enterprise (417–25 [321–7])
      1. Critique of Christian piety (417–24 [321–6])
      2. The (potential) value of Sebond's enterprise, or one like it (424–5 [326–7])
   B. Reply to the second objection: the wretchedness of our natural condition and the weakness of reason as a means to the discovery of truth (425–540 [327–418])
      1. The means of responding to this objection (425–7 [327–8])
      2. General attack on human pride; our inferiority to the heavenly bodies (427–30 [328–31])
      3. Our natural parity with the beasts (430–65 [331–58])
      4. Renewed attack on human presumption: the uselessness and impiety of philosophy; the presumption of religious speech (465–80 [358–70])

Armaingaud noted, to rely on evidence concerning Montaigne's religious practice (for instance, reports of his pious deathbed manner, or a reference in his *Travel Journal* to his attendance at mass while in Italy) as proof of his true belief, especially given the essayist's express distinction between the outward conformity of a wise person's behavior to social convention and his internal freedom of thought ("Etude," pp. 190–91; *Essais*, I, xxiii, 117 [86]; see also Gierczynski, "La Science de l'ignorance," pp. 12–13; Seillère, *Le Naturisme de Montaigne*, pp. 36–7). Nonetheless, Gierczynski's point about the need for a thorough and systematic analysis of the *Essays*, and particularly of the "Apology for Raymond Sebond," to settle the issue of Montaigne's religious belief remains valid. Gierczynski contributed substantially, but incompletely, to filling this need in his study "Le 'Que sais-je?' de Montaigne." That article does offer a systematic analysis of Montaigne's treatment of Christianity in the "Apology," but it treats only the first half (or less) of the chapter in detail. Moreover, Gierczynski fails to recognize the existence of a positive political and scientific project in the "Apology" (elaborated in the latter part of that chapter) and does not sufficiently acknowledge the distinction between Montaigne's putative skepticism and the doctrines of the classical Skeptics. Finally, even though Gierczynski highlights the antireligious thrust of Montaigne's argument, I do not believe that he adequately traces or analyzes the essayist's reasoning in the "Apology" in other respects; hence he is insufficiently appreciative of the rhetorical character of Montaigne's account of the capacities of animals and does not pay enough attention to the critical section of the chapter which describes the skeptical character of classical philosophy as a whole. Despite these flaws, Gierczynski's analysis (along with Craig Brush's *Montaigne and Bayle,* from a different point of view) remains the most systematic treatment of the "Apology" to have come to my attention. My interpretation largely accords with the conclusions of Armaingaud and Gierzcynski regarding Montaigne's religious thought but is somewhat closer to Armaingaud's analysis, inasmuch as he stressed the political implications of Montaigne's attack on Christianity. But I hope to demonstrate that Montaigne's political project was more far-reaching than Armaingaud realized, and that it involved not only a rejection of Christian theology but a transformation in the nature of philosophy, and of the relation of philosophy to the political community.

Sebond and His Book

As numerous commentators have noted, Montaigne often masks his boldest arguments with chapter titles of the most innocuous appearance.[6] This practice is exemplified in the "Apology for Raymond Sebond." At the outset, Montaigne purports to be undertaking an "apology" or defense of the fifteenth-century theologian's book *Natural Theology, or Book of God's Creatures,* which he had previously translated, against its critics. Yet Sebond and his book are barely mentioned beyond the first few pages. Montaigne instead uses his putative defense of Sebond's work, in which the author endeavored to support the essential tenets of the Christian faith by reference to our natural reason, to undertake his own systematic examination concerning the grounds and limits of human belief and knowledge. Not only does Montaigne set aside the task of defending Sebond, he directly contradicts a number of that author's arguments, including his central assumption that the truth of Christianity is susceptible of rational proof.

Modern commentators have interpreted Montaigne's relation to Sebond in diverse ways.[7] Sainte-Beuve (who was followed in this regard by Armaingaud, Gide, and Gierczynski, among others) read in the "Apology" a perfidious betrayal of Sebond and Christianity, barely concealed under a mask of piety.[8] A number of more recent scholars, beginning with the

[6]For example, II, iii, "A Custom of the Isle of Cea" (on suicide); III, vi, "Of Coaches" (criticizing European imperialism); III, xi, "Of Cripples" (on trials for witchcraft).

[7]For brief summaries of the major views, see Zeitlin, *Essays of Montaigne,* 2:487–94; Marcel Gutwirth, "Montaigne pour et contre Sebond," *Revue des Sciences Humaines* 34, no. 134 (1969): 177–9.

[8]Charles Sainte-Beuve, *Port-Royal,* ed. Leroy, 3 vols. (Paris, 1961), III, iii, 1:855–7.

Dutch cleric Herman Janssen, have attempted to defend Montaigne's piety by viewing the "Apology" as an expression of "fideism," a doctrine characterized as "typical of [Montaigne's] whole age," which holds that the truths of Christianity can be grasped only by faith, without necessarily implying any doubt about their validity.[9] They attribute Montaigne's failure to defend Sebond persuasively to the essayist's self-professed ignorance of theology (417 [321]),[10] his "forgetting" his original project,[11] or his moving on to other topics after making "the best apology he could honestly make" for Sebond in response to a friend's request.[12]

None of these hypotheses accounts for the title Montaigne gave this chapter. Why should he describe an inquiry in which Sebond plays so small an explicit role as an "Apology" for Sebond? Sainte-Beuve's interpretation is certainly compatible with the explanation that Montaigne chose to conceal the boldness of his argument with an inoffensive label.[13] But this is not sufficient by itself. Montaigne has indicated that the titles of his chapters give at least an oblique hint of their contents (III, ix, 973 [761]). Thus, beyond his caution, we need to discern why he chose this particular title, with a view to understanding the significance of Sebond for Montaigne's own argument.

The term *apology* brings to mind the most famous "apology" (literally, "defense"), the one given by Socrates at his trial.[14] It was a defense not

---

[9]Boase, *Fortunes of Montaigne*, p. xv; Janssen, *Montaigne fidéiste*, p. 78 and passim; Brush, *Montaigne and Bayle*, pp. 44–6 and passim.

[10]See Janssen, *Montaigne fidéiste*, pp. 41–5, 60, 62, 66, and passim; but cf. Gierczynski, "Le Fidéisme apparent de Montaigne," pp. 143–4, regarding the speciousness of Montaigne's pretended theological naïveté. Another critic, Grace Norton, explains that "Montaigne was no logician" and consequently "was not perturbed by the immense assumptions with which Sebond starts, or by the colossal leaps his argument makes in reaching his conclusions." Montaigne's recognition of the "heartfelt piety" of Sebond's book inspired him, she hypothesizes, "with a piety that made him its apologist." Although Montaigne's point of view gradually diverged from Sebond's, it is not surprising that he never revised his initial praise of the book, since "it can easily be believed that he never cared to review his conclusions—all the more because they took no formal or formulated shape to him." Thus Montaigne remained unaware that the central argument of his "Apology" "is fatal to Sebond's work" (Norton, in Ives, *Essays*, 3:1787–9).

[11]Villey, *Les Sources*, 2:183.

[12]Frame, ed., *Complete Works*, p. 319; cf. Frame, "Did Montaigne Betray Sebond?"; Zeitlin, *Essays of Montaigne*, 2:511.

[13]Zeitlin, *Essays of Montaigne*, 2:514–15, suggests such an explanation, as does Joseph Coppin, whom he cites.

[14]To preserve this resemblance I have followed the practice of most English translators of the *Essays* by rendering the word *apologie* as "apology" rather than "defense." In "Did Montaigne Betray Sebond?" Frame notes the similarity in form and intent of Montaigne's "Apology" to Henry Estienne's *Apologie pour Herodote,* published fourteen years before the *Essays.* Despite the title of Estienne's book, Frame notes, "Herodotus is mentioned just eight times," and his purported defense "is a mere pretext for a critique of the religion of the author's contemporaries" (p. 321). Although it is plausible that Montaigne modeled his "Apology" on Estienne's, this possibility is not incompatible with the hypothesis that he also had in mind, and intended his readers to recall, the much more famous *Apology of Socrates.* The significance of Montaigne's use of the term *apologie* is further suggested by the fact that he titles his chapter on Seneca and Plutarch (II, xxxii) a "Défense," not an "Apologie."

simply of himself but of his way of life. The *Essays* as a whole, we have seen, serves as Montaigne's own "apology," his "ironic and mocking confession" before unnamed accusers. But he has singled out the largest chapter of his book ostensibly to provide an "apology" for another author, a somewhat popular writer in his time, but surely not a thinker of the rank of Socrates (or, I believe, of Montaigne himself).[15]

A connection between Montaigne's "apology" for Sebond and Socrates' self-defense is further suggested by the opening remarks of the chapter, which concern the value of knowledge, including its relation to government, virtue, and happiness—the central themes of Socrates' speech at his trial. Montaigne begins by acknowledging that "in truth, knowledge is a great and very useful quality," observing that "those who despise it give evidence enough of their stupidity." Yet he disagrees with the "extreme" valuation placed on knowledge by those who identify it as "the sovereign good" and attribute to it the "power to make us wise and content," curiously citing the obscure Stoic philosopher Herillus, rather than Socrates, as a source of this opinion. As for the (Socratic) view "that knowledge is the mother of all virtue, and that all vice is produced by ignorance," Montaigne remarks, "If that is true, it is subject to a long interpretation" (415 [319]).[16]

The essayist goes on to distinguish his attitude toward learning from that of his father, who, "inflamed with that new ardor with which King Francis I embraced letters and brought them into credit, sought with diligence and expense the acquaintance of learned men," revering them all the more "as he was less qualified to judge them," since he had "no knowledge of letters."[17] Montaigne, while esteeming the learned, does not "adore" them (415 [319]).

Montaigne identifies his unlearned father as the cause of his own initial concern with Sebond. Sebond's book, he explains, had been presented and recommended to his father by Pierre Bunel, "a man of great *reputation* for learning in his time" (415 [319]).[18] Subsequently, the elder Montaigne,

---

[15]On Sebond's popularity, see pp. 416–17 [320] of the "Apology"; Zeitlin, *Essays of Montaigne*, 2:483; and Joseph Coppin, *Montaigne, traducteur de Raymond Sebon* (Lille, 1925), pp. 17–23, 31–4. Despite the appearance of a number of editions of Sebond's book in both complete and abridged forms between 1484 and 1566 (including a French translation that antedated Montaigne's), Montaigne remarks that Sebond's "name [was] little known" (417 [320]), a judgment evidently confirmed by the report of a learned contemporary, Etienne Pasquier, that "Sebond was unknown to us" before the publication of the "Apology" (Pasquier, *Choix de lettres*, ed. D. Thickett [Geneva, 1956], p. 44). No independent documentation has been discovered of either of the "objections" against which Montaigne purportedly set out to defend Sebond (Eva Marcu, "Les Dédicaces de Montaigne et 'l'Inconnue' de 'l'Apologie,'" *BSAM*, 3d ser., no. 27 [1963]: 40).

[16]Cf. Plato, *Apology*, 25c–26a. Note that Socrates would hardly have denied the need for such a "long interpretation."

[17]On the influx of men of learning from Italy under Francis I, see Busson, *Les Sources du rationalisme*, pp. 148–62.

[18]On Bunel, an early French disciple of the Paduan school, see ibid., pp. 57–8, 77–80, 96–105; also the article on Bunel in Pierre Bayle's *Historical and Critical Dictionary*, which

having come across the book "by chance," "some days before his death, . . . under a pile of other *abandoned papers* . . . commanded" his son to translate it into French (416 [320]).[19] Because there was no particular style in the book requiring reproduction, Montaigne found his task an easy one—so easy, in fact, that he was able to complete his translation of Sebond's lengthy tome in time for his father to pass a favorable judgment on it (and order its publication) within the "days" before his death (416 [320])![20]

It is unfortunate that most commentators, while noting that Montaigne must have underestimated the time he took to translate the *Natural Theology,* have been so humorless as to take this whole account as if it were seriously meant.[21] His entire description of how he came upon the book serves to indicate in a barely subtle manner the slight opinion he has of its merit. He alludes to its especial popularity with "the ladies," whose unfitness for judging theological matters he has already remarked (I, lvi, 307, 310 [233, 235]). Only at one point does Montaigne appear to concur in Bunel's judgment. The essayist praises him for having foreseen that the "malady" of Protestantism "would easily decline into an execrable atheism," from which fact Bunel deduced that books like Sebond's were needed to uphold orthodox belief. But Montaigne does not say that Sebond's book is likely to achieve that result, let alone that he would have chosen to translate it if not for his father's "command" (416 [320]). Moreover, the very horror Montaigne appears to express, in agreement with Bunel, at the

---

praises Bunel's learning and conduct. Whatever Montaigne's true opinion of Bunel, his explicit commendation is surely fainter than Bayle's subsequent one.

[19]The "compulsory" character of Montaigne's original concern with Sebond again reminds us of the circumstances governing Socrates' speech at his trial. See Plato, *Apology,* 18e–19a.

[20]By claiming that Sebond's book, which was actually in Latin, was written in "a Spanish scrambled up with Latin endings" (415–16 [319]), Montaigne further deprecates its style. On the irregularity of Sebond's Latin, see Coppin, *Montaigne, traducteur,* pp. 31–2.

[21]An extreme example is Norton, who asserts (in Ives, ed., *Essays,* 3:1786) that "the book was so warmly approved by his father that he begged Michel to translate it." See also Coppin, *Montaigne, traducteur,* pp. 25–8. Coppin points out that the dedication to the translation implies that Montaigne must have worked on it, contrary to his claim, for at least six months, since the dedication was dated June 18, 1568, but refers to the work of translation as having been imposed on him "last year." Similarly, he notes that Adrianus Turnebus, whom Montaigne reports having consulted about Sebond's work (417 [320–21]), died in 1565. And he questions how Montaigne's father (who the essayist says avoided imposing any "constraint" in his education—I, xxvi, 174 [129]) could have "commanded" his son to translate Sebond, since the younger Montaigne was then in his thirties, especially given the latter's professed disposition to "flee command, obligation, constraint" (II, xvii, 633 [493]; Coppin, *Montaigne, traducteur,* pp. 36–7). Yet Coppin refuses to disbelieve the essential sincerity of Montaigne's apologetic intention (pp. 141–2). Zeitlin, *Essays of Montaigne,* 2:511, does note the "slighting manner" in which Montaigne refers to Sebond's book; Brush comments that "Montaigne seems to be disassociating himself as much as possible from the translation," and observes that his estimate of the *Natural Theology* "is quite guarded" (*Montaigne and Bayle,* pp. 66–7). Gutwirth views Montaigne's approach to Sebond as the embodiment of an Oedipal conflict with his father ("Montaigne pour et contre Sebond," pp. 184–6). But Gierczynski, in "Le 'Que sais-je?' de Montaigne," pp. 39–40, straightforwardly charges that the entire introduction to Sebond in the "Apology" is filled with "artifice and falsity," "irony and contempt."

dangers of allowing "the vulgar" to judge and doubt received opinions, is so at variance with remarks he makes elsewhere in the *Essays* as to call its sincerity into question, as will be noted subsequently.[22]

More is at stake in the consideration of Sebond's argument, however, than one might think from Montaigne's deprecating account of him. "So firm and felicitous" does the essayist find Sebond's attempt "by human and natural reasons, to establish and verify against the atheists all the articles of the Christian religion" that he does "not think that it is possible to do better in that argument" or even that anyone "has equaled him" (417 [320]).[23] Montaigne reports having heard, in fact, that Sebond's argument was "some quintessence drawn from St. Thomas Aquinas," whose mind "was alone capable of such ideas [*imaginations*]" (417 [321]). Montaigne thus hints that in purportedly treating of the obscure Sebond, he will really be addressing the Thomistic attempt to reconcile the teachings of Christianity with the findings of natural reason. Herein, I believe, lies the true significance of Montaigne's "apology" for Sebond. Though the figure of Sebond is

---

[22]Considering that Bunel himself had been expelled from Toulouse "on suspicion of Lutheranism" (Zeitlin, *Essays of Montaigne*, 2:484), one is inclined to doubt Montaigne's representation of his aim in transmitting Sebond's book. Later, Bunel was in turn denounced in print by Calvin. In view of the Paduan-influenced Bunel's questioning intellect, Busson (*Les Sources du rationalisme*, pp. 104–5) judges it to be "hardly probable that . . . he found in Sebond's reasonings the bases of a more solid faith." Consider also Montaigne's account of Bunel's private motive in presenting the book to his father—"he hoped that with very little help he could make his profit of it" (416 [319])—in light of the suggestion, in "Of Pedantry," that the poor quality of French learning is due to the fact that "our study . . . has almost no other goal than profit" (I, xxv, 140 [103–4]).

Sebond himself had been censured by the ecclesiastical authorities for exaggerating the power of human reason; the *Natural Theology* was placed on the Index from 1558 or 1559 until 1564, and its prologue (which Montaigne toned down in his translation) remained on the prohibited list thereafter (see Zeitlin, *Essays of Montaigne*, 2:481; Frame, "Did Montaigne Betray Sebond?" pp. 316–18; idem, *Montaigne's Discovery of Man*, pp. 32–3).

Both Floyd Gray and Zbigniew Gierczynski have pointed out a striking parallelism between several aspects of Montaigne's introduction to Sebond in the "Apology"—including his account of his father's having come across it by chance in a pile of papers, as well as the belief he attributes to Bunel that it would be an antidote to atheism—and Henry Estienne's introduction to his Latin translation of the *Hypotyposes* (*Outlines of Pyrrhonism*), by the Greek Skeptic Sextus Empiricus, published in 1562. Given the significant role that Sextus' doctrine will play in the "Apology" and the fact that Montaigne is known to have employed Estienne's translation; given the similarity in title, noted previously, between the "Apology" and another work by Estienne; and given Montaigne's admitted habit of making unacknowledged borrowings from others' works, it is odd that Gray should judge this parallelism to be "undoubtedly coincidental" (Gray, "Montaigne's Pyrrhonism," in Raymond La Charité, ed., *O Un Amy!* [Lexington, Ky., 1977], pp. 121–2; Gierczynski, "Le Fidéisme apparent de Montaigne," pp. 150n, 159n). Rather, it would appear that Estienne provided the rhetorical model from which Montaigne borrowed in introducing, as I shall argue, the Trojan horse of skepticism into the city of the faithful.

[23]In this passage Montaigne emphasizes and even exaggerates the claims Sebond made on behalf of reason, whereas in his translation of the *Natural Theology* he had softened the author's most rationalistic remarks, which had earned the church's censure (see Coppin, *Montaigne, traducteur*, pp. 67–70; Janssen, *Montaigne fidéiste*, pp. 32–7).

quickly dropped from consideration,[24] the great body of thought that he symbolizes remains an object, in fact the chief focus, of Montaigne's concern.[25] The two criticisms of Sebond's book to which Montaigne's "Apology" is purportedly an answer are not limited in relevance, as we shall see, to Sebond. Rather, as Montaigne interprets them, they constitute a challenge to *any* attempt (of which Thomism is perhaps the most notable example) to support the truth of the Christian religion by reason; to any endeavor to demonstrate the existence, let alone the will, of God; and perhaps to any enterprise aimed at uncovering the true nature of the universe. By remarking that it is not possible for anyone to surpass Sebond in rationally demonstrating the truth of Christianity, Montaigne indicates that the criticisms he will suggest of Sebond's position are meant to apply, ipso facto, against the arguments of far more renowned theologians.

Socrates was compelled in his "Apology" to try to demonstrate the compatibility of philosophy with the piety demanded by the city. Aquinas sought to establish more specifically the harmony of philosophy with the tenets of the Christian faith. Both Christian theology and classical philosophy, as embodied in the Thomistic synthesis, are again "on trial" in Montaigne's "Apology."[26] By incorporating his ostensible defense of this body of thought in an "apology" for someone else, Montaigne disassociates himself from it. But by attributing that thought to the obscure Sebond rather than the revered Saint Thomas, Montaigne gains a much freer hand to suggest its weaknesses. To the extent that the criticisms he will state of "Sebond's" argument are left unrefuted by him, he will actually have revealed the need for a revision of fundamental principles that were long regarded as authoritative in the Christian world, and perhaps in post-Socratic Western thought generally.

Reply to the First Objection: The All-Too-Human Roots of Faith

The first objection against which Montaigne purports to defend Sebond's book is that it is harmful to Christianity to attempt to support it "by human

[24]This is not to deny the frequent occurrence of implicit allusions to Sebond's arguments in the "Apology" (as detailed by Coppin, *Montaigne, traducteur,* passim); but as Guizot notes, Sebond's thought is everywhere "deformed" and its sense twisted in these allusions (Guizot, *Montaigne,* p. 116). I shall point out some of the passages where this occurs.

[25]But why, then, should Montaigne have originally undertaken to translate the *Natural Theology?* The only answer I can suggest is that at the time he did the translation, Montaigne may already have been planning to write the *Essays* (if he had not actually begun to do so), and that he hoped by means of the translation to buttress his reputation as a defender of the faith, while preparing a hook from which to suspend his own future theological reflections.

[26]The existence of two classes of critics against whom Montaigne will purport to defend Sebond's argument is reminiscent of the two sets of accusers against whom Socrates defended himself in Plato's account of his trial.

reasons," because Christian belief "is conceived only through faith and through a particular inspiration of divine grace" (417 [321]). This argument corresponds to the "fideistic" position that numerous commentators attribute to Montaigne himself.[27] Since those who advance it seem to be motivated by "a certain pious zeal," Montaigne proposes to respond to them with "mildness and respect." He readily agrees with these critics, in fact, that human intelligence alone is not sufficient to grasp the "lofty" truths of Christianity. If it were, then the great minds of pagan antiquity would surely have realized those truths. Consequently, "it is quite necessary" that God "lend us his help, by an extraordinary and privileged favor," for faith to be conceived and lodged in us. "It is faith alone that embraces vividly and certainly the high mysteries of our religion." Although it is "a most fine and laudable enterprise to accommodate to the service of our faith the natural and human tools that God has given us," it must be "always with the reservation of not thinking that it is on us that [faith] depends, or that our efforts and arguments can attain a knowledge so supernatural and divine." If faith "does not enter into us by an extraordinary infusion; if it enters there . . . by human means, it is not there in its dignity or in its splendor" (417–18 [321]).

Orthodox readers could hardly find fault with Montaigne's assertion of the necessity of a divinely infused faith. Abruptly, however, he now challenges the assumption that Christians have ever received such an infusion and suggests rather that it is *only* by "human means" that they hold to their faith at all. If that faith had a divine source, it could not be so easily shaken as it is by "human accidents," such as "the love of novelty, the constraint of princes, the good fortune of one party, the rash and fortuitous change of our opinions." "We ought to be ashamed," in fact, that whereas "in human sects, there never was a partisan, whatever difficult and strange thing his doctrine maintained, who did not to some extent conform his conduct and his life to it," the faith of Christians is marked only by their speech. In

---

[27]The term *fideism*, it should be noted, is a late-eighteenth-century coinage, and one may question whether intellectual historians who apply this concept to the sixteenth century display proper caution. The chief source of the supposed fideism of the Renaissance was the teaching of Pietro Pompanozzi and other Averroists of the Paduan school, whose piety was— to say the least—highly suspect (Boase, *Fortunes of Montaigne*, p. xvi; Busson, *Les Sources du rationalisme*, pp. 40, 54–6, 97). Although it is claimed that fideism was subsequently adopted by sincere Christian thinkers as a means of defending their faith against philosophic onslaught, we cannot take for granted, in dealing with writers of that time, that the "inconsistency" that characterizes their works was "far more often" the reflection of a sincere attempt to reconcile opposed beliefs to which they were deeply attached than of "the intention of escaping disagreeable consequences" (Boase, *Fortunes of Montaigne*, p. xvi). Speaking of the somewhat analogous "double-truth" theory, Ernest Fortin remarks that "it is nearly certain that no one in the Middle Ages subscribed to such follies" (*Dissidence et philosophie*, p. 166). In his study of Montaigne's influence (p. 375), Boase fails to locate "a truly logical fideist" before Pascal. But although the sincerity of Pascal's piety is indubitable, it is not evident that he himself renounces reason to the extent the "fideist" position requires.

morality, which the essayist asserts is the only objective test of a religion's truth ("all other signs," such as "penitence" and "martyrs," being "common to all" faiths), he claims that Christians fall far short of Moslems and pagans. After recounting two anecdotes (one of them borrowed from Boccaccio) attesting to the "dissoluteness" of the Christian "prelates and people" in times past, Montaigne reflects that "some make the world believe that they believe what they do not believe. The others, in much greater number, make themselves believe it, unable to penetrate what it is to believe" (418–19 [321–2]).

The context of this remark invites us to identify the two classes of false believers, respectively, with the Christian "prelates and people" just mentioned; but Montaigne does not limit the application of his observation to the past. In conformity with his remark, later in the *Essays*, that it is easy to feign piety so long as one does not "conform his morals and life to it" (III, ii, 791 [617]), he proceeds to emphasize how widely that quality is counterfeited in the religious wars of his time. Only a handful of the combatants are motivated by pure religious zeal, or even by genuine loyalty to their prince or country. The changeability of each party's beliefs makes it doubtful that there is any substantive difference of opinion between them; rather than serving religion, both sides subordinate it to their private interests and passions. Hence, instead of extirpating vices, as it was made to do, Christianity "covers, nourishes, and incites them." The shamelessness with which Christians defy God's will demonstrates that, far from holding to Him by faith, they give even less credence to His promise of "immortal glory" than they do to other "histor[ies]" (419–21 [323–4]).

This condemnation of Christian practice, read by itself, might reasonably be interpreted as a pious exhortation to Christians to improve their conduct and thereby demonstrate the reality of their faith.[28] But Montaigne immediately relates several ancient stories about pagan religion that suggest an entirely different point. The philosopher Antisthenes, he reports, when told by a priest of the "eternal and perfect blessings" promised by the Orphic religion to its followers after death, responded, "Why, then, do you not die yourself?" Diogenes asked a priest of another sect who had described "the blessings of the other world" that would be attained by the members of his order, "Do you want me to believe that Agesilaus and Epaminondas, such great men, will be miserable, and that you, who are but a calf, will be blessed because you are a priest?" (421–2 [324]). Montaigne leaves it to the reader to ask these same questions of those who speak for Christianity. (Recall his remark, a few pages earlier, on the excellence of the great pagan souls who, according to Christian doctrine, are cut off from salvation—417 [321]).

---

[28]See, e.g., Strowski, *Montaigne*, pp. 158–63; Janssen, *Montaigne fidéiste*, pp. 45–9.

Resuming his emphasis on the weakness with which Christians adhere to their faith, Montaigne observes that "if we accorded the same authority" to that religion's "great promises of eternal beatitude" as we do to "a philosophic discourse, we would not hold death in such horror as we do." Whereas Christians merely "say" that they "would be dissolved . . . and be with Jesus Christ," the "power of Plato's discourse on the soul" actually "impelled some of his disciples to death, to enjoy more promptly the hopes he gave them." Hence Montaigne concludes "that we receive our religion only in our own way and with our own hands, and not otherwise than as other religions are received." Christianity, like other religions, is believed, not because of its uniquely manifest truth, but on account of custom, regard for "its antiquity or the authority of the men who have maintained it," or fear of its threats and (apparently lukewarm) hope of what it promises. Its foundation, in sum, is purely conventional: "We are Christians by the same title that we are Perigordians or Germans" (422 [324–5]).[29]

Montaigne proceeds to cite the opinion of Plato that few people are "so firm in their atheism that a pressing danger," or "old age or illnesses," will not restore their faith.[30] In fact, because of the unsalutary effect that the fear of "hell and future punishments" has on our souls, the Greek philosopher "forbids in his laws" the teaching that the gods can harm man, "except for his greater good and for medicinal effect."[31] Montaigne remarks that it "is not the role of a true Christian" to owe his belief to such fears, but he has just pointed out the key role that the fear of future punishments plays in inducing what passes for Christian belief. To mitigate such fears might, by his own account, give rise to an unvarnished atheism. While professing, indeed, to find atheism "unnatural and monstrous," Montaigne qualifies his condemnation by distinguishing between the superficial atheism of weak minds, which are quickly altered when faced with danger, and "a doctrine seriously digested"—as if it is inconstancy, not impiety, that he finds truly objectionable (422–3 [325]).[32]

Montaigne attributes to "the error of paganism, and ignorance of our sacred truth," the opinion of "that great soul Plato (but great with human

[29]Exhibiting the lengths to which some interpreters will go to defend Montaigne's piety, Marcel Conche takes this sentence to signify that the essayist truly regarded himself as a Christian, since he was indisputably a Perigordian ("La Méthode pyrrhonienne de Montaigne," BSAM, 5th ser., nos. 10–11 [1974]: 61–2). Conche neglects to consider whether belief in certain *doctrines* is not a more essential criterion of membership in a religion (especially the Christian one) than of membership in a geographic or ethnic group (which, by necessity, is ultimately conventional). Montaigne himself, in the immediate sequel to the quoted remark, denies that genuine Christian faith can derive from purely "human" or conventional sources.

[30]See Plato, *Laws,* 888c; *Republic,* 330d–e.

[31]See Plato, *Republic,* 379a–380c; but cf. *Laws,* 904c–905b.

[32]Contrast his seemingly unqualified concurrence in Bunel's reported judgment of atheism *as such* as "execrable" (416 [320]); cf. I, lvi, 304 [230] on the superiority of consistent dissoluteness to hypocritical piety.

greatness only) . . . that children and old men happen to be more suscepti-ble to religion, as if it were born and drew its credit from our imbecility."[33] This opinion, however, does not appear far removed from Montaigne's own observation in an earlier chapter of the link between "facility of belief" and "ignorance"; later in the "Apology" he will remark that ignorance is greatly "recommended to us by our religion as a quality suitable to belief and obedience" (I, xxvii, 177 [132]; II, xii, 423-4, 467-8 [325-6, 360]). In the sequel the essayist avers that "the knot that should tie our judgment and our will" and "bind our soul to our creator" should be derived not from varying human "reasons and passions" but from the uniformity of divine authority (424 [326]). But the diversity and inconstancy of Christian belief make it incredible, by his account, that Christianity has received such divine sanction. And throughout the *Essays* Montaigne indicates that he himself is unwilling to let his judgment be "bound" by any preconception or external authority (see, e.g., II, xvii, 641-2 [499])—further suggesting his own skepticism about the claims of Christianity or any other religious doctrine to represent the word of God.

Having all but forgotten Sebond during the foregoing pages, Montaigne now suggests that the Spanish theologian's enterprise has merit, inasmuch as it might assist us to gain insight into God's nature. He holds it incredible "that this whole machine [the world] should not have on it some marks imprinted by the hand of [its] great architect," or that worldly things should not embody "some picture . . . that somewhat represents" their maker. Only our "imbecility" prevents us from recognizing those marks. In seem-ing justification of Sebond's undertaking, he adds that "it would be doing wrong to the divine goodness if the universe did not consent to our belief" (424 [326]). Once again, however, it is instructive to compare the essayist's present argument with remarks he makes elsewhere. According to the argument of such chapters as I, xxvii ("It Is Folly to Measure the True and False by Our Own Capacity") and I, xxxii ("We Should Meddle Soberly with Judging Divine Ordinances"), as well as much of the "Apology," the assumption that the universe must conform to human beliefs is foolishly presumptuous. Thus we are driven to suspect that the "imbecility" that prevents us from deducing the nature of the world's architect from the study of perceptible phenomena is the same imbecility that Montaigne has just suggested (via his citation of Plato) lies at the root of religious credulity. By interpreting the world in accordance with received doctrines he had set out to defend, Sebond himself would appear to have obscured the reality of things, as do those historians Montaigne has condemned for wrongfully "assuming the authority to regulate our belief by their own" rather than

---

[33]Elsewhere, Montaigne will recommend "human" greatness as the *only* kind to which we should aspire; see, in reference to Plato, III, xiii, 1096 [856].

literally describing things as they appear.[34] To observe and study the world in a genuinely empirical manner, on the other hand, as Montaigne professes to do, might lead to conclusions quite at variance with the doctrines Sebond sought to uphold. This possibility is suggested by a quotation Montaigne inserts from the Roman astrological poet Manilius, which the essayist suggested (in the editions published during his lifetime) might have served as an appropriate "preface" (presumably, to his translation of the *Natural Theology*). The quoted verses express the un-Christian belief that God has a physical being that is displayed in the revolution of the heavens (424 [326]). By observing the movement of the physical universe, one may learn, as Manilius suggests, to understand its "laws"—without, however, becoming a more confirmed Christian as a result.[35] Perhaps Sebond's pious critics were well advised.

Montaigne concludes his response to those critics by saying that "faith" gives Sebond's arguments their strength. This devout conclusion will persuade only those readers who choose to ignore the import of Montaigne's preceding argument, reading it as a "sermon," the findings of which are irrelevant to his broader theme.[36] The essayist has just demonstrated, in fact, how little reason there is to think that Sebond's faith, or that of any Christian, is well grounded. "Human means," he has contended, cannot suffice to justify Christian belief. But that belief, he has found, rests solely on "human" grounds, since it lacks the moral force and intellectual certitude that would accompany a faith "infused" in us by God. Christianity, like other religions, owes its existence to human hopes and fears, customs and accidents. What reason is there, then, to think that Sebond's "faith" is anything other than "imagination" (the term by which Montaigne referred to the theologian's thoughts at pp. 416–17 [320–21])? In saying that Sebond's arguments derive their strength from faith, Montaigne really implies that they are likely to persuade only those readers who already accept the theologian's conclusions "on faith." So convincing does Montaigne now represent Sebond's book to be that, he reports, he can recall *one* man who was "brought back" to religion by it! If stripped of their "orna-

[34]Coppin, *Montaigne, traducteur,* p. 171, notes that although Sebond, like Montaigne, recommends the study of "experience," in his book he has already reduced such experience to fit a particular theory and system, in accordance with his apologetic aim—a procedure quite different from Montaigne's. Contrast *Essais,* III, xiii, 1056 [826], where Montaigne describes his book as a most useful source of experience regarding health because he presents it "pure, not at all corrupted and altered by art and by opinion." Cf. also I, xxxi, 202–3 [152].
[35]Cf. Gierczynski, "Le 'Que sais-je?' de Montaigne," p. 46; also, Bacon, *The Advancement of Learning,* bk. II, in *Works,* ed. Spedding, 3:349–50: "For as all works do shew forth the power and skill of the workman, and not his image; so it is of the works of God, which do shew the omnipotency and wisdom of the maker, but not his image. . . . Wherefore . . . out of the contemplation of nature, or ground of human knowledges, to induce any verity or persuasion concerning the points of faith, is in my judgment not safe."
[36]The term *sermon* is Janssen's: *Montaigne fidéiste,* p. 49.

ment" of faith and taken as "purely human fancies," he adds, Sebond's arguments "will still be found as solid and as firm as any others *of the same type* that may be opposed to them" (425 [327]). Faint praise!

The Wretchedness of the Natural Human Condition

Having defended Sebond most equivocally against the charge that it is harmful to Christianity to support it by "human reasons," Montaigne now turns to the second objection: that Sebond's arguments, in particular, "are weak and unfit to prove what he wants." Those who make this criticism, less pious and hence more "dangerous" than the first objectors, think, according to Montaigne, "that they are given an easy game when set at liberty to combat our religion by purely human arms, which they would not dare to attack in its majesty, full of authority and command." One might expect Montaigne to respond to them by giving some account of Sebond's arguments and showing that they are stronger than the objectors think. Instead, he appears to react with vehemence, as if it were improper to challenge *any* arguments that are used to uphold Christianity. Identifying the second group of critics as atheists—as if the validity of Christianity depended entirely on Sebond's case for it—Montaigne proposes to treat these critics "more roughly" than he did the first ones, so as to "beat down" their madness.[37] The means he will employ is "to crush and trample underfoot human arrogance and pride; to make them feel the inanity, the vanity, and nothingness of man; to wrest from their hands the puny arms of their reason; to make them bow their heads and bite the ground beneath the authority and reverence of the divine majesty" (425–6 [327]). Strong words, coming from a man who decries the habit of being overly sensitive to others' speech, and paradoxical ones, in view of Montaigne's avowal that *his* reason "is not trained to bend and bow" and his resistance to the "tyranny" of those who "beat you down with . . . authority" in discussions, obstructing the honest pursuit of truth.[38] Contrary to the argument he makes throughout the *Essays* in favor of freedom of inquiry and discussion (e.g., I, xxiii, 116 [84–5]; I, xxvi, 149–50 [110]), Montaigne appears to side here with those who demand utter submission to the claims of God's putative

---

[37]Grace Norton observes that "Montaigne seems to confuse somewhat those who declare the arguments of Sebond to be weak, with those who feel at liberty to fight against Christianity with merely human weapons" (Ives, ed., *Essays*, 3:1789). I believe the "confusion" is intentional.

[38]I, xxvi, 149 [110]; II, xii, 483–4 [373]; II, xviii, 650 [506]; II, xxxvii, 766 [597–8]; III, viii, 909–10, 913 [710–11, 714]. Cf. also III, xi, 1009 [789]: "He who establishes his argument by boasting and command shows that it is weak in reason"; those who dispute in this way give "much the advantage" to "their contradictors" in "the effectual consequence" of their argument. Cf. Gierczynski, "Le Fidéisme apparent de Montaigne," p. 151.

earthly representatives, regarding any questioning of the established religion as both foolish and vicious.

Saint Augustine, Montaigne goes on to remark, rightly reproaches the atheists for their "injustice" in holding "those parts of our belief to be false which our reason fails to establish." Augustine refutes them by citing "certain known and indubitable experiences into which man confesses he has no insight" in order to demonstrate that there are "plenty of things whose nature and causes our reason cannot possibly establish" (426 [320]).[39] But Augustine's response, the essayist implies, is insufficient: "We must do more." Rather than "sifting out rare examples" as Augustine did "to convict our reason of weakness," Montaigne proposes to demonstrate the weakness of human reason in dealing with any and all subjects. By revealing the puniness of "man alone, without outside assistance, armed solely with his arms, and deprived of divine grace and knowledge," he will ostensibly cut the ground out from under Sebond's critics, who rely on reason to disprove the theologian's arguments (426–7 [328–9]). And he will do so without actually having to defend those arguments!

Sebond's critics could hardly object, however, to the rules of debate that Montaigne adopts. By assuming—merely hypothetically, it seems—that human beings are "deprived of divine grace and knowledge," he grants those critics precisely the liberty they seek "to combat our religion by purely human arms," without having to fear its "authority" (that is, the danger of persecution). In the light of the argument that has preceded it, moreover, Montaigne's proposal to consider man "armed solely with his arms" turns out to be no hypothesis at all, but rather *the essayist's true view of the human condition.*[40] Whatever faith we possess, Montaigne has argued, comes from ourselves rather than from God. There is no reason to think that Christianity, or any other religion, embodies divine wisdom. Nor does the human situation exhibit divine governance. Rather than being a reason for blame to humanity, our ignorance and weakness constitute evidence, in

[39]The reference is to *The City of God*, XXI, chs. 5–6, where Augustine alludes to a variety of extraordinary natural occurrences reported in books. Zeitlin, who trusts the sincerity of Montaigne's approbation of Augustine's argument, comments: "Montaigne's acceptance of the 'indubitable experiences' and his commendation of the 'careful and subtle inquisition' of St. Augustine do not in this instance approve themselves to the modern critical mind" (Zeitlin, *Essays of Montaigne*, 2:522).

[40]Gierczynski comments: "For a sincere believer such a disassociation [as Montaigne proposes] between the 'truly human' qualities and 'supra-human' ones has no meaning and cannot be admitted. In fact it hides a trap and leads towards a new conception of man" ("Le 'Que sais-je?' de Montaigne," p. 52). Cf. Montaigne's explicit recommendation at I, xxv, 137 [101], and III, xii, 1015–18 [794–6], that people rely on their own "arms" or means rather than "foreign" assistance; Machiavelli, *The Prince*, ch. 6, pp. 22–3, and ch. 13, p. 56, with Mansfield's introduction, p. xxii. See also I, lvi, 308 [234], where Montaigne describes his own thoughts as purely "human and my own," to be considered "separately" from any theological considerations—thus justifying his use of such terms as *fortune*, which had been censured by the Vatican.

theological terms, of God's meanness to those who are thought to be his children. Much, if not all, human error and even vice, Montaigne elsewhere suggests, can be attributed to the defects of our natural condition (I, xvi, 70 [48]; cf. I, iii, 18 [8]; I, xxi, 100–101 [72–3]). To remedy the defects of that condition, as we shall see, we have no choice but to rely on our own "arms." But before we can be taught to arm ourselves, we must be led to recognize our true condition—both in order to see the need for relying on our own resources and to know the capacity of those resources. It is Montaigne's project in the *Essays* to reveal us as we are, stripped of the "armor" of false opinion that obscures our situation. Crucial to that project is the critique of false *religious* opinions that the essayist will set forth in the center of the "Apology."

To challenge the fundamental tenets of Christian dogma was, of course, a highly dangerous undertaking in Montaigne's time. The means by which Montaigne secures the freedom to do so safely is to present his description of the human condition *as if* it were entirely hypothetical, abstracting from the "divine grace and knowledge" that all good Christians know have been granted them. But Montaigne's introduction to his treatment of the second objection to Sebond is in fact a straight-faced parody of (what the essayist sees as) the Christian hostility to reason (cf. 477–8 [368]). No sooner were Sebond's arguments challenged than Montaigne denounced the challengers, without pausing to consider their arguments. It is, he claims, "a great consolation" for a Christian to recognize the frailty of human reason (426 [328]). Only the reader who bears in mind that Montaigne has already cast into doubt the divine grace on which the Christian relies, and who recalls Montaigne's frequent expressions of his own radical independence of judgment, will see this pretense of piety for what it is: an ironic posture by which the author gains the right, not merely for Sebond's anonymous (and probably fictitious) critics but for himself, to combat the Christian religion with "purely human arms." All the remaining argument of the "Apology" ostensibly rests on the assumption that divine grace has been granted to humanity through the Christian faith, and hence that the truth of Christianity is unaffected by anything Montaigne says in his entirely "hypothetical" discussion.[41] But the prop of faith upon which the structure of Montaigne's argument supposedly rests was kicked away by him at the outset; the structure will stand on its own if it stands at all.[42]

[41] Cf. Rousseau's analogous claim that his antibiblical history of human development, in the *Second Discourse*, is merely hypothetical: *Discourse on the Origin and Foundations of Inequality Among Men*, in Roger D. Masters, ed., *The First and Second Discourses* (New York, 1964), p. 103; Marc F. Plattner, *Rousseau's State of Nature* (De Kalb, Ill., 1979), pp. 18–25; the parallel to Rousseau's methodology is noted by Fleuret, *Rousseau et Montaigne*, p. 58.

[42] This integral relation between Montaigne's responses to the first and second groups of Sebond's critics is overlooked by such interpreters as Richard H. Popkin, who dismisses the essayist's account of the human roots of Christian faith as a "digression" (*The History of Skepticism from Erasmus to Descartes* [New York, 1968], p. 46).

Our Natural Parity with the Beasts

Montaigne commences his portrayal of humanity "deprived of divine grace and knowledge" with a lengthy attack on the pride that makes us place ourselves at the head of the visible universe. What ground does man have, Montaigne asks, for believing that the heavens and the seas were created for his service?

> Is it possible to imagine anything so ridiculous as that this miserable and puny creature, who is not even mistress of herself, exposed to the attacks of all things, should call herself mistress and empress of the universe, the least part of which it is not in her power to know, much less to command?[43] And this privilege that he attributes to himself of being the only one in this great edifice who has the capacity to recognize its beauty and its parts, the only one who can give thanks for it to the architect and keep account of the receipts and expenses of the world: who has sealed him this privilege? (427 [329])

A few lines later, partly imitating the argument of an Academic critic of Epicurean theology in Cicero's dialogue *On the Nature of the Gods*, Montaigne eulogizes "the incorruptible life of the celestial bodies, their beauty, their grandeur, their continual motion by so exact a rule," as well as "the dominion and power" they exercise not only over our lives and fortunes "but over our very inclinations, our reasonings, our wills." Why then, he asks, do we therefore deny "soul, life, and reason" to the heavens? Continuing to paraphrase the Ciceronian character, he seems to deny the relevance of the argument "that we have seen in no other creature than man the exercise of a rational soul." "If what we have not seen does not exist, our knowledge is marvelously shrunk: 'How narrow are the limits of the mind!' " (429 [330]).[44]

It is helpful, in attempting to understand this curious passage, to refer to a chapter of Augustine's *City of God* to which Montaigne alluded just previously, when he proposed to surpass that theologian's refutation of the doubters. In that chapter Augustine cites a dilemma posed for his argument by his critics, who contend that if he is willing to believe in the "miraculous" events cited in the pagan histories and to use them as evidence of the limits of human reason, he ought to be equally willing to accept the pagan theology contained in those books.[45] By suggesting that the visible, heav-

---

[43]Norton (in Ives, ed., *Essays*, 3:1808) remarks "the bitterly ironic effect of this description of man as of the feminine gender, made possible in French by the fact that *creature* is feminine."

[44]For the original source of this quotation, as well as much of the argument quoted in this paragraph, see Cicero, *On the Nature of the Gods*, I.31. This work, from which Montaigne made some forty-five borrowings, was a prime text for sixteenth-century freethinkers (Busson, *Les Sources du rationalisme*, pp. 16–19).

[45]*City of God*, I.6.

enly bodies are ensouled, Montaigne—while purporting to uphold Augustine's position—has in effect sided with his pagan opponents, implying that Augustine's mode of argument, if sound, would serve to uphold pagan theology just as well as Christianity. (It was precisely in order to challenge his interlocutor's belief in gods that the Ciceronian character Montaigne quoted questioned the interlocutor's ground for denying divinity to the heavens.)[46]

There is no reason to suppose that Montaigne adheres any more seriously than his Ciceronian source to the belief that the heavenly bodies are ensouled. Neither Montaigne nor his source provides any positive argument to support that belief. Nor is the negative argument he borrows from that source (involving a manifestly fallacious analogy between denying rational soul to the stars, because no creatures other than human beings have been seen to possess such a soul, and denying existence to the sun because nothing like it has been seen) very persuasive (429 [330]). At most, therefore, Montaigne's eulogy of the heavens serves to suggest that the scope of the human mind and its knowledge may be more limited than most people realize: although we do not know that the heavenly bodies are ensouled, neither, it seems, can we know that they lack souls. But more important, by tacitly siding with the ancient mockers of religion, Montaigne gives us further reason to doubt the pious intent of his reply to Sebond's second group of critics. Not only does the foregoing argument constitute evidence of Montaigne's disagreement with Augustine, it runs in even more direct opposition to the position of Sebond himself. The essayist's challenge to the notions that the world was made for our benefit, and that we alone among created beings can appreciate its beauty and order, contradicts Sebond's claim that we have been granted these privileges by God.[47] Having purportedly set out to support Sebond's assertion of the greatness of our debt to God, Montaigne actually launches into a refutation of that claim: contrary to Sebond, he proceeds to describe man as "the most vulnerable and frail of creatures," who "sees himself lodged here, amid the mire and dung of the world, fastened to the worst, the deadest and most stagnant part of the universe, on the lowest story and the farthest removed from the celestial vault," but who nonetheless "goes planting himself in his imagination above the circle of the moon and bringing down the sky beneath his feet,"

---

[46]Cicero, On the Nature of the Gods, I.31. In City of God, V.1–2, Augustine challenges the belief that our fate is determined by the stars and in the same work, XIII.16, withholds assent from the doctrine that the heavenly bodies are ensouled.

[47]See La Théologie naturelle de Raymond Sebon, translated by Montaigne, in Armaingaud, ed., Oeuvres complètes de Michel de Montaigne, 9: chs. 96–8, 117–18; Zeitlin, Essays of Montaigne, 2:522. As Norton points out, "to [Montaigne's] ironical questioning, who has persuaded man that he is of such immense importance? the immediate, natural answer of the reader of Sebond would be: Sebond has at least done his best to prove that the whole creation is for the benefit of man" (in Ives, ed., Essays, 3:1789).

thus demonstrating the "presumption" that constitutes "our natural and original malady" (429 [330–31]).[48] It is ostensibly to combat this presumption that Montaigne now initiates a lengthy critique of our unfounded belief that we are set apart from, and above, other animals: a critique of Sebond's own doctrine.[49]

Since the faculty of rational speech constitutes the most obvious mark of our apparent superiority to the beasts, it is appropriate that Montaigne commences his argument by challenging the uniqueness of that faculty. Lacking knowledge of "the secret internal stirrings of the animals," he suggests, we have no ground for attributing "stupidity" to them. As for the "defect that hinders communication between them and us, why is it not just as much ours as theirs?" The beasts, moreover, do communicate with one another as adequately as human beings do—even, Montaigne argues, with members of other species. Aside from the ability possessed by some animals to communicate vocally, others do so by gestures, just as "our mutes" do. Indeed, in view of its universal intelligibility and utility, the language of gestures rather than words "must . . . be judged the one proper to human nature" (430–32 [331–2]). (In other words, even if the human faculty of speech constituted an advantage, it would be an artificial one, not a mark of our natural superiority or preordained eminence in the cosmos.)

Not only do we lack any natural superiority to the beasts in the capacity for communication, according to Montaigne's argument; the essayist goes on to suggest that "in most of their works" the beasts surpass us. Their capacity to provide for their needs, and even (in the case of the bees) to maintain a naturally regulated social order, suggests the presence of "reason and foresight" in them, rather than the "natural and servile inclination" to which we attribute their accomplishments (432–3 [332–3]).[50] And indeed, in attributing such natural guidance to them,

> without realizing it, we grant them a great advantage over us, making nature, with maternal tenderness, accompany and guide them as by the hand in all the actions and commodities of their life; while she abandons us to chance and fortune, and to seek by art the things necessary for our preservation, and denies us at the same time the power to attain, by any education and mental straining, the natural resourcefulness of the beasts; so that their brutish stupidity surpasses in all commodities all that our divine intelligence can do. (433 [333])

[48]Sayce, *Essays*, p. 79, cites this passage as evidence of Montaigne's belief in an "old-fashioned" cosmology, but it is unwise to infer from the essayist's rhetorical use of a traditional notion that he himself accepted it.

[49]See Sebond, *Natural Theology*, chs. 99, 102, 103.

[50]Here again the view Montaigne criticizes is one adopted by Sebond (ibid., chs. 82, 103).

"Truly, by this reckoning," Montaigne concludes, "we would have good reason to call [nature] a very unjust stepmother. But this is not so . . . nature has universally embraced all her creatures; and there is none that she has not amply furnished with all the means necessary to the preservation of its being." He decries the "vulgar complaints . . . that we are the only animal abandoned naked on the naked earth, tied, bound, having nothing with which to arm and cover ourselves," while nature has granted to "all other creatures" a variety of clothing and arms, of which Montaigne provides an extensive list, "according to the need of their being."[51] If Montaigne truly disbelieves these complaints, he surely goes out of his way to give evidence for them. But contrary to those who assert the helplessness of the natural human condition—among them Lucretius, whom Montaigne quotes at some length—"there is a greater equality and a more uniform relation in the regulation of the world." Our skin naturally provides as adequate a protection against the weather as the beasts' does, as one may judge from the nations who have gone without much clothing even in cold climates, and from the fact that "all the parts of the body we see fit to expose to the air are found fit to endure it." Like us, the beasts feel helpless at birth, while "the habit of eating . . . is in us, as in them, natural and untaught." The earth, on the whole, produces enough food to meet our needs without our having to labor; only "the excess and unruliness of our appetite" causes us to demand a more varied diet than nature provides, "outstripping all the inventions by which we seek to satisfy it."[52] We possess natural "arms" as serviceable as, or more so than, those with which most animals are pro-vided. In addition, the skill we possess to "fortify and cover the body by acquired means" may properly be termed a "natural" instinct comparable to those of the beasts. Finally, even speech of a sort is provided to us by nature, like the vocal "language" by which the beasts express their feel-ings (433–6 [333–5]). Montaigne does not accuse nature of injustice, but wishes to show that she treats us equally with the other animals, and thus combats the "fancy" by which we assign a superior position to ourselves:

> I have said all this to maintain this resemblance that there is to human things, and to bring us back and join us to the majority. We are neither above nor below the rest; all that is under heaven, says the sage [Ecclesiastes, 9:2], incurs one law and a similar fortune. . . . There is some difference, there are orders and degrees, but it is under the aspect of one and the same nature. . . . Man must be constrained and forced into line inside the barriers of this order. The

[51]The source of these complaints is the prologue to Book 7 of Pliny's *Natural History*, a widely cited source during the Renaissance (Busson, *Les Sources du rationalisme*, p. 24).
[52]Contrast Sebond (*Natural Theology*, ch. 82), who says that labor is not only a necessity but our purpose on earth, and Gen. 4:17–19.

miserable being is in no position really to step beyond; he is fettered and bound, he is subjected to the same obligation as the other creatures of his class, and in a very ordinary condition, without any real and essential prerogative or preeminence. That which he accords himself through opinion and fancy has neither body nor taste. (436–7 [336])

Let us pause here to reconsider the thrust of the preceding arguments. Montaigne's ostensible purpose, we recall, is to reveal the human need of divine grace by demonstrating the misery of the human condition without it. Hence he describes the guidance exercised over us by "nature" rather than by God, since the "fact" of divine guidance is not known without faith. It cannot be said, however, that Montaigne's description of the natural human condition reveals it to be one of unmitigated deprivation. Much of his argument, we have seen, purports to defend nature against the charge that she has been "unjust" toward us and has failed to provide adequately for our well-being.

Yet we are unlikely to find our natural condition, as Montaigne describes it, to be attractive.[53] With all the "advantages" nature grants us, to counterbalance those she has given to the beasts, we would still live like the rudest of savages: eating a simple diet of uncooked food, naked, unable to communicate with our fellows except by grunts and gestures. If our natural condition is no worse than that of other animals, this equality seems to constitute a sharing in penury rather than a cause for rejoicing: hence Montaigne's remark that the "weeping" that most of our fellow creatures practice along with us "long after their birth" is "a demeanor most appropriate to the helplessness that they feel."[54] Nor—despite Montaigne's claim that nature "provided us in plenty with all we needed"—does she do so "at all times" [or "in all weather" or "seasons"], for us or other animals (434–5 [334–5]). Hence it is not surprising that Montaigne calls human beings "miserable."[55]

In the foregoing discussion Montaigne appears to hold humanity itself to be primarily responsible for its misery. By arguing at the same time that we are "in no position" to step beyond the natural order, and that we "must be

[53]Cf. Montaigne's later account of "Androdus" (Androcles), who left the company of a lion "weary of this wild and brutish life," despite the beast's generous treatment of him (456–7 [350–51]).
[54]Cf. Augustine, The City of God, tr. Marcus Dods (New York, 1950), XXI.14, p. 785: "Our infancy, indeed, introducing us to this life not with laughter but with tears, seems unconsciously to predict the ills we are to encounter." For Augustine, only the "future happiness" we are to enjoy in another life can redeem us from the "heavy yoke" that the Bible assigns to "the sons of Adam."
[55]The facts alluded to in this paragraph refute Gierczynski's claim that in this section of the "Apology" Montaigne idealizes the natural environment of animal life as "a terrestrial paradise" ("Le 'Que sais-je?' de Montaigne," pp. 49–50). If anything, his argument to this point imitates what Busson terms the "pessimism" of Pliny (as well as Lucretius) (Busson, Les Sources du rationalisme, p. 25).

constrained and forced" inside its barriers, the essayist seems to mean that although our real condition is essentially similar to that of the other animals, the imaginative freedom of our mind, combined with our natural "presumption," causes us to overlook this fact and hence to seek to transcend the animal condition. Our imaginative freedom makes us dissatisfied with nature's provision and hence engenders "unruly" appetites that we cannot satisfy. As Montaigne remarks a few pages later, in imitation of Plutarch, nearly all human desires are "superfluous and artificial" ones "which ignorance of the good and a false opinion have insinuated into us," thus driving out the "natural and necessary" appetites, which are quite few (450 [346]).[56] Montaigne's remedy for this situation, it would appear, is to seek to "constrain" our imagination so as to make us content with the goods that suffice to satisfy other animals.

Yet there are several difficulties with this argument. In the first place, if presumption is, as Montaigne has asserted, our "natural and original malady"—that is, something innate—it is not clear why we should be held responsible for it. Elsewhere, we note, Montaigne attributes to *nature* our "error" of "always gaping after future things" rather than contenting ourselves with "present goods" (I, iii, 18 [8]). Moreover, in Book III he challenges the distinction between natural and nonnatural desires, holding that "no great desire can be imagined that is so strange and vicious that nature does not apply herself in it," and adjusting the concept of nature to include the desires implanted in us by habit (III, xiii, 1065 [833]; III, x, 987 [772]). In an early passage he suggests that human beings should not be blamed for faults that arise from the "imperfection and weakness" in which nature left them (I, xvi, 70 [48]). And later in the "Apology" itself, in an ostensible reply to Plato, he blames human vices on the "faulty condition" in which the gods brought mortals forth (500 [386]). Thus—leaving aside the issue of whether it is possible to constrain our already liberated imagination and desires so as to make us contented with the goods that nature supplies—it is questionable whether the distinction this policy presupposes between humanly and naturally caused desires is a meaningful one in Montaigne's view. At the very least, the distinction is in need of a clarification and elaboration that he has not yet supplied.

A related difficulty concerns the possible use of art as a means of ameliorating the wretchedness of our natural condition, and the relation of art to nature. Montaigne's argument thus far has been equivocal on the latter point. At first he distinguished between the "plenty" provided by nature and the less adequate provision resulting from "our artifice." He proceeded, however, to describe as *natural* the practice of "arm[ing] ourselves with wood and iron," and similarly attributed to "natural instinct" our capacity

[56]See Plutarch, *That the Beasts Use Reason*, 989b–c.

to protect and clothe the body "by acquired means"—in apparent contradiction to his suggestion, a few lines earlier, that it is natural for us to go naked. Montaigne vindicates the description of the human use of "acquired" arms as natural by observing that this practice (as well as, according to a subsequent passage, "most of the arts") is carried on by the beasts (435, 442 [335, 340]). But in so doing, he appears to have clouded, if not entirely obliterated, the distinction between art and nature. In light of these remarks, it appears to be no more meaningful to condemn human beings for supplementing or supplanting "nature's" provision with their own artifice than to blame them for exceeding the "natural" limits of desire.

Having pointed out these difficulties, I must postpone attempting to resolve them until a later point in my analysis of the "Apology," which I now resume. Following his refutation of the charge that nature has treated human beings unjustly, Montaigne reiterates his challenge to those who dismiss the beasts' abilities as due merely to instinct. "There is no apparent reason," he holds, "to judge that the beasts do by natural and obligatory instinct the same things that we do by our choice and cleverness. We must infer from like effects like faculties, and consequently confess that this same reason, this same way that we have of working, is also that of the animals." Moreover, it is "more honorable, and closer to divinity, to be guided and obliged to act lawfully [regléement] by a natural and inevitable condition, than to act lawfully by accidental and fortuitous liberty; and safer to leave the reins of our conduct to nature than to ourselves." Only our vain presumption leads us to prefer to attribute our abilities to ourselves rather than to nature (437 [337]). (In questioning the value of free will, we note, Montaigne is again contradicting Sebond, who describes this faculty as the greatest privilege that can be found in nature, and one by which God has raised us far above all other creatures.)[57]

Montaigne continues his attack on this presumption by elaborating at great length the evidence of the beasts' manifold capacities and qualities, with a view to further demonstrating their parity with the human species. The major points he makes are as follows:

1. The animals demonstrate a remarkable "natural sense," rivaling our vaunted "science and knowledge," in choosing a path to follow, and in "distinguish[ing] the things useful" for life and health; if this sense is due to the "tutelage of nature," it is in any case a "better reason," because surer, than ours (437–41 [337–9]).
2. Yet the animals are also capable of "being taught in our way"; witness the birds we teach to speak, dogs who learn tricks, dancing elephants,

[57]Sebond, *Natural Theology*, ch. 3 (in *Oeuvres complètes de Michel de Montaigne*, ed. Armaingaud, 9:10); ch. 62 (9:101); ch. 234 (10:110); ch. 235 (10:114).

and the like. Indeed, oxen have been taught to turn a water wheel exactly one hundred times, whereas "we are in our adolescence before we know how to count up to a hundred, and we have just discovered nations which have no knowledge of numbers" (441–5 [339–42]).

3. Our capacity to make animals serve us cannot be taken as a sign of superiority to them, since human beings also enslave one another, and indeed take better care of their animal servants than of their human ones. The beasts are in fact more noble than human beings, in that no animal ever enslaved itself to another one on account of a "lack of heart" (438–9 [337–8]).

4. The animals can teach as well as learn; Democritus even "proved that the beasts taught us most of the arts" (442 [340]).

5. Observing the "ablutions and purifications" practiced by the elephants, and their habit of raising their trunks, gazing toward the rising sun, and standing still "a long time in meditation and contemplation at certain hours of the day," we "can . . . say" that they have "some participation in religion." Nor does our failure to observe "any such sign in other animals" enable us to "prove that they are without religion" (446 [343–4]).[58]

6. The animals' ability to do things "far beyond our capacity" and even our imagination—the chameleon's change of color; the torpedo fish's capacity to numb its prey; birds' migration and their flight patterns, from which the ancients drew their most "certain" auguries—suggests the presence in them of many other "properties and powers of which no signs come through to us" (447–8 [344–5]).

7. The animals demonstrate justice, friendship, sympathy, fidelity, gratitude, magnanimity, repentance, and clemency, and surpass human beings in moderation (449–50, 454–9 [346, 350–53]).

8. Yet they also exhibit envy, avarice, debauchery, "unnatural affections between one species and another," trickery, and warfare (450–52 [346–8]).

9. The capacity on which we pride ourselves to conceive things incorporeally is shared by the beasts, as Montaigne judges from the twitching of animals during their sleep, which he attributes to their dreaming (460–61 [354–5]).

10. Although human beings may surpass some animals in bodily beauty, they are surpassed in it by many other species; indeed, considering the human creature's "blemishes, his natural subjection, and his imperfec-

[58]Cf. Brush, *Montaigne and Bayle*, p. 81, n. 1: Jacques Amyot, in the introduction to his translation of one of the Plutarch essays from which Montaigne borrows in this section of the "Apology," had criticized Plutarch for "fail[ing] to realize that the privilege man has over the beasts is his knowledge of God, not simply his reason." Far from agreeing with Amyot, Montaigne "implies the opposite when he speaks semi-seriously of the elephants' religion."

tions, . . . we had more reason than any other animal to cover ourselves" (462–3 [356–7]).[59]

However disposed readers may be to share Montaigne's apparent admiration for the wondrous faculties distributed among the various animal
species, they cannot avoid noting that much of the evidence on which the
essayist bases the claims just listed is quite unreliable, and many of his
conclusions are wildly exaggerated. The bulk of his animal stories are
derived from such ancient sources as Pliny, Herodotus, and, above all,
Plutarch. For the most part these authors did not claim to have witnessed
personally the phenomena they described; and in some cases—notably
Plutarch's—it is clear that they did not intend these descriptions to be taken
seriously. As Jacob Zeitlin points out, the Plutarchean source on which
Montaigne drew most extensively here, *Whether Land or Water Animals
Are Cleverer,* "is little more than an amusing *jeu d'esprit*" in which the
speakers compete "to 'tell a better one' " and make no distinction between
factual and legendary evidence; a second such dialogue, *That the Beasts
Use Reason,* is similarly humorous and factually unreliable.[60] The essayist's
own attribution of religion to the elephants on the basis of the behavior he
describes is, of course, wholly implausible. Equally unpersuasive is his
assertion that the "foresight" displayed by ants who gnaw off the ends of
grains of wheat to prevent them from sprouting "surpasses anything imagined by human prudence" (452 [347]).[61]

From such facts Zeitlin inferred that Montaigne had "deliberately and
consciously abandoned his critical sense in writing this section" of the
"Apology," "unscrupulously" using unreliable evidence to support his "thesis . . . which called for the humiliation of human reason."[62] If, however (as
I have argued), the piety underlying Montaigne's project in the "Apology" is

[59]Each of the last two points embodies another implicit criticism of Sebond's argument.
Regarding no. 9, see Sebond, *Natural Theology,* ch. 217; on no. 10, ibid., ch. 99. Whereas
Sebond praises man's upright posture, Montaigne (p. 463 [356]) claims that many other
animals share or surpass it. On this point, see, however, Hans Jonas, *The Phenomenon of Life*
(New York, 1966), p. 155n.; Erwin W. Straus, "The Upright Posture," in *Phenomenological
Psychology* (London, 1966), pp. 137–65.
[60]Zeitlin, *Essays of Montaigne,* 2:496–7. Given his awareness of the unreliability of this
evidence, it is curious that Gierczynski should claim that in this section of his argument,
Montaigne undertook to found his philosophic system on "the vastest possible experience"
rather than on the "uncertain" testimony of reason ("Le 'Que sais-je?' de Montaigne," p. 51).
Also surprising is Géralde Nakam's taking the apparent "anthropomorphism" of this section
seriously (*Les Essais,* p. 93).
[61]In Montaigne's apparent source (Plutarch, *Whether Land or Water Animals Are Cleverer,*
968a), this example is said only to surpass any other human conception of the *ants'* intelligence.
[62]Zeitlin, *Essays of Montaigne,* 2:497. Norton (in Ives, ed., *Essays,* 3:1790) excuses Montaigne's "illogical deductions" by explaining that "he is not to be blamed for not being wiser
than his age on the matters that he here treats of."

also highly suspect, there is reason to doubt that the purpose underlying the present section of his argument is simply to humiliate human reason. That purpose can be illuminated by consideration of two passages interspersed among the animal stories in which Montaigne explains what he is doing and draws certain broader inferences from those stories, as well as a third passage that concludes this section of the "Apology."

The first of these passages begins as follows:

> We admire more, and value more, foreign [estrange] things than ordinary ones; and but for that I should not have spent my time on this long register. For, in my opinion, if anyone studies closely what we see ordinarily of the animals that live among us, there is material there for him to find facts just as wonderful as those that we go collecting in remote countries and centuries. It is one and the same nature that rolls its course. Anyone who could sufficiently have judged its present state could infer from this with certainty both all the future and all the past. (445 [342–3])

The initial two sentences of this quotation seem at first reading to be saying merely that familiar domestic animals possess abilities as remarkable as those of the beasts described in the ancient and exotic testimonies on which Montaigne has drawn. But the last two sentences (which did not appear in the editions of the *Essays* published during Montaigne's lifetime) indicate a broader concern, as is shown by their sequel, a passage in which Montaigne remarks how human beings wrongly denigrate foreign *peoples* whose customs differ from their own. "Everything that seems strange to us," he concludes, "we condemn, and that which we do not understand: as happens in the judgment we make of the beasts" (446 [343]). Our deprecation of our fellows' ways reflects the same bias that distorts our judgment of the beasts' capacities. Both sorts of misjudgment would be corrected, Montaigne suggests, if we recognized "one and the same nature" operating in all things.

Montaigne's denial of the need to search far afield for evidence of the beasts' capacities echoes his previous remark that "there is no need to go sifting out rare examples," as Saint Augustine did, to demonstrate the weakness of our reason. But the last two sentences of the passage embody a different understanding of nature, and humanity's place in it, from that of Sebond as well as Augustine. Sebond, in conformity with the doctrine of the Christian Aristotelians, views the human being as the most elevated creature in a natural order that is both hierarchical and teleological. Montaigne's remarks, on the contrary, suggest a deterministic and egalitarian conception of nature in which no creature, or class of human beings, stands higher, or closer to God, than any other. (Consider, in this regard, his attribution of religion to the elephants, and of the ability to conceive incorporeal things to other species: human beings, it is implied, are in no better position to conceive religious truth than other animals are.[63] Similarly, the attribution of "properties and powers" to the beasts of which we are unaware recalls the Skeptical argument, which Montaigne will later state explicitly, that we have no ground for assuming that our senses convey an accurate picture of the world to us.)

In this light it seems that the "long register" to which Montaigne refers in the first sentence quoted above may be not merely his account of the beasts' abilities in this section of the "Apology" but the *Essays* as a whole—which he later terms "a register of the essays of my life" (III, xiii, 1056 [826]). Similarly, "the animals that live among us" may be taken as a reference to humanity. In other words, the mass of "foreign" matter with which Montaigne fills the *Essays*—such as (in this instance) his account of the beasts— is an indirect means of causing his readers to examine themselves more closely than they customarily do. As he has just indicated, human beings are inclined to condemn all things that are foreign or strange to them, on account of their bias in favor of themselves; yet they also possess (as he remarked on the previous page) a countervailing disposition to admire foreign things in comparison with "ordinary" ones, because of their tendency to become jaded by anything to which they are accustomed (cf. II, xv, 597 [464–5]). By appealing to people's taste for hearing about "foreign" things—including his own life and attitudes, which are "foreign" to his readers—Montaigne may counteract the bias in favor of themselves and their kind which distorts their judgment, and thereby moderate their conduct toward one another. In sum, the real purpose of Montaigne's discourse on the beasts may be to combat people's misjudgment of *one another*, rather than their failure to appreciate the merits of other members of the animal kingdom. To see ourselves as insignificant units in an infinitely vast and ever-moving cosmos, rather than as elevated beings atop a fixed, meaningful, and purposeful order, would, he suggests, be conducive to greater tolerance in the way we treat each other. Such a mode of self-understanding might serve, in particular, to undermine the religious intolerance exemplified in France's civil wars, to which Montaigne alluded earlier—an intolerance rooted in the belief held by partisans on each side that they have a particular insight into God's will.

A similar purpose is suggested by the next passage with which Montaigne interrupts his account of the beasts. He begins this passage by questioning whether we should cite the example of warfare, "the greatest and most pompous of human actions," as evidence of our superiority to the beasts, since it seems rather to attest to "our imbecility and imperfection." Some animals do, indeed, fight wars, but the ridiculousness of such spectacles serves only to highlight the "absurdity and vanity" of human battles. It is

---

[63]Cf. Gierczynski, "Le 'Que sais-je?' de Montaigne," pp. 60–61.

remarkable, Montaigne observes, "by what inane causes" wars are incited among men. Warfare, he suggests, is the product of a foolish pride, by which man forgets what a "feeble, calamitous, and miserable" being he is, and aspires "to threaten heaven and earth" (452–3 [347–9]). In opposition to such pride, the essayist remarks,

> the souls of emperors and cobblers are cast in the same mold. Considering the importance of the actions of princes and their weightiness, we persuade ourselves that they are produced by some causes equally weighty and important. We are wrong; they are led to and fro in their movements by the same springs as we are in ours. The same reason that makes us bicker with a neighbor creates a war between princes; the same reason that makes us whip a lackey, when it happens in a king makes him ruin a province. Their will is as frivolous as ours, but their power is greater. Like appetites move a mite and an elephant. (454 [350])

Here again the assertion of parity between human beings and beasts serves to challenge the beliefs that set us at odds with members of our own species. Montaigne's use of the physical term *springs [ressors]* reminds us of the deterministic view of nature suggested by the passage discussed previously. By recognizing the similarity or identity of the causes that impel human and animal conduct, we discover at the same time the parity of the motives that direct the actions of both "great" and ordinary people. To recognize the kinship between emperors and cobblers, like that between human beings and ants, is to see the absurdity of "five hundred thousand men" risking their lives for their emperor's "enterprises" (453 [348]).

It is from this perspective that we may understand the import of Montaigne's seeming imputation of reason, intelligence, and virtue to the beasts. Nowhere, we note, does Montaigne make this imputation unambiguously. Rather, he asserts that our outward observation of the beasts' activities makes it *plausible* to attribute them to conscious intelligence and questions the soundness of the judgment that dismisses such activities as the product of mere instinct, while attributing our own doings to reason and free choice. The essayist places the burden of proof on those who would deny that the similitude of "effects" we observe between our conduct and the beasts' reflects a similitude of causes. At the same time, as we have seen, he argues that if the distinction between human and animal motivation really held, the beasts would be better off than we are, as they would be guided more surely to their well-being (433, 437, 440 [333, 336–7, 339]).

The animal stories Montaigne has retold surely do not demonstrate the presence of active reason or free choice, let alone virtue and vice, among the animals. The obvious fallacy in his attribution of such qualities to them is that his examples provide no insight into the intentions, if any, underlying the conduct he describes. "[A]ll . . . judgments founded on external appearances," he later remarks, "are marvelously uncertain and doubtful" (II, xvi, 609 [474]). To argue that we must attribute conscious intention to animal behavior that outwardly resembles human actions merely because we cannot positively disprove the existence of such an intention is no more persuasive than the analogous argument by which Montaigne previously purported to demonstrate that the heavenly bodies are ensouled.[64]

That the beasts are governed by reason and free will is not, I think, the real point of Montaigne's argument concerning their parity with humanity. Rather, I suggest, the aim of that argument is to call into question the assumption that *human* behavior is dictated by such causes. Just as the interpretation of the elephant behavior Montaigne described as a religious ceremony depended upon an unjustified anthropomorphism, he implies that the attribution of human deeds to such noble causes as reason, justice, and piety may be based on a false model of humanity. This is not to deny that a subjective piety may be present in human religious ceremonies, for instance, which is entirely lacking among the beasts. But as the essayist's analysis of the French religious wars earlier in the "Apology" suggested, to identify piety as the real *cause* of many, if not all, of the actions taken in its name may be an act of gross hypocrisy or self-deception, or both. Similarly, although human intelligence may be far more developed than that of the beasts, it does not follow that reason governs or motivates most people's actions, any more than it does those of the beasts.

Throughout the *Essays* Montaigne emphasizes how easily we are deceived about the motives underlying human conduct. "Most of our actions," he observes, "are only mask and make-up" (I, xxxviii, 229 [172]). Thus "a sound understanding" must "not judge us simply by our actions from without; one must probe within and see by what springs motion is impelled" (II, i, 321 [244]). Those actions that wear virtue's appearance "do not for all that have its essence; for profit, glory, fear, habit, and other such external causes lead us to perform them" (I, xxxvii, 226 [170]). Not only is it dangerous to trust what people say about themselves, or to judge their real feelings by the outward appearance of their behavior; each of us is liable to be deceived about our own motivation, unless we study ourselves closely, as few people do (548 [425]; II, xviii, 649 [505]; III, xiii, 1051–2 [822–3]). One primary error in judging a person is to attribute to grand or noble intentions what is actually the result of trivial or base motives and transient passions (II, ii, 328–9 [250]; III, v, 821 [641]). This error is particularly common when the individual being judged holds an eminent position (I, xlii, 252 [191]; III, viii, 913–14 [714]).

The teaching embodied in these passages squares with the observations

---

[64]Cf. Montaigne's remark, apropos of an anthropomorphic interpretation of ants' behavior, that "we are meddling foolishly by expressing our opinion" in such cases (447 [344]).

Montaigne has made about humanity while comparing us to the animals in the "Apology": people's vain tendency to overvalue themselves; the need for Montaigne to examine "foreign" materials in order to teach his readers the same lessons that the wise can acquire from looking into themselves; the parity of the "springs" impelling the conduct of emperors and cobblers; the triviality of the real causes giving rise to wars. The intention underlying that comparison is summarized in a particularly pithy manner by a remark near the end of this section of the argument, just after Montaigne's suggestion that human beings, far from being (as they think) the most beautiful of animals, are in reality the ugliest. "To cool love," Montaigne observes, "one need only see freely what one loves" (464 [357]). This observation may be taken to refer not merely to the physical appearance of the human body but to the rank of humanity within the natural order. By emphasizing our parity with the beasts, Montaigne has apparently sought to "cool" the excessive self-love that leads people to overestimate their cosmic importance—both as a species and as individuals.

That Montaigne intends his denial of human "beauty" to be taken metaphorically is confirmed by its sequel, where he professes to limit the bearing of the denial by asserting that "this discourse touches only our common sort, and is not so sacrilegious as to mean to comprehend those divine, supernatural, and extraordinary beauties that are sometimes seen shining among us like stars under a corporeal and terrestrial veil" (464 [357]). Without such a disclaimer, in other words, the preceding rebuff to our claims of transcending the animal condition could easily be interpreted as a rejection of the possibility of a link between humanity and God, such as Montaigne had purportedly set out to defend. We have already had substantial reason to doubt the piety of Montaigne's purpose, however, and consequently the sincerity of this disclaimer.[65] And the conclusion of Montaigne's comparison between human beings and beasts now points in an entirely different direction:

> Moreover, the very share of the favors of nature that we concede to the animals, by our confession, is quite advantageous to them. We attribute to ourselves imaginary and fanciful goods, goods future and absent, for which human capacity cannot answer, or goods which we attribute falsely to ourselves through the license of our opinion, like reason, knowledge, and honor; and to them for their share we leave essential, tangible, and palpable goods: peace, repose, security, innocence, and health; health, I say, the finest and richest present that nature can give us. (464 [357])

[65]Zeitlin (*Essays of Montaigne*, 2:493) observes that Montaigne inserts a "formula of submission, whenever he is about to utter some particularly dangerous opinion." The present passage is a prime instance—although the formula in this instance follows rather than precedes the "dangerous" statement. See, on Montaigne's critique of human claims to spiritual "beauty," Chapter Seven, below.

The original, ostensible aim of revealing the nullity of the human condition, as Montaigne has just finished doing, was to demonstrate our need for divine grace. Rather than concluding his comparison of human beings and the beasts by restating this need, however, the essayist instead now seems to recommend to us the goods that the beasts enjoy, and which our pride wrongly leads us to scorn. He goes on to assert that the philosophers themselves have recognized that bodily health is a greater good than the wisdom of which they boast, borrowing from Plutarch a report of a Stoic saying to that effect.[66] He somewhat obfuscates the point he is making by drawing from the same source a remark placing a higher valuation on the human bodily form than on wisdom, and using this remark as the starting point for a final condemnation of the "foolish pride and stubbornness" we display in setting ourselves above other animals. Yet he seems to exempt the philosophers themselves from the charge of vanity by adding that "they knew that those qualities about which we make so much ado are but vain fancy." Be this as it may, Montaigne's final example of "vanity" in this passage is that of believing that God must resemble us: a belief reminiscent not of philosophy but of the biblical teaching that God made us in his own image (464–5 [357–8]).

Montaigne's comparison of human beings to the beasts thus culminates in the lament that by foolishly believing ourselves to be elevated above other animals and claiming to possess such "future and absent" goods as reason, knowledge, and honor that we vainly think are appropriate to our lofty status, we deprive ourselves of the essential bodily goods of which we stand in need: above all, physical health. Yet Montaigne surely has not demonstrated that as a result of their claim of reason and knowledge, human beings are *less* healthy than other species. More generally, his entire portrait of the human condition, including the rather fantastic claim that our rational capacities are no greater than the beasts', has thus far been deficient inasmuch as no serious consideration has been given to the possible use of human art or knowledge as a way of ameliorating the miseries of our natural state. As previously noted, Montaigne hedges his argument in a confusing way regarding the relation between art and nature. The nature of this relation, and the reason for its previous obfuscation, will gradually become clearer in the remainder of the "Apology."

[66]See Plutarch, *Of Common Conceptions Concerning the Stoics*, 1064a. In the dialogue these arguments are cited as an objection to Stoicism in particular, whereas Montaigne presents them as if they represented a consensus of philosophers in general.

CHAPTER THREE

The "Apology," II: Critique of Religion and Philosophy

The Uselessness of Philosophy

From the outset of the next section of the "Apology," Montaigne silently drops the thesis that human beings' mental faculties in no way surpass those of our fellow creatures. That argument derived a superficial plausibility from the fact that Montaigne compared our capacities with those of other animals solely in terms of the extent to which their possessors were enabled to achieve tangible, earthly goods. Since human life is commonly characterized by such evils as war, poverty, and disease, he implied, there is no ground for assuming that any superiority we enjoy in respect to reason constitutes evidence of nature's special benevolence. The real issue, therefore, which Montaigne will now address, is not whether we possess a greater intellectual capacity than our fellow creatures—an undeniable fact—but whether, and (if so) how, that capacity may be used to ameliorate the wretchedness of the "natural" state that we share with the beasts.

Initially, Montaigne links his evaluation of the utility of reason to the problem of our unlimited desires and cares, which seem to be a necessary consequence of our intellectual or imaginative freedom. After a long list of human passions, evils, and defects of judgment, the essayist remarks that "we have strangely overpaid for this fine reason in which we glory, and this capacity to judge and know, if we have bought it at the price of this infinite number of passions to which we are incessantly a prey." Nor does it appear, he argues, that those who have cultivated their reason enjoy any resultant benefit in the form of freedom from pain or illness, or heightened enjoyment of sensual pleasure and health. It is furthermore doubtful that knowledge has made them more virtuous. Artisans and plowmen are commonly "wiser and happier than rectors of the university" (465–6 [358–9]).

Contrary to those who place great value on learning, Montaigne cites the cranes and ants, who "conduct themselves in a very orderly manner without erudition," and with few "offices, rules, and laws of living." We would be better off if, like the animals, we had our duty "prescribed" to us, rather than being left to determine it by our own choice and judgment. "Otherwise, judging from the imbecility and infinite variety of our reasons and opinions, we would finally forge duties for ourselves that would set us to eating one another, as Epicurus says" (467 [359]).[1]

Montaigne's questioning of the value of reason and his recommendation of simple obedience accord, he suggests, with the teachings of Christianity. "From obeying and yielding arise all other virtue, as from presumption all sin. . . . The plague of man is the opinion of knowledge. That is why ignorance is so greatly recommended by our religion as a quality proper to belief and obedience" (467–8 [359–60]).[2] But human nature, the essayist observes, resists the divine commandment of obedience. Rather than accepting the lowness of our condition, we presumptuously view ourselves as divine or even supradivine, precisely on account of our supposed wisdom. Thus Montaigne (echoing his initial profession of ire at the second group of Sebond's critics) must "tread this stupid vanity underfoot, and shake . . . the ridiculous foundations on which these false opinions are built," showing man the meagerness of his resources in order, ostensibly, to demonstrate "what he owes to his master" (468–9 [361]). The essayist mocks the philosophers' pretense of having overcome the misfortunes of earthly existence. The firmness with which the Stoics faced pain and illness was only a posture: they felt those evils no less than the ignorant multitude did. Knowledge shows itself inferior to ignorance as a means of "blunting and lessening the keenness of the misfortunes which pursue us." Active minds add to the "real," bodily ills to which all of us are subject, others that stem from "the sole power of the imagination." Philosophy itself has found the sovereign good to lie "in the recognition of the weakness of our judgment," and "sends us back to the examples of an athlete and a muleteer, in whom one ordinarily sees much less feeling of death, pain, and other discomforts, and more firmness than knowledge ever supplied" (470–71 [361–2]). The

[1]As Zeitlin (*Essays of Montaigne*, 2:529) points out, in the apparent source for Montaigne's reference (Plutarch, *Against Colotes*, 30), Colotes (not Epicurus) says that if established laws were taken away, human beings would live as beasts, ready to eat one another. For Colotes the danger lies not in the excessive duties we impose on ourselves but in the *insufficient* legal regulation of human conduct. Montaigne quotes Colotes' remark correctly (while still attributing it to Epicurus) at p. 541 [419] of the "Apology."
[2]Sebond holds that "all our ills came to us from disobedience" (*Natural Theology*, ch. 239 [10:122]), and that we must believe in God's word "simply, without proof, without argument, and solely because he has said it" (ch. 214 [10:38]).

Brazilians are carefree and happy, living "in admirable simplicity and ignorance, without letters, without law, without king, without any religion
whatsoever." The "subtlest wisdom" and "supreme virtue," on the other
hand, are dangerously close to "madness." To be "healthy" and "disci-
plined," Montaigne concludes, we would have to be wrapped in "darkness,
idleness, and dullness. We must become beastlike, and be blinded in order
to be guided" (471–2 [363]). To be made less sensitive to woes entails, it is
true,

> the incommodity of making us also consequently less keen and eager for the
> enjoyment of goods and pleasures; . . . but the misery of our condition makes
> us have less to enjoy than to avoid, and makes the most extreme pleasure not
> touch us so much as a slight pain. . . . Our well being is but the privation of ill-
> being. . . . To be free from evil is to have the most good for which man can
> hope. (472 [363–4])[3]

Montaigne's conclusion is tentative: "if simplicity leads us on the way to
having no pain," it is beneficial. But here his argument turns: "I do not at all
praise that insensibility that is neither possible nor desirable. . . . [I]f I am
[sick], I want to know that I am." These reflections then lead to a conclusion
seemingly opposed to the tenor of the preceding argument. "In truth, he
who would eradicate the knowledge of evil would at the same time extirpate the knowledge of pleasure, and in sum would annihilate man" (473
[364]).[4]

Following this shift, Montaigne resumes his criticism of the pursuit of
wisdom, but with a different thrust. Though reiterating the charge that the
philosophers have found no better way of dealing with human ills than to
imitate the attitude of the ignorant, he no longer claims that ignorance is an
adequate remedy. "Philosophy," he remarks, "should put arms in my hand
to fight fortune," rather than relying on such "ridiculous," "cowardly
dodges" as the (Epicurean) recommendation that we "take consolation for
present ills from the remembrance of past joys." Even if it were in our power
to do so, ignorance is still, as Seneca remarked, "a weak remedy for evils."
The sages' precepts lead us "to borrow frivolous delusions from the vulgar"
and to seek to live under a "hallucination," rather than showing us how to

---

[3]Montaigne's emphasis on the greater importance of avoiding evils than possessing goods
anticipates the "bourgeois" psychology of Hobbes and Locke: cf. Hobbes, *Leviathan*, ch. 13,
first paragraph; Locke, *An Essay Concerning Human Understanding*, ed. Peter H. Nidditch
(Oxford, 1979), II, xxi, secs. 31–4, with *Essais*, I, liii, and the discussion of the uncertainty of
the "sovereign good" at pp. 560–62 [434–5] of the "Apology."

[4]I have followed Frame's translation of *mal* variously as "ill," "pain," and "evil" in the
above quotations. Cf. ch. 299 of Sebond's *Natural Theology*, which justifies pain as a means by
which our souls are purified—not as an inevitable accompaniment of our capacity of experiencing pleasure.

better our real condition. And in advising us, finally, to kill ourselves if we cannot endure life, philosophy confesses its "impotence" (474–6 [365–6]).

Having denounced such impotence, however, Montaigne seems to have no alternative remedy to offer, but instead resumes his own eulogy of ignorance. He cites Saint Paul: "The simple and the ignorant raise themselves and take possession of heaven; and we, with all our learning, plunge ourselves into the infernal abyss." Paul is one of many who have denounced learning, among them Mohammed, two Roman emperors, and "the great Lycurgus," founder of "that divine Lacedaemonian government, so grand, so admirable, and so long flourishing in virtue and in well being, without any teaching or practice of letters." But the evil nature of curiosity is particularly well known to Christians, whose religion teaches that "the urge to increase in wisdom and knowledge was the first downfall of the human race" (477–8 [367–8]).

Repeating his denunciation of human presumption, Montaigne appears to lend support to the Christian teaching. Paradoxically, however, he buttresses his argument against curiosity by citing Socrates' belief that the greatest wisdom consists in awareness of one's ignorance (478 [368]). Socrates himself surely did not infer from this belief that the *quest* for wisdom is evil; quite the contrary.[5] Although Montaigne quotes Plato, moreover, as holding it impious to "inquire too curiously into God and the world, and the first causes of things" (479 [369]), his apparent source actually suggests the contrary view.[6]

By siding with Socrates and Plato, Montaigne indicates that the real presumption he is condemning is not curiosity but its opposite: the unwarranted presumption that we already know the truth. Far from justifying what Montaigne represents as the Christian hostility to the quest for knowledge, the Socratic view is juxtaposed with the Christian understanding of God in such a way as to make the latter appear the essence of presumption. "Superstition follows pride," Montaigne warns; but the particular superstition he has in mind becomes explicit only in the sequel. "To Christians it is an occasion for belief to encounter something incredible. It is the more according to reason as it is contrary to human reason." Christianity attributes to God qualities that the human mind cannot properly conceive. In ascribing power, truth, justice, fear, anger, love, wisdom, and virtue to the Deity, human beings presumptuously impose categories derived from human experience on a being who cannot be so bound (478–9 [368–9]).

As is his practice, Montaigne draws what looks like a pious conclusion from the preceding critique of Christian theology:

---

[5]See Plato, *Apology,* 23a–b, 37e–38a.
[6]See Plato, *Laws,* 821a ff. On Montaigne's misuse of a comparable Platonic quotation elsewhere in the "Apology," see Isidore Silver, "Man Humbled and Exalted: Montaigne's 'Apologie de Raimond Sebond' and a Passage of Plato's *Timaeus,*" in La Charité, ed., *O Un Amy!,* pp. 280–82.

The participation which we have in the knowledge of the truth, whatever it may be, has not been acquired by our own powers. God has taught us that well enough by the witnesses he has chosen from among the vulgar people, simple and ignorant, to instruct us in his admirable secrets: our faith is not of our own acquiring, it is a pure present of another's liberality. It is not by reasoning or by our understanding that we have received our religion, it is by authority and by foreign command. The weakness of our judgment helps us more in this than our strength, and our blindness more than our clear-sightedness. (479–80 [369])

Here again Montaigne superficially expresses a fideistic position but in fact says something quite different. Let us note, first, that the quotation does not even grant the truth of Christianity but speaks only of the origin of "whatever" participation in truth the adherents of "our faith" possess. Furthermore, the argument that preceded this passage did not merely deny that religious truth is knowable by reason but challenged the possibility of comprehending by *any* means the qualities that Christianity attributes to God. The superstition that follows pride is in fact exemplified, Montaigne implies, in those who believe most firmly what reason finds "incredible."[7] In responding to the first group of Sebond's critics, Montaigne indeed lent support to the notion that "our religion" is received "by authority and by foreign command"; but that authority and command belonged to human sovereigns and prelates, not God. And he has provided no evidence that he himself is more disposed to believe in doctrines insofar as their foundation lies in human "blindness" and "weakness of judgment."

Considering that Montaigne's denunciation of human presumption thus appears to apply at least as much against religion as against philosophy, we seem at this point to have reached a dead end. Both philosophy and religion evidently offer no better advice to alleviate our misery than to emulate the thoughtlessness and pure obedience that result from ignorance. But Montaigne has given no reason to think that the conventional authorities whom the multitude obey are themselves guided by wisdom, or that the "insensibility" of the ignorant is a desirable condition. Has he then, as Sainte-Beuve thought, led us into the farthest reaches of a labyrinth and extinguished any light by which we might find our way out?[8]

A reconsideration of the preceding arguments will correct that impression. Montaigne's condemnation of philosophy is not so thoroughgoing as it first appears. He does, indeed, question the practical value of philosophy as hitherto understood; but far from signifying his rejection of the philosophic enterprise, that questioning will serve as a propaedeutic to the

---

[7]As noted by Gierczynski, "Le 'Que sais-je?' de Montaigne," p. 64. Gierczynski also notes (p. 61) the fact that one of the reasons Montaigne gave a few pages earlier for the supposed happiness of the primitive Brazilians was the absence of religion among them.

[8]*Port-Royal*, III, iii, 1:861.

reconstruction of philosophy with a view to radically improving our piti-able condition.

Montaigne has raised two major nontheological objections to the utility of philosophy. In the first place, he mocks the sages for urging us to cultivate an attitude of Stoical endurance, or to find our happiness in memories, as a means of mitigating the evils that beset us. By such counsels philosophy merely tries to blind us to our real condition, thereby confessing its in-feriority to sheer ignorance. Second, Montaigne suggests that philosophy fails to promote the moral virtue that decent civil society requires and undermines the habit of obedience that is essential to civic order.

An exposition of Montaigne's final verdict on the latter issue must be postponed until his political teaching is examined thematically. We may note here, however, that his denial that human beings should endeavor to raise themselves above the beasts has already rendered questionable the value of moral virtue as traditionally understood. And as I have observed, Montaigne's recommendation of obedience in thought seems to conflict rather sharply with his frequent professions of his own intellectual free-dom.[9]

Montaigne has laid much more stress in the foregoing pages on the impotence or uselessness of philosophy as a means of easing the human condition. Even on this point, however, his argument is somewhat ambig-uous. Having questioned whether human reason is worth the price we have paid for it, he once more quotes a Ciceronian character to the effect that "it is a plague to many and salutary only to a few" (466 [358]).[10] Whether or not Montaigne agrees that humanity as a whole would have been better off without reason, he does not deny that it may be of benefit to some individ-uals. He proceeds to raise a number of seemingly rhetorical questions that imply that philosophy has not freed its adherents from pain, disease, and the fear of death. After asking whether it makes shame and poverty less troublesome, however, he inserts a quotation from Juvenal which sug-gests an affirmative answer (466 [359]). Also, when Montaigne questions whether Varro and Aristotle "were reconciled to death for knowing that some nations rejoice in it, and with cuckoldry for knowing that wives are held in common in some region" (466 [358]), the reasonably attentive reader will recall that the author himself has mentioned such facts earlier in the *Essays* (I, xiv, 50–54 [33–6]; I, xxiii, 113 [83]). We may presume that, if Montaigne is not talking nonsense, he finds such knowledge to have some

[9]Note that after his initial assertion of the incompatibility of wisdom and moral merit, Montaigne chooses to "leave this discourse, which would lead me *farther than I would wish to follow*" (467 [359]); when he resumes this point, with the words "as I was starting to say a while ago" (477 [367]), his argument soon turns into the condemnation of the *anti*philosophic attitude characteristic of Christianity which was discussed above.

[10]The source is *On the Nature of the Gods*, III.27.

value. Indeed he does, for he asserts that the variety of "humors, sects, judgments, opinions, laws, and customs teach us to judge sanely of our own, and teach our judgment to recognize its own imperfection and natural weakness, which is no small lesson" (I, xxvi, 157 [116]).[11] Although he remarks, moreover, that he would prefer to resemble many a plowman or artisan he has seen than a university rector, it is clear that Montaigne does not regard the scholastic "learning" taught in the universities of his time as identical with wisdom or philosophy in the true sense.[12]

Thus Montaigne has not simply denied that knowledge is superior to ignorance, or that philosophy may have value for at least some people. The main thrust of his argument, nevertheless, has stressed the philosophers' failure to benefit their fellows by helping them to secure "essential, tangible, and palpable goods." The sages' "vanity" led them, like the advocates of Christianity, to point us to the divine while ignoring our earthly weakness. We gain nothing, Montaigne argues, by pretending that human beings, like God, are unaffected by such corporal miseries as pain, hunger, and illness. It remains to be seen whether philosophy might be redirected or reconstituted so as to be of more substantial benefit.

Our Inability to Attain Knowledge

Up to this point Montaigne's critique of philosophy, despite its sharpness, has remained oblique, inasmuch as the essayist has questioned the practical utility of the philosophic enterprise but has not called directly into question the Socratic claim that wisdom in itself—without regard to any practical benefit it might produce—is the greatest good, and that the life dedicated to its pursuit is consequently the most rewarding one.[13] In the following section of his argument Montaigne confronts this claim more directly by proposing to investigate "whether it is in man's power" to find the knowledge he seeks. The apparent premise underlying this inquiry is that if the

[11]More specifically, he indicates elsewhere that an awareness that some people "knowingly have derived profit and advancement from cuckoldry" might overcome men's horror at this supposed evil, by demonstrating that its badness is due to convention, not to nature (I, xiv, 62 [42]; cf. III, v, 839–43, 863–4 [655–8, 675–6]).

[12]Cf. I, xxv, 132 [98] (quoting Rabelais): "The greatest scholars are not the wisest men," and the general contrast in that chapter between the learned men of Montaigne's time and the philosophers of antiquity; also III, viii, 910 [711]: the reason "why so many inept souls are seen among the learned" is that most of them are people of insufficient natural capacity. Such men, Montaigne observes, would have made better husbandmen, merchants, or artisans. Zeitlin, Essays of Montaigne (2:499), notes that Erasmus had used the ironic eulogy of ignorance in The Praise of Folly, on which Montaigne apparently drew in this section of the "Apology," as a means of attacking the schoolmen and the ecclesiastical hierarchy as a whole.

[13]See Plato, Apology, 37e–38a; Republic, 527d–e; Aristotle, Nicomachean Ethics, X.8; Metaphysics, 981b16–22, 982b11–983a11.

philosophic quest has thus far failed to provide us "with any new power and any solid truth," the quest ought to be recognized as fruitless and hence foolish, and therefore abandoned (480 [370]).

Montaigne opens this new stage of his argument with a sweeping assertion that the only profit man "has gained from so long a pursuit [of wisdom] is to have learned to recognize his weakness." He continues:

> The ignorance that was naturally in us we have by long study confirmed and verified. . . . [R]eally learned men . . . grow humble and lower their horns. Similarly, men who have essayed and sounded everything, having found in that pile of knowledge and store of so many diverse things nothing solid and firm, and nothing but vanity, have renounced their presumption and recognized their natural condition. (480 [370])

The quest for knowledge, it appears, teaches the same lesson of humility preached by Christianity. We have already seen, however, that to renounce presumption may entail rejecting rather than accepting the Christian teaching. That Montaigne is far from concurring in Paul's preference for "the simple and ignorant" is in any case reconfirmed by the language in which he now refers to the philosophers.[14] They represent "man in his highest estate": a "small number of excellent and select men" who have developed their unique natural ability, by "study" and "art," to "the highest pitch of wisdom that it can attain." Exemplifying "the utmost height of human nature," they have "regulated the world with governments and laws; . . . instructed it with arts and sciences; and instructed it further by the example of their admirable conduct." Yet Montaigne observes that even these wisest of men, by their admission, were unable to attain genuine knowledge. And he proposes to verify that admission by surveying their teachings. Since it is unlikely that anyone else can attain the knowledge that has eluded the greatest intellects, "the world may well boldly acknowledge" the "infirmities and defects" found among the philosophers "as its own" (481–2 [371]).

The "Verisimilitude and Utility" of Skepticism

At the outset of his analysis of the philosophers' teachings Montaigne borrows a distinction among three types of philosophy from the ancient Skeptic, Sextus Empiricus. "The Peripatetics, Epicureans, Stoics, and others," who "established the sciences that we have," believed they had found the truth. The Academics, on the other hand, who "had the greatest following and the noblest adherents," denied that human beings are capable of

---

[14]The significance of this passage and its connection to the opening sentences of the "Apology" are noted by Gierczynski, "Le 'Que sais-je?' de Montaigne," pp. 73–4.

conceiving the truth and inferred their inevitable "weakness and igno-rance." A third group, Pyrrho and his disciples the Skeptics, "say that they are still in search of the truth," regarding those who claim to have dis-covered it as "infinitely mistaken" but also condemning as "overbold van-ity" the Academics' claim to have proved the impossibility of attaining it. Doubting that we can determine the limits of our own powers, "a great and supreme knowledge," the Skeptics (or "Pyrrhonians") profess "to waver, doubt, and inquire, to be sure of nothing, to answer for nothing," refusing to incline their judgment for or against any proposition (482 [371–2]).

Montaigne proceeds to elaborate the advantages of the Pyrrhonian posi-tion. By keeping their judgment "straight and inflexible," the Pyrrhonians achieve "Ataraxy, which is a peaceful and sedate condition of life," free from the many passions, ills, and vices we receive "through the impression of the opinion and knowledge we think we have of things." Holding their own doctrine to be as open to challenge as any other, "they dispute in a very mild manner" and avoid trying to impose their beliefs on other people. Unlike those who "are carried along either by the custom of their country, or by their parental upbringing, or by chance . . . without judgment or choice" to adhere to a particular opinion or sect, the Pyrrhonians seek "to maintain their liberty and to consider things without obligation and servi-tude." This posture is superior, Montaigne suggests, to that of "dogma-tism," which "stupid[ly]" compels us to choose and forbids us "to be ignorant of that of which we are ignorant" (483–4 [372–3]).

In one of several borrowings in this section from Cicero's *Academica,* the essayist asks why a wise individual should not be allowed to doubt all things (484 [373]). He had seemed to answer this question only a few pages earlier: doubting received opinions and seeking truth independently makes us presumptuous and disobedient, undermining civic order as well as the Christian religion. Now, however, Montaigne suggests that Skepticism is fully compatible with order and even piety. Borrowing from Sextus' de-scription of his sect, he remarks that the Skeptics' actions are "of the common fashion," conforming to the laws and customs of their country as well as to "natural inclinations." Like any philosophic sect, the Pyrrhonians must "conform in a number of things that are not understood . . . or accepted" in order to live. Living well does not require that one "decide the true and false": many arts are founded on the mere appearance of things (485–6 [374–5]).[15]

Up to this point Montaigne's defense of Skepticism has been based largely on Sextus' own account; but now, in a seeming effort to demonstrate the salutariness of that doctrine, the essayist goes to such an extreme as to

---

[15]The bulk of the borrowings from Sextus cited in the foregoing paragraphs come from Book 1 of his *Hypotyposes,* chs. 1, 4, and 6–8.

blur its very meaning. Endeavoring to reconcile his praise of Skepticism with his earlier paean to ignorance and incuriosity, he downplays the questioning and independent aspect of the doctrine. His claim that a "soul guaranteed against prejudice" as the Skeptic aspires to be is all the more likely to submit docilely to "the laws of religion and . . . political laws" culminates in the following eulogy of Pyrrhonism as conducive to piety:

> There is nothing in man's invention that has so much verisimilitude and utility. It presents man naked and empty, recognizing his natural weakness, fit to receive from above some foreign power, stripped of human knowledge and all the more apt to lodge the divine [knowledge] in himself, annihilating his judgment to make more room for faith; neither disbelieving nor establishing any dogma against the common observances; humble, obedient, tractable, diligent; a sworn enemy of heresy, and consequently free from the vain and irreligious opinions introduced by the false sects. He is a blank tablet [*carte blanche*] prepared to take from the finger of God such forms as it shall please him to engrave there. The more we return ourselves and commit ourselves to God, and renounce ourselves, the better we are. (486–7 [375])

Thus does Montaigne implicitly encourage the religious authorities of his time to tolerate or even promote a Skeptical attitude among their flock. But were these authorities to act on his advice, it is almost certain that they would be admitting a Trojan horse through their gates. Montaigne's previous account of Skepticism hardly makes it plausible that a Skeptic could be a good Christian. The Skeptic who is an "enemy of heresy" is equally likely to be an enemy of Christianity.[16] However much the follower of this school may adapt his conduct to the common ways, he could hardly be willing to "annihilat[e] his judgment" in the sense of uncritically accepting received doctrines as true. "Acknowledging his natural weakness" as he does, the Skeptic could be expected to endorse the argument Montaigne made a few pages earlier, to the effect that God (if he exists) is beyond our power to conceive him, and hence is unknowable (479 [369]).

---

[16]Zeitlin, *Essays of Montaigne* (2:505), remarks of the above passage: "The phrasing here is coloured just sufficiently by Montaigne to make it applicable to Christianity, for the ancient Skeptics make no allowances for divine knowledge." Sextus Empiricus, in the eleventh chapter of the *Hypotyposes*, explains the Skeptic's regard for "piety" as simply a manifestation of his general, practical accommodation with the customs of his country. Cf. also Karl Löwith, "Skepticism and Faith," in his *Nature, History, and Existentialism* (Evanston, Ill., 1966), pp. 118–20. Gierczynski, in "La Science de l'ignorance," p. 59, notes the "hypocrisy" of Montaigne's purported derivation of an attitude of pious submission from his previous exposition of Pyrrhonism. See also idem, "Le 'Que sais-je?' de Montaigne," p. 72.

Marcel Conche has attempted to demonstrate that Montaigne's putative Pyrrhonism is compatible with a "sincere" Christianity but does so only by redefining Christianity so as to divorce adherence to it from any belief in the objective validity of its doctrines, or even in their superiority to the principles of Islam or cannibalism (Conche, "La Méthode pyrrhonienne," pp. 61–2). But not only does Conche himself fail to defend such a relativistic interpretation of religious belief, he also fails to demonstrate that Montaigne would have regarded such a belief as seriously Christian.

Having recognized that the "verisimilitude and utility" of Skepticism for Montaigne cannot lie in its conduciveness to Christian piety or to an attitude of unthinking docility toward authority in general, we must ask why he has gone out of his way to explain and defend the doctrine at such length. Despite his praise of the Skeptics' tranquility of soul and mildness of behavior, he has given us no reason to believe that the theoretical teachings of that school are true. Moreover, his description of the fundamental Skeptical principle—that the judgment should not be inclined for or against any proposition—contains more than a hint of ridicule: "Whoever will imagine a perpetual confession of ignorance, a judgment without leaning or inclination, on any occasion whatever, he conceives of Pyrrhonism. I express this fancy as well as I can, because many find it difficult to conceive; and the authors themselves represent it rather obscurely and diversely" (485 [374]).

Farther on in the "Apology" we shall see that Montaigne explicitly rejects Pyrrho's reported belief that it is desirable or necessary to suspend one's judgment in *practical* affairs. The key point he has stressed in commending Pyrrhonism, however, is the desirability of being free to doubt all things (whether or not such doubting leads to an *ultimate* suspension of judgment). This, I believe, is the central reason for his defense of that school. By describing the Pyrrhonian way of life as peaceful, orderly, and (potentially) pious, he suggests that a political community, even a Christian one, may safely allow its citizens to doubt and question all received opinions.

It is Montaigne's public advocacy of freedom to doubt and question all opinions, as something politically salutary rather than harmful, that constitutes the real novelty of his argument on behalf of Pyrrhonism. The notion that the wise should be conscious of their ignorance and should question, in their own minds, all received opinions, is not peculiar either to Pyrrhonism or to Montaigne. It is rather of the essence of all philosophy, which is strictly speaking a *quest* for wisdom.[17] Montaigne acknowledges

[17]Cf. II, iii, 330 [251] (first sentence); Leo Strauss, *On Tyranny* (Glencoe, Ill., 1963), pp. 209–10; idem, *What Is Political Philosophy?* pp. 38–40; idem, "Farabi's Plato," *Louis Ginzburg Jubilee Volume* (New York, 1945), pp. 392–3.
The failure adequately to appreciate the skeptical character of classical philosophy as a whole mars Gierczynski's otherwise acute analyses of the "Apology," causing him to misinterpret Montaigne's professions of openness toward all opinions as evidence of "his membership in the skeptical 'sect'" ("La Science de l'ignorance," pp. 69–70; note that the passage Gierczynski cites on the latter page from III, viii, if read in its context, is far from connoting that all human opinions are equally valid or invalid). Similarly, Gierczynski wrongly claims that "for Montaigne, Pyrrho was the model of the sage" (ibid., p. 35), disregarding not only his tongue-in-cheek summary of the Pyrrhonist "fancy" at p. 485 [374] but also the account of Pyrrho's ridiculous way of life at II, xxix, 683 [533]. Gierczynski's misconception of the relation between Pyrrhonism and classical philosophy generally also causes him to miss what is truly novel about Montaigne's public exposition of Skepticism: while ancient Skepticism may have been "the philosophy of an elite" ("La Science de l'ignorance," p. 8), to perpetuate such elitism can hardly have been Montaigne's intention, given the openness with which he professes, and encourages his readers to emulate, his own uncertainty. Gierczynski himself elsewhere expresses amazement at "the frankness with which Montaigne presents the secret

as much at the end of his discussion of Pyrrhonism, where he concludes: "That is how, of the three general sects of philosophy, two make express profession of doubt and ignorance; and in that of the dogmatists, which is the third, it is easy to discover that most of them have put on the mask of assurance only to look better. They have not thought so much of establishing any certainty for us as of showing how far they had gone in this pursuit of the truth" (487 [375]).

According to this interpretation of the philosophic tradition, the tripartite classification of philosophic doctrines that Montaigne had borrowed from Sextus breaks down almost completely. The philosophers as a whole agree on the uncertainty of human opinions, including their own. The only real difference between "dogmatists" and "skeptics" seems to concern the rhetorical issue of how the philosopher should represent himself before the public.

We may better understand how this conclusion relates to Montaigne's preceding discussion when we recognize that much of his ostensible exposition of Pyrrhonism is actually a description of *the philosophic way of life in general*. Such an interpretation is suggested by a peculiar vagueness in Montaigne's language, which otherwise would seem a mark of unusual carelessness. Through most of his seeming exposition of Pyrrhonism, running more than two and a half pages of text in the Pléiade edition, he avoids mentioning that sect or its founder by name. The subject of his sentences is commonly an indeterminate *they* (seemingly compelling the translator to substitute "the Pyrrhonians" or to add an explanatory footnote to that effect).[18] This practice of Montaigne's is particularly confusing when the *they* is preceded by the mention of other, non-Pyrrhonian philosophers, as happens at several points. Some of these instances, it is true, occur as the result of insertions that the author made in later editions. But when one notes that the conclusion I have quoted, which refers to *all* philosophic sects, belongs to the original edition, and that even the original text is quite vague in the manner indicated, bearing in mind the essayist's sweeping assertion that he never errs accidentally, it is reasonable to conclude that the

---

depth of this destructive [Skeptical] doctrine," yet he refuses to question the sincerity of Montaigne's agreement with the Skeptics regarding the need for outward submission to convention, and consequently regarding the permanent need for philosophic "esotericism" ("Le 'Que sais-je?' de Montaigne," pp. 68–9). In another passage Gierczynski remarks that "the 'Apology' . . . is not only a manual of skeptical philosophy, destined for the usage of an elite: it is also a work of propaganda," dedicated to undermining "religious dogmatism" and intolerance (ibid., pp. 82–3), but he seems to forget this when he argues that Montaigne "does not write his work for the people but for an elite" and denies that the essayist wished to undermine popular religious belief (ibid., pp. 90, 93).

[18]See, for instance, Frame, ed., *Complete Works*, pp. 372n, 373 (sixth par.), and 375n. Harvey C. Mansfield, Jr., in *Machiavelli's New Modes and Orders* (Ithaca, N.Y., 1979), p. 13, notes that a similar, pointed ambiguity in pronoun reference is characteristic of Machiavelli's writing.

ambiguity is intentional. Within the context of an apparent exposition of the doctrines of a particular philosophic sect, I suggest, Montaigne has actually sought to induce his readers to accept as legitimate the open pursuit of philosophic inquiry in general. His exposition of Skepticism masks the more daring aspect of his teaching: the suggestion that the political community can safely allow a sweeping freedom for philosophy, a "liberty . . . to consider things without obligation and servitude" (484 [373]). The true "dogmatists" whose confidence in their opinions Montaigne challenges are not a sect of philosophers but the political and religious authorities who refuse to tolerate deviations from the public orthodoxy. It is these authorities who demand, for instance, that the belief that "heavy things go down" (suggesting Aristotelian physics, an element in Scholastic doctrine) be accepted without question, and who "espouse, as [they] would [their] honor and life, Aristotle's belief about the eternity of the soul," a subject with respect to which Montaigne later remarks that "no one knows" that philosopher's true opinion (483–4, 534 [373, 414]), and on which the essayist himself will later boldly challenge the received views.[19] In reality, Montaigne (following Plutarch) asserts, Aristotle's teachings amounted to "Pyrrhonism in an affirmative form" (487 [376]). Nor did the Pyrrhonian uncertainty exceed that of Plato, for "never was a teaching wavering and noncommittal, if his is not" (489 [377]).

Even leaving aside what Montaigne suggests was the substantively "Pyrrhonian" character of the reputedly "dogmatic" philosophers' teachings, his description of the mildness and freedom of the Pyrrhonians' *manner* of argument would still more obviously apply to any true philosopher. To the extent that one is genuinely devoted to the quest for truth, as Montaigne later reports of himself along with Socrates (III, viii, 902–3 [705–6]), one will not fear contradiction but will welcome it as a means of progress towards one's goal. Not only are such individuals heedless of upholding their own reputation for wisdom, they feel no duty to defend that of their particular city, family, or sect in opposition to the evidence of reason. Like Cicero, they pursue their quest "without obligation to any party" (481 [370]; note the similarity to the ostensible description of the "Pyrrhonians" at 484 [373]).

It is eminently possible for two such persons to disagree without rancor or violence. But can a philosopher dare speak so openly in public? Can one expect most people to be so free from prejudice or envy that they will accept whatever conclusion follows from honest and rational investigation, or at least tolerate individuals who openly challenge their most cherished beliefs? Surely the history of civilization up to Montaigne's time suggested that

[19]Cf. also p. 521 [403]: "The god of scholastic knowledge is Aristotle: it is a religious matter to debate any of his ordinances"; and p. 542 [420], contrasting the ancient philosophers' liberty with the modern civil prescription of school doctrine.

the relation between the philosopher and political society was a tenuous one at best, with the fate of Socrates always a possibility for those who inquire too boldly and openly into the grounds of accepted opinions. The caution that Montaigne displays in his own writing demonstrates his awareness of that danger. In the sequel to his discussion of Pyrrhonism, moreover, Montaigne indicates how previous thinkers obscured their true beliefs, not only for their own safety but also out of consideration for the well-being of the public: "Some things they wrote for the need of political society, like their religions; and on that account it was reasonable that they did not want to bare common opinions to the skin, so as not to engender disorder in the obedience to the laws and customs of their countries" (492 [379]).

The apparent dogmatism of writers such as Aristotle, Montaigne explains, was only a cover they used to hide their uncertainty from the people. In reality, all the ancient philosophers raised questions more than they provided answers. But in presenting their views publicly, they thought it necessary to lay down, as if certain, principles which they knew to be questionable or false (487–92 [375–9]; cf. III, ix, 968 [757]; III, x, 983 [769]). Thus in stressing the uncertainty of things and openly recommending that individuals be left free to doubt and judge for themselves, Montaigne diverges from classical political philosophy, not so much (if at all) over the extent of human ignorance as over how far that ignorance should be revealed. If, as he suggests, it is unnecessary to conceal the uncertainty of human beliefs from the public, then philosophy might enjoy a new freedom, and authors such as Montaigne might be able to write without the need for protective rhetoric.

But to allow this kind of freedom is likely to involve much more far-reaching consequences for political society as a whole than Montaigne admits on the surface of his defense of Pyrrhonism. Let us consider, in this regard, the warning Montaigne gave at the outset of the "Apology" concerning the dangers of any sort of public challenge to accepted beliefs about religious matters, in supposed agreement with Bunel:

> For the vulgar, not having the faculty of judging things in themselves, let themselves be carried away by chance and by appearances, once they have been given the temerity to despise and examine the opinions that they had held in extreme reverence, such as those in which their salvation [or "welfare," "preservation"] is concerned; and when some articles of their religion have been put in doubt and upon the balance, they soon after throw into like uncertainty all the other pieces of their belief, which had no more authority or foundation in them than those that have been shaken; and shake off as a tyrannical yoke all the impressions which they had received from the authority of the laws or the reverence of ancient usage, "for eagerly is trampled what was

too much feared"; undertaking from then on to accept nothing to which they have not given their sanction and granted particular consent. (416 [320])[20]

Since Montaigne has observed that Christianity derives its sole force from political authority and reverence for ancient usage, he must expect that the public freedom of judgment he advocates would weaken or undermine that faith, if not all religions. It remains to be seen how such a weakening of religion, which Montaigne later describes as a human "invention" designed to bind society together (563 [436]), is compatible with the maintenance of civic order. At the very least, if his recommendation of public freedom to doubt all things is to prove viable, it is likely to require a fundamental reordering of political society.

The Vanity of the Other Philosophers' Pretensions

More immediately, Montaigne suggests the need for a change in the nature of philosophy itself. He relates the "difficulty" affected by "most philosophers" to the "vanity" of their pursuit, which led them to despise "most of the arts" while "amus[ing] their minds on things in which there was no profitable solidity" (488–9 [376–7]). Like the Pyrrhonians, the other philosophers, according to Montaigne, were aware of the impossibility of achieving the knowledge they sought. Yet, taking "pleasure in the chase," they amused themselves "in the pursuit of things we have no hope of acquiring." Montaigne illustrates the philosophers' vanity with a story (borrowed from Plutarch) that Democritus was angered when someone revealed the simple human agency that had produced an event whose "natural" cause he was seeking.[21] It is further illustrated by the claim of a speaker in Cicero's *Academica,* to the effect that the study of nature "uplifts and swells us, makes us disdain base and earthly things by comparison with higher and heavenly ones," and that "the very search for occult and great things is very pleasant, even to him who gains nothing from it but the reverence and fear of judging them." "The vain picture of this morbid curiosity" is exemplified, finally, in Eudoxus' prayer (reported by Plutarch) that he might "see the sun from close by so as to comprehend its form, its greatness, and its beauty," even at the cost of his life—being prepared, "for

---

[20]The quotation near the end of this passage comes from Lucretius' *On the Nature of Things,* V, 1139, where it refers to the overthrow of absolute monarchs at the dawn of civilization. Though it initially led to chaos, this event was the prelude to the establishment of more wisely framed governments and legal codes.

[21]According to Plutarch (*Table Talk,* I, x, 628c), Democritus was only feigning anger. Cf., on Bacon's treatment of "the mechanical arts," Hiram Caton, *The Politics of Progress* (Gainesville, Fla., 1988), pp. 39–40; contrast Plato, *Apology,* 22d–e.

the sake of this momentary and fleeting knowledge, to lose all other knowledge that he has and that he may afterward acquire" (490–91 [378–9]).

Several aspects of vanity are revealed in these examples. By looking for too sublime "causes" as Democritus supposedly did, the philosophers obscure the truth. They have, moreover, an overly high estimation of their pursuit, which leads them to forget their actual, "earthly" condition. Their pursuit is especially vain if, as they admit, its ultimate goal may be unattainable.

Once again, Montaigne—despite his praise of the philosophers' achievements only a few pages earlier—seems to have concluded that the pursuit of knowledge is a vain and valueless endeavor. But once more, on the verge of rejecting philosophy outright, he alters the direction of his argument. In the immediate sequel to his comment on Eudoxus, he explains the philosophers' enterprise as follows:

> I cannot easily persuade myself that Epicurus, Plato, and Pythagoras gave us as good coin their Atoms, their Ideas, and their Numbers. They were too wise to establish their articles of faith on anything so uncertain and so debatable. But into the obscurity and ignorance of the world, each one of these great personages labored to bring an image of light, such as it was, and exercised their minds on such inventions as had at least a pleasant and subtle appearance; provided that, false though they might be, they could maintain themselves against opposing ideas: "These are created by each man's imaginative genius, not by the power of his knowledge." (491–2 [379])[22]

Montaigne's description of the philosophers as "great personages" who endeavored to illuminate the world demonstrates anew his regard for their enterprise. The more particular interest of this passage, however, lies in the specific explanation it offers of what the philosophers were doing. This "skeptical" interpretation of the ancient philosophers' physical or metaphysical teachings may profitably be compared—and was, perhaps, intended by Montaigne to be compared—with the famous vision of the philosopher's quest and its relation to political society set forth at the beginning of Book VII of Plato's *Republic*. Socrates there represents ordinary human existence as taking place in a cave that is illuminated only by the light of a fire. The only things that prisoners within the cave see are the shadows of objects carried before the light by other, unseen individuals who effectively rule the prisoners' minds. This cave is open at one end, however, to the light of the sun. The rare human being who seeks after knowledge must somehow escape the bonds that hold him within the cave and ascend to the sunlit world. Those who completed that ascent not only would see

---

[22]The concluding quotation is from Seneca the Elder, *Suasoriae*, IV.3; the original is worded somewhat differently from Montaigne's version and forms part of a critique of *prophecies*, not of philosophy.

things as they truly are but would gaze at the very source of truth and being, represented by the sun. Having made this ascent, they could benefit their fellow human beings most greatly if they were compelled to return to the cave and rule there with the insight they had gained. They would try to turn the most naturally gifted of their fellows in the direction of the sunlight so as to induce them to make the ascent themselves. There is no suggestion, however, that the philosopher might bring the true light back into the cave, thus easing the quest for others. The pursuit of knowledge requires an effort that each human being must undertake alone.[23]

The world as Montaigne describes it in the passage under consideration is, before the philosophers undertake to alter it, even darker than Plato's cave; he does not mention its initially having any light to ease its "obscurity." Nor does it have any way leading out of it, toward the sun: human beings have no contact with the true light. As Montaigne remarks later in the "Apology," "You see only the order and government of this little cave you dwell in, at least if you do see it" (504 [389]). The only illumination attainable by us is an "image of light" that is *produced* out of the minds of a few "great personages." By this account, we owe our "light" entirely to human effort; nature furnishes us with nothing but the equipment for that production.[24] But since none of us can ever see the "true" light, or even know whether there is such a light outside the world in which our life is spent, we have no external standard against which to measure the "image of light" that we enjoy as a gift from a few of our fellows. Expressed non-metaphorically, this seems to mean that we can never attain a perspective on the world which we can know to be the true one. Human reason, by Montaigne's account, is capable of producing a variety of equally plausible interpretations of the world, reflecting what he will later stress is the infinite variety of phenomena in that world, without our ultimately being able to determine that one of those interpretations is objectively more valid than the others. This is not, it should be stressed, a vulgar relativism: Montaigne does not say that *all* world views are equally valid; he has distinguished sharply between the philosophers and the unthinking multitude "who leave most of their natural faculties idle," and he holds that an interpretation of the world, to merit being taken seriously, must be able to "hold its own" against rival theories—that is, withstand critical comparison with them. But in the end, it appears, our inquiries are blocked by a limit that we cannot transcend: the fundamental "obscurity" of nature.

Given Montaigne's acknowledgment of the "noncommittal" character of

---

[23]*Republic*, 514a–521c. My interpretation follows the analysis by Allan Bloom in his edition of *The Republic of Plato* (New York, 1968), pp. 403–7. Montaigne explicitly refers to the cave metaphor at I, xxiii, 106 [77].

[24]Cf. I, xxvi, 151 [112]: "It is the understanding, Epicharmus used to say, that sees and hears, it is the understanding that makes profit of everything, that arranges everything, that acts, dominates, and reigns; all other things are blind, deaf, and soulless."

Plato's teaching, and given the rhetorical, and somewhat misleading, character of Socrates' cave metaphor in particular,[25] it is impossible to say, on the basis of the foregoing discussion, how far Montaigne and Plato disagree about the actual character of the philosophic enterprise, or the attainability of knowledge. (It may not be accidental that the story Montaigne has recounted about Eudoxus recalls Plato's use of the sun as a metaphor for the ultimate object of knowledge—apparently evincing Plato's own doubt that the philosopher's quest can ever achieve its final goal.)[26] What obviously differentiates Montaigne's account of philosophy from that of Plato and other classical philosophers whom he cites is his rhetorical mode of representing it. In contrast to the claim that the philosophic enterprise somehow "elevates" its practitioner by comparison with other pursuits, Montaigne dismisses that claim as a "vain" and harmful delusion. While acknowledging that the philosophers were men of superior capacity, he implies that their gifts might have been better employed in pursuit of the same earthly goods that the lowly practical arts seek to develop—rather than in the pursuit of knowledge for its own sake.

Only in the later part of the "Apology," along with the concluding chapters of Books II and III of the *Essays* (to be examined, together, in Chapter Four), will Montaigne indicate how the philosophic enterprise might be reconstituted, with a view to securing the tangible and earthly goods whose importance he has stressed. Before we conclude our consideration of the present section of the "Apology," however, we should note that although Montaigne appears to mock his predecessors for their deprecation of the useful arts, he by no means represents them as having been unmindful of the public utility in a broader sense. It was with a view to "the need of political society," as we have seen, that they avoided undermining popular opinions about such matters as religion. And in the immediate sequel to that remark, Montaigne explains how Plato, finding it "so easy to imprint all sorts of phantasms on the human mind," filled his exoteric or political writings with "profitable lies" for the benefit of the multitude (492 [379]). But rather than endorsing this enterprise, Montaigne apparently judges such practices to constitute, at best, a regrettable necessity:

> It is easy to discern that some sects have rather followed truth, others utility; whereby the latter have gained credit. It is the misery of our condition that often what appears to our imagination as most true, does not appear to it as most useful for our life. The boldest sects, Epicurean, Pyrrhonian, and New Academic, are still constrained to bow to the civil law. (492–3 [380])

[25]See, on the latter point, Mary P. Nichols, *Socrates and the Political Community* (Albany, N.Y., 1987), pp. 117–19.
[26]As noted by Bloom, *Republic of Plato*, p. 409. Daniel Martin has pointed out to me that Montaigne put his quotation of Ronsard's poetic tribute to the sun (494–5 [381]) at the very center of the "Apology" in the 1580 edition. Cf. Plato, *Phaedo*, 99d–e.

This passage concisely expresses the fundamental difficulty that has characterized Montaigne's entire account of philosophy thus far. The last sentence reminds us of, and elaborates, Montaigne's earlier argument on behalf of freedom of philosophic inquiry. It turns out that not even the Pyrrhonians were fully able to enjoy such freedom; their investigations, like those of the other philosophic sects, were "constrained" by civil ordinances in a manner that Montaigne appears to regret. But why should Montaigne care whether philosophers are free to pursue the truth, considering his description of their enterprise as vain and valueless? To the extent that the laws, unlike philosophy, have the public utility as their primary aim, is not the subordination of philosophy desirable by Montaigne's own account? And is not Plato's enterprise, in this regard, at least more defensible than that of less politic philosophers, in that he did aspire, in part, to promote the good of the many, rather than devoting himself entirely to a "vain" amusement?

The questions just raised point us toward the core of Montaigne's project in the "Apology" (and, I shall argue, in the *Essays* as a whole). That project involves a transformation of both philosophy and political society, with a view to *overcoming* the apparent gap between truth and utility, and therefore between philosophy and politics. Montaigne aspires, I shall contend, to transform philosophy into a preeminently "useful" enterprise that will have the good of humanity as its chief goal (rather than a secondary by-product of the pursuit of wisdom, as it appears to have been for Plato). The transformation will enable philosophers to secure a historically unparalleled toleration and support from the political community, while freeing themselves from the necessity of propagating ostensibly salutary lies for the benefit either of themselves or of their audience. Whereas the classical political philosophers rhetorically sought to "elevate" the many in the direction of virtue, as they claimed to be elevated by the contemplation of nature, Montaigne, as we have seen, points his readers' vision downward, toward the earthly needs that we share with the beasts. It is only by an alteration of the philosophers' own ambitions that their pursuit can be fully harmonized with the good of humanity. This redirection of philosophy must go hand in hand, however, with a reorientation of the minds of the many. Having initiated this reorientation in the "Apology" through his highly rhetorical comparison of humanity with the beasts, Montaigne will now elaborate it through a more direct attack on the religious teachings that underlie the popular belief that we human beings enjoy an elevated rank in the cosmos. This attack will constitute an effectuation of the principle Montaigne has just advanced, to the effect that the wise should be allowed to express their doubts in public, but an effectuation masked just sufficiently to enable the essayist to protect himself against being prosecuted for heresy.

The Teachings of Reason Concerning God

If further evidence were needed of the disingenuousness of the title "Apology for Raymond Sebond," it would be worthy of note that the central portion of the "Apology" contains Montaigne's most extensive and direct attack on the grounds of Christian belief. As will be seen, the critique of philosophy serves here largely as a pretext for the critique of faith.

Ostensibly as part of his indictment of the "vanity" of the philosophic enterprise, Montaigne focuses attention on the particular vanity of "wanting to divine God by our analogies and conjectures," and "to use at the expense of the divinity" our little shred of natural ability.[27] The inconsistency and absurdity of the philosophers' opinions on this subject demonstrates that "these excellent and admirable souls" treated such topics only for "exercise," without claiming to establish any truth about them (493 [380]).

"Of all the ancient and human opinions concerning religion," Montaigne finds "most probable and most excusable"

> that . . . which recognizes God as an incomprehensible power, origin and preserver of all things, all goodness, all perfection, accepting and taking in good part the honor and reverence that human beings rendered to him, under whatever aspect, under whatever name, and in whatever manner: "Almighty Jupiter, of things and kings and gods, begetter and conceiver." (493 [380]; the quotation is from Valerius Soranus)

The ambiguity of the phrase "ancient *and* human" in this passage is in all probability intentional: a view that holds God to be almost infinitely tolerant is preferable, Montaigne implies, to *any* other religious opinion, that is, including the less liberal Christian doctrine (which is "human" but not only "ancient"). The pagan quotation in the last sentence, which implies a "Deistic" view, suggests the superiority of the ancient Roman religion in this regard.[28]

But Montaigne appears hesitant about ascribing even this much to God. Although he alleges that "this zeal has been regarded universally with favor by heaven," and that "all governments have reaped fruit from their piety," he says nothing of the sincerity of this piety, or of the kind of "fruit" it

[27]The critique of the theological use of analogical reasoning would apply with special force against Sebond, who relies heavily on analogy in his exposition of Christian doctrine (as noted by Coppin, *Montaigne, traducteur*, pp. 159–60).

[28]Cf. I, lvi, 308 [233], where Montaigne observes that "the pagans, such devout idolators, know nothing of their gods except simply their names and statues," shortly after noting the superiority of "pure ignorance" to "vain and verbal" theological "knowledge" (306 [232]). The remark about the pagans, like the passage quoted above from the "Apology," ends in an exhortation to Jupiter.

bore.[29] Elsewhere, indeed, he observes that "all lawgivers" have attempted to secure people's obedience to their laws by attributing them to the gift of a god (II, xvi, 613 [477]), but this demonstrates nothing more than the possible utility of a sham piety as a means to earthly benefits. Even more ambiguous is the essayist's statement in the present context that impious persons and deeds "have always come out appropriately" (493 [380]).[30]

Pythagoras, Montaigne continues, came closer to the truth in describing "this first cause" as indefinable, the product of each person's particular vision of perfection. But such a view, he adds, could not serve as the basis of a popular religion. The human mind requires some "definite picture after its own pattern" to worship. Hence "the divine majesty" must be represented corporeally, as in the ornaments and sacraments of Christianity, which "warm the people's soul with religious passion." But although Montaigne describes this passion as "very useful," he suggests no ground for believing that it leads us any closer to a true conception of God (494 [381]).[31]

He now provides a list of the multifarious opinions expressed by ancient philosophers about the nature of the gods, drawn largely from Cicero's dialogue so entitled. Such "confusion" has humbled and instructed Montaigne, he reports, so that he has grown tolerant of "morals and fancies different from mine" and sees little advantage in any choice other than one "which comes expressly from God's hand" (but of which he has provided no example) (494–7 [381–3]). His aim in cataloguing the laughable diversity of the philosophers' theological opinions seems to be to encourage his readers to wonder whether their own religious beliefs are any better grounded. Montaigne indicates this intent more directly by mocking those ancients who attributed a human form and human experiences to God: most of the qualities and experiences he lists are also given to the deity by the Bible (including, of course, God's human incarnation) (497 [383]).[32]

"When the philosophers dissect the hierarchy of the gods," Montaigne concludes, they cannot have been "speaking in earnest." Both Plato and Mohammed, in promising a life of sensual pleasure after death, "are mockers stooping to our folly to honey us and attract us by those opinions and

[29]Cf. p. 561 [435]: "Cleobis and Biton, Trophonius and Agamedes, having prayed . . . for a recompense worthy of their piety, got death for their present; so different are the celestial opinions of what we need from our own"; also I, xxxii, 215 [160–61].

[30]Cf. I, xix, 79 [55]: "God has willed it as he pleased; but in my time, three of the most execrable and most infamous persons I have known in every abomination of life have had deaths that were ordered and in every circumstance composed to perfection."

[31]Cf. p. 549 [426], on the power of emotion to incite belief; but also III, viii, 908–10 [710–11], where Montaigne avows his resistance to the "vain" external trappings "that delude our judgment through the senses" but on which governments and religions rely to secure people's respect. Recall also his mockery at p. 465 [358] of the "Apology" of the practice of modeling God on the human pattern. Cf. Weiler, *Pour connaître la pensée de Montaigne*, pp. 62–4.

[32]Antoine de Laval cited this passage as evidence of Montaigne's heresy (Zeitlin, *Essays of Montaigne*, 2:536). Cf. Gierczynski, "Le 'Que sais-je?' de Montaigne," pp. 94–5.

hopes, appropriate to our mortal appetite." Mohammed, however, was the founder of a religion rather than a philosopher. In the sequel, Montaigne's true concern emerges: the "similar error" of "some of our fellows." Plato and other philosophers, he has already intimated, would not have needed Montaigne to show them the falsity of their own public teachings. Once again in the present context, he expresses doubt that a person of "conceptions so celestial" as Plato's could have believed us capable of participating in "eternal beatitude or pain" (498 [384–5]). Hence, although Montaigne proceeds to address a refutation of that belief to Plato, the real addressee of this attack can only be the nonphilosophic multitude, whose theological prejudices derive from the public teachings of philosophers such as Plato and religious founders and lawgivers such as Mohammed.[33]

"On behalf of human reason," Montaigne denies that the pleasures of an immortal life can have anything to do with those we know on earth. "All contentment of mortals is mortal." The joys of an afterlife must be regarded as "unimaginable, ineffable, and incomprehensible." Moreover, to be made capable of enjoying such sublime pleasures, we mortals would have to be "reform[ed] . . . by so extreme and universal a change that, according to the doctrine of physics, it will no longer be ourselves. . . . It will be something else that will receive these rewards." Our bodies, insofar as they are ours, could not ascend to heaven; but if our souls alone are to enjoy an afterlife, "it will no longer be man, or consequently ourselves, whom this enjoyment will concern; for we are built of two principal essential parts, whose separation is the death and ruin of our being."[34] In sum, Montaigne's argument—which conforms, as he indicates, to the teachings of Epicurus and Lucretius—denies that the prospect of eternal life can reasonably be a human concern. Furthermore, he denies that it would be just for the gods to reward or punish us for our deeds, since they are responsible for our condition and consequently for our actions (498–500 [384–6]).[35]

---

[33]Cf. Zeitlin, *Essays of Montaigne*, 2:500–501: "Montaigne stabs the Christian teaching . . . through the body of Plato." This point is also noted by Weiler, *Pour connaître la pensée de Montaigne*, p. 58, and by Gierczynski, "Le 'Que sais-je?' de Montaigne," pp. 98–9.

[34]In opposition to Zeitlin's comment that this passage represents "a denial of personal immortality which it is impossible to mistake, no matter how much [Montaigne] may shelter himself behind Epicurus or utilize it as a proof of the impotence of human reason" (Zeitlin, *Essays of Montaigne*, 2:506), Brush cites "Montaigne's repeated belief that Christianity . . . correctly views human nature as a composite of body and soul equally" and quotes a remark from II, xvii, 623 [485], where the essayist seems to express approbation of the doctrine that "divine justice" subjects the body as well as the soul to eternal reward or punishment (*Montaigne and Bayle*, p. 93n). Brush, however, overlooks the significance of Montaigne's argument in the passage cited by Zeitlin, which I have summarized above, to the effect that our mortal bodies are inherently incapable of enjoying divine or infinite pleasures, whereas, if they were first to be "reformed," they would "no longer be ourselves." "If it is nothing but what cannot pertain to this present condition of ours, it cannot be counted" (499 [385]). Cf. Gierczynski, "Le 'Que sais-je?' de Montaigne," pp. 99–100.

[35]Grace Norton observes that this implicit "indictment of the Last Judgment" constitutes "the impeachment of the very corner-stone" of Sebond's work (*The Early Writings of Mon-*

Once again, Montaigne covers over the heresy of his argument by concluding that we should follow the path laid out for us by the church, in order not to go astray (501 [386–7]). But this conclusion hardly follows. "Man," the essayist has found, "can only be what he is, and imagine only what is within his reach" (501 [387]). Since it is beyond our capacity to comprehend the ideas of God or an afterlife, what reason have we to believe that the church's teachings embody his word?

Having launched an attack on popular religious belief in the guise of a critique of philosophy, Montaigne now elaborates his explanation of why such an attack is needed. In an earlier chapter he had charged that "all religions" have "universally embraced" the belief "that we gratify heaven and nature by our massacre and homicide" (I, xxx, 199 [149]). Now he twice quotes Lucretius regarding the crimes and evils religion has inspired and details the "inhuman vengeance" human beings have exercised on each other to propitiate the gods, as well as the foolish sacrifices they extract from their compatriots and themselves for that purpose. Though his examples are prudently drawn from foreign or ancient nations, he indicates that similar instances might be found among "our own."[36] One could indeed add to this list a number of stories of terrible cruelty and self-sacrifice in the name of Christianity as well as paganism which Montaigne incorporated (without overt criticism, and even with seeming admiration) in chapters xiv and xxxiii of Book I. The lesson of those examples, as Montaigne now indicates, is that insofar as religion teaches us to sacrifice our earthly happiness and that of our fellows for the sake of a God whose will and being we have "imagined," it makes this life—the only relevant one for mortals—miserable (501–3 [387–9]).

One might reply that to enumerate the most extreme cases of religious fanaticism is not to discredit religion as such. Montaigne's argument, however, is not merely against cruelty but also against any sort of religiously

---

taigne and Other Papers [New York, 1904], pp. 24–5).
    A more extensive critique of the biblical God's treatment of humanity is implicit in the eighth chapter of Book II of the Essays, titled "Of the Affection of Fathers for Children." In this chapter Montaigne—who elsewhere, following Sebond, has described God's relation to us as "fatherly," and here refers to the practice of calling God "Almighty Father" (I, lvi, 303 [230]; II, viii, 373 [284]; Sebond, Natural Theology, ch. 228 [10:88]; ch. 229 [10:94])—reports conversing with a "Lord" who "hoarded his riches" so as to "make himself honored and sought after" by his children. Montaigne, on the contrary, condemns the "father . . . who holds his children's affection only by the need they have of his help . . . if that is to be called affection." To avoid "furnish[ing] their life reasonably with what is in [his] power" is to "cast them into the despair of seeking by any means, however unjust, to provide their need" (II, viii, 367–9 [280–82]). Cf. also II, xxxi, 692–3 [539], concerning the folly of "abandon[ing] children to the government and responsibility of their fathers." The theological interpretation of II, viii, is supported by such remarks as a reference to the "reverence" of a father's "bones and relics" (368 [281]) and the mention of "scholastic" disputes and dishonest textual interpretations (374 [285–5]). Similar theological allusions recur in the chapter "Of the Resemblance between Children and Fathers" (II, xxxvii).
    [36]Cf. Gierczynski, "Le 'Que sais-je?' de Montaigne," p. 96.

inspired sacrifice of material goods, such as was made by several ancients he mentions. Among his examples is a tyrant who sought to gratify "fortune" by throwing away a "precious jewel." It is no more reasonable, Montaigne suggests, to seek God's favor through self-deprivation (however small) than to try to propitiate fortune by this means. We should not punish ourselves or each other for our sins, but should leave the matter entirely to God (503 [388]).

But Montaigne provides no reason to think that, if God exists, he punishes what we regard as sins. At the conclusion of his list of the philosophers' theological opinions, he appended a quotation from Cicero denying that human doings matter to the gods at all (496 [383]). In chapter xxxii of Book I, Montaigne himself had challenged the presumption of claiming to know God's will. His argument now buttresses that challenge by elaborating the previously expressed doubt whether any aspect of God is knowable.

Human beings, Montaigne argues, have nothing in them that "can be likened . . . to the divine nature" and consequently have no basis for knowing what that nature is like. To those who assert what God can or cannot have done, he replies,

> You see only the order and government of this little cave you dwell in, at least if you do see it: his divinity has an infinite jurisdiction beyond; this part is nothing in comparison with the whole. . . . It is a municipal law that you allege, you do not know what the universal one is. Attach yourself to what you are subject to, but not him. (504 [389])

In effect, Montaigne denies that we are "subject" to God at all. In any case, we are incapable of seeing beyond our own world, which is so small in comparison with the universe that (as a quotation from Lucretius further suggests) it is doubtful that God gives it much thought (504 [389]). This is the same sort of argument, we recall, by which Montaigne earlier denied that the human being, one among many creatures, is of special concern to "nature."

To indicate the bias and narrowness of the rules we apply to God in attempting to define his being, Montaigne argues that we know little of the universe itself. It is most plausible to believe in "the plurality of worlds, . . . inasmuch as in this structure that we see, there is nothing alone and single." He continues, "if there are many worlds . . . how do we know if the principles and rules of this one apply similarly to the others?" Even in this world, "we see . . . an infinite difference and variety due solely to distance. . . . [I]n times past, see in how many parts of the world they had no knowledge of either Bacchus or Ceres." Furthermore, "if we want to believe Pliny and Herodotus, there are species of men in certain places who have very little resemblance to our kind. And there are half-breed and ambiguous forms between human and brutish nature." If Plutarch's report of "men without mouths" is correct, "how many of our descriptions are false? [Man] is no longer capable of laughter, nor perhaps of reason and society" (504–6 [390–91]).

As Zeitlin has pointed out, Pliny and Herodotus admitted that most of these stories were "legendary or false." Pliny, indeed, cited one of them as an extreme example of "Greek credulity."[37] As was the case with the animal stories that Montaigne recounted earlier in the "Apology," these examples constitute a rhetorical, humorous surface beneath which lies a serious point. Despite his previously noted contention that all human conduct (and in a broader sense, that of the animals as well) is the product of similar causes or "springs," Montaigne emphasizes throughout the *Essays* the variousness of the particular customs, passions, beliefs, and behavior that result from those springs. So great does he find this diversity to be that he twice asserts (once in an earlier passage of the "Apology") that the differences from one man to another are greater than those between a given man and a given animal (444 [342]; I, xlii, 250 [189]). By means of his rhetorical use of (questionable) "evidence" from Pliny and Herodotus, Montaigne aims to challenge his readers' assumption that there is a fixed human nature, distinct from that of the animals, such that one could infer from it what the nature of a perfected being, or God, would be like. No one, it appears, is in a sufficiently "objective" position in relation to the world to comprehend its meaning, or consequently the nature of its creator.[38] Orthodox Christian doctrine would admit, of course, that God's ways and nature must remain ultimately mysterious to us, but Montaigne carries this point much further than orthodoxy would allow by arguing that it is presumptuous even to assert that God is immortal. To do so, he contends, is wrongly "to confine . . . the divine power under the laws of our speech" (508 [392]).[39]

The foregoing assertion leads Montaigne into a more general criticism of the way that the accepted rules of grammar produce errors in human thought. "Most of the occasions for the troubles of the world," he claims, "are grammatical." He gives several examples of such "grammatical" disputes but identifies one particular linguistic practice as the root of "all the delusions and errors with which the world is possessed": the endeavor to describe God's qualities in the terms of human discourse. When we speak of God's infinity, his virtue, or his power, "our words say it, but our intel-

---

[37]Zeitlin, *Essays of Montaigne*, 2:497, 538. Regarding Plutarch's report, Zeitlin points out that both Plutarch and Pliny (who cited the same claim) "cautiously cover themselves with the authority of Megasthenes" in relating it (II, 538).

[38]Cf. Brush, *Montaigne and Bayle*, p. 94: the idea of "the plurality of worlds . . . is a mockery of the whole Christian concept of the history of the creation and redemption of man." See also I, xxvi, 157 [116], regarding the theological effects of a cosmopolitan perspective.

[39]Coppin, *Montaigne, traducteur*, p. 160, notes that Montaigne contradicts Sebond on this point.

ligence does not apprehend it." This error is "grammatical" in the sense that because ordinary language "is wholly formed of affirmative propositions," we naturally, but wrongly, assume that the terms of our discourse refer to some objective reality. Language, in such instances, serves to obscure rather than reveal the nature of things: the ease with which it enables us to discuss the qualities of an infinite being deters us from questioning whether we understand what we are talking about (508 [392]).[40]

In opposition to such delusions, Montaigne seeks in the next few pages to show that the impressions people think they have of God can be only the creations of their own minds. This argument constitutes an elaboration of his earlier contention, in reply to the first objection to Sebond, that human beings receive their religions only from "their own hands."

In the first place, Montaigne denounces the "arrogance" that leads us "to attribute events of importance, by particular assignment, to God." This practice foolishly presumes that what is most important to us is thereby most important to God. On the contrary, Montaigne observes, it is equally easy for an omnipotent being "to move an empire or the leaf of a tree." God's government is a regular one: "The hand of his government lends itself to all things with the same tenor, the same force, and the same order; our interest adds nothing to it." God cares no more for human beings than for trees (509–10 [394]).

Montaigne advances his argument by citing the opinion of two ancients, ostensibly as another illustration of human "arrogance":

Because our occupations burden us, Strato endowed the gods with total immunity from duties, like their priests. He makes Nature produce and maintain all things, and with her weights and movements constructs the parts of the world, relieving human nature of the fear of divine judgments. "What is blessed and eternal has no business itself, nor gives any to another." Nature wills that in like things there be a like relation. (510 [394]; the quotation is from Cicero's *On the Nature of the Gods*)

Far from dismissing these opinions, Montaigne assents to them elsewhere. Later in the "Apology" he suggests that it was reasonable of the Epicureans "to discharge God of all care and solicitude of our affairs, inasmuch as the very effects of his goodness could not operate upon us without disturbing his repose by means of the passions" (551 [427]). If

---

[40]Cf. Locke, *An Essay Concerning Human Understanding*, III.ii.5; III.v.16; III.ix.6–9, 21; III.x.14, 30. Philip Hallie has pointed out the connection between Montaigne's grammatical "therapy" and contemporary "analytic" philosophy (*The Scar of Montaigne* [Middletown, Conn., 1966], pp. 89–93). Hallie fails, however, to appreciate the antireligious intent underlying Montaigne's critique of religious language; whereas Montaigne at least faced the religious issue directly, the very claim of revealed religion to truth is ignored when theological speech is treated merely as one "language-game" among many (pp. 90–92).

there is a perfect being, he cannot be concerned about us, and hence (as the above quotation from Cicero implies) we have no business worrying about him. (Recall the belief Montaigne attributed to Plato earlier in the "Apology" that it was desirable to liberate ourselves from the fear of divine judgment.) Montaigne has already lent support to Strato's view of nature by describing human beings as belonging to a deterministic natural order operating according to regular laws, in which like "springs" cause human and animal behavior. Hence there is no reason to resort to God to explain the events of the world; those that appear unusual merely indicate our ignorance of nature (cf. I, xxiii, 110 [80]; I, xxvi, 156–7 [116]).

The same theme is continued in Montaigne's mocking quotation of a number of arguments from Cicero's *On the Nature of the Gods*. One sequence of reasoning embodies a teleological "proof" of God's existence, part of which resembles an argument of Sebond's.[41] But the two quotations that follow show that the same logic would equally prove that "the world" itself has soul and reason, rather than owing its order and grandeur to God. Further quotations suggest the folly of assuming that God exemplifies moral perfection as we understand it. If he must embody "life, reason, and liberty, . . . goodness, charity, and justice" because we have or esteem these qualities, why should he not require food as we do? On the other hand, if God is assumed not to require "worldly goods," what reason is this for us to scorn them (511–12 [395–6])?[42]

Although Montaigne's purported intent in listing these philosophic arguments is to satirize their presumption, we note that two of the quotations on his list that seem to express the utmost in such presumption are left unrefuted, and at least one receives Montaigne's more explicit concurrence elsewhere. In chapter xxix of Book II he seems to agree in part with the assertion quoted here that man excels God in being good through his own effort rather than by nature (512 [396]; II, xxix, 683 [532–3]; cf. II, xi, 401 [307]). The quotation that follows in this list ranks human beings and God as "fellows" because their wisdom is the same, except for the fact that God's is eternal (512 [396]).

Thus it seems evident that the true intent underlying Montaigne's critique of theology is not to humble human beings before God, but to liberate us from the belief in gods to whose will we must subordinate ourselves. Montaigne's conclusion concerning our relation to God is simply that all the gods are a human creation—that is to say, the notion of God is a product of our imagination. It must be emphasized that he does not limit the application of this conclusion to the pagan deities, or to the philosophers' argu-

---

[41]See Coppin, *Montaigne, traducteur*, p. 161.

[42]The argument that God must have the virtues we esteem is another parody of Sebond. See Sebond, *Natural Theology*, ch. 99 (10:162). Cf. also *Essais*, II, xii, 479 [369]; Aristotle, *Politics*, 1323b21–5.

ments concerning them. Rather, he denies that anyone can truly conceive a divine being, and consequently that there can be a meaningful theology. Nor, he argues, does the rational contemplation of the world compel the supposition that gods exist; having cited philosophic opinions suggesting that the world might be its own creator, Montaigne goes on to suggest (contradicting his previous argument in defense of Sebond's project) that in this case, as in other "natural things," effects need not reflect their causes (512 [396]). As he observes in a later chapter, when we seek weighty "causes" of events, we miss the true ones, which "escape our view by their littleness" (III, xi, 1006 [787]): the true causes of the world's structure may be little rather than great ones.[43]

The relevance of the foregoing critique of theology to Christianity is signified by Montaigne in the least ambiguous way in the sequel, where he mockingly recounts stories of the gods' "cuckoldries" with women, as well as observing the multitude of "virgin" births to which Moslems attest (512–13 [396–7]).[44] A further step in his mockery of Christianity is to put into the mouth of a gosling the argument by which Sebond purported to prove that human beings are the specially favored creatures of God, only this time to the advantage of the gosling (514 [397]).[45] Finally, he satirizes the multitude of minor pagan deities and their alleged powers (515–16 [398–9]) in a passage from which (as Craig Brush observes) "a freethinking reader might well infer that he is speaking by indirection of the devil and the Catholic saints."[46]

The most general conclusion that Montaigne derives from his critique of theology seems to be indicated by his concurrence with a view he attributes to Socrates that "the wisest way to judge heaven [*ciel*] is not to judge it at all" (517 [400]).[47] We have no knowledge of what lies beyond our world, and reason demonstrates that the idea of God is a figment of our imagination. The only "excuse" for religion is the belief "that it is necessary that the people be ignorant of many true things and believe many false ones." This assertion of a pagan pontiff and theologian, to which Montaigne appends a quotation from Saint Augustine expressing a similar thought,[48] resembles

[43]Thus Zeitlin's assertion that Montaigne had at least the faith of "a high-minded deist" (*Essays of Montaigne*, 2:506) does not seem well founded. Cf., on causes, III, vi, 876 [685].
[44]Cf. Weiler, *Pour connaître la pensée de Montaigne*, p. 53; Gierczynski, "Le 'Que sais-je?' de Montaigne," pp. 93–4; François Tavera, *L'Idée d'humanité dans Montaigne* (Paris, 1932), pp. 130–31. Consider also the bearing of the story Montaigne reports having been told by an honorable lady at II, ii, 323–4 [246].
[45]See Coppin, *Montaigne, traducteur*, pp. 156–7.
[46]Brush, *Montaigne and Bayle*, p. 94; Gierczynski, "Le 'Que sais-je?' de Montaigne," pp. 97–8.
[47]The attribution is based on Xenophon, *Memorabilia*, IV.vii; but Xenophon's account must be interpreted in light of his apologetic intention: cf. Plato, *Apology*, 19.
[48]In its original context the quotation actually forms part of Augustine's critique of such deceptions (*City of God*, IV.27).

Plato's belief, cited earlier in the "Apology," that it is "necessary to trick men for their own good" (492, 516 [379–80, 399]). Montaigne will continue his attack on religion—in opposition to that principle—in the next section of his argument, the ostensible theme of which is the insufficiency of our knowledge of "human and natural things" (517 [400]).

The Teachings of Reason Concerning "Human and Natural Things"

There is a significant parallelism in form and structure between the next section of Montaigne's argument and the one I have just been considering. The two sections are approximately the same length. Each section contains an extended enumeration of the doctrines of various ancient philosophers on the matter in question, which leads Montaigne to infer in each case that these teachings cannot have been meant seriously. And in each section he proceeds to employ a purported critique of these teachings as the vehicle for an attack on popular religious beliefs.[49]

The only nonhuman part of nature that Montaigne considers in order to demonstrate our ignorance of "human and natural things" is the heavenly bodies. At the outset of this section of his argument, he mocks the poetic descriptions of the movements of the planets offered by Ovid, Plato, and Varro. The consideration of these writers' "dreams and fanatical follies" leads him to wish that nature would "one day open her bosom to us and make us see properly the means and conduct of her movements," so that the "abuses" and "miscalculations" of "our poor science" would be revealed (517 [400]).

By expressing this wish, Montaigne modifies the opinion he has just endorsed that it is best "not to judge" heaven at all. The real issue is not whether it should be studied, but how and to what end. The proper role of science, Montaigne suggests, is not to daydream about the gods who may

---

[49]The parallelism between the two sections is actually even greater than that noted above but is partly obscured by an overlap between them. As noted in the text, Montaigne's survey of our knowledge of "human and natural things" begins with a discussion of the heavenly bodies—the only nonhuman aspect of nature that he examines. This discussion, as I shall observe, issues in a recommendation of the physical study of the heavens which implicitly contradicts Montaigne's previous conclusion that it is best not to judge the heavens at all. Thus, even though the astronomical discussion occurs after Montaigne's announcement that he will turn to human and natural things, this discussion forms part of the preceding section as well. The overlap reflects the ambiguity of the term *heavenly*: divine, or astronomical (and hence "natural"). If Montaigne's astronomical survey is assigned to the previous section of his argument, the two sections will be seen to be even more closely parallel in structure (albeit less so in length), inasmuch as each section then ends with a lament (based on utterly insufficient evidence) of the philosophers' ignorance of the subject being discussed (the heavens in the first case, human nature in the second), followed by a hinted invitation to advance its study from a physical or mechanistic point of view.

dwell above but to discover the *forces* that impel the heavens, along with the rest of nature. Although he appears to mock the ancients for attributing "material, heavy, corporeal springs" to the planets, the essayist himself, we recall, had previously described nature as a vast "machine" and implied that even the movements of human beings and animals are determined by mechanical "springs" (424, 454 [326, 350]). The real error of philosophy, he implies, lay in its giving fantastic descriptions of those springs, instead of observing and studying the planets' mode of operation.

Already at the end of his demonstration of our ignorance of God, Montaigne had mocked the philosophers' ignorance of the composition of the sun and heavens (516–17 [399–400]). It is apparently on account of such ignorance, and the fabulous stories the philosophers provide in lieu of knowledge, that Montaigne now describes philosophy as "but sophisticated poetry." He goes on to suggest that the philosophers' ignorance is equally evident in their accounts of human nature, a subject much more "familiar" to us. In a reference that recalls Plato's *Republic* as well as Sebond, he mocks the philosophers for dividing man into so "many orders and stages . . . besides the natural and perceptible ones" and so "many functions and occupations" that "they make of him an imaginary republic" (518–19 [400–401]).[50]

Upon examining this condemnation of philosophy so far, one is struck by its unfairness. First, apparently on the basis of three poetic or quasi-poetic quotations, Montaigne inferred that philosophy has not discovered anything about the movement or constitution of the heavens. Then, simply by pointing to the various ways in which philosophers divided the human soul and alleging their inability nonetheless to comprehend it fully, he seems to have concluded that they know nothing of human nature either. In asserting that "every philosopher is ignorant of what his neighbor is doing, yes, and of what he himself is doing" (520 [402]), Montaigne appears to echo the grossest of popular prejudices.

There are several reasons for regarding this denunciation of philosophy as partly ironic. In the first place, the entire passage in which the words last quoted occur, including a story about how the philosopher Thales was rudely brought down to earth from his heavenly speculations, and a remark that the philosopher does not even know whether he and his neighbor are "beasts or men," has been borrowed by Montaigne, with slight modification, from Plato's *Theaetetus*—hardly an antiphilosophic source. The most significant modification Montaigne made in the passage is as follows: whereas Socrates describes the philosopher as hardly knowing whether his neighbor is a human being (because he is so preoccupied with his specula-

---

[50]See Sebond, *Natural Theology*, chs. 105 and 175, and Plato, *Republic*, 427d–445e. Cf. also Machiavelli's critique of the ancient philosophers' "imaginary republics" in ch. 15 of *The Prince*.

tions that he has no time to notice his neighbor),[51] Montaigne extends this criticism to imply that the philosopher lacks self-knowledge as well. But whatever the ground of this charge may be, it cannot be that Montaigne shares the popular view that philosophers lack the capacity for dealing with human affairs: in an earlier chapter, he argued at length against that view, pointing out that in ancient times, learning helped produce "able men in the handling of public matters, great captains and great counselors in affairs of state." The ancient philosophers, "great in knowledge," were "still greater in every [kind of] action." Although they sometimes ignored "common things," they did so because they regarded themselves as being above such things, not because they were incompetent to deal with them. Indeed, Montaigne demonstrated that point with specific reference to Thales, describing how the reputed founder of philosophy once made "his learning stoop . . . to the service of profit" and reaped enormous wealth as a result (I, xxv, 134–5 [99]).[52] At the very outset of the "Apology," we recall, Montaigne expressed his own belief in the utility of learning, and at the beginning of his critique of the philosophers' teachings he again noted their contribution to law and government (415, 481 [319, 371]). And Montaigne himself professes an unsurpassed ignorance regarding "vulgar things" later in the *Essays* (II, xvii, 636 [495]).

No less ironic is Montaigne's seemingly mocking reference to the philosophers as people "who find Sebond's reasons too weak, who are ignorant of nothing, who govern the world, who know everything" (520 [402]). As we have seen, Montaigne himself finds Sebond's arguments weak and has explicitly referred to the philosophers with evident seriousness as rulers of the world (481 [471]). As for the other two alleged philosophic pretensions, Montaigne has shown that the philosophers were aware of their ignorance but concealed it for prudential reasons.

The serious element in Montaigne's present critique of the philosophers is actually a continuation of his previous attack on their propagation of edifying myths—as well as their relative disregard of the genuine needs of humanity (including their own). By urging the individual "to look rather to himself than to the sky [*ciel*]" (519 [402]), he suggests that it is wrong to seek our model in what is "above" us, as both philosophers and divines have urged. This is also the serious implication of Montaigne's contention that the philosophers do not know whether they or their neighbors are "beasts or men." As we have seen, that issue is more debatable than it first appears to be: Montaigne suggests that we are not by nature different from the beasts and might do better to emulate them rather than the gods.[53] This

[51]*Theaetetus*, 174b.
[52]For the source, see Aristotle, *Politics*, 1259a5–21; cf. *Nicomachean Ethics* 1141b4–8, which expresses the contrary popular prejudice.
[53]Cf. also p. 527 [408], citing Plato's opinion that man is as difficult an object to understand as any other part of the universe.

suggestion explains, finally, the meaning of his critique of the philosophers' descriptions of the heavens. Montaigne is certainly aware that Plato's poetic description was meant as a salutary teaching rather than as a literal account of the structure of the heavens.[54] Though he may well believe ancient astronomy to be inaccurate and certainly holds the prior philosophic understanding of human nature to be inadequate, the real thrust of his argument is not that the philosophers were ignoramuses but that they sought to guide us in too high a direction. Montaigne supplements his advice to observe ourselves as we are, rather than look to the heavens for our pattern, by directing his readers' attention to what is lowest, or "at [our] feet" (519 [402]). In short, philosophy needs to take its bearings by the corporeal aspect of human nature.

What renders the passage I have just examined confusing—as has occurred elsewhere in the "Apology"—is Montaigne's practice of blending a serious philosophic argument with an ironic, popular attack on philosophy. A similar problem arises in the next stage of his argument, where he laments our failure to doubt received opinions, such as the belief that the body's movements are governed by a "spiritual" soul. A large section of this argument is explicitly directed against the doctrines of Aristotle, "the god of scholastic knowledge," whose "ordinances" it has been made a matter of "religion" to dispute, so that they may not be questioned despite their manifest implausibility (520–21 [402–3]). Yet earlier in the "Apology" Montaigne indicated that Aristotle was far from truly holding to such a dogmatic posture himself, despite the dogmatic appearance of his writings. In introducing his present argument, moreover, Montaigne again suggests that the philosophers in general were aware of the uncertainty of their teachings (520 [402]). Thus it once more appears that the true object of his attack is not the philosophers but the religious and political authorities of his time. It is thanks to them that "men's opinions are accepted in the train of ancient beliefs, by authority and on credit, as if they were religion and law," so that "the world is filled and soaked with twaddle and lies" (520–21 [403]; cf. 542 [420]).

But there is more to Montaigne's present argument than a protest against the antiphilosophic practice of Christian polities. As we have seen, although a large element of his previous critique of philosophy is ironic, he does seriously appear to hold the philosophers at fault for not having attained a sufficient understanding of humanity or the rest of nature. Montaigne now focuses his attention more directly on philosophy itself, suggesting that its deficiencies are due to the uniform acceptance of certain "presuppositions" that are taken to constitute the foundation of all inquiry. "Whoever is

[54]See Plato, *Republic*, 621b–c. Cf. p. 553 of the "Apology," where Montaigne acknowledges that Copernicus' highly successful astronomical system was founded on an ancient insight [429].

believed in his presuppositions," he remarks, "is our master and our God; he will plant his foundations so broad and easy that by them he will be able to raise us, if he wants, up to the clouds." (It is precisely such attempts to "elevate" us that Montaigne has just been attacking.) This barrier constitutes "the principal source of error"; yet anyone who crashes it is met with the reply "that one cannot argue with people who deny first principles" (521–2 [403–4]).

The reply to which Montaigne refers may be traced to Aristotle, who points out that all demonstration must proceed from principles that cannot themselves be proved (lest there be infinite regress), but that nonetheless must be more certain than the conclusions derived from them. The only proof one could give of the principle of contradiction, for instance, would be to show that it is necessarily presupposed in all thinking, even in the arguments of one who seeks to deny it. Similarly, there is no way of "proving" strictly speaking that our sense perceptions provide a generally reliable representation of the world; but all human behavior shows our belief that they do. Aristotle asserts that both the first principles of reason and our knowledge of ultimate particulars are given by *nous*, or "intuitive intelligence." Without this faculty, the world would be unintelligible to us.[55]

Montaigne implicitly denies that we have such a faculty. He later asserts that "the end and the beginning of knowledge"—the points at which *nous* provides us with our greatest certainty, according to Aristotle—"are equal in stupidity" (526 [407]). It will not do, Montaigne argues, for the philosopher to tell people who doubt that fire is hot to try throwing themselves into it. Whatever the practical utility of this answer, it is not an inference from reason. Montaigne proposes to challenge the tyrannical authority of "those who fight by presupposition" by "presuppos[ing] the opposite" of any axiom they assert. Only if reason demonstrates a difference between them is one presupposition to be preferred to another. Hence unless the philosophers can demonstrate that "what I think I feel, I therefore actually do feel," they must "abandon their profession" of accepting nothing that does not follow from reason (522–3 [404–5]).

The demand last quoted—that philosophy should provide a syllogistic demonstration that our senses are generally reliable—is manifestly impossible to satisfy, as Aristotle recognized. Yet it is not evident how the denial of that assumption could issue in any fruitful result. Moreover, as I shall observe, Montaigne himself subsequently admits the need for philosophers as well as other human beings to rely on their sense impressions in practice as if they were generally trustworthy. Thus it is not clear how seriously his

[55]Aristotle, *Physics*, 185a1–5; *Metaphysics*, 1036a1–7, 1073b8–11; *Nicomachean Ethics*, 1143b3–5; *Topics*, 105a3–8.

present demand is meant. In any event, Montaigne can hardly be said to have demonstrated that the dependence of philosophy on the presumption that our senses are trustworthy puts its conclusions on the same level as beliefs founded on purely arbitrary premises (for example, that fire is cold).

More plausible, and suggestive, are the remaining challenges Montaigne poses to the philosophers immediately after demanding that they prove the accuracy of his sense perceptions: "and if I feel [what I think I feel], let them next tell me why I feel it, and how, and what I feel. Let them tell me the name, the origin, the ins and outs of heat and cold, the qualities of that which acts and that which suffers (523 [405]). In effect, Montaigne proposes a research program for science, aimed at providing a more accurate knowledge of the efficient and material *causes* of our sense perceptions.[56] Having described such a program, he immediately drops the subject, proposing instead to survey the teachings of reason about itself and about the soul to which it belongs (523 [405]). The invitation that Montaigne has just laid down for a more thorough study of our bodily constitution and sensations will be revived, however, at the end of this discussion of the soul, and will be elaborated in a later section of the "Apology."

The Teachings of Reason about the Soul

Despite just having proposed to examine the teachings of reason about itself as well as about the human soul as a whole, Montaigne limits his explicit discussion to the latter topic. Apparently, what reason teaches about itself is to be inferred from this survey of what it teaches about the soul.

As he had done in examining the teachings of reason about the gods, Montaigne begins this subsection of his argument with a catalogue of the philosophers' varying and mutually contradictory opinions about the subject—in this case, the nature and location of the soul. As in the earlier case, the conclusion to which Montaigne at first points—the vanity and hopelessness of the philosophic enterprise when it attempts to deal with such topics—is succeeded by an inference that the philosophers' assertions cannot have been sincere. Conscious of their ignorance, Montaigne asserts, the philosophers concealed their uncertainty "so as not to frighten the children." They were guilty more of "imprudence" than of "ignorance" (527 [408]). By revealing their contradictions, Montaigne again shows that they were dishonest, even if with a noble intent.[57]

---

[56]Montaigne's proposal appears to reverse the transformation Socrates reports in his own inquiries, from pursuing such efficient and material causes to seeking truth through the medium of speeches, which led him to understand nature in the light of our primary political and moral concerns: Plato, *Phaedo*, 96a ff.

[57]Cf. I, ix, 38–9 [23], where Montaigne shows that the way to trap a liar is to catch him in a contradiction. The relevance of this point to the present discussion is noted by Hallie, *The Scar of Montaigne*, pp. 86–7.

A central issue between Montaigne and his philosophic predecessors, as we have seen, concerns the nature of philosophic "prudence," or the kind of public teaching that is truly salutary. Immediately after reminding his readers of the concealment that the philosophers practiced, the essayist asserts his own openness, thus highlighting this issue. Whereas they "obscure their natural opinions . . . to accommodate themselves to public usage," Montaigne professes a "natural" behavior. True, he may conceal the originality of his thought, letting fly his "caprices more freely in public" because he is confident that readers will explain them away as corresponding to "some ancient notion" (527–8 [408–9]). But though he thus considers his own safety, he does not cover over the truth for the sake of the supposed good of the public. As he remarked earlier, he does not falsify things out of "conscience" (I, xxi, 104 [76]).

These remarks about Montaigne's rhetoric supply the key to an understanding of his discussion of the soul, in the sequel. As in his treatment of the gods, Montaigne boldly attacks the popular beliefs and seeks to uncover the extent of human ignorance regarding the matter being discussed but protects himself by putting his argument in the form of a mocking exposition of "ancient notion[s]."

Just as in his discussion of the gods, Montaigne begins by singling out one opinion as more "plausible" than most. This view holds that the soul operates through "one single power" and by means of the body, and that it is located in the brain (528–9 [409]). The first point implies that the soul cannot properly be divided into a multitude of faculties, as was done in the philosophic schemes that Montaigne previously mocked. (Montaigne suggests that Plato's true opinion of the soul, despite appearances to the contrary, may have been similar to this one.) The second point seems to entail that the soul itself is an extended body, since only such bodies are capable of having spatial location (to locate the soul in the brain is different from asserting that the operation of the brain is the necessary condition for the presence of soul).[58]

Next Montaigne describes a variety of hypotheses concerning the origin of individual souls. Of these he selects one (which he asserts was believed by "most of the ancients") that holds that souls "are engendered from father to son, in a similar manner of production to that of all other natural things." He attributes to "the ancients" the view "that thereupon is founded divine justice, punishing in the children the fault of the fathers, inasmuch as the contagion of the paternal vices is to some extent imprinted on the soul of the children." They also held that souls must be produced by a "natural succession," along with the bodies to which they are attached, since the soul has no memory of any prior existence outside the body (529–30 [409–10]).

Montaigne points out that this view of the generation of souls conflicts

[58]Cf. Socrates' distinction between regarding "bones and sinews" as causes and as conditions of human action: Plato, *Phaedo*, 98b–99b.

with Plato's apparent doctrine "that what we learned was only a recollection of what we had known: a thing which each man, by experience, can maintain to be false." The view that "the corporeal prison stifles" the soul's faculties also contradicts the belief that the soul's operations in this life are so "admirable" that it is evidently divine and immortal. By means of a quotation from Lucretius, Montaigne suggests that the soul is in fact mortal; for even if it has merely lost all remembrance of the past, as a result of its purification, this is practically the same as its having died (530–31 [411]; cf. 498–9 [385]). He then argues that it would be unjust for the soul to be judged and have its entire future determined on the basis of a life in which its "resources and powers" were "cut short." But in fact, whether its powers are cut short is beside the point: "It would be an inequitable disproportion to receive eternal compensation in consequence of so short a life," in any event. Plato, Montaigne observes, took account of this difficulty by limiting the duration of "future payments" to "a hundred years" (531 [411]).[59] What is left unsaid is that orthodox Christian doctrine does not set temporal limits to the "future payments" it forecasts. As in his discussion of the gods, Montaigne again disguises an attack on the Christian teaching about the afterlife by pretending to refute Plato. If it is "inequitable" for us to suffer eternal punishment for sins committed during a finite lifetime in which the powers of our souls are limited, still more would it appear unjust for us to be punished for our "fathers'" sins—a doctrine not of "the ancients" in general, of course, but rather of biblical theology.[60] Indeed, as Montaigne suggested earlier, if God is our true "father" (as Sebond argues), it is he who is ultimately responsible for our sins.

Montaigne now continues to develop the position that both the life of the soul and its manner of generation follow "the common condition of human things." Although he appears to mock this view by referring to the "fine evidence" for it, Zeitlin rightly points out that this "affectation of irony" is followed by an elaboration of the "fine evidence" that runs for several pages, "with many quotations from Lucretius and with every symptom of adhesion."[61] Montaigne's argument stresses the utter dependence of the soul on the body's condition; one of his Lucretian quotations reiterates the thought that the soul is itself corporeal (532 [411–12]).

From the dependence of the soul on one's physical condition, Montaigne derives a consequence that he finds the philosophers "hardly touched." If the soul is greatly subject to the effects of passion and to corporeal "accidents" such as pain and disease, than the traditional remedies prescribed by

---

[59]Actually, according to *Republic* 615a–b, Montaigne's apparent source, such punishments are inflicted for a thousand years.

[60]See Exod. 20:5.

[61]Zeitlin, *Essays of Montaigne*, 2:508.

the philosophers for the miseries of human existence are of little value. "Patience" or suicide are not available ways out for the soul that is not "its own master," and Montaigne argues that the soul is almost never, if at all, in that condition. Thus "this soul loses the taste for the Stoic sovereign good, so constant and so firm." If the ancients recognized the soul's dependence on the body, they should have looked for a more adequate means of ameliorating its sufferings (532–3 [412–13]).

As for the soul's immortality, Montaigne concludes that it is a lesson neither of "nature" nor of "reason" (536 [415]). The ancients themselves treated this subject "with most reservation and doubt." Only two things made the notion of immortality "plausible" to them: the beliefs that it was a necessary support for our "vain hopes of glory," and that it is "useful" for us to think that the wicked, even if they escape human punishments, "will always remain a target for divine justice." But neither belief actually justifies the hope of immortality unless one first makes the assumption, which Montaigne has questioned, that there is a divine order in the world which answers our hopes and supports human justice. He suggests that the real reason for the belief in immortality is man's "extreme concern" to "prolong his being" (534 [414]), adding: "The soul, through its confusion and weakness being unable to stand on its own feet, goes questing everywhere for consolations, hopes, and foundations in external circumstances where it clings and takes root; and, flimsy and fantastic as its imagination may create them, it rests more assured in them than in itself, and more gladly" (535 [414]).

Having shown all religious beliefs to be "flimsy and fantastic" creations, Montaigne once more briefly renders lip service to them. He asserts the "vanity and folly" of "all that we undertake" without God's assistance, and the greatness of the debt we owe him for "the fruit of immortality, which consists in the enjoyment of eternal beatitude" (535–6 [415]). But neither of these claims has been substantiated by Montaigne's argument. What he has shown to be "vain" is, rather, the belief that we have any contact with or knowledge of what is immortal, as well as the hope of receiving any assistance other than that which comes from ourselves.

Montaigne's discussion of the soul's fate, like his treatment of the gods, concludes with a summary of various fantastic ancient beliefs on the subject at hand, followed by an observation of the link between the "mysteries of philosophy" and "those of poetry." Having considered "the fine and certain teachings that we derive from human knowledge on the subject of our soul," he remarks that "the human understanding los[es] its way in trying to sound and examine all things to the utmost" (538 [417]). But the phrase "fine and certain teachings," like Montaigne's earlier reference to the "fine evidence" for the soul's dependence on the body, is less ironic than it appears. Largely by means of a summary of the ancients' teachings, Montaigne has advanced a certain interpretation of the soul that he himself appears to accept. That interpretation stresses its essentially corporeal as well as mortal character. The proper way to study human nature, it appears, is therefore to observe our bodily constitution. Though knowledge of the eternal and infinite may lie beyond our grasp, we may yet achieve understanding of what is earthly and perceptible.

Despite having emphasized the need to investigate our corporeal nature, Montaigne touches only briefly here on what philosophy has taught about that subject. Having pointed out earlier the folly of seeking to know "first causes," he excuses the philosophers for not knowing the mode of our "first production." However, he mocks their inability to agree even about "from what matter men produce one another." He claims that this single example "is enough to prove that man is no more versed in the understanding of himself in the corporeal part than in the spiritual." Yet, he observes, self-knowledge is the prerequisite of all further knowledge (538–40 [417–18]).

Montaigne can hardly be said to have demonstrated that we have gained no knowledge of our physical constitution, any more than he previously "proved" the philosophers to be utterly ignorant of astronomy. But the very scantiness of his evidence is again significant. Whereas he made a serious effort to show the impossibility of demonstrating the existence of God and the immortality of the soul, he does not rule out the possibility of achieving knowledge of ourselves, and especially of our bodily constitution. The remarks that conclude this section of the "Apology" constitute, to the contrary, a renewed invitation to pursue such investigations, just as the conclusion of the preceding section led Montaigne to wish for a more accurate physical study of the heavens.

Contrary to Montaigne's initial statement of its intent, and contrary to the "pious" conclusion of his remarks on the soul, the foregoing survey of the philosophers' teachings has not demonstrated the fruitlessness of rational inquiry, or our need to throw ourselves on God for help. Montaigne has in reality argued only the folly of believing that we can know what is infinite and incorporeal—a belief that he has made it seem doubtful the philosophers shared. His argument has been based on reason, not its rejection. Far from rejecting reason, the foregoing critique of human beliefs has served to clear the ground, as we shall see, for what Montaigne hopes will be an infinite progress in our knowledge of physical nature, as well as a salutary reordering of political life. It is in this sense that the preceding discussion has taught us about reason as well as the soul, as Montaigne promised: by revealing the *limits* of reason—that is, its inability to describe, or even demonstrate the existence of, incorporeal substances—Montaigne prepares to teach us about the proper positive use of this faculty.

Conclusion of the "Defense" and Provisional Counsel to the Multitude: The Need for Moderation

Having completed his apparent demonstration that even the wisest individuals have been unable to achieve knowledge, Montaigne pauses to give a word of counsel to an unnamed addressee for whom, he says, he has "extended" his work. Because he speaks of the addressee's having an "authority" due to "greatness," and the ability "to command by the flicker of an eye whomever you please," and also of the addressee's receiving regular religious instruction (540–41 [418–19]), scholars have generally concluded that he must have written the "Apology" to please some woman of high rank.[62] Although his language seems intended to give that impression, it is certainly vague. Moreover, the scholars' interpretation conflicts with Montaigne's previous explanation that his defense of Sebond is meant not for one person's needs but for "many" with whom Sebond's book is popular (416 [320]). A consideration of Montaigne's counsel in the light of his foregoing argument may shed some light on the issue.

Montaigne first advises his addressee as follows: "You . . . will not shrink from upholding your Sebond by the ordinary form of argument in which you are instructed every day" (540 [418]). By speaking of "your" Sebond, he once more disassociates himself from both Sebond and his devotees.[63] He apparently regards the "ordinary" argument by which the latter are "instructed"—presumably, orthodox religious doctrine—as good enough or even best for them. It is unclear, however, whether Montaigne's "you will" is a piece of advice or merely a prediction.

Montaigne proceeds to warn of the dangers of his own mode of argument: it is "an extreme remedy . . . a desperate stroke in which you must abandon your arms to make your adversary lose his" (540 [418–19]). He admits, in other words, that to "refute" Sebond's critics as he has done entails abandoning both Sebond and his cause. If Sebond's reasoning is to be defended by pointing out that the human mind is incapable of understanding the things of which he speaks, and consequently that his critics could not outdo him in the enterprise of describing God and the soul's afterlife, one will have admitted that neither Sebond nor Christianity has any claim to be believed. This seems, indeed, to be the conclusion to which Montaigne's argument has led.

---

[62]See ibid., 509–11, with references. Eva Marcu has pointed out the difficulties in each of the attempted identifications of Montaigne's addressee and concludes that the addressee is fictitious, the apostrophe to her serving both a literary and a rhetorically defensive purpose ("Les Dédicaces de Montaigne," pp. 36–42).

[63]As noted by Zeitlin, *Essays of Montaigne*, 2:513. Contrast the reference at p. 469 [361] of the "Apology" to the opinion of "*my* Seneca . . . that God gave man life, but that he got the good life from himself."

But why, then, should Montaigne wish his addressee to uphold Sebond at all? He suggests, as he has done previously, that maintenance of the traditional faith is necessary for civic order. Because "our mind is a wandering, dangerous, and reckless tool," it must be given "the tightest possible barriers." "Few souls . . . can be trusted with their own guidance" to "sail with moderation and without temerity in the freedom of their judgments, beyond the common opinions." Thus the mind is bridled with "religions, laws, customs, science, precepts, mortal and immortal punishments and rewards." Apparently in conformity with such practices, Montaigne advises "moderation and temperance, and the avoidance of novelty and strangeness. All extravagant ways offend me" (541 [419]).

This apparent agreement between Montaigne and those who "bridle" the mind with religions, laws, and customs is highly problematic, if not simply misleading. The predominant thrust of his previous argument—as well as his general posture elsewhere in the *Essays*—has been in favor of freedom of judgment and toleration.[64] In fact, he has indicated that the need for "moderation" is greatest among those who profess the Christian faith. The two examples he now gives of immoderate and extreme sacrifices that some men made to destroy their enemies (540 [419]) reinforce that point: the implication is that Christians would do well to exercise more restraint in dealing with their opponents. He adds that the extremity of knowledge, as of virtue, is a vice. It is in opposition to the latter sort of extreme, I believe, that his advice to stay in the "common road" (540 [419]) is to be taken: those shining examples of Christian self-sacrifice are not to be imitated.[65]

By distinguishing here between the multitude who would do best to follow the "common road" and the few "orderly, strong, and well-born souls" who can safely be allowed to go beyond the "common opinions," Montaigne marks out the true addressee of his counsel. That addressee, I believe, is the nonphilosophic multitude as a whole.[66] The passage now being examined marks the conclusion of the work that Montaigne under-

[64]Contrast with the above profession of being offended by unfamiliar ways II, xxxvii, 766 [597–8], where Montaigne emphasizes his tolerant attitude toward opinions and humors that differ from his own; also III, viii, 901–2 [704–5]; III, ix, 950–51 [743–4].

[65]Cf. I, xxx, 195 [146], where a parallel remark identifying extreme "virtue" as vicious serves to introduce a critique of the immoderation of theologically inspired "moderation" regarding sensual pleasure. Montaigne further clarifies the meaning of his rejection of "extravagant" or eccentric ways by repeating it at the end of the book, in the context of a denunciation of "transcendental humors" that lead people to despise their earthly being (III, xiii, 1096 [857]).

[66]Montaigne's remarks about the addressee's power and authority could be applied to this class, which would include the political rulers themselves. Similarly, his allusion to "your courts," in which the "dangerous plague" he has undertaken to combat "spreads every day" (542 [420]), can be taken to refer to the public courts of law, or the courts of the rival claimants to the French throne, rather than the court of a particular noblewoman.

took for their sake—the "defense," actually the refutation, of Sebond and (more importantly) the faith he upholds.⁶⁷ The counsel that the essayist infers for them from his inquiry is simply to be moderate, that is, to avoid fanaticism.⁶⁸

What may be "enough" for the many to know, however, is not sufficient to resolve the problems of human life which, Montaigne has indicated, tend to generate religious fanaticism. Even if his repetition of ancient arguments against religion serves to weaken the people's attachment to Christianity, it is unlikely, by itself, to make them more moderate. Religion, he has shown, originates in certain fundamental human passions and needs. Evidently, if the people are to be prevented from adopting some new superstition that may be as harmful (or more so) than Christianity, their minds must be "bridled" in some manner. But Montaigne observes that none of the "bridles" heretofore applied have been successful (541 [419]). Moreover, it will do no good to deprive the people of the consolation that religion provides for their unhappy condition, however false it may be, unless their state is susceptible of an actual improvement by some other means. Furthermore, if the threat of divine punishments is to be removed, some alternative method must be found to fortify the people's obedience to civil law.

Montaigne's twofold solution to these problems embodies a new kind of science, dedicated to improving the human condition, and a reordering of political society, to promote the goals of toleration and civic peace. In the remainder of the "Apology," he will outline the foundations of this project.

⁶⁷Note that the explicit reference to Sebond in this passage is Montaigne's final one.
⁶⁸Cf. the first rule of the "provisional" morality adopted by Descartes before his scientific inquiries in *Discours de la méthode*, III: *Oeuvres et lettres*, ed. André Bridoux (Paris, 1953), p. 141.

The "Apology," III:
The Proper Use of Reason

A new beginning occurs in the argument of the "Apology" immediately after Montaigne's counsel of moderation to the multitude. Montaigne indicates this new beginning by challenging, at the outset, the two propositions he had proposed to demonstrate at the beginning of his reply to the second objection to Sebond, and to which he again alluded in his concluding counsel. These propositions are (1) the inevitable fruitlessness of all rational inquiry and (2) the consequent need for absolute submission to authority.

Regarding the latter point, Montaigne now laments that the ancients' "liberty and wantonness" of thought (previously described with such apparent scorn) have been replaced by a legally prescribed curriculum. As a result, people no longer judge the real merit of the doctrines they are taught; the only standard is "common approbation." Consequently, the grossest superstitions and most foolish studies "are accepted equally" with more solid sciences, such as geometry; "everything is admitted without contradiction" (542 [420]).

Thus, whereas Montaigne had previously denounced the absurdity and inconsistency of the exoteric doctrines propounded by the pagan philosophers, he now suggests that the relative freedom of debate these individuals enjoyed served to protect the public against the acceptance of far more absurd beliefs and practices, such as palm reading (542 [420]). Having reraised the issue of the desirability of freedom of philosophic inquiry, however, Montaigne immediately turns to the problem of the limits of inquiry in a different sense: the question of whether there are *intrinsic* bounds to the scope of human knowledge. While describing as "moderate and pleasant" the opinion of Theophrastus that we "could judge the causes of things to a certain extent" but had to stop upon reaching the "ultimate and first causes," Montaigne responds that "it is not easy to set limits to our mind." He goes on to suggest the possibility of infinite advancement in the arts and sciences, describing the pursuit of knowledge as a progressive enterprise in which each participant, building on preceding discoveries, makes it possible for the inquirer's successors to proceed still further (543 [421]). How far we have suddenly come from the seeming contempt for human reason that Montaigne expressed earlier!

The following pages of the "Apology" embody Montaigne's response to the issue of the "limits" of the mind, in both senses: the political question of how far the authorities should permit freedom of inquiry and debate, and the epistemological question of how much we are capable of knowing. This response constitutes the outline of his positive political and scientific projects. Although the political and scientific themes are intermixed, I shall depart from my serial reading of the chapter in order to treat them separately, beginning with the latter.

Skepticism and Science

Montaigne's reconsideration of the limits of knowledge begins with a seeming contradiction. Immediately after stating that "experience" has taught him the possibility of infinite advancement in the arts and sciences, he appears to revert to the Pyrrhonian denial that we can know anything.[1] If man is ignorant of "first causes and principles," he must "give up all the rest of his knowledge," for it lacks a foundation. The Academics, Montaigne points out, were inconsistent in believing "some things more probable than others" while denying that human beings are capable of knowledge. A judgment of probability can be founded only on a recognition of truth. Thus Montaigne professes to find the Pyrrhonian position "bolder" and "more likely." Emulating the Pyrrhonians, he argues that, since our perception of things varies with our physical condition, "things do not lodge in us in their own form and essence." Furthermore, the fact that every proposition can be debated and controverted demonstrates the absence of

[1]Hence Villey (*Montaigne et François Bacon*, p. 65) judges that the former argument was "only a sally" and that the sequel demonstrates Montaigne's real belief that the "progress" of science is illusory. Brush (*Montaigne and Bayle*, p. 103n) seeks to explain the shift by arguing that the words expressing a belief in progress "are not the essayist's own, but rather the expression of an apparently common sense idea that Montaigne wishes to reject"—despite the fact that they are stated in the first person and express what Montaigne professes to have "learned [*essayé*] through experience." Yet Brush also notes that the pages in which these remarks occur are the most "personal" in tone in all of the "Apology" (p. 105).

François Tavera is one of the few scholars to have taken seriously Montaigne's allusion in this passage to the possibility of infinite scientific progress (*L'Idée d'humanité*, pp. 74–5).

any "natural power" in us (such as Aristotle's *nous*) by which we can grasp the truth. Thus the earlier account of the futility of the pursuit of knowledge would seem to be confirmed (543–5 [421–2]).

But Montaigne now draws a quite different consequence from our necessary ignorance of nature's essential character. At the conclusion of his account of the philosophers' inquiries into "human and natural things," we recall, he observed that knowledge of human nature is the precondition of any other knowledge. He reiterates that thought here by asserting that "if the soul knew anything, it would first of all know itself." The Pyrrhonian argument suggests that we can know at least this much of ourselves: that we are necessarily ignorant of the true constitution of the things we perceive. From this fact, the Pyrrhonians themselves derived nothing fruitful, but only a complete suspension of judgment that leads to "infinite irresolution" (543 [421]). Montaigne, however, has described irresolution elsewhere as "the most common and apparent vice of our nature" (II, i, 315 [239]). He suggests a way out of this irresolution, therefore, based on the Pyrrhonians' own picture of human capacities. Our ignorance of the nature of things causes them, he argues, to "surrender to our mercy" and "dwell in us as we please" (545 [422]). It follows, according to the argument of an earlier chapter, that we have an opportunity to "dispose of them and arrange them to our advantage" (I, xiv, 50 [33]).[2] These remarks elaborate, and must be understood in the light of, the description of philosophy earlier in the "Apology" as an essentially constructive or creative enterprise. If we lack access to the essences of things, the way we view them is a product of ourselves, not of the objects. Our very ignorance, once we are aware of it, makes our minds free in a certain sense: it allows us to dispense with the vain quest to know things as they are, and enables us to understand them rather "as we please," by arranging the data derived from our sense perceptions into any forms we choose. We are free to choose our "presuppositions."[3]

To understand in what sense knowledge is possible on this basis, we must consider the difference between the attitude Montaigne adopts toward "appearances" and the stance of the Pyrrhonians. He points out how difficult it is to conceive of what the Pyrrhonians assert, that we are "no more assured of the movement of a stone that leaves our hand than of the eighth sphere" (544 [422]). However unreliable our everyday sense percep-

[2]The context of this earlier remark is a discussion of our capacity, by means of adopting a particular philosophic outlook, to ease the physical ills of human existence; but Montaigne's use of the identical phrase "surrender to our mercy" regarding our relation to external things, as well as the overall similitude of reasoning between that passage and the one being discussed in the "Apology," implies a link between them.

[3]On this and the following summary of Montaigne's conception of science, compare Leo Strauss's account of Hobbes's similar reasoning, in *Natural Right and History* (Chicago, 1953), pp. 174–5.

tions may be as a guide to what things truly are, he later observes that "there is no more extreme absurdity to us than to maintain that fire does not heat, that light does not illumine, that there is no weight or firmness in iron, which are notions that the senses bring us; *man has no belief or knowledge that can compare to this sort of certainty*" (572 [444]).[4]

The greatest certainty that is available to us, according to this passage, is of particular, constant *conjunctions* among our perceptions—for example, between the looks and the feel of iron. However groundless reason may show this certainty to be, as Montaigne has previously argued (523 [404–5]) (and as Hume will later stress), to attempt to live as if we did not have it is ridiculous. Pyrrho, who tried to live in accordance with his doctrine, had to be saved by friends from falling off precipices and being hit by carts, so Montaigne later reports (II, xxix, 684 [533]).[5] Thus Montaigne mocks the Pyrrhonians farther on in the "Apology" for "using their arguments and their reason only to ruin the appearance of experience and . . . combat the evidence of the facts."[6] As for himself, he "would rather follow facts than reason" (554 [430]). Although he has shown the weakness of the Academics' contention that we can know the "probable" *truth,* he later avows that he prefers "to hold to the solid and the probable" rather than believe what is obscure and incomprehensible (III, xi, 1008 [789]).[7]

In short, although the appearances we perceive may reveal nothing of the true essence of things, they provide us with a knowledge of utmost *practical* value, the "experience" that constitutes the only reasonable guide for our actions.[8] Unfortunately, experience alone provides only weak guidance, not

---

[4]Cf. I, xiv, 55 [37]: "Here [in perceiving pain] all does not consist in imagination. We have opinions about the rest; here it is *certain knowledge* that plays its part. Even our senses are judges of it"; II, xxxvii, 753 [587]: "Surgery seems to me much more certain [than other branches of medicine], because it *sees and feels* what it is doing"; III, xiii, 1074 [840]: "I judge myself only by actual feeling, not by reason." Cf. Tavera, *L'Idée d'humanité,* p. 71.

[5]In his earlier, more favorable presentation of Pyrrhonism in the "Apology," Montaigne had professed to find such stories (which derive from Diogenes Laertius) incompatible with a true interpretation of the Pyrrhonian principle (485 [374]). Sextus Empiricus, on whose exposition of Pyrrhonian doctrine Montaigne's previous account of it had been based, indeed denies that that doctrine entails a practical disregard of our sense perceptions (*Hypotyposes,* I, vii–x). Be this as it may, Montaigne's elaboration of the stories about Pyrrho in the later chapter without any accompanying expression of disbelief in them seems clearly to signify his own ultimate rejection of what he labels that thinker's "amusing science" (II, xxix, 684 [533]).

[6]Cf. Bacon, *Novum Organon,* I, aph. 37. Though I have followed Frame's translation of *effects* as "facts" in the above passage, it may also mean "effects" in English. The latter sense accords with Montaigne's recommendation that we concern ourselves with the "effects" we experience, rather than wonder about the essences of the things that cause them (see III, xi, 1003–4 [785]).

[7]The link between the "probabilism" of the Academics "and Montaigne's final acceptance of experience as a commonsense solution of the sceptical dilemma" is noted by Elaine Limbrick, "Was Montaigne Really a Pyrrhonian?" *Bibliothèque d'humanisme et Renaissance* 39 (1977): 75.

[8]Cf. the opening passages of II, vi, and III, xiii, where Montaigne recommends the study and use of experience, but ostensibly only as a supplement to the nobler instrument of reason. As

only because our perceptions vary with our physical state (569, 583 [441, 453]) but also because each person's experience is finite while nature's scope and variety are infinite. In the last chapters of Books II and III, however, Montaigne suggests that a science can be built upon experience that will marvelously improve the human condition. This science is what he calls "medicine."

Having described health, earlier in the "Apology," as the most valuable of goods (464 [357]), he refers to it in a later chapter as "a precious thing," and the only good that merits devoting one's life to its pursuit. He also expresses certainty that there can be an "art" of medicine, which would discover, "among so many works of nature," those that are "suited to the preservation of our health" (II, xxxvii, 744 [580]). While describing medicine as "the most important science within our use, being the one that is in charge of our preservation and health," he goes on to lament, however, that it is also the most "uncertain" and "confused" (II, xxxvii, 750 [585]).[9] Aside from the superstition and dissension by which it is bound, its fundamental weakness is that the "experience" on which its rules are grounded is unpersuasive. Most of the "medicinal virtues" of substances, Montaigne observes, are properties that can be discovered only through "usage." Apart from the possible "miracle" of demonic inspiration, the only way it is likely we could discover such curative properties is either by finding them accidentally in "things that often fall into our use for some other consideration" or by observing "the example of certain animals." But the essayist finds most of the physicians' claims to have discovered medicinal properties to be

---

Villey points out, despite this seeming disparagement of experience, he relies on it (as does Bacon) as the foundation of his teaching and demonstrates that it is foolish to despise it (*Montaigne et François Bacon*, pp. 88–9). Cf. also E. M. Curley, *Descartes against the Skeptics* (Cambridge, Mass., 1978), p. 15, which observes that other seventeenth-century scientific thinkers, "such as Gassendi and Mersenne, accepted a part of what Montaigne said, agreeing with him that we could have no genuine knowledge of the real nature of things, but arguing that a knowledge of appearances was sufficient for all practical purposes. What is important to us is not how things really are, but how they seem. So long as we can develop a science of appearances and a knowledge of what experiences may be expected to follow a given set of experiences, this is all that we require." I argue that this new conception of science was fully, not just partly, in accordance with Montaigne's teaching. Cf. Gierczynski, "Le 'Que sais-je?' de Montaigne," pp. 22, 70–71, 76; François Batisse, "Montaigne et les principes de la médicine expérimentale," in Palassie, ed., *Mémorial*, pp. 208–15; Will G. Moore, "L' 'Apologie' et la Science," ibid., pp. 200–203. See also *Essais*, III, xiii, 1053–4 [823–4], concerning Montaigne's practice, in contrast to the pretensions of "the scholars," of describing only what he has learned from experience, without attempting "to arrange this infinite variety of actions" and "aspects" into "certain types and sections"; and III, vi, 876–7 [685].

[9]Although Montaigne ascribes these opinions to "one of [the doctors'] friends" (i.e., Pliny, his source), he does not contradict them, and the body of his argument supports them. Tavera, *L'Idée d'humanité*, pp. 146–8, emphasizes the importance Montaigne attributed to the science of medicine and stresses that his criticisms are directed against the ignorance of its sixteenth-century practitioners, not against "medicine itself." See also François Batisse, *Montaigne et la médicine* (Paris, 1962).

incredible, since the circumstances in which a given cure was achieved are so numerous and variable that there is no way to identify its actual cause with any certainty. These circumstances include the patient's age, temperament, and particular malady; the time and place of the cure; the conjunction of the planets at the time; and the part of the body that was treated.[10] How can one know that a patient's return to health occurred because of the physician's treatment, and not "because the illness had reached its term, or [as] an effect of chance, or the operation of something else he had eaten or drunk or touched that day, or the merit of his grandmother's prayers?" (II, xxxvii, 762–3 [594–5]; cf. 752–3 [586–7]).

In the process of noting the obstacles to a science of medicine, however, Montaigne suggests a way to overcome them. He urges, first, that more people "record their experiences" as he has done, so that medicine will have a broader empirical foundation (II, xxxvii, 763 [595]; III, xiii, 1056 [826]). But a random record of various people's experiences will not suffice. In the first place, one must consider the observers' character and judgment. Montaigne frequently expresses distrust of reports ostensibly based on observation, such as accusations of witchcraft (III, xi, 1009–10 [789–90]; cf. II, x, 397–8 [304–5]). Most people are easily deceived by their imagination; hence it is unwise to rely on "popular belief" [foy] (I, xxi, 104 [76]). Nor does the mere number of witnesses prove anything: Montaigne remarks that "in a matter on which I would not believe one, I would not believe a hundred ones." In "researches" concerning medical "cures," "a very prudent, attentive, and subtle inquirer is needed, impartial and unprejudiced" (III, xi, 1006 [787]).[11]

Assuming a number of such inquirers could be found, they would have to follow a rigorous procedure in order to provide others with useful medical experience. Montaigne suggests that the curative properties of different substances be tested repeatedly, with the results being carefully recorded. In order to isolate the curative factor among the infinity of possibly relevant circumstances, these tests must be conducted by a "fortune" that is "perfectly artificial, regulated, and methodical" (II, xxxvii, 762–3 [595]). Fortune itself, Montaigne has observed, does not have these characteristics: its

[10]Montaigne's previous dismissal of "horoscopy" (II, xii, 542 [420]) makes it doubtful that he regards the position of the planets as a truly relevant factor; nor can his eulogy of the power of the heavens at the outset of his attack on Sebond's rationalistic critics (428–9 [329–30]) be assumed to represent his serious belief, in view of his subsequent critique of astrological doctrines (518 [401]). Cf. the remark of Kepler (Opera, ed. Frisch, VIII, 705), quoted in Edwin A. Burtt, The Metaphysical Foundations of Modern Science, rev. ed. (New York, 1954), p. 69n, suggesting the need for an astronomer to feign a belief in astrology for prudential reasons.

[11]Cf. Descartes's dismissal of others' experiments, on account of the multitude of "superfluous circumstances and elements" they contain, as well as the researchers' endeavor to make the results conform to their preconceptions: Discours de la méthode, VI, in Oeuvres et lettres, p. 176.

motion is inconstant and fluctuating (I, xxxiv, 217 [163]). His argument suggests the possibility of regulating fortune, however, by means of a process of controlled experimentation, of the sort relied on by modern natural science.[12]

It would be foolishly risky to test the properties of randomly chosen substances by applying each one to a human subject. But Montaigne has suggested that it may be almost as useful to observe the effects of different substances on certain animals (presumably, those that most resemble human beings); earlier in the chapter he reports having conducted such an experiment to test a treatment that "men of understanding" had recommended "for the protection and preservation of human life" (the result suggested they were wrong) (II, xxxvii, 759–60, 762 [592, 594]).[13] Moreover, one must bear in mind Montaigne's broad understanding of "medicine" as comprising "everything that is found to be salubrious for our life" (II, xxxvii, 745 [581]). This definition suggests that the process of controlled experimentation should be used to seek out *all* the potentially useful properties of things, not only their "medicinal" ones in the usual sense. Montaigne asserts "the power and fertility of nature and its application to our need" but laments the deficiency of "our science and art," which limit "the usage that we draw from nature" (II, xxxvii, 744 [580]). By remarking in the "Apology" that "what I say of medicine may be applied generally to all knowledge," in a context where he is decrying the inability of learning to "blunt and lessen the keenness of the misfortunes that pursue us" (470–71 [362]), he implies the need to reform science as a whole along the lines he has suggested are appropriate for medicine; that is, to put the quest for learning on an experiential, or experimental, basis.[14]

It would be insufficient to describe the scientific procedure Montaigne prescribes as simply experiential, however. In ordinary life we experience objects and events as wholes or members of classes, not merely as groups of

[12]Cf. Bacon, *Novum Organon*, I, aph. 100. Villey notes that the entire passage cited from II, xxxvii, constitutes a kind of invitation to Baconian experimental science, but he overlooks the significance of Montaigne's reference to an "artificial, regulated and methodical" fortune and hence denies that the essayist recognized "the possibility of guiding experience" as Bacon did (*Montaigne et François Bacon*, pp. 101–3). Lanson acknowledges Montaigne's awareness of the need "to organize experience" and to establish "an experimental method" but still underestimates the degree to which the essayist laid the foundations of such a method (Lanson, *Les Essais*, pp. 279–80). Tavera (*L'Idée d'humanité*, p. 70) points out the "extreme importance" Montaigne attaches to method, and the connection of his thought in this regard to that of Descartes. See also Batisse, "Montaigne et les principes de la médicine expérimentale," pp. 209–13; Moore, "L'Apologie' et la Science," pp. 202–3; Limbrick, "Was Montaigne Really a Pyrrhonian?" p. 74.

[13]Sayce, *Essays*, p. 186, comments that "we have here a true if elementary manifestation of the experimental spirit," reminiscent of Bacon's work.

[14]The French word *expérience* has the sense of "experiment" as well as "experience"; Montaigne appears to use the term in the former sense at II, xxxvii, 762 [594], with reference to Galen.

sense data.[15] In other words, as thinking beings, we deal with the world through the mediation of our concepts: the data of our senses reach our consciousness already "interpreted" by those concepts. Yet it is just here that the problem lies, according to Montaigne. Several chapters of the *Essays* recount manifestly absurd reports of events (such as many of the animal stories presented earlier in the "Apology") ostensibly based on "experience," which exemplify the tendency of the imagination to distort people's observations (see especially I, xxi; III, xi).

Classical philosophy sought to overcome this problem by means of dialectic: that is, the juxtaposition of opposed common opinions, with a view to extracting the element of truth that each embodies from the morass of prejudice and error in which it is naturally embedded.[16] Montaigne, however, has challenged the assumption that there is an underlying harmony between the human mind and the world, such that the truth about nature is accessible to an inquiry that begins at the level of common opinion.[17] The very fact "that no proposition can be seen that is not debated and controverted among us, or that may not be," demonstrates the insufficiency of our "natural judgment" as a guide to truth (II, xii, 545 [422–3]). To refound science on a firm and unquestionable base requires a radical break with common opinion. The means Montaigne proposes to achieve this goal is to restrict the definition of scientifically relevant "experience" to information derived from the senses, as validated by the perception of a number of unbiased observers under identical conditions. Such experience is the indubitable residue that was left by Montaigne's critique of human reason earlier in the "Apology," which indicated the uncertainty of all attempted descriptions of that which transcends the corporeal and sensible.

Experience in this altered sense, however, constitutes only the starting point of Montaigne's new science. The science of medicine, properly understood, comprises not merely a set of experientially founded precepts concerning the appropriate cures for various diseases but a broader set of generalizations concerning the rules by which nature as a whole appears to operate. How an understanding of this sort may be acquired is suggested by several remarks early in the last chapter of the *Essays*, titled "Of Experience."

Near the beginning of this chapter Montaigne asserts that no two natural

[15]Cf. Georg W. F. Hegel, *Phenomenology of the Mind*, tr. James Baillie, rev. 2d ed. (London, 1949), pp. 149–78; Aristotle, *Physics*, 184a25–26; *Posterior Analytics*, 100a15–b1.

[16]See, e.g., Plato, *Republic*, 514a ff., 523b ff., 531e ff.; *Phaedo*, 99e–100a; cf. Bloom, *Republic of Plato*, pp. 406–7.

[17]Cf. III, viii, 903–5 [706–7], regarding the limitations of "dialectical" inquiries; also the quotation from Cicero at I, xxiii, 109 [79]. Montaigne's rejection of the assumption of an underlying harmony between our mind and the world was also suggested by his critique of the Platonic doctrine of recollection, earlier in the "Apology" (530 [410–11]).

objects are exactly alike, and that the differences among them are greater than their resemblances. Thus "the inference that we try to draw from the resemblance of events is uncertain, because they are always dissimilar" (III, xiii, 1041 [815]). Taken in itself, this argument would seem to deny the possibility of a meaningful science of nature. In the sequel Montaigne does argue the difficulty of subsuming human actions under *prescriptive* laws that stipulate our duties. With regard to "the hunt for knowledge," however, he reiterates that an infinite progress is possible (III, xiii, 1045, 1047 [817, 819]). The seeming contradiction between the last two quotations is resolved in a third passage where Montaigne observes that although "no event and no form entirely resembles another, so none is entirely different from another." Even though, because of the diversity of things, "the relation that is drawn from experience is always faulty and imperfect," still "all things hold together by some similarity." Hence we always have "some corner" by which to "fasten comparisons together" (III, xiii, 1047 [819]).

The import of this argument is that even though nature's infinite variety constitutes an insuperable obstacle to science in the Aristotelian sense, which seeks to articulate the structure of Being by identifying the essential characteristics of each natural genus and species of things, that variety is compatible with another kind of science, which would recognize its generalizations to be *hypothetical constructs*. Though any randomly selected pair of objects will be sufficiently similar in one or more respects to enable the observer to classify them together for analytical purposes, it must be recognized that every such classification is arbitrary inasmuch as it disregards differences between the objects. The classification will reflect the focus of the observer's interest on one quality rather than another, but it can never attain the status of an account of the true structure of nature. Just as in the "Apology" Montaigne had denounced the "grammatical" error of assuming that our verbal categories reflect real entities, in "Of Experience" he mocks the Aristotelian and Scholastic practice of explaining things through such "purely verbal," general terms as "substance" (III, xiii, 1046 [818–19]).[18]

From the standpoint of everyday experience, Montaigne's claim that all classifications are equally arbitrary sounds absurd. It surely does not seem arbitrary to classify two horses (however different they may otherwise be) as belonging to a species separate in nature from that of a cow. Not only are the visible differences between these species much greater than those within them, but two horses have never been known to generate a cow. Montaigne's premise, however, is that we cannot know that we perceive all or

---

[18]Cf. Locke, *Essay Concerning Human Understanding*, III.iii, vi; also, with reference to Bacon's reinterpretation of "the concept of truth as knowledge of effects as revealed by experiment," such that there can be "no finished theory of the frame of the world," Caton, *Politics of Progress*, p. 39.

most of the qualities belonging to these animals, let alone the "essential" ones.[19] Moreover, the eternal variation of nature's "forms" makes even the argument based on generation inadequate, as Montaigne suggests elsewhere by describing a "monstrous" deformed child. He denies that such a case is "unnatural"; "what we call monsters are not so" in the light of the "infinity of forms" in nature that are unfamiliar to us. Indeed, "nothing is anything but according to nature, whatever it may be" (II, xxx, 691 [539]).[20]

Montaigne's assertion that all things are equally natural implies a rejection of the Aristotelian interpretation of nature in teleological terms. The latter had rested on a distinction between nature's "intention," which is realized in most cases, and deviations from that intention resulting from chance. According to this view, the occasional occurrence of individuals with characteristics that depart from the norm of their species would not in itself refute the existence of species.[21] Montaigne, on the contrary, cites such deviations as evidence of the arbitrariness, or at least the artificiality, of all human classifications of natural objects. While viewing nature as a vast "machine," operating according to fixed laws, he denies that there is any permanence or manifest order to the particular forms she produces. What is permanent, and hence a possible object of science, is simply matter and the laws according to which it is perpetually transformed.[22]

Montaigne's brief and scattered remarks about the character of nature cannot be said to constitute a serious refutation of the Aristotelian view. Moreover, these remarks appear to leave unresolved certain fairly obvious difficulties. (How can Montaigne himself continue to speak about human "nature" if there are no fixed boundaries between species?) However, the essayist's strategy in dealing with the Aristotelian view, as suggested earlier in the "Apology," is essentially a negative one: to challenge its underlying "presuppositions" by emphasizing that, however plausible they may seem

[19]Cf. I, l, 289 [219]: "For I do not see the whole of anything; nor do those who promise to make us see it. Of a hundred members or faces that each thing has, I take one."

[20]The "monstrous child" constitutes a more serious piece of evidence for the thesis Montaigne propounded earlier in the "Apology" (seemingly relying on spurious "evidence" from Pliny, Plutarch, and Herodotus) to the effect that human nature may be more variable than we commonly suppose. Cf. Locke, Essay Concerning Human Understanding, III.vi.23, 26–7. And consider the statement by a contemporary exponent of sociobiology that owing to the genetic diversity among individuals, " 'Man' does not exist"; although "humans have a nature, it is complex and changing" (Roger D. Masters, "Evolutionary Biology and Naturalism," Interpretation 17 [1989]: 113, 121).

[21]See Aristotle, Physics, II.5–8; On the Generation of Animals, 767b, 770b; Politics, I.5. One must note, however, that the "intention" Aristotle attributes to nature is not a conscious one; see Stephen G. Salkever, Finding the Mean: Theory and Practice in Aristotelian Political Philosophy (Princeton, N.J., 1990), pp. 43–4; and, more generally, Martha Craven Nussbaum, Aristotle's "De Motu Animalium" (Princeton, N.J., 1978), pp. 59–106.

[22]The eternity of matter is suggested at p. 507 [391] of the "Apology," where Montaigne refers to life as a brief interruption of "our perpetual and natural condition" and goes on to cite the opinion "that there is neither generation nor corruption in nature"; and at p. 586 [455], where he says that "all mortal things go on flowing and rolling unceasingly."

to common sense, they themselves cannot be proved. By demonstrating that the Aristotelian view—like all philosophic accounts of the whole—rests on inherently questionable foundations, Montaigne aims to liberate his readers from the belief that it *must* be accepted. Having shown that the facts of nature do not compel one particular interpretation, he suggests that the ground of the choice we make among views of nature be shifted from "truth" to utility: that is, the extent to which a particular view can facilitate our prediction, and even our manipulation, of nature's behavior, with a view to satisfying our physical needs. This point is expressed by a passage in the "Apology" wherein Montaigne discusses the changes that have previously occurred in our conceptions of natural phenomena. After citing the overthrow of the belief in the motion of "the heaven and the stars," he remarks that "in our day Copernicus has grounded" the doctrine of the earth's motion "so well that he uses it very systematically [*très-regléement*][23] for all astronomical deductions." Despite Copernicus' success, Montaigne suggests that his example should make us aware of the possibility that "a third opinion, a thousand years from now, will . . . overthrow the preceding two." Hence, he infers, "when some new doctrine is presented to us, we have great occasion to distrust it," knowing that however plausible it may seem, it too may some day be supplanted. Aristotle's principles, for instance, which "satisfy us at present . . . are no more exempt from being thrown out than their predecessors were" (553–4 [429]).

Given the outwardly skeptical tone of this passage, it is understandable that Richard H. Popkin (along with many other commentators) should interpret it to signify that Montaigne was unimpressed with the scientific discoveries of his time and "recommended abandoning scientific research along with other misguided efforts to find out what is really going on."[24] But this impression is mistaken. The remarks with which Montaigne concluded his accounts, earlier in the "Apology," of the philosophers' findings about the heavens and humanity, along with his previous eulogies of learning and of the philosophers, made evident his esteem for the pursuit of knowledge. And the language with which he describes Copernicus' discoveries is itself highly favorable. Rather than signifying a rejection of science, the passage under consideration reflects Montaigne's desire to encourage people to examine all scientific theories critically in the light of observable facts, and to hold to a given view only so long as available data bear it out—in contrast with the church's practice, which he has decried, of freezing scientific inquiry by turning chosen doctrines about nature into matters of "religion." The ultimate test of the value of any scientific theory, as Montaigne goes on to suggest with the example of explanations of "the nature

[23]Cf. Montaigne's demand in the passage cited previously from II, xxxvii, 762–3 [595], that medical experiments be conducted by a "fortune" that is perfectly "*reglée*" (translated then as "regular").

[24]Popkin, "The Sceptical Origins of the Modern Problem of Knowledge," in Norman S. Care and Robert H. Grimm, eds., *Perception and Personal Identity* (Cleveland, 1969), p. 14.

and movements of the winds," is its utility in enabling us to predict and hence make use of nature's mode of operation (in this case, in navigation) (554 [430]). Montaigne's comment, in discussing Copernicus' theory and its predecessor, that "we should not bother which of the two is so" (553 [429]), simply means that the truth of a theory is not a matter of concern *apart* from its utility.[25] His assault on the Aristotelian understanding of nature has been motivated by the belief that only if people are persuaded to forsake the aspiration of articulating the structure of Being can they be driven to focus their inquiries on the pursuit of "useful" knowledge of nature's mode of operation. Only by liberating ourselves from the assumption of an underlying harmony between our intellect and the nature of things can we be impelled to investigate with adequate care the lowly material and efficient causes of the phenomena we experience (cf. III, xi, 1006 [787]).[26]

Fundamental to Montaigne's conception of natural science is what we call "analysis," that is, the breaking up of the phenomena we ordinarily experience as complete entities into their material, perceptible elements.[27] Data about these qualities drawn from the process of controlled experimentation are reconstituted into new categories that enable the scientist to

[25]Similarly, the essayist's hesitancy to put his own life "to the test" of Paracelsus' medical discoveries (554 [430]) signifies no more than a prudent disinclination to serve as a guinea pig, at a time when medical science had a long way to go before becoming reasonably trustworthy. On the state of medical knowledge in Montaigne's time, see Vivian Nutton, "Montaigne in the Age of Medicine," in Keith Cameron, ed., *Montaigne and His Age* (Exeter, Eng., 1981), pp. 15–25.

[26]Cf. Sayce's comment on Montaigne's discussion of astronomy earlier in the "Apology": "All this is very close to the recent concept of models in science, not an exact picture of reality but an approximate representation of how it might be thought to work." Sayce infers that even though Montaigne's "empiricism and attack on merely verbal authority" helped "to lay the foundations for the [scientific] discoveries of the seventeenth century," the essayist's "scepticism is clearly more in tune with the doubts of recent science than with the confidence of the great period which immediately followed him" (Sayce, *Essays*, pp. 187–8). But perhaps Montaigne's rejection of what is now called scientific "realism" was implicit in modern science all along: consider Bacon's denial of the "false assertion that the sense of man is the measure of things" and his portrayal of the human understanding as "a false mirror" (*Novum Organon*, I, xli); also Kant's distinction—at the peak of the Enlightenment—between the "phenomenal" realm in which empirical science is constrained to operate and the "noumenal," truly intelligible realm. From this perspective the present-day "crisis" in the philosophy of science, in which the authority of reason itself has come to be doubted, may stem from a broader societal disillusionment with the modern project of mastering nature rather than from any new "discoveries" in philosophy or science. For a summary statement by a leading contemporary philosopher of science which partly reflects Montaigne's own account of the scientific enterprise but embodies a far more equivocal view of scientific progress, see Karl R. Popper, *The Logic of Scientific Discovery*, 2d Torchbook ed. (New York, 1968), pp. 278–81. See also Thomas Kuhn, *The Structure of Scientific Revolutions*, 2d ed. (Chicago, 1970), pp. 170–73, 206. On the link between modern scientific empiricism in its original form and the subsequent historicist critique of science, see Eugene F. Miller, "Locke on the Meaning of Political Language: The Teaching of the *Essay Concerning Human Understanding*," *Political Science Reviewer* 9 (1979): 165, 176–8, 191.

[27]Cf. Jonas, "The Practical Uses of Theory," in *The Phenomenon of Life*, pp. 200–202; Bacon, *The Great Instauration*, in *Works*, 4:25: "What the sciences stand in need of is a form of induction which shall analyse experience and take it to pieces."

advance our understanding of nature's mode of operation. Such categories (as instanced by the wave and particle theories of light employed by modern physicists) may deviate enormously from our everyday, "natural" way of looking at the world. Their very artificiality makes it unlikely, moreover, that any of them represents a literal account of the structure of nature. Any given theory constitutes a hypothesis designed to account for the data thus far acquired; no such theory should be taken to embody the ultimate truth. But this fact in no way reduces the utility of the partial knowledge we acquire of nature's operation: while knowledge of the ultimate causes of things may lie beyond us, "we have the perfectly full use of them, according to our nature, without penetrating to their origin and essence" (III, xi, 1003 [785]).

Montaigne's reconstitution of the purpose and method of scientific inquiry entails a transformation of our bearing or attitude toward nature, for which the earlier, "negative" or critical portion of the "Apology" prepared us. Even though the purported intent of Montaigne's comparison of humanity to the beasts was to humble human pride, its actual lesson was the penury of our natural condition, and the consequent need to improve that condition by means of our own "arms." Although the ancient philosophers were indeed vain in Montaigne's view in aspiring to rival the gods through their pursuit of knowledge, his argument entails that human beings should take the place of God in another sense, by achieving the *creative* power that the Bible attributes to the Deity. Montaigne observes (in a somewhat different context) that "the greatest miracles of nature" could be formed "from the most ordinary, commonplace, familiar things," if only we "put them in their proper light" (III, xiii, 1059 [829]). But to take advantage of nature's fertility and "set it to work," "we must subject it . . . for our service" (I, viii, 33 [20]). Although nature, in her "pitiless" way, cares no more for our species than for "fleas and moles" (II, xxxvii, 746 [582]), this defect of nature can be supplied by the compassion of such men as Montaigne (III, xiii, 1079 [844]), who will force nature to serve our needs. "There is nothing useless in nature" (III, i, 767 [599])—not because nature has provided for us but because we can compel her to do so if we know how.[28] Our proper posture toward nature is one of mastery, not gratitude.[29]

[28]Cf. also III, vi, 885–6 [692–3], where an admiring account of other civilizations' inventions is preceded and followed by a lament regarding the inadequacy of "our knowledge" of nature, implying that an increase in the latter could generate a vast development of devices to ameliorate the human condition. (This chapter opens with a mockery of ancient writers' explanations of various human bodily conditions, on account of their insufficient attentiveness to "experience," and their disposition to substitute edifying *literary* "invention" for reality—876–7 [685]). The passage cited from II, xxxvii, contradicts Starobinski's attribution to Montaigne of the belief that "even if we renounce the pride of knowledge, we still know that a benevolent Nature stands ready to meet our needs and deserves our docile obedience" (*Montaigne in Motion*, p. 301).

[29]Cf. Descartes, *Discours de la méthode*, VI, in *Oeuvres et lettres*, p. 168, regarding the individual's duty to advance the "general good" of humanity, which Descartes interprets as

In the light of the new attitude Montaigne proposes toward nature, it is possible to clarify the ambiguity in his earlier treatment of the naturalness of human desires and of arts designed to satisfy those desires. That ambiguity resulted from the intermixing of two distinct conceptions of nature—an older, teleological view, according to which nature embodies standards, which serve as limits (instinctive in the lower animals, intelligible in human beings), conformity to which is beneficial for each species, and an opposed view, which denies any such preexistent harmony between the natural and the good. Having given lip service to the former view when attacking human "presumption," Montaigne ultimately rejects it. What is truly presumptuous, he suggests, is the naive belief that God or nature has ordained such a benign or elevated status for us that we need not make great efforts to alleviate the miseries of our condition—but can dedicate ourselves, instead, to pursuing "higher" goods. In portraying the natural human condition as a purely animal one, Montaigne was in effect satirizing the teleological view. Once one grants that we must employ art to promote our well-being, given the penury of our condition without it, there is no "natural" limit that can be drawn to the need for such art—or to the desires that the arts both awaken and serve.[30] What needs limiting is not our desire for earthly comforts but our "vain" disposition to scorn such goods in pursuit of transcendent ones; since that disposition is itself natural (I, iii, 18 [8]), human nature must in this sense be constrained by art.

The redirection of human concern from transcendent things to earthly ones is the precondition of a science that—unlike previous philosophy—will be inherently, not accidentally, progressive. Of his philosophic predecessors Montaigne remarks, "The pride of those who attributed to the human mind a capacity for all things produced in others, through spite and emulation, the opinion that it is capable of nothing" (III, xi, 1013 [792]). The uncertainty of the teachings of previous philosophers, who aspired to comprehend the meaning, purpose, and order of the universe, left their findings vulnerable to the attacks of the Skeptics, who denied that any knowledge is possible. This uncertainty is traceable to the philosophers' concurrence, explicit or implicit, in Protagoras' assumption that "man [is] the measure of all things," that is, that the human perspective on the world is the "true" one (540 [418]).[31] If the quest for knowledge is not to remain

---

obliging him to contribute to the project of making us "masters and possessors of nature." Cf. also Jonas, *Phenomenon of Life*, pp. 192–3; Strauss, *Natural Right and History*, p. 175.

[30]Contrast Aristotle, *Politics*, 1256b7–58b8; but cf. Wayne H. Ambler, "Aristotle's Understanding of the Naturalness of the City," *Review of Politics* 47 (1985): 163–85, esp. 175. Cf. also, on Aristotle's treatment of the arts, Seth Benardete, "On Wisdom and Philosophy: The First Two Chapters of Aristotle's *Metaphysics* A," *Review of Metaphysics* 32 (1978): 215–25.

[31]Cf. Villey, *Montaigne et François Bacon*, p. 82. In its original form, Protagoras' remark appears to have been intended as a statement of conventionalism, and it is criticized as such both by Plato's Socrates and by Aristotle (Plato, *Theaetetus*, 161c ff.; *Cratylus*, 386a ff.; Aristotle, *Metaphysics*, XI.6). Montaigne, however, seems to cite the remark to impute an unjustified anthropocentrism both to Protagoras and to his more renowned critics.

futile, the human mind must be diverted from the unanswerable metaphysical questions with which previous philosophers as well as theologians were concerned.[32] The kind of "knowledge" Montaigne directs us to pursue—knowledge of the properties of things *as they appear* to us and affect us, and of the chain of efficient causes that produce them—is one in which progress can be made, since the findings of a series of properly conducted experiments can be refuted only by new findings that in turn broaden our knowledge and our capacity to predict nature's behavior. The arts and sciences, Montaigne remarks, "are not cast in a mold, but are formed and shaped little by little, by repeated handling and polishing"; the labors of each inquirer serve to advance the starting point of subsequent investigators (543 [421]). "It is only personal weakness that makes us content with what others or we ourselves have found out in this hunt for knowledge. . . . There is always room for a successor, yes, and for ourselves, and a road elsewhere. There is no end to our inquiries" (III, xiii, 1045 [817]).

As these passages suggest, the progressive character of natural science as Montaigne describes it makes it an essentially collective endeavor, unlike the individual ascent out of Plato's cave. The infinite vastness of the factual knowledge being sought of nature's operation dictates that "medicine" be subdivided into a variety of specialized fields (II, xxxvii, 754 [588]). The divisibility of this knowledge eliminates the need for each inquirer to reproduce previous investigations; instead, the inquirer builds on prior researchers' findings, following the rules of method to advance to further discoveries.[33] This divisibility reflects the fact that the knowledge being sought is valued not in itself, as a satisfaction of our deepest need, but for the uses to which it can be put.[34] Montaigne's teaching points toward the subsequent recruitment of an army of scientific laborers who supplement (and in a sense—whether or not Montaigne intended it—ultimately supplant) the work of philosophers: whereas "men of understanding" in Montaigne's sense are always rare (III, iii, 802 [625]; III, viii, 910 [711]), less natural talent or dedication may be required of a "prudent, attentive, and subtle" scientific researcher who has been properly educated in the presuppositions of science.[35]

---

[32]Cf. Villey, *Montaigne et François Bacon*, pp. 78–9; Strauss, *Natural Right and History*, p. 175 (Hobbes's "walls").

[33]Cf. Kuhn, *Scientific Revolutions*, pp. 19–20: "When the individual scientist can take a paradigm for granted, he need no longer, in his major works, attempt to build his field anew, starting from first principles and justifying the use of each concept introduced." There is an integral relation between this division of scientific labor and the questionable *rationality* of modern science as Kuhn articulates it.

[34]Cf. III, viii, 904–5 [707–8]: learning in itself is "a thing of almost indifferent quality"; only "in its true use"—in service to "the need of life"—is it "the most noble and powerful acquisition of man." Cf. Jonas, *Phenomenon of Life*, pp. 188–93.

[35]Cf. Descartes, *Discours de la méthode*, VI, in *Oeuvres et lettres*, pp. 175, 177, concerning the need and use of paid "artisans" to execute what Descartes represents (p. 169) as a vast collective undertaking. On the modern transformation of the pursuit of knowledge into a

During Montaigne's era a number of other, lesser known writers urged the pursuit of empirical, "practical" knowledge of nature, associated with the arts, in opposition to the traditional "aristocratic" contempt for such concerns and to the disposition to seek knowledge in books rather than in observation of the natural world.[36] Montaigne's attack on the pretensions of the learned and his encouragement of the pursuit of "useful" knowledge link him with this movement. At the same time, Montaigne appears to have gone beyond his contemporaries in articulating the principles on the basis of which a comprehensive *science* of nature could be built out of the information acquired from empirical observation. His scientific teaching combines elements borrowed from the teachings of various ancient inquirers into nature, in such a manner as to generate a fundamentally new orientation. Although such ancient scientists as Galen recognized the dependence of medical advance on empirical observation, they did not therefore deny the intrinsic value of "metaphysical" speculation. Similarly, the deterministic picture of nature that Montaigne sets forth has an ancient precedent in Lucretian atomism, but Lucretius did not use this doctrine to found a science aimed at the mastery of nature.[37] Finally, the skeptical arguments that Montaigne uses to attack the philosophers' claims are drawn almost entirely from ancient sources; but the original Skeptics, as Montaigne points out, never attempted to build a positive, practical science on that foundation. Thus Montaigne is not truly a skeptic in the Pyrrhonian sense at all: the ultimate intent of his skepticism is not to convince us that the pursuit of knowledge is futile but to direct and encourage us to seek an attainable kind of knowledge that will promote the good of humanity. Montaigne's specific contribution to the philosophy of science is to describe how a comprehensive science of nature can be based on information derived from the senses, without attempting to penetrate to the essences of things, or to cut off the realm of scientific inquiry from the orientation of the "natural" human consciousness.[38] Thus he accomplishes, as Gustave Lan-

---

collective, progressive enterprise, see Jonas, *Phenomenon of Life*, pp. 191–5; Paolo Rossi, *Philosophy, Technology, and the Arts in the Early Modern Era*, tr. Salvator Attanasio (New York, 1970), ch. 2; Henry Magid, "Mill and the Problem of Freedom of Thought," *Social Research* 21 (1954): 53–60. Cf. also Friedrich Nietzsche, *Beyond Good and Evil*, pt. VI, secs. 204–7, 211–12; Max Weber, "Science as a Vocation," in H. H. Gerth and C. Wright Mills, eds., *From Max Weber: Essays in Sociology* (New York, 1958), pp. 139–41.

[36]See Rossi, *Philosophy, Technology, and the Arts*, ch. 1; Nakam, *Montaigne et son temps*, p. 147.

[37]Cf. Lucretius' lament at the increase in our desire for material goods and comforts as detrimental to our happiness: *On the Nature of Things*, V, 1412–35; James H. Nichols, Jr., *Epicurean Political Philosophy* (Ithaca, N.Y., 1976), pp. 22, 171–6; Timothy H. Paterson, "Ancients and Moderns: The Case of Bacon and Lucretius" (paper presented at the 1982 meeting of the American Political Science Association).

[38]How far this contribution was entirely original with Montaigne is a question that cannot be resolved without inquiries into the history of science which I have not undertaken; but given the role that Bacon is commonly assigned as the originator of such a science, it seems safe to ascribe a considerable degree of originality to his precursor Montaigne in this regard.

son observes, the severance of science from metaphysics[39]—as well as its consequent divorce from theology, which Montaigne explicitly recommended in an earlier chapter (I, lvi, 308 [234])—a severance widely regarded as the precondition of the modern scientific revolution. In the words of the historian Jules Michelet, Montaigne's skepticism, far from being his ultimate resting place, "is but the provisional doubt that renders science possible."[40]

Many scholars have recognized a link between Montaigne's putative skepticism and the positive scientific enterprise subsequently articulated by Bacon and Descartes.[41] Yet, in spite of the similitude of many of his themes and arguments to theirs (as well as those of Hobbes and Locke), scholars have rarely attributed a positive scientific intent to Montaigne himself, portraying him rather as the source of doubts Bacon and Descartes had to overcome to facilitate scientific advance.[42]

[39]Lanson, Les Essais, p. 282.

[40]Cited by Sayce, Essays, p. 185. Cf. also Armaingaud, "Etude," pp. 180–81. To what extent the renunciation of metaphysics was in fact essential to the progress of modern science cannot be considered here; relevant to this question, however, are the discussions in Salkever, Finding the Mean, pp. 36–53, and Jonas, Phenomenon of Life, pp. 34–7, both of which call into question what Salkever terms the "myth of metaphysical neutrality." These scholars' analyses suggest that the link between the renunciation of metaphysics and teleology, or the dichotomy between the "natural" and "scientific" consciousness, on the one hand, and the subsequent progress of science, on the other, may have been historically contingent rather than essential. That is, the "co-optation" of classical philosophy by Christian theology may have rendered the attack on metaphysics a circumstantially necessary condition for liberating the pursuit of empirical knowledge of nature from the antiscientific presuppositions imposed by the church. This rejection was also motivated, as seen in the Essays, by the desire to redirect attention to the pursuit of "useful" knowledge.

See also, on the issue raised here, Kurt Riezler, Physics and Reality: Lectures of Aristotle on Modern Physics at an International Congress of Science (New Haven, 1940); David Lowenthal, "The Case for Teleology," Independent Journal of Philosophy 2 (1978): 95–105.

[41]See especially Villey, Montaigne et François Bacon, chs. 3–4; Hiram Caton, "Tory History of Philosophy," Independent Journal of Philosophy 5–6 (1988): 5–8; Harcourt Brown, Scientific Organizations in Seventeenth-Century France (New York, 1967 [1934]), p. 1. On the more general connection between Montaigne and Descartes, see Curley, Descartes against the Skeptics, pp. 16–20, 38, 59, 69, 173, 177, as well as the references cited in n. 3 to Chapter One, above. Note particularly the echo of Montaigne in Descartes's remark that health is "no doubt the first good and the foundation of all the others in this life," his emphasis on the dependence of the mind's condition on that of the body, and his contrast between the present sorry state of medical science and the almost infinite progress of which it should be capable: Discours de la méthode, VI, in Oeuvres et lettres, pp. 168–9.

It is possible that Montaigne and Bacon met; at any rate, Montaigne knew Bacon's brother Anthony, who lived twelve years in the south of France, and he continued to correspond with Anthony Bacon after the latter's return to England: Sidney Lee, The French Renaissance in England (New York, 1968 [1910]), pp. 171–4; cf. Montaigne's reference at II, xii, 563 [463] to the connections his "house" retains with the English. Norton, Early Writings of Montaigne, pp. 207–11, notes a possible reference in Francis Bacon's Historia Vitae et Mortis to his having met Montaigne; on this issue see Villey, Montaigne et François Bacon, pp. 10–11. Norton also compiled a list of parallel passages in Montaigne's and Bacon's works: The Spirit of Montaigne (Boston, 1908), pp. 3–48.

[42]See, e.g., Curley, Descartes against the Skeptics, pp. 12–20; Brush, Montaigne and Bayle, p. 167; Starobinski, Montaigne in Motion, pp. 160–64, 288–9; Gierczynski, "La Science de

It is easy enough to see how a reading of the *Essays* and particularly of the "Apology" could engender such an interpretation. Certainly the theme of skepticism is expressed far more frequently and manifestly, both in the "Apology" and elsewhere, than a belief in scientific progress. The last long section of the "Apology" embodies a restatement of Pyrrhonian arguments, apparently confirming Montaigne's intention of demonstrating our "necessary stupidity" (576 [447]). The most extensive remarks about scientific methodology elsewhere in the *Essays* are intermixed (as in the "Apology") with attacks on the pretensions of the learned.[43] And—aside from the "experiment" Montaigne reports having conducted in II, xxxvii, and his unmethodical record of his "experience" regarding bodily health in the last chapter—he provides no evidence in the *Essays* that he himself engaged in scientific research.[44] Nonetheless, Montaigne's emphasis in the "Apology" on our need for earthly or corporeal goods, especially health; the focus of his critique of philosophy on its failure to facilitate the acquisition of such goods, owing to the philosophers' "elevated" ambitions; his attestation of the value of learning; his express wish that philosophy should uncover the structure and mode of operation of the heavens, the causes of our sense perceptions, and the nature of our bodily constitution; and his explicit assertions of the possibility of scientific progress—all constitute powerful testimony that he did intend such a project. This testimony is buttressed by the multitudinous reminiscences of the *Essays* in the writings of Bacon and Descartes, among other architects of the scientific revolution.

To understand the reasons underlying Montaigne's peculiarly back-

---

l'ignorance," pp. 48–9; Popkin, *The History of Skepticism*, pp. 14, 21–4; Paul Stapfer, *Montaigne* (Paris, 1895), pp. 102–7; Philippe Desan, *Naissance de la méthode* (Paris, 1987), pp. 131, 133–4.

[43]The fullest and most important of these attacks is the denunciation of the practice of medicine in II, xxxvii. To understand the import of this denunciation, one must bear in mind Montaigne's use of the term "spiritual and bodily physicians" in an earlier chapter where he mocks the ascetic and painful "cures" such doctors prescribe for the respective diseases of soul and body (I, xxx, 198 [148]). Chapter II, xxxvii, includes a series of barely veiled references to practices of the church: the "physicians'" "mysterious and divine" choice of drugs; their "festivals" and bitter "contestations"; their "unintelligible," esoteric language; their ostensibly "celestial," "miracle" cures; the "tyrannical authority" they "usurp over these poor souls"; the dependence of their reputation on the "faith" of simple people in their "mysteries," "divinations," "supernatural arts," and "mumblings and magic formulas," etc. (748–9, 759 [583–4, 592]). Note also that Montaigne, even while professing a hatred for the teachings of "medicine," admits in this same chapter to having a doctor call on him when he is sick (760 [593]). In sum, although Montaigne had good reason to question the efficacy of the science of medicine practiced in his time, the real object of his attack is not the bodily physicians but the spiritual ones, who add imaginary sufferings to our "essential and bodily" ones (738 [575]).

[44]However, Dr. Batisse, in *Montaigne et la médicine*, pp. 199–252, finds Montaigne's detailed account in his *Travel Journal* of his attempts to treat his kidney stone through the use of mineral waters to constitute a rigorous and scientifically useful empirical record. Cf. also Montaigne's perhaps exaggeratedly self-deprecating account in the *Journal* of his having been called on for an important medical "consultation" while in Italy, an incident that he indicates was not unique: *Oeuvres*, p. 1285 [999–1000].

handed way of expressing his thoughts on science, we must remember that he expected the *Essays* to be read by two different kinds of audience, whom he aimed to influence in different, albeit complementary, ways: the few "men of understanding," who could be expected to read the book with sufficient care and insight to discern the author's true purpose; and the many who would read it cursorily and would recognize and be influenced by only the more obvious, surface teaching. In order to advance his scientific project at this early stage of its development, it was not necessary for Montaigne to present the project as such before the public. The effectuation of the project would depend above all on the efforts of "men of understanding," who would elaborate that project and gradually recruit a corps of assistants to help execute it. Only in a negative sense would the attitude of the public at large affect the success of the project at the outset: if they, through the acts of the political authorities that reflect their fundamental opinions, should continue to subject the pursuit of knowledge to a narrow censorship, science could make little or no progress.[45] Thus Montaigne's main need regarding the attitudes of his vulgar readers toward the scientific project is to weaken their attachment to dogmatic opinions that obstruct scientific inquiry. His attack on the "presumption" embodied in common opinions, especially religious ones, has been designed to produce such a liberating effect: even though most readers will not recognize the anti-religious intention that underlies Montaigne's skeptical argument, it is likely that the dominant impact of his challenge to all human beliefs about God and our "immortal" soul will be to weaken their acceptance of Christian dogma.[46] His putatively skeptical attitude toward the scientific discoveries of his time has similarly been expressly intended to deter his readers from committing themselves permanently to any particular scientific theory. Moreover, as will be noted later, Montaigne's critique of Christian

---

[45]Although the sixteenth century was an era of considerable scientific advance, the situation of inquirers into nature remained precarious. In the year Montaigne died, Giordano Bruno was arrested as a heretic by the Venice inquisition, to be burned at the stake eight years later. Consider also the church's condemnation of the Copernican system in 1616, and the subsequent fate of Galileo, to which Descartes alludes as a reason for his own prudence (*Discours de la méthode*, VI, in *Oeuvres et lettres*, p. 167); cf. Bacon, *Novum Organon*, I, aph. 89, and Caton, *Politics of Progress*, p. 50.

[46]A further reason for the contrast that scholars have erroneously drawn between Montaigne and Descartes is a failure to appreciate the ironic character of the latter's metaphysical "proofs" (see, e.g., Lanson, *Les Essais*, p. 282; Gierczynski, "Le 'Que sais-je?' de Montaigne," p. 14; Popkin, *The History of Skepticism*, ch. 9; Curley, *Descartes against the Skeptics*, pp. 19–20, 37–40). Despite its seeming opposition to Montaigne's skeptical argument, the Cartesian "metaphysics" actually serves an identical purpose: to liberate experimental, scientific reason from the restraints of church dogma, while protecting the liberator against persecution. See Richard Kennington, "René Descartes," in Leo Strauss and Joseph Cropsey, eds., *History of Political Philosophy*, 2d ed. (Chicago, 1972), pp. 402–6, 410–11; Hiram Caton, *The Origin of Subjectivity: An Essay on Descartes* (New Haven, 1973), pp. 121–30; idem, "On the Interpretation of the *Meditations*," *Man and World* 3 (1970): 224–43; idem, "Tory History of Philosophy."

theology in the "Apology" is complemented by an attack, elsewhere in the *Essays*, on the "ascetic" morality associated with Christianity as well as with Stoicism; one result of the new moral teaching that he substitutes will be to stimulate our appetite for the practical fruits of the new science.

The content of the *Essays* indicates that, as Pierre Villey stresses, the main focus of Montaigne's own work was the study of human rather than nonhuman nature.[47] This focus does not demonstrate that progress in natural science was unimportant to him, however, but suggests that he conceived himself in the scientific realm, as in the political one, as a kind of master architect, outlining and advocating a project that would be executed by others: just as it was not necessary for Montaigne to work for a particular monarch to become an "adviser" to kings, he did not need to dedicate his time to scientific experimentation in order to lay the theoretical and political foundations for scientific advance. In sum, even as Montaigne sought to encourage others to pursue knowledge that would be of practical benefit to humanity, philosophy remained *for him* a primarily reflective rather than "experimental" enterprise.[48]

If the scientific researchers who come after Montaigne will be following a theoretical and methodological path that he has blazed, there is also a deeper sense in which their work will be instrumental to his. Montaigne's project for the reformation and redirection of science is subordinate to his broader political project, which aims at transforming our understanding of the purpose of human life, the standards by which human conduct is to be judged, and the proper role of government. In the same section of the "Apology" wherein Montaigne begins to uncover his new conception of science, he sets forth a more extended argument embodying the theoretical foundations of his political project.

Skepticism and Toleration

At the outset of his survey of the philosophers' teachings, purportedly designed to demonstrate the inevitability of human ignorance, Montaigne

---

[47]Villey, *Montaigne et François Bacon*, pp. 65, 107.

[48]Cf. II, xvii, 636 [495], where Montaigne professes to be ignorant of "vulgar things," such as "the mechanical arts," after having mocked the philosophers' ignorance and contempt of such things in the "Apology"; II, vi, 355 [271], where a lesson of experience serves only to confirm, not to alter, Montaigne's previous judgment of the matter he is discussing; and III, ix, 964 [754], where he denies having traveled very far, despite having professed a taste for travel in this chapter, and recommending travel as an educative device for the young (I, xxvi, 152 [112]). (Montaigne's own extensive foreign journey of 1580–81 did not take place until after the first edition of the *Essays* had been published and the fundamental principles of his thought established.) Recall also the remark at p. 445 of the "Apology" that it is unnecessary to seek out "foreign" things to discover the truths Montaigne portrays. The emphasis in "Of the Education of Children" on the practical goal of such education, with philosophical study to be

had chosen to "leave the people aside" (481 [371]). It seemed reasonable to assume that no one else was capable of knowing that of which the wisest human beings proved ignorant. Montaigne's subsequent remarks, however, tacitly revealed that assumption to be partly false: the philosophers' failure to gain greater insight into the material constitution and operation of nature with a view to relieving the miseries of the human condition resulted from their unwarranted disdain for our earthly needs rather than from any inherent limitation of the human mind. Yet an awareness of the limits of the human mind in a more specific sense was presented by Montaigne as the precondition of the scientific progress he forecasts: only because "things do not lodge in us in their own form and essence" do they "surrender to our mercy," to be broken up and rearranged by the active, constructive operation of our understanding.

In the sequel to the remarks just quoted, Montaigne appears to reverse the procedure of his previous epistemological investigation. It is now the "infinite confusion of opinions" of "the philosophers themselves, and that perpetual and universal debate over the knowledge of things," that he will "leave aside." Instead, he directs the reader's attention to "the confusion that our judgment gives to our own selves, and the uncertainty that each man feels within himself," all of which demonstrates that our judgment "has a very insecure seat" (545–6 [423]). Having previously evaluated the capacity of the mind to achieve theoretical knowledge, and having concluded "that men . . . are in agreement about nothing" (545 [423]), Montaigne will now demonstrate the mind's weakness in its everyday operation, as a practical guide.

He begins by citing the frequency with which people who firmly believe something subsequently change their minds. This experience seems peculiar to the nonphilosophic, we observe, since Montaigne has shown that the philosophers knew better than to believe they had certain knowledge of anything. Once more indicating the theological bearing of his skepticism, he stresses that "whatever is preached to us" has a fallible, mortal source and recipient. Again he describes God's grace as the only source of truth, but he still provides no evidence that God has offered such insight to us. One can easily apply to the religious warfare and persecution that Montaigne has shown to be encouraged by people's erroneous belief that God is on their side his present plea: "At least our faulty condition should make us behave more moderately and restrainedly in our changes" (546 [423–4]).[49]

---

limited (I, xxvi, 162 [120–21]), may be taken to reflect the gap between his own way of life and the one toward which he directs humanity (see n. 76, below). Cf. also II, vi, 359 [274], where Montaigne suggests the superiority of thought to action and identifies his "essence" with the former; also the citation of Pythagoras at I, xxvi, 157–8 [117]. And cf. Caton, *Politics of Progress*, pp. 30–31, on the character of the contributions of Bacon and Descartes to the development of modern science.

[49]Cf. the explicit reference at p. 563 [436] to the recent changes of religious law in England.

To encourage such moderation, Montaigne elaborates a theme he has touched on earlier: the dependence of people's judgments on nonrational causes, particularly their bodily condition. It is significant that he uses the phrase "it is certain" in asserting that "our apprehension, our judgment, and the faculties of our soul in general suffer according to the movements and alterations of the body, which alterations are continual," such as the movement between sickness and health (547 [424]). This rare expression of certainty corresponds to Montaigne's previously quoted remark that we have no certainty that can compare with that of our sense perceptions (572 [444]). In both cases certainty is founded on a subjective, sensed experience. We can be surest of such sensations because our awareness of them does not depend on any (inherently questionable and controversial) assumption about the nature of the external world. The problem in each case is that we naturally tend to "objectify" and externalize the source of our sensations: assuming respectively that our sense perceptions or our judgments reflect some reality outside ourselves.[50]

In order to remedy our instability of judgment in practical affairs, it is again necessary for Montaigne to overcome this tendency toward objectification. Such overcoming will be more difficult than it was in the case of physical sense perceptions, inasmuch as it involves a direct challenge to people's understanding of their good, and it is hard for human beings to judge honestly any issue that touches their own interest (cf. III, vii, 896 [701]). Montaigne professes, however, by virtue of his dedication to self-study, to see into himself more clearly than others do with respect to themselves. Hence he recognizes, and invites his readers to appreciate, the dependence of human judgments on "fortuitous instinct," passion, and random circumstance (547–50 [424–6]).

Given the soul's subjection to the body, which undergoes "so many continual changes" and contains "so many springs of action," it is doubtful, Montaigne argues, that we are ever in a position to judge things objectively (548 [424–5]). But even more powerful than the body's passions are those of the soul, which "perhaps" are the only source of its "motion." Desires move us, he observes (following Cicero's *Tusculan Disputations*), to "useful ends." Cowardice causes penitence; compassion spurs clemency; and "no eminent and lusty virtue is without some unruly agitation." Yet it is also evident that such agitations can be dangerous. Their power biases our judgment. Thus, Montaigne implies, those human beings who exhibit the most eminent "virtue," being most agitated, are least able to judge soberly the ends for which they should act, as well as the means to them. Hence he suggests that it is "rashness in philosophy to consider that men produce

---

[50]Cf. Hobbes's definition of heresy: *Leviathan*, ed. C. B. Macpherson (Baltimore, 1968), ch. 11, p. 165; also, on morality, ch. 15, p. 216.

their greatest deeds and those most closely approaching divinity when they are out of their minds and frenzied and mad." Such a judgment reflects the entry of "enthusiasm" into the "philosophical spirit" itself (550–51 [426–7]).[51]

It is interesting to compare the foregoing description of the motives underlying virtue and piety with Montaigne's previous remarks about them. Earlier in the "Apology" he pretended to denounce Plato for holding religion to be generated by cowardice. He questioned whether such a "vicious passion" could "produce in our soul anything regulated" (422–3 [325]). As for virtue, he observed in an earlier chapter that she "will not be followed except for her own sake" (II, i, 320 [243]; cf. I, xxxvii, 226–7 [170]). Now, however, he suggests that "piety" and "virtue" are *always* produced by extraneous passions. Human beings are impelled to them not by a true grasp of divine or human perfection, respectively, but by the same sort of forces that lead others to vice and impiety. "By the dislocation that the passions bring about in our reason, we become virtuous; by [reason's] extirpation that is brought about by madness or the semblance of death, we become prophets and soothsayers." Montaigne warns that the "voice" people take to reflect divine inspiration "is a voice coming from the spirit which is a part of earthly, ignorant, and shadowy man, and for that reason an untrustworthy and unbelievable voice" (551–2 [427–8]).

The essayist appears to endorse the view of Pyrrho that we cannot know which state of our soul is more truthful. But from the very awareness of our ignorance, a certain attitude and mode of behavior emerge as most in accordance with reason. By being aware of his innate "mobility," Montaigne has achieved "a certain constancy of opinions," holding to his "first and natural ones" and not changing easily. Being unable to choose for himself, he professes to "accept the choice of others" and to conform to "the ancient beliefs of our religion" (552–3 [428–9]). (In this conformity he seems to emulate the Skeptics, whom he previously represented as accommodating themselves to established laws and customs.)

But Montaigne's conservative posture stands in need of further explanation. It is hard to see how following his "first and natural" opinions is compatible with letting others choose for him. Thus it is not surprising that Montaigne later denies ever having followed any opinions but his own. The "universal opinions" he has followed since childhood, he affirms, are those he established for himself (III, ii, 790, 793 [616, 618]). Nor is it credible

---

[51]The four possible sources cited by Zeitlin for this judgment (Plato, *Phaedrus*, 244; *Timaeus*, 71; Cicero, *Of Divination*, I, lvii, II, xlviii), associate divination or prophetic insight—not virtuous action—with madness (Zeitlin, *Essays of Montaigne*, 2:548). On the relation between philosophy and madness in Plato's thought, see Stanley Rosen, *Plato's "Symposium"* (New Haven, 1968), pp. 21, 239, 282. For Montaigne's view of divination, see I, xi (discussed in Chapter Five, below).

that his "natural" opinions include a belief in Christianity, in view of his previous demonstration that the foundations of that religion, like those of other faiths, are entirely conventional.

Montaigne's argument actually tends to show not that "the ancient beliefs of our religion" merit adherence but that it is unwise to give "magisterial and permanent authority" (559 [433]) to *any* set of beliefs about the universe. It is at this point that he refers to the changes in accepted opinions about astronomy and medicine, and argues that no scientific theory should be regarded as embodying the final truth. After elaborating the variety of ancient cosmological opinions, in a manner recalling his previous catalogues of the philosophers' opinions about God and the soul, he again asserts the plausibility of one particular view: the Epicurean opinion "that while things here are as we see them, at the same time they are exactly alike and of the same fashion in many other worlds" (556 [431]; cf. 505–6 [390]). In its support he cites "the coincidences between a great number of fabulous popular opinions and savage customs and beliefs, which do not seem from any angle to be connected with our natural reason," but many of which exhibit a striking "correspondence" to the beliefs and practices of Christianity. He asserts that "these empty shadows of our religion . . . testify to its dignity and divinity," since they suggest that Christianity shares with the "barbarous" religions "a common and supernatural inspiration." One might as easily infer, however, that Christianity has no more claim to be believed than any of the "barbarous" religions.[52] Indeed, if—as Montaigne goes on to suggest—religions, like other human beliefs, are produced by nature's "ordinary progress," there is nothing "supernatural" about any of them. No doubt Christianity will be supplanted by some other religion in the future (556–9 [431–3]).[53]

Not only our opinions, Montaigne argues, but our abilities and qualities of disposition and character vary in accordance with "the air, the climate, and the soil where we are born."[54] The change and variety inherent in nature seem to underlie what he cites as another token of "our imbecility," the fact that we cannot "agree about what we need for our contentment." People possessing different bodily constitutions and formed by different

[52]Cf. Weiler, *Pour connaître la pensée de Montaigne*, p. 54; Gierczynski, "Le 'Que sais-je?' de Montaigne," p. 27; Starobinski, *Montaigne in Motion*, p. 338, n. 58.

[53]Cf. Machiavelli, *Discourses on Livy*, II, v; also the Paduan philosopher Pietro Pomponazzi's theory of the natural cycle of religions, with his forecast of the imminent decline of Christianity: John Herman Randall, Jr., *The School of Padua and the Emergence of Modern Science* (Padua, 1961), pp. 102–5; Andrew Halliday Douglas, *The Philosophy and Psychology of Pietro Pomponazzi* (Cambridge, Eng., 1910), pp. 299–303.

[54]The passage in which Montaigne develops this theme embodies the germ of Montesquieu's doctrine of the effects of climate and geography on human character, dictating that laws and regimes be adapted to those forces: *The Spirit of the Laws*, XIV–XVIII. Cf. Thomas L. Pangle, *Montesquieu's Philosophy of Liberalism* (Chicago, 1973), pp. 161ff.; Starobinski, *Montaigne in Motion*, p. 338, n. 58.

conditions necessarily desire different things, and the changeableness of everything, including ourselves, prevents any one thing from being always good even for the same individual. Hence there seems to be no way of resolving the philosophers' most "violent" and "bitter" dispute, which concerns "the sovereign good of man."[55] By a quotation from Horace, Montaigne suggests that such disagreements simply reflect differences of taste.[56] He wishes someone would compile a "register" of "the opinions of ancient philosophy on the subject of our being and our mores," relating the lives of each doctrine's advocates to their precepts—implying that the doctrinal differences might be explained by the diversity of their respective adherents' temperaments and life histories (559–62 [433–6]; cf. II, xxxi, 693–4 [541]).

Montaigne's survey of the diversity of human beliefs and its ultimate cause—the flux inherent in nature—issues in a query: By what standard *ought* we to guide our conduct? To avoid attaching full credence to any set of beliefs while continuing to test them in the light of experience may be an adequate rule for the conduct of natural science; but human beings need some more stable principle by which to guide their lives, if they are not to fall into an unacceptable "confusion" and anarchy. "The most plausible advice that our reason gives" on this matter, Montaigne observes, "is generally for each man to obey the laws of his country," a precept that Socrates attributed to "divine counsel." But the essayist—who had seemed to endorse such a conservative posture a few pages earlier—now rejects it. Socrates' precept means that "our duty has no rule but an accidental one." But the truth (as Sextus Empiricus had argued) "must have one face, the same and universal." If there is a real, knowable standard of right, it cannot be identified with the customs and fancies of a particular people. "There is nothing more subject to continual agitation than the laws," as is particularly evident in Montaigne's time. Just as the variability of legal justice demonstrates its conventionality and arbitrariness, so Apollo's advice (according to Xenophon's Socrates)[57] that each man should follow his country's *religion* implies that religion is a human creation, instituted for purely political ends. Although Montaigne professes to thank God "for having freed our belief from the folly of these vagabond and arbitrary devotions, and having based it on the eternal foundation of his holy word," he has just finished suggesting that Christian beliefs and practices are no less arbitrary than those of other religions (562–3 [436–7]). As his previous remarks about the French religious wars indicated, Christianity fails even to secure the goal of civic unity for which other religions were instituted, but is rather the chief instrument of society's fragmentation.

---

[55]Cf. I, liii; Hobbes, *Leviathan*, ch. 11 (first para.); Locke, *An Essay Concerning Human Understanding*, I.iii.6 (first sentence); contrast Aristotle, *Nicomachean Ethics*, 1154b20–30.
[56]Cf. Locke, *An Essay Concerning Human Understanding*, II.xxi.54–5.
[57]Xenophon, *Memorabilia*, I.3.

Montaigne concludes that he cannot have his "judgment so flexible" as to follow Socrates' advice: "to follow the laws of our country" would mean conforming to "the undulating sea of the opinions of a people or a prince, which will paint me justice in as many colors, and refashion it into as many faces, as there are changes of passion in those men." He seems to wish for the discovery of a natural standard of justice, but he goes on to mock those who, "to give some certainty to the laws, . . . say that there are some which are firm, perpetual, and immutable, which they call natural, which are imprinted on the human race by the condition of their being." "The only likely sign" by which particular laws could be demonstrated to be natural is "universality of approval," since "what nature had truly ordered for us we would without doubt follow by common consent." But Montaigne challenges the exponents of natural law to show him one such rule. Customs and laws are the most variable things in the world: incest, infanticide, parricide, polygamy, theft, "license for all sorts of sensual pleasures, nothing in short is so extreme that it is not accepted by the usage of some nation." Montaigne finds it "credible," indeed, "that there are natural laws, as may be seen in other creatures," but contends that they are "lost" in us, owing to "that fine human reason" which "butts in everywhere, domineering and commanding, muddling and confusing the face of things in accordance with its vanity and inconsistency" (563–5 [437–8]).

In the last sentence quoted Montaigne resumes his earlier rhetorical posture of mocking human reason for making us worse off than the beasts. Once again, his argument actually suggests not the harmfulness of reason, but the need to use it properly. The inconsistency of human beliefs is due to nature's apparent failure to provide us with manifest "first principles" on which all can agree. "Things may be considered in various lights and from various viewpoints; it is principally from this that diversity of opinion is engendered" (565 [438]). The variety of possible points of view leaves justice uncertain, so that a judge may arbitrarily decide to favor whichever party he chooses (566 [439]). The need in the political sphere, as in the scientific one, is to provide a firm foundation for our reasoning.[58]

While lamenting our lack of such a foundation, Montaigne has told us where to look for it: among the beasts. Although in the "Apology" he claims that the natural law is "lost" in human beings, a discussion of the subject in an earlier chapter titled "Of the Affection of Fathers for Children" (II, viii) is less discouraging. There Montaigne offers a definition of natural law that differs slightly from the one propounded in the "Apology," in that it does not contain the requirement of universal consent: it is an "*instinct* that is found universally and perpetually imprinted in the beasts and us." If there are any such laws, "which is not beyond controversy," Montaigne remarks,

---

[58]Cf. II, xvii, 639 [497]: political disputes cannot be resolved except by reference to "plain and apparent" principles.

the first would be "the care every animal has for its preservation, and for fleeing what is harmful" (365 [279]). Although he adds as a second possible law "the affection that the begetter has for his begotten," he indicates that this affection not only has "weak roots" and is frequently overcome but actually conflicts with the first law (II, viii, 365, 379–80 [279, 290]; I, xxviii, 183 [136]). Its naturalness would therefore seem far more doubtful.[59]

In a multitude of other passages Montaigne refers to what he variously calls natural or universal laws or rules (beginning with the allusion in "To the Reader" to "those nations that are said still to live under the sweet freedom of nature's first laws"). So far as I know, he does not seriously identify any particular rules relating to the direction of human conduct, outside of the passage discussed above, with the specific terms "natural law" or "law of nature."[60] He does, however, use similar phrases to describe certain regularities in human and animal behavior which are related to the "law" described in II, viii. There is a "general habit of nature which can be observed in all that lives under heaven that we shall tremble under pain"; the instinctive fear of pain is the means by which nature impels all animals toward their preservation (I, xiv, 55 [37]; III, xii, 1032 [807–8]). Also among the "rules" that nature has "maternally observed" is "that the actions she has enjoined on us for our need should also be pleasant to us" (III, xiii, 1088 [850]). Both our disposition to fear pain and our finding necessary actions pleasurable thus appear to be elements of the more fundamental law of self-preservation. Montaigne extends the scope of the "law" ordaining indulgence in sensual pleasures beyond the demands of preservation, however, by describing the enjoyment of "drinking and feasting" as well as sex as "laws of the human condition," to which even the most virtuous should "meekly" submit (III, xiii, 1089 [851]). This extension reflects the essayist's questioning and ultimate rejection of the distinction between natural and unnatural pleasures (III, x, 987 [772]; III, xiii, 1065 [833]).

In identifying both the instinct for self-preservation and the desires to enjoy physical pleasure and avoid pain as natural, Montaigne is far from contending that human beings always follow them. He asserts, indeed, that a number of philosophers went out of their way to suffer pain and poverty, even cutting out their eyes and sexual organs, in order to "toughen" their

[59]There is also an ambiguity in the *object* of "parental" affection, which might be directed toward the offspring of one's mind rather than one's body (II, viii, 380–83 [291–3]).

[60]The one manifestly unserious case is his assertion, at III, v, 863 [674], that nature gives women a "law" that they should not "will or desire" sexual intercourse but should only "suffer, obey, consent." That claim is immediately refuted by an example of "Amazonian license" (863 [675]), as well as by the overall argument of the chapter in which it occurs (see esp. 832–3, 837 [649–50, 654]). Cf. also the story Montaigne reports having heard in Toulouse, at II, iii, 338 [257].

souls; and he remarks that "any opinion is strong enough to make itself espoused at the price of life" (II, vi, 350 [267]; I, xiv, 52 [35]; cf. II, xxxiii, 711–12 [555]). What makes the desires for preservation and sensual pleasure natural, however, is that they are apparently *present* in all human beings, even those who seem most strikingly to disregard them. Whatever endurance of pain the Stoics may display, they feel it just the same (I, xiv, 55 [37]). Similarly, we cannot help feeling the desire for sensual pleasure, even though we may limit its satisfaction (cf. III, xiii, 1088 [850]). And the instinct for self-preservation, Montaigne suggests, is powerfully present even in those who sacrifice themselves. It is really "fantastic and irrational humors," such as the hope of prolonging existence in an afterlife or through glory, that impel most such sacrifices (II, iii, 334–5 [254–5]; II, xvi, 476 [612]). The cheerfulness that some people display in the face of death is merely a "diversion" they use to avoid confronting it squarely (III, iv, 810–11 [632]).

Montaigne's restriction of natural law to an instinct toward self-preservation and the pursuit of pleasure which we share with the beasts must be understood in contradistinction to the traditional Christian natural law doctrine formulated by Thomas Aquinas, according to which that law is imprinted in our reason or conscience, and it ordains higher goals for us than preservation, stemming from our distinctive status as rational creatures.[61] But Montaigne is far from holding that animal instinct constitutes a simply adequate standard for human conduct: just after identifying the instinct for self-preservation as the most truly natural law, he observes that since human beings have "some capacity for reason . . . we should not be slavishly subjected to the common laws, like the beasts, but should apply ourselves to them by judgment and voluntary liberty . . . yield[ing] a little indeed to the simple authority of nature, but not let[ting] ourselves be carried away by her; *reason alone must guide our inclinations*" (II, viii, 366 [279]). We should submit "to reason, notwithstanding the force of nature"; indeed, the "predispositions that are born in us without reason . . . are

[61]See Thomas Aquinas, *Summa Theologica*, II, i, Qu. 94, Second Article, in Anton C. Pegis, ed., *The Basic Writings of Saint Thomas Aquinas*, 2 vols. (New York, 1945), 2:775. Thomas describes human sensuality as a "law" only in an indirect or metaphorical sense, as a punishment for Adam's sin: ibid., Qu. 91, Sixth Article (2:756–7). The contrast between Montaigne's view of natural law and Thomas's, the novelty of the essayist's challenge to natural law doctrine, and the parallel to his argument in Locke's *Essay* are discussed by Carol Clark in "Montaigne and Law," in Cameron, ed., *Montaigne and His Age*, pp. 55–61. Cf. also Leo Strauss, "Locke's Doctrine of Natural Law," in *What Is Political Philosophy?* pp. 199–200. An older precedent for Montaigne's identification of natural law as an instinct shared by all animals is found in Roman law: see Justinian, *Digest*, I.2; Michael P. Zuckert, " 'Bringing Philosophy Down from the Heavens': Natural Right in the Roman Law," *Review of Politics* 51 (1989): 76–7. However, Montaigne's formulation is distinguished from the Roman one by his hedonistic emphasis and his depreciation of the parental instinct, and by his apparent elevation of natural law thus understood over civil law (III, i, 773 [604]).

vicious; they are a kind of disease that must be combated" (II, viii, 366 [280]; II, xxxvii, 743 [580]).

The problem, then, is to determine how the guidance of reason may be combined with the recognition of natural necessity. Montaigne addresses this problem in the "Apology" just after his remark that human beings are no longer ruled by the laws of nature, by describing a way of life that he holds to be in accordance with both nature and reason: that of the philosophers. Since these people "weigh everything" by reason, "accept nothing by authority," and "take as their pattern the original image of nature," he observes, their judgments and opinions deviate sharply from "the common way," exemplified by the civil laws, which rest on "trivial and frail" foundations. The fundamental characteristic of the philosophers' moral opinions was their "freedom," or rather "license." Montaigne says that "there is no need to expand" on these opinions, and that some "are better hushed up than published to weak minds." Yet he proceeds to elaborate them without appearing to hush up anything out of concern for its effect on public morals. Indeed, he exaggerates the philosophers' shamelessness, as in his alteration of a story about Chrysippus.[62] He takes "a great and religious author" (Saint Augustine) to task for not believing that "the licentiousness of the Cynic" went as far as it did.[63] And he later criticizes interpreters of Plato who "make his meaning disavow customs that were licit in his century because they are illicit in ours" (presumably, homosexuality) (567–71 [439–43]).

That Montaigne goes out of his way to demonstrate the extent of the philosophers' license makes it unlikely that he was, as Zeitlin believes, "genuinely shocked" by it.[64] By his very revelation of their ways, he conforms to certain opinions he ascribes to them: that it is "stupidity" not "to do openly what it is decent for us to do in private" and vicious "to hush up . . . what nature, custom, and our desire publish and proclaim about our actions" (568 [440]). He portrays the philosophers as living without regard for the conventions of civil society, particularly the restraints it lays on sensual pleasures: "These philosophers set an extreme price on virtue and rejected all other studies but morals; yet in all actions they attributed sovereign authority to the decision of their sage, above the laws; and ordered no other bridle on sensual pleasures except moderation and the preservation of the liberty of others" (569 [441]). Not only does Montaigne describe the philosophers' conduct as in accordance with reason and nature, he explicitly calls that philosophy "soundest" which ordains an "excessive license" (567 [440]). Contrary to Zeitlin, he says nothing to indicate

[62]See Zeitlin, The Essays of Montaigne, 2:552 (note to p. 247).
[63]See ibid., p. 553 (note to p. 249).
[64]Ibid., p. 518.

that he regards such conduct as wrong (despite his putative concern for the effect that publicizing it might have on "weak minds").

The difficulty with this account of the philosophers' way of life arises in trying to reconcile it with Montaigne's portrayal of their attitude toward nature and convention elsewhere. Whereas the present account describes the philosophers as regarding efforts to obscure nature as foolish, earlier Montaigne had called attention to their practice of publishing "profitable lies" for the benefit of the vulgar. And in Book III, he will blame them for having "sophisticated" nature with so many "farfetched reasonings" as to hide her face, thus rendering it necessary to seek evidence of her among the beasts (III, xii, 1026–7 [803]; cf. III, xiii, 1050 [822]). The present account thus minimizes or denies the difference Montaigne elsewhere emphasizes between his own "free" and "natural" manner and the philosophers' "prudent" mode of speaking and writing. Moreover, this account omits mention of what Montaigne earlier represented as the philosophers' proud, or vain, dedication to the "elevating" pursuit of wisdom: the main fruit they derived from their wisdom, he now implies, was the liberation of their appetites from conventional restraints.

The relation between the present account of the philosophers' ways and the earlier one may be clarified by noting that this account omits any reference to the greatest classical philosophers, Socrates, Plato, and Aristotle (aside from the later allusion to Plato's acceptance of homosexuality). It is illustrated rather by a number of stories, borrowed from Diogenes Laertius, of the antics of relatively minor philosophers belonging to the Stoic and Cynic sects. Elsewhere, Montaigne points out that the doctrines of the Platonic and Peripatetic (Aristotelian) schools were more "civil" or "accommodated to civil society" than those of such sects as the Stoics (568 [440]; II, x, 393 [300]; II, xvii, 623 [485]; III, ix, 955 [747]). By basing his present account of the philosophic life on the activities and opinions of the less politic sects, Montaigne appears to emulate their disregard of the problem of the philosopher's relation to society. But in fact, this account exemplifies what I shall contend is Montaigne's new mode of addressing that problem. Though he is no less concerned with political things than Plato and Aristotle were, he has already called into question their manner of dealing with those things, that is, their concealment of truths that they thought would be harmful to the multitude. In contrast to the "elevating" interpretation that they gave to nature in their exoteric writings, Montaigne proposes to reveal its true character to the vulgar, and to derive a more adequate standard for political life directly from it. The apparent import of his account of the philosophers' "natural" way of life is that dedication to self-indulgence is entirely compatible with the constraints of moderation and respect for other people's liberty that a decent civil life requires.

It remains unclear from the "Apology" how civil society can be constituted on such a foundation. Montaigne's earlier counsel to the multitude evinced his awareness of the difficulty of achieving any modicum of moderation in their conduct. But the elaboration of this project takes place elsewhere in the *Essays*. At this point the argument of the "Apology" undergoes a descent.

The Intent of Montaigne's "Skepticism"

From discussing the philosophers' "excessive license," Montaigne abruptly returns to the inevitability of human ignorance. Following a brief excursus mocking his contemporaries for reading their own beliefs into ancient books, he launches into a lengthy restatement of the Pyrrhonian argument about the unreliability of the sense impressions on which human knowledge is founded (571–86 [443–55]). This section runs almost to the end of the "Apology," but—aside from a previously discussed remark that the senses provide the greatest degree of certainty that we can attain—it adds practically nothing of philosophic importance to what was said earlier in the "Apology."[65]

Observing that Montaigne has already appeared to transcend the Pyrrhonian position in the previous section of his argument, and noting that the present section is characterized by an impersonal and imitative style typical of the "early" essays, Zeitlin concludes that it must represent an earlier "stage" of Montaigne's thought than the previous section.[66] But in view of Montaigne's avowals of the consistency of his thought and the care with which he writes, I suggest another explanation, based on Montaigne's reference to the "Mannerist" technique of writing in I, xxviii. The section under consideration seems to constitute one of the "grotesques" with which Montaigne proposed to surround his most valuable productions. In other words, his extended transcription of the Pyrrhonian doctrines at this point is a kind of rhetorical window-dressing, designed to mitigate the shocking effect of the attack on Christianity and conventional morality that preceded it.[67] Just as Montaigne used the device of short chapters early in the *Essays* in order to conceal the systematic and serious character of his thought from vulgar readers, he has employed another kind of "diversion" here. Inattentive readers who remember mainly what they have read last are encouraged by this section to come away (as most readers seem to have done) with the

[65]Brush seems to concur in this judgment, since in his running commentary on the "Apology" he provides no specific analysis of this section, only a brief summary (*Montaigne and Bayle*, pp. 108–9).

[66]Zeitlin, *Essays of Montaigne*, 2:515–16.

[67]Cf. Armaingaud's observation of Montaigne's habit of placing his deepest conclusions in the middle of a chapter so as to "insinuate" them the more subtly into his readers' minds (*Montaigne pamphlétaire*, p. 129).

impression that the "Apology" is merely a shotgun attack on the weakness of human reason, typified or even climaxed by the "Pyrrhonian" critique of the senses. This is not to deny that the chapter will have had a more substantive effect on such readers, but it will be an effect of whose cause they will remain largely unconscious (in a manner that Guillaume Guizot seems to have had in mind when he termed Montaigne a "putter-to-sleep of consciences").[68] This section of the "Apology" thus typifies not the teaching but the rhetoric of the chapter as a whole, which masks a positive political and scientific project under the guise of an idiosyncratic "skepticism" that serves either a pious aim or none at all.

For a franker indication of the political intent underlying Montaigne's skeptical posture, we must turn—in accordance with the author's Mannerist procedure—to the numerically central chapter of Book II, "Of Freedom of Conscience." In this relatively short chapter, which opens with a criticism of the "unjust, violent, and even reckless" practices to which passion drives supporters of "the old religion and the old government" in France's civil wars, Montaigne undertakes to defend Julian the Apostate against the condemnations that Christians have heaped on him, merely because he opposed their religion. So excellent and, indeed, philosophic does Montaigne find the Roman emperor that he remarks (in accordance with the judgment of his source, Ammianus Marcellinus) that "there is *no* sort of virtue of which he did not leave very notable examples"—despite his being "vicious throughout," according to the essayist, "in the matter of religion" (II, xix, 651–3 [507–8]). Montaigne even represents Julian as rivaling or surpassing in certain respects all but one of the men he describes in a later chapter (II, xxxvi) as "the most excellent."[69] It is not surprising that this rehabilitation of Julian was censured in Rome.[70]

In contrast to those who surnamed Julian "the Apostate," Montaigne argues that it is more likely he never truly believed in Christianity but had to dissemble his unbelief "out of obedience to the laws . . . until he had the Empire in his hand." His dissimulation was not really the product of respect for law; rather, "because all his army was composed of Christians, he dared not reveal" his paganism until he had triumphed (653–4 [508–9]). Then,

> having found the people in Constantinople at odds and the prelates of the Christian Church divided, he had them come to him and earnestly admonished them to lull these civic dissensions and urged that each man should serve his own religion without hindrance and without fear. This solicitation he made with great care, in the hope that this license would augment the schisms and factions that divided them and would keep the people from uniting and

[68]Guizot, *Montaigne*, p. 52.
[69]Cf. Butor, *Essais*, pp. 132–4.
[70]See Montaigne, *Journal de voyage*, in *Oeuvres*, pp. 1228–9 [955].

consequently strengthening themselves against him . . . having learned by experience [*ayant essayé*] from the cruelty of some Christians that there is no beast in the world so much to be feared by man as man. (654 [509])[71]

In the conclusion of the chapter Montaigne observes that it "is worthy of consideration that the Emperor Julian uses, to kindle the trouble of civil dissension, that same recipe of freedom of conscience that our kings have just been employing to extinguish it" (apparently referring to a short-lived liberalization of royal policy toward the Protestants following the Peace of Beaulieu [1576]).[72] He appears uncertain regarding the likely effect of such a policy: although one might argue "that to give factions a loose rein to entertain their own opinions is to scatter and sow division," the result could also be "to soften and relax them." Montaigne prefers to believe, "for the reputation of our kings' piety, that having been unable to do what they would, they have pretended to will what they could" (654 [509]). In other words, it would be more favorable to the kings' reputation to say that they liberalized their policy only because they found themselves unable to impose the true religion on all their subjects than to believe that they secretly hoped to undermine Christianity, as Julian did.

We need not attempt to evaluate the extent of the French kings' piety to grasp the significance of "Of Freedom of Conscience." As Michel Butor remarks, "The *Apology* gains considerably in virulence by being thus subordinated [through its placement] to this extraordinary central chapter."[73] Such scant records as exist of Montaigne's political activity tend to suggest—as we would expect—that in the immediate circumstances of the civil wars, he did favor a policy of toleration, as a means of bringing those wars to an end, as well as avoiding needless persecution and cruelty.[74] The

---

[71]The last remark is actually a bit softer on Christianity than Ammianus' text, which observes "that no wild beasts are such enemies to mankind as are most of the Christians in their deadly hatred of one another" (*Ammianus Marcellinus,* ed. and tr. John Rolfe [Cambridge, Mass., 1937], XXII, v, 4).

[72]See Zeitlin, *Essays of Montaigne,* 2:579.

[73]Butor, *Essais,* p. 139.

[74]See esp. Armaingaud, "Etude," ch. 10; Nakam, *Montaigne et son temps,* passim. On the basis of a somewhat arguable interpretation of some recorded facts about his actions, such scholars as Frame, Armaingaud, and Dreano infer that Montaigne was originally opposed to the policy of toleration favored by his friend, the chancellor Michel de l'Hôpital (Frame, *Montaigne's Discovery of Man,* pp. 24–5; Armaingaud, *Montaigne pamphlétaire,* pp. 44–5; Dreano, *La Religion de Montaigne,* pp. 89–92). But Armaingaud shows that for most of his political career, at any rate, Montaigne acted in support of the principle of freedom of conscience, as well as the goal of civic peace; Dreano stresses the tolerant attitude expressed in the *Essays* (Armaingaud, "Etude," ch. 10; Dreano, *La Religion de Montaigne,* 2: chs. 2–3). For a sensible defense of Montaigne's apparent opposition to the Edict of January (1562) authorizing toleration for the Protestant religion, in light of the proximate political circumstances that had generated it, see Marcel Françon, "Montaigne et l'Edit de Janvier (1562)," *BSAM,* 5th ser., nos. 3–4 (1972): 17–26. Also relevant to an understanding of the reasons that may have led Montaigne—before the full outbreak of the religious wars—not to favor the establishment of toleration as a *principle,* even while opposing religious persecution, is Robert P. Kraynak, "John Locke: From Absolutism to Toleration," *American Political Science Review* 74 (1980): 53–69.

deeper significance of "Of Freedom of Conscience," however, is that it confirms the antireligious intent underlying Montaigne's skeptical posture in the "Apology."

Montaigne's own situation is, I suggest, analogous to Julian's.[75] He, too, harbors a project entailing the destruction (or at least an enormous weakening) of the Christian religion; but because his "army"—the multitude whose belief and conduct he hopes to guide—is "composed of Christians," he dare not openly reveal that project. As Montaigne acknowledges in Book III, he must "excuse" himself before "certain humors which I believe to be stronger in number than those that are on my side" (III, v, 867 [678]). Hence he couches his attack on Christianity in the "Apology" in the form of a skeptical argument purporting to show the uncertainty of all human beliefs, and hence the need (as he sometimes claims) for submission to the authority of the church, or (alternatively) for greater toleration of religious differences (such as Julian professed to practice). In reality Montaigne is following a policy he attributes to Epicurus of secretly opposing religion while "cover[ing] himself" with the claim "that it is impossible to establish anything certain about immortal nature from mortal nature" (500 [386]).

I have previously argued that Montaigne understands himself as a kind of legislator-founder who hopes to guide future generations by means of the influence of the *Essays*. In this connection it is plausible to regard the chapter "Of the Education of Children" (I, xxvi) as a summary of the ultimate effect he expects his book, and especially the "Apology," to have. (He refers to the multitude at one point as "the little ones"—III, xiii, 1079 [844]: from the perspective of the philosopher, all nonphilosophic human beings are "children.")[76] The most prominent positive feature of the scheme of educa-

[75]Cf. Gide, *Les Pages immortelles de Montaigne*, pp. 33–4.

[76]Cf. Plato, *Gorgias*, 521e–522a; Alexander Kojève, "The Emperor Julian and His Art of Writing," in Joseph Cropsey, ed., *Ancients and Moderns* (New York, 1964), p. 108; and Montaigne's reference at II, xii, 527 [408], to the philosophers' endeavor to avoid "frighten[ing] the children." Gierczynski ("Le 'Que sais-je?' de Montaigne," p. 20) erroneously claims that the plan of education outlined in I, xxvi, is intended to form "a philosopher." Montaigne specifies that the youth whose education he is prescribing owes all but the first fifteen or sixteen years of his life "to action" (I, xxvi, 162 [120–21]), unlike the "spectators" of others' lives whose pursuit Pythagoras defended (157–8 [117]—and contrary to the course that Montaigne himself pursued. The recipient of the proposed education is a son of the nobility, born to a high "degree of fortune" (148 [109]); but there is no necessary connection between "greatness of fortune" and natural ability (155 [114]), hence no reason to assume that such a youth would possess the rare natural capacity requisite in a philosopher (cf. III, viii, 910 [711]). The true intention of Montaigne's educational proposal is to turn gentlemen into *allies* of philosophy, overcoming their "contempt" for learning and what has wrongly been thought to be "the natural incompatibility that exists between the vulgar and people of rare and excellent judgment and knowledge" (I, xxv, 132 [97]). More generally, the popularization of "lessons" derived from philosophy will undermine the severe morality that young people have formerly been taught to follow: philosophy as Montaigne represents it "preaches nothing but merrymaking and a good time" (I, xxvi, 160 [118]), as typified by the "natural" way of life Montaigne attributed to the philosophers in the "Apology." See, on Montaigne's influence on the education of French gentlemen in the seventeenth century, including the popularization of "philosophy" at the expense of piety, Villey, *Montaigne devant la postérité*, II.ii.

tion Montaigne proposes is that the tutor (*gouverneur*) must accustom his pupil to judge all things independently (just as Montaigne himself claims to do elsewhere in the *Essays*), rather than accept others' authority (I, xxvi, 149–50 [110–11]). The pupil who is unable to choose should remain in doubt, knowing that "only fools are certain and assured" (I, xxvi, 150 [111]). Concomitantly, the most striking negative characteristic of the proposed education is the absence of any religious instruction.[77]

If the program of I, xxvi, is taken literally as a plan for the upbringing of children, its most obvious likely consequence would be, in the words of one commentator, to make "precocious skeptics" of them.[78] Montaigne highlights the antireligious (rather than merely neutral) orientation of this education by indicating how the pupil, by acquiring a cosmopolitan perspective, would learn to reject theological interpretations of particular events (156–7 [116]). This point reminds us of the emphasis Montaigne has placed in the "Apology" on the diversity of the world, and the way in which awareness of this diversity undermines the ground for belief in any particular religion (or therefore, in religion as such).

The most important passage in the "Apology" relating to this scheme of education, however, is the essayist's forecast, near the beginning, of the likely effect of the Reformation, if unchecked, on popular belief: that the many, having learned to doubt received opinions and to regard their own judgment as authoritative, would ultimately succumb to atheism (416 [320]). The tendency of the "Apology" is surely to encourage such doubts. But if this is the case, it would be wrong to say that Montaigne merely wishes to teach people to think for themselves, or that his intention regarding religion is simply to promote toleration. In professing to warn of the danger of allowing the vulgar to judge and cast off conventionally accepted opinions, Montaigne remarked that they lack "the faculty of judging things in themselves"; nowhere does he impute such a faculty to them.[79] Later in the "Apology," as we have seen, Montaigne stresses the need to "bridle" the minds of the many, so as to prevent them from adopting views "that would set us to eating one another" (541 [419]). Thus there is no reason to think that Montaigne believes the unphilosophic multitude, if simply allowed to judge for themselves, will thereby become capable of rational self-guidance.

We are now in a better position to define the relation between Montaigne's teaching and that of his ancient philosophic predecessors. Montaigne does not disagree with the belief he attributed to Plato, among

[77]As emphasized by Armaingaud, "Etude," pp. 184–5; Weiler, *Pour connaître la pensée de Montaigne*, p. 51; Guizot, *Montaigne*, p. 19.
[78]M. Félix Hémon, *Cours de littérature—Montaigne*, cited by Norton in Ives, ed., *Essays*, 3:1625; similarly, Gierczynski, "Le 'Que sais-je?' de Montaigne," p. 21.
[79]Cf. III, vii, 896 [700]: the common people are "an inexact judge, easy to dupe, easy to satisfy."

others, that since the minds of the many are inevitably ruled by some sort of prejudice, the wise should endeavor to guide popular thought in a salutary direction (492 [379]). The real issue between Montaigne and his predecessors concerns the kind of public teaching that is truly salutary. Montaigne's fundamental criticism of the ancients' teachings, we have seen, is that they endeavored to "elevate" the many rather than promote the satisfaction of their earthly, animal needs. He observes in Book III that "in all the barracks of ancient philosophy," the same sages who published "rules of temperance" for the multitude also published "amorous and licentious" writings (III, ix, 968 [757]); as we have learned from the "Apology," their private life was one of sensual "license." The sages' practice was "to preach things as they serve, not as they are"; they "thought to achieve a fine result" by teaching people to neglect their selfish interests, "presupposing that we were attached to ourselves only too much and by too natural a bond" (III, x, 983 [769]). But the ultimate result of such well-intentioned if hypocritical teachings has been the terrible bloodshed and needless asceticism that are sanctioned by Christian leaders in Montaigne's time; the essayist would agree with his nineteenth-century admirer Friedrich Nietzsche that Christianity is a vulgarized "Platonism."[80]

In place of the unsalutary "presuppositions" instilled in the multitude by the classical philosophers, as well as lawgivers and theologians, Montaigne seeks to instill a more beneficial set of attitudes. Let us recall, in this regard, his uncharacteristic use, late in the "Apology," of the phrase "it is certain" regarding the soul's dependence on the body, as well as his assertion, shortly before, that it is "very truly presupposed that men are in agreement about nothing" (545, 547 [423–4]). The controversy between Montaigne and his predecessors concerns not whether a public teaching should "presuppose" anything but *what* it should presuppose.

Contrary to appearances, it is thus not the case that Montaigne is truly more skeptical than the classical political philosophers. As previously noted, and as Montaigne himself acknowledged, skepticism in the original sense of the term—an inextinguishable awareness of the uncertainty of all putative solutions to "the fundamental and comprehensive problems" (in Leo Strauss's words)—was essential to philosophy from the outset.[81] To the extent that there is a difference between Montaigne and his predecessors in this regard, it is actually Montaigne's teaching—as Sainte-Beuve suggested[82]—that is more "dogmatic." The ancient philosophers' awareness of their ignorance led them, as Montaigne observed, to dedicate their lives to the *pursuit* of wisdom, even though they knew that goal could never be fully

[80]Nietzsche, *Beyond Good and Evil*, tr. Walter Kaufmann (New York, 1966), Preface, p. 3.
[81]Strauss, *On Tyranny*, p. 210.
[82]*Port-Royal*, III, iii, 1:853.

achieved. The public myths they propagated represented, in part, an attempt to provide the multitude with an ennobling substitute for the satisfactions of philosophy. We have no reason to doubt that Montaigne is just as dedicated as his predecessors to the pursuit of knowledge. His public teaching, however, amounts to a dogmatic denial that we are capable of insight into the true character of the whole. Although that teaching is motivated, in part, by the desire to encourage the pursuit of "useful" knowledge, its more fundamental aim is to undermine religion. Having witnessed the frenzy to which religious passion is capable of driving humanity, Montaigne is convinced that such dangers can be overcome only by persuading the multitude of the impossibility of acquiring the kind of knowledge to which the adherents of revelation lay claim. To achieve this goal, he popularizes the "negative" aspect of the philosophic enterprise—its doubting of all received beliefs, as distinguished from its dedication to the discovery of truth—into a new "dogma" of skepticism or relativism.

It thus seems appropriate to label Montaigne's teaching—without any pejorative intent—as one of dogmatic skepticism. Within that teaching lies a conception of humanity that since Montaigne's time has had an ever-growing influence on Western civilization (and now, indeed, on the entire world): the independent "self" or *moi*, which affirms its radical independence from established institutions, customs, and beliefs, and views itself as a sovereign creator rather than a part of an order embodying ends that are in some sense "given" by nature or by God.[83] Montaigne himself represents his teaching as a kind of liberation of the individual from prejudice and constraint. Yet, as I have tried to indicate, there is something deceptive about this "liberation": the freedom Montaigne aims to provide for the multitude of his readers is not identical with the intellectual liberty of a philosopher who has thought things through independently, but will rather result from their acceptance of a new dogma in place of the ones they have formerly been taught to accept.[84]

If the foregoing observations are correct, it is impossible to arrive at an adequate evaluation of Montaigne's teaching purely on the basis of a judgment of its theoretical accuracy—or on the ground of that teaching's ostensibly superior "frankness." Such an evaluation, rather, must be based on an analysis of the entire scheme for human life that Montaigne outlines in the remainder of the *Essays*. Before undertaking this analysis, one brief, remaining section of the "Apology" must be considered.

[83]Cf. A. J. Krailsheimer, *Studies in Self-interest from Descartes to La Bruyère* (Oxford, 1962), pp. 28–30; Allan Bloom, *The Closing of the American Mind* (New York, 1987), pp. 173–9.

[84]Note that in "Of the Education of Children," although the pupil is supposed to be learning to rely on his own judgment, "the authority of the tutor [*gouverneur*]" is to be "sovereign over him" (I, xxvi, 153 [113]). To the extent that human beings in general are Montaigne's "pupils," does he not become their "sovereign" *gouverneur*?

Conclusion of the "Apology"

At the end of the "Apology" Montaigne returns to the question of whether we can hope to raise ourselves above our earthly condition. Most of this section practically reproduces a passage from Plutarch which describes the gap that separates humanity from the only eternal thing, God (586–8 [455–7]). "To this so religious conclusion of a pagan" Montaigne appends a quotation from Seneca: " 'O what a vile and abject thing is man,' he says, 'if he does not raise himself above humanity' " (588 [457]).

Fortunat Strowski, among other commentators, has cited this concluding section as a confirmation of the sincerity of Montaigne's piety; despite its borrowed character, he contends that this passage expresses the deepest level, and ultimate conclusion, of the essayist's own thought in the "Apology."[85] I believe, on the contrary, that Sainte-Beuve was much closer to the mark when he alluded to the irony of the passage.[86] To clarify the issue, let us consider what Montaigne says in the immediate sequel to the remark last quoted. The desire to rise above humanity, he comments, is "absurd," for it aims at something "impossible and unnatural"; man "can see only with his own eyes, and seize only with his own grasp." In imitation of Sebond[87] he adds that no one can "raise himself" unless "God, by exception, lends him a hand"; man, Montaigne infers, must abandon and renounce "his own means." It is only "for our Christian faith, not [Seneca's] Stoic virtue, to pretend to this divine and miraculous metamorphosis" (589 [457]). Yet the "Apology," as we have seen, has emphasized the absurdity of expecting the uniform course of nature to be broken for our benefit. Nor has Montaigne given us reason to believe in the special beneficence toward the human species of whoever or whatever is responsible for the world's existence. He has portrayed the human condition as one of deprivation or neediness that can be mitigated only by the use of our "own means." Elsewhere in the Essays he explicitly suggests that to hope for outside assistance is unnecessary as well as vain: "We are each richer than we think, but we are trained to borrow and beg"; our "own resources . . . alone are sure and alone powerful, for the one who knows how to arm himself with them" (III, xii, 1015, 1022 [794, 799]). And at the conclusion of the book he represents the wish to transcend our nature as both vain and dangerous (III, xiii, 1095–6 [856–7]; cf. II, iii, 334 [254]).[88] If we dispense with the quest to "rise" to a

---

[85]Strowski, Montaigne, pp. 200–216.

[86]Port-Royal, III, iii, 1:861. Cf. also Armaingaud, "Etude," pp. 178–9; Weiler, Pour connaître la pensée de Montaigne, pp. 49–51.

[87]As noted by the Pléiade editors: Oeuvres, p. 1581 (n. 1 to p. 589).

[88]Donald Frame, who upholds Montaigne's piety in "Did Montaigne Betray Sebond?" nonetheless concedes that "in Montaigne's final scheme of things, escape from the man—even upwards—has no place" ("To 'Rise Above Humanity' and to 'Escape from the Man': Two Moments in Montaigne's Thought," Romanic Review 62 [1971]: 35). I have tried to show that

condition beyond our reach, we may improve our earthly condition infi-nitely. But the precondition of such improvement is the abandonment of the belief that we have or can have access to Being.

Montaigne's position throughout the "Apology" is consistent with his "final scheme of things."

Cf. the "fable" of Antaeus, retold by Machiavelli in *Discorsi*, II, xii, 308 (the same book and chapter number as Montaigne's "Apology"), with Strauss, *Thoughts on Machiavelli*, p. 207.

CHAPTER FIVE

Conservatism and "Reformation"

Montaigne: "Liberal" or "Conservative"?

I have argued that the "Apology for Raymond Sebond" points toward the need for a fundamental transformation of political life to bring it into greater conformity with the standard of nature and reason. That Montaigne could have intended such a project is denied, however, by most recent interpreters, who have typically viewed him as a more or less paradoxical combination of a theoretical skeptic and a practical ultraconservative. While recognizing that Montaigne harbored profound doubts about the wisdom and justice of many existing laws and customs, they attribute to him a proto-Burkean attitude according to which the very fact that laws have no deeper foundation than customary prejudice makes it extremely dangerous to change them, lest the entire structure of political order be undermined. Hence, although Montaigne himself is understood to have been a lover of freedom and to have exhibited an attitude of enlightened tolerance unusual for his age, it is denied that he favored any sort of political transformation designed to secure the benefits of freedom to the populace at large. The typical scholarly view is summarized in one commentator's remark that "Montaigne represents the paradox of a writer liberal in thought but conservative in action."[1] Perhaps the most notable

---

[1] Francis S. Heck, "Montaigne's Conservatism and Liberalism: A Paradox?" *Romanic Review* 66 (1975): 165. For representative statements that follow a similar line of interpretation, see Brown, *Religious and Political Conservatism;* Sayce, *Essays,* ch. 10; Dreano, *La Religion de Montaigne,* 2:i; Tavera, *L'Idée d'humanité,* ch. 4; Villey, *Les Sources,* 2:335–43, 495–6; Albert Thibaudet, *Montaigne* (Paris, 1963), pp. 304–19; Friedrich, *Montaigne,* pp. 206–10; Starobinski, *Montaigne in Motion,* pp. 250–56, 293–4; Quentin Skinner, *The Foundations of*

dissenter from this view is Arthur Armaingaud, who stresses Montaigne's practical political role in advancing the cause of religious toleration as well as his attack on Christian theology in the *Essays*. But even he treats Montaigne as a loyal monarchist who wished only to facilitate the accession of Henry IV to the throne so as to bring an end to the era of religious persecution and civil war, without altering the structure of the regime.[2]

Numerous passages of the *Essays* can be cited to support the view that Montaigne, however "liberal" (in the sense of favoring freedom) his thought may have been, was an archconservative in matters of political practice, whether out of a general opposition to change or out of a distrust of his own capacity (as well as others') to guide it in a salutary direction. But despite the surface plausibility of this interpretation, it embodies a number of difficulties. The most obvious, though not the most fundamental, is that the accepted interpretation would render Montaigne's political thought extremely shallow (even if few of the interpreters would put it that way). If Montaigne's professions of opposition to change are taken at face value, what we have is not a conservatism with the flexibility of Burke's doctrine (which allowed the British statesman to justify the American Revolution) but a position so extreme that it casts doubt on the desirability of changing *any* law, however irrational or unjust, and denies that it is ever proper to seek to change the form of government under which one lives (I, xxiii, 117–18 [86]; III, ix, 934 [730–31]). Yet these remarks occur right next to passages that describe existing legal customs as "barbarous" and express the author's "horror" at the monstrous "inhumanity" of the accepted mores (I, xxiii, 116 [85]; III, ix, 933–4 [730]). Given the manifest contradiction between Montaigne's frequently expressed longings for freedom and the extreme subordination that, by his testimony, the laws of his time imposed, Frieda Brown would seem to understate the case when she admits it as "permissible to maintain that Montaigne had made an error in judgment" in advocating "strict adherence to authority and the complete unity

Modern Political Thought, 2 vols. (Cambridge, Eng., 1978), 2:278–84; Nannerl O. Keohane, "Montaigne's Individualism," *Political Theory* 5 (1977): 378–81. A suggestive exception among recent studies is Colette Fleuret, "Montaigne et la société civile," *Europe* 50, nos. 513–14 (1972): 107–23; see also Nakam, *Les Essais*, ch. 3, and René Etiemble, "Sens et structure dans un essai de Montaigne," *Cahiers de l'Association internationale des études françaises* 14 (1962): 263–74.
That Montaigne was a theoretical skeptic but a practical conservative also appears to have been the view of Pascal: see "Entretien de M. Pascal et de M. de Sacy sur la lecture d'Epictete et de Montaigne," in Pascal, *Oeuvres complètes*, ed. Jacques Chevalier (Paris, 1954), pp. 565, 570. The authenticity of this work, however, is disputed: see Henri Gouhier, *Blaise Pascal: Commentaires* (Paris, 1966), ch. 2. See also sec. V of the *Pensées* (ed. Brunschvicg), parts of which (notably no. 294) largely reproduce Montaigne's apparent view that human justice can have no deeper support than custom, which must be obeyed for that very reason.
[2]Armaingaud, "Etude," pp. 208–9. Nakam, *Les Essais*, p. 268, provides a list of specific reforms favored in the *Essays* but does not fully relate Montaigne's practical recommendations to his theoretical project.

of Church and State," even as he sought to demonstrate "the possibility of living as a free and autonomous individual."[3] But is it likely that Montaigne, so revered for his judgment and good sense in other respects, was unaware of his "error" in this case?

Whatever judgment one is initially inclined to make regarding the sincerity of Montaigne's conservatism, it is noteworthy that most interpreters have judged the overall *effect* of the *Essays* on its readers to be far more revolutionary than conservative. Hence Richard Sayce, while holding that Montaigne's "temperament and personality" were predominantly conservative, nonetheless finds his "critique of conservatism . . . much more powerful in its expression and influence" than his "defence of conservatism" and observes that the essayist's putatively conservative position "is reached by a circuitous route which takes in all the potentially revolutionary themes which were eventually to find expression in action as well as thought" in later centuries. Thus, if one focuses not on "Montaigne in himself" but on "his influence and the later history of his subversive ideas, . . . it is the revolutionary side" rather than the conservative one that is "uppermost."[4] Jacob Zeitlin, drawing a similar dichotomy between Montaigne's personal inclinations and his influence, remarks that the essayist's "freedom of speculation . . . has encouraged radicalism in spheres of action where his own leanings were decidedly conservative."[5] And Colette Fleuret, taking issue with most contemporary interpretations of Montaigne's political thought, reminds us "that the philosophers of the eighteenth century unanimously saw in Montaigne a precursor, and that the [1789] Revolution . . . numbered him among the 'Saints' of its calendar."[6]

If it were true that Montaigne's own thought and inclination were conservative rather than revolutionary, one would have to conclude, given these accounts of his influence, that he made a poor advocate for his cause. This judgment would be surprising, in view of his recognized mastery as a rhetorician and stylist. But an even more telling objection is that Montaigne himself expressly acknowledges the tension between the liberty of thought and judgment he professes and the policy of absolute submission to established laws and customs. In "A Trait of Some Ambassadors" he claims that to a ruler, no quality is so valuable in subordinate officials as "artless and simple obedience." Borrowing from Aulus Gellius, he asserts that rulership is weakened when people "obey through discretion, not through subjection" (I, xvii, 73 [51]). Similarly, in the "Apology" Montaigne recommends that each person's duty "should be prescribed to him, not left to the choice of his reason," since "humility and submissiveness alone can make a good

[3]Brown, *Religious and Political Conservatism*, pp. 83, 91.
[4]Sayce, *The Essays*, pp. 237, 259.
[5]Zeitlin, *Essays of Montaigne*, vol. 1, "Introduction," p. lxiii.
[6]Fleuret, "Montaigne et la société civile," p. 110.

man." It is for this reason that he represents Christianity in particular, as we have seen, as praising ignorance and condemning curiosity (II, xii, 467, 477–8 [359, 367–8]). In a later chapter he reaffirms that "obedience is not pure or tranquil in a man who reasons and argues" (II, xvii, 640 [498]). Yet at the same time, he openly refuses to submit his own understanding to a king's dictates, avowing that "my reason is not trained to bend and bow, it is my knees" (III, viii, 913 [714]). Far from encouraging a thoughtless reverence toward kings, he explicitly challenges the claim that monarchs have any inherent superiority to their subjects (I, xlii, 252–3 [191]). And in criticizing the hypocrisy of the rules by which political societies have tried to restrain the sexual impulse, he makes clear that he intends his own example of freedom of judgment and behavior to be emulated by his readers: "God grant that this excess of my license may encourage our men to attain freedom" (III, v, 822 [642]).

These passages make it evident that far from maintaining a radical dichotomy between the spheres of thought and action, Montaigne recognized an ineluctable connection between them: the more freely people think about and judge political things, the less they can be counted on to practice an automatic obedience to established authority.[7] He surely cannot have been unaware that his denunciations of the stupidity and injustice of many existing laws and customs would tend to weaken his readers' disposition to maintain or accept them. I shall argue here that his periodic disclaimers of intending to promote any sort of political change have the same protective, rhetorical function as the affirmations of submission that he appends to his attacks on religious orthodoxy. When scrutinized more closely in their context, these disclaimers prove to have a sense quite at variance with their ostensible one.

The foregoing remarks are not intended to deny the seriousness or the sincerity of the aspiration Montaigne frequently expresses to see a stable legal order established, or his evident horror at the suffering and injustice that his compatriots endured during the religious wars. In these respects, contemporary interpreters are correct in viewing Montaigne as a law-and-order man. They err, however, in overlooking the fundamental changes Montaigne thought to be necessary in people's political beliefs and institutions, as well as in their religious and moral opinions, before a just, orderly, and lasting political system could be established. Though Armaingaud rightly emphasizes Montaigne's endeavors to bring about an end to the wars and promote a reign of peaceful toleration in his country, Montaigne's greater undertaking is to reconstitute the foundations of political life, so as to secure our well-being from dependence on such accidents as the royal succession or shifting religious currents.

[7]Cf. also the emphasis in I, xxv–xxvi, on the need to judge the value of an education by "the test [*essay*] of action" (I, xxv, 142 [105]).

"Of Custom": First Reading

The chapter in which Montaigne's ostensibly conservative posture is stated and developed thematically—I, xxiii, "Of Custom, and Not Easily Changing an Accepted Law"—opens with a lengthy discourse concerning the power of custom or habit[8] in shaping our thoughts and perceptions. With regard to this theme, Montaigne professes his agreement with Plato's metaphor of the cave in the *Republic*. But the denunciatory tone with which Montaigne speaks of habituation at the outset has no parallel in the Platonic passage: habit, he claims, is "a violent and treacherous schoolmistress" that, from unnoticed beginnings, "soon uncovers to us a furious and tyrannical face against which we no longer have the liberty of even raising our eyes"; everywhere she "force[s] the rules of nature." Montaigne's first examples, it is true, do not exactly support his denunciation: they include a woman who reputedly toughened her body to endure an unusual burden, and individuals and peoples who accustomed themselves to live on strange foods (I, xxiii, 106–7 [77–8]). (In his own prescriptions for the education of children, Montaigne explicitly recommends this sort of physical toughening and adaptability—I, xxvi, 152–3 [112–13].) Although the essayist goes on to observe "that our greatest vices take shape from our tenderest childhood," moreover, he refers to children's displays of "ugly inclinations" as signs of "nature speaking" (I, xxiii, 107–8 [78]). Hence some overcoming of "natural" inclinations by salutary customs would seem to be beneficial rather than harmful.

Be this as it may, Montaigne focuses most of his attention in this section of the chapter on demonstrating rather than evaluating the power of custom. In support of the thesis that there appears to be no "opinion so bizarre"—even "leav[ing] aside the gross impostures of religions"—"that custom has not planted and established it by law in the regions where she saw fit to do so" (109 [79]), he offers a long list of the seemingly fantastic customs practiced by various peoples. To readers who find this list (borrowed mostly from Francisco López de Gómara's reports about the New World) "marvelous," Montaigne responds in a manner reminiscent of the "Apology":

> Miracles arise from our ignorance of nature, not from the essence of nature. Habituation puts to sleep the eye of our judgment. Barbarians are no more marvelous to us than we are to them, nor for better cause; as everyone would admit if everyone knew how, after perusing these new examples, to reflect on his own and compare them sanely. Human reason is a tincture infused in about equal strength in all our opinions and mores, whatever their form: infinite in matter, infinite in diversity. (110 [80])

[8]The word *coutume* has both meanings.

At the conclusion of the list, having demonstrated that custom is rightly called "the queen and empress of the world," Montaigne reiterates the need to transcend the bias that she imposes on our judgment: to "return into ourselves to reflect and reason about her ordinances." It is most needful, albeit highly difficult, to overcome the tendency to identify "the common notions that we find in credit around us" as "the universal and natural ones"—as, for instance, in our inherited notions regarding the best form of government (114–15 [83–4]).

Up to this point Montaigne's argument has remained largely at the theoretical plane of the "Apology." But he now applies his analysis of custom to his own country. Having once been authorized "to justify one of our observances," he reports finding "its foundation so weak that I nearly became disgusted with it, I who was supposed to confirm it in others." Without identifying that custom, he goes on to note that the "fine [belle]" virtue of chastity, despite its well-known "utility," is as difficult to justify "according to nature" as it is easy to justify "according to customs, laws, and precepts." Because "the first and universal reasons are hard to scrutinize," Montaigne observes, "our masters" take refuge in "the protection of custom," whereby they "enjoy a cheap triumph."[9] He appears to balance this remark by holding that "those who will not let themselves be drawn out of this original source err even more and bind themselves to barbarous opinions, like Chrysippus," who made light of incest (115–16 [84]). Noting that the essayist's previous assertion that all customs are about equally reasonable was followed by a reference to countries where the practice of incest is accepted (113 [82]), we might wonder how seriously this criticism of Chrysippus is meant. In any event, Montaigne immediately proceeds to recommend the emulation of Chrysippus' liberation of his judgment from the bonds of custom:

> Whoever wants to get rid of this violent prejudice of custom will find many things accepted with undoubting resolution, which have no support but in the hoary beard and the wrinkles of the usage that goes with them; but when this mask is torn off, and he refers things to truth and reason, he will feel his judgment as it were all upset, and nevertheless restored to a much surer state. (116 [84–5])[10]

As a demonstration of how to do this, Montaigne now sets forth a forthright criticism of a number of French legal practices: the fact that the

[9]Compare the reference to those who establish the presuppositions of inquiry that others accept on faith as "our masters" at pp. 521–2 [403–4] of the "Apology." See also Montaigne's criticism of the "feverish solicitude" for female chastity at II, vii, 364 [278].

[10]The words with which this passage began in the pre-1592 editions—"And whoever wants to essay himself in the same way, and get rid . . ."—make even clearer the connection of the practice recommended here with Montaigne's own project.

laws are printed in Latin and thus are incomprehensible to most people; the "barbarous" custom of charging for legal judgments, thus denying justice to the poor; and the contradiction between the code of honor, which obliges noblemen to avenge personal insults, and the civil code, which punishes such vengeance with death (116–17 [85]).[11] After adding to this attack an observation of how French fashions in "indifferent things such as clothes" deviate from "their true purpose, which is the service and comfort of the body," however, Montaigne abruptly shifts direction. "These considerations," he cautions, "do not deter a man of understanding from following the common style." He then propounds a dichotomy between thought and action, according to which the wise man, while "withdrawing his soul from the crowd" and retaining his freedom of judgment, should nonetheless "wholly follow the accepted fashions and forms" in "externals." We may rightly withhold our thoughts from the public, but

> the rest—our actions, our work, our fortunes, and our very life—we must lend and abandon to its service and to the common opinions, just as that good and great Socrates refused to save his life by disobedience to the magistrate, even to a very unjust and very iniquitous magistrate. For it is the rule of rules, and the general law of laws, that each man should observe those of the place he is in. (117 [85–6])

Not only does Montaigne now insist on the obligation to obey the laws and government of one's country, however unjust or unreasonable they may be; he goes on to question even whether it is ever desirable to change defective laws or customs: "There is great doubt whether there can be such evident profit in changing an accepted law, of whatever sort it be, as there is harm in disturbing it; inasmuch as a government is like a structure of different parts joined to one another in such a relation that it is impossible to budge one without the whole body feeling it." Having described the efforts that ancient Thurian and Spartan lawgivers undertook to obstruct or prevent such change, Montaigne proceeds to express his own disgust with "innovation, in whatever guise," with particular reference to France's civil wars. He denounces not only the Protestant reformers, however, but also their Catholic opponents who profess to be defending the old order, for the "self love and presumption" they exhibit in so esteeming their opinions as for their sake to "overthrow the public peace and introduce so many inevitable evils and such a horrible corruption of morals as civil wars and

---

[11]These criticisms of the French judicial system, it has been noted, were not original with Montaigne, but were common to numerous writers of his time (Pierre Villey, "Les Sources des *Essais:* Annotations et éclaircissements," in Fortunat Strowski et al., eds., *Les Essais de Michel de Montaigne* [Bordeaux, 1920], 4:60 [note to p. 150]; Nakam, *Les Essais,* pp. 132–7). The central significance of this passage will be shown rather to lie in its relation to the overall argument of "Of Custom."

political changes bring with them." "Isn't it bad management," he asks, "to encourage so many certain and known vices in order to combat contested and debatable errors?" In contrast to such conduct, Montaigne praises the true Christian religion for recommending "obedience to the magistrate and maintenance of the government" (118–20 [86–8]).

If "Of Custom" ended at this point, its argument would seem fully to support the conventional interpretation of Montaigne as a theoretical skeptic and practical conservative. That interpretation is rendered questionable, however, by the concluding twist that his argument now takes. He modifies his general condemnation of innovation to indicate that political change, even in violation of the law, is sometimes necessary for the public good. He cautions, indeed, that anyone who seeks to bring about such change assumes a heavy responsibility, such as he himself disclaims wishing to undertake. Nonetheless, he observes that "Fortune . . . sometimes presents us with a necessity so urgent that the laws must give some place to it" and notes that such great men as Octavius and Cato "are still reproached . . . for having let their country incur all extremities rather than disturb things by rescuing it at the expense of the laws." It is especially dangerous to oblige oneself to remain within the laws when one is seeking to oppose an innovation that has already introduced itself by violence and in disregard of the laws. In such "ultimate necessities," Montaigne concludes, "it would be better to make the laws will what they can do, since they cannot do what they will."[12] Hence he completes the chapter by citing instances in which the Spartans, the Athenians, and other peoples found ways of changing the laws when necessary, or of letting the laws "sleep" so that illegal but necessary actions could be taken. Just as these examples moderate the thrust of the earlier discussion of the ancient lawgivers' hostility to change, Montaigne's citation, in the last sentence of the chapter, of the praise Plutarch gave to Philopoemen for knowing how to "command . . . the laws themselves, when the public necessity required it," seems to counteract his previous claim that the civil laws are "supremely the judges of their judges" (120–122 [88–90]).

The argument of "Of Custom" thus oscillates in an ambiguous manner: from a lament of our subordination to custom and the recommendation that unreasonable laws and customs be questioned to a denunciation of political innovation and a denial of the applicability of the wise person's reflections to political improvement, culminating in a statement of the need for political change on occasion, going beyond or against the laws, albeit prudently guided change. To determine the specific consequences Montaigne derived from his principles—and hence to arrive at a more concrete

[12]Note the similarity of this remark to Montaigne's preferred interpretation of the French kings' motives in instituting a policy of religious toleration in "Of Freedom of Conscience."

interpretation of "Of Custom"—requires the consideration of two passages in later books of the *Essays* in which Montaigne again reflects on his country's political condition and on the adequacy of an extreme conservatism as a response to that condition.

The Political Condition of France

The first of these passages occurs in chapter xvii of Book II, "Of Presumption." A few pages from the end of this chapter Montaigne elaborates the disclaimer he had expressed in "Of Custom" of wanting to undertake the responsibility for innovative political leadership, citing his distrust of his own capacities (638 [496–7]). We are compelled by several remarks earlier in the chapter to take this profession of incapacity as an ironic statement of Socratic ignorance, rather than an indication that Montaigne truly regards himself as inferior in political wisdom to others.[13] Be this as it may, he goes on to reassert his opposition to political changes that cause instability, remarking that "in public affairs there is no course so bad, provided it is old and stable, that it is not better than change and commotion." Thus even while noting that "our morals are extremely corrupt and lean with a remarkable inclination towards worsening," and that "of our laws and usages, many are barbarous and monstrous," he avows that "because of the difficulty in improving our state and the danger of everything collapsing, if I could put a spoke in our wheel and stop it [*l'arrester*] at this point, I would do so with all my heart." But in the sequel he indicates that France's situation does not allow of such a remedy, commenting that "the worst thing I find in our state is instability, and the fact that our laws cannot, any more than our clothes, take any settled [*arrestée*] form" (639 [497–8]). In other words, however much Montaigne might wish to stop France's decay by putting "a spoke in our wheel," he cannot do so: by virtue of their instability, further change in France's institutions is inevitable,[14] and if they continue in their present course, that change will be for the worse. It is thus not surprising that when Montaigne reiterates his doubts about reform, his

[13]See II, xvii, 617–19 [480–81]. Also, contrast Montaigne's profession of deference at II, xvii, 638 [497], to those who are "more assured of [their] opinions and wedded to them than I am to mine" with the remark at I, xxvi, 150 [111] that "only fools are certain and resolute," and with III, xi, 1007–8 [788]. And consider Montaigne's accounts of his success as mayor and his qualifications to serve as a royal adviser in III, x and xiii, respectively.

[14]Cf. III, ix, 935 [731], where, in the midst of another purportedly conservative passage that I discuss later in this section, Montaigne observes that "alteration and corruption [are] natural to all things." Cf. also the assertion at I, xliii, 261 [198] (following Plato, *Laws,* 797b–c) that "in all things except those that are simply bad, change is to be feared: change of seasons, winds, food, and humors." Since changes of seasons and winds, at least, are inevitable, a purely "conservative" posture once again seems inadequate, for it goes contrary to the nature of things.

conservatism is very much tempered. He no longer denies that a reformation might succeed but merely cautions that many people who have endeavored to bring about improvements have achieved nothing for their pains (639 [498]), thus reminding the reader, as he had done in the last part of "Of Custom," of the need for prudence in such matters. He implies that the true alternative to such ill-advised "reformations" as the Protestant one is not a diehard conservatism that is doomed to failure, but a wisely guided sort of change that would remedy both France's instability and its corruption.

Montaigne returns to the theme of political change and preservation in chapter ix of Book III, "Of Vanity." This chapter contains a lengthy account of the travels the essayist reports having undertaken for the sake of enjoyment. Despite having asserted in "Of Custom" that the wise, like all others, owe themselves (except their thoughts) to the public, and despite acknowledging here that "the most honorable occupation is to serve the public," Montaigne claims to stay out of political affairs and shamelessly explains his devotion to private pleasure by saying that he is "content . . . to live a merely excusable life, which will merely be no burden to myself or others" (929–30 [727]). He has traveled not only for the pleasure of seeing "new and unknown things" but also out of opposition to "the present morals of our state" and its "unruly . . . form of government," from which he has suffered excessively (925, 933 [723, 729]). Despite this striking criticism of the French political order, Montaigne proceeds to argue anew against trying to change it. He rejects "all those artificially simulated descriptions of government" that "prove ridiculous and unfit to put into practice" and disdains "these great, lengthy altercations about the best form of society and the rules most suitable to bind us." Even though "we are prone to be discontented with the present state of things," Montaigne distances himself from those "desiring the government of a few in a democratic state, or another type of government in a monarchy." He asserts, instead, what appears the most conservative political attitude possible: "The best and most excellent government for each nation is the one under which it has maintained itself" (934 [730–31]).

Once again, Montaigne's conservative posture proves on further examination to be misleading. In view of his previous observation of the instability of the French state and his present complaint of the riotous form of government under which he lives, it may be doubted whether he regards the existing regime as capable of "maintaining" the nation. He goes on to note that "the preservation of states is a thing that probably surpasses our intelligence," and that "in all the great states that we know . . . everything is collapsing"; "it seems the stars themselves ordain that we have lasted long enough beyond the ordinary term" (937–9 [732–4]).[15] At times Mon-

---

[15]Cf. I, xliii, 261 [197]: "The masonry [of the French regime] is crumbling." Although this passage occurs in the midst of another seeming argument against change, the same chapter

taigne appears to be imitating the "Stoical" counsels of his contemporary Justus Lipsius against despairing at the state of one's country, however bleak things may appear.[16] But the dominant thrust of his argument is in quite a different direction, for he not only expresses doubt that the French political order can be preserved in its present state but implies that "so unruly a form of government" is *unworthy* of being preserved, even if its preservation were possible. He marvels at, while detesting, the continuance of "morals in common and accepted practice, so monstrous, especially in inhumanity and treachery . . . that I have not the courage to think of them without horror" (933–4 [730]). He cites the preservation of the Roman Empire as a parallel case and calls attention to the spectacle of "all those nations . . . ruled with so little order and conquered so unjustly" under its hegemony (938 [733]). Such remarks hardly appear calculated to encourage support for the existing order.

Just as he did in "Of Custom," Montaigne has inserted into this purportedly conservative argument a bold critique of established institutions. And just as he concluded the former chapter with an emphasis on the need for change, he includes in "Of Vanity" a discussion of the proper aims and means of such change. Here he compares the wise political reformer who aims at a "general improvement" rather than a mere release from "present evil[s]" to a surgeon who looks beyond the destruction of "diseased flesh" in order "to make the natural [flesh] grow again [*renaître*], and restore the part to its proper state [*estre*]." He contrasts such prudence with the lack of foresight displayed by "Caesar's slayers," who found that they had "cast the republic into such a state that they had reason to repent of having meddled in it" (935 [731]). But far from inferring that all efforts at political reform are similarly doomed to failure, Montaigne concludes this discussion by counseling future reformers on matters of tactics, encouraging them by reference to the decay of present institutions and the astrologers' forecasts of "great and imminent alterations and mutations,"[17] and expressing the hope that the French state, after a purgation, may be "restored to a better condition" (938–9 [734]).

Although Montaigne expresses himself prudently, both the passages I have examined in this section suggest that he regards the contemporary situation of France as one that corresponds to those discussed in the last part of "Of Custom": a condition sufficiently dire to require a supralegal

contains a recommendation by Montaigne himself of a change in the practice of kings (259–60 [196–7]). Cf. also the reference to the "old age" of the French monarchy in "Of Custom," p. 118 [87].

[16]See Zeitlin, *Essays of Montaigne*, 3:379. Note that Montaigne concludes this section of his argument by criticizing the Stoics' practice (which he has just been imitating) of "restating ever anew the common and universal arguments and reasons" (939 [734–5]).

[17]Cf. Machiavelli's account of the "extraordinary things" he claims have taken place in his time, as an encouragement to those who would institute new modes and orders: *The Prince*, ch. 26, p. 103.

remedy, rather than being soluble through a restoration of the old order. We must now attempt to reconcile this inference with Montaigne's seeming denunciation of all political innovations earlier in that chapter.

Aristotle's View of Political Change

The key to resolving this problem is to compare the passage in "Of Custom" where Montaigne questions the desirability of ever changing the laws with the classical source on which it seems to be based. In introducing this passage, Montaigne remarks, "Here is something from another vat" (117 [86]). The vat to which he refers is, I believe, Aristotle's *Politics*, from which both Montaigne's central argument in this passage and the second part of the title of the chapter appear to have been borrowed.[18] Aristotle's warning about the danger of changing the laws emerges out of his critique of the proposals of an ancient political scientist, Hippodamus, who was guided in his approach to politics by his background in natural science and mathematics. Hippodamus attempted to rationalize political life by advocating a number of sweeping reforms designed to bring a quasi-mathematical orderliness into the polis. Aristotle demonstrates, on the contrary, that most of Hippodamus' proposals were either impracticable or pointless. He takes especial issue with what might be suspected as a rather self-serving proposal on Hippodamus' part: a system of rewards for political innovators.

In opposition to Hippodamus, Aristotle argues that politics is quite different from a technical art like medicine. The fundamental reason for this difference is the problem of consent. Sensible people generally obey a competent physician's orders, for they have no reason to doubt that the physician intends to serve their interest by offering advice in return for a fee. But such causes do not suffice to lead people to obey governments. Statesmen are not the possessors of a recognized technical knowledge like that of doctors, to which nonexperts readily defer. Nor do citizens have the same assurance about the government that they do about a doctor, to the effect that the orders they are given are meant to serve their well-being. Politicians and lawgivers, unlike doctors, may easily find ways of benefiting themselves at the expense of their constituents, rather than by serving them.[19] Consequently, citizens who are inclined to question the laws may readily find

---

[18]*Politics* 1268a25ff. The resemblance of Montaigne's argument to this passage has been pointed out by Villey, who believes it nearly certain that the essayist knew the *Politics* in La Roy's translation before 1580 (*Les Sources,* 1:68). Aristotle's argument had been restated by Montaigne's contemporary Jean Bodin in his *Les Six Livres de la République* (1576), IV, iii. Cf. also Thomas Aquinas, *Summa Theologica,* II, i, Qu. 97, Second Article.

[19]*Politics* 1287a32–b3.

reasons for not obeying them. It is not only their recognition of possible defects in the commands of government that may inspire them to disobedience, however; their own selfishness can supply a greater inducement. Whereas the physician's prescriptions are intended to promote the health of the individual, the statesman frames laws that are supposed to serve the political community as a whole. But what is good for the whole community will not always be most advantageous for every individual within it. Hence the citizen has a much greater incentive to disobey the government's orders than those of a physician.

It is because of this problem of securing obedience to the laws that punishments are attached to them and police forces instituted to enforce them. But a community held together exclusively or mainly by such force would be neither a tolerable place in which to live nor very long lasting. The more fundamental bond that holds political communities together and secures general obedience to the law, Aristotle argues, is custom or habit. The habitual morality that every child is taught, embodying such simple precepts as "don't steal," is "internalized" by us in our youth so that, as adults, we refrain from seeking unjust or illegal gains even when no one is watching to scold or punish us. Thus the teaching of custom develops (as Montaigne points out: I, xxiii, 114 [83]) into what we call "conscience." It is habit, rather than reason, that causes most people to act decently most of the time.[20] However useful it may be, from a philosophical point of view, for the individual to ask "why be just?" no well-bred person ever asks this question; such a person "knows" that justice and honorableness are their own justification. And because most people are not philosophers and hence not fully rational beings, the political community's survival depends, Aristotle suggests, on the inculcation of such a habitual morality of justice, honorableness, and obedience to law. Even though the habit of law-abidingness will lead citizens sometimes to conform to unjust laws, there is no higher standard than positive law which could adequately bind the citizenry to some modicum of justice. Hence Aristotle asserts that the true gentleman will conform not only to ordinances that prohibit what is wrong by nature but also to the purely conventional morality of his city.[21]

The contrast between politics and medicine with respect to the causes that lead the "patients" of each art to obey the orders they are given is the basis of Aristotle's cautionary remarks against lightly changing the laws. It is undoubtedly beneficial, he observes, for the rules of such arts as medicine to be altered in the light of new discoveries. It is similarly true that some changes in the laws have been salutary: as evidence, Aristotle cites some

---

[20]*Nicomachean Ethics*, I, iv, 1095b2–8; II.1.

[21]Ibid., 1128b22–26. Montaigne mimics this claim at III, ii, 784 [612] but renounces it through his denunciation of merely conventional rules at III, i, 773–4 [604] and III, v, 866 [677], among other passages.

"barbaric" old customs and a rather foolish old law that have subsequently been discarded. Hence he grants "that some laws must be changed at some times." But here the parallel between change in the laws and change in the arts and sciences ends: "since it is a bad thing to habituate people to the reckless dissolution of laws . . . some errors both of the legislators and of the rulers should be let go; for [the city] will not be benefited as much from changing them as it will be harmed through being habituated to disobey the rulers."[22]

Aristotle contends that the power of the laws to command habitual obedience can be given only by time. Every time citizens observe changes being made in some laws inherited from previous generations, they will be encouraged to question whether the laws that remain are worthy of obedience. Rather than having a divine or quasi-divine origin, such as their original authors may have attributed to them, the laws may now seem to represent the mere will of a ruling class, composed of people not essentially different from other citizens, who have aimed to advance their own interests through the law at the citizens' expense.[23] Once reverence for the laws has been undermined by frequent and obvious changes, it will be easy enough for people to find excuses for breaking the law when it conflicts with what they perceive to be their interest, assuming they can avoid being caught. Thus the bonds that hold a community together by deterring its members from injustice are weakened and ultimately destroyed.

"An Easy Reformation"

Having traced the reasoning that leads Aristotle to caution against frequent changes in the laws, let us compare this argument with Montaigne's adaptation of it in "Of Custom." The first fact that strikes one is that Montaigne has so rigidified Aristotle's argument as to make a travesty of it. Whereas Aristotle merely warns against excessive changes, Montaigne expresses doubt that the laws should *ever* be changed. He sets forth little reasoning to support this conclusion, however. Rather—as if a mere appeal to the authority of custom could settle the issue of the authority of custom—he limits himself to citing three examples of the ancients' hostility to change. And at least one of these examples, that of an ephor "who so rudely cut out the two strings that Phrynis had added to music," is presented in

---

[22]*Politics*, 1269a12–18; quoted from the translation by Carnes Lord (Chicago, 1984).
[23]Cf. *Rhetoric*, 1387a15–20; Plato, *Republic*, 338d–339a, 358c–359b. Recall Montaigne's remark in "Of Custom" concerning the effects of his having traced a widely accepted French practice "to its origin" (115 [84]); cf. II, xii, 567 [440]. Compare Alexander Hamilton, James Madison, and John Jay, *The Federalist*, ed. Jacob Cooke (Middletown, Conn., 1961), no. 49, p. 340.

such a manner as to make this posture appear wholly unreasonable: the ephor "does not worry whether [music] is the better for it or whether the chords are richer; for him to condemn them it is enough that they represent an alteration of the old fashion" (118 [86]).[24]

If Montaigne is indeed in agreement with Aristotle's point, one would have to judge that his renowned rhetorical ability has failed him in this case. But there is good reason to suspect that the weakness of Montaigne's "defense" of Aristotle's argument (like that of his defense of Sebond) is intentional. Not only is the defense so weak as to make Aristotle's point into a straw man, but by the very impersonality of his presentation of the argument, Montaigne severs himself from it. In remarking that this argument comes from "another vat," Montaigne means that it does not come from his own "vat" of thought and that he does not agree with it. The insincerity of Montaigne's criticism of changing the laws is further suggested by the fact that in other chapters of the *Essays*, he clearly contradicts some of the remarks concerning the absoluteness of one's obligation to obey the laws which had led up to it. In "Of Vanity," as already noted, he diverges from his claim in "Of Custom" that all citizens owe themselves to the public. In the "Apology," as we have seen, he disputes the principle expressed in "Of Custom" that everyone should obey the established laws, by protesting that he cannot have his "judgment so flexible" as to conform to the ever-shifting opinions of the ruling classes who enact them. And, contrary to his praise of Socrates' law-abidingness, Montaigne later criticizes the overly "tender" attitude Socrates displayed in "refusing to get out of prison by the intervention of others so as not to disobey the laws, at a time moreover when they were so thoroughly corrupt" (III, ix, 951 [743]). Far from being prepared to emulate Socrates' professed choice of death over exile, Montaigne would readily leave his country if its government or laws threatened him in the slightest way (III, xii, 1049 [821]).[25]

When we consider that "Of Custom" itself ends with a discussion of the need for political change and even for disregarding the law at times, we have no reason to assume that these remarks in later chapters represent an "evolution" of Montaigne's thought away from a conservative position.[26]

[24]Cf. Socrates' "purgation" of music in Plato's *Republic*, bk. III, esp. 397b–e and 399c–e.
[25]Cf. III, ii, 795–6 [620], for a different explanation of Socrates' choice.
[26]Zeitlin, *Essays of Montaigne*, 1:333, tries to explain the seeming disunity of "Of Custom" itself by reference to Montaigne's supposed evolution. But his claim that the first published version of the chapter was "consistently conservative" is belied by several passages in the original edition: Montaigne's denunciation of custom as a "violent and treacherous schoolmistress" that opposes "the rules of nature" (106 [77]); his recommendation of a liberation of people's judgment from customary prejudices, which would reveal the unsupportedness of many accepted things (116 [84–5]); his condemnation of several French laws and customs as "barbarous" (116 [85]); and his concluding discussion of the need to disregard the laws at critical times (121–2 [89–90]).

In fact, further comparison of the argument in "Of Custom" with the Aristotelian passage that it imitates will show that this chapter has the same revolutionary thrust as do the later remarks, although it is presented more subtly.

Let us recall at this point that Aristotle, like Montaigne, cites examples of "barbarous" customs and laws to demonstrate the occasional desirability of changing the law. But there is a significant difference between the examples that the two philosophers provide. Aristotle cites only barbarous practices of the past, refraining in this context from any criticism of present Athenian laws or practices. Such indirectness conforms with his contention that one ought not to weaken citizens' respect for the laws of their country. By contrast, Montaigne forthrightly denounces the unreasonableness and barbarity of many of his country's present laws and customs. None of his disclaimers of wanting to change the laws could possibly prevent his criticism of French laws and customs from having an effect on his readers. In short, Montaigne has sought by these criticisms to inspire precisely the sort of questioning attitude that he recommended earlier in the chapter; and he can be under no illusion about the fact that such questioning will weaken the kind of habitual respect for law that Aristotle recommends.[27]

Once the contrast between Montaigne's presentation and Aristotle's is recognized, the true point of the essayist's criticism of custom in general, earlier in I, xxiii, becomes clear. Whereas Aristotle represents moral habituation as the means by which nature's intention is realized, in the sense that such habituation helps enable people to actualize their natural *telos*,[28] Montaigne emphasizes the antithesis between nature and custom, describing custom as "tyrannical" and arguing that it "forces . . . the rules of nature" (106 [77]). Rather than viewing habituation as the means by which we acquire moral virtue, Montaigne argues that habit or custom is the source of our most dangerous vices. Whereas Aristotle suggests the need for laws to acquire a kind of permanence that will make them seem, to the citizen, like natural phenomena, Montaigne presents the reader with a panorama of various nations' contradictory customs in order to demonstrate the foolishness of identifying any one set of customs with the dictates of nature. Whereas Aristotle concludes his discussion of change in the laws by promising to discuss elsewhere when and by whom the laws should be changed—a promise that is not clearly kept in the *Politics*—Montaigne's conclusion in "Of Custom" expressly encourages such changes.

[27]Montaigne expressly repeats the classical view at the conclusion of I, xliii, by arguing that people do not fully honor laws unless they are so old that their origin, and hence their conventionality and changeability, are unknown (261 [198]). This statement demonstrates his awareness of the likely effects of his emphasis on the arbitrariness of human laws and customs in "Of Custom." Cf. also III, xiii, 1049 [821], regarding the flimsiness of the laws' foundation; II, xii, 567 [440].
[28]*Nicomachean Ethics*, II.1, X.9 (1179b20–1180a3); *Politics*, 1252b30–1253a40.

None of the foregoing evidence is meant to deny the seriousness of Montaigne's attack on one particular "innovation"—the Reformation. But considering that Montaigne applies his critique of the Protestants equally against their Catholic opponents, one must doubt that the reason for his opposition to the Reformation is its "innovative" character as such. Rather, the Reformation represents the wrong *kind* of innovation, one that can only exacerbate the defects of the old order.

An early hint as to what Montaigne regards as the right kind of innovation is supplied in the third chapter of the *Essays*. There he describes as "an easy reformation and a cheap one" that we should "avoid expense and pleasure the use and knowledge of which are imperceptible to us" (I, iii, 23 [12]). The immediate context in which this remark occurs—a discussion of funeral customs—might easily cause the reader to miss its significance;[29] but the same theme is picked up in "Of Custom," where, after denouncing the unreasonableness of France's laws, Montaigne suggests the need to restore "indifferent things such as clothes . . . to their true purpose, which is the service and comfort of the body" (117 [85]). The examples of "indifferent things" that follow this statement are indeed concerned only with fashions in dress. But the previous argument of the chapter suggested that many things more significant than clothing are in essence "indifferent," in that nature dictates no particular way in which they should be arranged.[30] By listing examples of the great variety of customs followed by different nations in such matters as sexual rules, family and property arrangements, religious beliefs, and marks of nobility, Montaigne aimed to show that the way in which one orders these things is an "indifferent" affair, in that any one way may be considered as inherently reasonable or "natural" as any other.

If Montaigne is correct in holding that such matters are by nature indifferent, then—as an earlier chapter suggests—an enormous range of freedom is opened up to anyone who would tear the "mask" from things, as proposed in "Of Custom," and refer them to "truth and reason." At the beginning of I, xiv, Montaigne argues that if human beings, as an "old Greek maxim" claims, "are tormented by the opinions they have of things, not by the things themselves," it "would be a great point gained for the relief of our miserable human condition. . . . For if evils have no entry into

---

[29]The significance of the remark is suggested, however, by its broader context: the central theme of I, iii, is our disposition to concern ourselves with things that will occur after our death. Note that Montaigne's denunciation of the error of pursuing "future things" to the neglect of present ones in this, the third chapter of the *Essays*, has a parallel in the third chapter of *The Prince* (p. 12), where Machiavelli alludes to the fact that people sometimes find themselves "deceived in their opinion of that future good which they had expected"; see ibid., pp. 18–19, for a hint of the theological implications of that remark.

[30]Cf. I, xliii, 260 [197], regarding the ease with which customs concerning "indifferent" things may be changed; also III, i, 781 [610], concerning the power of "time and example" in altering and possibly improving popular mores.

us but by our judgment, it seems to be in our power to disdain them or turn them to our good" (49–50 [33]). As the argument of this quasi-Stoical essay (which will be examined in detail in Chapter Seven) proceeds, it becomes doubtful that Montaigne can succeed (or intends to succeed) in demonstrating that such miseries as pain, disease, and poverty are not in fact evils. But he nonetheless reports that he is barely touched by some "common causes of affliction" that trouble others, giving as an example his near indifference to the death of his children (I, xiv, 61 [42]). The reason for his freedom from "repining" in such cases, as he later explains, is that he finds it easy enough to "bear misfortunes that do not affect me personally" (III, xii, 1023 [800]). More specifically, he distinguishes elsewhere between "the sufferings that affect us simply through the soul . . . which are almost indifferent to me," and "the really essential and bodily sufferings," which he abhors as much as anyone (II, xxxvii, 738 [575]).

The secret of Montaigne's contentment, therefore, is his near indifference to the alleged good of his soul, and his concentration on his own selfish, bodily well-being. Given that the soul is much more malleable than the body, he urges others similarly to adapt their souls to their bodies' needs, thus giving their souls an attitude "conducive to our repose and preservation" (I, xiv, 57 [39]). This remark dovetails with the recommendation in "Of Custom" that "indifferent things" should be arranged to serve our bodily needs. It also elaborates the ground on which Montaigne denounced the conduct of both the Protestant and Catholic parties in the civil wars: the "contested and debatable" things over which the two sides fight are *opinions about the good of the soul.* What is wrong with both the Reformation and the Catholic response to it is that they produce evils that are *undeniably* wrong (because of their perceptibly and unavoidably harmful effect on the body), such as torture and bloodshed, in the name of opinions that are indemonstrable (because they concern things that have no tangible reality). Herein lies the true meaning of the "reformation" Montaigne proposed in I, iii: to "avoid expense and pleasure the use and knowledge of which are imperceptible to us" is to forsake the concern with the divine and the transcendent, things of which we can have no true knowledge. Consequently, the essayist's recommendation concerning the reordering of "indifferent things" amounts to this: that our moral and religious opinions, being concerned with essentially "indifferent" matters (since there is no natural standard, accessible to reason, by which their rightness or wrongness could be established), should be revised to accord with our bodily needs, which are not at all matters of indifference. Our very malleability by custom makes it possible to revise our beliefs in such a way as to promote our contentment.

The teaching of "Of Custom" thus harmonizes with Montaigne's remark in the "Apology" suggesting that the "natural" law observable in the beasts constitutes a more appropriate standard for the governance of human beings than our fanciful opinions about incorporeal goods. To pursue that implication will require a detailed survey of Montaigne's moral teaching in other chapters. Before this survey is undertaken, however, a further passage in "Of Custom" should be considered for the light it sheds on Montaigne's political intention.

Montaigne: Republican?

Let us look back at the earlier section of the chapter, wherein Montaigne decries the tendency to identify the ways of one's own country with the true and natural ones. In this context he observes that "peoples bred up [*nourris*] to liberty and to ruling themselves consider any other form of government monstrous and contrary to nature. Those who are led to monarchy do the same" (114 [83]). Up to this point Montaigne's argument suggests that there is no real difference in merit among various regimes and appears to support the assertion in "Of Vanity" that it is equally foolish "to wish for the government of a few in a democratic state, or another type of government in a monarchy" (III, ix, 934 [731]). But in the immediate sequel he adds, "And whatever easy chance fortune offers them to change, even when with great difficulties they have rid themselves of the importunity of one master, they run to supplant him with another, with similar difficulties, because they cannot resolve to hate mastery" (114–15 [83–4]).

In this remark, it would appear, Montaigne discards his pretense of impartiality and indifference regarding the choice among regimes. Contrary to his almost universal reputation as a loyal monarchist, he speaks as if he were trying to move people to act permanently to overthrow their subjection to kings. Such an interpretation is further suggested by a later remark wherein Montaigne professes to be "disgusted with mastery both active and passive" (III, vii, 896 [700]). (This remark parallels, and hence qualifies, his claim in "Of Custom" to be "disgusted with innovation"—118 [86].) The chapter in which Montaigne professes his opposition to mastery concludes with a lengthy denunciation of the many "defects and vices" monarchs have been seen to exhibit, and of the tyrannical intolerance they have practiced toward philosophers and poets (III, vii, 898–9 [702–3]). It is followed by a chapter in which he reaffirms his hatred of "every sort of tyranny" while questioning the real superiority of "men of extraordinary grandeur" (III, viii, 910 [711]).

This same thought may be elaborated through reconsideration of the third chapter of Book I, "Our Feelings Reach Out Beyond Us"—the same chapter in which Montaigne proposed the "reformation" already alluded to. The most explicit theme of this chapter, indicated by its title, is our tendency to occupy our thoughts with what is beyond us—specifically, in accordance with the "commonest of human errors," "with what will be, even when we shall no longer be" (18 [8]). A secondary theme, however, is the relative merits of monarchical and popular government. With respect to the former type of regime, Montaigne indicates the inefficacy of popular praise and blame in checking monarchs' vices: the greatest good to which the docile subjects of a vicious monarch may aspire is the questionable gain of providing a "useful example" to posterity, by earning "the glory of having reverently and faithfully served a master whose imperfections were so well known to them" (19 [9]; cf. III, vii, 898 [702]). The two themes of the chapter are brought together in the following statement, which—along with Montaigne's proposal for a reformation—constitutes one of the two most politically significant remarks contained therein:

> I am almost ready to vow irreconcilable hatred against all popular rule, although it seems to me the most natural and equitable, when I remember the inhuman injustice of the Athenian people, who killed their brave captains without remission and without even consenting to hear them in their own defense, because after their victory over the Lacedaemonians in the naval battle near the Arginusian Isles—the most sharply contested and the greatest battle that the Greeks ever fought at sea with their forces—they had pursued the chances that the law of war presented them, rather than stopping to gather up and bury their dead. (23–4 [12–13])

The first two clauses of this sentence exhibit the rhetorical technique that a commentator on Machiavelli has termed "boldness hedged with caution."[31] By consigning the truly remarkable aspect of the statement to a subordinate clause ("although . . . equitable"), Montaigne lays a trap for the unwary reader, who is thereby induced to read it as a conventional expression of the antidemocratic sentiments of the French nobility.[32] Yet surely what is most noteworthy in this sentence is not the hatred Montaigne is "almost"—but not actually—ready to vow against popular rule, but the fact that this aristocratic subject of a monarchy explicitly holds popular government, *not* monarchy, to be "the most natural and equitable" regime. This remark, as well as the other criticisms of monarchy just cited, appear to confirm Montaigne's departure in "Of Custom" from his posture of political fence-sitting, and his agreement with those advocates of republican rule who regard alternative forms as "contrary to nature," if not "monstrous" (I, xxiii, 114 [83]).

But what, then, are we to make of the essayist's condemnation of the "inhuman injustice" displayed by the Athenian *demos* toward their vic-

[31]Mansfield, *Machiavelli's New Modes and Orders*, p. 27.
[32]Guizot, for one, is outraged by Montaigne's readiness to denounce popular government in general, and Athens in particular, on the basis of "one example" (*Montaigne*, pp. 33–4).

torious generals? In order to grasp the point of this remark, we must recall the reason that the burial of the dead sailors was a matter of concern to the *demos:* their belief that such an act was an obligation of piety, reflecting the more general concern with intangible goods which Montaigne has deprecated in I, iii. He calls the Athenians' belief an "importunate superstition" (24 [13]). It may be said, therefore, that according to Montaigne the chief defect of popular government, which would otherwise be the justest form of rule, is the people's proneness to *religious superstition,* which disposes them to commit acts of "inhuman injustice." We may thus reformulate Montaigne's judgment of popular rule by saying that if a way could be found to overcome the people's proneness to superstition, that form of government would be the best, simply.

Let us at this point take note of a fact about the trial of the generals which it is somewhat curious Montaigne does not mention: according to the testimony of Socrates at his own trial (as reported by Plato), he was the sole member of the Athenian Council to oppose the populace's illegal action of trying the generals as a group, rather than individually.[33] In view of the frequency with which references to Socrates occur in the *Essays,* one might have expected an allusion to him here. But there is perhaps a hint of such an allusion in the account Montaigne adds of the conduct of Diomedon, one of the condemned generals. "Coming forward to speak" after the condemnation had been pronounced, "instead of using this for his own cause and for exposing the evident injustice of so cruel a decision," Diomedon "expressed only concern for the continued safety of his judges," after which "he went directly and courageously to his punishment" (I, iii, 24 [13]). It may be suggested that this account of Diomedon's behavior—based on the report of Diodorus Siculus—is somewhat reminiscent of Socrates' behavior at his trial, as reported by Plato. After hearing the death sentence pronounced, although charging his *accusers* with "wickedness and injustice," Socrates refrains from denouncing the judges who issued the sentence but warns them that killing him will not save them from having to give an account of their lives. And he concludes that if his accusers and condemners should reproach his sons as he reproached the *demos* during his lifetime, he as well as his sons will have been "justly treated" by them.[34] Of course Socrates'

<hr/>

[33]Plato, *Apology,* 32b–c. Socrates' defense of the generals is explicitly mentioned in Amyot's translation of Diodorus Siculus, Montaigne's source for his account of the trial (*Oeuvres,* p. 1434 [n. 1 to p. 24]).

[34]Plato, *Apology,* 42a. Cf. Montaigne's paraphrase of Socrates' defense at III, xii, 1030 [806], where he has the Athenian urge the judges to acquit him for the sake of *their* "conscience," in accordance with his "habit of advising just and useful things." Although Socrates, in this paraphrase, does imply—unlike Diomedon—that his judges are "unjust and corrupt," his expression of trust in the gods, with the confidence that "they will do what is best for you and for me," bears some resemblance to Diomedon's prayer that the gods turn the Athenians' judgment "to their advantage," and his concern lest, by failing to fulfill his vows to the gods, the Athenians should incur their wrath. (Socrates' profession of acting out of concern for the

174 | The Political Philosophy of Montaigne

own manner of facing death, as recounted in Plato's *Phaedo* and *Crito* as well as the *Apology,* was no less steadfast than Diomedon's.

The significance of this possible allusion to Socrates may be seen in a subsequent chapter—I, xi, "Of Prognostications"—which is linked to I, iii, by a remark that the belief in divination reflects "the frenzied curiosity of our nature, which wastes its time anticipating future things, as if it did not have enough to do digesting the present" (42 [27]). Even while asserting that "our religion has abolished" the use of prognostications, Montaigne cites numerous instances of the persistence of various means of divination "among us," elaborating a recent case in which the belief by "a lieutenant of King Francis" in the "insane prophecies" of his country's ruin redounded "to his own great misfortune" as well as the injury of France (42–3 [27–8]).[35] This anecdote is succeeded by three quotations from Horace, the gist of which opposes not merely the belief in prognostications but also the sort of concern with the afterlife that Christianity demands. While citing the mockery that Diagoras the Atheist directed at the belief that the gods care about human affairs, Montaigne also quotes Cicero to the effect that "only Xenophanes of Colophon, out of all the philosophers who have acknowledged the gods, tried [*a essayé*] to eradicate every kind of divination." For

---

Athenians rather than himself is even more explicit in the original text of the *Apology* [30c–e].) A further parallel between Montaigne's accounts of the two cases is that he follows his description of each man's defense with a reference to the punishment that "fortune" (not the gods) subsequently meted out to the condemners (I, iii, 24 [13]; III, xii, 1031–2 [807]).

The foregoing remarks are not intended to deny the hubristic character of Socrates' defense as a whole, or what Thomas West terms the "impious arrogance" of his proposal that he be rewarded like the city's greatest heroes (West, *Plato's "Apology"*, pp. 79, 165, 211). But Socrates' lack of indignation at the verdict against him (*Apology* 35e–36a) appears to reflect a belief that the tension between philosophy and political society is inevitable, and hence that there is no lasting means of taming the disposition of the multitude toward superstition and spirited vengefulness. In "Of Custom," as previously noted, Montaigne cites Socrates as having "refused to save his life by disobedience to the magistrate, even to a very unjust and very iniquitous magistrate"—that is, the *demos*—owing to his belief that the wise must subordinate themselves, except for their thoughts, to the "common opinions" of their community.

[35]Cf. Machiavelli's discussion of divination, with special reference to Savonarola's prophecies of destruction, in *Discourses*, I, lxi. The Florentine's account of benign prognostic "intelligences" in that chapter (p. 259) should be compared with Montaigne's ambiguous reference to Francis's having sought "always to maintain some intelligences in Italy" (I, ix, 38 [24]), the country where the anti-French prophecies that inspired his lieutenant's treason were most widely accepted (I, xi, 43 [28]; cf. Mansfield, *Machiavelli's New Modes and Orders*, pp. 165–6; Strauss, *Thoughts on Machiavelli*, pp. 210–11). It may not be accidental that Montaigne, by a seeming historical "mistake," has Pope Julius II endeavoring to incite the English king to war against King Francis (rather than Louis XII) in the same chapter where he mentions Francis's maintenance of foreign "intelligences" in the pope's homeland (I, ix, 39 [24], and n. 3 to that page, p. 1438). Cf., regarding Julius's reliance on "foreign" support, Machiavelli, *The Prince*, ch. 13, p. 54. Cf. also *Essais*, I, xvii, 73 [50], where Charles V—the beneficiary of the treason of Francis's lieutenant—remarks that if his subordinates did not have a different "fidelity" as well as military capacity from that of Francis's men, he would immediately go to Francis "to ask mercy." Montaigne alludes to Savonarola's aborted trial of his word by fire at II, xxix, 688 [536].

this reason, he concludes, it is "less amazing that we have occasionally seen some of our princely souls linger on these vanities to their misfortune" (43–5 [28–9]). In other words, the persistence of (politically harmful) superstition is to be explained by the failure of philosophers forthrightly to attack it. Might not this remark be applied to the fate of Socrates—that he was condemned for impiety owing to a popular superstition that he had been unable or unwilling, previously in his life, to uproot?[36] Are we not also reminded of Montaigne's own project in the "Apology for Raymond Sebond" of undermining the popular religious belief that obstructs both scientific progress and civic peace and toleration? Is Montaigne's overall political enterprise one of so liberating people's minds from religious superstition that the popular rule that *would* be the most just form of government if not for that superstition may safely be established?

Though a definitive answer to the last question cannot be given at this point, it is nonetheless relevant to cite here two other passages from the *Essays* which attest to its author's republican sympathies. In "Of Friendship" (I, xxviii), where Montaigne eulogizes Etienne de la Boétie, he gives mildly qualified but nonetheless strong and significant praise to his friend's *Discourse of Voluntary Servitude,* also called *Le Contre un* (Against one man). Montaigne says that La Boétie wrote it "by way of essay in his early youth, in honor of liberty against tyrants." What Montaigne omits to mention is that the treatise literally reads as a condemnation of monarchical government per se, rather than merely of some kings denoted "tyrants." As I have noted, after promising earlier in the chapter to reprint La Boétie's treatise within the *Essays,* Montaigne curiously retracts this promise in the conclusion, on account of the misuse of the work by men of "evil intent." Nonetheless, he goes on to remark that his friend "would rather have been born in Venice than in Sarlat"—that is, in a republic, rather than in the French town of his birth—*"and with reason"* (193 [144]). Just as the first part of Montaigne's remark about his "disgust" with novelty in "Of Custom" was paralleled in a passage previously quoted from Book III expressing "disgust" with mastery, so the latter part of the remark—"and with reason"—is paralleled here. The two later passages, jointly expressing a preference for republicanism and a hatred of monarchy, thus significantly modify the putative conservatism of the earlier remark.

A further relevant passage occurs near the conclusion of "Of Vanity," where Montaigne expresses his pride in having received a certificate of

[36]Note the reference to Socrates' ostensible belief in the prognostic power of his *daimon,* at the conclusion of "Of Prognostications" (45 [29–30]). Cf. also III, xiii, 1078 [843], concerning the deference that Socrates, Xenophon, and Aristotle gave to the belief in divination, in contrast to Montaigne's avowed unbelief in that phenomenon (despite his opinion that dreams faithfully reflect the dreamer's particular *inclinations*—1077 [843]). Cf. Caton, *Politics of Progress,* p. 46, regarding Bacon's critique of classical philosophy.

176 | The Political Philosophy of Montaigne

honorary citizenship in the Roman Republic. Despite deprecating the pleasure he finds in this honor as a "silly humor," he imposes on the reader sufficiently to reprint the entire certificate (III, ix, 978–9 [764–5]); in his *Travel Journal* we learn that he went to considerable trouble to obtain it.[37] As Michel Butor observes, Montaigne's language implies that he takes at least as much pride in his Roman "citizenship" as he does in the "vain" titles he enjoys as a French nobleman (which are recounted in the bull of Roman citizenship).[38] It also signifies an attachment to Rome *qua* pagan republic rather than as the seat of the papacy.

We thus have substantial evidence of a preference on Montaigne's part, at least in principle, for republican over monarchical government. We have also seen, in "Of Custom," that his "conservative" posture masks a clear intention of promoting a new "reformation" that would mitigate, if not eliminate, the influence of religion in political life. And we have seen, in "Our Feelings Reach Out Beyond Us," how the latter project may be linked with the former attitude: how, that is, a weakening of civic piety might make it safer to introduce a popular form of government.

In the following chapter I undertake a deeper scrutiny of the grounds on which Montaigne seems to hold popular government to be juster, in principle, than monarchical rule. This theme is developed in three chapters of Book I: the famous essay "Of Cannibals" (I, xxxi) and the lesser known but more overtly political "Of the Inequality among Us" and "Of Sumptuary Laws" (I, xlii–iii). These chapters demonstrate that Montaigne's political thought is far more egalitarian, and that his egalitarianism has a more practical thrust, than has generally been recognized. I also endeavor to indicate how Montaigne's political egalitarianism is linked with the libertarian moral teaching that he elaborates most fully in Book III.

[37]*Journal de Voyage* (April 5, 1581), *Oeuvres,* pp. 1236–7 [962].
[38]Butor, *Essais,* p. 185.

Of Cannibals and Kings:
Montaigne's Egalitarianism

"Of Cannibals": First Reading

We have seen how Montaigne, in such essays as "Of Custom," conceals a potentially revolutionary political project under a guise of extreme conservatism. By contrast with the conservative appearance of "Of Custom," the chapter "Of Cannibals" contains several bold and forthright criticisms of the French, or European, political order—without any qualifying, conservative hedge. We may surmise that Montaigne expected the exotic theme of "Of Cannibals"—the ways of some natives of the New World—to deter most readers from appreciating the political seriousness of his remarks. If we may judge from the way contemporary interpreters typically have treated this chapter, the strategy appears to have succeeded. Insufficient weight, in particular, has been given to a remarkable passage near the end of the chapter, in which Montaigne reports the judgment that some New World natives made of the institutions of France upon visiting that country:

> They said that in the first place they thought it very strange that so many grown men, bearded, strong, and armed, who were around the king ... should submit to obey a child, and that one of them was not chosen to command instead. Second (they have a way in their language of speaking of men as halves of one another), they had noticed that there were among us men full and gorged with all sorts of good things, and that their halves were beggars at their doors, emaciated with hunger and poverty; and they thought it strange that these needy halves could endure such an injustice, and did not take the others by the throat, or set fire to their houses. (212–13 [159])

As Montaigne raises no objection to this judgment and has high praise for the New World natives elsewhere in this chapter and later in the *Essays,* this passage seems to express a strikingly radical criticism of the French order, embodying what one might easily take to be a revolutionary intention. Yet contemporary scholars tend to play down this implication in discussing the passage, denying either its seriousness or its practical intent.[1] Their interpretations presuppose a dichotomy in Montaigne's writing between theory and practice, such as he indeed asserts in "Of Custom"—but which, as we have seen, he ultimately repudiates. Contrary to these interpretations, I contend that the argument of "Of Cannibals," combined with that of two later chapters of Book I, sets forth the foundations of an egalitarian and libertarian political position that Montaigne indeed intended to have a substantial practical effect.

"Of Cannibals" opens with a point identical to that which was stressed at the outset of "Of Custom": the fact that custom commonly biases and overpowers our judgment, so that we mistake the conventional horizon of our nation for the universal and natural one. Montaigne first illustrates this point by noting how various Greek leaders, upon observing the formation of the Roman armies opposing them, were compelled to question the conventional attitude of their country that dismissed all foreigners as "barbarians." From these incidents he infers that "one should beware of clinging to vulgar opinions, and judge things by reason's way, not by popular say" (200 [150]).

Montaigne next mentions having had with him "for a long time" a man who had lived in the New World. He notes that the recent discovery of "a boundless country" there, by upsetting the claims of previous geographers, demonstrates how likely we are to be mistaken in thinking that our knowledge comprehends the world. Alluding to Plato's discussion of the lost island of Atlantis, Montaigne is led to reflect on the enormous changes wrought by natural movements such as floods, which further demonstrate the instability of the grounds on which our knowledge rests (200–202 [150–51]).[2]

After these reflections, Montaigne returns to the theme of his employee who had returned from the New World. This person, he reports, was "a simple, crude man" and consequently one "fit to bear true witness," inasmuch as stupid people who lack the capacity to "invent" facts describe

---

[1]See, e.g., Sayce, *Essays,* p. 259; Keohane, "Montaigne's Individualism," p. 371. Nakam, *Les Essais,* pp. 186–7, does cite the "incendiary" character of the cannibals' remarks, and Thibaudet, *Montaigne,* pp. 398–9, notes the "curious" connection between those remarks and the eighteenth-century literature that inspired the French Revolution. The remarks are paraphrased at the conclusion of Rousseau's *Second Discourse.*

[2]Cf. the similar reflection in Machiavelli, *Discorsi,* II, v, pp. 292–3, where the theological implication of this theme—the questionableness of the biblical account of the world's history—is suggested more explicitly; also, *Essais,* II, xii, 504–7 [389–91]; Plato, *Laws,* 676b ff.

their observations more reliably than cleverer ones who inevitably "interpret" and hence alter what they have seen. This thought inspires Montaigne to wish that topographers would "give us an exact account of the places where they have been," rather than claiming to know the whole world on the basis of their limited experience of a part of it. "I would like everyone to write what he knows, not only in this, but in all other subjects" (202–3 [152]).

The remarks I have just summarized serve as Montaigne's introduction to the general theme of "Of Cannibals." Before we proceed to that theme, it is necessary to observe the bearing on it of the introduction. Commentators have commonly failed to recognize the ironic or tongue-in-cheek character of that introduction, and the consequent implications regarding Montaigne's account of the cannibals.

The first ironic feature of the introduction which deserves comment is Montaigne's claim that stupid people are good reporters of events. This is an assertion that the essayist repeats elsewhere, in his discussion of historians (II, x, 396–7 [303–4]). But readers who reflect on their own experiences with people and events will surely recognize that the claim is false. And Montaigne himself indicates its falsity in other passages. In "Of the Power of the Imagination" he remarks: "It is probable that the principal credit of miracles, visions, enchantments, and such extraordinary occurrences comes from the power of imagination, acting upon the minds of the vulgar, which are softer. Their belief has been so strongly seized that they think they see what they do not see" (I, xxi, 97 [70]).

Montaigne repeats his observation of simple people's "facility in believing and letting themselves be persuaded" elsewhere (I, xxvii, 177 [132]). In the very chapter where he praises "simple" historians, he goes on to describe the difficulty of "this quest of truth" and the need for verification of "the slightest details of each incident" (II, x, 398 [305]). And he later protests reliance on the testimony of the vulgar to convict alleged practitioners of witchcraft (III, xi, 1003–10 [785–90]).

The irony of Montaigne's claim that his stupid employee was a trustworthy witness is buttressed by a further irony. Montaigne, as we have seen, urges in "Of Cannibals" that people should write only about things of which they have direct personal knowledge. Yet what he is about to do in this chapter is precisely the opposite: to describe a people he has never seen, inhabiting a territory he has never visited, merely on the basis of his employee's testimony.[3]

I suggest that the irony of Montaigne's introduction to his account of the

---

[3] As noted by Howard White in *Copp'd Hills towards Heaven: Shakespeare and the Classical Polity* (The Hague, 1970), p. 124. Montaigne does claim to have spoken with one of the three Indians who visited Rouen at the time they made the pronouncement cited at the outset of this chapter (212–13 [159]).

cannibals is meant to indicate to the thoughtful reader that this account is not intended to be empirically accurate. Indeed, contrary to the essayist's claim that the account derives from the testimony of his employee, scholars have discovered that considerable portions appear to have been borrowed from popular books written about the New World.[4] Given this fact, there is no reason to assume that any of Montaigne's information comes from an employee such as he describes; for all the reader can know, Montaigne, having borrowed some facts from available written reports about the American natives, made up the rest himself.[5] The possibility of such a fabrication becomes especially plausible when one takes note of the curious similarity (as I shall indicate) between some institutions Montaigne attributes to the cannibals and those described in Plato's *Republic*.

Why should Montaigne have chosen to pass off a largely fabricated (or at least unreliable) account of a foreign people as an empirically accurate one? A partial explanation is suggested by the following considerations. The essayist's opening remarks seem to indicate that his central intention in "Of Cannibals" is to overcome the ethnocentrism with which his readers judge the world and their own place in it. As Montaigne suggested in the "Apology," he can most easily advance such a project by describing things that are "foreign" to his readers' experience, since people admire strange things more than ordinary ones. Yet, as he remarks more than once, a thoughtful observer of his own self (such as Montaigne professes to be) would not need to go hunting up foreign examples in order to make the same discoveries, since "one and the same nature" is present in all things (II, xii, 445 [342–3]; I, xxiii, 107 [78]).

In sum, I suggest that Montaigne's didactic purpose in "Of Cannibals" is largely independent of the empirical accuracy of his account of the American natives' way of life. As I have noted, Montaigne is not, by his own testimony, a "simple" historian: rather than reporting facts at random, he selects those facts, or alleged facts, that he thinks will be most instructive to his readers.[6] It is on this ground, therefore, rather than on its empirical

---

[4]See Gilbert Chinard, *L'Exotisme américain dans la littérature française au seizième siècle* (Geneva, 1970 [1911]), ch. 9; Zeitlin, *Essays of Montaigne*, 1:378; Marcel Françon, "On a Source of Montaigne's Essays," *Modern Language Review* 48 (1953): 443–5; idem, "Montaigne et les Brésiliens," *BSAM*, 5th ser., no. 16 (1975): 73–4.

[5]A further indication by Montaigne of the factual unreliability of his account of the cannibals is his lament at the incapacity of the interpreter during his conversation with one of them (I, xxxi, 213 [159]). A faith in Montaigne's honesty nonetheless causes Zeitlin, who acknowledges the evidently "borrowed" character of parts of "Of Cannibals" (including "a resemblance" noted by other critics "in the terminations of the Greek and Brazilian languages" as Montaigne reports the latter which "is a little suspicious"), to assume that the remainder did come from the essayist's employee (Zeitlin, *Essays of Montaigne*, 1:378). On Plato's use of a device similar to Montaigne's purported reliance on an unreliable reporter, see Raymond Larson's introduction to his translation of *The Symposium and The Phaedo* (Arlington Heights, Ill., 1980), p. xiv.

[6]This point is noted, in the case of "Of Cannibals," by Zeitlin, *Essays of Montaigne*, 1:379. An excellent account of the rhetorical strategy of the chapter is Rendall, "Dialectical Structure."

accuracy that his account of the cannibals should be judged. Despite the borrowed character of much of what Montaigne reports about the cannibals, the reader must assume that the inclusion of this information reflects a conscious choice on the essayist's part, in conformity with his didactic aim.

Montaigne begins his description of the cannibals with a series of striking and sweeping judgments. Contrary to the typical European opinion that the cannibals are barbarians, he reports:

> I find . . . that there is nothing barbarous and savage in that nation, from what I have been told, except that each man calls barbarism whatever is not his own practice; for in truth it seems we have no other test of truth and reason than . . . the opinions and practices of the country we live in. *There* is always the perfect religion, the perfect government, the perfect and accomplished practice in all things. [The American natives] are wild, just as we call wild the fruits that nature has produced by herself and in her ordinary progress; whereas in truth it is those that we have altered by our artifice and turned away from the common order, that we should rather call wild. In the former the truest and most useful and natural properties are alive and vigorous, properties that we have debased in the latter in adapting them only to please our corrupted taste. (203 [152])

High praise, indeed, for a tribe of man-eaters; but there is more. Montaigne professes to be vexed that such great men of antiquity as Lycurgus and Plato did not know of them:

> for it seems to me that what we see by experience in these nations surpasses not only the pictures with which poetry has embellished the golden age and all its inventions in imagining a happy condition of men, but also the conceptions and the very desire of philosophy. They could not have imagined a naturalness so pure and simple as we see by experience; nor could they have believed that our society could maintain itself with so little artifice and human solder. This is a nation, I should say to Plato, in which there is no sort of trade; no knowledge of letters; no science of numbers; no name for a magistrate or for political superiority; no custom of servitude, of riches or of poverty; no contracts; no successions; no partitions; no occupations but leisure ones; no care for any but common kinship; no clothes; no agriculture; no metal; no use of wine or wheat. The very words that signify lying, treachery, dissimulation, avarice, envy, detraction, pardon, unheard of. How far he would find the republic he imagined from this perfection. (204 [153])[7]

The irony to which I have referred is clearly present in this passage, since what Montaigne claims that "we see by experience" among the cannibals is entirely foreign to the experience both of Montaigne and of the vast major-

[7]This passage is best known to English-speaking readers through Shakespeare's adaptation of it in *The Tempest* (II. 1. 143–67).

ity, if not all, of his readers. A further problem in the passage is the lack of clarity regarding the grounds on which the essayist regards the cannibals' society as superior to the utopias of Plato and the poets. Though some features of that society are undoubtedly attractive, others—the absence of literacy, of wine, and of pardon—are less so. Is it so clear, then, that the cannibals' way of life is a desirable one? And in what sense is this way of life "natural"?

In seeking to answer these questions, let us survey some other features of the cannibals' society as Montaigne describes it. He alludes to the pleasantness of their climate, the abundance of food, the apparent absence of illnesses, and the fact that aside from hunting and war, the cannibals spend their "whole day . . . in dancing." The cannibals' "ethical science," like their religion, is simple, and "contains only these two articles: resoluteness in war and affection for their wives." Yet this morality, to which the cannibals are exhorted by their "prophets," is apparently quite efficacious in maintaining their social order, perhaps because of the innate limitedness of the cannibals' desires: they remain "in that happy state of desiring only as much as their natural needs demand; anything beyond that is superfluous to them" (205–8 [153–6]).

The aspect of the cannibals' life which Montaigne discusses most extensively is their practice in war. He remarks the "astonishing . . . firmness of their combats, which never end but in slaughter and bloodshed." Lacking "neither anything necessary nor that great thing, the knowledge of how to enjoy their condition happily and be content with it," the cannibals fight not for material gain but only for glory. Hence "their warfare is wholly noble and generous, and as excusable and beautiful as this human disease can be." Montaigne suggests that the cannibals are more truly courageous than the soldiers of civilized countries, in that their victories depend solely on the strength of their will, not on agility, strength, or "trick[s] of art and knowledge" (207–10 [155–7]).

Mention of the cannibals' warfare brings to mind the custom that gives them their name. Montaigne readily acknowledges the "barbarous horror" of cannibalism. He makes use of his readers' horror, however, to lament their blindness to their own faults: there is more barbarity in torturing or burning living human beings, as Europeans do, "on the pretext of piety and religion," than in the cannibals' practice of eating them after they are dead. Montaigne extends this criticism of European ways by charging that "treachery, disloyalty, tyranny, and cruelty . . . are our ordinary faults." Hence, barbaric as Montaigne now concedes the cannibals to be (contradicting his earlier denial), when judged "in respect to the rules of reason," he contends, his fellow Europeans "surpass them in every kind of barbarity" (207–8 [155–6]).

By comparing the barbarism of European ways unfavorably with those of the despised cannibals, Montaigne conforms to the intention he had intimated of challenging the ethnocentrism that causes us to overvalue our own ways in comparison to alternative customs. The same intention obviously underlies the critique of the radical inequalities of European society which the essayist attributes to the American natives near the end of "Of Cannibals," which I quoted at the outset of this chapter. Immediately after this report, Montaigne concludes the chapter by contrasting these inequalities with the absence of a true political hierarchy within the cannibals' own society. The leading man among them, so one of their representatives told Montaigne, gains nothing from his superior position except "to march foremost in war" and to have paths cleared for him when he visits his people's villages (213 [159]).

This conclusion makes it seem that Montaigne regards the cannibals' egalitarian social order as inherently more reasonable than that of his own country. But he refrains at the end from any express judgment on this issue, aside from commenting ironically on his readers' prejudices by remarking, "All this is not too bad—but so what? They don't wear breeches" (213 [159]). This remark is certainly a much milder praise than Montaigne's previous claim that the cannibals' way of life surpasses the best societies imagined by poets and philosophers. Moreover, as we have seen, Montaigne did concede that the cannibals' man-eating is barbarous. It remains unclear, therefore, to what extent he really regards the cannibals' society as a desirable model. The first step one must take to elucidate this problem, I believe, is to compare Montaigne's account of the cannibals with an alternative philosophic understanding of the best social order to which he has claimed their way of life is superior: Plato's. Hence I turn, in the next section, to a survey of some relevant passages in the *Republic* and the *Laws*, with a view to evaluating Montaigne's claim that the cannibals' way of life surpasses anything that Plato could have imagined. I shall focus attention on two Platonic accounts of primitive life of which Montaigne must have been aware (given the frequency of his references to both dialogues), each of which seems to belie his claim regarding the ancients' ignorance of the possibility of a society like the cannibals'.

Montaigne and Plato on Primitive Society

One Platonic model of a primitive way of life to which Montaigne's account of the cannibals invites comparison is presented in Book III of the *Laws*. Here the Athenian Stranger attempts to describe how human beings lived immediately after one of the natural cataclysms that, he asserts, periodically destroy civilization and its attendant knowledge. These people are initially presented as being well disposed toward, while largely isolated from, one another. The abundance of food and the absence of gold or silver and consequently of wealth or poverty prevent conflicts of interest and feelings of jealousy and ill will from arising among them. Like Montaigne's cannibals, they lack knowledge of letters, metallurgy, or the sophisticated arts of war (although they do know the art of weaving). Lacking written statutes, they are guided instead by habits and ancestral laws. Although the Stranger at first contends that these people's simplicity made them braver, more moderate, and juster than their predecessors or successors, he implicitly modifies this praise a bit later by identifying them with the cannibalistic Cyclopes; nor does he dissent from a description of their ways as "savagery."[8] The savagery of these primitive human beings reflects a more fundamental defect in their way of life: whatever advantages their simplicity and consequent "innocence" may have given them are outweighed, the Stranger implies, by their inexperience in noble or beautiful things and their consequent inability to become truly virtuous (676b–680e). Hence their way of life is not truly a model to be emulated; the Stranger dedicates himself instead to constructing "in speech" a regime that would aim at the promotion of genuine human excellence.

Plato presents a somewhat more attractive account of a primitive society in Book II of the *Republic*. In seeking an understanding of justice by locating it within the political community, Socrates begins by constructing what he calls the "city of utmost necessity." This city is more clearly an organized society (as distinguished from a collection of isolated individuals or families) than the primitive one described in the *Laws*. Like the society of Montaigne's cannibals, this city is dedicated to the satisfaction of people's basic material needs; it is harmonious, lacking in any luxury, and apparently without any political organization or inequality. Its inhabitants, like Montaigne's cannibals, go naked "for the most part" in summer, although (presumably living in a colder climate) they are "adequately clothed" in winter. Also like the cannibals, they are accustomed to joyous feasting and drinking, despite the simplicity of their diet, which (like the cannibals' food) lacks any spice. But the inhabitants of this city are not cannibals; indeed, their diet is purely vegetarian. And they are peaceful, not warlike (*Republic*, 369b–372a).

Socrates describes the city he has constructed as the "true" or "healthy" city. A different judgment is expressed, however, by one of his young interlocutors, Glaucon, who compares it to a city fit for pigs. The express ground of Glaucon's dissatisfaction with the city is its lack of luxury. Socrates readily accedes to this complaint by describing how the first city

---

[8]That the first human beings were cannibals is indicated somewhat more explicitly in Book VI, at 782b–c. (I have employed Thomas Pangle's translation of the *Laws* [New York, 1980] and have benefited from Pangle's accompanying interpretative essay.) Cf. Aristotle, *Politics*, 1252b22–24, with its Homeric source.

may be transformed into a more luxurious and hence "feverish" one. This transformation requires the addition of numerous classes of people, including hunters, imitators, and servants. Moreover, the liberation of the desire for luxuries gives rise to the pursuit of "the unlimited acquisition of money," which Socrates describes as the greatest source of "evils both private and public." The necessity of acquiring more land for the satisfaction of the citizens' unlimited desires, and of protecting the land already gained against similarly aggressive neighboring cities, generates the need for a class of warriors. The disposition of these "guardians" is reminiscent of the morality of Montaigne's cannibals: they are loyal to their fellow citizens and hostile to foreigners (372c–375c).

Once having introduced the guardians, Socrates devotes his entire attention to their education and organization. In order to ensure their dedication to the common good, a community of property, and of women and children, is instituted. These institutions again remind us of the ways of Montaigne's cannibals, who are polygamous (although with fixed marriages, unlike the guardians), apparently have no private property, and like the guardians have "no care for any but common kinship" and "call those of the same age brothers [and] those who are younger, children" (208, 211 [156, 158]).[9]

The Spartan ways of the guardians in the *Republic* stand in stark contrast to the original reason for their introduction, the enhancement of the city's luxury. Paradoxically, the perpetuation of a city supposedly dedicated to the pursuit of luxury ultimately requires the "purgation" of all opportunities for selfish indulgence on the part of its guardians. Once the original condition that made social harmony possible—the limitation of people's desires to necessities—is undermined, harmony must be reestablished through a set of radically artificial limitations, notably the abolition of the family. (The artificiality of these limitations is demonstrated by their dependence on the inculcation of "a throng of lies and deceptions" [459c].) Only at the conclusion of Socrates' account of the development of the city—his creation of the best city—does the reason underlying these paradoxes, as well as the most serious justification for the transcendence of the "city of necessity," become clear. The true guardians, it emerges, are philosophers, whose activity constitutes the perfection of human nature, even though it does not fall within the category of "necessary" pursuits. The guardians' Spartan education served to wean them from the pursuit of bodily pleasures and hence prepared them to find their happiness in philosophic contemplation. Yet the pursuit of philosophy requires as its precondition a society of greater wealth, and consequently a greater development of the arts catering to the body, than the original "city of necessity." Only an economically

---

[9]Cf. *Republic* 461d–e (the parallel is admittedly inexact) and 463c–e.

developed society could afford the leisure necessary for a way of life that is not dedicated to the satisfaction of basic physical needs.

Despite the more attractive (albeit less realistic) character of the "city of necessity" as compared with the primitive way of life described in the *Laws*, Socrates' ultimate judgment of the former thus parallels the Athenian Stranger's judgment of the latter. Even though the liberation of human desires from their "natural" limitation to bodily necessities brings with it, as Socrates acknowledges, a host of evils, this introduction of "unnecessary" desires is the prerequisite of an excellence that transcends the bestial concerns of the "city of necessity." It is the absence of the possibility of such excellence that truly made the first city a "city of sows."[10]

In view of these passages in the *Republic* and *Laws*, it is evident that we cannot take literally Montaigne's claim that the cannibals' society "surpasses the conception and the very desire of philosophy." Especially in the *Republic*, Plato did describe a society of great simplicity in which people live together harmoniously without government or inequality, and with limited and easily satisfiable wants. In fact, by virtue of its peaceableness, the higher development of the arts within it, and its consequently higher standard of living, the "city of necessity" might well be thought more pleasant (as well as less barbaric) than the society of Montaigne's cannibals. We must therefore conclude that the real novelty of Montaigne's account of the cannibals lies not in any distinctive features of their way of life but in the sheer fact that, unlike Plato, Montaigne appears to regard such a primitive way of life as superior to civilization.

By praising primitive life as he does, Montaigne implicitly questions the desirability of the perfected regimes constructed in the *Republic* and *Laws*, and consequently their utility—by contrast with the primitive model—as a standard for judging actual regimes. Yet he can hardly be accused of having simply idealized the primitive condition. Whereas Plato plays down the most barbaric features of that condition (in the *Laws*, by only hinting initially at the fact that primitive people were cannibals; in the *Republic*, by making primitive life seem entirely peaceful), Montaigne emphasizes primitive people's warlikeness and cannibalism. For Plato, it would appear, the well-being of civilized societies requires a deemphasis or forgetting on the part of most human beings of the primitive origins out of which their politics arose: the principles on which civilization rests are only indirectly or partially related to the goals of primitive people.[11] By contrast, Montaigne seems to hold that a full awareness of the character of primitive life is

---

[10]I have been guided in my understanding of the reasons for the transcendence of the city of sows by the discussion in Bloom, *Republic of Plato*, pp. 345–8.

[11]Cf. Aristotle's distinction between the original reason for the establishment of political societies and the true purpose of a fully developed political order: *Politics*, 1252b29–31.

of decisive importance for determining the principles on which civilized polities rest; such awareness is not to be limited to a philosophic few.

There is ample evidence that Montaigne is far from regarding the cannibals' way of life *in toto* as a model that civilized people should strive to follow. As noted, he readily concedes the barbarity and horror of cannibalism itself. Although in "Of Cannibals" he professes to regard the cannibals' practice as less horrifying than the "civilized" custom of torturing living victims, this relative praise of the American natives is effectively negated by a passage near the end of the preceding chapter, "Of Moderation," which describes the Indians' cruelties:

> in these new lands discovered in our age, still pure and virgin compared with ours, this practice is to some extent accepted everywhere: all their idols are drenched with human blood, often with horrible cruelty. They burn [the victims] alive, and take them out of the brazier half roasted to tear their heart and entrails out. Others, even women, are flayed alive, and with their bloody skins they dress and disguise others. (I, xxx, 199 [149])

Montaigne further alludes to the cannibals' cruelty in I, xxxi, by indicating that they lack even a word for "pardon" (204 [153]). The disposition to cruelty is natural to human beings, or at least to some, as the essayist has suggested elsewhere (I, xxiii, 108 [78]; II, xi, 412 [316]); primitive peoples exemplify this disposition in the most manifest way, while "innocently" seeing nothing wrong in it. Their attitude is far from that of Montaigne, to whom cruelty is "the extreme of all vices" (II, xi, 408 [313]).

A further reason for doubting that Montaigne regards the cannibals' society as a desirable model is that, despite his seeming praise of the simplicity of their way of life, he expresses at many other points in the *Essays* a taste for luxury and softness that is manifestly in contradiction with such Spartan ways. In "Of Moderation" he denounces the so-called human wisdom that "very stupidly exercises its ingenuity to reduce the number and the sweetness of the sensual pleasures that belong to us" (I, xxx, 198 [148]). And whereas he presents the cannibals as being concerned only with the barest of "natural" needs, in Book III—as I have previously noted—he expresses his own unwillingness to rest content with such necessities and his desire to continue enjoying those non-"natural" goods to which he has become accustomed (III, x, 987 [772]). Indeed, far from trying to limit the desire for corporeal pleasures, he urges that the soul should "hatch and foment" them (III, v, 871 [681]).

Even if the cannibals' society did not suffer from these defects of cruelty and penury, Montaigne suggests that it would be wholly impractical to expect civilized people to return to such a condition. He predicts that now that the cannibals have been "tricked by the desire for novelty" into gaining knowledge of European corruption, they will ultimately lose their "repose and happiness" (212 [158]); indeed, such "curiosity" has already caused the downfall of some American natives who came into contact with Europeans (III, vi, 888 [694]). It would seem, therefore, that in addition to being of doubtful overall superiority to civilization, the cannibals' social order is incapable of maintaining itself once its isolation from more developed nations has ended. Perhaps the capacity to be satisfied by a primitive condition is a "knowledge" that, once lost, can never be regained. There seems to be no way in which civilized peoples, having had their desire for unnecessary goods awakened and developed, could return to the innocence of the American natives.[12]

Aside from its use as a way of criticizing his fellow Europeans' "barbarity," what, then, is the positive import of Montaigne's praise of the cannibals? Two points are made in "Of Cannibals" that direct us toward an answer. First, Montaigne cites the cannibals as an example of how human society may be held together with "little artifice and human solder" (204 [153]). Second, as we have seen, he contrasts the cannibals' equality with the arbitrary inequalities that characterize civilized societies. These two points are closely related, for by asserting that society needs little "human solder" to bind it, Montaigne implies that there is less need for government, and consequently for political inequality, than his fellow Europeans believe.

While suggesting the unnaturalness of the inequalities of French society in "Of Cannibals," Montaigne does not make clear in this chapter the substantive reason for his objection to them. To understand the point of his criticism, we must turn to another chapter that treats the subject of inequality thematically: "Of the Inequality among Us" (I, xlii; hereafter cited as "Of Inequality"). Not only do the title and theme of this chapter bear an obvious relation to the conclusion of "Of Cannibals," but the two chapters are also linked in other ways. In both, Montaigne urges that we judge man by "his own" qualities, rather than by "borrowed" advantages or external appearances (209–10 [157]; 251 [190]). And the essayist's contention in "Of Inequality" that the difference between individuals and among classes often lies "only in their breeches" (252 [191]) recalls the last sentence in "Of Cannibals," in which Montaigne commented ironically on the European tendency to despise the American natives merely because "they don't wear breeches."

Montaigne's Critique of Inequality

Montaigne begins "Of Inequality" by remarking the magnitude of the differences among people, such that "there is more distance from a given

---

[12]That the fragility of the American natives' way of life when confronted with European society constitutes a fundamental defect of the former in Montaigne's judgment is demon-

man to a given man than from a given man to a given animal" (250 [189]). He laments, however, that human beings, unlike other animals, are commonly judged by parts not truly their own, such as "riches and honors" (251 [190]). The true test of a human being is the quality of his soul, not external goods that depend on fortune.

Although Montaigne claims that there are extreme differences in the quality of people's souls, his argument in support of that claim is not very persuasive. Having quoted Horace's description of a man who is wise, "master of himself," and secure against fortune's blows, and Lucretius' remark that "nature" desires "a body wholly free from pain" and a mind without care, Montaigne contrasts the people described in these passages with "the common run of our men, stupid, base, servile, unstable, and continually tossed about by . . . diverse passions: depending entirely on others" (252 [191]). But to cite poetic descriptions of the best possible human condition is hardly to demonstrate that there have often, if ever, been people answering to these descriptions, or consequently that "our men" are much worse than others. Nor can freedom from bodily pain be said to prove the quality of a person's soul. Indeed, Montaigne expressly denies elsewhere that even a wise individual can "overcome our natural limitations," including susceptibility to pain and passion (II, ii, 328 [249]; II, xii, 532–3 [412]).

Having unpersuasively asserted the existence of vast natural inequalities among people, Montaigne launches into a more extensive, and more serious, argument concerning the unreality of many of the *supposed* human differences. He laments that although "our practice" takes "little or no account" of the natural distinctions among human beings, nonetheless, "if we consider a peasant and a king, a nobleman and a plebeian, a magistrate and a private man, a rich man and a pauper, there immediately appears to our eyes an extreme disparity between them, though they are different, so to speak, only in their breeches" (252 [191]).

Part of Montaigne's objection to this tendency to judge people by their rank is that the outward superiority of a king may mask a soul "viler than [that of] the least of his subjects." But the main thrust of his argument concerns the parity of all people's "natural and original condition"—their universal susceptibility to illness, old age, and bitter passions (253–4 [191–2]).

At this point Montaigne's argument makes another subtle shift. From the question of the degree of natural inequality among human beings, he turns to the issue of whether those who enjoy a conventional political superiority derive any real benefit from their position. Those whose "body and mind are in a bad state," he argues, can receive no gain from "these external ad-

strated by Dain A. Trafton in "Ancients and Indians in Montaigne's 'Des Coches,'" *Symposium* 27 (1973): 76–88.

vantages." Furthermore, in the light of "the great and troublesome charges incumbent on a good king" and the "difficulty of choice" that a ruler must face, Montaigne expresses the "opinion, that it is much easier and pleasanter to follow than to guide . . . and to be answerable only for oneself" (254–5 [192–3]).

Most monarchs do not share Montaigne's opinion, it would appear, since unforced abdications are relatively infrequent.[13] But the essayist goes on to cite the tyrant Hiero (from Xenophon's dialogue of the same name) concerning the miseries of rulership. Whereas in Xenophon's account Hiero laments only the unhappiness of being a tyrant, Montaigne—who calls him "King Hiero"—extends these complaints to the situation of all kings.[14] The very "ease and facility" of kings' pleasures, as Hiero argues, take the "bittersweet tang" from them; hence kings are bored from "satiety." Hiero also laments that he "cannot go about and travel freely, being like a prisoner within the limits of his country," and that "in all his actions he finds himself surrounded by an annoying crowd." Hiero's greatest regret, however, is "that he finds himself deprived of all mutual friendship" by his position, since he cannot trust the sincerity of any love or honor that his subjects, who live in fear of his power, may render to him (255–8 [193–5]).

The tyrant's laments in the *Hiero* are in fact rather disingenuous, since Hiero shows no disposition to want to throw off his burdens by returning to a private status.[15] Montaigne's presentation of these complaints makes their irony even more apparent. Seemingly adding to the tyrant's litany, the essayist actually suggests some advantages of supreme power:

> And, I know not why, [the great] are more obliged than we to hide and cover up their faults. For what in us is indiscretion, in them the people judge to be tyranny, contempt, and disdain for the laws; and it is true that besides the inclination to vice, it seems that they take *an added pleasure* in insulting public observances and trampling them underfoot. Indeed, Plato, in his *Gorgias,* defines a tyrant as one who has license to do *anything he pleases* in a city. (256 [194])

[13]I refer here to monarchs who truly rule their countries, not to contemporary "constitutional" monarchs whose positions are essentially symbolic, so that they are less reluctant to abdicate for personal reasons. Montaigne does allude to one voluntary abdication (Diocletian's) near the conclusion of I, xlii (258 [196]). At III, vii, 894 [699] he denies that the "essence" of "greatness" is so obviously "advantageous" that "it cannot be refused except by a miracle"; hence he holds that "the resolution of those . . . who have despised it or laid it down of their own accord" is overvalued; in a manuscript note in his copy of Nicole Gilles's *Annales et croniques de France,* he observed that although such renunciations "are miracles to us . . . they were sometimes known to happen" in the past (Zeitlin, *Essays of Montaigne,* 3:370).

[14]Machiavelli similarly confers legitimacy on Hiero by calling him a "prince": *The Prince,* ch. 6, p. 25.

[15]*Hiero,* VII.11–13; Strauss, *On Tyranny,* pp. 45–7, 57–8.

Rulers enjoy a freedom to do as they please which others envy. Nor does the popular scrutiny of their actions to which Montaigne alludes hamper this freedom to any considerable extent: as he notes elsewhere, the people are "an inexact judge, easy to dupe, easy to satisfy" (III, vii, 896 [700]). Whatever their private feelings, the people are obliged to treat any ruler with respect; hence wicked kings are honored equally with good ones (258 [195]; I, iii, 19 [9]).

The other arguments by which Montaigne purports to show the disadvantages of rulership are no more persuasive. The fact that princes sometimes "delight . . . to disguise themselves and stoop to a low and plebeian way of living" (256 [193]) hardly demonstrates that they would prefer such a life as a full-time occupation. Elsewhere, in fact, Montaigne remarks that "greatness has this evident advantage, that it can step down whenever it pleases, and that it almost has the choice of both conditions" (III, vii, 894 [699]). That "the weight of sovereignty scarcely touches a French gentleman twice in his life" (257 [195]) may show that noblemen are almost as free as kings, but this point is not established with respect to most of the citizenry. Nor, when Montaigne—once more emulating Hiero—contends that "all the real advantages that princes have are shared by men of moderate fortune," does he specify what such a fortune must amount to, or how many people possess it (258 [195]).[16]

Montaigne's account of the disadvantages of rulership, then, is hardly convincing.[17] Though the task of "a good king" may indeed be more troublesome than a merely private life, the bulk of the essayist's argument suggests that bad kings may enjoy all the advantages of their more virtuous counterparts with little or none of the trouble. As Montaigne indicates even more forthrightly at the end of chapter vii of Book III, "Of the Disadvantage of Greatness," the monopoly of power that kings enjoy prevents their subjects from criticizing their many "defects and vices." As a result, kings are seen to display not only "lechery . . . and every sort of dissoluteness" but also cruelty, the vice most abhorrent to Montaigne (III, vii, 898 [702]).

In this light we may understand why Montaigne gives the title of king to the tyrant Hiero. Montaigne obliterates the distinction between kings and

---

[16]See Strauss, *On Tyranny*, pp. 49–50, regarding a similar ambiguity in the *Hiero*.

[17]This is not to deny that they would be disadvantages *for Montaigne*, who disdains the pleasure of command as too bothersome, by comparison with those of freedom (III, vii, 896 [700]; III, ix, 925 [723]). Montaigne particularly emphasizes his love of travel, a pleasure that Hiero laments is denied him (III, ix, passim; I, xlii, 256–7 [194]). The theme of travel is best understood in this connection as a metaphor for the intellectual "journey" of the philosopher (see III, iii, 806 [628]); from his perspective, conventional rulership is not worth the trouble it entails. See I, xxv, 134 [99], for the classical view; but cf. III, x, 998–1002 [781–4], for Montaigne's account of a manner of governing which did not require him to forsake his freedom.

tyrants because he denies that the distinction has much practical substance. Given the freedom that any monarch enjoys to deceive his subjects and evade the law, he has an overwhelming temptation to pursue his private interest at his subjects' expense. Consequently, whereas Aristotle distinguished between kings and tyrants on the ground that the former pursue the common good, Montaigne suggests that kingship so defined is purely a fiction, which imitates a popular prejudice.[18] As he remarks elsewhere, titles and offices, regardless of professions to the contrary, are "sought out to gain private profit from the public" (I, xxxix, 232 [174]).

If this interpretation is correct, it may help us to understand the relevance of a seemingly unrelated remark near the end of "Of Inequality." "In the opinion of Anacharsis," Montaigne reports, "the best government would be one in which all other things being equal, precedence was measured out according to virtue, and rejection according to vice" (259 [196]). At first reading, this remark seems to signify that virtue is of the utmost importance in allocating offices. But its literal meaning, I believe, is almost the opposite: if all other things must be equal before virtue comes into consideration, it is the least important criterion.[19] This interpretation is confirmed, and the meaning of the statement elaborated, by a parallel remark in a later chapter wherein Montaigne specifically endorses the policy of taking "nobility" into account in filling offices only when the "merit" of rival applicants is "entirely equal." In that context, he distinguishes between nobility and "virtue" properly understood but notes at the same time that others have tended to collapse this distinction (III, v, 828 [646]). The relation between Anacharsis' remark and the overall argument of "Of Inequality" emerges in the light of that tendency. Having shown how easily people misjudge others' virtue, being misled by outward appearances, and having indicated the abuses that inequality of rank, based on a *supposed* inequality of virtue, engenders on the part of rulers, Montaigne suggests the desirability of moderating or eliminating those class differences.[20] Whatever the natural

[18]Aristotle, *Politics*, III.7; cf. Strauss, *On Tyranny*, pp. 22–3 and 110, n. 1, citing the questioning or denial of the king/tyrant distinction by Machiavelli, Hobbes, and Montesquieu. On the connection between Montaigne's exposure of the nature of princes in "Of Inequality" and the political teaching of Machiavelli, see Alexander Nicolaï, "Le Machiavélisme de Montaigne," *BSAM*, 3d ser., no. 9 (1959): 18–30, esp. 26–30.

[19]Montaigne's version of the remark slightly alters the sense of the original, which refers to the determination of the better and the worse, rather than "precedence," by virtue and vice, respectively. The original context of the remark is also significant: it is made in response to a question concerning the best form of popular or republican (as opposed to monarchical) rule (Plutarch, *Banquet of the Seven Sages*, 154d–e). Cf. also *Essais*, III, ix, 959 [749]: "I should find myself more at home in a country where these orders [of rank] were either regulated or despised." Nakam, *Les Essais*, pp. 222–3, offers a contrary interpretation.

[20]Cf. III, iii, 799 [623]: "The administrations which admit the least disparity between servants and masters" are "the most equitable"; also I, iii, 19–20 [9–10], lamenting the attribution to rank of "the praise that belonged to merit."

inequalities among human beings, he has intimated, these differences have no relation to the conventional distinction between ruler and ruled. Quite the contrary: Montaigne elsewhere asserts that "the chief places are commonly seized by the least capable men, and . . . greatness of fortune is rarely found in combination with ability" (I, xxvi, 154–5 [114]). The obscurity and inefficacy of the true human inequalities explain why Montaigne asserted in I, iii, that popular rule (which presupposes human equality rather than inequality) is the "most natural and equitable" form of government, despite the defects that such rule has thus far exhibited. The essayist's emphasis, early in "Of Inequality," on the parity or equality of our natural condition, in the sense of the most fixed and visible aspect of that condition—our equal susceptibility to such physical ills as pain and disease—seems intended to justify such egalitarianism.[21]

That Montaigne's critique of inequality has a practical intent becomes even more evident in the following chapter, "Of Sumptuary Laws." His explicit aim in this chapter is to criticize laws that "try to regulate vain and insane expenditures for the table and for clothes" by limiting the use of luxuries to royalty.[22] Montaigne argues that such limitations, far from "engendering in men contempt for gold and silk as vain and useless things," serve "to give prestige to such things and increase everyone's desire to enjoy them." It would be better, Montaigne contends, for kings to "abandon those marks of greatness" themselves and for the law to forbid "gold ornaments and crimson" to anyone but "mountebanks and courtesans." By such a device, as an ancient example shows, the people's "corrupted manners" may be reformed and the citizenry "diverted . . . from pernicious superfluities and luxuries" (I, xliii, 259–60 [197]).

Montaigne's argument in "Of Sumptuary Laws" may be seen, as Sayce observes, as expressing an attitude of "middle-class thrift."[23] But this apparent thrust of the chapter masks a deeper point. In treating sumptuary laws as if their primary purpose were "to regulate vain and insane expenditures," Montaigne downplays their more political goal: visibly to distinguish people of the highest rank, so as to encourage the vulgar to venerate them.[24] There are, he contends, "enough better ways of distin-

[21]Cf. also III, v, 855 [668–9]: through the sexual act nature makes all of us equal, and "put[s] on the same level the fools and the wise, and us and the beasts." Hobbes's argument for natural equality similarly emphasizes people's parity in physical strength, while denying the naturalness of differences of knowledge and passing over the issue whether there are natural inequalities in the capacity for attaining knowledge: Leviathan, ch. 13, pp. 183–4; cf. ch. 15, p. 211, and Aristotle, Politics, 1254b27–33, with 1332b15–27.
[22]Sumptuary laws had been enacted in France in 1549–50 and were a continuing theme of discussion in the 1570s (Nakam, Montaigne et son temps, pp. 46, 50).
[23]Sayce, Essays, p. 240.
[24]As noted by Zeitlin, Essays of Montaigne, 1:400.

guishing ourselves and our rank externally (which I truly believe to be very necessary in a state)" (260 [196]). But this is bare assertion; Montaigne provides no illustration of any such alternative means to the same goal. And in "Of Inequality" he contended that it is often only their clothing that distinguishes kings from their subjects. Thus, by following Montaigne's recommendation to avoid such expenditures, kings would make their natural equality more visible to all. (Indeed, one of the other reforms that Montaigne recommends in this chapter is the abandonment of a kind of clothing that "makes us [look] completely different from what we are"— 261 [197]). The metaphorical sense in which Montaigne's advice should be taken is indicated not only in "Of Inequality" but also by the wish he expressed in his foreword to be able to present himself "wholly naked" before the public (9 [2]). Such an intention is in conformity with the hatred Montaigne expresses in Book III for the "tyranny" of vain external appearances by which governments seek to maintain the respect of the populace. "Keeping a close watch" on eminent men, he adds in this context, "I have found that they are for the most part like the rest" (III, viii, 910 [711]). And as he remarked in the "Apology," "the souls of emperors and cobblers are cast in the same mold" (II, xii, 464 [350]).

"Of Sumptuary Laws" ends on a putatively conservative note that seems to belie the foregoing interpretation. After citing Plato's opinion that changes of fashion lead to corruption and the disdain of ancient institutions, Montaigne remarks that "no laws are held in their true honor except those to which God has given some ancient duration, so that no one knows their origin or that they were ever different" (261 [198]). But to take this conclusion (like his earlier remark acknowledging the need for external class distinctions) as a demonstration that Montaigne's intention is truly conservative is to ignore what he has been doing in this and the preceding chapter. Both the reforms Montaigne advocates and, more important, his arguments in their favor would tend, by his admission, to weaken people's veneration for established authorities. By his argument in these chapters and elsewhere, he has endeavored to "unclothe" monarchs: that is, to undermine the conventional opinions that obscure our natural equality. Thus he implies that the inequalities that distinguish civilized polities from the cannibals' society have their ground in convention rather than nature. The question of political obligation that Montaigne attributed to the cannibals' spokesman therefore remains open: why should people who are naturally equal or even superior to the rich and powerful agree to obey them? We have seen that Montaigne agrees with the spirit of the cannibals' challenge to civic inequality; but it remains to be seen whether and how civilized societies might be reformed so as to eliminate or at least mitigate those inequalities, without at the same time incurring the admitted disadvantages of the cannibals' existence.

The Significance of "Of Cannibals"

In seeking to resolve the issue just stated, let us consider the other key point for which Montaigne praises the cannibals' society—the scant quantity of "artifice and human solder" by which it is held together. What Montaigne means by "human solder," I suggest, is the various moral, religious, and political conventions that civilized societies have instituted in an attempt to bind a number of self-interested individuals into a social whole. The example of the cannibals ostensibly demonstrates the possibility of holding a people together with few of these restraints.[25] The cannibals' morality and religion are limited to two precepts that serve to unite them: affection (founded on natural erotic attraction) for their spouses, and courage (founded in natural spiritedness) in battle against enemies. It is the simplicity of these social rules, as well as the limitedness of their individual desires, that prevents the cannibals from feeling a conflict between their respective self-interests and the good of the community. This absence of conflict between individual and common interests, in turn, enables the cannibals to do without government or political hierarchy.

In order to understand more precisely the relation between the cannibals' egalitarianism and their lack of reliance on "human solder," it is useful to bear in mind the classic justification of political inequality given by Aristotle. Aristotle links his defense of such inequality with the notion that it is the purpose of government to promote human excellence. If a polis were merely an association formed for purposes of mutual defense, he implies, then all its members might, like the signatories to a treaty among independent nations, be regarded as having an equal share in it. It is because the purpose of government is a comprehensive one, however, its laws being intended "to make the citizens good and just," that the claims of the virtuous are entitled to a special weight.[26]

Montaigne, we have seen, suggests that the pretense of rewarding "virtue" serves merely to enable kings and nobles to oppress other citizens. It is thus that he presents as a model a society—that of the cannibals—the purposes of which go scarcely beyond that of mutual defense. It is by jettisoning the notion that the aim of government is the moral improvement of its citizenry, he implies, that the practice of political oppression can be ended.

The import of Montaigne's praise of the cannibals' lack of "artifice and human solder" can be seen more fully in the light of his remarks in the ninth and tenth chapters of Book III, some of which were cited in Chapter Four. In both of these essays Montaigne argues that the ancient sages set forth

---

[25]Cf. Fleuret, "Montaigne et la société civile," pp. 118–19.
[26]Politics, III.9.

public teachings that demanded an unrealistic degree of public-spiritedness, self-sacrifice, and temperance regarding physical pleasure. He objects to "these lofty points of philosophy on which no human being can settle, and these rules that exceed our practice and our strength." And he censures the laws themselves for demanding too much of human beings, observing that "since our licentiousness always carries us beyond what is lawful and permitted to us, the precepts and laws of our life have often been made strict beyond universal reason"; he wishes "that there should be more proportion between the command and the obedience," since "a goal that we cannot reach seems unjust" (III, ix, 967–9 [756–7]; cf. III, x, 983 [769]).

Just as, in the "Apology," Montaigne exposes the philosophers' deference to popular religious beliefs as a sham, so, elsewhere in the *Essays,* he aims to expose the hypocrisy of their exoteric political and moral teachings. Hence the significance of Montaigne's portrayal of the cannibals' society as a "natural" one: the way of life that is natural for human beings is not that of moral virtue, but one dedicated purely to the satisfaction of animal wants and to victory in the struggle for survival against other creatures.

The significance of Montaigne's account of the cannibals can be further seen if we recall three vices from which he claims they are free: "lying, treachery, dissimulation" (204 [153]). Each of these vices is a form of dishonesty. The cannibals are apparently free from it because they perceive no conflict between private and public interests. Having limited desires, and not being subject to a morality that interferes with those desires, they see no gain in deceiving one another.

Montaigne's attribution of a total honesty to the cannibals links them to his self-portrayal. Throughout the *Essays* Montaigne professes a frankness and honesty the lack of which he laments in others. The connection between this honesty and that of primitive peoples was established in the foreword, where, after professing his "good faith," Montaigne said that he would have spoken even more frankly had he "been placed among those nations that are said to live still in the sweet freedom of nature's first laws" (9 [2]). This connection is further intimated in a later discussion of the New World natives in the chapter "Of Coaches" (III, vi). There, lamenting the brutality that native Americans suffered from their European conquerors, Montaigne remarks that these people's very virtues—"devoutness, observance of the law, liberality, loyalty, and frankness"—caused their defeat by the less scrupulous Europeans (III, vi, 887 [694]). This remark is reminiscent of Montaigne's account of his own relation to his society: his best qualities—"easygoing ways," "fidelity and conscience," "frankness and independence"—are "useless in this century," a "very depraved time" (II, xvii, 629 [490]). Montaigne's virtues, like those of the American natives, are insufficiently appreciated by his European contemporaries. At the same time, they disdain him for aiming at no higher goal than that which the American natives pursue: to pass one's life "happily and pleasantly." Whereas Montaigne is content to lead a "merely pleasant" life, his contemporaries insist that he owes duties to others and condemn his "idleness" (I, xxvi, 175–6 [130]; II, xvi, 605 [471]; II, xvii, 626 [487]; III, iii, 807 [629]; III, v, 821 [640]; III, vi, 889 [695]).

Montaigne's fellow Europeans pride themselves on the civilization that elevates them above the "barbarians" of the New World. But their conduct toward the American natives—as well as, in the religious wars, toward each other—is even more barbaric, according to Montaigne, than that of the cannibals. The Europeans' actions thus belie the claim that the elevated conception of duty they profess has served to improve them (cf. II, xii, 419 [322]). Hence Montaigne asks us to consider whether people would not be better off in a society where their professed duties, like those of the cannibals, were fewer, and their aspirations less transcendent. The Europeans use the pretext of "zeal for religion" to justify a shameful cruelty (III, vi, 891 [697]). Montaigne suggests that the multitude of duties that civilized people have added to the truly natural ones serve, similarly, as an excuse for worse vices than those committed by the "savages":

> For there is danger that we dream up new duties to excuse our negligence towards the natural duties and mix them up. As proof of this: we see that in places where faults are crimes, crimes are only faults; that in nations where the laws of propriety are rarer and looser, the primitive and common laws are better observed: for the innumerable multitude of so many duties smothers, weakens, and dissipates our concern. (III, v, 866 [677])

Of course, one may well doubt that the natives of the New World possessed all the virtues Montaigne attributes to them. As we have observed from his remark in "Of Moderation," he is fully cognizant of the barbaric cruelty practiced by the barbarians themselves. There is no reason to assume, therefore, that in his eulogistic account of the cannibals Montaigne has fallen victim to a fashion for exoticism which swept away his customary critical faculties. Rather, I suggest, his portrayal of the cannibals is a consciously created "utopia" analogous to the cities Plato constructs in the *Republic* and *Laws* and having a similar function: to provide a standard against which existing regimes may be judged.

Montaigne's utopia has a further purpose than this theoretical one, however, which is signified by the fact that unlike Plato, he claims that his model regime actually exists. This claim is related to the denunciation, in "Of Vanity," of "all those imaginary, artificial descriptions of a government [which] prove ridiculous and unfit to put into practice" (III, ix, 934 [730]). By portraying his primitive utopia as an existing society, Montaigne implies that—unlike the "best" or even the second-best regimes sketched by

Plato—this society, on its most important aspects, is actualizable. Hence it is meant to have a greater practical relevance than Plato's model regimes to the possible reformation of the European society of which Montaigne is a member.

The serious meaning of Montaigne's claim of actuality for his utopia is that, unlike Plato's best regime, it is not based on the assumption of the perfection of human nature through reason. Whether or not a society like that of the cannibals Montaigne portrays ever existed, he regards the essential features of this society as capable of being actualized because they are founded on the most basic and universal human instincts, rather than on a perfection that is rarely if ever found in a single individual. That the "naturalness" of the cannibals' society is susceptible of application in other contexts is suggested by Montaigne's account of the policy that Julius Caesar, "the sovereign model of the military art" (II, xxxiv, 713 [556]), followed in directing his army. Caesar, the essayist reports, was so "scarcely scrupulous . . . that he required no other virtue in his soldiers than valor, and scarcely punished any other vices than mutiny and disobedience" (II, xxxiv, 714 [557]). The rules that Caesar employed in leading an army of civilized men are analogous to those Montaigne attributes to the cannibals: to demand nothing more of the individual than loyalty or attachment to his own side and hostility to enemies. While employing his libertarian policy, Caesar achieved infinite military successes. But if the natural relation of human beings is (as the cannibals' example suggests) one of conflict (cf. I, xxii; III, vii, 896 [701]), the true rules of "the military art" may have a considerable relevance to politics.[27] Caesar's example suggests how the lessons learned from the cannibals can be applied with advantage to civilized society. By reducing the demands that society makes on people to the minimal, "natural" ones, one may not only mitigate political oppression but enhance the society's ability to preserve itself.

Contrary to Montaigne's initially exaggerated praise of the cannibals, we have seen that he is far from regarding their overall way of life as simply good, or even unambiguously superior to the ways of his European contemporaries. But it is equally doubtful that Plato regarded the "best city" that Socrates sketches in the *Republic* as simply desirable.[28] Rather than constituting a model of a good society, Montaigne's account of the cannibals is intended only to indicate the *direction* that efforts at political reformation should follow. In this light, what is most significant about Montaigne's "solution" to the political problem is that it points in a direction opposite to Plato's. Plato suggests in the *Republic* that to resolve the tension between

---

[27]Cf. Machiavelli, *The Prince*, ch. 14.

[28]Cf. Bloom, *Republic of Plato*, pp. 408–12; Nichols, *Socrates and the Political Community*, pt. II.

the good of the individual and that of the community would require an education that radically reformed our nature by overcoming our attachment to selfish, bodily goods. Montaigne, on the other hand, argues that the most harmonious solution to the political problem is found at the lowest level of human existence, at a point where people's minds are undeveloped and their life barely different from that of beasts. The effort to transcend the cannibals' situation in behalf of a common good based on the suppression of selfishness does not overcome human antagonisms, but merely provides tyrants like Hiero with an excuse and an opportunity to oppress others.

We have seen that Montaigne's apparent intention of reestablishing political life on a more egalitarian foundation is linked with, or presupposes, a transformation of the morality of European societies: one that would reduce the demands that society makes on the individual. At the same time we have observed that the evident defects of the cannibals' way of life—notably their cruelty, ignorance, and penury—make it unlikely that Montaigne regards their morality as a simply desirable model. A significant remark bearing on the purpose of his account of the cannibals is found in "Of Coaches." There, while eulogizing the virtues of the American natives and deploring their treatment by the Spaniards, he laments:

> Why did not such a noble conquest fall to Alexander or to those noble Greeks and Romans, and such a great change and alteration of so many empires and peoples fall under hands that would have gently polished and cleared away whatever was wild [sauvage] in them, and would have strengthened and fostered the good seeds that nature had produced in them, not only adding to the cultivation of the earth and the adornment of cities the arts of our side [of the world], insofar as they would have been necessary, but also adding the Greek and Roman virtues to the original [virtues] of that country! What an improvement that would have been, and what an amelioration for the whole world [machine], if our first examples and conduct presented there had called those peoples to the admiration and imitation of virtue and had set up between them and us a brotherly fellowship and understanding! How easy it would have been to make good use of souls so fresh, so famished for learning, and having for the most part such fine natural beginnings! (III, vi, 888–9 [694–5])

Even though the Indians being described here are *not* referred to as cannibals, and hence are presumably less barbaric than the natives described in I, xxxi, Montaigne makes it explicit that their morality is not sufficient in itself. Rather, their virtues, such as they are, constitute only a beginning, which could have been completed if they had been supplemented by the virtues of the pagan Greeks and Romans (rather than by the pseudo-virtues of the Spanish, exemplified by their use of religious pretexts to massacre the natives). But such a combination of the virtues of the Indians and the ancients would have represented an improvement for "the whole world," not just for the Indians: Western morality, even at its highest, stands also in need of correction.

In this passage Montaigne intimates the need to reconstitute morality by returning to its "natural" beginnings in the lives of primitive human beings, then recapitulating the process of moral development that made Greek and Roman civilization possible—but while averting the characteristic defects of their understanding of morality; above all, so guiding the understanding of morality that it cannot evolve, as the pagan view did, into a recipe for tyranny or fanaticism. What makes such a project urgent is the danger that the pernicious effects of Christian fanaticism on political life—manifested not only in the French religious wars but even more obviously in the Spaniards' treatment of the Indians—may otherwise lead to a degeneration of European civilization into a barbarism worse than that of the cannibals. At the other extreme, if Montaigne's intended reconstitution of morality is successful, it may lead to the elevation of human well-being to a historically unparalleled level. As previously noted, Montaigne's remarks about the French political order in II, xvii, and III, ix, suggest that it is in a state of decay and near collapse, such that only a fundamental reordering might save it (or make it worth saving). At the same time his reference to America as a "new" but eminently teachable world (III, vi, 886, 888 [693–5]) implies that its discovery may serve as the inspiration for a fundamental amelioration in the condition of "the whole world."[29] Montaigne's intention to reconstitute human moral and political life may amount to the almost literal re-creation of the world, the creation of a world more truly "new" (in the sense of being unprecedented) than America itself.

Montaigne's account of the cannibals exemplifies the first step that he indicated in "Of Custom" must be taken by anyone who wishes to judge human ways and conventions rationally: to return to "nature," and to "the first and universal reasons" for things (I, xxiii, 115 [84]). But the gap between the "natural" goods with which the cannibals are contented and those that civilized people demand is enormous. To bridge this gap requires an analysis of the European conception of morality and the reasons for its particular character, an understanding of the passions that underlie human conduct, and a consideration of how those passions might be rechanneled so as to promote human contentment.

[29]Note Montaigne's remark concerning the vanity of "infer[ring] the decline and decrepitude of the world . . . from our own weakness and decay," just after lauding the human capacity for invention, which is bounded only by the present limitedness of our knowledge (III, vi, 886 [693]).

CHAPTER SEVEN

The Good, the Beautiful, and the Useful: The Natural History of Morality

As noted in Chapter One, most twentieth-century interpreters of Montaigne's ethical thought have followed Pierre Villey and Fortunat Strowski in presupposing that the essayist underwent an evolution from an early, Stoical outlook toward a later attitude that has variously been described as hedonistic, libertarian, and Epicurean. The most prominent opponent of this interpretation, Arthur Armaingaud, argued that many of the passages cited by Villey to show that Montaigne was originally a Stoic are actually more reflective of Epicureanism.[1] Yet Armaingaud's own attempted demonstration that Montaigne's thought was consistently Epicurean is not free from difficulties. Since Armaingaud admits that Montaigne's encouragement of indulgence in corporeal pleasures violates Epicurus' rigorous strictures of moderation in that regard, he must maintain that the essayist's modification of Epicurean doctrine was faithful to its "spirit" even while deviating from its letter.[2] Aside from the questionableness of that claim, Armaingaud's interpretation fails to do justice to the *appearance* of evolution that many readers besides Villey and Strowski have noted in the book. Here again, Armaingaud sometimes hedges by attributing changes in the author's tone to his experiencing "moments of discouragement" or "pessimism," and by alluding to the consistency Montaigne displayed in "his life and his actions" in order to demonstrate "the unity of his ideas"—as if the latter were not sufficiently evident in the *Essays* itself.[3] Finally, Montaigne himself supplies reason for doubting the importance of determining

---

[1] Armaingaud, "Etude," pp. 114–28. See also idem, *Montaigne a toujours été épicurien* (Paris, 1908).
[2] "Etude," p. 158.
[3] Ibid., pp. 89, 153.

whether he was a Stoic or Epicurean by denying that the two ancient doctrines are fundamentally opposed (II, xi, 401 [307]).[4]

As I have indicated, my own challenge to the Villey-Strowski interpretation is a more fundamental one than Armaingaud's—and extends to Armaingaud's own position. Contrary to Armaingaud, I believe that Montaigne's true position is distinct from both Stoicism and Epicureanism—even though it has certain features in common with each doctrine, particularly the latter. Given the deviations that Armaingaud recognizes Montaigne made from the Epicurean position—not only by challenging the limits Epicurus set to indulgence in physical pleasure but by manifesting a direct concern with political affairs[5]—it is questionable whether the Epicurean label is much more appropriate than the Stoic one. In any event, there is substantial evidence that Montaigne himself thought of his moral teaching as revolutionary, rather than as a return to any of the ethical doctrines of antiquity.

Any interpreter of the *Essays* who aspires to refute the view that Montaigne was either a Stoic or an Epicurean for at least some period must explain what I shall call (*pace* Armaingaud) the "Stoical" appearance of several chapters of Books I and II, or major portions thereof, including chapters xiv, xix, xx, xxxvii, and xxxix of the first book and i and xi of the second. Of these chapters, Richard Sayce has singled out two—I, xiv, "That the Taste of Good and Evil Depends in Good Part on the Opinion We Have of Them," and I, xx, "That to Philosophize Is to Learn How to Die"—as presenting "something like a standard model of Stoic opinions."[6] The title of each chapter is derived from an ancient maxim: the first is based on a saying of the Stoic thinker Epictetus, and the second, although attributed by Montaigne to Cicero (who took it from Plato's Socrates), is consistent with the thrust of both Stoic and Epicurean doctrine. I shall consider the first of these chapters here, reserving detailed consideration of the second to Chapter Ten.

Montaigne's "Stoicism"

Just as Montaigne had softened Raymond Sebond's rationalistic claims in translating the *Natural Theology,* the title of I, xiv, significantly qualifies (with the phrase "in good part") the thrust of the Stoic maxim that it is Montaigne's ostensible purpose to examine. Whether or not this qualification signifies a divergence in attitude between Montaigne and the Stoics, he does proceed to quote the maxim in its absolute form in the first sentence:

[4]As noted by Sayce, *Essays,* pp. 166–7. Cf. *Essais,* II, ii, 329 [251].
[5]On the latter point, see Armaingaud, "Etude," pp. 171–2.
[6]Sayce, *Essays,* p. 163.

"Men . . . are tormented by the opinions they have of things, not by the things themselves."[7] Without expressing any initial judgment of the maxim's validity, Montaigne emphasizes how conducive to "the relief of our miserable human condition" it would be if the maxim *were* true:

> For if evils have no entry into us but by our judgment, it seems to be in our power to disdain them or turn them to good. If things surrender to our mercy, why shall we not dispose of them and arrange them to our advantage? If what we call evil and torment is neither evil nor torment in itself, if it is merely our fancy that gives it this quality, it is in us to change it. And having the choice, if no one forces us, we are strangely insane to tense ourselves for the course that is more painful to us, and to give sicknesses, indigence, and contempt a bitter and unpleasant taste if we can give them a good one and if, fortune furnishing merely the material, it is up to us to give it form. (I, xiv, 49–50 [33])

The thought that things "surrender to our mercy" and consequently allow us to view them as we please, presented here as a hypothetical possibility, is asserted by Montaigne as a truth, derived from the Pyrrhonian doctrine, in a passage from the "Apology" that I discussed in Chapter Four (II, xii, 545 [422]). The context of the later passage appears to give it a broader signification, relating to human knowledge as such, rather than only to the knowledge of things affecting human well-being, the overt theme of I, xiv. At the same time, the reasoning with which Montaigne supports the position being asserted is more restrained, in one respect, in the earlier passage. In the "Apology," as we have seen, Montaigne infers from the diversity of human opinions and judgments that "things do not lodge in us in their form and in their essence," but that our conceptions of them are rooted in convention or artifice. In I, xiv, on the other hand, while similarly judging that things "enter us only by mutual agreement," he adds that "one man perchance lodges them in himself in their true being, but in a thousand others they are given a new and contrary being" (I, xiv, 50 [33]). According to this passage, we are not absolutely barred from knowing the nature of things, as it seems we are according to the "Apology." The difference between the two statements may reflect the difference in their subject: that is, knowledge of the true character of *human ills* may be available to us in principle, even though knowledge of the essences of external objects is absolutely inaccessible.[8] (We shall observe that Montaigne himself tacitly professes to possess the former knowledge.)

In the long passage quoted above, Montaigne's three examples of the

[7]This maxim, drawn from the fifth section of Epictetus' *Enchiridion*, was one of the sentences that Montaigne had inscribed in Greek on the ceiling of his library. For similar statements, see also *The Discourses of Epictetus*, I, xix, in Whitney J. Oates, ed., *The Stoic and Epicurean Philosophers* (New York, 1940), p. 258; and Seneca, *Epistles*, lxxviii, 13.

[8]Montaigne draws such a distinction between the knowability of human nature and of other things at p. 540 [418] of the "Apology."

evils that it might be possible to transform to good were "sicknesses, indigence, and contempt." In proceeding to test the Stoic maxim, however, he observes that "we consider death, poverty, and pain our principal adversaries" (50 [33]). While "poverty" corresponds to "indigence" and "pain" may include the suffering of illness, we note that "death" replaces "contempt" in the list. Although death may indeed be generally regarded (by those lacking a strong sense of honor) as a greater evil than contempt, this substitution would seem to make the case for the Stoic maxim all the harder to establish—since, of the four evils listed, it would appear easiest to demonstrate that the painfulness of contempt is purely a matter of opinion.

In conformity with the outline he has suggested, Montaigne devotes the bulk of the remainder of I, xiv, in roughly equal parts (in the final edition) to considering our capacity to overcome death, pain, and poverty, respectively, by adopting particular opinions or attitudes about them. Taking up death first, he observes:

> Now this death, which some call the most horrible of horrible things, who does not know that others name it the only haven from the torments of this life, the sovereign good of nature, the sole support of our freedom, and the common and prompt remedy for all evils? And even as some await it trembling and afraid, others endure it more easily than life. (50 [33–4])

Even "leav[ing] aside these men of glorious courage," Montaigne asserts, "most philosophers have either deliberately anticipated or hastened and abetted their death," while "many low-born people [*personnes populaires*]" have displayed "such assurance, some through stubbornness, others through natural simplicity" while being "led to death" that they "yield[ed] in nothing to Socrates." In illustration, he recounts a series of stories of people joking on the way to the gallows, choosing to be executed rather than face a variety of seemingly less fearsome alternatives, and "blithely" obeying a custom consigning them to death by fire after their spouse or their king has died. Remarking that "any opinion is strong enough to make people espouse it at the price of life," Montaigne cites the contemporary instance of those who "accept a cruel death rather than abandon circumcision for baptism," "an example of which no sort of religion is incapable." He then offers a lengthy account of the abuse meted out by the Portuguese kings to the Jews exiled from Spain, which culminated in a royal plan to remove all Jewish children from their parents, "to be brought up in our religion." This action reportedly "produced a horrible spectacle, the natural affection between fathers and children, and also the [Jews'] zeal for their former belief, fighting against this violent ordinance. It was common to see fathers and mothers doing away with themselves, and, what is a still more austere example, through love and compassion throwing their children into wells to escape the law." To this report Montaigne adds the example of a friend of his whom he saw "chase death with a real affection, rooted in his heart by various seeming reasons of which I could not rid him." And after noting "many examples in our time of people, even children, who, for fear of some slight inconvenience, have given themselves up to death," Montaigne finally cites "Pyrrho the philosopher," who encouraged his fellow passengers in a boat to overcome their fear during a storm by referring to the example of a contented pig who accompanied them. In seeming accord with Pyrrho's point, and in anticipation of the "Apology," Montaigne questions the value of the reason on which we pride ourselves if it deprives us of "the repose and tranquility we should enjoy without it," and "puts us into a worse condition than Pyrrho's pig" (51–5 [34–6]).

It is significant that Montaigne's treatment of death in this chapter ends with a series of rhetorical questions, rather than a definitive conclusion. These questions may well suggest that Montaigne agrees with Pyrrho that it is foolish to spend our lives worrying about death; but they evince no evidence that he believes that a change in attitude could eliminate the undesirable character of death—or that death is a purely conventional, not a natural, evil. To the contrary, Montaigne strove to talk his friend out of seeking to die; he describes a people's craving for death as "frenzied" [furieux]; and he refers to the "spectacle" of the Jews' killing themselves and their children as "horrible" (52–4 [35–6]). Nor is the mode of argument by which Montaigne purportedly demonstrates that death is not to be feared, strictly speaking, a Stoical one: his emphasis on the capacity of unlearned and unphilosophical human beings, and even pigs, to overcome the fear of death can hardly be said to demonstrate the necessity of Stoical self-cultivation, while his query regarding the goodness of knowledge if it costs us our "repose and tranquility" calls into question the utility of philosophic contemplation.[9]

The example of the Jewish exiles is particularly instructive in revealing the underlying intent of the foregoing argument. If Montaigne's primary aim were to demonstrate how easily the fear of death can be overcome, then most of his account of the "inhumanity" the Jews endured before being driven to mass suicide and infanticide would be irrelevant.[10] But could not this example, along with several other cases recounted in the chapter of people's being killed in the name of religion, be taken rather to illustrate another point, with which we are familiar from the "Apology," "Of Cus-

---

[9]Cf. Boön, "Emendations des emprunts," pp. 155–6; also the conclusion of I, xx, where Montaigne asserts that people of "low condition" display "far more assurance" in the face of death than others do (p. 94 [68]). Contrast Epictetus, Enchiridion, sec. 21: "Keep before your eyes from day to day death and exile and all things that seem terrible, but death most of all" (Oates, Stoic and Epicurean Philosophers, p. 473). I discuss Montaigne's critique of previous philosophic attitudes toward death thematically in Chapter Ten.

[10]See Nakam, Montaigne et son temps, p. 230.

tom," and other chapters—the folly and horror of "the belief universally embraced in all religions" "that we gratify heaven and nature by committing massacre and homicide" (I, xxx, 199 [149])?

Although Montaigne refers several times in the *Essays* to his father, he says nothing specific about his mother (who outlived him).[11] Whatever the reason for this silence, the essayist's account of the Jews' fate gains deepened impact when we note that his mother is believed to have been descended from a family of Spanish Jews, many of whose members—including her great-great-grandfather—were burned at the stake during the Inquisition. In Montaigne's time the Bordeaux area was heavily populated with Marranos—former Spanish and Portuguese Jews and their descendants, ostensibly converted to Christianity, who were nonetheless suspected of continuing to practice their religion privately. Some Marranos, including Montaigne's great-uncle, achieved positions of wealth and prominence in the area; but there, as elsewhere, their very success exposed them to intolerance and harassment (despite the protection given them by the local parlement, on which Montaigne had served, and which included numerous members of Jewish ancestry).[12] Especially significant regarding Montaigne's attitude toward the Marranos and the suffering of their ancestors is a remark in I, xiv, about the beliefs of the Portuguese Jewish converts. Having quoted the explanation of the Portuguese king's rationale for persecuting them given by "Bishop Osorius, the best Latin historian of our era," Montaigne goes out of his way to question the bishop's judgment that the Jews who converted rather than kill themselves became sincere Christians. Rather, he remarks, "of their faith, or of that of their descendants, even today, a hundred years later, few Portuguese are sure, though custom and length of time are far stronger counselors than any other compulsion" (54–5 [36]). Not without reason does Frame surmise that Montaigne's "remarks about the Portuguese marranos may have applied in his mind to those of Bordeaux," including his relatives, or that the awareness of his ancestors' martyrdom may have helped to inspire his protests against the cruelty practiced and encouraged by the church.[13]

[11]As noted by Frame, *Montaigne*, p. 16.

[12]Ibid., pp. 19–20, 23. For a fuller treatment of the evidence concerning Montaigne's mother's ancestry, see Roger Trinquet, *La Jeunesse de Montaigne* (Paris, 1972), ch. 5. Montaigne's travel journal describes his visits to synagogues in Verona and Rome, and includes a detailed account of a Jewish circumcision he observed (*Oeuvres*, pp. 1180, 1214–16 [918, 944–6]).

[13]Frame, *Montaigne*, pp. 17, 19, 21. Despite the relatively restrained or indirect manner in which Montaigne expresses his criticism of the Iberian mistreatment of the Jews, Géralde Nakam finds it unparalleled in the work of any of the essayist's contemporaries, except for the Jewish historian Joseph Ha-Cohen (*Montaigne et son temps*, p. 215). Leo Strauss observes that earlier in the sixteenth century Machiavelli had been "the only non-Jew of his age" to object to this mistreatment; the Florentine's comment (in a posthumously published book) is far more concise than Montaigne's (Strauss, *What Is Political Philosophy?* p. 44; Machiavelli, *The Prince*, ch. 21, pp. 88; cf. Nakam, *Les Essais*, pp. 368–77).

I have suggested that the primary intention of Montaigne's account of the Jews' persecution is to demonstrate the barbarism that Christianity has engendered. But we should also note how his criticism of religion applies against the Jews themselves. From his allusion to religious opinions in "Of Custom" as "indifferent" things, we may infer that Montaigne's description of the Jews' killing their children to save them from forced conversion as reflecting "love and compassion" is ironic. The same irony is present, in the form of black humor, in a later chapter titled "To Flee from Sensual Pleasures at the Price of Life." There Montaigne recounts the "singular joy" that Saint Hilary experienced at the death of his daughter, an event for which he had prayed as a means of saving her from the unholy fate of marriage. Montaigne's remark that this occurrence imbued Hilary's wife with "such a lively sense of eternal celestial beatitude" that she begged to die herself ought sufficiently to convey his opinion of the saint's belief, although the point has typically escaped commentators (I, xxxiii, 216–17 [162]).[14]

Beneath the purported "Stoicism" of Montaigne's treatment of death in I, xiv, there thus lies a more radical thought, having a direct bearing on the theologico-political issues facing sixteenth-century Europe. Yet there is an underlying connection between the theme of Stoicism and the religious issue. Montaigne makes that connection explicit in his account of Saint Hilary. He ironically calls the saint's prayer for his daughter's death an instance of "Christian moderation" *in comparison* with the "Stoical harshness" of the advice that both Epicurus and Seneca gave their friends to kill themselves rather than pursue a "voluptuous and pompous life." In the sequel, however, Montaigne tacitly retracts that relative judgment[15] by noting that Saint Hilary "seems to outdo the others, in that he addresses himself from the first to this means [of death], which the others adopt only as a subsidiary [that is, in case the addressee is unable to reform his life]; and besides, it concerns his only daughter" (I, xxxiii, 216 [162]). In other words, the Christian contempt for worldly pleasures—even to the extreme of preferring death to indulgence in them—is an extension of the Stoic and

---

[14]"Montaigne is indeed in a Stoical mood when he can recount Saint Hilary's prayers for the death of his wife and only daughter without expressing amazement at the inhumanity of it" (Zeitlin, *Essays of Montaigne*, 1:383). Zeitlin points out that the essayist "enriches the unction of the pious narrative, giving an emotional colour to it that is not in" his source: "it is his own imagination" that invents Hilary's "singular joy," his wife's "extreme insistence" on dying, and the "singular contentment" with which her death was received. Cf. II, ii, 328 [250]: "Even that Plutarch of ours, so perfect and excellent a judge of human actions, on seeing Brutus and Torquatus kill their children, came to doubt whether virtue could go that far, and whether these personages had not rather been agitated by some other passion. All actions outside the ordinary boundaries are subject to sinister interpretation." Consider also the discussion of the church's reverence for women who killed themselves to avoid being raped, with Montaigne's own recommendation on how they should act in such circumstances, at II, iii, 337–8 [257].

[15]As noted by Zeitlin, *Essays of Montaigne*, 1:383.

208 | The Political Philosophy of Montaigne

Epicurean attitude. Even though, from an orthodox Christian point of view, Stoicism is a heretical doctrine, inasmuch as it teaches human self-sufficiency, without any need for divine redemption,[16] Montaigne represents Christianity as a radicalization of the "presumption" that underlay classical philosophy as a whole. Far from being in accordance with either Stoicism or Christianity, the real teaching about death which is implicit in I, xiv, and I, xxxiii, is consistent with the following anti-Stoical and anti-Christian passage from Book II of the *Essays*—almost of all of which dates from the first edition of a chapter that Villey attributes to the early stage of the author's "development":[17]

> And the opinion that disdains our life, it is ridiculous. For after all, life is our being, it is our all. Things that have a nobler and richer being may accuse ours; but it is against nature that we despise ourselves and care nothing about ourselves. It is a malady peculiar [to man], and not seen in any other creature, to hate and disdain himself. It is by a similar vanity that we wish to be something other than we are. . . . A man who wishes to be made into an angel does nothing for himself; he would never benefit from the change. For when he is no more, who will feel and rejoice in this improvement in him? . . . The security, the repose, the impassibility, the exemption from the ills of this life, that we purchase at the price of death, bring us no advantage. (II, iii, 334 [254–5])

So much for those who, according to I, xiv, "have given themselves up to death" to avoid "some slight inconvenience," "to flee the ills of this life," or out of "the hope of a better condition elsewhere" (54 [36]).

I have argued that the true thought underlying I, xiv, is quite at variance with the "conspicuous imitative quality" that Zeitlin observes in its argument, and which he takes (following Villey) to typify Montaigne's original "moral attitude."[18] Admittedly, the entire passage about the Jews derives from the posthumous edition of the *Essays* (whereas Montaigne's remark about trying to dissuade his friend from running toward his death dates from the 1588 edition). But on the other hand, nothing in the 1580 text of the chapter contradicts the essayist's later argument, and the very "impersonality" of that text serves, as previously noted, to distance him from it. Moreover, Zeitlin's endeavor to explain the Stoical appearance of the

---

[16]See the discussion of Augustine's critique of Stoicism in Louis Hippeau, "La Notion de fausse vertu chez Montaigne," *BSAM*, 5th ser., nos. 3–4 (1972): 8–9; also Strowski, *Montaigne*, p. 110; Frame, *Montaigne's Discovery of Man*, p. 55. There was, indeed, a controversial movement of "Christian Stoicism" in Montaigne's time, including such writers as Justus Lipsius and Guillaume Du Vair, which purported to reconcile the two doctrines: see Fortunat Strowski, *Pascal et son temps* (Paris, 1907), ch. 2; Léontine Zanta, *La Renaissance du stoicisme au seizième siècle* (Paris, 1914). The sincerity of this purported reconciliation would need to be determined by a detailed examination of each writer's arguments.
[17]Villey, *Les Sources*, 1:356–8.
[18]Zeitlin, *Essays of Montaigne*, 1:308.

chapter as reflective of an early stage in its author's evolution is belied by his admission that what he takes to be its "central idea" is "adhered to" "faithfully" by Montaigne in his later additions to it.[19]

To a reader of the 1580 edition, most of the text of I, xiv—constituting a little over a third of the final version of the chapter—could indeed have appeared dry and "imitative," not to say downright boring. But I suggest a different explanation of the character of the text, and its subsequent alteration, from Zeitlin's. Rather than reflecting an early stage in Montaigne's "evolution," the original text, an apparently pointless collection of borrowed material, was another of the essayist's "grotesques," which he set down with every intention of *filling in* his real views in subsequent chapters, and in subsequent versions of the same chapter that he intended to include in later editions. That Montaigne was planning such additions at the time the 1580 edition was published is suggested by the fact, noted by Sayce, that even though Montaigne seemed to promise in the first edition of I, xiv, to deal with poverty, "poverty is hardly mentioned [in the original version] and is only fully treated in the later interpolations."[20] Here again, prudence dictated that the revolutionary character of Montaigne's teaching be revealed only gradually—both textually and chronologically—to the public.

Let us now examine the second stage in Montaigne's evaluation of the Stoic thesis in I, xiv: his consideration of our capacity to triumph over pain by adopting the right attitude toward it. The lengthy passage, dating almost entirely from the first edition, with which Montaigne initiates this examination provides manifest evidence against the claim that Montaigne was ever a Stoic *or* an Epicurean. He begins by asserting not only that "most of the sages" have thought pain "the ultimate evil," but also that "those who have denied it in word have admitted it in practice." He illustrates this point by describing how the Stoic philosopher Posidonius, while being "extremely tormented by an acute and painful malady," boasted of his triumph in refusing to admit that pain was an evil. This story was recounted "with full

[19]Ibid., p. 309; see also Sayce, *Essays,* pp. 165–6.

[20]Sayce, *Essays,* p. 18. Strowski explains Montaigne's failure to discuss poverty in the first edition by surmising that the essayist was so "sick with avarice" at the time he originally composed the chapter that he was "too sensitive" on that score to touch the subject: "He therefore waited to be cured [of the fear of indigence] to make fun of himself" for it. By contrast, his willingness to confront pain and death in the first edition suggests that these fears "were not too sharp" at the time he composed it (*Montaigne,* pp. 33–4). To list only the two most obvious difficulties in Strowski's interpretation: first, the claim that Montaigne was less fearful of pain than of poverty when he composed the original text is belied by the essayist's explicit assertion, in the first edition, that among all people, he hates and flees from pain "the most" (I, xiv, 56 [38]). Second, Strowski's assumption that Montaigne had to wait to confront poverty until after he had been "cured" of the fear of it contradicts his claim that Montaigne turned to Stoicism as a remedy for his fears: apparently he did not find the Stoics' arguments to be a particularly efficacious remedy if he could not even bear to repeat them until he had already overcome by other means the ill they were supposed to cure!

approval," as Sayce points out, by a near contemporary of Montaigne's, Guillaume Du Vair, who was an exponent of Christian Stoicism.[21] Montaigne, on the other hand, mocks Posidonius' pretension by remarking: "This tale that they make so much of, what has it to do with contempt of pain? He is only arguing about the word; and meanwhile if these pangs do not move him, why does he interrupt his talk for their sake? Why does he think he is doing a lot by not calling pain an evil?" (55 [37]).

In contrast not only to Stoicism but also to the teaching of Epicurus, Montaigne goes out of his way to emphasize the badness of pain, remarking that it is undoubtedly something real, not an imaginary worry, calling it "the worst accident of our being," and professing to be, of all people, the one "who bears it the most ill will and who flees it the most" (55–6 [37–8]).[22] (This entire passage dates from the first edition.) He goes on to assert, it is true, that it should be "in us, if not to annihilate it, at least to lessen it by patience, and, even should the body be disturbed by it, to maintain nevertheless our soul and reason in good trim." But the immediate sequel to this assertion is far from an unambiguous endorsement of Stoicism:

And if this were not so, who would have brought into credit among us virtue, valor, strength, magnanimity, and resolution? Where would these play their role, if there were no more pain to defy? "Courage is greedy of danger." If we need not sleep on hard ground, sustain fully armed the heat of noon, feed on a horse and an ass, watch ourselves being sliced open and a bullet torn out from between our bones, let ourselves be sewn up again, cauterized, and probed, how shall we acquire the advantage that we wish to have over the vulgar? It is far indeed from fleeing evil and pain to what the Sages say, that among equally good actions, the most desirable to do is the one in which there is the most trouble. . . . And for that reason it has been impossible to persuade our fathers that conquests made by main force with the risks of war were no more advantageous than those made in complete safety by diplomatic maneuvers. (56–7 [38])[23]

This passage moves from the straightforward assertion of a utilitarian and hedonistic criterion for virtue—the capacity of a particular quality to mitigate pain—to an indication that neither "the Sages" nor "our fathers," in their moral prescriptions, adhered to that criterion. What underlies their praise of a "tough" form of virtue, it appears, is at least as much the desire to win some advantage over "the vulgar" as the aim of contributing to people's ultimate ease or tranquility.

At this point Montaigne does not yet specify whether the criterion for

[21]Sayce, Essays, p. 164.
[22]Contrast Epicurus, Fragments (Vatican Collection), "Epicurus' Exhortation," IV (in Oates, Stoic and Epicurean Philosophers, p. 40); Epictetus, Discourses, III, xx (ibid., p. 374).
[23]The passage in quotation marks is from Seneca, Of Providence, IV.

virtue he has suggested, if pursued, would generate a different understanding of the substance of virtue from the prescriptions of the sages or "our fathers." Indeed, he appears to endorse the Stoic view by citing some maxims from Cicero that "should console us": violent pains are also shorter ones; if evils become unbearable, we always have suicide as a remedy. And he proceeds to assert that "what makes us endure pain so poorly is that we are not accustomed to find our principal contentment in the soul." Yet here again his argument deviates somewhat from the Stoic position: he stresses the need not for the soul to master the body, but rather to mold the soul— which, unlike the body, is infinitely malleable—into a particular form "conducive to our repose and preservation." And he cites as a model of tranquility not the Stoic sages, but "the beasts, who keep [their minds] on a leash" (57 [38–9]).

There follows a train of anecdotes, paralleling the earlier list of instances of people's apparent indifference to death, of individuals who have borne extreme pain with equanimity. It extends from the incredible story, borrowed from Plutarch, of a Spartan boy who allowed a fox to eat out his entrails, to the more commonplace case of women who undergo all sorts of tortures for cosmetic purposes. Like the earlier list, this one culminates in a series of cases of endurance motivated by religion (or, in one case, of avarice making use of religion) (58–61 [39–41]).

Here Montaigne proceeds to stray once more from his ostensible theme. He begins by tacitly broadening the definition of the pain to be overcome to include psychological pain, of the kind occasioned by the death of one's children, and emphasizes that in the face of *this* sort of pain, he—despite his horror of pain in general—has maintained his equanimity. More generally, he reports observing "enough other common occasions for afflictions which I should scarcely feel if they happened to me," and having "disdained some, when they came to me, to which the world has given such an atrocious appearance that I wouldn't dare boast of my indifference to them to the people without blushing" (61 [42]). (Commentators have indeed taken Montaigne task for appearing to have been so untouched by the deaths of all but one of his children, at an early age, that he is unsure how many there were.)[24]

The transition from corporeal to psychological pain serves as a bridge to a point seemingly even more remote from Montaigne's original theme: the power of "opinion" to motivate actions that radically violate the interest of people's comfort and preservation. His examples include men who killed themselves rather than be deprived of the right to bear arms; others who

[24]See Zeitlin, *Essays of Montaigne*, 1:313–15, for an account of some readers' reactions, and a not entirely persuasive attempt to soften the essayist's meaning. Cf. III, ix, 926 [724], where Montaigne expresses his gratitude to Fortune for having "rid me of the need to multiply my riches to provide for a multitude of heirs," thereby facilitating his pursuit of an easy life.

forsook "the sweetness of a tranquil life" to seek out "humiliation, degradation, and contempt," or who "conceived a mortal hatred" for their most pleasurable and useful organs, "merely because they were too likable"; and a cardinal who lived in a particularly austere manner. Apparently even farther from the point are Montaigne's observation that some men "have derived profit and advancement from cuckoldry, the mere name of which frightens so many people," and his assertion that a lack of children is a no less fortunate situation than the abundance of them that most people consider desirable. But Montaigne has not forgotten his point; rather, the point has changed. The conclusion of this section of his argument has nothing directly to do with the contempt of pain, but concerns the fact that "our opinion gives value to things," and that people for some reason consider things more desirable merely because they are harder to attain. Hence "purchase gives value to the diamond, and difficulty to virtue, and pain to piety, and harshness to medicine" (61–2 [42–3]).

How does this conclusion bear on the ostensible theme of the chapter? Again, we have been presented with a critique of Stoicism masquerading behind a putative defense of that doctrine. Whatever may have been the intentions of the Stoic sages, the foregoing remarks and examples demonstrate that people have *not* consistently judged virtue, as they should, in terms of what is instrumental to their ultimate ease and pleasure, but—perversely—have commonly valued just those qualities likely to cost them the greatest pain and trouble, or even to end their lives. This is far from giving their souls an attitude "conducive to our repose and preservation" as Montaigne recommended.

Rather than endorsing the Stoic attitude toward pain, Montaigne's argument thus suggests that this doctrine has exacerbated our troubles by encouraging people needlessly to seek out difficulties so as to demonstrate their "virtue." In this respect the teaching of Stoicism regarding pain—which indirectly helped generate Christian asceticism—is as pernicious in its effects as we have seen its teaching about death to be. Only in one area does Montaigne appear sympathetic to Stoic (and Epicurean) doctrine: the notion that one should avoid grieving over the death of others, or fearing to be condemned by public opinion.[25] But Montaigne's distinction between the manner with which one should regard corporeal and psychological pains rests on a principle distinct from either Stoicism or Epicureanism, which he makes explicit in the last chapter of Book II, according to which only bodily pain—as distinguished from "the sufferings that affect us simply through the soul"—is truly "essential" (II, xxxvii, 738 [575]). (This remark appears to confirm the intimation in I, xiv, that the essential charac-

---

[25]See Epictetus, *Discourses*, III, xix (Oates, *Stoic and Epicurean Philosophers*, p. 372); Epicurus, "Letters to Unknown Persons," no. 43 (ibid., p. 49).

ter of human ills, unlike that of external, natural objects, is knowable.) Whereas both Stoics and Epicureans aspire to cultivate an attitude that will enable them to mitigate or overcome the pain of corporeal ills as well as those that arise purely from convention, Montaigne emphasizes *only* our capacity to overcome the latter, not the former, by giving our soul the right disposition—that is, the right opinions. Again, Montaigne's teaching in I, xiv, accords with his treatment of "indifferent" things in "Of Custom," and with his distinction between the noetic status of sense perception and opinion in the "Apology." Far from conflicting with the later chapters, the argument of I, xiv, sets the stage for them.

We need not tarry long over the third major part of Montaigne's argument in I, xiv, which ostensibly was to show that poverty, too, is merely a matter of opinion. It suffices to note that the essayist's putatively autobiographical treatment of this theme demonstrates, at most, that it is better to live off the gifts or loans of friends, without giving thought for the morrow, than to suffer the life of a fearful miser. But far from confirming that "ease and indigence depend on each man's opinion," the account suggests that the best situation of all is the last one Montaigne reports finding himself in—having plenty of money coming in, *and* spending it "to buy pleasure" as soon as it arrives. Though professing a readiness in spirit to emulate a rich man who gave away his possessions, he is conspicuously unready to do so in deed; and he praises "the fortune," but not the virtue or prudence, of "an old prelate" who ignorantly allows others to supervise his affairs and his purse (63–8 [43–6]).

There is no parallel in Montaigne's teaching to the Stoic and Epicurean doctrine that one should limit the desire for material goods and enjoyments so as to minimize one's dependence on fortune.[26] To the contrary, Montaigne remarks that it is hard to "set fixed limits" to avarice; what needs to be limited is not acquisitiveness but thrift (65 [45]). And he suggests that the dependence of most people's economic well-being on the vicissitudes of fortune reflects an exaggerated trust in "the liberality of heaven"—in place of a recognition that we must combat "fortune" with our own "arms" (63–4, 66 [43–5]).[27] The treatment of poverty in I, xiv, is thus consistent with the more explicit rejection of the Stoic attitude in Book III, where Montaigne professes to "hate poverty as much as I do pain" (of which he has indicated himself to be the greatest of haters) (III, ix, 931 [728]).[28]

The conclusion of I, xiv, is, on the surface, a paean to the Stoic position;

[26]See, e.g., Epicurus, "Principal Doctrines," XV (ibid., p. 36); idem, Fragments (Vatican Collection), XXV (ibid., p. 41); idem, "Letters to Unknown Persons," no. 37 (ibid., p. 48); Epictetus, *Discourses*, III, xxvi; Lucretius, *On the Nature of Things*, V, 1430–35.

[27]Recall the exhortation for philosophy to enable people to do this in the "Apology," p. 474 [365].

[28]Cf. also the rejection of the "sages'" teaching in this regard at III, x, 986–7 [771–2], apparently in particular reference to Seneca, Epistles, xvi.

but closer reading supports a contrary interpretation. Ostensibly in support of the Stoic view, Montaigne asserts that "things are not that painful or difficult in themselves; it is our weakness and cowardice that makes them so" (68 [46]). But if "weakness and cowardice," typified by Montaigne's fear of pain, are natural to human beings—as is suggested by his later remark that his self-portrait is intended to represent the entire "human condition" (III, ii, 782 [611])—it may be pointless to lament this fact. The rhetorical question that Montaigne poses a few lines later—"why, out of so many arguments which in various ways persuade men to despise death and endure pain, do we *not* find one that will do for us?"—in any case suggests the incapacity of Stoicism to overcome human weakness (68 [47]).

The last lines of the chapter cite three "unanswerable replies" of philosophy to anyone who complains of "the sharpness of pain and the weakness of men." The thrust of each reply is that anyone who finds life unbearable can always commit suicide (68 [47]). But Montaigne's more authentic opinion of these arguments is indicated not only by the remark already quoted from II, iii, where he argues *against* turning to suicide as a respite from ills, but also by the passage in the "Apology" where he denounces this "last remedy" as a confession of philosophic "impotence" (II, xii, 476 [366]). If philosophy is to have any greater value than sheer ignorance, as he argues there, it must do better than this.

We have seen that I, xiv, contrary to its "Stoical" appearance, embodies a critique of both Stoicism and Epicureanism as means of ameliorating the three sources of human fear and suffering that Montaigne cited. In addition, however, the chapter lays the foundation on which Montaigne will elsewhere proceed to reconstruct morality in a way more genuinely conducive to human well-being. The two key elements of that foundation are, first, the assertion that the true value of virtue lies in its capacity to mitigate pain and suffering; and, second, the charge that most people—including "the sages"—have erroneously deviated from that criterion in their moral judgments, valuing particular qualities merely on account of their rarity or difficulty. Montaigne's assertion that the soul is so malleable that it can and should be reshaped into a form conducive to our "repose and preservation" demonstrates that he does after all agree with the Stoic maxim in the chapter title—but in a sense different from the original. For the elaboration of this point we must turn to some later chapters of the *Essays*.

Virtue, Valor, and Beauty

The hedonistic approach to judging the purpose and the content of virtue which underlies the argument of I, xiv, is restated by Montaigne with remarkable explicitness in several later chapters of Book I, including the quasi-Stoical ones. At the outset of I, xx ("That to Philosophize Is to Learn How to Die"), he maintains that "all the opinions in the world agree . . . that pleasure is our goal, although they choose diverse means to it," and that "in virtue itself the ultimate object of our aim is voluptuousness." Hence he laments that "we should have given virtue the name of pleasure, a name more favorable, sweet, and natural; not that of vigor, as we have named it." And he criticizes "those who go on teaching us that the quest of [virtue] is rugged and laborious, [although] the enjoyment of it is agreeable," for making virtue itself appear "always disagreeable" (80 [56]). This theme is resumed in "Of the Education of Children," where Montaigne rejects the portrayal of philosophy as "inaccessible to children, with a surly, frowning, and terrifying face," since "she preaches nothing but merrymaking and a good time." Contrary to the claims of the schoolmen, virtue "is not . . . set on the top of a steep, rugged, inaccessible mountain"; "he who knows the way can get there by shady, grassy, sweetly flowering roads, pleasantly, by an easy, smooth slope." Hence children should be taught "this new lesson, that the value and height of true virtue lies in the ease, utility, and pleasure of its practice, which is so far from being difficult that children can master it as well as men, the simple as well as the subtle" (I, xxvi, 160–61 [118–20]).

Despite the hedonistic character of these remarks, they are stated in such general terms that it remains unclear whether Montaigne is proposing a substantive reinterpretation of virtue, or merely a new rhetorical representation of it.[29] That his "new lesson" is indeed a substantive one is made clear, however, in the following passage from the quasi-Stoical chapter "Of Solitude" (I, xxxix), all of which dates from the first edition:

> to anticipate the accidents of fortune; to deprive ourselves of the commodities that are in our hands, as many have done through piety and some philosophers through reason; to wait on ourselves; to sleep on the hard ground; to put out our eyes; to throw our riches into the river; to seek pain, some in order to win bliss in another life by torment in this, others to make themselves safe from a new fall by settling on the lowest step—these are the acts of an excessive virtue. (237 [179])

It will be noted that several of the steps that Montaigne rejects here—needlessly sleeping on hard ground, blinding oneself, casting away one's riches—correspond to those he cited in I, xiv, as actions that some might think necessary for the sake of toughening themselves against pain, or as instances of the "immoderate" power of opinion to induce people to pursue

---

[29]Strowski maintains that the original opening of I, xx, was consistent with Stoicism, but that the post-1588 additions I have quoted transform its sense in the direction of Epicureanism (*Pascal et son temps*, pp. 242–3). Cf. Plato, *Republic*, 363e–364a.

hardship (56, 62 [38, 43]). The ambiguity in the earlier chapter regarding Montaigne's evaluation of such conduct is erased here. His labeling such actions as "excessive virtue"—which he elsewhere identifies with vice (I, xv, 68 [47]; I, xxx, 195 [146])—confirms Montaigne's consistent rejection of both Stoic and Christian morality. And since he attributes the same unreasonable quest for difficulty to Epicurus (II, ii, 329 [251]; II, xi, 401 [307]), his argument amounts to a rejection of Epicureanism as well.

But if the identification of virtue with the endurance of pain and hardship is erroneous, how did it arise and became widely accepted in the first place? The most important passage in the *Essays* bearing on this question occurs in chapter vii of Book II, "Of Honorary Awards" (or "Of the Rewards of Honor"), which explicitly discusses how to replace one "order" of evaluation with another (363 [277]).[30] In the immediate sequel to that discussion Montaigne considers the relation between valor and other forms of virtue. After alluding to Plutarch's frequent discussions of that theme, he adds:

> It is worth considering that our nation gives valor [*vaillance*] the highest rank among the virtues, as its name shows, which comes from value [*valeur*]; and that, according to our usage, when we say "a very valuable man," or "a worthy man," in the style of our court and our nobility, we are saying nothing else than "a valiant man," as in the Roman fashion. For the general term "virtue" among them derives etymologically from "strength." The proper, the only, the essential form of nobility in France is the military vocation. (363 [277])[31]

I interrupt the quotation to point out that earlier in this chapter, Montaigne had *denigrated* the military virtue that the French—following the Romans—identify as the essence of virtue and nobility, by noting that despite the putative "rarity" of virtue, "there is no other virtue that spreads so easily as military valor," and by explicitly distinguishing it from true, "philosophical" valor (362 [276]). In the sequel to the passage quoted above Montaigne speculates on the original reason for the identification of virtue with military courage:

> It is probable that the first virtue that manifested itself among men and gave some the advantage over others was this one, by which the strongest and most

---

[30]Although the "order" in question is ostensibly the Order of Saint-Michel, a French order of nobility, Montaigne's reference to the system that is to be replaced by a "new order" is indefinite ("this one") and follows a discussion of the difference between the vulgar kind of courage that the Order of Saint Michel rewarded and true, philosophical courage (II, vii, 362 [276]). Here, as elsewhere, one must bear in mind the essayist's warning about the hidden implications of his discussions (I, xl, 245 [185]). Compare Machiavelli's discussion of the establishment of "new modes and orders" (e.g., *The Prince*, ch. 6; *Discourses*, I, proem and xviii).

[31]Cf. Plutarch's comment on the early Romans' equation of virtue with valor in his "Life of Coriolanus," *Lives*, tr. John Dryden, rev. Arthur Hugh Clough (New York: Modern Library, n.d.), p. 263.

courageous made themselves masters of the weaker and acquired particular rank and reputation, whence it has retained this linguistic honor and dignity; or else that these nations, being very warlike, gave the prize and the worthiest title to the one virtue which was most familiar to them. (363–4 [277])

Nowhere in the *Essays,* so far as I know, does Montaigne favor one of these explanations of the etymology of "virtue" over the other. Both, in fact, receive support elsewhere. But I suggest it is less important to choose between the two explanations than to consider what the two, taken together, teach about the equation of virtue with valor. In the first place, the above passage suggests that valor was originally valued for its political utility, as a source of "advantage" over other people, rather than as something intrinsically good (this point is explicit in the first explanation and it is implicit in the second: presumably the most warlike nations recognized courage as a virtue because of its conduciveness to their military success). Second, it links the understanding of virtue as valor with injustice—that is, with the oppression by the strong of the weak, for whom Montaigne elsewhere professes his compassion (III, xiii, 1079 [844]). And third, it suggests that the identification of virtue with valor reflects the attitudes of primitive human beings, whose minds were insufficiently developed and characters insufficiently civilized to perceive the possibility of a higher sort of excellence (such as the "philosophical" courage to which Montaigne alluded). The last point is confirmed by the fact that valor is the virtue most highly prized by the cannibals, who believe that the victor in war demonstrates his "master[y] in valor and virtue" (I, xxxi, 209 [156]). However Montaigne may have seemed in I, xxxi, to admire the cannibals' fortitude and simplicity, he makes clear the inadequacy of their identification of virtue with valor in the sequel to the passage quoted from II, vii, which constitutes the conclusion of the chapter, where he compares that conception of manly virtue to the equation of womanly virtue with chastity, an equation that disregards the importance of other feminine qualities and that seems to give women "free rein for every other fault" (II, vii, 364 [278]).

At this point two seeming difficulties must be faced. In the first place, it may appear illegitimate to relate Montaigne's discussion of the etymology of virtue in II, vii, to the treatment of Stoical virtue in I, xiv, since he expressly distinguishes in II, vii, between military and philosophical courage. Since the Stoics and Epicureans were philosophers, one might expect their virtue to be of the "philosophical," not the vulgar, kind. But this is not Montaigne's view. The Stoic disposition to seek out "trouble" was presented in I, xiv, as a manifestation of a general human tendency to identify virtue with rarity. At the same time the examples Montaigne provided there of unphilosophical individuals, and even whole nations, who displayed a courage or endurance rivaling the Stoics' demonstrated that such "virtue" is really a matter of custom. In II, vii, Montaigne makes these same points about military virtue as distinguished from philosophical courage: its essence is "rarity," and custom can easily make it "common," thereby reducing its impressiveness (362 [276]). Thus the military courage that is depreciated in II, vii, is integrally related to, if not identical with, the Stoical courage described in I, xiv: both are forms of endurance that can be justified only by demonstrating their conduciveness to our "repose and preservation." But that justification, as we have seen, is called into question by Montaigne.

A further seeming difficulty is that Montaigne's suggestion in II, vii, that valor was prized by the first human beings as a source of advantage or utility would seem to be belied by his assertion in I, xxxi, that the cannibals seek no other gain in their wars but glory and the opportunity to demonstrate their superiority, since—given their limited desires—"they have no use for the goods of the vanquished," or any desire to increase their territory (209 [156]). A response to this objection is suggested, however, by the chapter "Of Glory," wherein Montaigne asserts that "all lawgivers" have encouraged their peoples to pursue glory—despite the emptiness of this good, in Montaigne's view—in order "to keep the people in their duty" (II, xvi, 613 [477]). Thus, even though the cannibals are the most primitive people described by Montaigne, or the closest approximation to the "natural" human condition, they do not represent the human mind in its most naive, or unformed, state. Though a warlike disposition may be natural to human beings, it would seem that the cannibals' tendency to *honor* military courage as the essence of virtue, and to pursue glory through it, reflects the work of some lawgiver, who inculcated in them a morality that would equip them to preserve, if not to expand, their dominions—and to keep from serving as some other tribe's repast.

If the foregoing interpretation is correct, then the criterion that "all lawgivers" followed in formulating the morality of their societies is identical with that which guides Montaigne's judgment: that of utility. But this is not the criterion that people who are customarily judged, or judge themselves, to be virtuous typically apply in choosing how to act. Rather, virtue "aspires . . . to a reward that is purely her own, and more glorious than useful" (II, vii, 361 [276]). To a truly virtuous human being, virtue is its own reward (II, i, 320 [243]; although some people—not including Montaigne—might hope for "honor and glory" as a fitting, though supplemental, recompense (II, xvi, 607 [472]), no one would regard an action motivated purely by gain as one of genuine virtue. The specific motivation of the virtuous individual, it appears, is the desire to demonstrate one's intrinsic superiority to one's fellows. It is in seeming praise of such virtue, as exemplified by the cannibals' warfare, that Montaigne asserts that the "worth and value of a man is in his heart and will." Yet even if we assume the truth of that premise, the validity of the cannibals' inference from it—that victory in open combat is the criterion of virtue—is belied by Montaigne in the immediate sequel. He asserts that "valor is the strength, not of legs and arms, but of heart and soul"; but do not the former play at least as great a role as the latter in physical combat? And he goes on to emphasize that "the most valiant are sometimes the most unfortunate" (I, xxxi, 210 [157]): there is no necessary link between valor and victory.

With this discussion in mind, let us turn to a pair of chapters (I, v–vi) wherein the issue of the relation between virtue and political (as distinguished from personal) utility is joined even more directly. In the first of these chapters, ostensibly concerned with "Whether the Head of a Besieged Place Should Go Out to Parley," Montaigne initially seems to endorse the scruples of "the old men of the [Roman] Senate," who—"remembering the mores of their fathers"—condemned the ruse successfully practiced by a Roman general as "hostile to their old way, which was, they said, to fight in virtue, not in trickery." Of the old Romans' "scrupulousness," Montaigne remarks, in a manner reminiscent of his eulogy of the cannibals:

> These were truly Roman ways, not those of Greek subtlety and Punic cunning, according to which it was less glorious to conquer by force than by fraud. Deceit may serve for the moment; but only that man considers himself overcome who knows he was downed neither by trick nor by luck but by valor, man to man, in a fair and just war. (I, v, 27 [16])

This claim—along with Montaigne's expression of agreement with the Stoic philosopher Chrysippus' condemnation of cheating and his professed admiration for the great Alexander's "generous" refusal to "steal" a victory—must be read in the light of a fact revealed in the next chapter: "*in the age of the justest captains* and the most perfect Roman military order," the Romans freely took advantage of their enemies' "stupidity" to seize a town, during a parley, by surprise (I, vi, 30 [18]). This fact belies the senators' claim that their ancestors were too scrupulous to stoop to trickery. Those senators exemplify the disposition of old age to "praise the past and blame the present" (II, xiii, 589 [458]), evidently forgetting what the past was really like; like other conservatives, they try to make the beginnings of their regime look better than they were.[32] In opposition to their posture—and to

[32]Cf. Machiavelli, *Discorsi*, II, proem, p. 271. That all regimes originate in acts of injustice and that subsequent rulers endeavor to obscure the memory of them but ultimately must imitate those injustices to maintain their rule is a central theme of Machiavelli's: see, e.g., *Discourses*, I, ix, xxvi; III, i; *The Prince*, ch. 7, pp. 29–30. Montaigne alludes to the unjust origins of existing regimes in a chapter titled "Of Evil Means Employed to a Good End": overpopulated nations send their surplus inhabitants "to accommodate themselves elsewhere at the expense of others"; "there are hardly two or three corners of the world that have not felt the effect of such a movement" (II, xxiii, 663 [517]). Cf. *Discourses*, II, viii; Locke, *Second Treatise*, ch. 8, secs. 102–3, with Richard Cox, *Locke on War and Peace* (Oxford, 1960), pp. 42–4, 99–103.

his own seeming endorsement of it in the preceding chapter—Montaigne goes on to justify the practice of deceit, remarking that it is no less legitimate to benefit from the stupidity of one's enemies than from their cowardice. While professing to be "astonished at the range" that Xenophon gives to these "privileges" of warfare, considering his "marvelous weight as a great captain and a philosopher among the first disciples of Socrates," he does not dissent from the Greek's counsel beyond remarking that he does "not agree to the extent of his dispensation in all things and throughout" (I, vi, 30–31 [18]). He does not inform us of any points on which he disagrees with Xenophon. In fact, we find confirmation of his agreement in a remark in the preceding chapter which distinguished between those people, including "barbarians," who scorn to use deceit and "us, who, less superstitious, hold that the man who has the profit of war has the honor of it, and who say, after Lysander, that where the lion's skin will not suffice we must sew on a bit of the fox's" (I, v, 28 [17]). In view of the manner in which the argument of I, vi, undermines the case against trickery, there is no reason to assume that the use of the first person in this passage is ironic. Nor should we suppose that Montaigne does not mean it when he calls the following remark of Virgil a "fine saying":[33] "Courage or ruse—against an enemy,

[33]Contrary to the opinion of such interpreters as Thomas M. Greene and Frieda S. Brown, who consider both this judgment and the remark previously quoted from I, v, to be ironic. (Greene, "Dangerous Parleys—*Essais* I:5 and 6," in Defaux, ed., *Montaigne: Essays in Reading*, p. 8; Brown, "'Si le chef d'vne place assiegée doit sortir povr parlementer' and 'L'hevre des parlemens dangerevse': Montaigne's Political Morality and Its Expression in the Early Essays," in La Charité, ed., *O Un Amy!* pp. 75–6.) Greene does note that the Virgilian quotation blurs the claim of "the integrity of antiquity" by comparison with the supposed moral degeneracy of Montaigne's time (p. 6). But both he and Brown disregard the significance of Montaigne's account of the Romans' practice in I, vi, as well as his comments on Xenophon. Brown judges that because Montaigne describes Chrysippus, who condemned trickery, as a "philosopher" (I, vi, 31 [19]) and ends the chapter without contradicting Chrysippus' judgment, his profession of agreement with that Stoic thinker (who was criticized in "Of Custom") must be sincere (" 'Si le chef . . . ,'" p. 84). She does not explain why Montaigne would be more likely to respect the opinion of Chrysippus than that of Xenophon, given the explicit praise he gives to the latter but not the former. See also III, ix, 948 [741], where Montaigne refers to Xenophon as "a very good captain and still better philosopher."
   Three other passages from the *Essays* further illustrate the point I have drawn from I, v–vi. At III, i, 767 [599], Montaigne describes Tiberius, who ostensibly relinquished the opportunity to defeat an enemy by trickery, thereby giving up "the useful for the honorable," as "an impostor." At II, xxvii, 676 [527], we learn how the old French nobility, disdaining "the *reputation* of good fencers as injurious," since fencing is "a trade of subtlety, derogating from true and native virtue," "*learned it furtively.*" By contrast, Montaigne—in a passage dating from the first edition—openly recommends that we not despise "any bodily suppleness, nor any move with hand weapons . . . if it serves to protect us" (I, xii, 46 [30]).
   The readiness of Brown and other commentators to praise the "pure" political morality of honesty and honorableness that Montaigne purports to espouse in I, v–vi, constitutes another manifestation of the apolitical or unworldly character of much recent criticism of the *Essays*. It is unlikely that these scholars, if consulted by Allied commanders during World War II, would have condemned the use of trickery (for instance, the elaborate deception that was employed to disguise the intended location of the D-day landings) to defeat Hitler, on the ground that such practices are immoral. Nor would most Americans be likely to endorse such a rule of warfare even in combating foes less venal than the Nazis.

who cares?" (I, v, 27 [16]). (Both passages exemplify the double-edged, or reverse, irony described in Chapter One.)

A consideration of the Machiavellian implications of this defense of trickery—which are suggested by the reference to emulating the lion and the fox[34]—must be postponed to Chapter Twelve. Its implications for my present theme, however, are as follows. We have seen that Montaigne believes valor originally to have been valued for its utility, but that legislators—with utility as their real motive—have encouraged people to pursue and honor valor (along with honesty) as if it were something good in itself. The argument of the two chapters in Book I that we have just considered, however, challenges the notion that considerations of political utility justify the valuation people have been taught to place on valor. Combining the teaching of these chapters with that of "Of Cannibals" and "Of Honorary Awards" suggests that although valor may have been the most obvious source of "advantage" to primitive people, the development that the human mind has undergone now provides people with superior means of procuring advantages—here represented by the practice of trickery. It is hardly a novel teaching, of course, that people who are willing to stoop to dishonesty can gain advantages over opponents bound by a stricter code of honor. It can also be argued that although war, by its nature, excuses us from following such conventional moral rules as that which forbids dishonesty, it would be most dangerous to extend license for trickery to ordinary civil life. The thrust of Montaigne's argument, however, emphasizes the overall utility of perfidy, rather than limiting its practice to war; in a later chapter (III, i), he will suggest that such violations of conventional morality are essential to political success. What is distinctive about his treatment of trickery is not that he recognizes its utility but that the core of his argument stresses that utility, rather than its immorality. To be sure, that core is covered over, here as elsewhere in the *Essays,* with a pretense of moralism—a pretense sufficient to convince Zeitlin that I, v, expresses the author's "antipathy to treachery and double-dealing," even though that antipathy is not developed "with the same warmth and animation as in other places," and the argument is qualified in the following chapter.[35] But a reader who traces Montaigne's reasoning, rather than being seduced by his rhetoric, will recognize that the reasoning contradicts and undermines the premises of the rhetoric.

To avoid shocking admirers of Montaigne's moral character more than is necessary, let me reassure them that I do not think that the point of these chapters is that the world currently suffers from an insufficiency of treach-

[34]See *The Prince,* ch. 18, p. 69; also Machiavelli's account of the policy of Castruccio Castracani, who "if he was able to win by fraud . . . never attempted to win by force, because he said that the victory, not the method of gaining it, brought glory to the victor" ("Life of Castruccio Castracani," in Allan H. Gilbert, tr., *"The Prince" and Other Works* (New York, 1964), p. 205, par. 40).

[35]Zeitlin, *Essays of Montaigne,* 1:300.

ery and double-dealing. There is no reason to doubt the sincerity of Montaigne's denunciation of such vices, elsewhere in the *Essays,* as practiced by prominent political and religious figures in his time. The lesson of these chapters amounts rather to this: given the necessity of a choice between using force and fraud, there is no ground to regard the former as morally superior to the latter. Underlying the preference for the former is an irrational, atavistic belief that the true test of our worth is our "guts," a belief perpetuated and encouraged by lawgivers who mistakenly thought such a teaching necessary for the sake of encouraging military success and domestic morality.[36] In opposition to that belief, Montaigne elsewhere asserts that his "essence" consists in his thoughts rather than his actions, which "would tell more about fortune than about me" (II, vi, 359 [274]). The ultimate criterion of human excellence, he implies, is the profundity of one's thought rather than the fearlessness of one's actions.

Implicit in Montaigne's defense of political trickery is the suggestion that to replace the morality of valor with an alternative moral code honoring intelligence over toughness would serve to benefit humanity as a whole, rather than merely providing would-be conquerors with an additional means of victory. That implication may be brought out by a comparison of Montaigne's seeming praise of Alexander in I, vi, for "generously" refusing to win by subterfuge with his portrayal of Alexander in some other chapters. Despite purporting to rank Alexander among "the most excellent men," Montaigne emphasizes his cruelty, exemplified by "the ruin of Thebes, the murder of Menander and of Hephaestion's doctor, of so many Persian prisoners at one stroke, of a troop of Indian soldiers not without prejudice to his word, and of the Cosseians even to their little children" (II, xxxvi, 733 [571]). Although Montaigne attests in the same passage to "the kindness of [Alexander's] nature" and elsewhere terms him "very gracious to the vanquished," the context of the latter remark, as I shall observe in a later chapter, undermines these claims. Hence it is not surprising that Montaigne elsewhere denounces Alexander's "violent and indiscriminate injustice" (II, i, 320 [243]), and—near the end of the book—mocks the exaggerated self-estimation that may have been responsible for Alexander's so distancing himself from concern with mere mortals (III, xiii, 1096 [856–7]). Had Alexander not valued toughness and valor as a measure of transcendent excellence, humanity might have been better off. The morality of valor, however advantageous to the Greeks who followed the Macedonian conqueror, can hardly be said to be adequate from the cosmopolitan perspective to which Montaigne adheres (III, ix, 950 [743]).

[36]See Plato, *Laws,* 824a, for a (provisional) statement of this attitude. But cf. Plato, *Republic,* 430c, for a qualification; *Laches,* 195ff., and *Republic* 442c for Socrates' apparent equation of true courage with knowledge; and, on Aristotle's partial sympathy with that view, Aristide Tessitore, "Aristotle's Political Presentation of Socrates in the *Nicomachean Ethics,*" *Interpretation* 16 (1988): 8–10.

The defense of trickery in I, v–vi, thus confirms Montaigne's intention of uprooting the morality of valor and toughness, to replace it with one more genuinely conducive to human contentment. But although Montaigne has located the origin of the old morality in the utilitarian judgment of law-givers and their establishment of public honors to encourage its support, this analysis does not suffice to explain the appeal of the morality of valor to civilized people—which poses an obstacle to any project of moral recon-struction. The root of that appeal is suggested by the following passage from the chapter "Of Presumption," wherein Montaigne offers a different explanation of the origin of hierarchical distinctions among human beings from the one asserted in II, vii: "The first distinction that existed among men, and the first consideration that gave some men preeminence over others, was probably the advantage of beauty" (II, xvii, 623 [485]). On its face this remark contradicts the claim in II, vii, that strength, not beauty, was "the first virtue that manifested itself among men and gave some the advantage over others." But the quotation from Lucretius with which Montaigne supports the remark in "Of Presumption" harmonizes the two assertions by stating that both beauty *and* strength, along with intellect, were valued and rewarded by the first societies (ibid.).

The connection between beauty and virtue is in turn made explicit in the penultimate chapter of the *Essays,* "Of Physiognomy." There Montaigne describes beauty as a most "powerful and advantageous quality," adding that "we have no quality that surpasses it in credit. It holds the first place in human dealings; it presents itself at the forefront, seduces and prepossesses our judgment with great authority and a wondrous impression." He goes on to offer a linguistic observation that parallels the etymological analysis of virtue in II, vii: "One and the same word in Greek embraces the beautiful and the good.[37] And the Holy Ghost often calls good those whom he means to call beautiful" (III, xii, 1035 [810]). Although Montaigne does not say so

[37]Editors have generally taken this word to be the compound *kaloskagathos* (literally, "noble [or beautiful] and good"). In support of that interpretation the Pléiade editors cite the discussion in Xenophon's *Oeconomicus,* as translated by La Boétie and published by Mon-taigne (Montaigne, *Oeuvres,* p. 1667, n. 8 to p. 1035; see *La Mesnagerie de Xenophon,* tr. La Boétie, in Paul Bonnefon, ed., *Oeuvres complètes de Estienne de La Boétie* [Paris, 1892], pp. 93–4). I suspect, however, that the word Montaigne has in mind is simply *kalos* (fine, noble, beautiful, hence in a general sense "good"). I base this interpretation on the following sentence of Montaigne's text cited above, referring to the Holy Ghost's "often call[ing] good those whom he means to call beautiful [*beaux*]." The word *kaloskagathos* could hardly give rise to this confusion, since it distinctly connotes both nobility or beauty *and* goodness. Moreover, there are numerous instances in the New Testament where *kalos* is evidently used in the sense of goodness rather than beauty or nobility: see George V. Wigram and Ralph D. Winter, *The Word Study Concordance* (Pasadena, Calif., 1972), pp. 2564–5. (This concor-dance does not list any instances of *kaloskagathos* in the Bible.) That the ambiguity of *kalos* is what Montaigne has in mind is further suggested by his subsequent reference to Aristotle's attribution of the right of command to the *beaux,* which plays on that ambiguity. Socrates plays on the same ambiguity in the passage from the *Oeconomicus* cited above: see the note by Carnes Lord in Leo Strauss, *Xenophon's Socratic Discourse* (Ithaca, N.Y., 1970), p. 28n.

explicitly, a similar ambiguity persists in the French word *beau*, which can connote nobility or fineness as well as physical attractiveness; the word is frequently used by Montaigne, as I shall shortly observe, in the former senses.

As in II, vii, Montaigne's analysis of classical linguistic usage in "Of Physiognomy" points (if only tacitly in this case) to the influence that the classical understanding of human excellence continues to exercise on the thought of modern Europeans. Once again, he proceeds to question whether that influence is salutary. On the one hand, he lists numerous ancient figures, including philosophers, who attached great importance to beauty and apparently regarded it as a reliable sign of human excellence: he cites Aristotle in particular as holding "that to the beautiful belongs the right to command," and that men of godlike beauty are entitled to veneration. This passage culminates in the puzzling, if not outlandish, assertion that "most philosophers, and the greatest, paid for their schooling, and acquired wisdom, by the mediation and favor of their beauty." On the other hand, while admitting the advantage that beauty gives to its possessor, because of the way it influences others' judgment, he challenges the belief that it constitutes a trustworthy indicator of merit. He cites an ancient woman who "corrupted her judges" by revealing "her dazzling beauty" to them. More important, he emphasizes the "injustice" that nature did to Socrates by concealing the beauty of his soul behind a remarkably ugly face and body (III, xii, 1034–5 [809]).

At first glance it might seem that there is no real difference between Montaigne and the classical political philosophers on this point. It is, after all, from Plato himself that we learn of the disharmony between Socrates' soul and his physiognomy. And the passage that Montaigne cites from Aristotle's *Politics* clearly indicates that it is to the beauty or excellence of the soul, rather than the body, that veneration and authority are due. Aristotle explicitly notes in the same context the frequency with which people's bodily appearance and capacity belie the quality of their soul, terming this a failure of nature to realize her "intention."[38]

But the passage we have been examining points to a more fundamental issue between Montaigne and his classical predecessors: the question how far the "beauty" of the soul itself is a proper criterion for judging human character and conduct. Neither Plato nor Aristotle, it should be understood, simply equates the good with the beautiful. It is evident that many things that seem beautiful may prove, upon reflection and analysis, to be harmful. Indeed, judgments of beauty are ordinarily less reliable than judgments of utility, since (as Stanley Rosen points out in summarizing the classical understanding) they are "more closely conditioned by the body."[39]

---

[38]*Politics*, 1254b25–1255a1.
[39]Rosen, *Nihilism: A Philosophical Essay* (New Haven, 1969), p. 168.

Nonetheless, the everyday awareness of beauty—which originates in the perception of sensibly appealing objects but may ascend to the appreciation of incorporeal excellence—constitutes, in the classical view, a critical element in our understanding of the good, since this awareness demonstrates the inadequacy of the otherwise tempting identification of the good with the useful. Just as the perception of beauty in other people or objects can compel disinterested admiration, acts of nobility or justice induce our admiration, even though neither we nor those who perform them may derive any advantage from them. The goodness of many of the actions and attributes that characterize the morally virtuous human being cannot, in other words, be entirely explained in utilitarian terms. Yet the universal, disinterested admiration of moral virtue constitutes powerful evidence that such actions and attributes are in fact good. However inaccurate the popular or vulgar perception of virtue may be, the admiration for virtue points toward the true excellence of the philosopher; it is in the philosopher's goal, wisdom, or the understanding of nature that the ultimate unity of the good, the true, the beautiful, *and* the useful may be recognized.[40] The excellence of the philosopher's life, in turn, serves as a justification for the praise of virtue (albeit vulgar virtue) by the political community, and its consequent refusal explicitly to identify the good with the useful.[41]

In contrast to the classical teaching, Montaigne's argument in "Of Physiognomy" overtly challenges the claim that there is an essential harmony between beauty and genuine goodness.[42] Despite his initial assertion that "there is nothing more likely than the conformity and relation of the body to the spirit" (1035 [809]), all his evidence contradicts that claim. As we have seen, his emphasis is on the manner in which the perception of beauty *distorts* our judgment. Particularly important is his observation that beauty powerfully "seduces and prepossesses [*preoccupe*] our judgment," in view of his remarks elsewhere that all such nonrational predispositions "are a kind of disease that we must combat," and (in the chapter just preceding "Of Physiognomy") that he himself refuses to let his "judgment be throttled much by preconception [*preoccupation*]" based on a person's physical appearance (II, xxxvii, 743 [580]; III, xi, 1010 [790]). Also significant is his

---

[40]Cf. Socrates' account of the "lessons" he learned from Diotima: Plato, *Symposium*, 201ff.; also, *Hippias Major*, 297b; Rosen, *Nihilism*, p. 168; Strauss, *Natural Right and History*, pp. 128ff.

[41]Cf. Aristotle, *Politics*, VII. 1–3, where the philosopher's way of life serves as the basis for refuting the opinion upon which existing cities act (as distinguished from the moral opinions they profess), according to which virtue is valuable only as a means, not an end. The superiority of the philosopher's life to that of the tyrant similarly underlies Socrates' refutation of the praise of injustice in Book IX of Plato's *Republic*. See also Rosen, *Nihilism*, pp. 167–73; Strauss, *Thoughts on Machiavelli*, pp. 295–6.

[42]My interpretation is opposed to that set forth by Abraham C. Keller in his essay "The Good and the Beautiful in Montaigne," in Frieda S. Brown, ed., *Renaissance Studies in Honor of Isidore Silver* (Kentucky Romance Quarterly 21 [1974], suppl. no. 2), pp. 225–37.

assertion that "the Holy Ghost often calls good those whom he means to call beautiful," which implies that the Christian religion embodies a confusion between goodness and (spiritual) "beauty" which ultimately derives from Greek thought and language. Earlier in "Of Physiognomy," Montaigne expressly warned *against* "call[ing] . . . good what is only beautiful" (1016 [795]).

The passages I have examined from "Of Physiognomy" suggest that the classical linkage of goodness and beauty engendered a misapprehension regarding the nature of human excellence. But we have not yet discovered how this charge is related to the substantive indictment of the classical understanding of virtue on hedonistic and utilitarian grounds which Montaigne set forth in the chapters of Books I and II previously examined. The starting point for comprehending that relation is "Of Cruelty" (II, xi), which contains Montaigne's fullest analysis of the classical understanding of moral virtue at its peak. The key to understanding "Of Cruelty" is a grasp of the relation between its contents and its initially puzzling title.

CHAPTER EIGHT

From God to Beast: Montaigne's
Transvaluation of Values

"Of Cruelty"

Montaigne begins "Of Cruelty" by distinguishing "virtue" strictly understood from "the inclinations towards goodness that are born in us," calling
the former "finer" (*plus beau*) than the latter. Even though souls that are
"self-regulated and well born follow the same path, and show the same
countenance in their actions, as virtuous ones," he asserts, virtue nonetheless "means something greater and more active than letting oneself, by a
happy disposition, be led gently and peacefully in the footsteps of reason. . . . For it seems that the name of virtue presupposes difficulty and
contrast, and that it cannot be exercised without opposition." Indeed, since
the virtuous human being must overcome natural inclinations to the contrary, his excellence, Montaigne implies, in a way surpasses God's.[1] Among
those who have striven to practice such virtue are many "Stoic and Epicurean philosophers," who "seek pain, need, and contempt in order to
combat them and to keep their soul in trim." (Montaigne goes out of his
way to defend the Epicureans against the charge that their teaching was less
demanding than that of the Stoics, and to indicate that a similar firmness
characterized other ancient sects as well—II, xi, 400–401 [306–7]).
   Having set forth this account of virtue, Montaigne immediately discovers
difficulties in it. In the first place, although he regards the soul of Socrates as
"the most perfect that has come to my knowledge," by the criterion of

---

[1]This point is made more explicitly at II, xxix, 683 [532–3]; it follows Seneca, *Of Providence*, VI. Cf. the citation of Seneca at II, xii, 469 [361]. Cf., on Machiavelli's distinction
between virtue (somewhat differently understood) and goodness, Thomas Pangle, *The Spirit of
Modern Republicanism* (Chicago, 1988), pp. 62–3; Strauss, *Thoughts on Machiavelli*, p. 257.

virtue thus understood it would deserve little commendation, since it is impossible to conceive any "vicious lust" even being present to oppose Socrates' all-powerful reason (402 [308]). There are other difficulties as well:

> If virtue can shine only by clashing with opposing appetites, shall we say then that it cannot do without the assistance of vice, and that it owes to vice its credit and honor? What would become also of that brave and generous Epicurean voluptuousness, which undertakes to bring up virtue softly in her bosom and make it frolic, giving it as its playthings shame, fevers, poverty, death, and tortures? If I presuppose that perfect virtue makes itself known in combating pain and bearing it patiently . . . if I give it unpleasantness and difficulty as its object: what will become of the virtue that has climbed so high that it not only despises pain but rejoices in it and feels tickled by the pangs of a bad colic, the kind of virtue established by the Epicureans, of which many of them by their actions have left us most certain proofs? As have many others, who I find have surpassed in practice the very rules of their discipline. (402–3 [308])

The problem Montaigne has uncovered in the understanding of virtue as involving self-struggle, he implies, points to a difficulty or contradiction inherent in Epicurean doctrine (and, it would appear, even more manifestly in Stoicism). He has previously identified this difficulty in the prescription of "physicians" whose remedy for our spiritual "diseases" is "torment, misery, and pain" (I, xxx, 198 [148]). In order to excel, people are taught to seek out and endure unpleasantness; but if they succeed so well that pain itself becomes pleasurable, wherein lies their excellence?[2] To illustrate this problem in "Of Cruelty," Montaigne cites Cato the Younger, whom he elsewhere allows to "suffice for every example of virtue" (II, xiii, 594 [462]):

> When I see him dying and tearing out his entrails, I cannot be content to believe simply that he then had his soul totally free from disturbance and fright; I cannot believe that he merely maintained himself in the attitude that the rules of the Stoic sect ordained for him, sedate, without emotion, and impassible; there was, it seems to me, in that man's virtue too much lustiness and verdancy to stop there. I believe without a doubt that he felt pleasure and voluptuousness in so noble an action, and that he enjoyed himself more in it than in any other action of his life. . . . I seem to read in that action I know not what rejoicing of his soul, and an emotion of extraordinary pleasure and manly voluptuousness, when it considered the nobility and sublimity of its enterprise. (403 [308–9])

[2]Cf. the story Montaigne recounts about Diogenes at III, x, 992 [776], from which he infers that "to measure the constancy [a person has displayed] we must necessarily know the suffering [the person has endured]."

In the light of Socrates' example as well as that of Cato, Montaigne proceeds to revise his account of virtue. He asserts that it is doubtless

> finer [*plus beau*] to prevent the birth of temptations by a lofty and divine resolution, and to have so formed oneself to virtue that the very seeds of the vices are rooted out [as Socrates and Cato appear to have done], than to prevent their progress by main force, and, having let oneself be surprised by the first commotion of the passions, to arm and tense oneself to stop their course and conquer them; and that this second action is still finer [*plus beau*] than simply to be provided with an easy and affable nature and having an innate distaste for debauchery and vice. For it certainly seems that this third and last way makes a man innocent, but not virtuous; exempt from doing ill, but not apt enough to do good. Besides, this condition is so close to imperfection and weakness that I do not very well know how to separate their confines and distinguish them. (405 [310])[3]

Seemingly to justify this ranking, Montaigne observes that "the very names of goodness and innocence are for this reason terms of contempt." He goes on to note, however, "that several virtues, like chastity, sobriety, and temperance, can come to us through bodily failing," and that "firmness in dangers (if firmness it should be called), contempt for death, endurance in misfortunes, can come to men, and are often found in them, through failure to judge such accidents rightly, and not conceiving them as they are" (405 [310]). If Montaigne's aim is to demonstrate the inferiority of "goodness" to "virtue," he seems to have proved too much: not only innocence but also what people take to be virtue may be the result of imperfection.

At this point Montaigne redirects his attention "to say a word about

---

[3]I believe that such interpreters of "Of Cruelty" as Philip Hallie and Floyd Gray err in holding that Montaigne means to assign the first of the three ranks of virtue in this hierarchy to Socrates alone, while consigning Cato to the second (where virtue involves the struggle of reason against passion) (Hallie, "The Ethics of Montaigne's 'De la cruauté,'" in La Charité, ed., *O Un Amy!* pp. 160–61; Gray, "The Unity of Montaigne," p. 84). Montaigne introduces Cato's suicide *after* citing Socrates and after his reference to "Epicurean voluptuousness," with the word "witness" (*tesmoing*): Cato is presented as a further instance of the type of self-induced virtue that is so perfect that, once acquired, it frees its possessor from the need to struggle against the passions. Montaigne represents both Cato and Socrates not merely as being free from fear but as experiencing pleasure and cheerfulness, respectively, in the face of death. (Contrary to Hallie, p. 160, he does not describe Cato's suicide as "painful.") The essayist does judge that Socrates' death was even "more beautiful" than Cato's, which *by comparison* appears "more tragic and tense"; but he assigns both cases to the highest rank. This fact is evidenced most clearly by the immediate sequel to the comparison of their deaths, wherein Montaigne describes both ancients as exemplifying "so perfect a habituation to virtue that it has passed into their nature"; both men, "by a long exercise of the precepts of philosophy," immunized their souls against feeling the slightest temptation to vice (403–5 [308–10]). Later Montaigne will indeed contrast Cato and Socrates, holding the way of the latter to be more "natural," the former more "strained" (III, xii, 1013–14 [793]). But that conclusion is the result of a further development of his argument, not to be confused with the explicit or surface teaching of II, xi, with which I am concerned here.

myself." He places himself at the lowest of the three ranks of excellence: he neither possesses habitual virtue nor has "put myself to great effort to curb the desires by which I have found myself pressed." He possesses only a "virtue, or, to put it better, innocence, that is accidental and fortuitous," and that results from the mildness of his natural disposition. Although Montaigne "hold[s] most vices in horror," his freedom from vice is due "more to my fortune than to my reason," in that his "reasonings, having in some things broken away from the common road, would easily give me license for actions that this natural inclination makes me hate." He cites two philosophers, Aristippus and Epicurus, who similarly displayed more restraint in their actions than in their opinions (406–7 [311–12]).

Montaigne continues his confession by describing the "softness" manifested in his distaste for cruelty, which he "cruelly hate[s], both by nature and by judgment, as the extreme of all vices." He adds that the pleasure other men find in hunting is a more unruly passion than physical pleasure, although "those who have to combat" the latter argue that "at its greatest pitch it masters us to such an extent that reason can have no access" (408–9 [313–14]).[4]

Montaigne relates his abhorrence of cruelty to his sympathy for others' suffering, which would readily cause him to weep "if I could weep for any occasion whatever." Having expressed his shock at the torments and persecutions that some people inflict on others, he explains how a "Latin author" (Suetonius) indirectly indicated his own horror at the cruelty practiced by "the Roman tyrants." And, in a passage that incurred the censure of some latter-day rulers of Rome,[5] Montaigne objects to torture by remarking that "even in justice, all that goes beyond plain death seems to me pure cruelty, and especially for us who ought to have some concern about sending souls away in a good state; which cannot happen when we have agitated them and made them desperate by unbearable tortures." After recommending a more humane substitute for this practice ("torturing" the criminals' corpses instead), he remarks the frequency of cruelty that results from "the license of our civil wars." And, noting how the Romans progressed from "the spectacle of the slaughter of animals . . . to that of men," he infers that "nature herself . . . attaches to man some instinct for inhumanity" (410–12 [314–16]).

Having observed how the wars fought by Christians in the name of religion promote inhumanity toward human beings, Montaigne now re-

[4]Cf. *Nicomachean Ethics* 1152b17–18, where Aristotle mentions, as one of the objections that are made to the goodness of pleasure, the fact that sexual pleasure, in particular, interferes with our capacity to think. More generally, Montaigne's argument constitutes a critique of Aristotle's claim (ibid., 1149a25–b4) that anger or spiritedness is more rational than appetite. On Montaigne's understanding of the relation between *eros* and spiritedness, see Chapter Nine, below.

[5]See Montaigne, *Journal de voyage*, in *Oeuvres*, pp. 1228–9 [955].

marks that piety ought to encourage gentleness even toward other animals, thus justifying his own sympathy for them: "Theology herself orders us to show some favor in their regard; and considering that one and the same master has lodged us in this place for his service, and that they, like ourselves, are of his family, she is right to enjoin upon us some respect and affection toward them" (412 [316]).

The theological teaching expressed in this remark conforms to an argument by Raymond Sebond,[6] whose "defense" by Montaigne occupies the next chapter of the *Essays*. Montaigne chooses, however, not to dwell on the conduciveness of Christianity to sympathy for the animals but refers instead to pagan theology to support his position. He cites the belief of various peoples in the doctrine of metempsychosis and notes that "many nations, and notably some of the most ancient and noble, have not only received beasts into their society and company, but given them a rank far above themselves," some even deifying them. While disclaiming any belief in the "cousinship between us and the beasts," Montaigne remarks the "close resemblance" between us and them. He then introduces one of the central themes of the "Apology for Raymond Sebond" by professing to "beat down a lot of our presumption" and to "willingly resign that imaginary kingship that people give us over the other creatures" (cf. II, xii, 426–9 [328–30]). He asserts the existence of "a general duty of humanity, that attaches us not only to the beasts, who have life and feeling, but even to trees and plants." He concludes the chapter by recounting the honors and services bestowed on animals by various ancient peoples and the contemporary Turks (413–16 [317–18]).

Having completed this survey of "Of Cruelty," let us look back over it. Considered as a whole, the chapter seems to be divided into two parts, only tangentially related: a discussion of virtue and a discussion of cruelty, with particular reference to the animals.[7] To understand Montaigne's argument, we must grasp the underlying connection between the two parts. Their relation becomes more evident when we consider the overall movement of the chapter from "high" things to "low" ones. "Of Cruelty" almost begins with a reference to the virtuous human being's surpassing God; it ends with an account of the "resemblance between us and the animals," and even trees and plants, which challenges humanity's claim to superiority over other living matter (let alone God). In between these poles, the chapter moves from a seeming praise of "tough" virtue, to the observation that such virtue can frequently be a sham, to Montaigne's account of his own easygoing ways, to his admission of softness, and finally to his criticism of people's cruelty both toward each other and toward the beasts.

---

[6]As the Pléiade editors note: *Oeuvres*, p. 1542 (n. 5 to p. 412).
[7]The discontinuity between the parts is noted by Zeitlin, *Essays of Montaigne*, 2:474–5.

I suggest the following interpretation of this movement. By linking "hard" virtue to the quest to surpass or at least emulate God, and "soft" goodness to the recognition of humanity's kinship with the beasts, Montaigne wishes to indicate—as he elaborates in the "Apology"—that it is more *salutary* to understand human beings in the light of their kinship with the beasts than to view them as rivals of the gods. Why this should be so is suggested by a passage in an earlier chapter, "One Is Punished for Stubbornly Holding On to a Place without Reason," wherein Montaigne refers to the disposition of conquerors who "have so great an opinion of themselves and their power that, since it seems unreasonable to them that there should be anything worthy to stand up against them, they put everyone to the sword wherever they find resistance, as long as their fortune lasts" (I, xv, 69 [48]). Pity being a passion that results from the painful perception of an undeserved evil befalling someone else which we might expect to befall ourselves,[8] it follows that the greater people think themselves to be in comparison with others, the less prone they will be to experience pity or compassion for others' sufferings. Hence the Stoical understanding of virtue as a kind of self-conquest, by means of which the virtuous human being rivals or surpasses God, amounts—as the title of II, xi, suggests—to an education in cruelty.[9] The archetype of people so convinced of their transcendent greatness that they display a cruelty unmitigated by compassion, for Montaigne, is Alexander the Great. Alexander's significance is highlighted by the fact that two passages illuminating his character and disposition occur respectively in the first and last chapters of the *Essays*—chapters in which Montaigne emphasizes his own inclination toward compassion. In the first chapter the essayist describes Alexander's incredible, pitiless cruelty and suggests that the Macedonian conqueror's "hardihood" made him all the less prone to regard others' lives as worthy of respect (13–14 [5]). And near the end of the last chapter he observes that "nothing [is] so humble and so mortal in the life of Alexander as his fancies about his immortalization" and praises the reproof that Philotas directed at him when an oracle "had lodged him among the gods," to the effect that "there is reason to pity the men who will have to live with and obey a man who exceeds and is not content with a man's proportions" (1096 [856–7]).

Just as Montaigne juxtaposes his compassionate nature in these chapters with Alexander's pitiless one, in "Of Cruelty," as we have seen, he sets forth his compassion for comparison with Cato's cruel "virtue." Although he does not portray Cato as having practiced cruelty toward others, he does link Cato's cast of mind with Alexander's in a seemingly insignificant

[8]Aristotle, *Rhetoric*, 1385b12–24.
[9]The chapter "Of Virtue" (II, xxix) is correspondingly filled with stories of self-inflicted cruelty. Cf. Descartes, *Discours de la méthode*, I, in *Oeuvres et lettres*, p. 130: "Often what [the ancient writers] call by such a beautiful name [as that of virtue] is nothing but insensibility or pride, or despair, or parricide."

chapter titled "Of Sleep." There he remarks how both Alexander and Cato slept deeply on nights before they were to face dangers. After recounting two such incidents in Cato's life, he asserts that "the knowledge we have of the greatness of this man's courage from the rest of his life enables us to judge with complete certainty that his behavior proceeded from a soul elevated so far above such accidents that he did not deign to let them worry him any more than ordinary accidents." Yet he follows this remark by citing the reproach that Mark Antony directed at Augustus for having slept deeply "on the point of going into battle," to the effect that he lacked "the courage . . . to look with open eyes at the array of his army" (I, xliv, 262–3 [198–9]). That Montaigne—who is himself accustomed to facing all dangers "with open eyes" (III, vi, 877 [686])—intends Antony's reproach to be applied to Cato as well, despite the latter's "Stoicism" (and hence also, by implication, to Alexander), is further hinted near the conclusion of "All Things Have Their Season." There he alludes to Cato's having read "Plato's discussion of the eternity of the soul" on the night before his suicide, as if—despite Montaigne's denial that he sought thereby "to ease his death"—it was the hope of immortality that gave him strength to carry out his resolve (II, xxviii, 682 [532]). The implication, in sum, is that the valor of such men as Cato (or Alexander, with "his fancies about his immortalization") is a fundamentally irrational disposition, unlike the properly "philosophical" courage to which Montaigne alluded in II, vii. Their way of life is rooted not in an open-eyed awareness of the human condition but in pleasing yet dangerous illusions about their "godlike" status.[10]

This analysis of Montaigne's understanding of Cato is confirmed by his remarks about the Roman's motivation in other chapters. As we have seen, in "Of Cruelty," after purporting to admire Cato's courage, the essayist casts a shadow of doubt over it by remarking how easy it is for an outside observer to misjudge such qualities.[11] A similar hint of doubt is present in a chapter titled "Of Cato the Younger," where Cato is cited as an example of "how far human virtue and firmness could go." Montaigne purports to denounce the corrupt judgments of the wits of his time, who use "their ingenuity to obscure the glory of the beautiful [belles] and noble actions of

[10]With respect to Montaigne's claim in "Of Sleep" that Cato's soul was "elevated so far above such accidents" as death that "he did not deign to let them worry him," consider also the mockery of such claims to transcend "accidents" by means of "Stoic virtue" at II, ii, 328 [250]. Amyot's translation of Plutarch refers only to Cato's having read "the dialogue of Plato in which he treats of the soul" on the eve of his suicide; the reference to the soul's "eternity" is an addition by Montaigne, which highlights the implication that Cato's suicide was inspired by the hope of immortality. Cf. Essais, II, iii, 342 [260], and xii, 422 [324], for reference to other ancients who are said to have been inspired to suicide by the Phaedo's apparent promise of eternal life. On the inferiority of Alexander's valor, the most extreme "of its kind," to "full" and "universal" courage, see II, i, 320 [243].

[11]The problematic character of courage in this regard is indirectly acknowledged by Aristotle: see Nicomachean Ethics, III.8; Harry V. Jaffa, Thomism and Aristotelianism (Chicago, 1952), p. 56.

antiquity, giving them some vile interpretation and conjuring up vain occasions for them." Several points cast doubt on the sincerity of this denunciation. First, purporting to be satiric, Montaigne places himself among the unbelievers: "Give me the most excellent and purest action, and *I* will plausibly supply fifty vicious motives for it." Second, he proceeds to carry out his offer in a way, by calling attention to the belief of some ancients that Cato's suicide was motivated by his fear of Caesar, or by ambition. Third, although he counters such criticisms by asserting that Cato "would actually have preferred to perform a beautiful [*beau*], noble, and just action with ignominy than for the sake of glory," he precedes and follows this remark with the suggestion that the praise of a virtue such as Cato's may be the result of passion or a poetic frenzy that transcends reason (I, xxxvii, 226–8 [170–71]). Although Montaigne appears to endorse such enthusiasm here, it stands opposed to his own endeavor to judge people soberly (cf. II, xii, 545–53 [423–8]; III, xiii, 1051–2 [822–3]).

The doubt about the true cause of heroic virtue which Montaigne attributes to others in I, xxxvii, is explicitly endorsed by him in the second chapter of Book II, "Of Drunkenness." Here he reports that Plutarch, "so perfect and excellent a judge of human actions, on seeing Brutus and Torquatus kill their children, came to doubt whether virtue could go that far, and to wonder whether those personages had not been motivated by some other passion." Montaigne himself adds that "all actions outside the ordinary limits are subject to sinister interpretation." He cites the Stoics' contempt for sensual pleasure, the Epicureans' extreme endurance, and the boasts of "our martyrs" as evincing a "runaway courage" akin to that which the heat of combat instills in "high-souled soldiers," or to poetic *mania*. He contrasts such conduct with the way of reason, which consists in "an orderly management of our soul" (II, ii, 329–30 [250–51]; cf. II, xxix, 683 [533]).

As Book II proceeds, Montaigne continues to question the motives that underlie virtue such as Cato's. At one point in the "Apology" he observes "how imperceptibly near madness is to . . . the effects of a supreme and extraordinary virtue" (II, xii, 471–2 [363]). Later, in a passage already cited, he remarks the "rashness" of philosophy's having taught "that men produce their greatest deeds and those most closely approaching divinity when they are out of their minds and enraged and mad" (II, xii, 551 [427]). After noting Cato's calmness (a quality not necessarily incompatible with madness) on the night before he killed himself, Montaigne questions the uniqueness of such resolution by citing a woman who killed herself to escape her husband's brutality, having meditated on the plan overnight; the Indian practice of suttee, to which widows go "with a gay countenance"; and a whole order of men "in this same country" who kill themselves after "constant premeditation through a whole life" (II, xxviii, 682 [532]; II, xxix, 685–6 [534–5]). In the same chapter—titled "Of Virtue"—he re-counts stories of men lesser known than Cato who cut off their sexual organs for petty reasons, adding, "If this had been done through reason and religion . . . what should we not say of so sublime an enterprise?" (II, xxix, 684–5 [534]).

Each of these remarks leads the reader to wonder whether Cato's suicide, despite the "elevated" purpose that seemingly justified it, was not in fact motivated by the same self-destructive passion that shocks one in Mon-taigne's other examples. The resemblance between Cato's motivation and that of "lesser" human beings is further suggested in the chapter "That Our Desire Is Increased by Difficulty." After remarking that "our will is whetted by opposition" and that "difficulty gives value to things," Montaigne ob-serves, "that great Cato found himself, just like the rest of us, weary of his wife as long as she was his, and desired her when she belonged to another man." He adds that a similar attitude can be found among horses (II, xv, 597 [464–5]).[12]

Montaigne's account of Cato's attitude toward his wife induces us to suspect that the same desire for difficulty lay at the root of the Roman's virtue. Just as Cato's wife lost her attraction when she was his, other objects and activities that are easily available lacked savor for him. Cato was driven by a passion to distinguish himself from others, to demonstrate that he had surpassed the ordinary human condition. But by asserting that Cato must have "enjoyed himself more" in his suicide "than in any other action of his life" (II, xi, 403 [309]), Montaigne invites doubt about whether he should be admired for it. If Cato did what he did because it was pleasant to him, how was he truly different from other people who do more commonplace things for the same reason? And as for the original process of self-training that enabled Cato to find pleasure in what to others is most painful, how much greater an accomplishment was it than that of women who, as Montaigne remarked previously, accustom themselves to being "tortured" for the sake of beauty? Montaigne's analysis of Cato's motivation accords with his assertion in I, xiv, that people value qualities as virtuous merely on account of their difficulty, and with his demonstration, in the same chapter, that the acquisition of quasi-Stoical "virtue" is not nearly so difficult, or therefore so admirable, as it seems.[13] It also harmonizes with his remark in

[12]Plutarch attributes no such motivation to Cato to explain his giving up his wife to his friend Hortensius. See Plutarch's "Life of Cato the Younger," in *Lives*, pp. 932, 948; Grace Norton, *La Plutarque de Montaigne* (New York, 1906), p. 127. On the other hand, the incident as Plutarch recounts it is rather remarkable and seems to invite some sort of additional explanation, if not that suggested by Montaigne, then the one Plutarch attributes to Caesar (*Lives*, p. 948).

[13]Cf. also II, xxxiii, 712 [555], where Montaigne denies "the prize of difficulty" to those who mutilate themselves or adopt an ascetic way of life in order to overcome the temptations of vice: "It is in a sense dying to escape the trouble of living well."

"Of Honorary Awards" that the "principal essence" of virtue, understood as vulgar courage, lies in its "rarity," and his observation of how fragile or deceptive this rarity is (II, vii, 362 [276]).

Not only does Montaigne's analysis of Cato's virtue thus support his attack on the moral appeal of Stoicism elsewhere; it accords with his emphasis on the political inutility of "tough" virtue in the fifth and sixth chapters of Book I. In "Of Cruelty" he suggests, even while professing not to believe, that Cato was really uninterested in his country's well-being, as compared with his own glory: Cato might have been "grateful to fortune for having put his virtue to so beautiful [*belle*] a test" by enabling Caesar to destroy "the ancient liberty of his country" (II, xi, 403 [309]). Regardless of the degree to which Cato's motivation was patriotic, Montaigne elsewhere questions the utility of his conduct for his country. He observes that although the younger Cato's virtue was "much more spotless" than that of Cato the Censor, the latter "excelled the other in military exploits and in the usefulness of his public services."[14] This remark occurs in the chapter "All Things Have Their Season"; Montaigne elaborates the chapter title in the text with the phrase "good ones and all" (II, xxviii, 680–81 [531]). In other words, what are popularly regarded as bad things are sometimes necessary ones (as Montaigne will argue at greater length in III, i), and the most spotless virtue is not always most beneficial in its effects. Montaigne relates this point more explicitly to Cato the Younger in a later chapter: "Life in society should have some relation to other lives. The virtue of Cato was vigorous beyond the measure of his time; and for a man who took a hand in governing others, a man dedicated to the public service, it might be said that his was a justice, if not unjust, at least vain and out of season" (III, ix, 969 [758]).

The Problem of "Extreme" Virtue

An adequate understanding of the issue raised by the last quotation—the tension between extreme "virtue" and political prudence—requires a consideration, once more, of the teaching of the classical political philosophers. At the outset it should be emphasized that the classical thinkers whom

[14]Interestingly, the three anecdotes of human regard for animals with which Montaigne concludes "Of Cruelty" all derive from Plutarch's "Life of Marcus Cato" (Cato the Censor), although none of the incidents involves Cato. Plutarch's point in these stories, like Montaigne's in "Of Cruelty," concerns the connection between sympathy for animals and compassion toward human beings, qualities apparently lacking in Cato the Censor, to whom Plutarch attributes "an over-rigid temper" and a disposition to treat his servants like beasts (*Lives*, p. 415). Despite Montaigne's representation of Marcus Cato's accomplishments as more useful to his country than those of his namesake, he can hardly constitute a much more desirable moral model by the essayist's criteria.

Montaigne acknowledges to have concerned themselves with political things (unlike the Stoics and Epicureans) were far from blind to this problem. Plutarch, in the "Life" of Cato the Younger on which Montaigne drew, while presenting a generally more favorable picture of the Roman than Montaigne's, provides evidence tending to support the judgment that he was excessively severe and uncompromising.[15] Cato's contemporary Cicero similarly criticizes him for adhering to unrealistically high standards in his political conduct.[16] And in his "Life" of Coriolanus—in which one finds the remark about the derivation of "virtue" from "valor" to which Montaigne refers in II, vii—Plutarch castigates that Roman commander's excessive pride and contentiousness, his unwillingness to tolerate the inevitable injustices of political life, and his imprudence.[17]

To arrive at the root issue in this matter, we must consider two passages wherein Montaigne directly alludes to the problem of "excessive" virtue. At the beginning of I, xv, "One Is Punished for Stubbornly Holding On to a Place without Reason," he asserts that "valor has its limits, like the other virtues; and these limits transgressed, we find ourselves on the path of vice; so that we may pass through [valor] to temerity, obstinacy, and madness, unless we know its limits well—and they are, in truth, hard to pick out near the borderlines" (68–9 [47]). And near the beginning of I, xxx, "Of Moderation," he elaborates: "We can grasp virtue in such a way that it will become vicious, if we embrace it with too sharp and violent a desire. Those who say that there is never any excess in virtue, inasmuch as it is no longer virtue if there is excess in it, are playing with words." In the sequel to this remark Montaigne cites instances of the "excessive" pursuit of justice or lawabidingness and piety, and seems to endorse the scriptural warning against excessive wisdom (195 [146]).

The most notable source for the opposed doctrine that Montaigne dismisses as merely wordplay—the claim that since virtue, by definition, is something good, there can never be too much of it—is Aristotle's *Nicomachean Ethics*. Aristotle defines moral virtue as a mean between two extremes—courage, for instance, being intermediate between rashness (excessive fearlessness) and cowardice (excessive fearfulness). It follows that there can never be such a thing as excessive courage; what looks like it is really rashness, not courage in the strict sense.

On the surface, Montaigne's charge that this Aristotelian doctrine amounts to verbal trickery has an obvious plausibility. If one understands moral virtue, as Aristotle represents it, as a state of character disposing the individual to choose and follow the right course of action in particular circumstances, and if each person's character is largely (or wholly) the

---

[15]*Lives*, pp. 918, 920–21, 932–5, 942–3, 946–7.
[16]Letter to Atticus, 60 B.C., in *Letters of Cicero*, tr. L. P. Wilkinson (New York, 1968), p. 39.
[17]*Lives*, p. 272.

result, as he asserts, of the habits inculcated during childhood, it is not evident that the disposition of the courageous individual, for instance, is *qualitatively* different from that of the rash one. The very term *mean,* with its mathematical connotation, suggests the intermediate point on a yard-stick that measures a single quality—in this case, fear or fearlessness—rather than a distinction among qualitatively different dispositions. As Aristotle acknowledges, it is difficult to determine the true mean with respect to a given quality. He also observes that in the case of such virtues as courage and moderation, the mean is not equally opposed to both extreme states: courage is closer to rashness than to cowardice; moderation is closer to insensibility than to self-indulgence.[18] Hence—given the difficulty of arriving at the mean—Aristotle recommends, as a second-best course that is probably the best most people can achieve, that we choose the lesser evil among vices: that is, that we "drag ourselves away to the contrary extreme" from the one toward which we naturally tend to be tempted. In practice, this means leaning in the direction of rashness to avoid the more obvious vice of cowardice, and leaning toward insensibility, if that were possible, to safeguard oneself against self-indulgence. Aristotle's provisional advice, in a nutshell, is to steer ourselves away from pleasure: "in everything the pleasant or pleasure is most to be guarded against; for we do not judge it impartially. . . . If we dismiss pleasure . . . we are less likely to go astray. It is by doing this, then . . . that we shall best be able to hit the mean."[19]

From Montaigne's point of view, Aristotle's denial of the possibility of an extreme in virtue is not only misleading, it is dangerously so. In "Of Moderation" he adduces two ancient examples to illustrate its dangers: "the mother of Pausanias, who gave the first information and brought the first stone for her son's death, and the dictator Posthumius, who had his son killed because his youthful ardor had driven him successfully against the enemy a little in advance of his rank" (I, xxx, 195 [146]). If either of these examples can be said to manifest some semblance of virtue, that virtue would seem to be justice. It is very unlikely that Aristotle would represent either action as simply virtuous.[20] Nor does Montaigne assert that classical thinkers in general would have approved of these actions. His charge against the classical doctrine, however, amounts to this: by encouraging people *in practice* to identify the more virtuous course with the one more opposed to that toward which their natural instinct inclined them (the

[18]*Nicomachean Ethics,* tr. W. D. Ross, in *The Basic Works of Aristotle,* ed. Richard McKeon (New York, 1941), 1108b30–1109a11.
[19]Ibid., 1109b1–13.
[20]At ibid., 1110a4–8, Aristotle implies that it would be excusable to perform a base action at a tyrant's behest in order to save one's parents and children; at 1110a27–8 he suggests that it "perhaps" would never be excusable to slay one's mother. On the importance Aristotle attributes to the family, see Arlene W. Saxonhouse, "Family, Polity, and Unity: Aristotle on Socrates' Community of Wives," *Polity* 15 (1982): 202–19; Stephen G. Salkever, "Women, Soldiers, Citizens: Plato & Aristotle on the Politics of Virility," *Polity* 19 (1986): 242–53.

instinct, in this case, being the natural "affection that the begetter has for his begotten"—II, viii, 365 [279]), Aristotle and his successors helped inspire such fanaticism as is typified by these "savage and costly" examples (I, xxx, 195 [146]).

This point may be elaborated by consideration of a passage from the tenth chapter of Book III, a portion of which I quoted in Chapter Four:

> Most of the rules and precepts of the world take this course of pushing us out of ourselves and driving us into the market place, for the benefit of public society. They thought to achieve a fine [bel] result by redirecting us and distracting us from ourselves, presupposing that we were attached to ourselves only too much and by too natural a bond; and they have spared no words to that end. For it is not new for the sages to preach things as they serve, not as they are. . . . We must often be deceived that we may not deceive ourselves, and our eyes sealed, our understanding stunned, in order to redress and amend them. . . . When they order us to love three, four, fifty degrees of things before ourselves, they imitate the technique of the archers who, to hit the mark, take aim a great distance above the target. To straighten a bent stick you bend it back the other way. (III, x, 983 [769])

The thrust of this passage conforms to Montaigne's discussion in the "Apology" of how the ancient philosophers propagated "profitable lies" for the people's edification. What is most interesting about the passage for our present purpose, however, is the fact that the last image in it—bending a stick back to straighten it—reproduces the image used by Aristotle in advising people to pull toward the extreme that is opposed to the vice to which they are naturally susceptible, so as better to approximate the mean.[21]

In the passage as I have quoted it, Montaigne's attitude toward the sages' practice seems to be either neutral or mildly favorable—although the overall argument of III, x, will challenge it. Montaigne takes issue with the sages' teaching more directly, however, in "Of Moderation." There, in the context of emphasizing the dangers of excessive virtue, he remarks: "The archer who overshoots the target misses as much as the one who does not reach it" (I, xxx, 195 [146]). In other words, Aristotle and his successors were wrong

---

[21]*Nicomachean Ethics* 1109b3–7. As Zeitlin, *Essays of Montaigne*, 3:402, notes, the image is also found in Plutarch, *Of Flatterers and Friends*, xxv. The previous image in the above quotation (the archers) is more loosely reminiscent of a passage in the second chapter of the *Ethics* (1094a23–4). Cf. Montaigne's reference at II, i, 320 [243], closer to the sense of the latter passage, to people's need to emulate archers by determining the target or aim of their actions in order to give them a suitable pattern; this passage follows shortly after the criticism of Alexander's extreme but blemished "virtue." See also, however, *Ethics* 1172a28–1172b7, where Aristotle—in harmony with Montaigne—rejects as futile the attempt to counteract an excessive appetite for pleasure by means of untrue arguments that deprecate it. Machiavelli uses the simile of archers who aim higher than their target in *The Prince*, ch. 6, p. 22.

to steer people away from pleasure and toward the endurance of pain and hardship, and self-sacrifice: the true mean, contrary to Aristotle, is (at most) no closer to the latter extreme than to the former. In Montaigne's view, it appears, Aristotle underestimated the malleability of human nature, in the sense that he failed to appreciate the unnatural extremes of self-sacrifice, asceticism, and even pursuit of pain to which some people, encouraged to transcend their selfish and bodily needs, might go. Although the Stoics represent Montaigne's most obvious instances of such "excessive" virtue, his ultimate referent, as I suggested in analyzing I, xiv, and I, xxxiii, may be Christian asceticism. As we have seen, it is people's indifference, putative or real, to their own earthly well-being that lies at the root (according to Montaigne) of their shameful abuse of their fellows. We were reminded of the theological bearing of this problem in "Of Cruelty" by Montaigne's reference to the (church-sanctioned) practice of torture and the "license" of the civil wars.

Up to this point Montaigne's criticism of the philosophers' moral teaching may appear to be a matter of mere common sense, typifying the down-to-earth humanist ethic of moderation and sanity which he frequently professes—and which countless commentators have considered to represent the core of his thought. But more is at stake in the controversy between Montaigne and Aristotle than we have thus far recognized. It seems sensible, at least to us moderns, to say that people should realistically accept their natures and their limitations, rather than model themselves on gods. But why must Montaigne go on—in the latter part of "Of Cruelty," and in a major portion of the "Apology" which almost immediately succeeds it—to teach people to understand themselves instead in light of the beasts? Is it not at least as distorting to emphasize our subhuman qualities in this way as to exaggerate our suprahuman capacity? Why should the goal of rendering human relations more pacific and compassionate necessitate such a step?

The answer to these questions—which relate to the very foundations of modernity—is suggested by Leo Strauss's explanation of Machiavelli's comparable recommendation that princes emulate first Chiron (a legendary figure representing a combination of man and beast) and then, more radically, two beasts:

[Machiavelli's] model is half beast, half man. He urges princes, and especially new princes, first to make use of both natures, the nature of the beast and the nature of man; and in the repetition, simply to imitate the beast, i.e., to use the person of the fox and the lion, or to imitate those two natures. The imitation of the beast takes the place of the imitation of God. We may note here that Machiavelli is our most important witness to the truth that humanism is not enough. Since man must understand himself in the light of the whole or of the origin of the whole which is not human, or since man is the being that must try to transcend humanity, he must transcend humanity in the direction of the subhuman if he does not transcend it in the direction of the superhuman. *Tertium*, i.e., humanism, *non datur.*[22]

As Strauss emphasizes, we human beings are distinguished from the rest of nature by our essential openness or indeterminacy, by our consequent need to define ourselves in terms of something beyond ourselves, and by our resultant striving to transcend our present condition in one direction or another. If the outlook of humanism can be summed up in the slogan "Be yourself," the insufficiency of that doctrine is apparent once we recognize that it provides us with no information about what it means to be a "self." Montaigne may legitimately be regarded, as I shall later argue, as one of the philosophic architects of modern humanism and our consequent chatter about "selfhood." But he was more appreciative than all but a handful of his successors of the radical, underlying presuppositions and implications of that doctrine.

To shed the fullest light on those presuppositions, let us return once more to Aristotle. As I have noted, on the surface Aristotle's claim that there can be no extreme with respect to virtue seems highly misleading and hence open to the criticism that Montaigne levels against it. But I have thus far stated that claim only in the provisional form in which it appears in the earlier books of the *Ethics*. A critical turning point in that work occurs in Book VI, which treats the intellectual virtues. In the first chapter of Book VI, Aristotle acknowledges that the doctrine of the mean, as heretofore stated, is deficient, inasmuch as it leaves undetermined the nature of the standard or object by reference to which the mean is to be identified. In other words: how much, or how little, *for what?*[23] Later in the same book Aristotle distinguishes between mere "natural" virtue, a nonrational disposition toward certain qualities, of which children and beasts as well as adults are capable, and virtue strictly understood, which entails practical wisdom or prudence.[24] It is prudence, according to Aristotle, that enables the virtuous man both to determine the right end of conduct and to choose the appropriate means to it. But what, then, *is* the ultimate end, the need for knowledge of which was stated in the first two chapters of the *Ethics?* Not until the last book is the answer supplied: our ultimate goal and greatest good is wisdom; the best, and most truly human, way of life is that of the philosopher. Only wisdom, among the goods people seek, is choiceworthy purely for itself, without regard to ulterior consequences. By contrast, the "practical" or moral virtues exemplified by the statesman and warrior are ultimately instrumental to some good (power, honor, happiness) separate from themselves. Hence, if human beings were gods—that is, lacking

[22]*Thoughts on Machiavelli*, p. 78; see *The Prince*, ch. 18, p. 69.
[23]*Nicomachean Ethics*, 1138b20–34.
[24]Ibid., 1144b1–32.

bodies—they would pass their time wholly immersed in contemplation. Such a life of unconcern with external goods is admittedly "too high for man," given his "composite" nature. But it remains the case that reason is not only the "divine" element in us but also in the truest sense our "self": the more we dedicate ourselves to contemplation, or philosophizing, the more truly human (as opposed to bestial) we are.[25]

Herein, I believe, is the real ground of Aristotle's denial that there can be an extreme of virtue. That claim is true, strictly speaking, only of the philosopher, whose virtues are inseparable from wisdom and reflect it, rather than being irrational, habit-induced dispositions of the sort Aristotle described in his earlier account of moral virtue. The philosopher's courage, in other words, results from a true estimation of the extent to which things should be feared, and of how much life itself should be valued—not of an irrational disposition toward boldness or harshness. Of philosophic courage there truly can be no excess—just as one cannot have too much wisdom.

Of course, it remains true that what the generality of people understand as courage—the kind of disposition that is, in general, responsible for the actions of heroism and self-sacrifice on which a nation's salvation may ultimately depend—is susceptible to excess. But here we arrive at a fundamental difference between Aristotle's and Montaigne's rhetorical treatments of virtue, which helps to illuminate the nature of the essayist's project. Though fully cognizant of the inferiority of moral virtue to intellectual excellence, Aristotle endeavors to endow the former with a kind of independent dignity, despite its ultimately instrumental status. Hence, through most of the *Ethics* (as well as in the *Politics*) he tends to blur rather than stress the difference between moral and intellectual virtue. This mode of representing moral virtue reflects not only an awareness of the need to direct people toward public-regarding modes of conduct—along the lines of Montaigne's account of the ancient sages' practice—but also his belief, as suggested by Strauss's remarks, that human beings need to pursue a goal "higher" than themselves if they are not to sink "beneath" themselves. By contrast, as we have seen, Montaigne's analysis of courage in "Of Honorary Awards" emphasizes the opposition between true, philosophical courage and its vulgar form, eulogizing the former while devaluing the latter. And throughout the *Essays,* despite a pretense of admiration for classical heroism and Christian piety, Montaigne repeatedly deprecates both qualities. His emphasis on our animal nature reflects a conscious rejection of the Aristotelian enterprise of teaching human beings to understand themselves in the light of the "divine."

The contrast between Aristotle's and Montaigne's rhetorical emphases is

[25]Ibid., X.7; IX.8, 1168b28–1169a18.

most fully evident in their treatment of pride. The peak of moral virtue, for Aristotle, is great-souledness: the disposition of the man "who thinks himself worthy of great things, being worthy of them." Humility is no virtue to Aristotle, for when we think insufficiently well of ourselves, we tend to accomplish less then we might, regarding ourselves as unworthy of noble actions; undue humility or "small-souledness" is both a commoner and a worse vice than the opposite defect of vanity.[26] In "Of Presumption," by contrast, Montaigne expressly favors those ancient views "that despise, humiliate, and nullify us most," thus combating "the over-good opinion man has of himself" (II, xvii, 617 [480–81]). In the "Apology," as we have seen, he attacks presumption as the source of our most dangerous illusions. And in an earlier chapter titled "Of Democritus and Heraclitus" he prefers Democritus' "mocking" attitude toward the human race over the weeping and compassionate one of Heraclitus, since "it seems to me that we can never be despised as much as we deserve. Pity and commiseration are mingled with some esteem for the thing we pity; the things we laugh at we consider worthless" (I, l, 291 [220–21]).

To regard people as worthless is, it would seem, the attitude of a misanthrope. Yet Montaigne denies this consequence. He distinguishes between the disdain and contempt toward human beings that he recommends and a hatred of them, which signifies that the hater takes humanity seriously (I, l, 291–2 [221]). In the first and last chapters, as well as in "Of Cruelty," he affirms his own disposition toward compassion and mercy (I, i, 12 [4]; II, xi, 409 [314]; III, xiii, 1079 [844]). And in another passage, quoted in Chapter Seven, Montaigne argues against both the Stoic and the Christian contempt for earthly life, asserting that such hatred and disdain for one's very being are stupidly vain, "ridiculous," and unnatural (II, iii, 334 [254]).

Just as Raymond Sebond served in the "Apology" as a stand-in for Thomas Aquinas, I suggest that Democritus and Heraclitus, in the chapter named after them, are symbolic representatives of more fundamental bodies of thought. Montaigne's adoption of the Democritean, comic view of humanity may be taken to represent the outlook of Socratic philosophy; whereas the sentiment of "pity and compassion" that he professes to disdain when attributing it to Heraclitus, but elsewhere adopts as his own, constitutes a modified form of Christian compassion or *pietà*. Montaigne's project involves, at the broadest level, a synthesis of the Socratic and Christian outlooks, the product of which will be different from either of its constituent elements. What is taken over from the Socratic teaching is the comic view of the disproportion between the pretensions of the individual human being and the magnitude of the whole, which leads Socrates to say,

---

[26]Ibid., 1123a36–b2, 1125a16–33.

for instance, that a philosopher will not regard human life as anything great.[27] What is omitted from the Socratic view is the conception of the philosophic pursuit itself as an ultimately serious one, and as the means by which we might transcend our particularity and corporeality, achieving, in thought, a kind of oneness with the whole.[28] Such a claim embodies the "presumptuous" disregard for our earthly, corporeal needs for which Montaigne mocks the ancient philosophers in general. It is in his mockery of our pretensions to self-achieved greatness, and his preference for those opinions "that despise, humiliate, and nullify us most," that Montaigne comes closest to the Christian doctrine of humility. Yet by rejecting the "weeping" attitude he attributes to Heraclitus—a rejection that is confirmed in an early chapter titled "Of Sadness," wherein Montaigne professes to be "freest from this passion" and describes it as always "harmful" and "insane" (I, ii, 15 [6]), as well as by the generally comic tone of the Essays—Montaigne indicates that his compassion rests on a different ground from the Christian one.[29] Despite his disposition to sympathize with others who suffer, he disdains to "weep" for them (II, xi, 409 [314]) because he does not take them "seriously," as Christianity does. Although Christianity rejects as impious the Stoic notion that we can rival God's excellence, it takes human life seriously because of our kinship with our Creator. By contrast, Montaigne's sympathy for his fellows does not rest on any esteem for their rank in the scheme of things. In "Of Presumption" he suggests that there is no incompatibility between having "little esteem" for oneself and holding a "singular affection" for oneself (II, xvii, 641 [499]). By the same token, it appears, one need not esteem others highly to experience a generalized philanthropic affection toward them. In this respect Montaigne's compassion or "humanity" presupposes a more radical break with the classical understanding of human life than Christian *pietà* does. Precisely because it emphasizes our relation to God, Christianity attaches too little importance, in Montaigne's view, to the alleviation of our earthly sufferings: for a Christian, damnation, not corporeal pain, is the greatest form of suffering, whereas bodily hardship may be regarded as a salutary means of leading us toward faith and hence salvation. In "Of Cruelty," by contrast, Montaigne grounds his compassion on our kinship with the beasts and even with trees and plants. Compassion, as Montaigne portrays it, has the same root as self-love:[30] it is a natural instinct of pain and revulsion at the infliction of suffering on a fellow being, ungrounded in esteem for the merit of the

---

[27]Plato, *Republic*, 486a; cf. *Laws*, 803c–804b.

[28]Consider, e.g., Socrates' speeches in the *Phaedo* and *Symposium*.

[29]On life as comic, see also I, xix, 78 [55]; I, xx, 92 [65]. Cf. the remarks of Auerbach, *Mimesis*, pp. 255, 273, concerning the absence of tragedy in Montaigne's thought; Guizot, *Montaigne*, pp. 59–60; Strauss, *Thoughts on Machiavelli*, p. 292.

[30]Hence it is unnecessary to represent Montaigne's "goodness" and "horror at cruelty," as Armaingaud does, as "effac[ing]" the "apparent egoism" the essayist expresses elsewhere (Armaingaud, ed., *Oeuvres complètes de Michel de Montaigne*, 3:235n). Montaigne evidently

sufferer. Only if we are deterred from attempting to furnish a rational ground for our self-love can we be prevented from adopting "transcendent" opinions of ourselves which ultimately make us indifferent to the sufferings of others, if not our own. Paradoxically, to be "humane" in Montaigne's sense requires not only that we recognize our susceptibility to suffering and hence our nondivine character but that this animal susceptibility be regarded as more important than the capacity to strive after nonbodily goods which makes us distinctively "human."[31]

Virtue and Poetry

In his study "The Ethics of Montaigne's 'De la Cruauté'" Philip Hallie describes the point of II, xi, as the replacement of an "Inward Government theory of ethics," in which the agent's ability to control passion by reason is the primary basis of evaluation, by an alternative ethic in which the primary focus is on the effect an action has on other human beings.[32] Otherwise put, Montaigne's initial emphasis on the "beauty" of the virtue that Cato exemplifies is supplanted, later in the chapter, by a stress on social utility as the proper criterion of moral evaluation. As Montaigne's subsequent comparison of Cato the Younger with Cato the Censor makes evident, these two criteria are likely to engender very different sorts of judgments.

As Hallie recognizes, it was characteristic of classical moral philosophy to focus on the goodness of the agent rather than on the utility of the effects of the agent's actions.[33] In Aristotle's account of moral virtue, for instance, the political utility of courage is downplayed: the truly courageous man's

understands his natural compassion as an extension of his "egoism" and sensitivity to pain rather than as a limitation on proper self-love. Cf. I, xxi, 95 [68], where he acknowledges his sensitivity to others' suffering but indicates that his preferred remedy is to seek the company of "healthy and gay" people; III, xii, 1023 [800], on the link between compassion and pleasure; but also III, i, 768 [599], on the "malicious pleasure" we feel "in the midst of compassion . . . in seeing others suffer"; Starobinski, *Montaigne in Motion*, p. 249. See, on the relation of secularized pity to Christian *pietà*, Clifford Orwin, "Machiavelli's Unchristian Charity," *American Political Science Review* 72 (1978): 1222–6; on the compatibility of "humanity" with "a certain contempt for most men," Strauss, *Thoughts on Machiavelli*, p. 290.

[31]Contrast Hegel's argument on behalf of capital punishment: *The Philosophy of Right*, I, 100.

[32]In La Charité, ed., *O Un Amy!* pp. 156–71.

[33]Ibid., pp. 158–9. Hallie exaggerates this dichotomy, however, by claiming that the classical view "would concern itself, for example, with the impulsiveness or orderliness of Hitler's mind, not with the humiliations, tortures, and deaths of his victims" (p. 159). He also seems to overlook the fact that Montaigne agrees with the classical philosophers in viewing people's actions as at best an imperfect reflection of their merit (ibid., p. 158; *Essais*, II, vi, 359 [274]; Aristotle, *Nicomachean Ethics*, 1177a12–19, 1177b29–1178a4). Finally, it should be emphasized, in contradistinction to Hallie's argument, that the notion of virtue-as-struggle typified by Cato does not represent the Platonic-Aristotelian understanding of virtue in the strict sense: the model of human excellence is the philosopher, whose virtue is a function of his reason, not of his willpower. The Socratic thesis that "no one does wrong knowingly" implies that the love of wisdom makes the philosopher quasi-immune to the temptations of vice.

goal is said to be honor or nobility, not the good of his country.[34] Similarly, the emphasis in his description of the virtues connected with expenditure is on the agent's capacity to discern fitting (appropriately noble) objects, not on the use of money to alleviate the lot of the neediest individuals.[35] Analogously, in Plato's *Republic*, political justice, or the justice embodied in deeds, is treated as a simulacrum of the true "justice" which consists in a right ordering of the individual soul.[36]

Hallie, I think, rightly perceives that it is classical thought as a whole, or at its most profound, rather than Stoicism and Epicureanism in particular, that is the true focus of Montaigne's critique in "Of Cruelty." Nowhere is this fact more pointedly or hilariously brought out than in a remark near the middle of the chapter, where the essayist refers to "Epicurus, whose doctrines are irreligious *and delicate*" (*delicat:* also weak, dainty, effeminate) (II, xi, 407 [312]). Only a few pages after defending Epicureanism against the popular opinion that regards it as softer than Stoicism, and attributing a "firmness and rigor of opinions and precepts" to it (II, xi, 401 [307]), Montaigne defers to that same popular opinion![37] In this way he suggests that the comparative evaluation of Stoicism and Epicureanism is in truth a matter of indifference to him; his real concern is with a movement of thought that encompasses and transcends them both.

I have already observed that Montaigne's calling into question the conjunction between spiritual "beauty" and goodness points toward a fundamental issue between him and the classical political philosophers. The root of that issue is suggested by his charge in the "Apology," repeated elsewhere, that the philosophers' teaching was "poetic" rather than strictly rational (II, xii, 518 [401]; III, ix, 974 [761]). An important related passage is his account of Homer's influence in the chapter "Of the Most Excellent Men." There he observes, in attestation of Homer's greatness, that the Greek poet's thought served to guide "all those who have since taken it upon themselves to establish governments, to conduct wars, and to write about either religion or philosophy, of whatever sect they might be, or about the arts." Yet in the very act of praising Homer, Montaigne indirectly calls into question his adequacy as a guide. Although he claims that Homer "made the infancy of poetry and of several other sciences mature, perfect, and accomplished," despite the fact that "things at birth are ordinarily imperfect," he significantly does not indicate that the poet's influence was equally sound on all the sciences of which he laid the foundations. Indeed,

---

[34]*Nicomachean Ethics*, 1115b10–24.
[35]Ibid., IV.1–2.
[36]*Republic*, 368e–369a, 592a–b.
[37]Cf. also III, xiii, 1060 [829], where Montaigne suggests that a putatively austere practice of the Stoic Seneca could equally well be viewed as exemplifying "softness" or effeminacy (*mollesse*).

that soundness must be doubted in at least some cases, since Homer lived "before the sciences were reduced to rules and certain observations" (II, xxxvi, 730–31 [569–70]). Perhaps the incompleteness of the knowledge available in his time prevented Homer from adequately grasping or conveying the true rules of *political* science.

The classical political philosophers understood their teaching to constitute a fundamental departure from the horizon of the poets, including Homer. As is evident in Book X of the *Republic,* in the corrections of the poets' theology in Book II of the *Republic* and Book I of the *Politics,* and in Socrates' account of his examination of the poets in the *Apology,* both Plato and Aristotle thought the poetic understanding required decisive modification if it was to promote true individual excellence and political well-being. Yet Montaigne's argument suggests that they did not adequately break with that understanding. Insofar as they continued to identify virtue with "beauty" of soul, they retained the poets' tendency to understand human beings in a misleadingly idealized way, and to view the universe itself, at least in their public teachings, in an anthropocentric manner that exaggerates its beneficence. As a result, he suggests, they transmitted a conception of human excellence which originally derived from the minds of primitive people, major elements of which had been carried over in the poets' works: a conception that equates such excellence with "beauty" and valor.[38]

At the deepest level, Montaigne's attack on the "poetic" character of his predecessors' work reflects his criticism of the dialectical method, whereby philosophers beginning with Socrates endeavored to ascend to the truth by starting at the level of common opinion. Such a starting point, he implies, underestimates the degree to which "nature" imprints "many . . . false notion[s]" on our minds (I, iii, 18 [8]), errors then confirmed by custom. Hence in "Of Custom" Montaigne approvingly cites the remark of an Academic spokesman in Cicero's *On the Nature of the Gods* criticizing natural philosophers, who should observe nature directly, for "brazenly seek[ing] the proof of truth from minds imbued with habit" (I, xxiii, 109 [79]).[39] In that chapter, as already noted, he suggests that our failure adequately to question accepted notions is responsible for perpetuating unjust and irrational codes of law. As he puts it elsewhere, what people call

[38]Cf. Hobbes's complaint that the ancients' "Morall Philosophy is but a description of their own Passions": *Leviathan,* ch. 46, p. 686. Note the connection between Homer and Alexander, in contrast with the wily Scipio's attachment to Xenophon: *Essais,* II, xxxiv, 713 [556]; II, xxxvi, 731 [570]. See also III, vi, 876 [685] on the disposition of "great authors, writing of causes," to cite "not only those they think are true, but also those they do not believe in, provided that they have some novelty and beauty."

[39]Cf. also III, viii, 903–4 [706–7], regarding the futility of "dialectical" exchanges with incompetent interlocutors; and Montaigne's questionable compliment to Socrates at III, xii, 1014 [793], for having produced "the most beautiful effects of our soul" out of "the pure imaginings of a child, without altering or stretching them." Cf. Plato, *Phaedo,* 99d–100a.

justice is merely "the hodgepodge of the first laws that fall into our hands, and their application and practice, often very inept and iniquitous" (II, xxxvii, 744 [580]).

In the "Apology" and in "Of Custom," as we have seen, Montaigne holds that the truth about justice can be discovered only by means of a fundamental break with common opinion. An essential facet of common opinion about morality is the distinction and opposition it embodies between honor and utility, such that "it calls dishonorable and foul some natural actions that are not only useful but necessary" (III, i, 773–4 [604]). By contrast, Montaigne endeavors, as I have noted, to conjoin honor with utility, so that the qualities we praise as virtuous will be those that are truly advantageous. His project amounts to, and may be the paradigmatic case of, what Nietzsche was to call a "transvaluation of values": a radical and intentional alteration of the valuation we place on different goals and ways of life.[40]

Judgments of virtue, according to Montaigne's intention, are henceforth to be *explicitly* based on considerations of utility rather than beauty.[41] But here an irony presents itself: Montaigne can accomplish this aim only if he can persuade people to regard the new sort of valuation as itself "beautiful" and hence attractive. As he emphasizes in "Of Glory" (II, xvi), popular admiration for acts of "tough" virtue and self-sacrifice reflects the efforts of countless lawgivers, poets, philosophers, and religious founders, who have spared no effort at employing "vain ceremony or . . . lying opinion to serve as a curb to keep the people in their duty" (613 [477]). To counteract their efforts, Montaigne must make the kind of virtue they praised appear ugly and the humane way of life he advocates, despite its unimposing character, beautiful. Herein lies the core of the rhetorical intention underlying Montaigne's putative self-portrait in the *Essays*. It is noteworthy that the foregoing account of the efforts that previous lawgivers and philosophers undertook to glorify a self-sacrificing kind of virtue is immediately juxtaposed with a chapter (II, xvii) that embodies Montaigne's fullest account of himself. It is here that he lays claim to a set of attractive, if unimposing, virtues—"fidelity and conscience," "frankness and independence"—to which he laments his age has been inhospitable, while confessing to such

[40]See Robert Eden, *Political Leadership and Nihilism: A Study of Weber and Nietzsche* (Gainesville, Fla., 1984), pp. 59–61.

[41]In the "Apology" and in "Of Glory," as I have noted, Montaigne represents previous philosophers and lawgivers as having aimed at a *kind* of utility, the common good of a polity; but he holds that their judgments were nonetheless colored by considerations of beauty, and that they concealed the utilitarian foundation of their moral codes from the populace. Moreover, in teaching people in general to pursue virtue as if it were choiceworthy in itself, rather than a means to pleasure and contentment, these thinkers diverted individuals from a consideration of what was most directly useful to them. Montaigne's intention is that people should henceforth be taught to act in ways that are manifestly advantageous in terms of their real, essentially corporeal interests. I discuss the broader political implications of this liberation of self-interest from moral restraint in Chapter Twelve.

"vices" as forgetfulness, uncertainty, and an unwillingness to endure constraint and obligation, which enhance his appeal. The same rhetorical contrast was present in I, xiv, where Montaigne disarmingly contrasted his fear of pain with the Stoics' pretense of overcoming it, and may be found in such chapters as III, x, where he provides an account of his mayoralty that suggests he accomplished far more for the public good, in his "unambitious" way, than other officials who aspired to glory and greatness (999–1002 [781–4]).

That Montaigne intended his self-portrait to be contrasted to his advantage with the examples he provides of "Stoical" virtue is suggested by his remark that it is "the duty of good men to portray virtue as being as beautiful as possible" (I, xxxvii, 227 [170]). That remark—in a chapter devoted to the ways in which poets eulogized Cato's excellence—should be compared with the picture of Cato that the essayist chooses to represent "every example of virtue": the image of the Roman "in his proudest posture . . . *all bloody, tearing out his own bowels,* rather than sword in hand, as did the statuaries of his time" (II, xiii, 594–5 [462]). In light of this portrayal, we are not surprised by Montaigne's judgment that "so beautiful an action[!] would have been unbecomingly located in any other life than Cato's" (II, xi, 404 [309]).[42] By contrast, Montaigne presents his own way of life as one that *is* to be imitated by the generality of human beings (e.g., III, v, 822 [642]). Hence, in contrast with his presentation of Stoical virtue, which—when it does not emphasize the savagery of that quality, as in the portrait of Cato—is dry and impersonal, Montaigne describes his habits and temperament in the most attractive way. .

Nowhere is the contrast between Montaigne's unassumingly seductive (or seductively unassuming) self-portrait and his representation of the alternative understanding of human excellence more manifest than in "Of Cruelty." The rhetorical intent underlying the essayist's self-deprecatory account of his aversion to cruelty has been noted by Zeitlin, who observes that by referring "somewhat guiltily . . . to the trait as a mark of [his] softness and weakness," Montaigne is able to launch a far more telling and persuasive attack on cruelty before an audience that "regarded the courage of the soldier as the greatest virtue" than if he had advanced his view "with positive and solemn formality." Precisely because he does not seem to be claiming any genuine superiority to his readers, hence provoking their *amour-propre,* Montaigne can more effectively stimulate them to reflect on their vices.[43]

---

[42]Although Montaigne represents this statement as a previous judgment of "philosophy," it is actually a considerable exaggeration of what his apparent source (Cicero, *On Duties,* I, xxxi) says: Cicero judges that a suicide like Cato's would be fitting only for a person with a character *like* Cato's.

[43]Zeitlin, *Essays of Montaigne,* 2:476–7.

Such readers of "Of Cruelty" as Zeitlin and Hallie have rightly empha-sized the humanizing, and humane, intention that runs through the chapter. Unfortunately, their readings tend to obscure the more fundamental project that underlies Montaigne's references to his own "natural" gentleness and his appeal to fellow-feeling toward the beasts as a ground for compassion toward human beings. Recognizing (as Hallie acknowledges) that the senti-ment of cruelty is no less "natural" to us than compassion is, Montaigne can hardly have thought it sufficient to appeal to what Hallie terms "man's healthy, realistic life in nature" as a remedy for inhumanity. Nor is Hallie correct in attributing to Montaigne the view that reason is responsible for the cruelty to which he objects.[44] Reason, as we learned from the "Apol-ogy," is a tool to be used to ameliorate the human condition. Nowhere does Montaigne allege that the most truly rational individuals, philosophers, were advocates of cruelty in its literal sense, the sort of tortures inflicted on others by both the cannibals and the contemporary church. He nonetheless objects to their doctrines on the ground that the standard of excellence to which they taught people to aspire, thinking it most conducive to our political as well as personal well-being, lent itself to abuse by others—political and religious tyrants—who professed to be acting in its name. Although Montaigne frequently admonishes his readers to follow "nature," that admonition presupposes the acceptance of a particular understanding of nature, with which he aims to supplant previous philosophic accounts; his representation of nature is itself the fruit of reason, not of any naive faith in the inherent goodness of people's "true" inclinations.

[44]Hallie, "The Ethics of Montaigne's 'De la Cruauté,'" pp. 164, 169–70. Hallie's reading of the passage in which Montaigne cites Aristippus and Epicurus as examples parallel to his own, of how one's behavior can be more restrained than one's opinions (II, xi, 407 [312]), though following the apparent sense of the passage, misses its real point. That point—as is suggested more manifestly in the description of the philosophers' "licentious" way of life in the "Apology" and in the account of Montaigne's own ways in several chapters of Book III—is not that natural instinct is a safer guide than reason, but that reason provides no particular mandate for the restraints on sensual pleasure to which Aristippus and Epicurus conformed in practice. In the sequel to this passage in "Of Cruelty," as noted, Montaigne expressly defends sensual indulgence against the charge that it is incompatible with the maintenance of one's reason. And even while claiming that the overall "goodness" of his nature derives from an artless innocence rather than from reasoning or training, Montaigne expressly grounds his abhorrence of cruelty in "judgment" as well as in "nature" (408 [313]). In other words, Montaigne rationally judges that whatever inherent antipathy to cruelty he possesses is a salutary disposition; he does not judge his avoidance of other so-called vices to be any more reasonable than indulgence in them would be. Indeed, as I argue in the next chapter, he holds that to encourage people to indulge in putative vices such as drunkenness is a useful means of diverting them from more dangerous and genuinely vicious pursuits. In regard to the relation between "reason" and "nature," cf. I, ii, 17–18 [8], where Montaigne reports endeavoring to increase his natural resistance to "violent passions" by means of reasoning; also II, viii, 366 [279–80]). Consider also II, ii, 324 [247], and II, viii, 368 [281], where he describes himself as being less opposed by reason than by temperament to the vices of drunkenness and theft.

CHAPTER NINE

Eros, Spiritedness,
and Ambition

"By Diverse Means . . ."

Even though the opening chapter of the *Essays,* "By Diverse Means We Arrive at the Same End," articulates, in a way, the nerve of Montaigne's project, I have postponed treating that chapter until now because its obscurity and "impersonality" seem to necessitate familiarity with the whole of the book if it is to be understood. The opening chapter, along with two others to be considered here (I, xxiv, and II, xxxiii), is among the most mysterious parts of the *Essays* and has received relatively little scholarly analysis. The following, provisional interpretation is offered partly in the hope that others may refine and develop my findings.

The maxim that constitutes the title of I, i, would have a familiar ring to a Christian reader in Montaigne's time. Such a reader who had no previous acquaintance with the *Essays* might reasonably expect the chapter to concern the well-worn theme that whatever course of life we choose and whatever fortune we achieve, all of us will ultimately arrive at the same "end," that is, death. Such a reflection on the vanity of earthly achievements would constitute the greatest of incentives to concern oneself with the pursuit of eternal salvation.

This is not the sense in which Montaigne interprets the maxim, however. His explicit concern, as stated in the opening sentence, is instead with the achievement of *earthly* salvation from those who threaten one's life. The "end" he addresses is that "of softening the hearts of those we have offended, when, vengeance at hand, they hold us at their mercy." The two means considered to this end are "the commonest way," which is "by submission to move them to commiseration and pity," and the "entirely contrary means" of "audacity and constancy," which "have sometimes served to [produce] this same effect" (11 [3]).

In its form, as Zeitlin observes, the opening chapter typifies what is thought to have been "the earlier group of Montaigne's writings": it consists of a "simple reflection followed by a series of historical examples," in imitation of the "popular compilations" of the time. Hugo Friedrich notes more specifically that the style of the chapter imitates that of a Scholastic disputation, in which two principles, in this case equally "banal"—the alternative modes of softening a conqueror's heart—are compared and weighed; but unlike the Scholastic investigations, Montaigne's inquiry appears not to end in any "synthesis" or resolution. Neither Zeitlin nor Friedrich (nor, to my knowledge, any other commentator) has found in this chapter any more concrete or controversial lesson than that (as Montaigne puts it) "man is a marvelously vain, diverse, and undulating object" on whom "it is hard to found any consistent and uniform judgment" (13 [5]).[1]

Typical readers perusing the *Essays* for the first time could not be expected to dissent from the critics' judgment of the opening chapter's imitativeness or "banality." Having fresh in mind Montaigne's prefatory warning against expecting to find anything of particular value in the book, they might be jarred by the abrupt manner with which Montaigne introduces his odd topic and put off by his suddenly impersonal tone, but they might well conclude that the warning was indeed one "of good faith." It is only after reading the *Essays* through, having studied it with sufficient care to become aware of the profundity of its author's thought as well as the subtlety of his rhetoric, that readers may be led to reconsider their first impression. Why would an author who, by his testimony, provides such weighty food for thought as Montaigne does, who scorns the practice of the "compilers," and who is, to boot, a master stylist and rhetorician open his book with such a rambling and apparently insignificant pastiche of anecdotes in support of such a trivial thesis as we find in the first chapter? Must there not be more here than meets the eye?[2]

In pursuit of a deeper understanding of the chapter, let us begin by considering the significance of the passion of vengeance, with which Montaigne is concerned. Vengeance is, of course, a product of anger. In the

---

[1]Zeitlin, *Essays of Montaigne*, 1:291–2; Friedrich, *Montaigne*, p. 161; similarly, Marcel Gutwirth, "By Diverse Means . . . (I:1)," in Defaux, *Montaigne: Essays in Reading*, p. 186.

[2]A further reason for such suspicions is a similarity noted by Friedrich between this essay and chaps. 19–22 of Book III of Machiavelli's *Discourses* (the first four-fifths of what Leo Strauss labeled the "Tacitean subsection"). As Friedrich notes, the theme of the relative merits of toughness and softness as means of preserving oneself, which Montaigne treats from the point of view of the conquered, is treated by Machiavelli from the perspective of the conqueror or ruler. Friedrich observes that Montaigne, unlike Machiavelli, fails to draw a substantive conclusion from his analysis; but perhaps his conclusion is only less overt, albeit equally metaphorical (Friedrich, *Montaigne*, pp. 162–3; Strauss, *Thoughts on Machiavelli*, p. 160).

fourth chapter of the *Essays*, "How the Soul Discharges Its Passions on False Objects When the True Are Wanting," Montaigne discusses the often irrational nature of both anger and vengeance. Just as "beasts are carried away by their rage to attack the stone or the metal that has wounded them, and to take revenge tooth and nail on themselves for the pain they feel," Xerxes and Cyrus sought to punish rivers for interfering with their will, "and Caligula ruined a very beautiful house for the pleasure that his mother had had there."[3] But "those surpass all madness who," in seeking "causes . . . for the misfortunes that befall us," "turn their blame against God himself, or against Fortune, as if she [or he!] had ears susceptible to our assault" (I, iv, 25–6 [14–15]). And in a later chapter titled "Of Anger," while alluding to Aristotle's belief that this passion "sometimes serves as a weapon for virtue and valor"[4] and noting that it is unavoidable in certain military affairs, he remarks that it is "always an imperfection" (II, xxxi, 696–8 [543, 545]).

The root phenomenon that Montaigne addresses in these remarks, *thumos* or "spiritedness," constituted a major theme of classical political philosophy. *Thumos* is a passion that originates in self-concern—the desire to preserve and defend oneself, one's property, one's family and honor—but may ultimately issue in a transcendence of self, such that the spirited individual is driven to sacrifice life itself. The poetic exemplar of *thumos* is Achilles, who withdraws from battle as the consequence of an injury to his honor, returns to combat to avenge the death of his friend, and knowingly goes to his own death, only to discover that it would have been preferable to live as a slave on earth than rule over all of Hades. Owing to its self-centeredness and to its potentially self-contradictory character (sacrificing oneself in defense of oneself), *thumos* is a fundamentally irrational disposition. Yet it constitutes an essential foundation of the political community. It is their spirited attachment to the city (seen as an extension of themselves) that inspires people to risk their lives in its behalf. And it is their thumotic concern with their own dignity that inspires the performance of noble deeds that redound to the city's benefit in other respects. *Thumos* also lies at the core of the religious instinct: the belief in gods who avenge injustices that may escape the knowledge or the power of human beings to punish reflects our need to find cosmic support for our deepest concerns.

Given the demand of spiritedness to avenge wrongs, this passion presupposes that the persons who inflicted wrong or injury did so willfully and are

---

[3]Frame sensibly suggests that "pleasure" is an error for "displeasure," since "Caligula's mother had been a prisoner" in the house (Frame, ed., *Complete Works*, p. 15n). But what was Caligula's mother up to in that house? Consider the story Montaigne reports having heard in Toulouse (II, iii, 338 [257]). (In view of the theme of "sublimation" developed in I, iv, one is led to suggest that Freud may not have been the first to consider why a son might be angry at his mother's pleasures.)

[4]Apparently in reference to *Nicomachean Ethics* 1116b30–1117a4. Cf. the critical discussion of this passage in Seneca, *Of Anger*, I, xvii, which Montaigne partly mimics.

capable of feeling the pain of being injured in return. As Aristotle explains, anger, unlike hate, "is always concerned with individuals"; the angry man, unlike the hater, "aims at giving pain," as distinguished from harm, to the object of his ire, wanting "his victims to feel," whereas the hater is indifferent as to whether they do or not.[5] But so powerful is the capacity of spiritedness to overcome reason that at times we treat irrational or even lifeless objects from which we have suffered harm as if they possessed reason and will, and endeavor to "punish" them as well—as in the case of Achilles' doing battle with a river.[6]

Because spiritedness leads people to overvalue their particular selves and the things connected with their selves—including their city and their gods—it is the element of the soul most opposed to philosophy. It was the Athenians' spirited moral indignation that led them to execute Socrates for questioning their beliefs about the most important things and the value they attached to themselves and what belonged to them. Yet while recognizing the threat that *thumos* posed to philosophy, the classical political philosophers also appreciated its necessity both to the defense of the city and to the virtue of nonphilosophic human beings. Hence the response of Plato and Aristotle was not to attack spiritedness as such but to try to moderate or tame it so as to render it more amenable to the guidance of reason. Their representations of *thumos* as a disposition more closely allied to reason than to the irrational bodily desires exemplify this rhetorical intention.[7] But the very contexts of those statements point to the difficulty, if not impossibility, of achieving any lasting solution to the problem.[8]

There is substantial evidence that Montaigne agrees with the classical understanding of spiritedness on almost all the points I have just summarized. His examples of Xerxes' and Cyrus' attempts to punish rivers parallel Plato's use of Achilles' action to illustrate the irrationality of *thumos*. His explanation of religion, in the same chapter, as a consequence of our need to "invent" causes for our misfortunes, so as to have something "to blame," similarly imitates the classical understanding. In Book II, in a

[5]*Rhetoric*, tr. W. Rhys Roberts, in *The Basic Works of Aristotle*, ed. Richard McKeon (New York, 1941), 1382a2–13.

[6]Homer, *Iliad*, XXI, 265–6; cf. Plato, *Republic*, 391a–b; Bloom, *The Republic of Plato*, p. 356. The penal code in Plato's *Laws*, as Thomas Pangle points out, accommodates this disposition "to assign complete responsibility to that which frustrates desire" by including punishments for animals and stones (*Laws* 873e–874a; Pangle, "The Political Psychology of Religion in Plato's *Laws*," *American Political Science Review* 70 [1976]: 1063). My account of *thumos* is indebted to the discussions in Pangle, pp. 1062–5; Bloom, *Republic of Plato*, pp. 353–8, 375–8, 436; Strauss, *City and Man*, pp. 110–12, 129, 138; and Carnes Lord, *Education and Culture in the Political Thought of Aristotle* (Ithaca, N.Y., 1982), pp. 160–76, 192–96. See also Catherine H. Zuckert, ed., *Understanding the Political Spirit* (New Haven, 1988); and, on the irrational fear of divine vengeance, *Essais* I, xviii, 76–77 [53].

[7]*Republic*, 439e–440e; *Nicomachean Ethics* 1149a25–b4.

[8]See the discussions by Bloom, *Republic of Plato*, pp. 375–8; Pangle, "Political Psychology," pp. 1062–4; Lord, *Education*, pp. 162–4; Tessitore, "Aristotle's Political Presentation of Socrates," pp. 10–11.

manner reminiscent of Aristotle's distinction between anger and hate, he remarks that "the appetite for vengeance is . . . better assuaged" when we defeat an enemy without killing him, since this appetite "aims only at making itself felt," an aim that can no longer be achieved once its object is dead. For the same reason, he asserts, "we do not attack a beast or a stone when they hurt us, because they are incapable of feeling our revenge"—even though, in I, iv, he observed that people do become so irrational in their anger as to vent it on lifeless or nonexistent objects (II, xxvii, 672 [524]).

On only one point does Montaigne obviously depart from the Platonic and Aristotelian treatment of spiritedness. That point concerns the evaluation of the effects of this passion, or the degree to which *thumos* can be made the ally of reason. In "Of Anger," as noted, he questions Aristotle's claim that anger can serve as an instrument of "virtue and valor," calling it "always an imperfection" and remarking that unlike other "arms," it guides us rather than allowing us to control it (II, xxxi, 696–8 [543, 545]). And in "Of Cruelty," in a passage cited in Chapter Eight, he challenges the contention that *thumos* is more amenable to reason than erotic pleasure is (II, xi, 408–9 [313]).

Montaigne's criticism of spiritedness in later chapters attests to the importance he attaches to the theme of I, i, the means of moderating this passion. Let us now survey the argument of that chapter to determine whether any substantive teaching may be found to underlie its inconclusive or "banal" surface. At the outset, an ambiguity in the previously quoted statement with which the chapter begins should be noted: although Montaigne says that the policy of audacity and constancy has "sometimes served to produce the same effect" as that of submission, he is silent about what that effect is; that is, he does not explicitly state that either course has generally proved successful. Nor is the ambiguity entirely removed by the three examples with which he purports to illustrate the less common course. The central example is that of a soldier who found that "humility and supplication" failed "to appease" a prince who was seeking to kill him and hence "resolved in the last extremity to await him sword in hand," with the result that the prince, "having seen him take such an honorable stand, received him in grace." "This example," by Montaigne's admission, "may suffer another interpretation from those who have not read about the prodigious strength and valor of that prince." In other words, those who have not read such things—or who may disbelieve what they read, knowing how writers are prone to exaggerate rulers' virtues (III, vii, 898–9 [702–3]; cf. II, x, 393 [300])—might suspect that the prince's change of heart was the product of fear rather than admiration. Nor are the other two examples free of ambiguity: in one, Montaigne exaggerates the "mercy" displayed by a conqueror in the face of the "incredible boldness" of three enemy soldiers;[9] the other

[9]See *Oeuvres*, p. 1431 (n. 1 to p. 11).

exemplifies a kind of artful casuistry in addition to the "courage" to which the essayist calls attention[10] (I, i, 11–12 [3]).

At this point Montaigne interrupts his argument (in a 1588 addition) to describe the effect that the alternative modes described would have on him. Either one, he reports, "would easily win me, for I am wonderfully lax [*lache*] in the direction of mercy and gentleness"; but he would be "likely to surrender more naturally to compassion than to esteem"—in contrast to the Stoic view of pity as a "vicious passion." He then raises, without explicitly resolving, the question whether "to surrender simply to reverence for the sacred image of virtue," as in his three examples, is a sign of greater strength of soul than that displayed by those who yield to "commiseration," as "women, children, and the vulgar" (along with Montaigne himself) commonly do. But his next point—that "in less lofty souls, astonishment and admiration," such as Epaminondas' "haughty and arrogant manner" at his trial produced in the people of Thebes, may "engender a like effect"— suggests a negative answer (12 [4]).

Up to this point the unifying thread of Montaigne's argument has seemed to be that "audacity and constancy" may often be more effective than submission in deterring people (other than Montaigne) from vengeance. But almost all the remaining half of the chapter weakens that claim. The bulk of the text details the shocking cruelty with which two ancient rulers, Dionysius the Elder and Alexander the Great, punished valorous individuals who had resisted them. The chapter concludes with an account of the massacre that Alexander—whom Montaigne, without proffering any evidence, calls "very gracious to the vanquished"—inflicted on the Thebans (who appear for the second time in the chapter, this time as victims rather than judges). "In truth," if Alexander's anger "could have been bridled," the essayist remarks, "it would have been in the capture and desolation of the city of Thebes, at the sight of so many valiant men, lost and without any further means of common defense, cruelly put to the sword":

For fully six thousand of them were killed, of whom not one was seen fleeing or asking for mercy. . . . Not one was seen so beaten down with wounds as not to try even in his last gasp to avenge himself, and with the weapons of despair to assuage his death in the death of some enemy. Yet the distress of their valor found no pity, and the length of a day was not enough to satiate Alexander's revenge. This slaughter went on to the last drop of blood that could be shed, and stopped only at the unarmed people, old men, women, and children, so that thirty thousand of them might be taken as slaves. (14 [5])

[10]According to Bodin, the source of this anecdote, it exemplifies faith or piety (*Method for the Easy Comprehension of History*, tr. Beatrice Reynolds [New York, 1945], "Preamble," p. 12).

Since not even this spectacle could restrain Alexander's anger, we may infer that there is no reliable means of resisting such men's vengeance other than defeating them. As Montaigne sensibly remarks at the conclusion of a later chapter: "Thus above all we must beware, if we can, of falling into the hands of an enemy judge who is victorious and armed" (I, xv, 69 [48]).

Having scanned the argument of I, i, let us consider whether it points toward any conclusion more substantive than that people are diverse and unpredictable. It is true that Montaigne does not explicitly draw such a conclusion: the chapter's close is as stark as its beginning was abrupt. Yet a reconsideration of his various anecdotes does suggest some not insignificant conclusions.

The first conclusion to be drawn is that despite Montaigne's claim that the course of submission and softness is "the commonest way" of moderating a conqueror's vengefulness, that policy is an unpromising one. In each of the first three anecdotes an appeal for mercy failed, whereas "audacity and constancy" succeeded. Similarly, Epaminondas' "haughty and arrogant manner" at his trial proved more successful in dealing with the Theban people than Pelopidas' "pleas and supplications"—although the latter managed "just barely" to save himself (12 [4]). Montaigne cites only himself as a person who is more likely to yield "to compassion than to esteem"; but as he elsewhere denies ever having experienced the "sweet passion" of vengeance (III, iv, 812 [634]), he is hardly an example of the vengeful conqueror.

With respect to the overall utility of the policy of "audacity and constancy" the evidence is more ambiguous. As I have noted, the first and third examples given in the chapter somewhat exaggerate the effects to be attributed to such a policy, and in the second case, Montaigne suggests that its success is due to the conqueror's fear rather than to his esteem for virtue. In dealings with the people at large, the example of Epaminondas suggests— and Montaigne confirms in a later chapter (I, xxiv, 129–30 [95–6])—that an audacious course is best. But on the other hand, it appears, if one falls into the clutches of a Dionysius or an Alexander, there is no hope: although the valor of their victims' resistance failed to move them, their very harshness makes it seem unlikely that appeals for mercy would have succeeded any better. (Recall the list of Alexander's victims, including "the Cosseians even to their little children," previously quoted from II, xxxvi, 733 [571]).

This survey of Montaigne's examples, especially the concluding account of Alexander's cruelties, suggests that the major unresolved problem of the first chapter is how to deal with such men as Dionysius and Alexander. To shed some light on this problem, it is useful to note a parallel between this chapter and chapter 25 of *The Prince*, "How Much Fortune Is Able to Do in Human Affairs, and in What Mode It May Be Opposed." In the middle of that chapter Machiavelli remarks how men proceed "variously" or by "diverse modes" to "the end that each has before him," which Machiavelli identifies as "glory and riches." Not only does this observation, including the interpretation of the human "end" in worldly terms, remind us of the title of Montaigne's opening essay; the chapter contains a discussion of the variability of human nature which parallels the essayist's observation of that point (13 [5]).[11] There is admittedly a considerable difference in the manner in which Machiavelli and Montaigne discuss human variability: whereas Montaigne merely alludes to that fact, Machiavelli expressly teaches the *necessity* that individuals bent on worldly success should some-how manage to change their "nature" in order to adapt to, and hence overcome, the varying character of Fortune. Yet the significance of this difference may be outweighed by the following further link between the two texts: "obstinacy"—the quality opposed by Machiavelli to the variability that he recommends[12]—is also a quality that Montaigne attributes to Dionysius' and Alexander's victims (13–14 [4–5]). Although the essayist does not expressly describe these victims' obstinacy as the cause of their deaths, we are reminded of the chapter "One Is Punished for Stubbornly Holding On to a Place without Reason," wherein Montaigne identifies the excess of valor with "temerity, obstinacy, and folly" and remarks that people who display such obstinacy in opposing haughty and powerful conquerors are often massacred as a result (I, xv, 68–9 [47]). Hence we may infer a Machiavellian lesson from the fate of the victims of Dionysius and Alexander in I, i: the need to cultivate the quality opposed to "obstinacy," which Montaigne will elsewhere label "adaptability," as a means of mitigating or overcoming the cruelty of tyrants. Considering that obstinacy (the determination to defend one's position, dignity, or opinions at all costs) is a form of spiritedness, we may reformulate this lesson to mean that the spiritedness of rulers and conquerors, which issues in vengefulness, can be mitigated or overcome only by the modification or redirection of the spirited obstinacy on which those who resist them have heretofore relied.[13]

Let us now consider the relation of this lesson to the other point that has been suggested by I, i, the inefficacy of "pleas and supplications" in soften-ing a conqueror's heart. I suggest that in showing that remedy to be ineffec-tual, Montaigne was rejecting the Christian response to spiritedness: the endeavor to encourage compassion by humbling people and teaching them to emulate Christ's charity. In another passage, which I discuss later in this

[11]*The Prince,* ch. 25, p. 147. The opening lines of this chapter practically equate divine providence with Fortune, just as Montaigne does in I, iv, in connection with spiritedness.
[12]Ibid., pp. 148–9.
[13]Cf. "Of Constancy" (I, xii), where Montaigne represents constancy in enduring evils as a last resort; it is preferable, and "laudable," to employ "all honorable means of safeguarding oneself," such as moving so as to evade them (pp. 46–7 [30]).

chapter, Montaigne alludes to the ineffectuality of teaching a ruler "that we must turn our cheek to the man who has just struck the other one, for charity's sake" (III, iv, 813 [634]). And it is noteworthy that the three examples Montaigne set forth initially in I, i, to show the superiority of "audacity and constancy" to "submission" as a way to mollify a conqueror concerned Christian rulers, whereas the remaining anecdotes are drawn from pagan antiquity.[14] Evidently, Christian rulers have something in common with the ancient *demos*, as typified by the Theban people, who yielded more readily to firmness than to "pleas and supplications," and by the rank and file of Dionysius' soldiers, who, unlike their leader, "were softened by astonishment at such rare virtue" as his obstinate captive displayed (13 [4]). Both Montaigne's comment on the central one of his first three examples and his intimation, in discussing Alexander, that people are impressed with valor to the degree that they lack it (14 [5]) suggest that to the extent that Christian rulers moderate their vengefulness at all, they do so out of weakness rather than compassion. Yet, as Montaigne argues in II, xxvii—with particular reference to the tortures perpetrated by the authorities of his time—such "cowardice" is also "the mother of cruelty"; and other chapters of the *Essays* are filled, as we have seen, with instances of Christian bloodthirstiness. Hence it appears that in the opening chapter Montaigne rejects *both* the "obstinacy" of the classical hero and the Christian appeal to compassion as modes of securing our earthly well-being against the spiritedness of the powerful.

A further dimension of Montaigne's argument in I, i, is seen in the contrast between the demeanor of Epaminondas at his trial and the behavior of Diomedon in Montaigne's account of the Athenians' unjust trial of their captains two chapters later. In Chapter Five I observed that Montaigne's account of Diomedon's conduct may be taken as an allusion to the trial of Socrates, and that it points to a criticism of the ancient philosophers for having failed to challenge popular superstitions more openly, as indicated in "Of Prognostications." In this regard Montaigne's account of Epamonindas' success, in contrast with the failure of Diomedon-Socrates, suggests the need for a more forthright defense of *philosophy* against popular spiritedness than any of its ancient practitioners undertook.

How that goal might be combined with the defense of the people's own interest against the spiritedness of vengeful conquerors is suggested by the first of a pair of anecdotes about two-thirds of the way through I, i. Just

---

[14]Zeitlin, *Essays of Montaigne*, 1:293, points out that Montaigne's apparent source for the central example of those three (Paolo Giovio, *Commentarii delle Cose de' Turchi*) does not state, as Montaigne does, that the soldier in that anecdote "tried by every sort of humility and supplication to appease" the prince before resolving to defend himself. Since—contrary to Zeitlin—it is not "generally safe to assume that [Montaigne] did not deliberately alter the stories which he used," we may surmise that the essayist modified this story in order to identify the unsuccessful course with the Christian policy.

after remarking the variability of human nature, Montaigne illustrates it
with two examples from Plutarch's *Political Precepts:*

> Here is Pompey pardoning the whole city of the Mamertines, against which he
> was greatly incensed, in consideration of the virtue and magnanimity of the
> citizen Zeno, who took the public's fault [*la faute publique*] upon himself, and
> asked no other favor but to bear the punishment alone. And Sulla's host, who
> displayed similar virtue in the city of Perusia, gained nothing from it, either for
> himself or for the others. (13 [5])

Plutarch himself explains the different results of virtue in these two cases
in terms of the difference in character between the two conquerors involved.[15] Hence his account of them does appear to bear out Montaigne's
claim that people are so diverse as to render it difficult to form a uniform
judgment on them. But let us take note of a seemingly trivial change that
Montaigne made in transcribing the first anecdote. The name of the citizen
whose virtue impressed Pompey was not Zeno, according to Plutarch, but
Stheno. Montaigne's editors have generally assumed that this alteration is a
simple mistake.[16] But if we take seriously Montaigne's denial, in "Of
Presumption," that he has made any unintentional errors, we may be
inspired to seek a reason for the emendation.

By means of his substitution, Montaigne has given the successful practitioner of virtue the name of two famous ancient philosophers, one of whom
was the founder of the Stoic sect. That it is the Stoic whom Montaigne has
in mind is suggested by a mention of that sect earlier in the chapter,
concerning the school's dismissal of pity as "a vicious passion" (12 [4]).[17]
Interestingly, the references to the Stoics and to Zeno are placed in such a
manner as to divide the text of the chapter into approximately equal thirds.

Let us now consider another modification that Montaigne made in Plutarch's account. According to Plutarch, Stheno moderated Pompey's anger
by telling him "that he would be doing wrong if he should destroy many
innocent men for the fault of one: for, he said, it was he [Stheno] himself
who had caused the city to revolt by persuading his friends and compelling
his enemies."[18] By contrast, Montaigne makes Zeno's action appear a
purely gratuitous act of charity: Zeno does not represent himself as the
original cause of the people's "fault." Are we not reminded by this action, as
Montaigne recounts it, of a God-man who assumed the burden of human-

[15]Plutarch, *Political Precepts,* XIX, 815e–816a.
[16]E.g., *Oeuvres,* p. 1431 (n. 1 to p. 13); Frame, ed., *Complete Works,* p. 5 (where "Stheno" is substituted); Villey, "Les Sources des Essais," in Strowski et al., eds., *Les Essais,* 4:3.
[17]The *Essays* contains some two dozen references to this Zeno (of Cittium) and only two to the other (of Elea); both of the latter occur in the lists of philosophers' opinions in the "Apology."
[18]*Political Precepts,* tr. Harold North Fowler, 815e–f, in *Plutarch's Moralia,* vol. 10 (Cambridge, Mass., 1936).

ity's sins, despite his own blamelessness, and gave up his life, under the Roman regime, for their salvation?[19]

In this light, I suggest the following explanation of Montaigne's substitution of Zeno for Stheno. Through his transformation of the anecdote, Montaigne supplants a Christlike figure with a philosopher as a model of compassion toward humanity. Zeno himself would not properly fit that role, given the Stoics' previously cited contempt for pity. But by juxtaposing his own compassion with the Stoics' attitude, Montaigne prefigures the overall rhetorical movement of the *Essays,* in which, as I argued in Chapter Eight, he endeavors to supplant the Stoic model of virtue typified by Cato with his own self-portrait. If we applied that principle to the present case, we would be led to substitute *Montaigne himself* for Zeno. In other words: Montaigne indirectly suggests that the Christian model is to be replaced with his own, more effectual mode of compassion, the nature of which I have considered in the preceding chapter. It is precisely the degree of his compassion for humanity that distinguishes Montaigne from previous philosophers, including the Stoics, but it is the philosophic form of that compassion that renders it more effectual than the Christian variety. In this way, Montaigne introduces the project enunciated in the "Apology" of harmonizing philosophy and political society by turning the philosopher into the benefactor of humanity. Montaigne emulates Christ in undertaking to defend the people against oppression by excessively spirited rulers, but this project will require a "diversion" of the *popular* spiritedness that underlies Christianity itself and that has thus far rendered the people hostile to philosophy and hence to reason. The alliance he proposes with the multitude (III, xiii, 1079 [844]) requires that philosophers openly acknowledge the truth that they have "stubborn[ly]" obscured until now: that whatever the means we adopt, our true "end" is earthly pleasure (I, xx, 80 [56]).[20]

---

[19]Note that Zeno, in Montaigne's account, seeks "grace." Cf. "George Sechel, leader of those Polish peasants who, under pretext of a crusade, did so much harm"; in dying, Sechel prayed for his brother's "salvation" [*salut*], "drawing upon himself all the hatred for [his followers'] misdeeds"; the others were driven to drink his blood and feed on his body (II, xxvii, 680 [530]). This anecdote follows shortly after another concerning crucifixions (679 [530]). Cf. also Machiavelli's discussion of the customary modes of acquiring "grace" from a prince, in the Epistle Dedicatory of *The Prince.*
Another "error" of Montaigne's in the first chapter, his reference to Perusia (rather than Praeneste) as the site where the virtue of Sulla's guest-friend failed to move that conqueror to clemency, may well be due, as Montaigne's editors have supposed, to the fact that Amyot had made this error in the first edition of his translation of Plutarch (*Oeuvres*, p. 1431 [n. 4 to p. 13]). On the other hand, it may be significant that Perusia (= Perugia) was the site of a celebrated incident involving Pope Julius II, to whom Machiavelli alludes in the same chapter of *The Prince* that I have previously cited in connection with I, i (*The Prince,* ch. 25, pp. 100–101; *Discourses,* I, xxvii).
[20]Note that the quality of stubbornness (*opiniastreté*) that Montaigne attributes to the philosophers in this passage is the same one (*s'opiniastrer à une place*) that he identifies as the cause of people's being "punished" in I, xv; perhaps the "place" to which certain individuals

The theme of spirited vengefulness and the massacres it may engender had an obvious timeliness for the immediate audience of the *Essays,* who had already suffered through eighteen years of almost continuous, bloody civil war by the time the book was first published. Montaigne's decision to illustrate this theme in the opening chapter with the massacres inflicted by Alexander, rather than those committed by the French religious partisans, no doubt reflects his prudence.[21] But the connection to contemporary events will be made explicit in an essay that is linked with I, i, by its title, its theme, and its ostensible lesson: I, xxiv, "Various Outcomes of the Same Plan." The title of this chapter constitutes a mirror image of that of I, i: whereas the earlier chapter asserted that various courses may lead to the same result, this one purports to demonstrate that the same course may produce various results. The theme of I, xxiv, also provides a kind of reverse image of its predecessor: instead of considering how a conqueror's victims might soften his heart, it treats how a ruler or leader might deter his subjects from attacking him. And in both chapters, Montaigne's ostensible conclusion is that human affairs are too variable and unpredictable, or dependent on "Fortune," to permit any reliable practical rule to be laid down concerning the matter in question.[22] Consideration of key examples discussed in I, xxiv, as in I, i, suggests a more concrete and substantive conclusion.

---

have adhered with foolish stubbornness is a philosophic position. Cf. *The Prince,* ch. 20, regarding the superiority of popular support to reliance on "fortified" positions.

[21]The connection of the theme of I, i, to the religious wars is noted by Nakam, *Montaigne et son temps,* p. 100. In the very first anecdote of the chapter, Montaigne refers to "our Guienne" (9 [3]).

[22]I, i, and I, xxiv, actually constitute the first two-thirds of a triptych of chapters, numerically equidistant from one another, in which this ostensible lesson is suggested both in the title and in the body of the text. The third member of the group is I, xlvii, "Of the Uncertainty of Our Judgment." Without undertaking a comprehensive interpretation of that chapter here, I suggest that it should be understood in light of the twelfth chapter of Book II of Machiavelli's *Discourses,* the theme of which—"Whether It Is Better, When Fearing to Be Attacked, to Bring On War or Await It"—is the sixth and last question considered by Montaigne in I, xlvii. Both chapters are, as Leo Strauss observed of the Machiavellian text, parodies of Scholastic disputations, applied to non-Scholastic subjects (*Thoughts on Machiavelli,* p. 41). By using the word *terre* (land) four times in discussing his last topic, Montaigne reminds us of the "poetic fable" of Antaeus that Machiavelli had retold in *Discourses* II, xii, which suggests that people's strength depends on their remaining attached to their earthly home, rather than allowing themselves to be drawn "away from the earth [*terra*]." Earlier in I, xlvii, Montaigne deals with another Machiavellian theme, that of insults, which Machiavelli uses as a metaphor for the Christian "calumny" against humanity; Montaigne's conclusion suggests the need to find some means *other* than insults to make men resolute by "depriv[ing]" them of "all hope of grace" (I, xlvii, 273–6 [206–9]; Machiavelli, *Discorsi,* II, xii, 308; II, xxvi; Mansfield, *Machiavelli's New Modes and Orders,* pp. 222, 275–6).

The importance of the metaphorical teaching that I believe is contained in the "military" discussion of I, xlvii, may be signified by the fact that this chapter marked the halfway point of the first edition of the *Essays* (which had ninety-four chapters), and that its number was identical with the age Montaigne had just reached according to the date in "To the Reader." Of particular significance in this regard—and also reminiscent of Machiavelli—is the discussion in the center of the chapter of the need to find a way "to safeguard the leader of an army" by

"Various Outcomes of the Same Plan"

The core teaching of I, xxiv, may be gleaned from a comparison of two anecdotes purportedly exemplifying opposite outcomes of the same plan which Montaigne recounts at the beginning of this chapter. The first anecdote he claims to have been told by "Jacques Amyot, Grand Almoner of France . . . to the honor of one of our princes." From the facts contained in the anecdote, as well as its sequel, it becomes clear that the prince in question was Francis, Duke of Guise, one of two militant Catholic brothers, members of a leading noble family, who together rose to dominant political influence following the death of Henry II in 1559.[23] According to the story, "during our first troubles, at the siege of Rouen"—that is, at the outset of the civil wars in 1562—the prince "was warned by the Queen Mother [Catherine de' Medici] of a plot against his life and particularly informed by her letters of the person who was to carry it out." His response was to confront the man and compel him to "confess" his plan. Rather than allow the man to "pray for grace and mercy," the prince asked his reason for wanting to kill him, since the prince hardly knew him and had done him no harm. When the man responded that he had planned the assassination for "no personal cause" but rather for that of "his party," since he had been persuaded that it would be "an execution full of piety to extirpate by any means whatever so powerful an enemy of their religion" (presumably, the Protestant one), the prince responded by purporting to demonstrate "how

___

disguising him, while enabling him to signify his "presence" to his followers (273 [207]): this is in a sense Montaigne's own rhetorical problem (cf. II, xix, 654 [509], regarding Julian's relation to his army, with the discussion of that passage in Chapter Four, above; Machiavelli, *Discorsi*, III, xxxix, 492, with Mansfield, *Machiavelli's New Modes and Orders*, p. 423).

A full interpretation of I, xlvii, would also need to relate that chapter's consideration of whether King Francis should have remained "at home" at the time of Charles V's expedition into Provence, as he did, or gone "before him in Italy" (274–5 [208]), to the question raised in I, xiii, "Ceremony of Kings' Interviews," whether one ought to remain "at home" when someone "however great" "had notified you that he was to come," or should "go before the person who is coming to find him," despite the risk of his thereby "losing his way": perhaps the great personage whose "coming" Montaigne has in mind is Christ (I, xiii, 48–9 [33]; cf. also II, iv, 344–5 [262–3], concerning the "indiscretion" of "abandon[ing]" all things to speak with [or 'support'] a newcomer"). Both Francis and Charles figure in the related discussion in I, xiii, of whether the lesser personage should be first at a meeting with someone greater or "more apparent" (ostensibly, in both cases, the pope); according to the "noble response" of Eumenes in an earlier chapter, one need not regard anyone else as "greater," and so feel obliged to come before him, as long as one remains armed (I, xiii, 48–9 [32]; I, v, 29 [17]). Cf. Montaigne's lament that, owing to our concern with "future" things, "we are never at home" (I, iii, 18 [8]); and his affirmation that his own existence lies only "at home," not in a future life (II, xvi, 610 [474–5]); also, Francis's endeavor "to maintain some intelligences in Italy," with its deleterious result (I, ix, 38 [24]; I, xi, 43 [27–8]; see n. 35 to Chapter Five, above).

[23]The identification of the prince is made by numerous editors. On the Guises' political role, see James Westfall Thompson, *The Wars of Religion in France, 1559–1576* (Chicago, 1909), chs. 1–7, passim.

much gentler is the religion I hold than the one that you profess. Yours has advised you to kill me without a hearing, having received no harm from me; and mine commands me to pardon you, convicted though you are of having wanted to murder me without reason." Hence he let the man go free (122–3 [90–91]). Unfortunately for the prince, we learn farther on, "his mildness was not able to protect him from falling later into the toils of a similar treason" (125 [92])—an apparent reference to the assassination of the Duke of Guise a few months later.[24] Considering that a plan seemingly identical with the prince's had once been effected, with complete success, by the emperor Augustus, Montaigne concludes that "human prudence" is "a vain and frivolous" thing, subject to the whims of Fortune. In such cases where "the diverse accidents and circumstances" of the matter have so perplexed us that we are unable "to see and choose what is most advantageous" (by implication, not necessarily in other cases), he holds, the "surest" course is that in which there is "more honesty and justice." In the instances of Guise and Augustus, it was doubtless "finer and more generous for the man who had received the offense to pardon it"; Guise is not to be blamed if he "came to grief," for who knows whether he would have averted his fate had he chosen the less glorious course (125, 127–8 [92–4])?

But was the failed policy of the modern prince truly identical with that of his ancient predecessor? Montaigne's account of Augustus' "clemency" toward a conspirator summarizes a passage in Seneca's essay "Of Clemency." In the account Augustus, who had unsuccessfully relied on a policy of "severity" until then (according to Seneca, his actions in the pursuit of power had been vicious),[25] does confront the conspirator with his knowledge of the plot but then allows him to go free, just as Montaigne's modern prince did. What is lacking in the ancient example, however, by contrast with that of Guise, is any reference to religion as the real or ostensible motive of the ruler's clemency (or of the planned assassination). Augustus, moreover, does not limit himself to setting a more salutary moral example for the conspirator's edification; he shows the conspirator that the attainment of his presumed goal—imperial power—would be detrimental to the latter's own *interest*. As he points out, the conspirator lacks the capacity to defend his own house and recently lost a lawsuit; the various other claimants to power, "and such a great host of nobles," could not be expected to endure his rule (125 [92]). Hence the comparison between this anecdote and the previous one does not necessarily demonstrate that human affairs are too unpredictable to allow us to know what course to choose. Rather— if we recall Montaigne's account of himself as a "historian" who selects the

[24]Montaigne refers to that assassination as a "lofty execution" at II, xxix, 689 [538].
[25]Seneca, *Of Clemency,* I, ix.

facts he recounts in order to guide his readers' belief—it is reasonable to suspect that he intends the underlying differences in the outwardly similar courses pursued by the two leaders to explain their differing outcomes.

The full point of Montaigne's modern example becomes apparent only when we consider the character of the Duke of Guise, whom he represents as a spokesman for Christian charity and forgiveness. It was Guise, the Catholic champion, who set off the civil wars by leading a massacre of Protestant worshipers at Vassy in 1562.[26] The siege of Rouen ended in an even bloodier massacre of the city's Huguenot and English defenders by the Catholic forces, for which Guise was held chiefly responsible; he is reported to have urged, as a first priority, the "execution of man, woman, and child" by the victors.[27]

Since we have no independent documentation, so far as I know, of the story of Guise's clemency which Montaigne attributes to Amyot—and since, even if the story were true, its evidence of the duke's character would be outweighed by that of his actions at such places at Vassy and Rouen—the irony of Montaigne's anecdote is enormous. That irony is deepened by his understated reference to "our first troubles"—as if Guise had had no connection to those troubles![28]

[26]See Thompson, *Wars of Religion*, pp. 134ff.; for a pro-Guise account, Henry Dwight Sedgwick, *The House of Guise* (Indianapolis, 1938), ch. 17.

[27]Thompson, *Wars of Religion*, p. 169.

[28]In "Of Presumption" Montaigne ranks Francis of Guise among "the most notable men that I have judged by external appearances . . . in point of war and military ability"; but not only is this commendation limited to the duke's military capacities, it is undermined by Montaigne's remark in the preceding chapter that "all these judgments that are founded on external appearances are marvelously uncertain and doubtful" (II, xvi, 609 [474]; II, xvii, 644 [501]).

Also indicative of Montaigne's attitude toward the Guises is a passage in the chapter "Defense of Seneca and Plutarch" professing to esteem Francis's brother, the Cardinal of Lorraine, for his capacity, zeal, and loyalty, as well as "his good fortune to have been born in a century where it was so novel and so rare, and at the same time so necessary for the public good, to have an ecclesiastical personage of such nobility and dignity competent and capable of his charge" (II, xxxii, 699 [545]). Champion is scandalized by this seeming praise of a harsh religious partisan, believing it to reflect "a violent partisan spirit, a sort of fanaticism" from which Montaigne had suffered earlier in his life (*Introduction aux Essais*, pp. 27–8). But the immediate sequel to the passage subtly retracts its flattery. After observing that the pamphlets circulated by the Protestants "sometimes come from good hands," Montaigne cites one that had drawn a parallel "between the government of our late poor King Charles IX and that of Nero," and consequently between Lorraine and Seneca as the two rulers' chief advisers. Such a comparison, in Montaigne's opinion, "does great honor to the said Lord Cardinal" (contrary to the presumable intention of the pamphlet's author), since the cardinal's capacity was not "nearly so great, nor his virtue so clear and entire and firm as Seneca's." He follows this assertion with an ostensible refutation of the pamphleteer's "very insulting description of Seneca," which, however, is so backhanded as to deepen the insult. In response to the charge that Seneca was "avaricious, usurious, ambitious, effeminate, voluptuous, and playing the philosopher on false pretenses," Montaigne asserts that "Seneca's virtue shows forth so live and vigorous *in his writings,* and the defense is so clear there against *some* of these imputations, as that of his wealth and excessive spending, that I would not believe any testimony to

These facts about the Duke of Guise suggest that even if he did display clemency toward one particular opponent, his overall profession of practicing a "religion" of gentleness and forgiveness was hypocritical. The charge of hypocrisy is one that Montaigne will level explicitly against both parties in the religious wars in the "Apology for Raymond Sebond" (II, xii, 419–21 [322–4]). Considered in relation to the theme I have been examining—the means of moderating human spiritedness and vengefulness—Montaigne's comparison between the policies of the Duke of Guise and Augustus appears to deepen his implicit critique in I, i, of the effectiveness of Christian "compassion." Not only did the profession of Christian gentleness fail to protect Guise from being assassinated, it failed to moderate his own overall conduct toward his opponents. In the case of Guise as well as his assassins, the Christian religion appears to have furnished a motive for violence less susceptible of moderation than the openly self-interested motives of earthly ambition for which the ancient pagans (represented by Augustus' would-be assassin) attacked one another. (Note that the account of Guise follows by only a few pages Montaigne's denunciation in "Of Custom" of the "self-love and presumption" displayed by both parties in the religious wars.)

Not only does Augustus' success in deterring a conspiracy contrast with

---

the contrary. And, moreover, it is much more reasonable in these matters to believe the Roman historians," such as Tacitus, "who speak very honorably of both his life and death," than "the Greeks and foreigners," such as the historian Dion, the source of the Protestant's portrait of Seneca (II, xxxii, 699–700 [545–6]).

This defense of Seneca, relying largely on his writings, must be read in the light of Montaigne's discussion, in the preceding chapter, of the disharmony between people's sayings and their conduct. As the wicked may "preach" things they do not believe, it is "an easy game" "to attack the truth of our Church through the vices of her ministers" (II, xxxi, 693 [541]). (Compare Montaigne's claim there that the church "draws her testimony from elsewhere" than its ministers' conduct with his assertion in the "Apology" that goodness of conduct is the *only* objective test of religious truth; and cf. Machiavelli's reference to the "learning, prudence, and virtue" of Savonarola's mind, as reflected in "his writings," followed by an account of the friar's hypocritical and harmful conduct: *Discorsi*, I, xlv, 233.) In Book III Montaigne accuses Tacitus, his witness on Seneca's behalf, of numerous errors of judgment, including his judgment of Pompey—a point on which he had taken Dion to task in II, xxxii, so as ostensibly to discredit Dion's condemnation of Seneca (III, viii, 919–21 [719–20]). In regard to Montaigne's own judgment of Seneca, one should consider not only the passage in "Of Physiognomy" alluding to "the trouble to which Seneca puts himself to be prepared for death" (III, xii, 1016–17 [795]), thus giving weight to Dion's claim concerning the falsity of his philosophic pretensions, but also a remark in "Of Books" that Seneca "concedes a little to the tyranny of the emperors of his time," thus demonstrating the inferiority of his teaching to Plutarch's as a guide to civil affairs (II, x, 393 [300]). And in II, xxxii, not only does Montaigne juxtapose his backhanded defense of Seneca with a more powerful, and extended, praise of Plutarch; he specifically defends the latter's comparisons between the lives of the most famous Greeks and Romans against the charge that he was unjust to the latter—hence counteracting his claim, in reference to Dion's judgment of Seneca, that Roman historians are more trustworthy than "Greeks and foreigners" in judging Roman affairs (700, 704 [546, 549]). In sum, in saying that the Protestant pamphleteer did "great honor" to Lorraine by comparing him with Seneca, Montaigne really meant that the Protestant hadn't insulted the cardinal enough: despite his numerous defects, Seneca was still far superior! (See also, on the backhandedness of Montaigne's seeming eulogy of Lorraine, Nakam, *Montaigne et son temps*, p. 67.)

Guise's failure to do so; it also differs from the attitude that Montaigne describes other ancient rulers as having adopted toward such conspiracies. Having asserted that "most" people who "have followed the course of running to meet conspiracies against them with vengeance and punishment" have failed to secure themselves, he sets forth, by contrast, examples of three ancient rulers (Dion, Alexander, and Caesar) who disdained to investigate such conspiracies, choosing to face the risk of assassination with noble resolution. But of these three rulers, the first and third were killed as a result,[29] and Montaigne implies that the preservation of the second was due merely to chance (128 [94]). Even though Montaigne praises the beauty and nobility of such a posture of indifference regarding one's security, rulers will hardly be inspired to emulate it by its apparent likely consequences. They might find more useful Montaigne's account (borrowed from Plutarch) of the stratagem that the tyrant Dionysius learned from a stranger "to keep his enemies in fear" (paying the stranger on the public pretense that he had learned "a singular secret" from him), as well as the essayist's criticism (echoing Machiavelli)[30] of the stupidity of a modern tyrant, the Duke of Athens, in killing a man who had informed him of "the conspiracies that the people were forming against him" (131 [96–7]). Both anecdotes confirm the need Montaigne elsewhere attributes to rulers to acquire "good advice" from a wise and frank counselor (I, li, 293 [222])—a role for which, as we have seen, he recommends himself. Such advice as Montaigne has offered to princes in I, xxiv, amounts to the recommendation that they emulate Augustus in demonstrating that their rule is conducive to their subjects' security and well-being, rather than rely on either religion or terror to secure their position. At the same time, in advising rulers on how to deal with frenzied popular passions that endanger the public peace, he recommends (in the spirit of Machiavelli) a policy of "gracious severity" rather than "submission and softness" or "penitence" (129–30 [95]).[31] The teach-

---

[29]Montaigne explicitly refers to Caesar's assassination (p. 131 [96]). He borrows his account of Dion's attitude toward the conspiracy against him from Plutarch, *Sayings of Kings and Commanders,* 176–7; Plutarch discusses Dion's death as a result of that conspiracy in his "Life of Dion," *Lives,* pp. 1184–5. Cf. Machiavelli's interpretation of Dion's behavior as a failed stratagem, *Discorsi,* III, vi, 412. Regarding Alexander, compare *Essais,* II, i, 320 [243], criticizing him for "worry[ing] so frantically when he conceives the slightest suspicion that his men are plotting against his life," and "behav[ing] in such matters with such violent and indiscriminate injustice, and with a fear that subverts his natural reason."

[30]Machiavelli, *Discorsi,* III, vi, 412. Cf. Dionysius' treatment of his "obstinate" opponent in *Essais,* I, i, 13 [4].

[31]Cf. Montaigne's remark in this passage that one can calm an agitated populace only by instilling "reverence and fear" in them, not by "humanity and softness" or "penitence," with Machiavelli's account of two similar incidents in which a "grave" man succeeded in restraining a mob by employing, respectively, words "partly loving, partly menacing" and the people's reverence: *Discorsi,* I, xiii, 168; I, liv, 253; also *The Prince,* ch. 7, pp. 29–30, and ch. 17, p. 65, on the nature of effectual "compassion." Cf. also Montaigne's recommendation of a policy of "severe gentleness" in the education of the young (I, xxvi, 165 [122]).

ing Montaigne addresses to princes in I, xxiv, thus accords with the lesson of I, i, that earthly salvation can best be achieved by a mode other than those of (Christian) "softness" or (pagan) "obstinacy." Montaigne, like Machiavelli, can advise both princes and peoples without contradicting himself, inasmuch as his teaching aims to harmonize the interests of the two sides.

"Diverting" People from Vengeance

In the two chapters that have been considered thus far, Montaigne's critique of the classical and Christian modes of dealing with spiritedness or vengefulness is stated by indirection, in the form of a series of examples from which the reader must infer the lesson. In accordance with the generally "franker" character of Book III, the lesson is stated more overtly in a passage in the fourth chapter of that book, titled "Of Diversion," of which I have previously quoted one portion:

> Vengeance is a sweet passion, the impact of which is great and natural; I see this well, even though I have no experience of it. Recently, in order to distract a young prince from it, *I did not tell him that we must turn our cheek* to the man who has just struck the other one, *for the duty of charity; nor did I represent* to him *the tragic results that poetry attributes* to this passion. I let it [the passion] alone and applied myself to making him relish the beauty of a contrary picture, the honor, favor, and goodwill he would acquire by clemency and goodness; I turned him away towards ambition. *That is how it is done.* (III, iv, 812–13 [634])

The second sentence of this passage makes unmistakably clear, I believe, Montaigne's rejection of the Christian teaching of humility and charity as an ineffectual antidote for vengeance. At the same time, the second clause of that sentence appears to constitute a rejection, as well, of Aristotle's teaching that tragedy can serve as a means of "purging" or purifying such politically dangerous passions as vengefulness—a teaching reflecting his endeavor to make spiritedness an ally of reason.[32] Montaigne elsewhere alludes to the ineffectuality of such purgations by citing "Alexander, tyrant of Pheres," who "could not bear to hear tragedies played in the theater for fear that his citizens might see him groaning at the misfortunes of Hecuba and Andromache, he who, without pity, had so many people cruelly murdered every day" (II, xxvii, 671 [523–4]). Montaigne's criticism of tragedy is linked with his critique of Christianity, inasmuch as the Christian reli-

[32]See Aristotle, *Politics*, 1342a12–14; *Poetics*, 1449b24–29; Lord, *Education*, pp. 159–64, 169–73.

gion, as I observed in Chapter Eight, embodies a serious or "tragic" view of human life that he finds conducive to cruelty. The anecdote about Alexander of Pheres occurs near the beginning of the chapter titled "Cowardice, Mother of Cruelty"; toward the close of that chapter Montaigne repeats verbatim the sentence condemning torture from "Of Cruelty" which earned the church's censure; and he follows that remark with a criticism of the "old fashion" of killing people by crucifying them, as well as an anecdote borrowed from Josephus which suggests a naturalistic explanation of Christ's resurrection (II, xxvii, 679 [530]).[33] The apparent implication is that Christianity originated out of a desire for "just revenge" against pagan tyranny, but only engendered new "tragedies" for the entertainment of "foreigners" (675, 678 [527–8]). We can overcome the self-perpetuating cycle of cruelty and vengeance (678 [527]) only by adopting a new and nontragic attitude toward the soul which Montaigne, in the passage I quoted from III, iv, labels "diversion."

Although the passage from "Of Diversion" makes explicit Montaigne's rejection of previous remedies for the spirited vengefulness of rulers, it leaves the positive nature of his own remedy less clear. The explicit course he claims to have adopted with the young prince—to redirect him toward ambition—seems to mirror the appeal that Augustus' wife made to him, which inspired that emperor's act of "clemency," according to the story Montaigne borrowed from Seneca in I, xxiv (124 [91]). Seneca employs a similar appeal, in the work in which the story is recounted, to persuade Nero of the popular goodwill he will gain by clemency.[34] But in view of Seneca's evident failure to moderate the cruelties of "his fine disciple," as Montaigne calls Nero in discussing the death sentence the emperor imposed on his preceptor (II, xxxv, 725 [566], and of the essayist's criticism of Seneca for toadying to the emperors of his time (II, x, 393 [300]), it is unlikely that Montaigne can regard the appeal to ambition as a simply adequate remedy for vengefulness. The root problem is that ambition can take a variety of forms, not all of them conducive to clemency. Although a given ruler, such as the mature Augustus, or the young prince with whom Montaigne reports having dealt in "Of Diversion," might be moved to overcome his vengefulness in the hope of obtaining the "honor, favor, and goodwill" of his subjects, other rulers, whose ambition leads them to demand grander rewards, may be led by that same passion toward cruelty

[33]Compare Montaigne's condemnation in this chapter of his contemporaries' practice of introducing a third party into their quarrels, rather than relying on their own virtue (II, xxvii, 674 [526]), with Machiavelli's warning against allowing a "powerful foreigner" to gain influence in one's domain (The Prince, ch. 3, p. 11), and Montaigne's Machiavellian recommendation that we combat fortune with "our own arms" (I, xiv, 67 [45]); cf. also the concluding anecdote of II, xxvii, cited in n. 19, above.

[34]Of Clemency, I, i, 5–6. Cf. Montaigne's recommendation of "clemency and magnanimity" in his 1590 letter to Henry IV (Oeuvres, p. 1398 [1092]).

or harshness. Alexander the Great, in Montaigne's depiction of him, is a prime example: according to an anecdote in III, x, the Macedonian conqueror's ambition led him to be dissatisfied with the opportunity to inherit an "easy and peaceful" dominion from his father; he would not have wanted even to enjoy the governance of the whole world "softly and peaceably" (1000 [782]). What differentiates Alexander's ambition from that of other men is its immoderate quality, or its directedness toward immortal glory, which leads him, like Caesar, to seek out "unrest and difficulties" with the same ardor with which others pursue "security and repose" (I, xiv, 61 [42]), in order thereby to demonstrate his suprahuman character. It is this very belief in his superiority, as we have seen, that makes Alexander all the less inclined to pity others' sufferings, or to moderate his vengefulness against those who dare to resist him. It would appear, in other words, that as a prerequisite for the appeal to ambition to succeed in moderating a ruler's cruelty—as it did in the case of Augustus—the ruler's ambition must have already been moderated to "human" dimensions.

These considerations suggest that in order to clarify Montaigne's response to the problem of "softening the hearts" of rulers, we must further examine his understanding of ambition. One chapter that seems particularly relevant to this theme, since it not only discusses the extent to which such passions as ambition can be moderated but expressly relates ambition to a form of cruelty, is an odd essay titled "The Story of Spurina" (II, xxxiii). The "story" concerns "a young man of Tuscany" who,

> being endowed with a singular beauty, so excessive that the most continent eyes could not continently endure its brilliance . . . entered into furious spite against himself and against those rich presents that nature had made to him, as if these should be blamed for the fault of others, and deliberately slashed and disfigured with many wounds and scars the perfect proportion and symmetry that nature had so carefully observed in his visage. (II, xxxiii, 712 [555])

It is in the immediate sequel to this anecdote that Montaigne, having remarked that "these excesses are enemies of my rules," suggests that Spurina's action might be attributed to "a frantic ambition" (ibid.).

"The Story of Spurina" is one of those chapters wherein the relation between the title and the bulk of the text is most obscure.[35] Although the chapter begins and ends with a discussion of the extent to which reason can or should be given "mastery" over our appetites—a theme of which Spurina's act might be said to represent an extreme instance—its core concerns the character of Julius Caesar, more specifically three aspects of that character: his erotic desires, his ambition, and his clemency. Recalling Mon-

[35] As noted, for instance, by Sayce, *Essays*, p. 268.

taigne's remark that the titles of his chapters denote their theme by some "sign," however indirect, there is reason to suspect an underlying relation between his account of Caesar and the topic that the story of Spurina exemplifies. We have an incentive to seek out such a relation, in view of the connection that Montaigne suggested in III, iv, might exist between ambition—the one specific characteristic that Caesar and Spurina may have in common—and clemency or mildness.

The question with which Montaigne opens "The Story of Spurina" is whether, as some assert, the appetites engendered by love are hardest to restrain, inasmuch as they "affect both body and soul," or whether, "on the contrary, . . . the commingling of the body brings them some abatement and weakening," since "such desires are subject to satiety and capable of material remedies." Though Montaigne purports to favor the latter opinion, his argument suggests the contrary: of the two sorts of "material remedy" he discusses, one—the use of hair shirts "to torture [one's] loins"—is shown to be ineffectual; the other, and only reliable, one is to burn one's sexual organs (II, xxxiii, 705–6 [550–1]). It thus appears that so long as human beings remain whole, there is no way of effectively constraining their erotic appetites.[36]

Contrary to the thrust of his examples, Montaigne nonetheless concludes that "the passions that are all in the soul, such as ambition, avarice, and others, give reason much more to do" than love does, "for it can find no help for them except in its own means," and such appetites are also insatiable, growing sharper and increasing "through enjoyment." In order to demonstrate "the disparity of these appetites," Montaigne introduces "the sole example of Julius Caesar." He claims that "never was a man more addicted to amorous pleasures" than Caesar, citing numerous instances of the Roman's indulgence in them. Nonetheless, "the other passion of ambition, with which he was also infinitely wounded, coming into conflict with this one, incontinently made it give way"; Caesar's "pleasures never made him steal a single minute of time, or turn aside one step, from the occasions that presented themselves for his aggrandizement" (II, xxxiii, 706–8 [551–2]). After recounting several of Caesar's virtues—his learning, clemency, and justice—Montaigne laments that "all these fine tendencies were spoiled and stifled by the furious passion of ambition," which turned him into a "public robber" and led him to boast "that he had made the great Roman Republic a name without form and without body . . . and to allow himself to be worshiped and have divine honors paid him in his presence" (708–11 [552–4]; cf. II, x, 396 [303]).

[36]Cf. III, v, 833 [650]: "There is no passion more pressing" than sexual desire; "even those of us who have tried to get the better of it have sufficiently admitted what difficulty, or rather impossibility, there was in cooling off the body by material remedies"; also III, v, 864 [675]: sexual desire "still lives after satiety; no constant satisfaction or end can be prescribed to it."

Suetonius' life of Caesar, from which Montaigne drew most of the facts he relates about that emperor, fully confirms the strength of the two dominant passions the essayist attributes to him. What is more specifically worthy of note in Montaigne's account, however, is the judgment he places on the two passions, and the manner in which he represents their relationship. In portraying ambition as the "single vice" that ruined Caesar's other "fine inclinations" (711 [554]), Montaigne implies—contrary to the judgment he attributes to Cato (709 [553])—that Caesar's erotic indulgence is *not* to be regarded as a vice; perhaps it was itself one of his "fine" qualities. At the same time, contrary to his claim that Caesar's ambition uniformly compelled his erotic desire to "give way," Montaigne presents not a single instance in which it did so. In fact, having asserted that Caesar's "pleasures never made him steal a single minute" from the pursuit of his aggrandizement, Montaigne proceeds to cite an instance when Caesar's participation in an important debate in the Senate was interrupted by his receipt of a love letter from Cato's sister (709 [552–3]). Hence the example of Caesar is not necessarily contrary to those of "many . . . great personages whom voluptuousness made to forget the conduct of their affairs." Nor is this implicit vindication of the strength of eros contradicted by Montaigne's assertion that "where love and ambition were in equal balance and clashed together with equal forces," the latter would triumph (711 [554–5]): the assertion is meaningless, since what is in question is precisely whether, or how often, love and ambition clash, or whether the strength of ambition rivals that of erotic desire.

The direction in which these facts seem to point is as follows. Not only is the strength of erotic desire greater than those who tried to restrain it by "material remedies" believed; that desire is not simply opposed to such nonbodily passions as ambition. We may grasp the meaning of all this, I suggest, by referring back to the discussion in I, iv, of "How the Soul Discharges Its Passions on False Objects When the True Are Wanting." Taken in conjunction with "The Story of Spurina," that chapter suggests a proto-Freudian explanation of the ambition that leads such men as Caesar to become tyrants: when their "loving part" lacks "a legitimate object," it "forges itself a false and frivolous one"—such as glory, which Montaigne portrays as an "imaginary and fanciful" or insubstantial "good" (I, iv, 25 [14]; II, xii, 464 [357]; II, xvi, 601–2, 612 [468, 476]). And perhaps the same "frantic ambition" that turned Spurina against erotic pleasure was itself a product of eros.

The notion that tyranny has its roots in eros is hardly unique to either Montaigne or Freud; such a view was suggested by both Plato and Aristotle.[37] What is peculiar to Montaigne's account, however, by contrast with the classical one—and what makes his position more akin to Freud's—is

[37]*Republic,* 571a–575a; *Politics,* 1267a10–14.

his presentation of the sexual, bodily form of eros as its true one, with the "higher" manifestations of that passion appearing as inferior substitutes for, or sublimations of, the "real thing." Montaigne himself points out the difference between his understanding of eros and the Socratic one in Book III: whereas for Socrates "love is the appetite for generation by the mediation of beauty,"[38] to Montaigne, "leaving books aside and speaking more materially and simply . . . love is nothing else but the thirst for [sexual] enjoyment in a desired object, and Venus nothing else but the pleasure of discharging our vessels" (III, v, 855 [668]).

It would surely be going too far to infer that Montaigne believes that if only men fornicated enough to satisfy their erotic desires, they would give up wishing to be tyrants: to judge by the list Montaigne provides of Caesar's amours, this man who "willed to seek his glory in the ruin of his country" did not lack or pass up opportunities for sexual gratification. Nor is the essayist's putative demonstration of Caesar's "mildness and clemency" unambiguous: in "Of Cruelty" he interprets in an ironic sense Suetonius' reference to the emperor's having killed his enemies without torturing them as evidence of the mildness of his "revenges" (II, xi, 410 [314]); while an instance that Montaigne himself cites of the Roman ruler's "justice"—his having "put to death a servant of his of whom he was particularly fond, for having slept with the wife of a Roman knight, although no one made any complaint" (II, xxxiii, 710 [554])—was understandably taken by Suetonius to exemplify Caesar's "severity."[39] It nonetheless seems significant that in depicting Caesar and Alexander, whom he represents as rivals for classification among "the most excellent men," Montaigne emphasizes the disposition of the former toward both sexual indulgence and clemency while repeatedly describing the massacres inflicted by the latter.[40] Despite his lament that Caesar's ambition had "for its abominable object the ruin of his country and the general detriment of the world," he observes that that ambition "had in itself more moderation" than Alexander's (II, xxxvi, 734 [572]); and it is Alexander, not Caesar, whose valor he depicts as "extreme"

[38]The reference is to Socrates' speech in Plato's *Symposium,* 206ff.; the whole of that speech embodies an understanding of *eros* which contrasts with the one set forth by Montaigne.

[39]Suetonius, *Lives of the Caesars,* I, xlviii. At *Essais* II, xi, 410 [314], where Montaigne takes Suetonius to task for "dar[ing] to allege as evidence of [Caesar's] clemency the mere killing of those by whom [he had] been injured," he surmises that Suetonius was indirectly suggesting his horror at "the ugly and horrible examples of cruelty that the Roman tyrants put into practice." We may suppose that Montaigne—whose denunciation of torture in the same chapter was censured by the Vatican—is motivated by a similar horror at the practices of the "Roman" tyrants of his own time when he identifies Caesar's less shocking severity as "justice." Cf. Machiavelli, *Discorsi,* I, x, 157, regarding the practice of writers living under Caesar's successors.

[40]The only instance Montaigne recounts of sexual indulgence on Alexander's part—his extended liaison with an Amazon queen—was evidently motivated at least as much by ambition (the desire to produce "something great and rare for the future") as by sexual desire (III, v, 863 [675]).

and blemished by "violent and indiscriminate injustice," "fear," "superstition," and "pusillanimity" (II, i, 320 [243]).[41] Similarly, though he praises both Caesar and Alexander in the last chapter of the *Essays* for their readiness, "in the thick of their great tasks, so fully [to enjoy] natural and therefore necessary and just pleasures," he alludes later in that chapter to Alexander's "fancies about his immortalization," just after condemning the inhuman "wisdom" that causes people to try to transcend their corporeal nature (III, xiii, 1088, 1095–6 [850, 856]). In sum, the apparent linkage between Caesar's sexuality and his clemency in II, xxxiii, suggests that it was the Roman's disposition to indulge in earthly pleasures that moderated his ambition and hence his cruelty, by comparison with Alexander. By remarking, in the last chapter, that Caesar and Alexander would have been wiser to regard indulgence in "natural" pleasures as "their ordinary vocation," and "violent occupations and laborious thoughts" only an "extraordinary" one (III, xiii, 1088 [850]), Montaigne expresses his more general intention of moderating human ambition by directing people toward earthly pleasures rather than transcendent greatness. His goal is not to eliminate ambition—the characteristic motive of all political individuals—but to moderate or tame it more effectively than classical thinkers did. He confirms this intention in the chapter immediately following "The Story of Spurina," titled "Observations on Julius Caesar's Means of Making War," by retracting his claim in the earlier essay that such desires as ambition are incapable of satiety: he now suggests that "there may be some just moderation in [the] desire for glory, and some satiety in this appetite as in others" (II, xxxiv, 719 [561]). If, as the passage I quoted previously from "Of Diversion" suggests, Montaigne's remedy for the vengefulness of rulers is to "divert" them toward ambition—more specifically, to encourage them to pursue their subjects' "honor, favor, and good will" by means of "clemency and kindness"—that remedy presupposes that the rulers' ambition will be satisfied with the love of their contemporaries, rather than being directed toward "immortal" glory, a pursuit that (as in the case of Alexander) makes them indifferent to others' sufferings. Such a remedy also presupposes that the people at large will learn to judge rulers' merit by their promotion of the

[41]The "extreme" of valor, it will be remembered, is tantamount to vice (I, xv, 68–9 [47]; I, xxx, 195 [146]). Montaigne's account of the "blemishes" on Alexander's valor in II, i, contradicts his claim in "Of the Most Excellent Men" that the Macedonian's glory was "exempt from blemish" (II, xxxvi, 733 [572]). Similarly, the putative defense of Alexander in the latter chapter against criticisms of some of his particular misdeeds—"such men deserve to be judged in gross, by the master purpose of their actions"—is undermined by a subsequent remark that "all judgments in gross are loose and imperfect" (III, viii, 922 [721]; cf. II, xxix, 683 [533]). Alexander's recompense for the murder of Clytus, which Montaigne cites as evidence of his "goodness," was previously described as exemplifying "the unevenness of his temper" (II, i, 320 [243]); while the saying that Alexander derived "his virtues from nature, his vices from fortune" is almost immediately contradicted by Montaigne's remark that "there is more of his own in Caesar's exploits, more of fortune in Alexander's" (II, xxxvi, 733–4 [572]).

people's earthly security and well-being (as suggested by Augustus' remarks in I, xxiv), rather than by their military conquests or their piety.

My survey of Montaigne's treatment of spiritedness has been intended to indicate how that treatment harmonizes with his more general critique of, and response to, classical and Christian morality. I believe that the points made in this and the preceding chapters can be confirmed, and the practical meaning of Montaigne's recommendation that human beings emulate the beasts brought out more concretely, by considering two more essays that are linked by their seemingly opposed titles, but which set forth the same teaching: "Of Moderation" (I, xxx) and "Of Drunkenness" (II, ii).

"Moderation" and "Drunkenness"

Of all the chapters of the *Essays*, perhaps none more concisely typifies Montaigne's mode of blending serious thought with satire than "Of Moderation." It will be recalled that this chapter begins with a discussion of the problem of "excessive" virtue. Early on in the chapter Montaigne expresses a preference for "temperate and middling natures" and an astonishment at or antipathy toward "immoderation, even in the direction of the good." After illustrating such "savage and costly" "virtue" with the examples of two ancients who brought about the deaths of their own offspring, and citing the opinion of "Callicles, in Plato . . . that the extremity of philosophy is harmful," he focuses more extensive attention on the endeavor of "theology" to "bridle and restrain" even the "legitimate" affection that men bear toward their wives. Purporting to defend "theology and philosophy" against the complaint that they "enter in everywhere," even into men's most "private and secret" affairs, he advises husbands, "on behalf" of those sciences, "that even the pleasures they get in making love to their wives are condemned, if moderation is not observed therein." To assist men in thus respecting the sanctity of marriage, "a religious and holy bond" the "principal end" of which is generation, he offers an outlet for their excessively licentious desires: "Let them at least learn shamelessness from another hand" by practicing their "excesses" on women other than their wives, as the Persian kings did. The proper remedy for "immoderation," it appears, is adultery (I, xxx, 195–7 [146–7])!

The most abrupt break in the argument of "Of Moderation" occurs about two-thirds of the way through the chapter, just after Montaigne has observed that "there is no sensual pleasure so just that excess and intemperance in it are not a matter of reproach." At this point he interjects: "*But, to speak in good earnest,* isn't man a miserable animal? Hardly is it in his power, by his natural condition, to taste a single pleasure entire and pure, and still he is at pains to curtail that pleasure by reason; he is not wretched enough unless by art and study he augments his misery" (198 [148]). Our suspicion that, in purporting to warn men against excessive indulgence in sensual pleasure, Montaigne was *not* speaking in earnest is confirmed by the sequel, wherein he mocks "human wisdom" for "very stupidly exercising its ingenuity to reduce the number and the sweetness of the sensual pleasures that belong to us" and denounces "our spiritual and bodily physicians" for "find[ing] no way to a cure, no remedy for the diseases of the body and the soul, but by torment, misery, and pain," such as "vigils, fasts, hair shirts, remote and solitary exiles, perpetual imprisonments, scourges, and other afflictions." Despite the passing, rhetorically protective reference to medicine in the literal sense, the real object of Montaigne's attack is the "spiritual physicians," the theologians and philosophers he had previously purported to represent. He makes this fact clear when he observes the relation of the attitude he has been denouncing to "this other very ancient one, of thinking to gratify heaven and nature by massacre and homicide, [a belief] universally embraced by all religions." The chapter closes with an elaboration of that theme (198–200 [148–9]).

Zeitlin's observation that although moderation "is an important feature of Montaigne's wisdom . . . its treatment in this essay is rather light, not to say frivolous,"[42] is correct but misses the point. Although the essayist has made abundantly clear his opposition to "immoderation," the only instances he has criticized as such in this chapter exemplify "immoderation . . . in the direction of the good," that is, "excessive" virtue. His failure seriously to denounce immoderation in its root sense—the overindulgence in bodily pleasures—coupled with his satire of the theological attempt to "restrain" this putative vice suggests that it is the spiritual physicians' denunciations of sensual pleasure, rather than overindulgence in such pleasure, that are truly immoderate.[43] And his concluding discussion of the relation between religious asceticism and religious cruelty suggests that by opposing the former disposition, one might uproot the latter as well.

This same point is elaborated—but with explicit emphasis on philosophic rather than religious asceticism—in "Of Drunkenness," a chapter that similarly blends the satiric and the serious. Not only does this title denote a vice opposed to the virtue treated in "Of Moderation"; the argument of the chapter begins at the opposite pole: having introduced "Of Moderation" by suggesting the need to refine our judgment of virtue, so as to differentiate real moral excellence from the "excessive" virtue that amounts to vice, Montaigne begins "Of Drunkenness" by stressing the importance of precisely ranking different *vices*. In contrast to Socrates, who thought it the principal function of wisdom "to distinguish good things

---

[42]Zeitlin, *Essays of Montaigne*, 1:376.

[43]Cf. III, ii, 793–4 [619], where Montaigne expresses his unwillingness in old age to restrain his indulgence in sensual pleasure out of consideration for his spiritual, as distinguished from his bodily, health.

from bad," Montaigne remarks, "we others, who even at our best are always tainted with vice," have an equal need for a "science of distinguishing among the vices." He proceeds to denounce drunkenness as a "bodily and earthly" and hence "brutish" vice, in contrast with other vices that seem "noble" (*généreux*). Yet after this denunciation the status of drunkenness rises in the chapter with amazing rapidity, culminating in Montaigne's recommendation that "we should refuse no chance to drink, and have this desire always in our head" (II, ii, 322, 325 [245, 247]).

Montaigne indirectly suggests the reason for this shift. At first he asserts that drinking interferes with another supposed vice, lechery (II, ii, 325 [247]). In "The Story of Spurina," however, he denied this claim, noting that "Venus and Bacchus are prone to go together" (II, xxxiii, 709 [553]). But he proceeds in "Of Drunkenness" to introduce a less corporeal yet more politically significant form of intoxication: the "madness" of people who—driven by "the high opinion [they] have of [them]selves"—think that they can overcome our "natural limitations" and carry "virtue" to such an extreme as to kill their own children, or to profess a preference for physical pain over pleasure. It is in this context that Montaigne expresses the doubts about the true cause of heroic "virtue" to which I referred in Chapter Eight in connection with the analysis of Cato's character, and suggests that such virtue—as manifested in the doctrines of the Stoics and Epicureans—is really a kind of illness (II, ii, 329–30 [249–51]). The lesson of the chapter, in other words, is that if such people indulged their simply coarse and "brutish" appetites, such as for drinking, more freely, they would be less prone to treat themselves and others, as we say, "like brutes." The true "erotic" activity that greater physical indulgence would serve to check is not sex but what the Platonic Socrates interpreted as a higher manifestation of eros: the longing for greatness and glory. In fact, in light of Montaigne's interpretation (in "The Story of Spurina") of Cato's denunciation of Caesar as a "drunkard" as a reference to Caesar's amorous preoccupations (II, xxxiii, 709 [553]), it is reasonable to interpret his encouragement of drinking as a further recommendation of sexual indulgence as well.

That Montaigne—at least in what is thought to have been the final stage of his "evolution"—favored a loosening of the moral restrictions on sexual indulgence has often been recognized. The most obvious evidence of this intention is the long chapter "On Some Verses of Virgil" (III, v), which Sayce terms almost a "hymn to pleasure."[44] But although such interpreters as Sayce have properly stressed the significance that Montaigne attributed to sexuality as an aspect of "the human condition,"[45] I have sought to demonstrate that the essayist's advocacy of sexual "liberation" reflects a broader political aim—as is suggested by the fact that "On Some Verses of Virgil" immediately follows "Of Diversion." Montaigne's argument, near

[44]Sayce, *Essays*, p. 151.
[45]Ibid., p. 128.

the beginning of "Of Drunkenness," that we need to judge human beings by a lower standard than that of virtue is grounded in his belief that people's excessively high opinion of themselves is responsible for their irrational disposition toward cruelty and vengefulness. It is particularly worthy of note in this regard that the movement of "Of Drunkenness" from a reference to the bestial character of drunkenness to an account of the excessive "virtue" that results from an overly high self-estimation mirrors (in reverse) the movement of "Of Cruelty" from godlike virtue to our kinship with the beasts. The practical meaning of the latter emphasis is the elimination of legal and moral restraints on indulgence in corporeal pleasures—even the restraint of "moderation," broadly interpreted, by which Montaigne reported the ancient philosophers limited their licentiousness in the "Apology." Precisely because most human beings lack the concern for the pacific pursuit of wisdom which engendered the philosophers' moderation, it is the more needful to encourage the unbridled pursuit and enjoyment of bodily pleasures so as to divert the multitude from cruelty and religious frenzy. What Montaigne initially cited as the most serious objection to drunkenness, its "bestial" character, is in fact its greatest recommendation, inasmuch as focusing on our animal needs is the only adequate way to counterbalance our dangerous "presumption."

There remains to be considered one further aspect of Montaigne's reinterpretation of humanity in the light of our essentially animal nature. In Chapter Two, in analyzing the account of the parity of the natural human condition with that of animals in the "Apology," I noted that Montaigne's implausible suggestion that the beasts' conduct is guided by reason and free will actually seems intended to challenge the notion that *human* behavior is determined by such faculties. In a chapter titled "Of the Power of the Imagination" (I, xxi), Montaigne develops that hint into an open attack on the (Christian) notion of free will, the heterodoxy of which is masked only by its humorous form. This issue has a fundamental bearing on the problem of moderating spiritedness, since it is the essence of spiritedness or anger to blame and therefore punish others for having "willfully" chosen to injure oneself or violate one's dignity. Reason dictates that we not seek to inflict vengeance on an irrational thing, such as "a beast or a stone," when "it hurts us" (II, xxvii, 672 [524]). But whether it is more rational to avenge oneself against human beings for injuries they have inflicted seems to depend on whether they are truly more responsible for those injuries than beasts are.

"Imagination" and Free Will

"Of the Power of the Imagination" opens with a series of anecdotes illustrating the theme stated in the title; the more farfetched of these—

stories purporting to show how human imaginings or practices may induce radical changes of bodily form (for example, a girl who changed into a boy by jumping)—do so by demonstrating how people can be brought to believe almost anything. After boldly suggesting that the belief in miracles may similarly be due to the power of the imagination,[46] Montaigne turns to the theme of the "comical bindings by which our world is so fettered"— apparently referring to the belief of some of his contemporaries in the power of spells or enchantments to cause impotence.[47] In support of his opinion that the effect of these constraints is due to "apprehension and fear," Montaigne relates several anecdotes indicating how people can be liberated from them. The first story concerns a man so "tyrannized" by the fear of impotence that he became impotent. He found a "remedy for this fancy by another fancy": "by admitting and speaking about this subjection of his in advance, he relieved the tension [contention] of his soul, for when the trouble had been presented as expected, his constraint [obligation] diminished and weighed upon him less." As Montaigne observes in conclusion, "this mishap is to be feared only in enterprises where our soul is immoderately tense with desire and respect." In order to illustrate further how such fear may be overcome, he tells of another man "who was helped when a friend assured him that he was supplied with a counterbattery of enchantments that were certain to protect him." Montaigne then describes how he himself, in a similar case, protected a friend against the fear of such "sorceries" on the friend's wedding night. In describing his remedy, Montaigne represents himself as a "miracle" maker and as the issuer of an "ordinance" that he obliged his friend to "execute," involving the saying of "certain prayers" and the use of a medal "engraved with some celestial figures." Summarizing the lesson of this example, he remarks that "these monkey tricks are the main part of the business, our thought being unable to get free of the notion that such strange means must come from some abstruse science" (97–9 [70–71]).

As the metaphorical language quoted in the last two sentences suggests, Montaigne may have in mind a broader problem than sexual impotence.[48]

[46]Characteristically, Montaigne alternately plays to and pricks the prejudices of his aristocratic readers: here he attributes the belief in miracles to the softness of the minds of "the vulgar," from whom aristocratic readers can be expected to distinguish themselves; but only two or three pages earlier the essayist had attributed greater fortitude in the face of death to "villagers and humble folk" than to others (I, xxi, 97 [70]; I, xx, 94 [68]). Given Montaigne's remarks about the vulgar character of aristocratic "valor" (II, vii, 362–4 [276–7]) and about the general pliancy of the human mind (II, xii, 548 [425]), it is doubtful that he takes seriously any such moral or intellectual distinctions among "classes" in the conventional sense; the decisive difference, for Montaigne, is between the philosophic few and the generality of human beings, all of whom—rich or poor—are "vulgar" by comparison. This very fact, as I argued in Chapter Six, constitutes the ground of his political egalitarianism.

[47]Oeuvres, p. 1454 (n. 5 to p. 97).

[48]Cf., on "impotence," Machiavelli's charge that Christianity has contributed to the weakening of the world: Discorsi, I, proem, p. 124.

In the sequel he brings such a broader theme to the fore, by means of a forensic address on behalf of the penis, which men might plausibly accuse of exercising an "unruly liberty" in defiance of "our will."[49] In defense of this organ's "rebellion," Montaigne remarks that he might accuse "our other members, his fellows," of the same fault: "For I ask you to think whether there is a single one of the parts of our body that does not often refuse its function to our will and exercise it against our will. They each have passions of their own which rouse them and put them to sleep without our leave." Montaigne highlights the theological bearing of this argument by citing a claim made by Saint Augustine in order "to vindicate the omnipotence of our will," to the effect "that he knew a man who commanded his behind to produce as many farts as he wanted" (100–101 [72–3]). After setting forth a contrary example to challenge Augustine's inference, Montaigne launches his counterattack:

> But as for our will, on behalf of whose rights we set forth this reproach [against the penis], how much more plausibly may we charge it with rebellion and sedition for its disorderliness and disobedience! Does it always will what we would will it to will? Doesn't it often will what we forbid it to will, and that to our evident disadvantage? Is it any more amenable than our other parts to the decisions of our reason? (101 [73])

Underlying the wordplay of this passage is a serious point, to the effect that the very notion of free will is an incoherent one. If to will and do the good is by definition good, why would anyone ever will to do evil? If we accuse a man of "willing" to do evil, might he not plausibly respond, as Montaigne suggests, by saying that he didn't want to will evil, but that his will willed as it did despite his wishing or willing it to will otherwise? Why should anyone be held responsible for evildoing, since no one created his own self, or, consequently, his will?[50] It is along these lines that Montaigne concludes his "defense" of the penis by charging its accusers with a "manifest animosity and illegality." The law he accuses them of ignoring or violating is that of "nature," which "will meanwhile go her own way" (101 [73]). Neither political nor theological laws can maintain sovereignty over that most powerful "law" that expresses itself in human instincts and passions, and that directs us above all to seek our preservation and pleasure, and to avoid what is physically harmful or painful. Saint Augustine's denial of this fact on behalf of the will is itself, Montaigne implies, a manifestation of "the power of the imagination."

[49]Cf. III, v, 837 [654], citing Plato's reference (in the *Timaeus*) to the gods' "hav[ing] furnished us with a disobedient and tyrannical member, which, like a furious animal, undertakes to subject everything to itself."

[50]This argument appears to undermine the premise on which "all the rules of man's duty" are founded, according to I, vii, 32 [20], to the effect that each person is responsible for his will.

We may elaborate the political intent underlying Montaigne's argument by recalling his suggestion, a few pages earlier, that one may liberate people from being "tyrannized" by "constraint" by encouraging them to admit their weakness, thus alleviating the tension or struggle within their souls (97 [70]). We are reminded, in this connection, of the cannibals, whose natural freedom and equality reflect the absence of "artifice and human solder"—that is, religious and moral constraint—within their society. The present discussion confirms that by freeing our "natural," corporeal instincts from the moral constraints that have been imposed on them, Montaigne intends to liberate humanity from subjection to the political tyranny that has been imposed in the name of religion. But it also relates directly, as I have suggested, to the theme of moderating spiritedness or anger. This relation is brought out in "Of the Punishment of Cowardice" (I, xvi).

"Of the Punishment of Cowardice" immediately follows the chapter "One Is Punished for Stubbornly Holding On to a Place without Reason," wherein Montaigne alluded to the problem of "excessive" virtue, and specifically to excesses of valor, which at some point become indistinguishable from vice (I, xv, 68–9 [47]). By contrast, in I, xvi, he defends instances of the putative vice opposed to courage, namely, cowardice, against the disposition to punish it. After citing the opinion of "a prince and very great captain" that soldiers "could not be condemned to death for faintheartedness," he remarks:

> In truth it is right to make a great distinction between the faults that come from our weakness and those that come from our malice. For in the latter we have knowingly tensed ourselves against the rules of reason that nature has imprinted in us; and in the former it seems that we can call on this same nature as our warrantor, for having left us in such imperfection and weakness; so that many people have thought that we could not be blamed except for what we do against our conscience; and on this rule is partly founded the opinion of those who condemn capital punishment for heretics and unbelievers, and the belief that an advocate or judge cannot be held responsible for having failed in his charge because of ignorance. (I, xvi, 70 [48])

So far as it goes, this passage suggests that it would be an improvement on present practice for justice to treat differently people who committed wrongs out of "malice," for which they may legitimately be held responsible, and those who erred out of "weakness," for which nature is to blame. But—to say nothing of the practical difficulties involved in applying such a distinction—the grounds of the distinction are undermined by other remarks Montaigne has made about human responsibility and its relation to nature. In "Of the Power of the Imagination," as we have just seen, he suggests that human beings are impotent to control their "natural" corporeal desires by the exercise of will or reason. Nor is it possible, strictly speaking, to distinguish natural desires from artificial ones, according to Montaigne's denial in "Of Experience" that any "great desire can be imagined that is so strange and vicious that nature is not involved in it" (III, xiii, 1065 [833]).[51] And his assertion that nature has implanted "rules of reason" in us, for the violation of which we may justly be blamed, is undermined by the remark in I, iii, that nature, "more zealous for our action than for our knowledge," has "imprint[ed]" many "false" notions in our minds (18 [8]): how, given that fact, can we be held responsible for our inability to distinguish the true rules of reason from false but no less "natural" beliefs? Far from supporting even a modified form of the theological or legal distinction between faults for which human beings are and are not responsible, Montaigne's argument points toward the Socratic view to which he alluded at the beginning of the "Apology for Raymond Sebond," to the effect that all vice, strictly speaking, is a product of ignorance (and hence is involuntary), since we would not choose what we knew to be bad for ourselves. Indeed, in other chapters, Montaigne comes close to expressing explicit agreement with the Socratic thesis. In "Of Democritus and Heraclitus" he remarks, "I do not think there is . . . as much malice [in us] as stupidity: we are not so full of evil as of inanity" (I, l, 291 [221]). In "Of Repentance" he states, "perhaps the people are right who say that [vice] is principally the product of stupidity and ignorance" (III, ii, 784 [612]). And although the conclusion of "Of the Punishment of Cowardice" unexpectedly suggests that extraordinarily "gross and apparent ignorance or cowardice" might justly be taken "as sufficient proof of wickedness and malice" and "punish[ed] as such" (I, xvi, 71 [49]), it leaves unresolved what the appropriate punishment might be: according to Socrates, the ignorance that issues in vice would best be "punished" by education.[52]

In order to clarify Montaigne's understanding of the relation between vice and ignorance, it will be necessary first to consider the Socratic view of that matter in a bit more detail. Socrates' assertion that vice is the product of ignorance, if carried to its conclusion, constitutes a challenge to the legitimacy of all criminal laws, since it not only appears to deny that we are responsible for our vicious deeds but entails that the proper governmental response to such deeds is, as just noted, to "educate" their perpetrators rather than inflict suffering or deprivation on them. The manifest implausibility of the latter proposition to the political community's defenders, typified by Socrates' accuser Meletus, reflects their suspicion that those who act unjustly do so not out of ignorance of their interest but out of a clearer

[51]Cf. III, x, 987 [772] ("If what nature exactly and originally demands of us for the preservation of our being is too little . . . let us also call the habit and condition of each of us 'nature'"); III, xii, 1094 [855] ("I seek [nature's] trail everywhere"); the account of the philosophers' "natural" way of life in the "Apology" (567–9 [439–41]); and the discussion of this issue in Chapter Four, above.

[52]Plato, Apology, 25d–26a, 42d–e; cf. Republic, 337d.

perception of that interest than is contained in the city's laws and conventions. That is, although believing that general law-abidingness is the prerequisite of the "common" interest, they share the suspicions expressed by Glaucon in Plato's *Republic* that a truly superior human being would pursue personal gain at the expense of the community.[53] Socrates, of course, represents himself as a champion of justice rather than injustice and purports to refute Glaucon's suspicions by eulogizing the happiness of the just individual. What he actually demonstrates, however, is that the greatest happiness is that of the philosophers, whose goal of wisdom does not require them to act unjustly, in the sense of depriving others of the lowlier goods they seek to protect against thieves, murderers, or tyrants.[54] Socrates' view is in harmony with Aristotle's thesis that the best human beings are most truly "selfish," since they seek the things that are truly good for themselves, as distinguished from the vulgar goods that most people pursue, thereby giving selfishness a bad name.[55] If all people "knew" their interest, they would be philosophers; being totally concerned with the pursuit of knowledge, they would have no desire to rob or tyrannize over one another, and there would consequently be no need for penal sanctions to deter them from injustice.

Socrates' thesis, understood in this way, may be correct; but it cannot be said to resolve the problem of how to lead most people to act justly. The obstacle to such a resolution is that most human beings, as Socrates acknowledges, are too powerfully moved by narrowly selfish desires originating in their corporeal and particularistic natures to be satisfied with the pursuit of wisdom. (Nor would it be possible, indeed, to maintain a civilized political community—including the economic surplus that philosophy itself presupposes—were it not for the strength of such desires among the generality of human beings.) Hence Socrates himself admits—in apparent contradiction to his thesis—the need to threaten people with otherworldly as well as earthly punishments in order to promote just conduct.[56] His thesis cannot serve in practice to justify the abolition of penal laws; rather, it serves to illuminate the problematic nature of law, and hence of the political community, and points toward the philosophic life as the only truly rational one. Of all human beings, only philosophers are truly free, and hence responsible for their actions, in the sense that their way of life is the product of fully rational choice rather than of irrational desires and passions. In a sense, therefore, the actions of unphilosophic individuals, for which the law holds them accountable, are "involuntary": they did not choose their particular conception of the good, which results from the

[53]*Republic*, 358e–359b.
[54]Ibid., 580d–587b.
[55]*Nicomachean Ethics*, IX.8.
[56]*Republic*, 380b, 613d–616a.

combination of their nature and their upbringing. Yet governments must nonetheless treat them *as if* they were responsible for what they do, and punish them for violating the laws, if some semblance of justice and the common good are to be preserved. In this sense the assumption of individual responsibility for one's own character is a necessary legal fiction, or—to use the Socratic term—a "noble lie."

The relation of Montaigne's view of moral responsibility to the teaching of the Platonic Socrates is suggested by the critique of the free will doctrine in "Of the Power of the Imagination." As we have seen, Montaigne ridicules the notion that we should be held responsible for the inability to restrain our corporeal desires, or for "willing" to do what is evil. But unlike Socrates, he does not contend that the sole remedy for such unfreedom lies in dedicating one's life to philosophizing—a pursuit of which few people are capable. Instead, he suggests that simply to admit our "weakness" and relieve ourselves of "tyrannical" demands that impose an unrealistic "obligation" on us, filling our souls with "tension" or struggle, would serve to promote human freedom in an important way. As the following, previously quoted remark from "On Some Verses of Virgil" suggests, his Rabelaisian exhortations on behalf of self-indulgence in such chapters as "Of Moderation" and "Of Drunkenness" have been intended to have such a liberating effect: "God grant that this excess of my license may draw our men to liberty, rising above these cowardly and hypocritical virtues born of our imperfections; that at the expense of my immoderation I may draw them on to the point of reason!" (III, v, 822 [642]).

Unlike Socrates, Montaigne—at least in his public rhetoric—appears to understand human freedom *only* in contradistinction to the constraints of conventional legal and moral restrictions on the individual's conduct, not as something opposed to the "constraint" of our natural appetites themselves. In fact, he seems to hold that we can best advance the cause of human freedom by emphasizing the *inevitability* of our subjection to "the laws of our condition," as these laws manifest themselves in our physical sensations and appetites (III, xiii, 1067; 1050, 1074 [835; 821, 840]). It is evidently for this reason and in this sense that, in the "Apology" and elsewhere, he propounds the doctrine of determinism or fatalism as a politically salutary hypothesis, if not a theoretically demonstrable one. As previously noted, his comparison of human and animal nature in the "Apology" suggests that human beings—or at least most of them—are inevitably driven by the same sort of nonrational instincts and passions that govern the beasts' conduct. Later in Book II he observes that among the Turks, "the conviction . . . of the fatal and inflexible prescription of their days" is said to help provide "assurance in danger" (II, xxix, 689 [537]); in Book III, in a more personal vein, he reports having freed himself from the "pain" of repentance by adopting the view that things "were bound to happen thus, and now they are in the great stream of the universe and in the chain of Stoical causes" (III, ii, 793 [619]). As the last passage suggests, such an attitude is opposed to the Christian one; it reminds us of Strato's endeavor to attribute "all things" to the "weights and motions" of "nature" so as to "discharg[e] human nature from the fear of divine judgments" (II, xii, 510 [394]).[57]

Although one passage in the "Apology," in which Montaigne asserts that anyone who could adequately determine nature's present state "could infer from this with certainty both all the future and all the past" (II, xii, 445 [343]), seems to express a determinism of the most comprehensive and thoroughgoing sort, it is unlikely that he seriously adhered to such a doctrine in that form.[58] As we have seen, his teaching with respect to how we should deal with the "accidents" that oppress us is far from an attitude of Stoical acceptance or passivity. And he speaks of reason as a faculty that should help free us from being, "like the beasts, slavishly subjected to the common laws"; reason, not simply instinct, should "guide our inclinations" (II, viii, 366 [279]). But it is the chief function of reason, in turn, to determine the true character of nature; only a few human beings, according to the "Apology," possess the capacity to do so. Their most beneficial service to their fellows is not, as previous thinkers believed, to represent nature in a morally elevating or "sophisticated" fashion, so as to cover up the tension between nature and morality, but rather to uncover nature's mechanical, purposeless, and amoral character. Montaigne intends this uncovering of nature to have a directly political effect, in that emphasizing the inevitable strength of our natural appetites and the absence of any inherent limit to them will serve to justify a revision of the civil laws in order better to accommodate them to nature. In other words, the use of reason liberates us from slavish subjection to nature not by enabling us to master our corporeal appetites but rather by freeing our minds from the false *opinions* (identified in I, iii–iv) that nature has imprinted on our minds, which lead us to despise "present goods" out of a concern with (nonexistent) "future" or otherworldly ones, and to attribute to human beings a responsibility for their actions, and for the desires that generate those actions, that they do not possess.

The foregoing account of Montaigne's critique of the notion of moral responsibility is not intended to suggest that Montaigne would favor abolishing criminal punishments. To deny that we are responsible for our actions, in the Christian sense—that is, responsible for choosing or "will-

---

[57]Cf. Hobbes's use of the deterministic thesis to undermine specious political arguments based on the notion of free will: *Leviathan*, ch. 21, pp. 263ff.; and cf. Caton, *Politics of Progress*, p. 63, regarding the rationale underlying Descartes's endorsement of determinism.

[58]Cf. Machiavelli, *Discorsi*, I, xxxix, 222, where a less radical formulation of the same principle points to the need to study the lessons of the past in order to *alleviate* future evils. Montaigne shares Machiavelli's esteem for the study of history: see *The Prince*, ch. 14, p. 60; *Essais*, I, xxvi, 155–6 [115]; II, x, 396 [303].

ing" to do evil—is not to deny that we are capable of modifying our conduct in response to the incentives and disincentives meted out by the law for good and bad behavior (just as other animals modify their behavior in response to changes in external stimuli). To the extent that crime is the product, as Montaigne teaches, of our natural desire for selfish advantage vis-à-vis our fellows, it would be all the more necessary to divert the quest for gain into less harmful directions. But by denying that we are any more responsible for our behavior than other animals are, Montaigne endeavors to sever the practice of punishment from the passion of anger or vengeance that inspires punitive authorities to go to unjust excesses—a passion rooted in our irrational need "to have something to blame," and one that leads those who experience it to be "vexed even at truth and innocence" (II, xxxi, 692–3, 695 [540, 542]; I, iv, 25 [14]). At the same time, his argument undermines the legitimacy of laws directed at perfecting our character by restraining our indulgence in corporeal pleasures, when such indulgence would *not* directly injure others' interests. The punitive policy that his argument suggests is one that would penalize only vicious actions that directly injure "public society" (II, ii, 324 [247]), unlike drunkenness and what are now called "victimless" crimes, and that would make allowances, as Hobbes will later urge, for our natural weakness.[59] Such a policy was suggested by Caesar's practice of "scarcely punish[ing] any other vices" among his soldiers "than mutiny and disobedience," giving them "free rein for any sort of licentiousness," while nonetheless exercising an appropriate "severity in keeping them in check" (II, xxxiv, 714–5 [557]). Caesar's custom of having his soldiers "richly armed" with gold and silver, "so that care for saving their arms might make them fiercer in self-defense" (ibid., 715 [557]), further suggests the desirability of relying on the "carrot" of self-interest as opposed to the "stick" of punishment, wherever possible, to induce people to act as they ought; this lesson was also suggested by the Augustus anecdote in I, xxiv.[60] Montaigne, then, endeavors to practice a more effectual form of compassion than the Christian one by reducing the scope and extent of human moral responsibility. Although, in theory, the Christian doctrine that human beings are made in the image of God might

---

[59]Cf. the conclusion of III, xii, where Montaigne juxtaposes his distaste for participating in "legitimate actions . . . against those who resent them" with his willingness to take part in "illegitimate" ones "towards those who consent to them" (1041 [814]), which suggests the contemporary liberal standard exempting actions among "consenting adults" from governmental restraint. Hobbes, *Leviathan*, ch. 21, p. 270; ch. 26, pp. 344–6.

[60]Cf. Montaigne's citation of Seneca's opinion "that punishments whet vices rather than dulling their edge, that they do not engender a concern to do well, which is the work of reason and discipline, but only a concern not to be caught doing evil," to which he adds, "this I know by experience, that never was any civil morale [*police*] reformed in that way" (II, xv, 599 [466]). In "Of Experience" Montaigne expresses the wish that the law would reward good deeds as well as punish bad ones (III, xiii, 1048 [820]).

have been expected to increase their compassion for their fellows, in practice, he suggests, it had the opposite effect: instilling in such men as Guise a confidence that God is on their side, thus giving them license to vent their vengeful passions on their opponents, and excusing the sins of "murderers, traitors, tyrants" by reference to others' alleged "sins" of idleness, lasciviousness, or impiety (II, ii, 322 [244–5]). Rather than rely on the Christian remedy of "submission" as a means of softening people's spiritedness, or emulate the futile "obstinacy" of the ancient hero who relied on his own "virtue" for his preservation, Montaigne endeavors (as the juxtaposition of the Augustus and Guise examples in I, xxiv, suggested) to "divert" people from anger toward a concern with their earthly interests. But such a policy of diversion presupposes a prior weakening of the exaggerated sense of their own importance or "dignity" which lies at the core of spiritedness. Montaigne's continual attack on our "over-good opinion" of ourselves and his emphasis on the similitude of our motive passions to those of the beasts are intended to have this effect. In terms of the alternative policy to "submission" which Montaigne proposed in I, i—a course of "audacity and constancy"—the essayist's policy is "audacious" in embodying a sweeping challenge to the dominant thought and institutions of his time. And it is a policy of "constancy" according to his remark in II, xvii, that "the lowest step" is "the seat of constancy" as well as "security" (628 [488–9]). That is, it relies on emphasizing the lowest, animal or corporeal, aspect of human nature, rather than our aspirations toward divinity. Rather than condemn people for indulging in such "brutish" pastimes as drinking and sex, and demanding that they subordinate their physical appetites to their "will," we ought to accept such indulgence as a legitimate manifestation of our animal nature and a harmless outlet for passionate energies that might otherwise be exercised in violence, cruelty, and tyranny. It is noteworthy, in this connection, that the title of I, i, is almost recapitulated in the text of I, xx, where Montaigne openly asserts that our true "end" is sensual pleasure and argues that the means to that end, which is what the term "virtue" properly connotes, ought equally to be pleasant (80 [56]). Recalling Montaigne's implicit comparison of himself with Christ in I, i, and considering how his version of compassion is grounded in an emphasis on our animal nature and the denial of our link with the divine, we may say of his enterprise what Leo Strauss said of Machiavelli's: "he replaces the imitation of the God-Man Christ by the imitation of the Beast-Man."[61]

In teaching us to understand ourselves in light of the animal rather than the divine, Montaigne endeavors, as Machiavelli had done, to make us wholly "at home" on the earth, renouncing the attempt to transcend it. This teaching presupposes the attack on the *truth* of the Christian religion which

[61] *Thoughts on Machiavelli*, p. 78.

Montaigne set forth in the "Apology for Raymond Sebond." Yet my analysis so far leaves unresolved a problem to which the "Apology" itself pointed without appearing to settle: how can we be brought to regard the earth as our exclusive "home," forsaking any transcendental longings, given the transitoriness of our residence here?

CHAPTER TEN

"To Philosophize Is to Learn How to Die": Montaigne, Socrates, and Christianity

"To Philosophize Is to Learn How to Die"

Although the theme of death and our bearing toward it recurs frequently in the *Essays*, three chapters—one in each book—stand out in connection with this topic, because in each of them Montaigne quotes or alludes to the maxim that philosophy is a preparation for death: I, xx, "That to Philosophize Is to Learn How to Die"; II, vi, "Of Practice"; and III, xii, "Of Physiognomy." The three chapters are numerically equidistant from each other. Although the seeming contrast in attitudes among these chapters has generally been viewed as reflecting the evolution of their author's thought, I suggest that the external evidence of careful planning on Montaigne's part—the repetition of the maxim and the placement of the chapters—substantiates the suspicion that the appearance of evolution is a contrived rhetorical device. (As will be noted, the "lesson" of III, xii, is presaged, albeit in a less explicit form, in the original version of II, vi, and is also hinted at in I, xx; thus an acute reader might have surmised Montaigne's true position from the 1580 edition, before III, xii, itself appeared.)

The first sentence of I, xx, constitutes another manifestation of Montaigne's practice of using philosophical "stand-ins" in such a way as to mask the ultimate or most profound source of an argument that he is interpreting or criticizing. In this case he attributes the maxim "that to philosophize is nothing other than to prepare oneself for death" to Cicero rather than to Cicero's acknowledged source, Socrates.[1] He suggests two alternative interpretations of the maxim: it means either that "study and contemplation

---

[1]Cicero, *Tusculan Disputations*, I, xxx, 74; Plato, *Phaedo*, 64a, 67d–e.

draw our soul out of us to some extent and keep it busy outside the body, which is a sort of apprenticeship and semblance of death," or that "all the wisdom and reasoning in the world boil down finally to this point: to teach us not to be afraid to die." In support of the latter interpretation, and in harmony with the central thesis of I, xiv, he remarks that "either reason is a mockery, or it must aim solely at our contentment, and all its work must tend to make us live well and at our ease, as the Holy Scripture says."[2] He then sets forth the argument, quoted in Chapter Seven, that everyone agrees that the goal of life is pleasure, their differences arising only over the best means to it; that the ultimate goal of virtue itself is sensual enjoyment; and that the pursuit as well as the enjoyment of virtue ought to have been portrayed as pleasant rather than "rugged and laborious" (I, xx, 79–81 [56–7]).

Montaigne's interpretation of virtue as a means to pleasure obviously raises more problems than his abrupt and heavily rhetorical dismissal of alternative views at the outset of I, xx, would suggest; I have explored some of the reasoning that underlies it in previous chapters. In the present context he offers little by way of demonstration of the principle; but having more or less presupposed it, he proceeds to employ it in ostensible support for the maxim quoted in the title. "Among the principal benefits of virtue," he asserts, "is disdain for death," since such disdain enables us to live far more pleasantly than we could if we feared it. Indeed, given the inevitability of death, a contempt for it is more important than the scorn of such other evils as "pain, poverty, and other accidents" treated in the latter part of I, xiv (I, xx, 81 [57]). Hence the contentment that is the virtuous human being's goal requires, Montaigne suggests, that we contemplate the fact of our mortality throughout our life, since only by ridding death of its "strangeness" can we hope to overcome our fear of it. The alternative and opposite remedy of "the vulgar," which is to avoid thinking about death at all, he appears to dismiss as the product of "brutish stupidity" (despite having represented such thoughtlessness, as exemplified by Pyrrho's pig, as a model to be emulated in I, xiv). He observes that because they have not accustomed themselves to face death squarely, the vulgar take fright at its mere mention and abstain from making out their wills until "the doctor has given them their final sentence." In opposition to their attitude, and in imitation of Stoic doctrine, Montaigne asserts that forethought about death is the precondition of freedom, since "there is nothing evil in life for one who has well understood that the deprivation of life is not an evil" (82–5 [57–60]). He describes the contempt for life as the surest human foundation of "our religion" (90 [64]). And he almost concludes the chapter with a lengthy paraphrase of arguments from Lucretius and Seneca, designed to teach us to accept our mortality (91–4 [64–7]).

[2]The reference is apparently to Eccl. 3:12.

From the passages just cited, it is easy to understand why most commentators have interpreted I, xx, as a whole as embodying a restatement of the Stoic teaching.[3] That interpretation is rendered questionable, however, by other remarks scattered through the chapter which contradict the dominant thrust of the argument. After noting that he has just reached the age of thirty-nine, for instance, Montaigne asserts that "to be bothered . . . by the thought of a thing so far off [as death] would be folly" (82 [58]). He follows this remark, it is true, by remarking the uncertainty of anyone's term of life, citing the variety of circumstances in which a number of individuals' lives unexpectedly ended; but he immediately reverts to a nonchalant attitude, holding that the manner of a person's death does not matter, so long as one avoids worrying about it: for Montaigne it is sufficient "to spend my life comfortably" (84 [59]). Again, after seeming to reject such "brutish nonchalance" as he has professed as insufficient, he goes on to note that death "catches you just the same, whether you flee like a coward or act like a man" (84 [59]). If the ultimate purpose of virtue is to promote our ease and comfort, would it not be just as well to choose the easier course of cowardice?

Elsewhere in the chapter, Montaigne appears to laud the Egyptians' practice of having a "reminder" of death brought before them even "in the midst of their feasts"; but a few pages later he makes clear that the point of this reminder was not to lead people to meditate on their mortality but to encourage them to eat, drink, and be merry while there is still time (85, 88 [60, 62]). With respect to himself, the essayist expresses a readiness to "move out" of life, "without a regret for anything at all unless for life, if I find that the loss of it weighs on me" (87 [61]). In other words, although Montaigne is free from the concern for such goals as military victory, glory, and his children's education, the failure to achieve which adds (as he notes here) to others' regret of their impending death, he makes no claim to have forsaken a concern for the preservation of his life itself.

The final evidence casting doubt on Montaigne's acceptance of the view that we must prepare by forethought to meet death courageously is supplied by the conclusion of I, xx, where he remarks that "villagers and humble folk" commonly display "more assurance" in the face of death than other people do (94 [68]). This passage stands in marked contrast to the scorn he earlier seemed to express for common people's thoughtlessness about their mortality. Here he attributes the fearsomeness of death not to the event itself but to the "dreadful faces and trappings" with which people surround it, including the presence of "preachers." He concludes that a happy death is one that "leaves no leisure" for such ceremonies. This

---

[3]Strowski, *Montaigne*, pp. 98–101; Frame, *Montaigne's Discovery of Man*, pp. 43–4; Sayce, *Essays*, pp. 133–4; Zeitlin, *Essays of Montaigne*, 1:320–22; Lanson, *Les Essais*, p. 122; Norton, in Ives, ed., *Essays*, 3:1585–6.

conclusion accords with the last sentence of the previous chapter, in which Montaigne expressed a wish to die "quietly and insensibly" (I, xix, 79 [55]). (The heretical implication of that wish—that he disdained the opportunity for final repentance—was discerned by Pascal and other Christian apologists.)[4]

The foregoing summary of I, xx, demonstrates that—despite the "Stoical" overall appearance of Montaigne's argument—the chapter embodies an unresolved dialectic between two opposite attitudes toward death: those that are suggested, respectively, by the title and the conclusion. Adherents of the evolutionary interpretation explain the inconsistency by surmising that the anti-Stoical remarks scattered through the chapter constitute additions made at a later stage of the essayist's intellectual development; Zeitlin expresses "no doubt at all" that the conclusion of the chapter constitutes such an addition.[5] One difficulty with the evolutionary interpretation in this case is that the contradiction it is intended to explain was fully present in the original, 1580 text, rather than resulting from additions made to the later editions: the first edition contains such strikingly anti-Stoical remarks as the assertions that it would be foolish for Montaigne to worry about a thing so far off as death, and that the manner of one's death does not matter so long as one avoids worrying about it, as well as the concluding lines of the chapter. Several other aspects of the text do appear to support the evolutionary thesis, however. Montaigne's reference to his age as thirty-nine suggests that he wrote at least part of the chapter at a relatively early point (that is, 1572). On the other hand, the seeming contradiction between two references to the state of his health, both published in 1580—in one passage he professes to have enjoyed health "in great vigor and with little interruption" (86 [61]); in the second he reports "hav[ing] found that when I was healthy I had a much greater horror of sicknesses than when I felt them" (89 [63])—constitutes weighty evidence, *if* the essayist's "artless" manner is to be trusted, that some part of the chapter was written at a later date. (Grace Norton takes the latter remark to refer to Montaigne's kidney stones, the first attack of which he is not supposed to have suffered until 1573.)[6] Further evidence of the late composition of portions of the 1580 text is cited by Villey: an allusion to Caesar's *Gallic War*, which—to judge from two dates Montaigne wrote in his copy of that work—he began to read in 1578.[7]

Despite the foregoing evidence, I believe that the evolutionary interpretation of I, xx, is undermined by a fact noted by Zeitlin himself: almost all the

---

[4]Pascal, *Pensées*, ed. Brunschvicg, no. 63. Cf. *Essais*, III, ix, 956 [747]: "I would forget just as willingly to bid that great and eternal farewell."

[5]Zeitlin, *Essays of Montaigne*, 1:321.

[6]Norton, in Ives, ed., *Essays*, 3:1586. Frame believes that Montaigne did not experience his first stone until 1578, although he had suffered from a mild kidney illness since 1573 (*Montaigne*, p. 190).

[7]Villey, *Les Sources*, 1:91, 342.

additions Montaigne made to the chapter from 1588 on *harmonize with,* rather than contradict, his "original," Stoical position.[8] Though the evidence cited by commentators shows that Montaigne goes out of his way to invite an evolutionary interpretation of the chapter, the fact that he was fully capable of expressing Stoical thoughts in later editions of the same chapter (as in I, xiv, and elsewhere) again belies the supposition that Stoicism represented an early stage in his "development." Nor is ostensible evidence of the chronology of the chapter drawn from explicit references to dates (in the text or even in the inscriptions in Montaigne's library) to be relied on: Norton notes the essayist's "frequent inexactness about personal dates."[9] As elsewhere, I believe that the inconsistencies present in I, xx, reflect Montaigne's rhetorical subterfuge rather than his evolution. Though he will not openly articulate his new teaching about death until later chapters, the anti-Stoical remarks he inserts in his first treatment of that subject serve to indicate to more attentive readers that his initial posture is only a pretense.

"Practicing" for Death

The second stage in the purported evolution of Montaigne's attitude toward death is represented in "Of Practice." Like I, xx, this chapter opens with a discussion of the conception of virtue and the means of its attainment held by previous philosophers, but the initial emphasis here is quite different from the hedonistic point of view that was expressed at the beginning of the earlier chapter. Since "reasoning and instruction," Montaigne remarks, cannot suffice to move the soul to action without the training provided by "experience," some philosophers have voluntarily cast themselves into difficult or painful situations, impoverishing themselves or even "depriv[ing] themselves of the most precious parts of the body," for fear that their souls would otherwise grow too soft. Although, in such chapters as "Of Drunkenness," Montaigne has cast doubt on the wisdom or even the sanity of such a course, he refrains from casting a judgment on it here beyond remarking that since we can die only once, the philosophers' course of "practice" cannot help us to prepare for this, "the greatest necessity with which we have to deal" (II, vi, 350 [267]).[10]

[8]Zeitlin, *Essays of Montaigne,* 1:322. An exception is the remark, near the beginning of the chapter, "that pleasure is our goal," and Montaigne's argument that virtue ought to be interpreted in hedonistic terms (80–81 [56–7]). But this passage does not directly concern the theme of death.

[9]Norton, *Early Writings of Montaigne,* pp. 5–6. For instances of the unpredictability of Montaigne's references to historical events in chronological relation to the time of his writing, see Nakam, *Montaigne et son temps,* p. 228.

[10]Contrast Socrates' claim (*Phaedo,* 67e, 80e) that philosophizing *is* such a means of "practicing" for death.

In the sequel, however, Montaigne indicates that there is indeed "a certain way of familiarizing ourselves with death and trying it out [*l'essayer*] to some extent." The analogue to death, which enables all of us to "experience" what dying is like, is the loss of consciousness we undergo in falling asleep or, even more manifestly, in fainting. The ease with which this loss of consciousness occurs indicates that death (as Montaigne had already suggested in I, xx, 89 [63]) may be one of those things that "seem to us greater in imagination than in fact" (351–2 [268]). To elucidate this point, he provides a lengthy account of a loss of consciousness he once experienced, stemming from a collision on horseback. Having found that the fainting sensation he felt was pleasant rather than painful, he infers that "we pity [the dying] without cause, supposing that they are agitated by grievous pains or have their soul oppressed by painful thoughts."[11] In the process, he also hints at the meaninglessness of the last rites administered by the church, remarking that the answers made by those losing consciousness, in response to "the last words" spoken to them, "have more of fortune than of sense"; indeed, "the short and incoherent words and replies that are extorted from them by dint of shouting about their ears and storming at them, or the movements that seem to have some concordance with what is asked them," do not even prove that they are "fully alive" (354–5 [270–71]). (This point harmonizes with the conclusions of I, xix, and I, xx.)

The central point of "Of Practice," obviously, is to undercut the claim, to which Montaigne had seemed to assent in I, xx, that we must prepare for death by forethought. If dying is a painless or even a pleasant experience, there is no need to steel oneself in advance to face it bravely; those whose lives have not yet reached their end would therefore do well to turn their thoughts to more urgent and potentially fruitful matters. Purportedly, Montaigne's retreat from the Stoical position of I, xx, is the product of his "experience" of falling from a horse. Thus experience is shown to be not merely a supplemental guide for the conduct of life, as the philosophers thought (according to the beginning of the chapter), but a superior one. Once again, however, it would be erroneous to take Montaigne's ostensibly autobiographical account as a literal record of the development of his thought—as Sayce does in judging that "we have here one of the finest examples of the modification of Montaigne's theoretical positions by the impact of lived experience."[12] That interpretation is belied by a remark in

[11]The apparent contradiction between this passage and Montaigne's remark in "Of Cruelty" that "I very greatly pity the dying" (II, xi, 409–10 [314]) may be explained by the context of the latter remark, a condemnation of the use of torture, by which the process of dying is indeed made painful. In that context Montaigne also expresses unease at the practice of capital punishment itself, but his pity for its victims appears to be due to their premature loss of life and their having to undergo the "painful" anticipation of their execution (III, iv, 812 [633]) rather than to any painfulness directly attached to the moment of death.

[12]Sayce, *Essays*, p. 134.

the middle of the chapter, in which—just after suggesting that the dying lack consciousness of their condition—Montaigne professes "no doubt," in the light of his having "tried out [*essayé*]" what it is like to lose consciousness, that he "judged [this matter] rightly all along" (II, vi, 355 [271]). In other words, Montaigne did not decide as the result of his "experience" that dying need not be feared; rather, that experience conformed to, or at most confirmed, a belief that preexisted it.[13] Montaigne's account of his fall from horseback must be understood as a rhetorical device for persuading his readers that they need not fear or prepare for death rather than a step in the development of his own thought. There is no reason, by Montaigne's testimony, to suppose that his view of death would have been different had he never suffered such a fall; indeed, there is no reason to assume he is telling the truth in claiming to have had this experience! (This is not to deny that Montaigne's understanding of death is ultimately derived in part from experience; but that experience might just as well have been the universal one of falling asleep.)

Although the lesson of Montaigne's purported experience in "Of Practice" undercuts the Stoical view espoused in I, xx, the essayist does not yet make his rejection of Stoicism fully explicit. Indeed, his initial presentation of the problem in "Of Practice" retains an element of the Stoical view, in its reference to death as the greatest "necessity" that we have to face. (Norton takes this remark to signify that Montaigne had not yet fully renounced his "earlier" attitude.)[14] Montaigne directly challenges the Stoical teaching, however, while raising a more fundamental set of issues, in "Of Physiognomy."

Montaigne and Socrates

Although "Of Physiognomy" treats a greater variety of subjects than either of the two chapters I have thus far considered (including the relation between beauty and goodness, which I discussed in Chapter Seven), its unifying theme is the juxtaposition and comparison of Socrates—to whose "sayings" Montaigne refers at the outset (III, xii, 1013 [792])—with Montaigne himself. The chapter title alludes to the comparison of Socrates' unattractive appearance with Montaigne's more "favorable" bearing, to which he is indebted for his own preservation (1037–40 [811–14]).

Montaigne initially praises Socrates in "Of Physiognomy" for his "natural and common" manner, in contrast to the "strained" pace of Cato.

[13]Cf. Plato, *Apology*, 40c–e, where Socrates presents a similar possible view of death as a simple loss of consciousness.
[14]Norton, in Ives, ed., *Essays*, 3:1757.

He imitates Cicero in observing that Socrates "brought human wisdom back down from heaven"—"where [Montaigne adds] she was wasting her time"—"and restored her to man, with whom lies her most proper and laborious and useful business."[15] Having attributed to Socrates the view that each of us has the natural "learning" we need in order to live "at ease," and after adding that supernatural knowledge is practically "vain and superfluous," he urges his readers to find in themselves "nature's" true arguments against death—"the ones that make a peasant, and whole nations, die as steadfastly as a philosopher"—rather than turn to such works as Cicero's *Tusculan Disputations.* Whereas Montaigne himself had drawn extensively on Seneca in I, xx, as a source of arguments designed to reconcile us to our mortality, he now remarks that the very trouble to which Seneca put himself to prepare for death shows that he was hard pressed by it. Whatever courage Montaigne himself possesses in the face of death, as he draws closer to it, is the fruit of "nature," not of "books" (1013–17 [793–5]).

Following a seemingly irrelevant excursus on the evils of the French civil wars and on his own conduct amidst the general ruin, Montaigne returns, midway through "Of Physiognomy," to his anti-Stoical argument. In opposition to the course he had attributed to some philosophers in "Of Practice" of trying to prepare in advance for the inevitable misfortunes of life, he asserts it to be "certain that for the most part, the preparation for death has produced more torment than the suffering [of death]."[16] To the command of philosophy that we "have death always before our eyes" and the description of the philosopher's life (which he cites for a second time, in Latin) as a continuous meditation on death, Montaigne responds that although death is indeed the "end" in the sense of the limit [*bout*] of life, it is not its "end" in the sense of purpose [*but*]: life should be its own purpose. Nature teaches one "not to think about death except when he is dying." Hence Montaigne approvingly alludes to "Caesar's opinion that the least premeditated death is the happiest" (1028–9 [804–5]). (This opinion too is cited for a second time[17]—as if in answer to the second citation of the maxim that philosophizing means preparing to die.)

Let us recall that the original source for the maxim just cited, which Montaigne attributed to Cicero in I, xx, is Socrates. Let us also note that the

[15]Cf. Cicero, *Academica,* I, iv.

[16]Cf. the similar reflection on "the doctrines of the philosophers" in Bacon, *Advancement of Learning,* II (*Works,* ed. Spedding et al., 3:427), cited by Norton in connection with I, xx, in Ives, ed., *Essays,* 3:1587.

[17]The first reference to Caesar's opinion occurs in the chapter "Of Judging the Death of Others" (II, xiii, 592 [460]), where Montaigne adds, "If Caesar dared say it, it is no longer cowardice [*lacheté*] for me to believe it." The essayist's agreement with Caesar's view had already been indicated by the wish he expressed in I, xix, to die "quietly and insensibly." His denial that death is the goal of life retracts the claim he had made at I, xx, 82 [57].

work in which Cicero repeats that maxim—the *Tusculan Disputations*—is the very one the utility of which, as a means of preparing oneself for death, Montaigne has challenged in "Of Physiognomy." It would therefore seem that, despite the eulogy of Socrates with which Montaigne began that chapter, his point of view on the matter at issue is opposed to that of Socrates. Surprisingly, however, the essayist claims to be agreeing with Socrates, describing him as one of the foremost "interpreters of natural simplicity." Just as, in the "Apology for Raymond Sebond," Montaigne had cited Socrates and Plato to support his attack on the "presumption" of curiosity, here he proposes Socrates as a faculty member for a "school of stupidity," which would teach us to avoid the discontent that arises from our curiosity about death and other evils. As evidence, he provides a lengthy paraphrase of Socrates' testimony in Plato's *Apology*, including his counsel against fearing death. As if he were wholly persuaded by Socrates' disclaimer, at the outset of that dialogue, of using rhetoric in his defense,[18] Montaigne praises the Athenian's speech for the "unstudied and artless boldness . . . and childlike assurance" it embodies, reflecting "the pure and primary impression and ignorance of nature" (1029–32 [805–7]).

There is clearly something amiss in an interpretation of Socrates as a champion of ignorance and incuriosity. Montaigne's paraphrase of the *Apology* omits all reference to Socrates' account of his positive purpose in life—his quest, motivated by the belief that "the unexamined life is not worth living," to *overcome* his ignorance by acquiring knowledge. (The distortion is particularly evident in Montaigne's unqualified attribution to Socrates of an opinion that the latter derives from the supposed attitude of the Persian king—the sort of person whom the vulgar envy—according to which, if death is merely a kind of dreamless sleep, it is "an improvement" in our condition—1030 [806].[19] That this alteration of the Socratic teaching is intentional is suggested by Montaigne's allusion, a few pages later, to his practice of sometimes "disguising and altering" the passages he borrows from other authors' works "for a new service" (1034 [809]).

But what, more precisely, is the new service to which Montaigne has put Socrates' words? Let us take note of a later passage in III, xii, where Montaigne boasts of having "a favorable bearing . . . that makes a contrary

[18]Plato, *Apology*, 17a–c.
[19]Plato, *Apology*, 40c–e. Although Socrates professes in that context to adopt the opinion as his own, the view of dreamless sleep as the pinnacle of human happiness is contradicted by his previous representation of himself as a gadfly who strives to induce the greatest possible *awakeness* among his fellows, thereby making them truly happy (30e, 36d–e). Similarly, in alluding to Socrates' belief that if death were "a transmigration from one place to another," it would be "an improvement to go and live with so many great personages who have passed on and to be exempt from having any more to do with unjust and corrupt judges" (III, xii, 1030 [806]), Montaigne omits to mention the hope Socrates expresses in that case to "examine" such great men—i.e., to continue philosophizing (*Apology*, 41a–c).

impression to that of Socrates," shortly after emphasizing the power of beauty to influence our judgment (1035 [810–11]). In the sequel Montaigne describes how his trustworthy appearance, which causes others to believe in his "frankness" and the innocence of his intentions, has enabled him to preserve his life amidst the violence of his country's civil wars (1037–40 [811–14]). Montaigne's success in preserving himself and retaining the goodwill of all parties stands in implicit contrast to Socrates' failure to save himself from being executed (although Montaigne intimates that Socrates may not have been trying to save himself: III, ii, 795–6 [620]; III, xii, 1031 [807]).

We may take the comparison of Montaigne's and Socrates' physiognomies as a metaphor for the broader theme of the way in which a philosopher ought to present himself before the public. In this light we may better understand the purpose underlying Montaigne's transformation of Socrates' defense speech. Montaigne has omitted from Socrates' account of himself that facet of his way of life which rendered him (as he admits in the *Apology*) offensive to others: his disposition to challenge their most deeply held opinions about the good, the just, and the beautiful.[20] Montaigne's Socrates emphasizes instead his utility to the public: his "habit of advising just and useful things," to the "profit" of many of his fellow citizens (1030 [806]). Montaigne, I suggest, has assimilated Socrates to his own model of how philosophers should represent themselves, so as to promote their personal security and well-being, as well as those of the public.

Let us consider how the issue of the philosopher's bearing before the public relates to the problem of our attitude toward death. We recall that in initiating his consideration of whether "to philosophize is to learn how to die" in I, xx, Montaigne interpreted this maxim to mean that the ultimate purpose of wisdom is to teach us not to fear death. Interpreted in this way, the maxim does indeed appear subject to Montaigne's refutation of it as developed in the three chapters I have examined: might it not be more conducive to our contentment to discourage people from thinking about death at all?

When we examine the Socratic maxim in its original context in the *Phaedo,* however, we recognize that Montaigne's interpretation is really a caricature. Whatever Socrates may have meant by asserting that "true" philosophers spend their lives preparing for death, it is clearly not that their primary concern is with the moment of dying. Rather, he represents philosophy as an endeavor to transcend the body, for the sake of liberation from

---

[20]See Plato, *Apology,* 21b–23a. Though I have attributed to Montaigne himself the intention of undertaking a more direct challenge to popular beliefs on these subjects than Socrates did, what differentiates his project from that of Socrates in that regard, as I argue later in this chapter, is that it is intended to prepare the way for an *ultimate* harmony between philosophic and popular opinion, eliminating the need for philosophic concealment.

concerns that, he asserts, obstruct the acquisition of knowledge. He tries to overcome his listeners' fear of death by giving them reason to hope that a properly "purified" soul, at least, will "collect the greatest rewards" rather than simply perish once it is separated from the body. His apparent intent is to overcome both people's unreasonable resentment at the fact of their mortality and—more fundamentally—the hatred of reason itself that this fear might engender.[21]

Returning to the alternative interpretations Montaigne offered of the Socratic maxim at the beginning of I, xx, we observe that the meaning of this maxim, as propounded by Socrates, is closer to the interpretation that Montaigne disregarded, to the effect that philosophizing is a kind of "apprenticeship" for death because "study and contemplation draw our soul out of us . . . and keep it busy outside the body," than to the one he adopted, according to which the essential *value* of wisdom lies in enabling us to overcome the fear of death. The reason underlying his disregard of the former interpretation, as we learn from other chapters of the *Essays,* is that he regards it as a dangerously "idealized" account of the philosophic enterprise which serves as an unsalutary model for the direction of the lives of the unphilosophic multitude. Throughout the *Essays* Montaigne opposes the teaching that we should seek to sever our soul from our body, favoring the former at the expense of the latter. Whereas Plato, he remarks, "fears our hard bondage to pain and pleasure, since it obligates and attaches the soul too much to the body," Montaigne fears that bondage, "on the contrary, because it detaches and unbinds it" (I, xiv, 58 [39]; cf. III, xiii, 1091 [852–3]). In the education of youth, one should remember that "it is not a soul, it is not a body, that one is training, it is a man; one should not divide him" (I, xxvi, 164 [122]). Contrary to those who would denigrate the body by comparison with the soul, Montaigne stresses that "the body has a great part in our being, it holds a high rank in it; thus its structure and composition are very worthy of consideration. Those who want to separate our two principal parts and sequester them from each other are wrong. On the contrary, we must couple and rejoin them" (II, xvii, 622 [484]). Rather than force the body to conform to the soul's demands, we should take advantage of the soul's malleability, accommodating it to the body's needs so as to produce the requisite harmony between them (I, xiv, 57 [39]). As we have seen, the ultimate effect of Montaigne's denial of the supremacy of the soul over the body is to subordinate it to the body: to understand ourselves primarily in the light of what is animal and corporeal in us rather than what is incorporeal or "divine."

It is on the issue of whether the primary goal of human life is the perfection of the soul or the enjoyment of earthly pleasures that Mon-

---

[21]*Phaedo,* 63e–68b, 82b–83b, 89c–90e, quoted from the translation by Raymond Larson.

taigne—despite his profession of agreement with Socrates—diverges from Plato's account of his mentor's teaching. In the concluding chapter of the *Essays,* where Montaigne represents Socrates as exemplifying "the true balance" between bodily and spiritual concerns, he qualifies that judgment by professing to be "frighten[ed]" by his "transcendental humors"—"his ecstasies and daemonic possessions" (III, xiii, 1087, 1096 [850, 856]). In his eulogies of Socrates in the last two chapters Montaigne presents the reader with an entirely "humanized" Socrates—one devoid of any ambition to transcend "merely" human concerns.[22]

The linkage between Montaigne's treatment of death and his "correction" of Plato's account of Socrates' teaching is confirmed by a lengthy passage at the end of "Of Practice" in which the essayist discusses his practice of portraying himself. As in "Of Cruelty," the second part of this chapter (added in the final edition) seems on the surface to have only a remote connection to the theme of the first part.[23] Once again there is an underlying, and important, relation.

In this concluding section of "Of Practice," Montaigne defends the enterprise of writing about himself against the "custom" that condemns it as presumptuous. In reply to that condemnation, he not only suggests the utility of his self-study to others but cites Socrates' example as a precedent: "What does Socrates treat of more fully than himself? To what does he lead his disciples' conversation more often than to talk about themselves . . . ?" Farther on, in more direct response to the condemnation of self-praise, he remarks: "To say less of yourself than is true is stupidity, not modesty. To pay yourself less than you are worth is cowardice and pusillanimity, according to Aristotle. No virtue is helped by falsehood, and truth is never subject to error" (II, vi, 358–9 [273–4]; cf. III, viii, 921 [720]).

I believe that the passage last quoted is intended as a critique of Socratic irony—the means by which Socrates, even while speaking of himself before others, endeavored to moderate their hostility and mitigate the overt conflict between his beliefs and those of the multitude by concealing his true thoughts and his awareness of his superiority. This interpretation is suggested by Montaigne's allusion to Aristotle's discussion of truthfulness about oneself in the *Nicomachean Ethics.* In that context Aristotle describes irony as the vice opposite to that of boastfulness, both being opposed at the same time to the virtuous mean of speaking truthfully about oneself. He specifically cites Socrates as a practitioner of irony. At the same time he observes that irony is less offensive than boastfulness. And he

---

[22]Note that Montaigne modifies Socrates' disclaimer of being born "of wood or stone" by adding the words "any more than others"—thus seemingly turning the Athenian philosopher into a materialist (III, xii, 1030 [806]; cf. Plato, *Apology,* 34d).

[23]According to Norton, the concluding pages "are another Essay" having "nothing to do with death," the theme of the rest of the chapter (in Ives, ed., *Essays,* 3:1758).

alludes to the possibility of employing irony, as well as boastfulness, for the sake of some ulterior end; though he fails to specify the end to which irony might be a means, he may well have Socrates' conduct in mind—and may regard the Socratic form of irony as morally justifiable.[24]

Montaigne's denial in "Of Practice" that virtue can be promoted by falsehood is reminiscent of his critique, in the "Apology for Raymond Sebond," of the "profitable lies" that Plato and other philosophers set forth for the edification of the multitude. The essayist's rejection in the "Apology" of the philosophers' belief that there is a necessary disjunction between truth and political utility was tied, as we saw, to an attack on their endeavor to "elevate" humanity by means of edifying teachings. The same point, I believe, underlies his critique of Socratic irony in "Of Practice." The specific aspect of such irony that Montaigne has in mind in this context, I suggest, is Socrates' practice of feigning credence in such doctrines as those that Montaigne attacked in the "Apology": that there are gods who care for human beings, and that the soul lives on in some sense after death. This is not to deny that Socrates radically reformulates the traditional theology in such a way as considerably to reduce the gods' role in human affairs, or that the true meaning of his teaching concerning the soul's immortality is quite different from its surface appearance.[25] But in light of Montaigne's discussion of Diomedon in I, iii, and of his remarks about the philosophers' failure to eradicate the popular belief in divination in I, xi, there is reason to suspect that he holds Socrates to blame, so to speak, for his own fate: he failed to initiate a project like Montaigne's for rationalizing political life by rationalizing the beliefs of the populace. Insofar as Socrates deferred to the endeavor of lawgivers to elevate the many by encouraging them to strive for virtue, to moderate their bodily desires, and to transcend selfishness, he perpetuated the dichotomy between truth and utility, or (in other words) between philosophy and political society—to the detriment of both philosophers and the populace. Despite Montaigne's allusion to Socrates' pursuit of self-knowledge as a precedent for his own enterprise, he transforms the Socratic quest by modifying its outcome: at the conclusion of II, vi, he alleges that the Athenian, as a consequence of his self-knowledge, came "to despise himself" (360 [275]). Contrary to this claim, Socrates actually professed to have learned only to devalue so-called human wisdom; his examination led him not to self-contempt but to a recognition of the need to pursue genuine wisdom.[26] It is Montaigne more than Socrates

[24]*Nicomachean Ethics*, IV.7; Tessitore, "Aristotle's Political Presentation of Socrates," pp. 12–13. Cf. Aristotle's account of the virtuous man as one who demands less than his share of the goods that most men value, while claiming some greater good for himself: ibid., 1136b20–23; IX.8.
[25]On the latter point, see Ronna Burger, The *"Phaedo": A Platonic Labyrinth* (New Haven, 1984), esp. ch. 11.
[26]Plato, *Apology,* 23a–b, 38a.

who seeks to lower the value human beings put on themselves, by renouncing all claims to an "elevated" status. It is vain, he holds, for philosophers to pretend that whatever wisdom they acquire liberates them from the physical needs they share with their fellows. To recapitulate a central point of the "Apology for Raymond Sebond": if the value of knowledge is seen to lie in alleviating the common miseries of the human condition rather than enabling some individuals to transcend that condition, the hostility of the people to philosophy will evaporate.

Christianity and Death

I have noted that the surface argument of the three chapters dealing with our bearing toward death is misleading in several respects. Let me now take note of the final and most politically significant layer in this tissue of rhetorical deception and hidden suggestion. To introduce this layer, let us recollect the importance of the theme of this chapter for Montaigne's project. The most obvious difficulty confronting Montaigne's enterprise of combating the "transcendental" humors to which human beings are prone and making them wholly "at home" on the earth is the fact that our earthly residence is transitory. It is, as Montaigne observes, man's "extreme concern with prolonging his existence" beyond the moment of earthly life that constitutes the root of religion and of the concern with "future" goods which the essayist has attacked as irrational. How then can we be persuaded to dispense with that concern, so as to give ourselves wholly over to the concern with making earthly life more comfortable and peaceful?

Merely to restate this issue is to recognize what has been lacking in the surface teaching of each of the three chapters in which Montaigne deals with the fear of death. Just as Montaigne caricatured the Socratic maxim that he quoted in the title of I, xx, he has trivialized the more general issue of how, or whether, we need to prepare for death by making it seem that it was the mere momentary experience of dying that most people feared. But as he observes in III, xii, death is "too momentary" an event—"a mere quarter-hour of suffering"—to call for a lifetime of preparation (1028 [804]). It is not in truth for the experience of dying but for the fact of their mortality that human beings have most often sought consolation[27]—whether, as some did, in the doctrines of the Stoics and Epicureans; as did others, in the

---

[27]Augustine does claim that the "violence with which body and soul are wrenched asunder" at the moment of death "brings with it a harsh experience, jarring horridly on nature so long as it continues" (*City of God*, XIII.6, p. 416). Against *this* limited aspect of Augustine's argument, Montaigne's teaching of "experience" might be said to offer reassurance. Cicero himself, in the *Tusculan Disputations* (I, xxxiv, 82) had already dismissed the pain that might be engendered by the event of dying as a trivial concern.

pursuit of a glory that might outlive them; or, as did the multitude of Europeans in Montaigne's time, in the religious promise of undying life. How blithely does Montaigne pass over the significance of death for a Christian by reassuring his readers that it is an event "without consequence" (ibid.)![28]

The theological significance of Montaigne's initial, putative adherence to Stoicism was recognized by Fortunat Strowski:

> Montaigne calls himself a Catholic. Nonetheless death has no mystical meaning at all for him. While, in spirit, he confronts it, he does not even ask himself whether it is followed by another life, and what this other life will be. Suffering, in his eyes, is merely suffering; no more, no less. And as for the motives of the detachment he practices, they have nothing religious about them; they are absolutely secular. How can it happen that, having the succor of religion in his reach, Montaigne should so totally have dispensed with it?[29]

As Strowski discerns, the fact that Montaigne professes to turn to Stoicism in certain "early" chapters as a remedy for the fear of pain and death while entirely disregarding the solace offered by Christianity demonstrates that "he had no religion" at the time he wrote them. But there is no reason to suppose, as Strowski does, that this irreligion was a passing phase in Montaigne's development, to which he was driven by the excesses of the religious wars; or that his failure subsequently to articulate the Stoic position reflects the return of his faith, so that he no longer needed the support of Stoicism.[30] In fact, in "Of Physiognomy" his attack on the Stoical teaching about death is conjoined with a more subtle attack on the Christian teaching as well, reminiscent of the argument of the "Apology for Raymond Sebond." Just as, in the "Apology," Montaigne had attributed to people's desire to prolong their existence beyond the grave their disposition to seek support in religious "inventions," and to compensate for the soul's inability "to stand on its own feet" by "looking elsewhere" for imaginary "consolations," in "Of Physiognomy"—shortly after lamenting the evils of the religious wars—he remarks: "In all things men cast themselves on the resources of others to spare their own, which alone are sure and alone powerful, if we know how to arm ourselves with them. Everyone rushes

---

[28]Cf. also I, xix, 78–9 [55], where—in contrast to the claim that "all the other actions of our life must be tried and tested" by the manner in which we die—Montaigne remarks that "three of the most execrable and most infamous persons that I have known in every abomination of life have had deaths that were ordered and in every circumstance composed to perfection." Hence, it appears, one need not have a conscience that is "composed" in the Christian sense in order to die "well." Of course, Montaigne's entire treatment of death in the chapters I am examining here passes over the possibility that human beings will be punished for their sins in an afterlife—a possibility that was disposed of in the "Apology for Raymond Sebond."

[29]Strowski, *Montaigne*, p. 110. Cf. also Friedrich, *Montaigne*, pp. 278–9.

[30]Strowski, *Montaigne*, pp. 112–13.

elsewhere and into the future, because no one has arrived at himself." By contrast, Montaigne professes to have recognized that in time of trouble "the surest thing was to entrust myself and my need to myself," rather than to trust to "fortune" (III, xii, 1022 [799]).[31] This recommendation of human self-reliance—which, as I noted in Chapter Four, contradicts the rhetorical conclusion of the "Apology"—serves as a link between the essayist's purported critique of Stoicism and the antireligious argument of the "Apology"; it suggests that the real object of his attack on focusing one's mind on death is not the teachings of the Stoics (who had, after all, relatively few adherents in Montaigne's time) but those of Christianity. That interpretation is substantiated by the antireligious thrust of several passages in the earlier chapters on death: Montaigne's wish to go to his death "insensibly" at the end of I, xix; his suggestion at the end of I, xx, that the presence of "preachers" at deathbed scenes serves only to make the event more frightening; his remark in that same chapter that the surest foundation of "our religion" is contempt for life, an attitude that he elsewhere condemns as irrational; and his implicit mockery of the last rites in II, vi. In sum, just as Montaigne masked an attack on the Christian doctrine of the afterlife in the "Apology" as a criticism of Plato, his purported critique of the Stoic and Epicurean teaching about death in other chapters has similarly been directed against Christianity.[32]

Montaigne seeks a remedy for the popular terror of death which will not entail religious superstition and the consequent hostility to reason. Yet nowhere in the three chapters on death that I have examined does he indicate how our seemingly natural disposition to pursue immortality through such means is to be overcome. Montaigne's solution to that problem is suggested in another chapter, part of which I quoted in Chapter Nine: III, iv, "Of Diversion." Even a learned friend of the essayist, Etienne Pasquier, confessed that he found the theme of this chapter incomprehensible.[33] Pasquier's puzzlement may be explained by the oblique style of argument of the chapter, in which Montaigne never explicitly states some

[31]Cf. also the denunciation of the French armies' reliance on "foreign" aid (III, xii, 1018 [796]), which recalls Machiavelli's metaphorical attack on the Italian use of "auxiliary" and "mercenary" troops (*The Prince*, chs. 12–13; Harvey C. Mansfield, Jr., "Machiavelli's Political Science," *American Political Science Review* 75 [1981]: 302–3).

[32]Further reason for reading a deeper meaning into Montaigne's attack on the Stoic view of death is the following bit of mumbo-jumbo: in III, xii, he mocks Seneca for being preoccupied with death, despite his feigned indifference to it, just after quoting the Roman philosopher *in support* of his denial that we need much learning to prepare for death; in the same context he urges people to seek out "nature's arguments against death," rather than philosophical ones, whereas in I, xx, he had presented arguments borrowed from Seneca and Lucretius *as* those of "nature" (III, xii, 1016–17 [795]; I, xx, 91–4 [64–7]). Note also the contrast between Montaigne's account of the philosophers in II, vi, as having gone out of their way to accustom themselves to hardship and his representation of their way of life as hedonistic and licentious in the "Apology."

[33]Pasquier, *Choix de lettres*, p. 44.

unifying intention or concern that would relate the various kinds of "diversion" of which he speaks. Yet the chapter does contain, I believe, such a unifying concern—one that not only explains Montaigne's ultimate response to the problem of death but also serves in a sense to summarize his political intention. Having touched on one aspect of Montaigne's policy of diversion in the preceding chapter—his endeavor to redirect political leaders from anger to eros—I now give more extensive consideration to the argument of "Of Diversion" in order to uncover the overall teaching of which that endeavor represents a particular application.

Diversion

Although Montaigne discusses a variety of types of diversion in III, iv—including its use as a military and political tactic and in mythology—most of his attention is focused on the practice of diverting people from troublesome thoughts and passions. Of the causes of grief from which we need to be distracted, the one he treats most extensively is the specter of death. (It is with particular reference to people's inability to confront their mortality that Pascal took over the notion of *divertissement* to characterize the general condition of humanity if it were deprived of faith.)[34]

Among commentators on the *Essays*, such diverse interpreters as Zeitlin, an adherent of the evolutionary interpretation, and Armaingaud, its foremost opponent, have agreed in seeing in this chapter a teaching opposed to the Stoical one. Zeitlin argues that the chapter evinces Montaigne's rejection of the Stoic precepts on which he had previously relied for alleviating the soul's distress, owing to his recognition that to meditate and look bravely on "the inevitable troubles of life," including death, was too difficult for most people in the light of "the conception of human nature which he has now arrived at."[35] Armaingaud cites the chapter as evidence of Montaigne's Epicureanism: it is "entirely consecrated," he argues, "to the application of the Epicurean method," which consists in distracting the soul from its present sufferings "by the memory of past pleasures and the anticipation of future pleasures."[36]

Montaigne makes his rejection of Stoicism clear at the outset of "Of Diversion" by remarking that "one proceeds badly when one opposes" the passion of sadness, which is just the policy he had attributed to the Stoics in the second chapter of the *Essays* (III, iv, 808 [630]; I, ii, 15 [6]). Yet neither Zeitlin's nor Armaingaud's interpretation adequately explains the ground

---

[34]*Pensées*, ed. Brunschvicg, nos. 139–43, 168–72.
[35]Zeitlin, *Essays of Montaigne*, 3:337–8.
[36]Armaingaud, ed., *Oeuvres complètes*, 5:99n.

of this rejection. On the one hand, although Montaigne indeed recommends the policy of diversion as suited to the weakness of soul that characterizes most human beings, it should be noted that two chapters later he describes himself as having faced "with open eyes" all the dangers he has encountered (III, iv, 810 [632]; III, vi, 877 [686]). In view of the fact that Montaigne had described himself as "weak-backed" in I, xiv, it seems unlikely that his recommendation of an easier policy in III, iv, reflects an evolution in his attitude—contrary to Zeitlin's explanation. On the other hand, contrary to Armaingaud, when Montaigne describes his policy of diversion, he distinguishes it from the use of "the various sayings that philosophy prescribes for consolation," *including* the Epicurean recommendation "that we should transfer our thoughts from unpleasant to pleasant things." Montaigne does assert that Epicurus' recommendation is "closer to my style" than that of other philosophers; and since his reported practice of diverting the thoughts of a grieving woman to other subjects (III, iv, 808–9 [631]) seems to conform to that recommendation, Armaingaud concludes that his disavowal of reliance on Epicurus means merely that he sought to console the woman with "ordinary conversational resources" rather than by directly citing Epicurus.[37] But that interpretation runs into two further textual difficulties. In the first place, in the "Apology" Montaigne had mocked the policy of "tak[ing] consolation for present ills from the remembrance of past joys" as a sign of the impotence of philosophy (II, xii, 473–4 [364–5]). Second, the essayist's report of the ultimate result of his emulation of Epicurus' policy in "Of Diversion" seems to confirm the judgment of the "Apology": even though Montaigne managed to keep the woman "in good spirits and entirely soothed for as long as I was there . . . those who followed me in the same service found no improvement in her, for I had not laid the axe to the roots" (III, iv, 809 [631]).

From Montaigne's admission of the long-term failure of his quasi-Epicurean policy in "Of Diversion," along with the criticism of such a policy in the "Apology," I infer that the Epicurean method is not the sort of diversion he favors as a remedy for human miseries. In pursuit of an understanding of what he means by "diversion," let us look to the apparent core of the chapter, his discussion of the way in which people face death. At the outset of this section he remarks that "it belongs only to a Socrates to become acquainted with death with an ordinary countenance"; this policy of "mak[ing] the soul meet troubles head on" is "too high and difficult" for most human beings. Montaigne illustrates that proposition by pointing out how numerous people who appear to be facing death directly are really diverting themselves from it. Among them are the "disciples" of the Cyrenaic orator Hegesias, who, "inflamed by the fine arguments of his lectures,

[37]Ibid.

starve themselves to death";[38] in Montaigne's interpretation they "do not consider death in itself"; "the goal to which they run" and on which they "fix their thoughts" is "a new existence." Similarly, the "poor people whom we see on the scaffold, full of ardent devotion . . . are to be praised for religion, but not properly for constancy," since their minds are focused on something other than death. And "the man who dies in the melee, arms in hand," appears to face death courageously only because he is carried away by "the heat of the battle" so that he need not reflect on the danger. "Even Epicurus," Montaigne adds, "consoles himself at his end with the eternity and utility of his writings." And indeed, the very "arguments of philosophy," such as Zeno's purported demonstration that death is not an evil, merely sidestep the issue; it is amusing "to see these leading souls unable to shake off our common lot" (III, iv, 810–12 [632–4]).

Reflecting on the relation of these examples of diversion to the argument of the other chapters in which Montaigne deliberates over how and whether we should prepare ourselves for death, we are led to the following conclusion: contrary to the claim made in I, xx, it is not the case that there is a sharp distinction between the attitude that most philosophers adopt toward death and that of "vulgar" people. Nor do pious individuals, who claim to confront their mortality directly and call on others to emulate them, do so either. Rather, philosophy (at least in its Stoic and Epicurean forms) and religion are themselves means by which people "divert" themselves from death—no less so than the attempted forgetfulness of the vulgar, which Montaigne had previously purported to scorn. In sum, just as Montaigne's analysis of Cato's motivation undermined the claim that there is a true moral difference between his pursuit of difficulty and others' softness, the essayist's analysis of the minds of philosophic and pious individuals challenges the belief that they are truly more steadfast or courageous than those whose thoughtlessness or irreligion they condemn. As in the other case, the intention underlying this equalization or homogenization of human motives is to prepare Montaigne's readers to accept the substitution of an easier and more salutary attitude for the harsh one that previous philosophic, moral, and religious preceptors have propagated. The need for such a reconstruction of the soul is indicated once more by a quotation from Propertius with which Montaigne concludes "Of Diversion," which laments that in shaping man, Prometheus failed to order the mind prudently, as he did the body (817 [638]).

The conclusion of "Of Diversion" must be read in the light of Montaigne's attribution to "nature" in I, iii, of people's misguided inclination to pursue "future" goods rather than to satiate themselves with "present"

---

[38]According to Cicero, *Tusculan Disputations,* I, xxxiv. Recall also the account of Cato's suicide in *Essais,* I, xliv, and II, xxviii.

ones; and of his account in the following chapter of how the soul, when it lacks "a legitimate object" for its passions, forges "a false and frivolous one" rather than remain idle (I, iii, 18 [8]; I, iv, 25 [14]). As he remarks in "Of Idleness," unless people's minds are occupied "with some definite subject that will bridle and constrain them, they throw themselves in disorder hither and yon in the vague field of imaginings" (I, viii, 33 [21]). The term "diversion" is actually a label for the enormous project, of which Montaigne developed the theoretical foundation in the "Apology for Raymond Sebond," of redirecting human concerns from transcendent goods to earthly ones, so as to leave our souls with no leisure, so to speak, for the former. It is the same project as the "reformation" he proposed later in I, iii, according to which we should learn "to avoid expense and pleasure the use and knowledge of which are imperceptible to us," and as was suggested by his recommendation in I, xiv, that we give the soul an attitude most "conducive to our repose and preservation." Underlying this project, as the context of the last-cited passage indicates, is a confidence in the almost unlimited malleability of the human soul. Even though our disposition to pursue future and "imperceptible" goods is due to nature, the soul (unlike the body) is sufficiently flexible to lend itself to an enormous remaking by human art. That remaking is to take the form, literally, of a "diversion," in the same sense in which a hydraulic engineer diverts a stream from its "natural" channel to an artificial one.[39] In other words, Montaigne intends the energy of the passions which has previously been drawn in the direction of transcendental strivings to be redirected toward earthly concerns. Hence Montaigne's solution to the problem of preventing the awareness of our mortality from generating transcendental strivings is ultimately the same as his remedy for spiritedness: to stimulate the desire for earthly goods, to the exclusion of concern with transcendental ones.[40] Such a redirection of human concerns will constitute the "bridle" to restrain our imagination, the need for which Montaigne alluded to in both the "Apology" and "Of Idleness." To accomplish this redirection Montaigne proposes a kind of philosophic propaganda directed at the multitude (along the lines of "Of Physiognomy") which will teach people: "Why worry about death?" con-

[39]Montaigne uses a hydraulic metaphor at I, x, 41 [26] to illustrate the need to relieve the soul's "tension" lest it become "impotent"; cf. the treatment of "tension" and impotence at I, xxi, 97 [70], discussed in Chapter Nine; also Machiavelli's reference to "dikes and dams," *The Prince*, ch. 25, pp. 98–9.

[40]Note that among the various instances of "diversion" that Montaigne recounts in III, iv, the only two cases in which he describes *himself* as having applied this remedy to other people's illnesses of soul are those of the young prince he distracted from anger and the woman he sought to divert from mourning. This fact seems to confirm the dual intention of his teaching about diversion in the *Essays:* to divert political actors from the spirited vengeance that results from their excessively grand self-estimation and their concomitant strivings for immortal glory, and to divert the multitude from the religious superstition generated by the terror of death.

joined with the development of a science of "medicine" and a relaxation of the legal and moral restraints on sensual enjoyment which will make life so pleasant and "diverting" that to concern oneself with one's mortality will ultimately be seen as a kind of idiosyncratic pathology, for which the remedy is simply to plunge oneself anew into the "diversions" of life. It is the intended mass appeal of Montaigne's doctrine, combined with his advocacy of technological development and encouragement of unrestricted sensual indulgence, that distinguishes the kind of diversion he advocates from what he represents as the ineffectual methods of Epicurus.[41] Such a vast project as I have attributed to Montaigne would seem incredible had we not witnessed its practical completion in much of the Western and Westernized world during the past four centuries. If I am not mistaken, the philosophic roots of the contemporary phenomenon that Philippe Ariès has labeled "forbidden death"—a social attitude according to which "death, so omnipresent in the past that it was familiar, would be effaced, would disappear" from view[42]—are to be found as far back as 1580.

Montaigne's "Honesty" Reconsidered

Montaigne's distinction in "Of Diversion" between the Socratic way of dealing with death and the attitude that he prescribes for most people invites us to reconsider, in conclusion, the implicit contrast he presented in "Of Practice" between his mode of rhetoric and that of Socrates. Despite the claim he makes in the latter chapter—as elsewhere—to speak more frankly and honestly than earlier philosophers, we have seen ample evidence that Montaigne himself practices a kind of deceptive rhetoric, particularly in the first two books, in order to protect himself against persecution. The teaching of "Of Diversion," however, calls into question the honesty or openness of Montaigne's teaching at a more fundamental level. Having distinguished individuals with the psychic strength of Socrates from the multitude who need to be diverted in one way or another from the specter of death, Montaigne acknowledges two chapters later, as I have noted, that he himself has habitually confronted dangers "with open eyes."

---

[41]Cf. Nichols, *Epicurean Political Philosophy*, p. 207: "because of the bitter aspects of the truth as seen by Lucretius [in his exposition of Epicureanism], few men will come to know and accept it; it can therefore not be the source of a reformation of politics." Montaigne's emphasis on "diversion" in his sense anticipates Hobbes, who differs from Lucretius (and Epicurus), Nichols observes, in "adopt[ing] the opinion of the common man" on the nature of happiness, identifying it with the endless pursuit of new pleasures rather than with the moderation of one's desires and a philosophic acceptance of the limitations of the human condition. Hence Montaigne's moral doctrine shares the "fundamentally egalitarian" character of Hobbes's teaching (ibid., p. 184).

[42]*Western Attitudes toward Death*, tr. Patricia M. Ranum (Baltimore, 1974), p. 85.

This remark suggests that he assigns himself to the rank of the strong-souled minority, alongside Socrates. In other words, Montaigne does not personally rely on the remedy of diversion that he prescribes for the generality of people.[43] But if this is the case, it is open to question how far Montaigne provides his readers with a greater awareness of truth than Socrates did. As I noted in Chapter One, numerous passages in the *Essays* hint at the existence of substantial differences between the literary persona "Montaigne"—an easygoing, unambitious, even lazy fellow—and his real nature. That Montaigne should think it necessary to prescribe for the multitude a different way of life, including a different way of looking at death (that is, not looking at it), from the one he himself practiced suggests that he ultimately agrees with Socrates that it is impossible to convey a true understanding of philosophy to those who are not philosophers.[44] And one may wonder whether Montaigne leads people closer to the truth about their situation by encouraging them not to think about their mortality at all than Socrates did by setting forth "noble lies" designed to harmonize with, and in some sense reflect, the truths that only a philosopher can apprehend. The precondition of "diversion" is the propagation of the doctrine of dogmatic skepticism which Montaigne expounded in the "Apology." Perhaps the deepest justification of this enterprise arises, in Montaigne's eyes, from the previous corruption of philosophy by its incorporation into Christian theology—which leads him, in "Of Physiognomy" as well as in "Of Pedantry," to disparage "learning" even as he eulogizes Socrates.

Given that political philosophy, as Leo Strauss noted, was understood from its inception to be political in its function as well as its theme,[45] its pursuit was seen by its founders as being inseparable from the practice of rhetoric: a rhetoric that would convey to the multitude a distillation of the truth presented in the most politically salutary way. What differentiates Montaigne's rhetoric from that of the classical political philosophers, however, is the extent of its positive, or propagandistic, function: a popularized teaching derived from philosophy is now to be employed to accomplish a radical transformation in the beliefs, and consequently in the way of life, of the multitude.[46] This propagandistic function is particularly manifest in the more "open," and extended, chapters of Book III, where Montaigne advertises his putative way of life as a model to be emulated and frankly expresses

---

[43]This is not to deny the sincerity of Montaigne's wish to go to his death "quietly and insensibly," or of his claim to avoid "looking" at death when confronted with "mortal dangers" (III, ix, 949 [742]). But as the *Essays* as a whole make evident, Montaigne has surely devoted considerable thought to the fact of human mortality and its significance.

[44]See Plato, *Republic*, 493e–494a, 517d–518a; *Apology*, 37e–38a; *Essais*, III, viii, 910, 916–17 [711, 716]).

[45]*What Is Political Philosophy?* pp. 10, 93–4.

[46]Armaingaud, "Etude," p. 88, applies the term "moral propaganda" to Montaigne's rhetoric.

his opinions on such varied practical concerns as sexual mores, trials for witchcraft, and the Spaniards' treatment of the American natives. In surveying the positive elements of Montaigne's political and moral teaching in the two remaining chapters of this study, I shall focus attention more extensively than I have previously done on Book III. Though my account of the moral teaching embodied in the third book will in some respects accord with that of other interpreters—for whom the disarmingly "personal," easygoing, and seemingly commonsensical character of this book often appears to make it the highlight of the *Essays* as a whole[47]—I shall endeavor to stress the dependence of that teaching on an underlying philosophic understanding of the human situation, the very success of which has tended to obscure its controversiality.

[47]Consider, for instance, the conclusion of Frame's *Montaigne's Discovery of Man,* p. 168: "We may still call [Montaigne] a humanist in his late years. If we do, however, we are in fact declaring that he has changed the meaning of the term. He has given it a breadth and scope it never had before. He has made it, even as he has made himself, fully human."

CHAPTER ELEVEN

Selfhood, Conscience, and Individualism

Montaigne's Focus on His "Self"

If there is one point on which practically all interpreters of the *Essays* can be said to agree, it is the centrality of the "self" (*moi*) as the object of Montaigne's investigations. To portray himself was Montaigne's sole intention in writing the *Essays*, according to both the foreword and the description of the book which he gave to Henry III in 1580. It is the focus on himself that, by its author's testimony, makes the *Essays* unique (II, vi, 358 [273]; II, viii, 364 [278]). While denying that the original text of the *Essays* conformed strictly to the author's description, Villey aptly expresses the scholarly consensus by remarking, "It is in the portrayal of the self that [Montaigne] fully manifested his originality as a moralist, and he created a form of art marvelously well fitted to express it."[1]

Not only is the self generally recognized to constitute Montaigne's central theme; his greatest and most beneficial influence on his readers is seen to have been to encourage them, in accordance with the advice he cites from Plato (I, iii, 18 [8–9]), to come to know themselves and their proper business in life. Yet Montaigne's implicit analogy between his mode of self-examination and that of Socrates is, as I noted in Chapter One, at least partially misleading. This analogy does not take account of Montaigne's practice of confessing to various putative vices and describing particular

---

[1] *Les Sources*, 2:546. Though he suggests that scholars may have gone too far in representing Montaigne's self-portrait as "the sole centre" of his book, Sayce observes that the external objects of the author's reflection "can in their turn be subsumed in the unity" of his self-portrait, inasmuch as his thoughts and experiences all contribute "to the total picture of himself" (*Essays*, p. 50).

aspects of his life (such as his bodily functions) which are normally thought to be private—as if the essence of his self were somehow to be found in these things. Nor does it sufficiently explain his emphasis on the need to learn what one "owes" to oneself, in opposition to the duties that political society endeavors to impose on the individual. The distinctive political implications of that emphasis have been noted by Nannerl Keohane:

> Montaigne . . . presents a picture of a life centered in the self, a life in which all other obligations besides obligation to the self are peripheral, carefully mea-sured, kept in their places. It is not a life of retreat or isolation, but a life in which the self discovers itself by reflection upon other selves and other matter, and establishes its claims within and against the world. Montaigne succeeded better than any other writer in making such a self-centered life attractive, in teaching men to think of this individualism as a satisfactory and appealing moral norm. He provided for modernity an alternative ideal, to be set over against the ancient ideal of the engaged citizen and the medieval ideal of the self-sacrificing saint.[2]

Keohane properly contrasts Montaigne's elevation of the self with the dominant political ideals that the Western world had previously been taught to value. Yet she downplays the radical character of this teaching by denying "that Montaigne foresaw or desired the full-fledged morality of bourgeois individualism" and by claiming that he merely wished "to redress the balance" between public and private concerns, which he found to be excessively weighted toward the former in his time. And she softens the political import of Montaigne's "individualism" by comparing it with the essentially apolitical teaching of Epicurus, whose "counsel of regulated pleasure" she believes Montaigne found most attractive.[3]

Montaigne invites readers to understand his goal as the reestablishment of a balance between private enjoyment and public duty (for example, III, x, 981–5 [767–70]). But as I have suggested previously, the notion of a balance among competing goods is in itself no more meaningful than Aristotle's initial doctrine of the mean: everything depends on the relative weight one attributes to various goods, and consequently on the standard by reference to which they are evaluated. Given the purposive character of human life, it is inevitable that one goal or another will predominate, the others being regarded as (at most) ancillary to it. In the case of the cor-poreal/spiritual dichotomy, we have seen that although Montaigne pro-fesses merely to aim at a balance, he emphasizes the corporeal aspect of human nature, making the beasts rather than the gods the model for emulation. There is every reason to suspect that, with respect to the related

---

[2]"Montaigne's Individualism," pp. 365–6.
[3]Ibid., pp. 366, 387.

dichotomy between public and private, his emphasis on the latter similarly reflects a specific political intention. In this chapter I explore the way of life toward which Montaigne sought to direct humanity through his emphasis on the self, distinguishing between the "moral propaganda" of his rhetoric and the philosophic reasoning on which it rests.

When we consider Montaigne's teaching about the self, it is particularly necessary to avoid reading subsequent interpretations of this concept, or our own preconceptions, into the *Essays*. Despite Montaigne's emphasis on describing "himself" and his admonition that others seek to know "themselves," he still uses these pronouns reflexively, to refer to the identity of particular persons, rather than using *self* as an independent, substantive noun, as is commonly done today.[4] Whereas the term *self* is now employed as a substitute for *soul*, Montaigne still conforms to the older usage; references to the soul, as distinguished from the self, abound in the *Essays*. Yet, I shall suggest, Montaigne's particular mode of portraying himself paves the way for subsequent developments.

Although Montaigne claims in "To the Reader" that the delineation of his particular "conditions and humors" will constitute the sole "matter" of the *Essays*, it is not until the third chapter that he begins to discuss the significance and importance of such self-study. Following his lament at people's natural tendency to spend their time "gaping after future things" instead of focusing attention on "present goods," he cites Plato's "great precept . . . 'Do your job and know yourself,'" and adds, "Each of its two parts generally includes our whole duty, and similarly includes its fellow. He who would do his job would see that his first lesson is to know what he is and what is proper for him. And he who knows himself no longer takes foreign business for his own; loves and cultivates himself before anything else; refuses superfluous occupations and useless propositions." He appends a quotation from Cicero according to which the wise human being will always be contented with things as they are, and an allusion to Epicurus' having "dispense[d] his sage from foresight and concern for the future" (I, iii, 18 [8–9]).

As Montaigne's reference to Plato indicates, to say that people should seek to know themselves is not, in itself, to specify any particular limit to their inquiries: Socrates sought self-knowledge *by* considering his relation to the universe.[5] Nor need the injunction to do one's job be taken in any restrictive sense: all depends on what we understand our proper "work" to be. It is noteworthy that, immediately after proffering this advice in I, iii, Montaigne turns to an examination of "the laws that concern the dead" (18

[4] As noted by Jerome Schwartz, "'La Conscience d'un homme': Reflections on the Problem of Conscience in the *Essais*," in La Charité, ed., *O Un Amy!* p. 269.

[5] Cf. Marvin Zetterbaum, "Self and Subjectivity in Political Theory," *Review of Politics* 44 (1982): 59–60; Bloom, *Closing of the American Mind*, p. 174.

[9]), without explaining how it pertains to his role as a private citizen to judge such public ordinances.[6] Evidently, despite his later claims that no one spends less time ferreting into others' affairs than he does (II, iv, 345 [263]) and that he has "not much business elsewhere" than with himself (II, xii, 548 [425]), Montaigne understands *his* proper vocation in an extremely broad sense, perhaps one no more limited than Socrates' quest was.

Montaigne's allusion to Epicurus' having liberated the sage from a concern with future things does suggest a more concrete limitation to the sphere of self-concern which develops later in I, iii, into the recommendation (discussed in Chapter Five) that people avoid concerning themselves with intangible (that is, spiritual) goods. But to understand the political implications of Montaigne's focus on the self, we must further explore the manner in which his recommendations deviate from the Epicurean and Stoic teaching. A starting point is provided by the chapter "Of Solitude" (I, xxxix), wherein the essayist purports to follow, but significantly modifies, the ancient moralists' recommendation that the wise should withdraw themselves, both literally and figuratively, from public and external concerns.

Self-Ownership

Although "Of Solitude" is commonly interpreted as reflecting Montaigne's early "Stoicism," the text is far from consistently supporting that doctrine. The title and the first part of the chapter, as well as a lengthy passage based on Epicurus and Seneca at the conclusion, appear (as Zeitlin observes) to imitate "the comparison of the active and the contemplative life" which was "a commonplace" among ancient moralists.[7] Montaigne seems, in these passages, to mimic the Stoic and Epicurean counsel to withdraw from society so as to free oneself from dependence on external things, and to purify oneself of vices that obstruct contentment. Yet the remainder of the chapter contains passages so at variance in style and content with these "famous commonplaces" as to render the overall text "incoherent," in Zeitlin's judgment, unless one reads it in the light of our (supposed) knowledge of Montaigne's evolution. One element of incoherence is supplied by a post-1588 addition that "recommend[s] retirement for those who have given their years of active vigour to the world"; this posture, as Zeitlin observes, "implies approval of the active life," in contradiction to the putative theme of the chapter, and trivializes that theme, since retirement in old age "calls for no justification before the world." But even

---

[6]Cf. his subsequent complaint that "too many heads" judge public affairs (III, x, 998 [781]).
[7]Zeitlin, *Essays of Montaigne*, 1:389.

aside from that problem, Zeitlin notes, the original version of the chapter embodies "two sharply distinguishable attitudes": one seeming to favor a quasi-Stoical "austere aloofness from the common interests and affections of mankind," and another that encourages a regard for health and the enjoyment of external goods up to the limits of pleasure, while rejecting as "excessive virtue" the self-denial practiced by ancient sages and Christian monastics.[8] As elsewhere, I shall try to show that Montaigne's underlying thought is consistent, despite the surface inconsistencies.[9]

Since the anti-Stoical arguments of I, xxxix, essentially imitate those expounded in I, xiv, a brief summary of this aspect of the chapter will suffice here. All the advice of the ancient moralists concerning the need to free oneself from dependence on material goods and to train oneself to endure hardship and pain, which was subtly challenged in I, xiv, is forthrightly rejected as "excessive virtue" in a passage in the latter part of "Of Solitude" which I quoted in Chapter Seven (I, xxxix, 237 [179]). As in the earlier chapter, Montaigne ultimately endorses liberation from external concerns only to the extent of deprecating the pursuit of goods whose essence lies purely in "opinion"—notably, glory—and of denying that one's happiness should be dependent on the welfare or survival of other human beings, even one's own family.[10] While purporting to omit from his rejection of asceticism the withdrawal from earthly pleasures which is motivated by piety, Montaigne retracts that exception by including religiously inspired self-deprivation among the varieties of excessive virtue (237, 239–40 [179–81]). In sum, though Montaigne shares the Stoic and Epicurean goal of mitigating our dependence on the vicissitudes of fortune, it does not appear he ever thought that goal could best be achieved by "solitude" in the Stoical, let alone the Christian, sense.

The more serious aspect of the self-withdrawal that Montaigne advocates in "Of Solitude" is suggested by the latter part of the first sentence:

> as for that fine statement under which ambition and avarice take cover—that we are not born for our private selves, but for the public—let us boldly appeal

[8]Ibid., pp. 389–91.

[9]Zeitlin's claim that "the evidence is fairly positive" in this case that Montaigne composed the 1580 text in more than one stage (ibid., p. 389) is remarkable, since there is no such evidence whatsoever aside from the inconsistencies of argument that the evolutionary interpretation purports to explain. Indeed, in the very first sentence of the chapter, dating from 1580, Montaigne proposes to "leave aside the usual long comparison between the solitary and the active life" (I, xxxix, 232 [174]); this remark indicates that the imitation of such comparisons which follows does not represent his serious concern.

[10]At p. 235 [177], Montaigne asserts that "we should have wives, children, goods, and above all health, if we can, but we must not bind ourselves to them in such a way that our happiness depends on them." In subsequent pages, however, he effectively drops his qualification to the pursuit of the latter two goals by remarking that health "should be our chief consideration" and recommending that we "hold on, tooth and nail," to the enjoyment of corporeal pleasures and comforts (240, 241 [181–2]).

to those who are in the midst of the dance; let them cudgel their conscience as to whether, on the contrary, the titles, the offices, and the hustle and bustle of the world are not sought out rather to gain private profit from the public. (232 [174])

This passage bears an obvious relation to Montaigne's description in III, x, of the sages' practice of "diverting and distracting" people from themselves and encouraging them to live for the sake of the community, in the belief that only by exaggerating citizens' public duties could they overcome people's naturally excessive selfishness. Just before that passage Montaigne cites his father as one who, having "heard it said that we must forget ourselves for our neighbor, that the individual was not to be considered at all in comparison with the general," sacrificed his comfort and health in pursuit of the public good.[11] Unlike those who seek private profit from public office, Montaigne's father, a most "charitable and public-spirited [*populaire*] soul," did subordinate his interest to that of the public. But his way is far from the one that Montaigne recommends: "he who abandons healthy and gay living of his own to serve others thereby takes, to my taste, a bad and unnatural course." Whereas his father let his soul be "cruelly agitated" by public turmoils, Montaigne doubts he can "decently admit at what little cost to the repose and tranquility of my life I have passed more than half of it amid the ruin of my country," owing to his "patience" in enduring misfortunes that do not directly affect him (III, x, 983–4 [769–70]; III, xii, 1023 [800]).

Further light on what Montaigne means by solitude is provided in III, iii, "Of Three [Kinds of] Associations," wherein he distinguishes himself from men of "private, retiring, and inward natures," remarking that his "essential pattern is suited to communication and revelation." The solitude he advocates, he explains, is in no sense antisocial, but entails "leading my feelings and thoughts back to myself . . . abandoning solicitude for outside things, and mortally avoiding servitude and obligation" (801 [625]). These passages (along with Montaigne's account of his political activities) confirm that to return to oneself in his sense does not entail avoiding public action or association with others[12]—any more than it requires one to renounce "unnecessary" corporeal pleasures. But in order to grasp what is truly distinctive and radical about the doctrine of "Of Solitude," we must consider one particular theme in that chapter and observe the use that Mon-

[11]For one philosophic source of the principle by which Montaigne reports his father was influenced, see the paraphrase of Plato's *Laws* (923a–c) at II, viii, 378–9 [289–90], to the effect that all individuals, their families, and their goods "belong to the public," and that "the private interest must yield to the common."

[12]Cf. I, lvii, 312–13 [237], where Montaigne opposes early retirement, on the ground "that our employment and occupation should be extended as far as possible, for the public advantage."

taigne makes of it in a later chapter titled "A Custom of the Island of Cea" (II, iii).

The specific theme meriting our attention is that of self-ownership: the notion that all of us are our own proper "owners," having the right to dispose of ourselves as we wish. This principle is suggested at two points in "Of Solitude": one where Montaigne urges that we "repossess ourselves" (234 [176])—implying that we have wrongly been deprived of, or forsaken, an original condition of self-ownership; and another where he remarks that "the greatest thing in the world is to know how to belong to oneself" (236 [178]). Taken by themselves, these remarks might be understood as a recapitulation of Stoic doctrine.[13] But Montaigne's terming the knowledge of how to belong to oneself "the greatest thing in the world" suggests, to say the least, that this point is of particular importance for him. He brings out a critical political implication of this premise in his discussion of the justifiability of suicide—the Cean "custom" to which the title of II, iii, alludes. In that chapter, after quoting the Stoics' defense of suicide—"that it is living in conformity with nature for the sage to part with life even in full happiness, if he does so opportunely"—he adds:

> This does not pass without contradiction. For many hold that we cannot abandon this garrison of the world without the express commandment of him who has placed us in it; and that it is for God, who has sent us here not for ourselves alone but for his glory and the service of others, to give us leave when he pleases, not for us to take it. We are not born for ourselves, it is said, but also for our country; the laws demand of us, for their interest, an accounting of ourselves, and can take action for homicide against us. Otherwise, as deserters from our post, we are punished in both this and the other world. (332–3 [253])

This passage makes clear that in arguing *against* the policy of living for the sake of others in III, x, Montaigne was not merely taking issue with the teaching of anonymous "sages" but was opposing the doctrine of Christianity—as well as that of Plato, whose condemnation of suicide in the *Laws* he goes on to cite (334 [254]).[14] Although Montaigne does not explicitly judge between the Stoic position and the Christian-Platonic criticism of it in the immediate context of this passage, his verdict is indicated at the conclusion of II, iii, where he cites "unendurable pain and the fear of a worse death" as

---

[13]The Pléiade editors cite Seneca's twentieth epistle as the source of the latter remark, apparently referring to the opening sentence wherein Seneca addresses Lucilius as one "who one time might become your own."

[14]*Laws*, 873c–d; cf. *Phaedo*, 61e–62c. On the sixteenth-century church's total proscription of suicide, including the denial of Christian burial, see Albert Bayet, *Le Suicide et la morale* (Paris, 1922), pp. 541–2, 556–8. For a thorough analysis of the structure of II, iii, which emphasizes the heterodoxy of some of the thoughts Montaigne expresses on suicide and the prudent manner in which he conveys them, but without attributing a definite conclusion on the issue to him, see Henry, *Montaigne in Dialogue*, ch. 2.

"the most excusable motives" for suicide (342 [262]). This conclusion should be juxtaposed with a previous passage in the same chapter where Montaigne—in contrast with the judgment of "ecclesiastical history"—dissuades women from killing themselves to avoid being raped: "Enough for them to say No while doing it"[!] (338 [257]). That considerations of duty to one's creator are not the ground on which Montaigne determines the justifiability of suicide is confirmed by a still earlier passage that links with the "ridiculous" disdain for life which led some people to kill themselves the "vanity" of wishing "to be made into an angel": one who performs such an action "does nothing for himself; he would never benefit from the change. For when he is no more, who will feel and rejoice in this improvement for him?" (334 [254]). In sum, whereas Plato and Christian thinkers opposed suicide on the ground of one's duty to others or to God, Montaigne opposes it, as a general (but not inflexible) rule, purely in terms of the individual's gain and pleasure.

The theme of self-ownership has implications that range far beyond the issue of suicide. The principle that the individual "belongs" to the political community was given support by Aristotle as well as Plato. Aristotle infers from it not only that citizens should be educated to devote themselves to their country but that there is a general presumption against the freedom of individuals to live as they please: "what the law does not expressly permit it forbids."[15] By contrast, the principle of self-ownership that Montaigne enunciates is the ground of the liberal natural rights teaching subsequently formulated by Hobbes and Locke: the individual is "by nature" free; one is properly subject to no obligations other than those that can be said to derive from one's consent, motivated by gain to oneself; in all areas of life where no demonstrable harm to the rights of others can be shown to result, individuals should be left free to do as they like. The connection to Locke's teaching is particularly manifest in the English thinker's doctrine that each of us possesses a "property" in himself.[16]

We have already seen how in "Of Cannibals" Montaigne hints at the desirability of reducing the conventional restraints that laws impose on human behavior, and how, in "Of Cruelty," he suggests that our natural disposition toward inhumanity might be moderated if we were taught to understand ourselves in light of our kinship with the animals. Yet he is far from literally advocating that we live like savages or beasts. It remains to

[15] *Politics*, VIII.1; *Nicomachean Ethics*, 1138a5–7.
[16] See Locke, *Second Treatise*, ed. Peter Laslett, rev. ed. (New York, 1963), ch. 5, sec. 27, ll. 2–3; sec. 44, ll. 2–5. For Locke's view of suicide, see ibid., ch. 2, sec. 6, ll. 11–16 (restating the Christian view, in tacit contradiction of Locke's property doctrine), with ch. 4, sec. 23, ll. 15–18, and Laslett's note to the latter passage on p. 325; George Windstrup, "Locke on Suicide," *Political Theory* 8 (1980): 169–82. See also, on the connection between the right of suicide and the grounding of government in individual consent, Montesquieu, *Persian Letters*, no. 76; Marshall Berman, *The Politics of Authenticity* (New York, 1972), p. 34.

clarify, therefore, how Montaigne intends to promote the necessary civility in human behavior, in view of our natural self-interestedness, in the absence of the "elevated" moral teachings he has rejected.

On the surface it seems that Montaigne's remedy is to appeal to a conscience that he believes to be inherent in human nature. At various points throughout the *Essays,* especially in Book III, he refers to the conscience, or to an internal "pattern" or "form" that we may discover by looking into ourselves, as a guide to right conduct superior to laws, religions, or other people's approbation. Yet, as a number of scholars have recognized, there is an obvious problem with these appeals to conscience as *opposed* to law or conventional opinion. That problem arises from the remark in "Of Custom" that "the laws of conscience, which we say are born of nature, are born of custom" (I, xxiii, 114 [83]). If the dictates of conscience are themselves conventional in origin, it is hard to see how such a faculty could provide us with moral guidance superior to that of conventional opinion. And given the bizarre variety of customs that Montaigne described, many of them manifestly unreasonable and unjust, one may wonder how a conscience derived from custom could serve as an adequate guide at all. Not without reason did Rousseau apparently interpret Montaigne's emphasis on the diversity of customs as a denial of the very existence of conscience.[17] But why, then, should Montaigne appeal to it?

Numerous scholars have grappled with this difficulty without satisfactorily resolving it. Sayce, for one, leaves open the question of how far the passage from "Of Custom" "contradicts the erection of conscience into supreme moral authority" elsewhere in the *Essays.*[18] Alan Boase finds it "interesting that Montaigne did not more completely abandon the idea of conscience," in view of the "utilitarian" cast of his moral teaching, and infers "that to some extent his views on the relativity of customs and laws were merely a much-needed argument for tolerance" rather than an adoption of ethical relativism *tout court.*[19] Zeitlin, by contrast, stresses "the primacy of conscience" in Montaigne's thought, contending that "the arresting originality and importance of Montaigne's outlook lies in the boldness with which he has enunciated the idea that every person is an independent moral being, completely responsible to himself, and to himself only, for the regular conduct of his life."[20] While terming the notion that the laws of conscience are born of custom an "arresting" idea,[21] he does not explain how it can be reconciled with the supremacy of conscience. Jerome Schwartz, in a more recent study, depreciates the significance of the remark

---

[17]*Emile,* tr. Allan Bloom (New York, 1979), p. 289.
[18]Sayce, *Essays,* p. 197.
[19]Boase, *Fortunes of Montaigne,* p. xxxiii.
[20]Zeitlin, *Essays of Montaigne,* 1:xc–xci.
[21]Ibid., 1:335.

from "Of Custom" on the ground that this "post-1588 addition" is atypical of Montaigne's numerous contemporaneous references to conscience in all three books. To read it, as Sayce does, as a " 'devastating reflection' " is erroneously to attribute to Montaigne a "profoundly revolutionary ethical relativism in advance of his time." Yet since Schwartz also denies that Montaigne held to "an ontological view of conscience as an unchanging absolute," it is not clear how he would resolve the difficulty; he ends up describing "two opposite conceptions of conscience" between which he believes "Montaigne hesitates," without clearly choosing between them.[22]

Though Schwartz does not satisfactorily reconcile Montaigne's disparate remarks about the conscience, he properly stresses the importance of the chapter "Of Repentance" with respect to this issue. Of all the chapters in the *Essays*, "Of Repentance" contains the most moving and apparently sincere appeals to the conscience as the proper source of moral guidance. As Zeitlin comments, the chapter "abounds in phrases redolent of a pure and sweet-smelling morality."[23] But here, as elsewhere, the reader who wishes to understand Montaigne's reasoning rather then being lulled by his "sweet-smelling" rhetoric should bear in mind the essayist's counsel against equating beauty with truth. The appeals to conscience in "Of Repentance" cannot be understood outside of their context in the chapter, which includes remarks of a rather different hue concerning the status and the dictates of people's moral judgment.

Conscience and Repentance

"Of Repentance" opens with one of Montaigne's periodic discourses concerning his enterprise of self-study. The first two sentences are particularly pregnant with a broader meaning: "Others form man; I tell of him, and portray a particular one, very ill-formed, whom I should really make very different from what he is if I had to fashion him over again. But now it is done" (III, ii, 782 [610]).

At first glance this passage expresses Montaigne's recognition of and resignation to his particular defects as an individual. But a broader interpretation is suggested by the sequel, in which—after remarking the instability of the "subject" he is portraying—he remarks: "I set forth a humble and inglorious life; that does not matter. You can tie up all moral philosophy with a common and private life just as well as with a life of richer stuff. Each man bears the entire form of the human condition" (ibid. [611]).

[22]Schwartz, " 'La Conscience d'un homme,' " pp. 246–7, 255, 268.
[23]Zeitlin, *Essays of Montaigne*, 3:331.

In the light of these remarks—as well as other, previously quoted passages from the *Essays* in which Montaigne indicates the didactic purpose of his self-portrait—I suggest that the opening statement of III, ii, must be taken as referring to the defects of humanity as a whole, or of "the human condition." Understood in this way, the essayist's remarks that he is "ill-formed," and that he would make himself differently if he were to do the job over, constitute (assuming the doctrine of divine creation) a criticism of God's handiwork.

The defectiveness of the natural human condition had already been suggested by Montaigne's comparison between human beings and beasts in the "Apology for Raymond Sebond," as well as by the Propertius quotation in "Of Diversion." The particular interest of the opening statement of "Of Repentance," however, lies in the brief second sentence: "But now it is done." Taken in conjunction with Montaigne's disparagement, in such chapters as "A Custom of the Island of Cea," of the wish "to be something other than we are" (II, iii, 334 [254]), this remark suggests that whatever *moral* deficiencies we find to exist in our nature, as measured by some ideal standard, there is no point in lamenting them, let alone endeavoring to eliminate them: human nature must be accepted as it is. It is this view that underlies the entirety of Montaigne's treatment of the theme of repentance in III, ii, and that sets his understanding of the human condition at odds with the Christian one.

From an orthodox Christian standpoint, repentance or penitence is a lifelong obligation of every human being, in view of the "fallen" human condition that results from Adam's sin. Montaigne, by contrast, admits that he "rarely repent[s]" and that his "conscience is content with itself—not as the conscience of an angel or a horse, but as the conscience of a man" (III, ii, 784 [612]). (The avowal of submission to "the common and authorized beliefs" with which he follows this admission highlights its heretical character.)[24] The sequel makes clear that Montaigne's disavowal of repentance is

[24]Cf. Champion, *Introduction aux Essais,* pp. 199–200; Zeitlin, *Essays of Montaigne,* 3:329–30. Cf. also Montaigne's renunciation of efforts at moral self-reformation at III, ix, 924 [722], and III, x, 987 [772]. In the last sentence of "Of Repentance" Montaigne describes himself as having "fallen" from the healthier condition of his youth—when his sensual appetites had not yet abated (796 [621]). The self-"reformation" that Montaigne has undertaken, and which he recommends that others emulate, is to strive to regulate his conduct in the light of the discovery of the weakness of his understanding and its susceptibility to bias arising from his passions. Such a reformation entails a recognition that the passions themselves may not be susceptible to amendment (III, xiii, 1051–2 [822–3]). Marianne S. Meijer seeks to defend Montaigne's orthodoxy and sincerity by arguing that his position conforms to that of the fourth Lateran council (1215), which had obliged the faithful to confess their sins only once a year. Although the Council of Trent had imposed a more rigorous obligation in 1551, she argues that Montaigne need not have regarded himself as bound to accept it, since the council's decrees were neither formally registered by the French king and parlement nor recognized and published by the French clergy until 1615 ("De l'Honnête, de l'utile, et du repentir," *Journal of Medieval and Renaissance Studies* 12 [1982]: 265–9). Meijer perhaps

not due to the cognizance of any particular virtue or innocence on his part, but is intended as a posture that human beings in general might reasonably emulate. While contending that "a wellborn nature" is necessarily pleased by "goodness," he suggests that repenting one's vices is not only ineffectual but harmful:

> We can disown and retract the vices that take us by surprise, and toward which we are swept by passion; but those which by long habit are rooted and anchored in a strong and vigorous will cannot be denied. Repentance is nothing but a disavowal of our will and an opposition to our fancies, which leads us about in all directions. It makes this man [Horace, whom Montaigne proceeds to quote] disavow his past virtue and his continence. (785–6 [613])

Not only does a disposition toward repentance make us prone to instability, without ensuring that the new course of conduct on which we resolve will be better than the old one; it also serves as a mask and an excuse by which evil people disclaim responsibility for their deeds:

> There are some impetuous, prompt, and sudden sins: let us leave them aside. But as for these other sins so many times repeated, planned, and premeditated, constitutional sins, or even professional or vocational sins, I cannot imagine that they can be implanted so long in one and the same heart, without the reason and conscience of their possessor constantly willing and intending it to be so. And the repentance which he claims comes to him at a certain prescribed moment is a little hard for me to imagine and conceive. . . . These men make us believe that they feel great regret and remorse within; but of amendment and correction, or interruption, they show us no sign. Yet it is no cure if the disease is not thrown off. (790–91 [616–17])[25]

That repentance and sadness are characteristic of some of the most cruel and vicious individuals, such as Nero, has been one of the recurrent themes of the *Essays,* including the chapter just preceding "Of Repentance" (II, xxvii, 671 [523–4]; II, i, 315 [239]; III, i, 775–6 [605–6]). In the present context Montaigne highlights the theological bearing of that theme, re-

---

interprets "repentance" too narrowly, however, by identifying it with formal confession. Nor does she sufficiently explain Montaigne's disavowal of frequent repentance by attributing it to his "sincerity." Given the evident thoughtfulness with which the *Essays* as a whole was composed, Montaigne must have recognized that his deprecation of repentance would tend to encourage others to imitate his posture. As I argue in the text, it is doubtful that the overall argument of "Of Repentance" is intended merely to promote a more sincere piety. See also Henry, *Montaigne in Dialogue,* pp. 21–3; Sainte-Beuve, *Port-Royal,* III, iii, 1:851–2.

[25]See also, on the hypocrisy of pious "repentance," I, lvi, 304–5 [230–31], especially Montaigne's remark that "the state of a man who mixes piety with an execrable life seems to be rather more damnable than that of a man consistent with himself and dissolute throughout." Cf. Machiavelli, *Discorsi,* I, xxvii, 195, and context, concerning men's inability to be either "honorably wicked or perfectly good."

marking that there is "no quality so easy to counterfeit as devotion, if conduct and life are not made to conform to it" (III, ii, 791 [617]). But his point is not merely that genuine repentance entails an improvement in one's conduct; rather, he suggests that the very disposition to repent often reflects a judgment that is inferior to the one that concurred in certain putative sins. At the conclusion of the chapter he denounces the "accidental repentance that age brings," as exemplified by the disposition of old people to decry the sensual indulgence of youth, motivated by "envy, injustice, and malignity" (793–5 [619–20]). In contrast to the traditional view, which Aristotle endorses, that youths must be educated so as to control their passions,[26] Montaigne stresses the need to educate *old* people to counteract their disposition toward sourness and disdain for "present" pleasures (795–6 [620–21]).

The argument of "Of Repentance" as I have thus far surveyed it buttresses the principle of individual self-ownership by denying that ordinary human life should be understood as the incomplete manifestation of some particular excellence that people should strive to achieve and toward which governments should endeavor to guide them. The policy that Montaigne propounds instead is one of pure self-acceptance: "My actions are in order and conformity with what I am and with my condition. I can do no better" (791 [617]).

Precisely because the putative "vices" that Montaigne has previously admitted are such innocuous or even attractive ones, readers whose own judgments are not strongly colored by Christian doctrine are likely to find his attitude of self-acceptance reasonable and sensible. Yet the very examples cited in "Of Repentance" of vicious individuals who hypocritically profess to repent their misdeeds suggest that it is not sufficient as a general rule to "accept" human nature as it is. Whether or not all human beings should be regarded as sinful by nature, Montaigne clearly recognizes the existence of some who are truly vicious and affirms the natural roots of such ugly vices as cruelty and inhumanity. If repentance and reformation, sanctioned by religion and law, are not the remedy for such vices, what is?

It may seem that despite his renunciation of repentance, Montaigne holds that all human beings of healthy natures possess a conscience that offers sufficient *positive* incentives to good behavior, as well as guidance in how to act, if they will only listen to it: "There is . . . no goodness that does not

---

[26]*Nicomachean Ethics*, 1095a3–10; 1179b32–1180a3. Cf. the praise of the capacities of youth in "Of Age," the last chapter of Book I (I, lvii, 313–14 [237–8]), with the last chapter of Book I of Machiavelli's *Discourses* (I, lx); Mansfield, *Machiavelli's New Modes and Orders*, p. 179. Montaigne's criticism of the bias that age gives to people's judgments in III, ii, and at II, xiii, 589 [458], imitates the proem to Book II of the *Discourses* (*Discorsi*, pp. 271–2). Fleuret, "Montaigne et la société civile," p. 122, speaks of a "cult of youth" in Montaigne's thought, which she relates to his hopes for a world transformation to be brought about by future generations.

rejoice a wellborn nature. Indeed there is a sort of gratification in doing good which makes us rejoice in ourselves, and a generous pride that accompanies a good conscience" (784 [612]). Not only does Montaigne claim to judge his own actions by his private "laws and court," he asserts that anyone who "listens to himself" will similarly discover "a ruling pattern [*forme*]," "all his own," "which struggles against education and against the tempest of the passions that oppose it"; he implies that such an internal pattern constitutes a surer guide to moral improvement than the "external, arbitrary reformations" that others espouse. Hence he urges us to act for the sake of "conscience" rather than "glory" (785, 787–9 [613–15]). This emphasis on moral self-guidance is echoed in "Of Physiognomy," where Montaigne applauds "the virtue that laws and religions do not make but perfect and authorize, that feels in itself enough to sustain itself without help, born in us from its own roots, from the seed of universal reason that is implanted in every man who is not denatured," in contrast to "a certain image of scholastic probity, a slave to precepts, held down beneath fear and hope," which constitutes the dominant contemporary understanding of virtue; he concludes by emphasizing the "enormous distinction" between following one's conscience and mere conventional piety (III, xii, 1037 [811]).

It is phrases such as these that give "Of Repentance" what Zeitlin terms its "sweet-smelling" character. Yet when we scrutinize Montaigne's argument more carefully, we are again compelled to question the seriousness of his appeal to conscience. In the first place, nothing said in the chapter refutes the assertion in "Of Custom" that the dictates of conscience are rooted in convention. Indeed, the very arguments Montaigne uses to demonstrate the superiority of conscience to law or conventional opinion suggest the unreliability of most people's moral judgment:

> To found the reward of virtuous actions on the approbation of others is to choose too uncertain and shaky a foundation. Especially in an age as corrupt and ignorant as this, the good opinion of the people is a dishonor: whom can you trust to see what is praiseworthy? God keep me from being a worthy man according to the descriptions I see people every day giving of themselves in their own honor. . . . [T]o speak of it now in all conscience, I have often found in [his friends'] reproach and praise such false measure that I would hardly have erred to err rather than to do good in their fashion. (785 [612–13])

If the generality of human beings, including Montaigne's own friends, possess such a weak understanding of what is truly praiseworthy or honorable, it is not evident that their conscience can be relied on to identify their duty correctly. Nor do those who sin necessarily suffer the pangs of conscience as a result. Even though Montaigne claims that the "ugliness and disadvantage" of vice are "so apparent" as necessarily to make them hateful to "a sound judgment," he later observes that some people, "either from being glued to vice by a natural attachment, or from long habit, no longer recognize its ugliness." Similarly, despite his claim that goodness is necessarily a source of gratification to "a wellborn nature," he notes that on some people, including himself, "vice weighs heavily, but they counterbalance it with pleasure or some other consideration, and endure it and lend themselves to it for a certain price." While professing to find such conduct vicious, Montaigne goes on to suggest that a sufficient degree of pleasure or gain from a given action "might justly excuse the sin" (784, 789 [612, 616]). It may thus appear that his own freedom from repentance is due more to the laxness of his conscience than to its rigor—even though he elsewhere claims that his conscience is "tighter and more severe" in matters of personal obligation than the judgment of the magistrates (III, ix, 944 [738]).[27]

We may suppose that the vices for which Montaigne excuses himself are the merely conventional ones that, he remarks, are condemned by "false and erroneous opinion" in conformity with "laws and customs," as opposed to "those that reason and nature condemn" (784 [612]). But the unreliability of conscience as a source of internal retribution for more serious and politically significant crimes is further suggested by "Of Conscience" (II, v).

On the surface, the most politically important aspect of this chapter is the conclusion—most of it added in 1588—in which Montaigne denounces the judicial torture of accused criminals. With irrefutable, if not wholly original,[28] logic he points out that a disposition to confess under torture is a function of the limits of one's fortitude and endurance rather than cognizance of guilt; "whence it happens that the man whom the judge has tortured so as not to make him die innocent, is made to die both innocent and tortured" (II, v, 349 [266]). I wish, however, to call attention to the broader, underlying premise of this argument, as it is suggested earlier in the chapter. The first half of the text attests to "the power of conscience" to make people "betray, accuse, and fight" themselves, and to avow their guilt "in the absence of an outside witness" (346 [264]). Contrariwise, a good conscience "fills us with assurance and confidence"; Montaigne professes to have walked through "many perils . . . with a much firmer step by virtue of the secret knowledge I had of my own will and the innocence of my intentions" (347–8 [265]). He illustrates this power with three incidents from the life of the great Roman military commander Scipio Africanus the Elder.

[27]Note that Montaigne immediately precedes and follows this claim by describing how he therefore strives to avoid incurring "burdens and obligations."

[28]Villey, Les Sources, 1:237–8, and Nakam, Les Essais, pp. 322–8, among others, note the similarity of Montaigne's argument to that of the Spanish humanist Juan Luis Vives. Cf. also Augustine, City of God, XIX.6.

Each of the stories Montaigne recounts about Scipio concerns his manner of responding to public accusations. In none of these cases did Scipio refute the accusations. Rather, he boldly refused to answer or evaded the charge. In conclusion, Montaigne doubts that "a cauterized soul" could have "counterfeit[ed] such assurance" as Scipio displayed and cites Livy's judgment that the Roman leader "had a heart too great and accustomed to too lofty a fortune . . . to know how to play the part of a criminal and stoop to the depths of defending his innocence" (348 [265–6]). But he offers no opinion as to whether Scipio was really guilty or innocent of the charges!²⁹

Regardless of whether Montaigne had any opinion regarding Scipio's guilt, his refusal to assert the Roman's innocence clearly distances him from the Christian teaching—to which he lent lip service earlier in the chapter—according to which the evildoer will necessarily be punished by the pangs of conscience. To the contrary, his account of Scipio suggests that a sufficiently strong-souled individual can commit misdeeds while fully retaining both internal and apparent equanimity. Such an interpretation is buttressed by Montaigne's previous reference to the strength of his own conscience—in view of the questionableness of his professed "innocence." And it seems to be confirmed by the fact that the immediate sequel to the account of Scipio is Montaigne's attack on the use of torture as a means of compelling the conscience of the guilty to speak. There is, in sum, no necessary correlation between a "good" conscience and a strong one: a person's equanimity may just as likely be the result of inner strength and confidence—despite many

²⁹Neither of Montaigne's apparent sources for these anecdotes expresses a clear judgment as to Scipio's guilt. But both accounts embody a somewhat more explicit praise of the Roman's character (Livy, *History of Rome*, XXXVIII, 50–52; Aulus Gellius, *Attic Nights*, IV, xiv, 1–2).

At II, xxviii, 681 [531], Montaigne accuses Cato the Censor of being motivated by "envy and ambition when he dared to attack the honor of Scipio, [a man] in goodness and in all sorts of excellence far greater than he or any other man of his time"; but this remark no more refutes the specific charges Cato brought against him than the discussion in "Of Conscience" did. The remark is immediately preceded, moreover, by a passage in which Montaigne, while judging Cato the Censor's virtue less "spotless" than that of his younger namesake, stresses the greater utility of his public services. As I have noted, Montaigne elsewhere suggests that there is a tension between the purity of a man's virtue and his capacity to serve the public (III, ix, 969–70 [758]). In ascribing Cato's accusation against Scipio to selfish motives, Montaigne follows the suggestion of Machiavelli, who describes Cato as "*reputedly*" holy (*Discorsi*, I, xxix, 200). Elsewhere Machiavelli portrays Scipio as adept at manipulating the people and implies that his very "goodness" may have been a calculated means to winning their favor (ibid., I, xi, 160; I, liii, 251; III, xx, 445; III, xxix, 479–80). This portrayal must be read in the light of Machiavelli's emphasis on the danger that an individual's excessive popularity poses to the preservation of liberty in a republic, and his teaching that public accusations, whatever their motive, are an essential means of protecting liberty (ibid., I, vii–viii; III, xxii, 452). In sum, as Strauss puts it, "tutored by Machiavelli, we must assume that Cato's good conscience in acting as he did is indistinguishable from his envy of Scipio's fame" (*Thoughts on Machiavelli*, p. 192): envy and ambition, which Montaigne attributes to Cato more explicitly than Machiavelli did, are motives necessary to the health of the political community. (Cf. ibid., pp. 264–5; Mansfield, *Machiavelli's New Modes and Orders*, pp. 105–6; Strauss, *What Is Political Philosophy?* pp. 42–3.) The relation between motives of private interest and the public good in Montaigne's thought will be elaborated in Chapter Twelve.

sins—as of moral innocence; whereas weakness or "cowardice" in the soul, as Montaigne remarks in the "Apology," may dispose its possessor to "penitence and repentance," despite his relative innocence (II, xii, 550 [427]).[30] Thus conscience may indeed cause people to "betray, accuse, and fight" themselves—but it is the weak, not the guilty, who are most likely to suffer these consequences. If such is the case, one may doubt that the *belief in* the authority of conscience as traditionally understood is truly salutary. If such a belief disposes the weak to penitence and self-doubt, without mitigating the criminal conduct of the greatest evildoers, does it not facilitate the oppression of the former by the latter? It is for this reason, I suggest, that Montaigne, in "Of Repentance," set a public example of *non*repentance. If repentance, on the one hand, means regretting one's "sinful" nature, and the harmless sensual and corporeal pleasures that our natures cause us to pursue, then it is a vain and pointless disposition. If the term refers, on the other hand, to the regret that such tyrants as Nero experience for their great misdeeds—which they nonetheless have every intention of repeating—it is hypocritical. In neither case is the disposition toward penitence an effectual check on the truly hateful human vices. In fact, such a disposition induces the many all the more docilely to endure the perpetration of injustices against them, in the belief that slavery and tyranny, as the Augustinian and Thomistic teachings respectively assert, must be regarded as a divinely imposed punishment for their sins.[31] In "Of Drunkenness," we recall, Montaigne warned against "confusion about the order and measurement of sins," since "murderers, traitors, tyrants gain too much by it." "Even our teachers," he asserted, "often rank sins badly" (II, ii, 322 [245]). In opposition to the Christian teaching that brands all human beings as sinners, Montaigne, as we have seen, seeks to lower the moral standard by which people are judged, so that they will not be made to feel guilty and deserving of punishment for indulging in such harmless enjoyments as drinking. Only by means of this "science of distinguishing among the vices" may "the virtuous and the wicked" be properly differentiated (ibid.).[32]

The foregoing inquiry into Montaigne's understanding of the conscience demonstrates that his assertion that the "laws" of conscience originate in custom is not an aberration from his considered view but is amply supported elsewhere. Seen in this light, it is the appeals to conscience in "Of Repentence" and elsewhere, rather than the statement in "Of Custom," that require explanation. But we cannot conclude that Montaigne's refer-

---

[30]Cf. Montaigne's reference earlier in the "Apology" to "fear," "cowardice," and "faintheartedness" as the root of religious credulity (II, xii, 422 [325]).

[31]See *City of God,* XIX.15; Aquinas, *On Kingship,* I, vi, 52.

[32]Cf. also III, v, 839 [655]: "Iniquitous appraisal of vices!" and its context; and III, ix, 969 [758], regarding the folly of modeling our duties on those of "another being," with the result that we are "necessarily at fault."

ences to the conscience, or to the "ruling form" that he claims all of us may find within ourselves, are merely rhetorical in the sense that his specious professions of Christian piety are. In contrast with those professions, the essayist's exhortations to his readers to act out of regard for conscience rather than in pursuit of glory are presented with a forcefulness and an apparent sincerity that have made them a prime source of his book's moral appeal and influence.[33] As in other cases, there is reason to suppose that the overall rhetorical effect of Montaigne's argument reflects his intention. Our problem is to ascertain the serious meaning and intent that underlie his appeals to the conscience, in light of the fact that he does not share the traditional view of it as an innate and inherently trustworthy faculty of moral self-guidance. A particularly significant passage, in this regard, occurs in "Of Glory," wherein Montaigne attests to "the contentment that a *well-regulated* conscience receives in itself from well-doing" (II, xvi, 607 [472]). Given that "the laws of conscience," as most people conceive them, derive from what they have been taught to believe, it follows that the conscience cannot be the source of its own regulation. Rather, to guide people's consciences in a salutary direction is the responsibility of those rare individuals like Montaigne himself whose wisdom entitles them "to regulate our belief by their own" (II, x, 397 [304]). It is apparently part of Montaigne's moral project to retain people's belief in conscience but to revise their understanding of its sanction and dictates.

When we pursue an understanding of Montaigne's doctrine of conscience, it is helpful to bear in mind that the root meaning of the term is "knowledge." There is a close relation in the *Essays,* as Schwartz observes, between the moral conscience and "the idea of conscience as a form of self-consciousness."[34] That relation is particularly apparent in the first chapter of Book III, wherein Montaigne asserts that as a negotiator he "would rather fail in my mission than [fail] towards myself," remarks that "he who is unfaithful to himself, is excusably so to his master," and recommends that all people emulate the pledge once required of Egyptian judges not to "disavow their conscience for any command" (III, i, 769, 772, 775 [600, 603, 605]). Taken together, these remarks suggest that to follow one's conscience *means* being true to oneself, which in turn presupposes self-knowledge. To elucidate Montaigne's doctrine of conscience, we therefore need to survey his more general teaching about what it means to be, or be faithful to, oneself. We have previously learned that we are our own rightful owners and ought to "repossess" ourselves from those external authorities that have wrongfully claimed sovereignty over us; but what is the nature of the self to which we are encouraged to regain title?

[33]Cf. G. W. F. Hegel, *The History of Philosophy,* tr. Haldane and Simson, 3 vols. (London, 1955), 3:146 (pt. 2, sec. 3, C).
[34]" 'La Conscience d'un homme,' " p. 260.

The Road to Tranquility

As previous quotations will have made apparent, a major theme of the *Essays*, beginning with the third chapter, is that people need to learn to stay "home," that is, to settle in "themselves," rather than concern themselves with "foreign" things. In arguing against the pursuit of glory, Montaigne asserts that "our soul should play its role . . . at home within [us], where no eyes enter but ours"; he "hold[s] that I exist only at home," not in other people's opinion of him (II, xvi, 607, 610 [472, 474–5]). Elaborating the theme of self-reliance in "Of Vanity," he remarks that "we ourselves . . . are our most proper and surest resource," and that "I have nothing that is mine but myself"; at the beginning of the next chapter, he describes the care he takes to augment his natural "insensibility" to external concerns and reports that "as much as I can, I employ myself entirely on myself" (III, ix, 946 [740]; III, x, 980 [766]).

All well and good, the reader may reply; but how can one learn to stay within "oneself," given the admitted naturalness of our disposition to look beyond ourselves? This appears to be not at all an easy goal to attain, despite the ease that is supposed to result from its attainment. In "Of Idleness" Montaigne reports that after retiring to his home with the intention of leaving his soul "in full idleness, to entertain itself, and stay and settle in itself," he found "that, on the contrary, like a runaway horse, it gives itself a hundred times more trouble than it took for others, and gives birth to so many chimeras and fantastic monsters" that he has undertaken "to put them in writing, hoping with time to make it ashamed of itself." His experience demonstrates that unless people "occupy" their mind "with a definite subject, that will bridle and control them, they throw themselves in disorder [*desreiglez*] hither and yon in the vague field of imaginings" (I, viii, 33–4 [21]). Precisely in order to prevent the mind from losing itself elsewhere, it appears to be necessary, paradoxically, to occupy it with some particular concern.

Nor is imagination the only obstacle to keeping people's concerns "within themselves." The chief cause of the soul's being thrown "out of itself" is the passions; "to judge a man really properly, we must chiefly examine his common actions," rather than the extraordinary deeds that result from temporary flights of passion (II, xxix, 683 [533]). Yet so strong is the grip passion holds on us that it is "perhaps" the only source of the soul's acting at all. Consequently, it appears that the soul "never go[es] except with a forced and borrowed pace" (II, xii, 550–51 [426–7]). Similarly, Montaigne emphasizes in the "Apology" how corporeal accidents and diseases prevent a soul from "belong[ing] to itself" (II, xii, 532–3 [412–13]). At the same time, he identifies "health" as the cause of the mind's "extraordinary flights" (III, v, 821 [641]). In sum, however desirable it may be for the soul to be "straight and composed," it is questionable, given its "natural condition," whether even "the best regulated soul in the world" can achieve such a state (II, ii, 328 [249]).

The difficulty of locating or establishing a foundation that will keep the soul within its proper bounds appears to reflect, in turn, the difficulty of identifying any essential structure or order to the soul. Given the flux of our passions, it is wrong to try to compose a continuous "body" out of them, or "obstinately to insist on forming a constant and solid arrangement out of us"; our "arrangement [is] so unformed and diverse that each piece, each moment, plays its own game. And there is as much difference between us and ourselves as between us and others" (I, xxxvii, 231 [174]; II, 1, 315, 321 [239, 244]). "Man, in all things and throughout, is but patchwork and motley" (II, xx, 656 [511]). Nor can a hierarchy be established among the soul's faculties or activities: "every movement reveals us" equally; "each of my parts makes me myself just as much as every other one" (I, l, 290 [219]; III, v, 866 [677]). Hence Montaigne's amusement at the multiplicity of "orders and stages," "functions and occupations" into which the philosophers "divided our soul" to "accommodate the impulses they see in man" (II, xii, 519 [401]). We would do better, he concludes, "to trace [our actions] to the neighboring circumstances" than to seek some deeper cause for them (II, i, 317 [241]).

In light of the diverse and fluctuating nature of human motives and dispositions, Montaigne emphasizes the need to establish some overall "form" in one's head, a "definite goal" with reference to which people may order their actions, as an archer sets his sights by the target (II, i, 320 [243]). But it is just the nature of the goal that is most the subject of controversy. In the "Apology" Montaigne remarked that "there is no combat so violent among the philosophers, and so bitter, as that which concerns the question of the sovereign good of man" (II, xii, 561 [435]). He elaborates this point in "Of a Saying of Caesar's," citing as "a singular evidence of our imperfection that we cannot establish our contentment in any one thing," as manifested by "the great dispute that has always gone on among the philosophers over the sovereign good of man, and that still goes on and will go on eternally, without solution and without agreement" (I, liii, 296 [224]). Yet both of these remarks seem to be contradicted by another passage in the "Apology," wherein Montaigne asserted that "there is general agreement among all the philosophers of all sects, that the sovereign good consists in tranquility of soul and body" (II, xii, 468 [360]). The real issue, he indicates there, is not what the sovereign good is but how to attain it. The same point—but with a different specification of the end—was expressed in the remark in I, xx, that "all opinions in the world agree on this, that pleasure is our goal, though they choose different means to it" (80 [56]).

The difficulties that these remarks raise are resolved, I believe, by the following passage from "Of Glory":

> All the glory that I pretend to in my life is to have lived it tranquilly: tranquilly not according to Metrodorus or Arcesilaus or Aristippus but according to me. Since philosophy has not been able to find any way to tranquility that is good for all [en commun], let everyone seek it on his own! (II, xvi, 605–6 [471])

The attitude of tolerant relativism that Montaigne professes and recommends here corresponds to the unfettered way of life, grounded in "reason" and "nature," and hence respectful of "the liberty of others," which he attributed to the philosophers in the "Apology." The premise of this attitude is that we are so variously constituted, and so fluctuating within ourselves, that there is no way to tranquility, and consequently no single best way of life, that is appropriate for all of us, and toward which governments should seek to guide us. That premise in turn presupposes the overall teaching of the "Apology," which denied that we are capable of achieving any goal higher than earthly tranquility. In light of that argument, it would be misleading to say that Montaigne leaves the question of the good life entirely open-ended: only some ways of life—that is, those that aim at earthly pleasure rather than glory or immortality—are fully compatible with an uncritical tolerance of other people's ways. Since the unstable nature of the human soul prevents us from achieving a settled contentment in the possession of some particular good, and since the soul needs to be occupied with the pursuit of some object outside itself, the closest we can come to tranquility is to immerse ourselves in the pursuit of harmless sensual pleasures, emulating the way of life that Montaigne professes most prominently in Book III. In other words, in order that people in general should *achieve* tranquility, it is essential that they be encouraged to *seek* the "end" of sensual pleasure—each of us pursuing the particular pleasures, or "way to tranquility," that we find most attractive.

The import of Montaigne's argument may be clarified, once more, by comparison with Aristotle's moral teaching. In Book VII of the *Nicomachean Ethics* Aristotle acknowledges that the strength of the "animal" element in human nature makes us incapable of finding complete satisfaction or pleasure in any single object: the animal nature being constantly in motion, the objects of its pursuit are necessarily variable. Moreover, the bipartite character of human nature makes even the distinction between "natural" and "unnatural" pleasures ambiguous, since the pleasures that are "natural" to one part of our constitution are "unnatural" to the other. Yet—on the premise that our capacity for reason and contemplation, which most distinguishes the human species from the rest of nature, is more properly constitutive of our "self" than are our strictly animal desires and

characteristics—Aristotle concludes that human virtue entails pursuit of
the goods of the soul rather than those of the body, so far as it is in our
capacity to pursue them.[35]

Montaigne, unlike Aristotle, portrays the human soul nonhierarchically
and argues that it is unreasonable to favor the spiritual element in human
nature at the expense of the corporeal one (III, v, 871 [681]). In "On Some
Verses of Virgil" he alludes to the tension between those elements, remarking that "nature" is responsible both for the strength of our sexual appetites
and for our disposition to "accuse and shun" indulgence in them "as
shameless and indecent" (III, v, 856 [669]). But his way of resolving this
tension, as I have noted, is to accommodate the soul to the body's appetites,
rather than to subordinate the latter to the former. It is for this reason that
he interprets human nature in the light of animal nature, arguing that only
in the beasts can we find evidence of nature that is free from the "diversity of
opinions" that human imagination has engendered (III, xii, 1026–7 [803]).
It is also for this reason that he professes and recommends a way of life that
is guided by physical pleasure: the "laws of nature" are best known through
sensation rather than reasoning.[36] Such is the message of the concluding
chapter of the *Essays:*

> In this universality, I ignorantly and negligently let myself be led by the general
> law of the world. *I shall know it well enough when I feel it.* (III, xiii, 1050
> [821])

> Both in health and in sickness, I have readily let myself follow the appetites that
> pressed me. *I give great authority to my desires* and propensities. . . . Since
> there is a risk of making a mistake, let us risk it rather in pursuit of plea-
> sure. . . . *I have never received harm from an action that was really pleasant* to
> me. (III, xiii, 1064 [832–3])

> *I judge myself only by actual feeling,* not by reasoning. (III, xiii, 1074 [840])

The conception of a universal "law" that Montaigne states here corresponds to his teaching about "natural law," which I examined in Chapter
Four. It is in this light, I believe, that his remarks about the "natural"
goodness of human beings must be understood. When Montaigne praises
the "natural" virtue that is born of the "universal reason that is implanted

[35]*Nicomachean Ethics*, 1154a26–b30; X.7–8; *Politics*, VII.1.
[36]Cf. Starobinski, *Montaigne in Motion*, p. 157; and cf. Locke's emphasis on people's
capacity to judge their well-being by sensation rather than reasoning: *Second Treatise*, secs.
94, 168, 225; Robert Goldwin, "John Locke," in Strauss and Cropsey, eds., *History of
Political Philosophy*, pp. 480–81. In "Of Repentance" Montaigne follows his affirmation of
the consistency of his conduct throughout his life and the internal harmony of his soul with an
expression of his willingness to continue his indulgence in sensual pleasures, to the extent his
bodily condition permits (III, ii, 790, 793–4 [616, 619]).

in every man who is not denatured," in contrast to the virtue that "laws and religions" promote, he cannot be referring to an innate disposition to obey particular *moral* laws, or to pursue the well-being of others in preference to one's own, since he denied that such universal moral laws exist (II, xii, 563–7 [437–9]). Our natural goodness has approximately the same meaning for Montaigne as it does for Rousseau: before the awakening of our *amour-propre* and consequently of the desire to compete for glory and mastery with others, our desires are narrowly selfish but largely harmless to others because of their limitedness.[37] Hence the "ruling pattern" that Montaigne claims each man may "discover in himself," which "struggles against education and against the tempest of the passions that oppose it" (III, ii, 789 [615]), is not a conscience but simply the prerational disposition to pursue one's own good as determined by physical sensation.[38]

Montaigne is no more desirous than Rousseau of restoring humanity to a condition of primitive stupidity. But neither does he favor Rousseau's political remedy of minimizing human conflict by using law and education to moderate or restrain the acquisitive passions that civil society has generated. As we have seen, Montaigne encourages the pursuit of material comfort and physical pleasure as a means of "diverting" people from the more politically dangerous quest for mastery, glory, and salvation. But he also seeks to inculcate a positive morality that is intended to deter people from cruelty and inhumanity and to encourage compassion for their fellows. The essence of this morality is a kind of "sincerity," or honesty about oneself.

As I have noted, the characteristic by which Montaigne repeatedly distinguishes himself from previous moral and religious preceptors is his sincerity or "good faith." In "Of Presumption" he identifies this quality as the core of moral goodness: "A generous heart should not belie its thoughts; it wants to reveal itself to its inmost depths. . . . [Truthfulness] is the first and fundamental part of virtue" (II, xvii, 630–31 [491]).[39] Later in Book II he suggests that it was the unwillingness of previous moralists to reveal themselves truthfully that rendered their teachings ineffectual: although "a man of good morals may have false opinions, and a wicked man may preach the

[37]Cf. Montaigne's Rousseauean judgment that the "disposition to live with reference to others" is more harmful than beneficial (III, ix, 932 [729]).
[38]Contrast the account in Plato's *Republic* of how a philosophic ruler would shape human souls in accordance with an external "pattern" (484c, 500e, 540a). Note also that Montaigne's claim, in the second of the three quotations given above from III, xiii, that it is better to run a "risk" in the pursuit rather than the avoidance of pleasure constitutes a direct response to Aristotle's provisional advice in the *Ethics* that people should steer themselves *away* from pleasure.
[39]Contrast this statement with the account in the preceding chapter, "Of Glory," of how "all lawgivers" used "vain ceremony" and "lying opinion . . . to keep the people in their duty" (II, xvi, 613 [477]); though Montaigne professes to accept this practice if it truly accomplishes its aim (612 [477]), he has devoted the bulk of that chapter to undermining it through his critique of glory.

truth, yes, even a man who does not believe it," still, "it is no doubt a beautiful harmony when doing and saying go together, and . . . words are of greater authority and efficacy when actions follow"; "the man who says what he thinks strikes home much more forcefully than the man who pretends"; and Montaigne himself "never read[s] an author, especially those who treat of virtue and duties, that I do not inquire curiously what kind of a man he was" (II, xxxi, 693–4 [541]). More than once Montaigne stresses the need to relate an author's precepts to his life and character (II, x, 394, 396 [302–3]; II, xii, 562 [436]); by presenting his own teaching in the form of an ostensible self-portrait, he endeavors to demonstrate the harmony between his precepts and his life.

As Hugo Friedrich has pointed out, at the core of Montaigne's self-portrait is a posture of "self-abasement" and "self-depreciation": a depreciation of humanity that serves as the prelude not to contrition and penitence but rather to self-acceptance.[40] The self-deprecatory portrait Montaigne offers of himself accords with his intention of challenging the "over-good opinion" that people in general hold of themselves, thereby mitigating the moral demands that they make on others as well as themselves. Recalling the etymological link between *conscience* and (self-)*consciousness,* I suggest that the sort of conscience the essayist seeks to inculcate is one that is grounded in the lowered, ostensibly more honest self-understanding he advocates. To be "true" or "faithful" to oneself is to recognize and admit the triviality of one's own motives rather than to cover them with high-sounding pretensions; to appreciate that our temptation to espouse what look like noble or divinely sanctioned causes is really a reflection of the strength of our passions, and thereby to recognize our kinship with our fellows. The conscientious human being, in Montaigne's sense, rather than being ashamed to admit his lowliness, will be ashamed to hide it: accustomed to see himself for "what he is," he will be constitutionally unable to conceal it from others. This very habit of openness, the essayist suggests, may inspire a common trust—a trust rooted not in a common goal but in recognition that the other fellow is no greater than oneself, and that the pleasures one person seeks need not be incompatible with others' enjoyment.[41] The appreciation of the animal needs we hold in common and our vulnerability to disease and other "accidents" may in turn generate an attitude of mutual compassion.

[40]Friedrich, *Montaigne,* p. 226.

[41]Perhaps it is in this sense that we may understand Montaigne's remark that "facility of access" has helped "to protect my house from the violence of our civil wars" (II, xv, 600 [467]), as well as an anecdote illustrating how "my face and my frankness . . . disarmed" a would-be captor (III, xii, 1039 [813]). Cf. Tocqueville, *Democracy in America,* tr. George Lawrence (New York, 1966), II, iii, ch. 2, p. 541, regarding the "natural, frank, and open" character of social intercourse in America, owing to the general equality of social position; Bloom, *Closing of the American Mind,* pp. 175–6. On Montaigne's contribution to the reformulation of the gentlemanly ideal of the *honnête homme* so as to emphasize sociability and tolerance rather than honor and piety, see Villey, *Montaigne devant la postérité,* 2:ii.

Contrary to Friedrich's claim, Montaigne's departure from the moral teachings of previous philosophers does not result from his discovery of aspects of human nature that were unknown to them.[42] One need only examine Aristotle's account of the nature, causes, and effects of the various passions in Book II of his *Rhetoric,* or survey the divergent character types with whom Socrates converses in Plato's dialogues, to see that the classical political philosophers were fully cognizant of the diversity of human beings and of the passions that move them. What distinguishes Montaigne's examination of humanity from theirs is not any new discoveries about human nature, but a new mode of *interpreting* the phenomena that make up that nature. It is not that Montaigne views human beings as being any more diverse than his predecessors thought them to be: he remarked in the "Apology" that "the souls of emperors and cobblers are cast in the same mold" and are moved by like "springs." What is distinctive about his interpretation is that he portrays the differences in motives and ways of life *nonhierarchically,* as if no pursuit or activity (aside from cruel and inhumane ones) were objectively better or worse than any other. Even his seemingly most extreme statement of human diversity—the remark in "Of the Inequality among Us" that "there is more distance from a given man to a given man than from a given man to a given beast"—actually connotes not that people are utterly different but that their common animality is more significant than the differences among them.

In I, xiv, Montaigne emphasized the contrast between the relative fixity of the body and the almost infinite variability of the soul's dispositions. Precisely for that reason, he aims through his teaching to *give* an optimal "form" to the human soul. Although Montaigne attends to that task throughout the *Essays,* what Armaingaud termed his "moral propaganda" is particularly prominent in the three longest chapters of Book III: "On Some Verses of Virgil" (III, v), "Of Vanity" (III, ix), and "Of Experience" (III, xiii). Although the argument of these chapters appears on the surface to ramble, we have evidence of careful planning in the following facts: the three chapters, which are the longest ones after the "Apology for Raymond Sebond," are numerically equidistant from one another; they are close to one another in length; and their collective length in the final version nearly approximates that of the "Apology."[43] A brief survey of these chapters will

[42]Friedrich, *Montaigne,* p. 220.

[43]In the Courbet-Royer edition of the *Essais* (Paris, 1872–1900), which reprints the original 1595 edition and—like that edition—lacks paragraph divisions, the three chapters respectively run 78, 78, and 76 pages, for a total of 232; the "Apology" fills 236 pages. No other chapter comes close to III, v, ix, or xiii in length. I have not been able to examine the 1595 text itself; but since that text deviates at a number of points from the "Bordeaux copy" (the copy of the 1588 text on which Montaigne inscribed his final additions and revisions, either in the margins or on separate slips of paper), and since Montaigne did not live to supervise the printing of his final text, absolute precision in these matters is presumably impossible. (In the 1588 edition, the three chapters from Book III respectively numbered 53, 54, and 52 pages; see Martin, "En comptant les pages," p. 27.)

provide a clearer picture of what it means to live "within" oneself in Montaigne's sense.

Moral Propaganda

The central theme of "On Some Verses of Virgil" is sexual enjoyment, indulgence in which Montaigne encourages in opposition to those "who think they honor their nature by dishonoring themselves" (III, v, 857 [670]). The essayist trumpets his dedication to the "unambitious" pursuit of sensual pleasure, remarking that he has "no other aim but to live and enjoy myself" (820–21 [640]). He delights in emphasizing the corporeal aspect of love, observing that in this action nature "equalize[s] us," putting on the same level "the fools and the wise, and us and the beasts," so as to disabuse us of "pride" (855 [668–9]). This attack on hierarchical distinctions also manifests itself in the secondary theme of the chapter, the defense of women's rights in opposition to the tyranny men seek to impose on them; Montaigne concludes the chapter by remarking of the sexes what he had earlier asserted of emperors and cobblers, that they "are cast in the same mold," and asserting that most of the differences between them are due to "education and custom," not nature (875 [685]).

Like "On Some Verses of Virgil," "Of Vanity" stresses the (ostensible) aimlessness of Montaigne's life: his lack of an overarching, serious purpose beyond that of enjoyment. The unifying theme of this chapter is travel, which the essayist employs as a metaphor for the "journey" of life (III, ix, 955 [747]; III, iii, 806 [628]); to the charge that " 'there is vanity . . . in this amusement,' " he responds that the precepts of "wisdom" that denounce such idle pleasures are themselves "vanity," and that life itself is "a material and corporeal movement, an action that is imperfect by its very essence, and irregular [*desreglée*]" (III, ix, 967 [756]). Contrary to those who would limit or condemn "vain" and idle amusements as distractions from the serious business of life, Montaigne advances an account of life as circular rather than following "a straight line" (III, x, 988 [773]): life has no specific, ultimate purpose. In light of such a view, no "humor" is "too vain" as long as it is "pleasant" (III, ix, 976 [763]).

Montaigne's representation of aimless amusement as the central concern of life contrasts with Aristotle's tripartite distinction among business, recreation, and "leisured," intrinsically choiceworthy activity, wherein the former two are ministerial to the latter.[44] The essayist's denial that life has a serious purpose is a reflection of his "comic" view of human existence. A further consequence of that view is that he treats all particular human occupations as "roles" with which individuals need not identify themselves

---

[44]*Politics*, 1333a20–1333b3; 1337b33–1338a1.

338 | The Political Philosophy of Montaigne

(III, x, 989 [773]; cf. I, xx, 80 [56]: to see the world as a stage is to remind ourselves that in the end, there is no goal the attainment of which ultimately "matters."[45] It is also this view of life that underlies Montaigne's emphasis on the charm of diversity, the enjoyment of which he represents as a chief motive of his travels: rather than evaluate the merit of alternative beliefs, customs, and ways of life against some objective standard of human excellence, Montaigne encourages an appreciation of "the pleasure of variety" that they exhibit, a pleasure answering to the need that our unstable nature gives us for change and novelty (III, ix, 950, 964 [743, 753]). Aside from this benefit, acquaintance with the variety of human laws and customs promotes tolerance by leading us to recognize that there is nothing sacrosanct about our own ways (I, xxvi, 156–7 [116]; II, xxxvii, 766 [597–8]; III, ix, 964 [753–4]). While professing to emulate Socrates in regarding himself as a citizen of the world (III, ix, 950 [743]; I, xxvi, 156 [116]), Montaigne adheres to that attitude more consistently than his model apparently did, since he would "never . . . be so broken or so narrowly habituated to my own country" as to consider a sentence of exile to be worse than death, as Socrates professed to do. He deprecates the spurious "friendships" to which we are bound merely by "community of climate or of blood," by contrast with those that are "purely of our own acquisition" (III, ix, 950–51 [743]). By describing himself as a "citizen [bourgeois] of no city," Montaigne emulates the posture of Aristippus (the founder of the Hedonist sect of philosophers), who "liked to live as a stranger everywhere" (III, ix, 965, 979 [755, 766]; cf. Journal de Voyage, 1236 [961–2]).

Here again, the truly distinctive aspect of Montaigne's teaching consists not in his discovery of a fact about humanity which was unknown to the ancient philosophers but rather in his popularization of a principle that his predecessors thought suitable only for the guidance of philosophers. Montaigne himself elsewhere attributes Socrates' acceptance of death to his old age and his desire to set a salutary example, rather than to an excessive patriotism (III, ii, 795–6 [620]; III, xii, 1031 [807]). The classical political philosophers understood themselves to be "aliens" from the political community, inasmuch as they did not share its fundamental beliefs and commitments.[46] Yet in practice—as typified by the life of Socrates, the "citizen-

[45]Cf. the assertion at the beginning of III, iii, that "[our] principal talent is the ability to apply ourselves to various practices. It is existing, but not living, to keep ourselves bound and obliged by necessity to a single course" (796 [621]). The attitude that Montaigne recommends resembles the life of the "democratic" man caricatured in Plato's Republic, 561a–e. It also prefigures the inhabitant of Marx's communist society, who engages in hunting, fishing, cattle rearing, and criticism as desire dictates, "without ever becoming hunter, fisherman, shepherd, or critic" (The German Ideology, pt. I, in Robert C. Tucker, ed., The Marx-Engels Reader, 2d ed. [New York, 1978], p. 160). Cf. Friedrich, Montaigne, p. 231: Montaigne "does not establish a hierarchy among the distinct spheres of his life, any more than among his different states of mind. He finds the smallest trifles worthy of representing what one paradoxically must call the amorphous shape of his individuality."

[46]Cf. Plato, Republic, 327a, 592a–b; Apology, 17d; Bloom, Republic of Plato, pp. 310–11.

philosopher"—they endeavored to cover up rather than publicize the tension between philosophy and the city's conventions, not only for their own protection but to avoid undermining the city itself. Montaigne, in contrast, emphasizes the gap between nature and convention, lamenting our disposition to "imprison" ourselves through rigid civic attachments at the cost of our natural freedom (III, ix, 950 [743]). His goal is not a world of philosophers—a possibility he would have thought no more realistic than Plato did—but the liberation of humanity from the "tyranny" of custom and convention, with a view to promoting external peace and internal "tranquility."

The last of the three great tracts of pseudo-autobiographical moral propaganda in Book III is the concluding chapter, "Of Experience." In the first part of this chapter Montaigne renews his emphasis on human diversity and remarks the consequent difficulty of framing uniform laws to govern human conduct. Given the incommensurability between "our actions, which are in perpetual mutation, and fixed and immutable laws," he infers that "the most desirable laws are those that are rarest, simplest, and most general," that is, those of "nature"—which, as we have seen, are best known through feeling rather than by reasoning (III, xiii, 1042–3 [816]). It is in light of that claim that the lengthy account of his own way of life with which Montaigne concludes the chapter—ostensibly to instruct his readers with respect to "bodily health"—must be understood. Montaigne introduces that account by approvingly citing the opinion of Tiberius "that whoever had lived twenty years should be responsible to himself for the things that were harmful or beneficial to him, and know how to take care of himself without medical aid" (1056 [826]). The way of life Montaigne professes to have followed is noteworthy primarily for its freedom from reliance on the sort of "medical" assistance offered by the moral and religious preceptors he has described as "spiritual physicians." That is, Montaigne has guided his life by the criterion of pleasure rather than that of duty; and he has sought to shape himself "for change and variation," to the extent of recommending that one "plunge often into excess" and "dissipation" rather than being bound "to certain particular ways" (1061 [830]). In contrast to the older view that favors accustoming the body to endure hardship, Montaigne endeavors to give our souls the quality of "adaptability" by freeing them from the attachment to particular, restrictive *moral* rules. His account of his indulgence in bodily pleasures and his concern for physical comfort (his habits and tastes with respect to eating, drinking, and sleeping; his manner of dealing with the kidney stone) again suggest that this way of life is most conducive to toleration and the "moderation" of the soul. The "delicacy" he condemns is not a sensitivity to physical pleasure and pain but the moral *rejection* of hedonism which makes people unsociable: an attitude exemplified by the "vain" and unseasonable disposition of Cato (III, xiii, 1061 [830]; III, ix, 969 [758]). If people can be persuaded to dedicate themselves to the pursuit of earthly pleasures, Tiberius' proposal for individual self-government can be effectuated in a sense broader than the narrowly "medical" one.[47]

Bourgeois Morality

In light of the foregoing analysis, I believe that the conception of human life that Montaigne espouses may legitimately be viewed as embodying—in Keohane's phrase—the "morality of bourgeois individualism." I use the term *bourgeois* not in its Marxist sense but in its broader and, I think, more authentic one, to denote the typical inhabitant of the modern liberal, commercial regime as portrayed by Montesquieu and Tocqueville: one whose aspirations are earthly and moderate, whose disposition is pacific rather than warlike, whose concerns are focused primarily (though not exclusively) on himself and his immediate family and friends, and who—precisely on account of the private character of his concerns—is disposed to be tolerant of the ways of his fellow citizens. In this sense, Montaigne deserves to be recognized (as Colette Fleuret has suggested) as one of the key philosophic architects, and perhaps *the* original architect, of what we know as "bourgeois" morality.[48]

To view Montaigne as such an architect is by no means to identify *him* as a merely "bourgeois" individual. If there is a "class" to which Montaigne could be said to belong, on the basis of his own self-understanding, it is, as I have argued, that of the philosophers. Surely, no one of merely bourgeois capacities, tastes, or aspirations could have written such a book as the *Essays*. In contrast to his philosophic predecessors, Montaigne indeed dedicates much of his rhetoric to depreciating the difference between his way of life and that of others—professing to seek no goal beyond harmless pleasures; remarking that he, like all human beings, is "full of inanity and nonsense" (III, ix, 979 [766]; and asserting that "we are all of the vulgar [sort]" (II, xii, 554 [429]).[49] But despite his "unambitious" and self-

[47]Cf. III, x, 984 [769]: "The principal responsibility of each of us is his own conduct."

[48]Fleuret, *Rousseau et Montaigne*, p. 80. See also Sayce, *Essays*, pp. 239–40.

[49]Donald Frame cites this remark, added to the final version of the *Essays*, as evidence of Montaigne's having freed himself, in his later years, from the "humanist" contempt for "the vulgar" in which he had been schooled; Frame notes that in general, "after 1580, Montaigne has less criticism, and much praise, of the *vulgaire*" (*Montaigne*, pp. 300–301; see also *Montaigne's Discovery of Man*, pp. 3–4). Contrary to Frame, I interpret this development as another instance of Montaigne's having gradually expressed more openly an attitude that he had maintained from the outset of his writing. Recall the striking praise of the bearing of common folk toward death at the end of I, xx, dating from the first edition; and consider on the other hand the passage in "Of Presumption," dating from the last edition, wherein Montaigne *distinguishes* himself from people of "the common sort" on the ground that unlike them, he recognizes his membership in that class (II, xvii, 618 [481]). Consider also the

deprecating posture, Montaigne is no less dedicated to the pursuit of wisdom and no less grand in his ambitions than such subsequent philosophic propagators of the bourgeois way of life as Hobbes and Locke, Montesquieu and Adam Smith—all of them men of vast capacity and broad public concerns. As Allan Bloom observes, these philosophers, in establishing a political alliance between themselves and the multitude, had no illusions about the character of the human beings who would tend to dominate a society that had as its express purpose the alleviation of its members' earthly and predominantly corporeal needs.[50] But they, like Montaigne, were convinced that the price of vulgarity was worth paying for the benefits of peace and toleration, liberty and comfort. The seeming fascination, mixed with horror, with which Montaigne views such "great" souls as those of Cato and Alexander suggests that he was not insensitive to the "aesthetic" appeal of the older models of human greatness. But given his emphasis on utility rather than beauty—the reflection of his "compassionate" desire to alleviate the miseries of existence for the generality of human beings, along with his less disinterested desire to win greater popular support and toleration for philosophy—he was prepared to sacrifice the endeavor to promote such greatness for the sake of more "substantial" goods.

Montaigne's emphasis on compassion establishes a further link between him and his liberal philosophic successors. His encouragement of kindness toward animals in "Of Cruelty" as a means of overcoming the otherwise "natural" instinct of inhumanity is echoed by Locke's prescriptions for the upbringing of children—as is his recommendation that servants be treated with humanity rather than contempt (III, iii, 799 [623]).[51] As for Montesquieu, one of his chief reasons for favoring the commercial way of life is its effect in softening people's attitudes and mores: making human beings not only more tolerant and pacific but also more prone to appreciate their common neediness, and consequently more humane.[52] Montaigne's critique of Cato's "unseasonable" virtue and his assertion that all people including himself are "vulgar" anticipate the bourgeois renunciation of pride for the sake of peace exemplified in the fifth and ninth of Hobbes's

---

resemblance of the passage quoted in the text to the following remark of Machiavelli's: "the vulgar are taken in by the appearance and the outcome of a thing, and in the world *there is no one but the vulgar*" (*The Prince*, ch. 18, p. 71). The context of that remark brings out its underlying political ramifications. Cf., on Montaigne's independence from the interests and viewpoints of particular classes, Nakam, *Les Essais*, pp. 81, 84–5.

[50]"Commerce and 'Culture,'" *This World* 3 (1982): 16.

[51]Locke, *Some Thoughts Concerning Education*, secs. 116–17, in James L. Axtell, ed., *The Educational Writings of John Locke* (Cambridge, Eng., 1968), pp. 225–8.

[52]See *Spirit of the Laws*, XX, i–ii; Pangle, *Montesquieu's Philosophy of Liberalism*, pp. 204–9, with references. Cf. also Tocqueville, *Democracy in America*, II, iii, ch. 1, and, on the compatibility between individualism and charity, ch. 4.

laws of nature, which dictate respectively "that every man strive to accommodate himself" to his fellows and that he acknowledge his natural equality with them.[53]

Perhaps the chapter wherein Montaigne appears most sharply to distinguish himself from the bourgeois "individualist" is "Of Friendship" (I, xxviii). In that chapter he provides a moving, if somewhat mawkish (and quite possibly fictitious)[54] account of the affectionate union that bound him to Etienne de la Boétie, a union that embodied such a "complete fusion of our wills" that the essayist regarded his friend as "a second [self]" (189, 192 [141, 143]). Yet even Montaigne's account of friendship is presented in such a way as to emphasize its *antipolitical* and in this sense "individualistic" aspect. At the outset he professes to agree with Aristotle's teaching that human beings are naturally sociable, citing his remark that "good legislators have had more care for friendship than for justice" (I, xxviii, 182 [136]). But whereas Aristotle treats our natural sociability as a ground of the political community, Montaigne overtly deprecates all merely "civil bonds" by comparison with true friendship (II, viii, 375 [287]). Not only does he disparage associations rooted in "public or private needs" (I, xxviii, 182–3 [136]), he devotes a major part of "Of Friendship" to stressing the particular limitations of the various elements of the familial relation. The community between fathers and children, between brothers, and between husbands and wives is in each case radically incomplete: the former two cases are characterized by a conflict rather than community of interests, and marriage "is a bargain to which only the entrance is free—its continuance being constrained and forced, depending otherwise than on our will," and consequently a relationship that falls short of the freedom that genuine friendship requires (I, xxviii, 183–5 [136–8]). In fact, given Montaigne's claim that true friendship between the sexes is almost impossible, the only association that would meet his definition of a perfect community—an association "in which not only would the souls have this complete enjoyment, but the bodies would also share in the alliance, so that the entire man would be engaged"—is homosexual friendship. Despite professing to believe that such "Greek license is justly abhorred by our morals," his account dwells almost completely on its advantages. The only substantive defect he finds to have existed in Greek homosexuality was that "it involved . . . such a necessary disparity in age and such a difference in the lovers' functions" as to fall short of "the perfect union and harmony that we require here" (185 [138]). The implication is that a homosexual friendship embodying a parity of age as well as function between the lovers—a parity such as existed

---

[53]*Leviathan*, ch. 15, pp. 209, 211.
[54]For a summary of the inconsistencies as well as literary borrowings in this account, all of which cast doubt on its veracity, see Floyd Gray, "Montaigne's Friends," *French Studies* 15 (1961): 204–8.

between himself and La Boétie—is the only relationship in which men's natural sociability could fully be realized.

Nowhere does Montaigne explicitly state that his friendship with La Boétie was a homosexual one—although the juxtaposition of his defense of pederasty with the account of that friendship surely suggests such a possibility.[55] But whether Montaigne and La Boétie actually had a homosexual relationship, or whether his hints in this regard are another of his autobiographical distortions, is a point of no particular theoretical interest. What is of such interest is that Montaigne's account of friendship has the effect not only of challenging the Christian sexual morality but also of deprecating all merely "accidental" unions among human beings (that is, those that do not originate and continue purely as the result of the free choice of those involved), most significantly the political community itself.[56] The latter point is brought out by Montaigne's defense of the willingness of a Roman citizen, Caius Blossius, to set loyalty to his friend Tiberius Gracchus over loyalty to his country's laws: "They were friends more than citizens, friends more than friends or enemies of their country" (187–8 [140]). We may infer that the friendship between Montaigne and La Boétie similarly transcended all conventional civic or legal obligations; the essayist's denial that his friend intended his antimonarchical treatise *Voluntary Servitude* to be put to any revolutionary use mirrors his somewhat unpersuasive denial that Blossius and Gracchus were "friends of ambition and disturbance" (188 [140]).

As in other cases, Montaigne's account of friendship constitutes a radicalization of, rather than a simple break with, the teachings of the classical political philosophers: although Aristotle similarly represents the union of friends as superior to the political association, he does not highlight the antipolitical implication of this teaching as Montaigne does. In this respect Montaigne's account of friendship represents the obverse side of his professed cosmopolitanism: he portrays the political association as less natural than either the ties that link friends, on the one hand, or those that link humanity as a whole, by virtue of their common nature, on the other.

Of course, to the extent that Montaigne's praise of friendship serves to disparage the family, its spirit would seem to be distinct from that of bourgeois morality: the bourgeois (as portrayed, for instance, by Tocqueville) is above all a family man. Yet, even here, the underlying connection between Montaigne's teaching and the bourgeois spirit may be more significant than the seeming differences between them. The bourgeois family is

---

[55]This possibility is considered by William J. Beck in "Montaigne face à l'homosexualité," *BSAM*, 6th ser., nos. 9–10 (1982): 41–50. Beck lists a number of twentieth-century works wherein it is assumed that the Montaigne–La Boétie friendship was a homosexual one (p. 42n).

[56]On the connection of the elevation of the claims of love over political bonds with the bourgeois spirit, cf. Irving Kristol, *Two Cheers for Capitalism* (New York, 1978), p. ix.

distinguished from the premodern or traditional one, above all, by its "individualistic" spirit: that is, the relations among its members are no longer grounded in respect or reverence for the ancestral, or in a recognition of the father, in particular, as sovereign authority. The typically modern attitude toward the family is capsulized in Locke's *Second Treatise,* which denies that fathers are necessarily entitled to any obedience from their children, once the latter have reached the age of maturity, beyond that which might be motivated by the children's hope of obtaining an inheritance.[57] Montaigne, similarly, denies that there is a natural harmony between the interests of parents and children; protests exercises of paternal authority that violate the interests of the latter, as well as the tyranny that men exercise over their wives; and proposes, as we have seen, a system of education in which children would be encouraged to judge the truth for themselves and be led by their own taste for pleasure, rather than to be guided in their belief and action by reverence for the traditional or ancestral (I, xxvi, 149–52 [110–12]; I, xxviii, 183–5 [136]; II, viii, 366–7, 379–80 [280, 290]; II, xxxi, 691–2 [539–40]; III, v, 832 [649]). The ultimate ground and limit of all human associations—political, familial, and friendly—is the individual's free consent.

One might argue that the connection between Montaigne and the bourgeois spirit is belied by the contrast between his admonition that human beings turn their attention within themselves and the characteristic "other-directedness" of bourgeois life: the tendency of people in an individualistic society, bereft of the sense of unity between their own interest and the common good that animated the citizenry of ancient republics, and also bereft of profound religious faith, to live merely for the sake of popular reputation and in accordance with "mass" opinion. But once again, the contrast is deceptive. As we have seen, Montaigne suggests that it is impossible literally to occupy the soul with itself, given its overwhelming tendency to throw itself into "external" preoccupations. Hence his remedy for people's vain disposition to concern themselves with "future and absent" goods is to "occupy" and "bridle" their minds with the pursuit of "present" ones—that is, material comforts and sensual enjoyments. Even while urging people to derive the law of conduct from themselves, he emphasizes that most people lack the capacity to study themselves fruitfully as he has done,

[57]*Second Treatise*, ch. 6, secs. 70–74. See, on Locke's reconstruction of the family, Pangle, *The Spirit of Modern Republicanism*, ch. 18; on the freedom of the democratic family, Tocqueville, *Democracy in America*, II.iii.8–9. The relation of Montaigne's criticisms of civil laws regarding the family, including the treatment of inheritances and the right of divorce, to subsequent legal reforms in France is discussed by Jean-Eugène Bimbenet, *Les Essais de Montaigne dans leurs rapports avec la législation moderne* (Paris, 1863), pp. 21–32. Bimbenet remarks that Montaigne's principles favoring the liberation of the citizen from subservience to paternal authority "are absolutely those of the modern family" (p. 21).

or to construct adequate rules of conduct for themselves.[58] Hence his repeated allusions to the need for individuals like himself to guide popular belief in a salutary direction. His moral teaching is derived from self-examination, in the sense that by examining himself, Montaigne uncovers the "springs" that impel the conduct of people in general; that teaching encourages individual "self-government" in appealing to selfish instincts that Montaigne holds to lie at the core of human nature. But it presupposes that people in general will be guided by an understanding of "themselves" which they have learned from Montaigne, rather than directly from themselves. Here again we may look to Tocqueville for clarification and confirmation: he attributes to the American people a Cartesian (we might equally say Montaignist) philosophical attitude, ordaining that people "seek by themselves and only in themselves for the reason for things," yet observes at the same time that there is "no country in which . . . there is less independence of mind and true freedom of discussion than in America," owing to the tyranny of majority opinion.[59] The fundamental elements of that dominant opinion derive, in turn, from the liberal political philosophy-cum-propaganda of Montaigne and his successors.

As Tocqueville affirms, there is no necessary incompatibility between popular acceptance of the doctrine of "individualism," such as Montaigne espoused, and a general sameness among individuals' opinions and way of life. We may find the roots of the homogenizing influence of individualism in Montaigne's own teaching. By stressing the importance of bodily health and physical pleasure, Montaigne emphasizes what separates people from one another rather than what unites them; such an emphasis on the bodily aspect of human nature is perhaps the source of our modern tendency to speak about the "self" rather than the "soul." But paradoxically, to stress the private, bodily character of human nature is ultimately to deny the significance of the characteristics that truly distinguish human individuals from one another. Such a result is implicit in Montaigne's remark, cited earlier, that the sexual act "equalizes" human beings, both with one another and with the beasts, and that imagining the "most contemplative" of human beings engaged in sex refutes their claim to superiority (III, v, 855 [668–9]). Similarly, to depreciate national, class, and sexual distinctions (III, v, 875 [685]; III, ix, 950 [743]) is to homogenize the human species. Montaigne's very emphasis on the diversity of human ways has the effect, as we have seen, of relativizing them, and hence of denying that any particular

[58]Cf. III, iii, 797 [621–2]: "Meditation is a powerful and full study for anyone *who knows how* to examine and exercise himself vigorously"; most people, according to the "Apology," "are not conscious of themselves . . . do not judge themselves . . . [and] leave most of their faculties idle" (II, xii, 481 [371]).
[59]*Democracy in America*, II, i, ch. 1, p. 393; I, ii, ch. 7, p. 235.

custom or way of life is inherently superior, so long as no direct harm to others is involved. His teaching underlies both the modern quest to express one's "individuality" and the essential sameness of ends which forever stimulates that quest.[60]

I have described Montaigne's endeavor to moderate people's treatment of one another by inculcating a doctrine of "conscience" that lowers their self-estimation and their ambitions. The limitations of that doctrine were suggested, however, in "Of Conscience": appeals to the conscience, however understood, are unlikely to moderate the behavior of strong-souled, political individuals like Scipio. The limited effectuality of conscience in the public sphere is further indicated in the chapter just preceding "Of Repentance," titled "Of the Useful and the Honorable,"[61] where Montaigne argues that the public good requires political actors to undertake "vicious" offices on its behalf, and consequently recommends that such offices be assigned to "the more vigorous and less fearful citizens, who sacrifice their honor and their conscience" for their country's welfare (III, i, 768 [600]). These facts suggest the need for a reordering of political *institutions* that will induce political leaders concerned with their own well-being to act in ways that benefit the public.

[60]Cf. ibid., II, iii, ch. 3, pp. 544–5, and ch. 17. Recall Friedrich's remark about the "amorphous" character of Montaigne's own "individuality" (cited in n. 45, above).

[61]As noted previously, the word translated as "honorable" (*honnête*) also has the meaning of "honest."

CHAPTER TWELVE

Liberal Politics

Montaigne and Machiavelli

I have previously noted several connections between Montaigne's political teaching and that of Machiavelli—most significantly in their emphasis
on the "animal" rather than the "divine" element of human nature. That
there is also a relation between the two men's thought with respect to
politics in the narrower sense has been recognized by numerous commentators, who cite the "Machiavellian" conception of political life which Montaigne espouses in "Of the Useful and the Honorable."[1] With rare excep-
tions, however, their analyses have generally represented the differences
between Montaigne and Machiavelli to be more important than any agreement between them. Typically, Montaigne is viewed as far less interested in
political affairs than Machiavelli: Friedrich observes that Montaigne never
provided the kind of systematic analysis of politics that Machiavelli did; he
was, according to Villey, essentially a "moralist," not a "politician."[2] The
essayist's avoidance of a more active role in politics was a reflection,
according to Villey, of his moral attitude: because he recognized the necessity for political officials to act dishonorably, he abstained from political
activity so as to keep his own conscience pure.[3]

---

[1]Brown, *Religious and Political Conservatism*, pp. 73–4; Villey, *Les Sources*, 2:358–62;
Alexander Nicolaï, "Le Machiavélisme de Montaigne," *BSAM*, 3d ser., no. 4 (1957): 16–18.
On other parallelisms between Machiavelli and Montaigne, see Nakam, *Les Essais*, pp. 245–
50.
[2]Friedrich, *Montaigne*, p. 196; Villey, *Les Sources*, 2:362.
[3]Villey, *Les Sources*, 2:362. Nakam, similarly, distinguishes Montaigne's attitude toward
political deceit from Machiavelli's (*Les Essais*, pp. 250–51).

In contrast to the classical writers whom Montaigne cites so frequently, Machiavelli is mentioned by name only twice in the *Essays* and is never directly quoted. Both references embody seemingly loose or ambiguous judgments of the Florentine's work. In "Of Presumption" Montaigne purports to illustrate the debatability of political propositions by remarking that while "the discourses of Machiavelli . . . were solid enough for the subject . . . it was very easy to combat them; and those who did so left it no less easy to combat theirs" (II, xvii, 638 [497]). And at the outset of "Observations on Julius Caesar's Methods of Making War," discussing the popularity of particular books among military leaders, he remarks that "it is said that in our time Machiavelli is still in repute elsewhere," but adds that "the late Marshal Strozzi, who took Caesar as his choice, undoubtedly chose much better," given Caesar's status as "the true and sovereign model of the military art" (II, xxxiv, 713 [556]).[4] Of these two references, the second would appear to be of lesser weight in representing Montaigne's opinion of Machiavelli as a political philosopher, since the essayist compares him unfavorably to Caesar only as a guide to military affairs. Concerning the former reference, however, wherein Montaigne appears on the surface to adopt a more or less neutral stance regarding Machiavelli's merits, the following remark of Sylvia Sanders is to the point: "At a time when the very name of Machiavelli was anathema to so many, Montaigne's moderation on the question of the value of Machiavelli's arguments is particularly striking."[5] Indeed, one may go further and note that the judgment that Machiavelli's discourses "were solid enough for the subject" of politics, taken by itself, could be read as remarkably unambiguous praise. That it was "easy to combat" his arguments would have come as no surprise to Machiavelli himself, who wrote in a manner so shocking as to invite attack and condemnation; but this remark need not imply that Montaigne thought the attacks were justified. His overall discussion of the uncertainty of political propositions in this context recalls his discussion of the debatability of astronomical theories in the "Apology"; his praise of Machiavelli's arguments more specifically parallels his judgment of Copernicus' theory. In neither case does Montaigne's observation that the doctrines of the thinker he has praised are vulnerable to attack necessarily entail his disbelief in those doctrines. With respect to astronomy, Montaigne con-

---

[4]Another instance of numerical symmetry in the *Essays*, which perhaps highlights Machiavelli's significance: the two references to the Florentine occur in chapters that divide the text of Books II and III, taken as a whole, into three equal groups of chapters.

[5]Sanders, "The Political Thought of Montaigne" (Ph.D. diss., Yale University, 1971), p. 213. On attitudes toward Machiavelli in France at the time, see Villey, *Les Sources* 2:358; Nicolaï, "Le Machiavélisme de Montaigne," *BSAM*, 3d ser., no. 4 (1957): 12–15; Albert Chérel, *La Pensée de Machiavel en France* (Paris, 1935), ch. 4; Nakam, *Les Essais*, pp. 246–7. According to Nakam, Machiavelli was read with enthusiasm in France until about 1570 for his illumination of the "effectual truth" of political life; his works then came to be vilified by Catholic and Protestant partisans on account of his irreligion, and by the nobility for his republicanism.

cluded that the value of a theory depends on its demonstrated utility or predictive capacity when measured against the "palpable" facts of experience—a criterion by which he ranked Copernicus' hypotheses quite high. In the sequel to his remark about Machiavelli, Montaigne similarly suggests the need to discover principles sufficiently "plain and obvious" as to set limits to the field of political debate (II, xvii, 638 [497]). The question remains open how far Machiavelli himself may have supplied such principles.

Montaigne explicitly considers the utility of Machiavelli's advice to princes—albeit without mentioning the Florentine by name—in an earlier passage in "Of Presumption," to which I alluded in Chapter One:

> Those who, in our time, have considered, in establishing the duty of a prince, only the good of his affairs, and have preferred it to caring for his faith and conscience, would have something to say to a prince whose affairs Fortune had so arranged that he could establish them forever by a single breach and betrayal of his word. But that is not the way it goes. One often falls into the same bargain again; one makes more than one peace, more than one treaty in his life. The gain that lures them to the first disloyalty (and almost always [gain] is present in it, as in all other wicked deeds: sacrileges, murders, rebellions, treasons are undertaken for some sort of fruit), this first gain brings after it infinite losses, casting this prince out of all relations and means of negotiation as a result of the example of this infidelity. (II, xvii, 631–2 [492])

Given the unique quality of Machiavelli's ostensible advice to princes, as compared with the traditional "mirrors" of princes,[6] this passage can only be taken as a reference to *The Prince*—as commentators have generally recognized. With the exception of Sanders, however, they have typically interpreted the passage as a refutation of Machiavelli's teaching. Villey, for instance, praises Montaigne for having refuted Machiavelli in an effectual, realistic way: rather than denouncing Machiavelli's immoralism, or attempting to prove that virtue is always rewarded and vice always punished, Montaigne demonstrates the disadvantageous consequences that an act of betrayal is likely to produce for the prince.[7] Sayce likewise interprets the passage as a refutation of Machiavelli; while acknowledging that the refutation is couched "in strictly Machiavellian and pragmatic terms," he finds the initial reference to "faith and conscience" suggestive of a "concealed indignation" on the essayist's part.[8]

---

[6]As noted in this connection by Sylvia Sanders, "Montaigne's Prince" (paper presented at the 1980 meeting of the American Political Science Association), pp. 29–30; Nicolaï, "Le Machiavélisme de Montaigne," *BSAM*, 3d ser., no. 9 (1959): 21–2.

[7]*Les Sources*, 2:357–62; similarly, Nakam, *Les Essais*, pp. 254–5.

[8]Sayce, *Essays*, p. 256. Friedrich denies the presence of moral indignation in this passage and emphasizes that Montaigne's response "does not leave the pragmatic terrain of the Machiavellian principle," but he nonetheless denies that Montaigne was truly a "Machiavellian" (*Montaigne*, p. 198).

In order to elicit Montaigne's true attitude toward Machiavelli from this passage, we need not debate whether his language conveys any connotation of indignation. The more fundamental fact, noted by Sanders, is that the passage *is no refutation of Machiavelli at all*. Turning to *The Prince*, we find that Machiavelli explicitly takes account of, and responds to, the difficulty raised by Montaigne—the danger that a prince who breaks his word once will find people unwilling ever to trust him again. He points out that in order to be a successful deceiver, a prince must know how "to color his inobservance"—that is, to excuse or deny it. He adds that "men are so simple, and so obedient to present necessities," that a deceiver will always find suitable victims.[9] Given Montaigne's account of the people's susceptibility to being deceived by the "profitable lies" inculcated by philosophers, lawgivers, and religious founders, there is no reason to suppose that he would dissent from this judgment. Indeed, he explicitly states, in connection with the people's evaluation of their rulers' conduct, that the populace is "an inexact judge, easy to dupe" (III, vii, 896 [700]). And in full accordance with Machiavelli's advice, he recommends that "the Prince, when an urgent circumstance and some sudden and unexpected accident of state necessity makes him deviate from his word and his faith or otherwise forces him from his ordinary duty, should attribute this necessity to a blow from the divine rod"; he denies that such a breach of faith should be viewed as vicious (III, i, 777 [607]).

The parallelism between Montaigne's advice and that of Machiavelli extends to the remark in the passage from "Of Presumption" concerning the possibility of a prince's "establish[ing]" his affairs by "a single breach and betrayal of his word." It is simply not the case that Machiavelli, as Villey claims, advised rulers "to *constantly* make use of ruses and lying."[10] Rather, in *The Prince* he explains how some princes "after infinite treacheries and cruelties could long live safe in their fatherland" by distinguishing between "cruelty [and, it would seem to follow, treachery] badly used [and] well used": vicious deeds are well used if they "are done at a stroke, out of the necessity to secure oneself, and then are *not persisted in* but are turned to as much utility for the subjects as one can," rather than permitted to "grow with time."[11] The correct use of treachery and cruelty is exemplified by Agathocles, who, after a single betrayal and massacre of his rivals, "held the principate" of Syracuse "without any civil controversy."[12] Hence a

[9]*The Prince*, ch. 18, p. 70. As Sanders points out, Machiavelli would certainly have agreed with Montaigne that it is foolish for a prince "to make a profession of covering up" and boast of his dishonesty (*Essais*, II, xvii, 631 [491]), in such a way that he prevents people from believing his promises in the future ("The Political Thought of Montaigne," pp. 234–5).

[10]*Les Sources*, 2:360 (emphasis added).

[11]*The Prince*, ch. 8, pp. 37–8 (emphasis added). The relevance of this passage is pointed out by Sanders, "Political Thought of Montaigne," pp. 232–3.

[12]*The Prince*, ch. 8, p. 35.

prince's readiness to undertake "a single breach and betrayal of his word" at the right time may actually mitigate his need to commit further betrayals— or to depend on other people's trust—in the future.

The underlying agreement between Montaigne and Machiavelli regarding the utility of political deception is but one of a multitude of parallels between the two men's thought—both in their general views of human nature and in their understanding of the tactics essential to political success—which have been noted by Sanders and Alexander Nicolaï. These parallelisms cover such diverse points as the nature of princes, the inutility of royal "liberality," and the value of the study of history. Yet while attributing a common conception of politics to Machiavelli and Montaigne, Sanders nonetheless subscribes to the view of previous commentators that Montaigne's personal attitude toward political life differed from that of his Florentine predecessor, in that he chose to stay out of politics because of his concern with morality.[13] And Nicolaï, without differentiating so sharply between the attitudes of Montaigne and Machiavelli, blurs the significance of this comparison by representing the Florentine's thought as morally scrupulous and even pious.[14] I believe that the connection between Montaigne's political thought and that of Machiavelli is even closer than Sanders has represented it to be, and that this connection can be established without any effort to soften the "immoralism" and impiety of Machiavelli's teaching. This point can be demonstrated through an examination of Montaigne's essay "Of the Useful and the Honorable."

Political Ethics

Given the unusually irregular, sometimes contradictory manner in which the argument of "Of the Useful and the Honorable" moves, it will be helpful to begin with an outline:

1. Prologue: disparagement of the seriousness and the value of the following reflections (767 [599])
2. The hatefulness and utility of treachery and vice (767–8 [599–600])
   a. The significance of the renunciation of treachery by Tiberius, "an impostor" (767 [599])
   b. The political utility and necessity of vice (767–8 [599–600])
3. Montaigne's own attitude and conduct (768–73 [600–603])
   a. His hatred of trickery (768 [600])
   b. His frankness as a negotiator (768–9, 771–2 [600–601, 603])
   c. The justifiability of neutrality (769–72 [601–2])
   d. His avoidance of public life (772–3 [603])

[13]"Political Thought of Montaigne," p. 232; "Montaigne's Prince," p. 26.
[14]Nicolaï, "Le Machiavélisme de Montaigne," BSAM, 3d ser., nos. 5–6 (1958): 35, 43.

The prologue of III, i, in which Montaigne professes to offer proof (that is, the remarks that follow) that the "silly things" he says have been produced "nonchalantly" rather than with care, may refer to the text of Book III as a whole (which this passage introduced when that book was first published in 1588) rather than to this chapter in particular. Be this as it may, the prologue does bear a specific relation to the argument of the chapter, in that Montaigne's initial profession of artlessness or openness in his writing is mirrored by his subsequent remarks about his conduct as a negotiator. Yet one of the later remarks almost directly contradicts the initial profession, inasmuch as Montaigne says that as a negotiator he has "carefully [*curieusement*]" avoided letting the people with whom he deals "be mistaken about me and deceived by my outward appearance [*masque*]," whereas in the prologue he implied that he does not write "*curieusement*" (767–8 [599–600]. As I noted about the later passage in Chapter One, a "carefully" produced openness must be distinguished from openness in the literal sense. At the least, therefore, the opening remarks in III, i, should put us on our guard regarding the honesty of the discussion of honesty which follows.

Immediately after these remarks Montaigne introduces the central theme of the chapter by asking, "To whom should perfidy not be detestable, since Tiberius refused it at such great sacrifice [*interest*]?" Tiberius scorned to make use of an opportunity to have his country's "most powerful enemy" poisoned, remarking that "the Roman people were accustomed to avenge themselves on their enemies by open ways, arms in hand, not by fraud and surreptitiously." Hence, according to Montaigne, "he gave up the useful for the honorable" (767 [599]).

Tiberius' reply is reminiscent, we note, of the spurious claim made by "the old men of the Senate," according to I, v, regarding the Romans' honesty in dealings with their enemies. And Montaigne immediately charges that Tiberius himself "was an impostor" (cf. II, xvii, 631 [491]). He nonetheless insists that "the acknowledgement of virtue carries no less weight in the mouth of the man who hates it, inasmuch as truth wrests it from him by force, and if he will not receive it within, at least he covers himself with it as an ornament" (767 [599]). Yet this claim would seem to have been contradicted by the remark in "Of Anger" (quoted in Chapter Eleven) that "words are of greater authority and efficacy when actions follow" (II, xxxi, 693 [541]), and by Montaigne's frequent attacks on hypocritical notions of "virtue" that obscure the reality of human selfishness. And in the immediate sequel to his account of Tiberius, rather than elaborate the hatefulness of treachery, Montaigne dwells on the naturalness and *utility* of vice. "In every government," he holds, "there are necessary offices which are not only abject but also vicious"; vices are made "excusable" by "the common necessity" that requires them. In the spirit of Machiavelli (as Sanders notes),[15] he reverses the traditional counsel according to which princes should sacrifice their private interest for the sake of their honor *and* the public good, holding instead that "the more vigorous and less fearful citizens" must "sacrifice their honor and their conscience . . . for the good of their country" (767–8 [599–600]). This whole argument reads, therefore, less as a defense of the "virtue" to which Tiberius lent lip service than as a justification of the sort of perfidy that the Roman emperor purported to renounce!

Montaigne, it is true, professes to be incapable of undertaking the role he assigns to more vigorous individuals: "We [who are] weaker, let us take parts that are both easier and less hazardous. The public welfare requires that a man betray and lie and massacre; let us resign this commission to more obedient and subtler people." He proceeds to elaborate his hatred of the trickery used by judges to lure criminals into confessing, remarking that "it would serve justice well, and Plato himself, who favors this practice, to furnish me with other means more suited to me." He then offers the account of his practices as a political negotiator to which I alluded in Chapter One, wherein he attributes his success to the "freedom" of his manner, by which he exempts himself "from any suspicion of dissimulation" (768–9 [600–601]). As previously noted, Montaigne's remarks about his negotiating technique actually suggest the speciousness of his professions of innocence: they indicate that he succeeded in causing other people to *believe* in his honesty, not that he was scrupulously honest. Later in the chapter (3e in my outline) Montaigne himself alludes to the charge "that what I call frankness, simplicity, and naturalness in my conduct [*moeurs*] is rather prudence than goodness, artifice than nature, good sense than good luck," and answers it only by challenging anyone artfully to "reproduce this natural movement and maintain an *appearance* of liberty and license, so constant and inflexible on such tortuous and varied paths," as he has done (773 [603]); this is hardly a refutation of the charge. Nor does he deny that the challenge of successfully maintaining a "counterfeit and artificial liberty in practice" could be met; he merely observes that it has "most often" failed (773 [604])—perhaps because its practitioners lacked his own thespian skills (I, xxvi, 176 [131]). Indeed, a few sentences earlier in III, i, Montaigne suggests that dishonesty is the only means by which a political negotiator could succeed: "innocence itself could neither negotiate among us without dissimulation nor bargain without lying" (772 [603]). And later in Book III he reports that after having "formerly tried to employ in the service of public dealings opinions and rules of living as crude, green, unpolished or unpolluted, as they were born in me or derived from my education, and which I use, if not commodiously, at least surely, in private [affairs]," he came to recognize that they were "inept and dangerous" for such dealings; political life requires that one "leave the straight way" and adapt to the character of the people with whom one must deal (III, ix, 970 [758]). We may infer that Montaigne's success as a negotiator was not due to any strict adherence to "the straight way."[16]

From an account of his "honest" manner, Montaigne moves on to describe the equable and disinterested temper with which he approaches public affairs. So disinterested, indeed, is his attitude that he professes his readiness to "carry . . . in case of need, one candle to St. Michel and another to the dragon," endeavoring to accommodate both sides so as to prevent himself from being "engulfed in the public ruin." There follows a complex and somewhat confusing passage in which the essayist weighs the moral respectability of such a stance. "To keep oneself wavering and half-and-half, to keep one's allegiance motionless and without inclination in the troubles of one's country and in a civil division" is, he admits, "neither handsome [beau] nor honorable." He adds, however, that such neutrality "may be permitted in regard to the affairs of our neighbors"—apparently referring to the adoption of a neutral posture by the ruler of one country in a conflict involving other countries, with a view to siding ultimately with the victor, as was done by "Gelo, tyrant of Syracuse" (769–70 [601]). He then remarks:

> It would be a sort of treason to do this in our own, domestic affairs. But not to involve oneself, for a man who has neither responsibility nor express command that presses him, I find that more excusable (and nevertheless I am not using this excuse for myself) than to keep out of foreign wars, even though, according to our laws, no one need be involved in them who does not want to be. (770 [601])

By remarking in this passage that it is even more excusable to avoid involving oneself in a civil conflict than to avail oneself of the opportunity that French laws allowed to gentlemen of staying out of foreign wars, Montaigne—who elsewhere professes "to live a merely excusable life" (III,

---

[16]Cf. also his remark at III, i, 769 [600–601], that he does not refrain "from saying anything, however weighty and burning, I could not have said *worse*" when not in the presence of those he is negotiating with—an outright admission that he does dissimulate his thoughts while negotiating.

ix, 930 [727])—surely weakens his previous condemnation of such neutrality as "neither handsome nor honorable." And he adopts an even bolder stance on behalf of neutrality (if one may speak of bold neutrality) by remarking, "Nothing keeps us from getting along commodiously and loyally among men who are enemies to one another" (771 [602]). Lest readers be left in any doubt about how Montaigne applies this principle to his own situation, they need only recall the later passage wherein the essayist admits the "repose and tranquility" he has enjoyed amid his country's ruin, owing to his "patience" regarding "misfortunes" that do not directly affect him (III, xii, 1023 [800]). Montaigne's defense of a posture of noninvolvement in one's country's quarrels is a reflection of his more general teaching that the individual ought to focus attention on personal well-being rather than sacrifice it for others' sake.[17]

Montaigne's "Machiavellianism" might seem to be belied by the sequel to his defense of political neutrality in III, i, wherein he claims to have avoided "public occupations" on account of the incompatibility between his honest ways and the "dissimulation" that political negotiations require. But a closer reading again sheds a different light on Montaigne's attitude. He does not, in the first place, claim simply to have abstained from political activity but remarks that "what my profession requires, I perform in the most private manner that I can."[18] This is to say no more than that his political actions have been undertaken secretly rather than openly. He goes on to explain, moreover, that to the extent that he has avoided involvement in public affairs, this avoidance is the result rather of "fortune" than of choice, "for there are ways less hostile to my taste and more suited to my capacity, by which, if [fortune] had formerly called me to public service and to my advancement towards worldly reputation, I would have passed over the arguments of my reason to follow it" (772–3 [603]). The claim that "fortune" has excluded him from political office is reminiscent, as I noted in Chapter One, of Machiavelli's rhetoric in the epistle dedicatory of *The Prince*. Just as the Florentine's complaint invites the reader to speculate on how the author might nonetheless, by means of his book, achieve the ruling authority he merits, the remark just quoted directs us toward the passage in the final chapter of the *Essays* wherein Montaigne describes his competence to serve as a royal adviser. It is perhaps this sort of political activity, undertaken in the unofficial capacity of author, to which Montaigne is referring when he speaks of pursuing a political role "in the most private

---

[17]Cf. Machiavelli's discussion of whether a prince should remain neutral in others' quarrels, which begins by opposing such a posture but gradually reveals the limitations of that advice: *The Prince*, ch. 21, pp. 89–91; Strauss, *Thoughts on Machiavelli*, p. 82.

[18]On Montaigne's "profession," see n. 24 to Chapter One. I interpret this remark to refer metaphorically to Montaigne's indirect or private "political" activity on behalf of philosophy, undertaken by means of his book, discussed below.

manner possible." His reference a few lines later to the "appearance of liberty and license" he has maintained surely reminds us of the rhetoric of the *Essays*.

Insofar as the passages I have surveyed suggest that Montaigne's professed honesty is deceptive, they provide further confirmation of my argument in Chapter One; but their particular interest at present lies in their bearing on the overall theme of political ethics, or the relation between honor and utility. Immediately after the foregoing discussion Montaigne takes up that theme directly. After qualifying his professed abhorrence of trickery by remarking that "I do not want to deprive deceit of its rank; that would be misunderstanding the world," and that "it has often served profitably and . . . it maintains and feeds most of men's occupations," he asserts that "there are lawful vices, as there are many actions, either good or excusable, that are unlawful." At this point he enunciates one of his most important statements on the subject of natural right and its relation to positive law:

> Justice in itself, natural and universal, is regulated otherwise and more nobly than that other, special, national [justice], constrained to the need of our governments . . . so that the sage Dandamis, hearing tell of the lives of Socrates, Pythagoras, and Diogenes, judged them to be great personages in every other respect, but too enslaved to reverence for the laws, to authorize and support which true virtue has to give up much of its original vigor; and not only by their permission, but even by their persuasion, many vicious actions take place. . . . I follow common language, which distinguishes between things useful and honorable, so that it calls dishonorable and foul some natural actions that are not only useful but necessary. (773–4 [604])

This passage clearly recalls Montaigne's rejection in the "Apology" of Socrates' reputed advice that each of us should conform to our country's laws, on the ground that the laws are too unstable and fluctuating a guide, and merely reflect the prejudices of the ruling classes who enact them. Montaigne's solution to this problem, I have suggested, is that the laws should be revised so as to accord with those of "nature," and be limited to prescribing what each person's preservation requires. But let us consider how Montaigne's understanding of natural justice relates to the overall theme of III, i.

The most significant part of the passage just quoted is the last sentence, wherein Montaigne alludes to the distinction that "common language" makes between the useful and the honorable. In Chapter Seven we saw how Montaigne seeks to challenge this dichotomy between goodness or honorableness and utility, so as to engender a harmony between the goods that people's natures compel them to seek and the moral standards of praise and blame that they apply to one another's conduct. His attack, in such chapters as I, v–vi, and II, ii, on the moral hypocrisy by which people purport to forsake the useful for the sake of the honorable, or to disdain lowly goods in the name of transcendent ones, is integrally related to the argument he has made in III, i, that what are popularly denoted as "vices" are essential instruments of political governance. It should be added that this attack on the dichotomy between morality and utility also reflects Machiavelli's emphasis on "the effectual truth" of political life, according to which many things that are reputed to be virtuous are ruinous to a prince's welfare, and other, reputed vices are essential to the well-being of his subjects as well as himself.[19] In this light the argument of III, i, provides further evidence of Montaigne's agreement with Machiavelli not only in his empirical understanding of how political life operates but in his prescriptive moral teaching: that is, with Machiavelli's aim of redefining "virtue" so that the things that are morally honored are those truly conducive to our earthly welfare. As Clifford Orwin has stressed, it is this redefinition of morality, rather than his recognition of the disjunction between conventional morality and political utility, that constitutes the real novelty of Machiavelli's teaching.[20]

The parallelism between Montaigne's teaching and that of Machiavelli becomes even more apparent in the next pages of "Of the Useful and the Honorable," which include several examples of "treachery" reminiscent of anecdotes recounted in chapters 7 and 8 of The Prince. Particularly significant is Montaigne's discussion of the sort of "remorse" or penitence with which those who profited from the wicked actions they had commanded their subordinates to carry out purported to atone for their evildoing. Typical of these examples is "Jaropelc, a Russian duke," who, having "suborned a Hungarian nobleman" to betray the latter's country, "began to feel such remorse and revulsion" for having slaughtered the inhabitants of a Hungarian town with the nobleman's aid "that he had the eyes of *his agent [son executeur]* put out and his tongue and private parts cut off." Similarly, Mohammed II, induced by his hunger for power to have his half-brother murdered, "*in expiation* of this murder delivered the murderer into the hands of the dead man's mother," who killed him in a particularly hideous manner (775–6 [605–6]). These stories demonstrate the power of conscience or remorse in the same sense that it is manifested in Machiavelli's anecdote of how Cesare Borgia, having brought law and order to the Romagna by giving "the fullest power" to Messer Remirro de Orco, "a cruel and ready man," "purge[d]" the people's mind of the anger Orco's cruelties had generated by having Orco executed, a spectacle that "left the people at once satisfied and stupefied."[21] In other words, they show conscience and repentance to be politically ineffectual except as a popular

---

[19]The Prince, chs. 15–18.
[20]"Machiavelli's Unchristian Charity," pp. 1218–19.
[21]The Prince, ch. 7, p. 30.

prejudice that rulers must accommodate, and that clever ones can manipulate so as to perpetrate their cruelties all the more successfully.

Ostensibly, the difference between Montaigne's presentation of these stories and Machiavelli's is that Montaigne professes to be repelled by such treachery and consequently declines to be employed "to lie, to betray, and to perjure myself" (774 [605]), whereas Machiavelli ordinarily refrains from any express condemnation of actions such as those he attributes to Borgia, even remarking of the latter that "he did all those things which ought to be done by a prudent and virtuous man" who finds himself in a similar situation.[22] But there is no reason to assume that this difference between Montaigne and Machiavelli is other than rhetorical. Both Sanders and Nicolaï, in fact, have cited a passage in the *Discourses on Livy* wherein Machiavelli adopts a rhetorical stance identical with Montaigne's. There the Florentine remarks that the cruel methods a new prince must employ are so inimical to Christian and humane standards that it "behooves any man to shun them, and to prefer rather to live in private than as a king with so much ruin for men."[23] According to Machiavelli's public teaching, it is only if one is determined to succeed in the political arena that one is obliged to liberate oneself from ordinary moral standards. Montaigne concurs. He holds that perfidy is "excusable . . . only when it is employed to punish and betray perfidy" (775 [605]); but his examples—along with his remark in III, ix, that a statesman must "leave the straight way" and adapt to the character of the people he deals with—suggest that people in general are so prone to perfidy when it serves their interest that there are few occasions when his rule would not correspondingly serve to justify treachery.[24] As we have seen, he expressly denies that it is a "vice" for the prince to "deviate from his word and his faith" out of a recognition of political necessity, and openly advises princes, in the spirit of Machiavelli, to attribute such instances of faithlessness to "divine" causes.[25]

As his argument proceeds, Montaigne appears to reverse gears once again, expressing sympathy with those princes whose consciences are too tender to permit them to break their word for any reason whatever. "If there should be" such a prince, he remarks, "I would not esteem him the less." He continues:

[22]Ibid., p. 42.
[23]*Discorsi*, I, xxvi, 194; Sanders, "Montaigne's Prince," pp. 26–7; Nicolaï, "Le Machiavélisme de Montaigne," *BSAM*, 3d ser., nos. 5–6 (1958): 35. Machiavelli illustrates these un-Christian and inhumane methods with a quotation from the New Testament, referring to the works of God: *Discorsi*, I, xxvi, 194; Mansfield, *Machiavelli's New Modes and Orders*, p. 99.
[24]Cf. *The Prince*, ch. 17, p. 66; ch. 18, p. 70.
[25]One should compare Montaigne's advice at p. 777 [607] that a prince who finds himself compelled by circumstances to break his word should attribute his action to "a blow of the divine rod" with his claim in "Of Custom"—in a context where he purports to be arguing against endeavors at political reformation—that deviations from "the rules to which [divine providence] has necessarily constrained us" are "blows of the divine hand" not to be imitated by mortals (I, xxiii, 120 [88]). Cf. Machiavelli's account of how Numa used religion to impress a "new form" on the Roman people: *Discorsi*, I, xi, 62.

He could not ruin himself more excusably or becomingly. We cannot do everything. Do what we will, we must often commit the protection of our vessel . . . to the sole guidance of heaven. . . . For what juster necessity is he preserving himself? What is less possible for him to do than what he cannot do except at the expense of his faith and his honor, things which *perhaps* should be dearer to him than his own safety, yes, and even than the safety of his people? When with folded arms he simply calls God to his aid, may he not hope that the divine goodness is not such as to refuse the favor of its extraordinary hand to a hand pure and just? (777–8 [607])

We are almost overwhelmed by the apparent piety of these sentiments—until we recall that Montaigne devoted the longest chapter of his book largely to demonstrating how foolish it is to hope for any such "extraordinary" divine aid; and that, in imitation of Machiavelli once more, he later admonishes people not to "cast themselves on the resources of others," but to rely on "their own, which alone are sure and alone powerful, if we know how to arm ourselves with them" (III, xii, 1022 [799]). Given these facts, it is hardly likely that Montaigne would regard as a genuinely open question whether a prince ought to keep his conscience pure at the expense of his country's preservation as well as his own. The essayist's overall argument suggests rather—as he explicitly recommends in "Of Vanity"—that anyone who has "morals established and regulated above his time" and is unwilling to "twist or blunt his rules" should "withdraw" from public life (III, ix, 972 [760]); overly scrupulous princes should abdicate rather than be the cause of their country's ruin.[26]

Following the passage last quoted from III, i—and after explicitly resolving the issue left open by the "perhaps" in that passage by affirming that the public "utility" justifies a prince in violating his conscience, provided that that utility is "very apparent and very important"—Montaigne adds several casuistical refinements to the general principle he has laid down. He holds that the purpose in the name of which Timoleon committed the "lofty" deed of killing his brother—that of liberating his country from the brother's tyranny—"is excusable if any could be so." It would be unjustifiable, however, to practice perfidy merely for the sake of "augmenting the public revenue," as the Romans did. He further laments such "false and lax" philosophical rules as that which would exempt one from keeping an oath that robbers had extracted by force, to pay them a sum of money: "What fear has once made me will, I am bound still to will when without fear" (778–9 [607–8]). (By limiting his objection in such cases to breaking one's word for reasons of "private utility," Montaigne tacitly concurs, so far as the *public* utility is concerned, with Machiavelli's judgment that it is

---

[26]Cf. also III, ix, 970 [758]: "The annals to this day reproach one of our kings for having given in too simply to the conscientious persuasions of his confessor. Affairs of state have bolder precepts."

"not shameful" to break promises that were extracted by force.[27] We must also wonder how seriously this objection to philosophical laxity is meant, in view of the essayist's later complaint that the philosophers have often made "the precepts and laws of our life" unreasonably *strict,* and his recommendation that ethical rules be softened to accommodate our condition—III, ix, 967–9 [756–8].)

The argument of "Of the Useful and the Honorable" culminates in a concluding section that poses, on its face, the most serious obstacle to a "Machiavellian" interpretation of the chapter as a whole. The first half of this section consists of a paean to the Theban political and military leader Epaminondas, whom Montaigne had ranked first (ahead of Homer and Alexander) among the three "most excellent men" in II, xxxvi (734 [572]). He now elaborates the reasons for his esteem of Epaminondas:

> To what a height did he raise consideration for his private duty, he who never killed a man he had vanquished, who even for the inestimable good of restoring liberty to his country scrupled to kill a tyrant or his accomplices without due form of justice, and who judged anyone a wicked man, however good a citizen he was, who among his enemies and in battle did not spare his friend and host. There is a soul of rich composition. To the roughest and most violent of human actions he married goodness and humanity, indeed the most delicate that can be found in the school of philosophy. (779–80 [609])

After completing his portrait of the "extreme gentleness and goodness" of Epaminondas' disposition and the "pure innocence" of his ways, Montaigne concludes:

> Let us not fear, after so great a preceptor, to consider that there are some things illicit even against the enemy; that the common interest must not require all things of all men against the private interest . . . and that not all things are permissible for an honorable man in the service of his king, or of the common cause, or of the laws. (780 [609])

In view not only of the moving language of this eulogy but also of Montaigne's repeated expression of his own antipathy to cruelty and inhumanity, there seems little reason to doubt the sincerity of his admiration for Epaminondas and the lesson he represents. But there are obvious problems in reconciling this passage with the teaching of the rest of the chapter, as I have interpreted it; as well as with passages in other chapters of the *Essays,* notably the lengthy denunciation of unrealistic standards of virtue in "Of Vanity," wherein Montaigne remarks, for instance, that "the virtue as-

---

[27]*Discorsi,* III, xlii, 496. Champion, *Introduction aux Essais,* pp. 215–16, notes that Montaigne's position violates the church's doctrine, which maintained that agreements with heretics need not be kept. Cf. Hobbes, *Leviathan,* ch. 20, pp. 251–2.

signed to the affairs of the world is a virtue with many bends, angles, and elbows, so as to join and adapt itself to human weakness; mixed and artificial, *not straight,* clean, constant, *or purely innocent"* (III, ix, 970 [758]). One might attempt to explain the contradiction by saying that the world has declined so greatly in virtue since Epaminondas' time that what worked for him can no longer succeed in contemporary France. Montaigne does, indeed, assert in "Of Vanity" that it is impossible to employ "a pure and sincere virtue in the service of the world" in "a sick age like this" (III, ix, 971 [759]). Such an interpretation is belied, however, by his express refusal to emulate those who, in "old age," "praise times past and blame the present" (II, xiii, 589 [458]), and his profession of "esteem[ing] this age just as if it were another that is past" (III, xiii, 1059 [828]). It is also belied by what we learned in I, vi, of Roman military conduct in the time of "the justest captains and the most perfect" army discipline. And in "Of Vanity" Montaigne indicates that his professed attitude toward politics mirrors that of the philosopher who, according to Plato's *Republic,* would find no actual government worthy of his participation (III, ix, 970 [759]).[28]

The first step that must be taken to grasp the meaning of Montaigne's account of Epaminondas is to recognize that however sincere his admiration for the Theban leader may be, it is not unmixed. Epaminondas' deficiency, from Montaigne's point of view, is signified in III, i, by the seemingly laudatory remark that the Theban set such high store by his "private duty" that he scrupled to violate the ordinary rules of justice *"even for the inestimable good of restoring liberty to his country."* (This remark is an allusion to Epaminondas' hesitation to join the conspiracy in which his friend Pelopidas took a leading role, and which aimed to liberate Thebes from a tyranny imposed by the Spartans—II, xxxvi, 736 [574].)[29] However laudable Montaigne may think Epaminondas' scrupulousness to have been in the abstract, his remark that the goal at which the conspiracy aimed was an "inestimable good" suggests a doubt not only about whether such an attitude is politically beneficial but even about whether it is morally defensible. The doubt is deepened when we recall the essayist's argument, in the latter part of "Of Custom," that laws must sometimes be bent or ignored in the face of urgent "necessity," and his remark that such "great personages" as Octavius and Cato *"are still reproached* for having let their country incur the last extremities rather than disturb things by rescuing it at the expense of the laws" (I, xxiii, 121–2 [89]). This same questioning of the adequacy of positive law as a standard of conduct recurred in "Of the Useful and the Honorable," in the passage where Montaigne distinguished between natural and legal justice and cited Dandamis' criticism of the Greek sages' excessive regard for law-abidingness.

[28]Cf. Plato, *Republic,* 496b–497b.
[29]See Plutarch, *On the Daimon of Socrates,* III, 576–7.

Further confirmation that Montaigne does not regard Epaminondas simply as a model of correct political conduct may be found in "Of the Most
Excellent Men," where he calls the Theban's goodness "excessive" and
concludes by remarking that "the prosperity of his country died, as it was
born, with him" (II, xxxvi, 736 [573–4]). As Sanders has pointed out, the
latter remark mirrors the implicit criticism that Machiavelli levels at Epaminondas in the *Discourses:* although Epaminondas' virtue enabled his country to maintain "a republican form of government as long as he lived . . . on
his death, [it] returned forthwith to its former disorderly state." Although
Machiavelli initially attributes this result to the lack of a sufficiently virtuous successor to complete the reformation of the Thebans' morals, he
later indicates that an adequately knowledgeable and unscrupulous individual might have succeeded where Epaminondas failed.[30]

In view of Montaigne's emphasis in "Of the Useful and the Honorable"
on the necessity of perfidy as a condition of political success; in view of his
recommendation in "Of Vanity" that people of excessively pure morals
should withdraw from the political arena; and in view of his criticism, in the
former chapter, of the distinction between utility and honorableness, there
is every reason to conclude that he agrees with Machiavelli's judgment of
Epaminondas.[31] But how, then, are we to reconcile this judgment with the
essayist's apparently sincere admiration for Epaminondas' goodness and
humanity?

To answer this question we should begin by reminding ourselves of the
distinction Montaigne draws, as I suggested in Chapter Nine, between
compassion or goodness as an end and the reliance on the same quality as a
policy. Montaigne represents himself, as we have seen, as a man of the
utmost compassion toward humanity; but he criticizes the "compassionate" *stance* of Christianity—its appeal to people to act docilely in the face
of evil, and to renounce selfishness—since its "effectual truth," as person-
ified by Manuel of Portugal or Francis of Guise, is cruelty. This is the same
criticism of Christian compassion rendered by Machiavelli—notably in his
distinction between the benign effects of Cesare Borgia's "cruelty" and the
spurious "pity" of the Florentine people.[32] Montaigne and Machiavelli
agree that the first step in constructing an *effectually* "compassionate"
policy is to enunciate a realistic view of human nature. To this end, human

[30]*Discorsi,* I, xvii, 179; I, xviii, 182; Sanders, "Montaigne's Prince," p. 20. The modern
counterpart to Epaminondas is Piero Soderini, whose excessive "patience and goodness," or
"humanity and patience," led to the loss of his office and his reputation "together with his
fatherland" (*Discorsi,* III, iii, 386–7; III, ix, 418).
[31]One may also interpret a remark about Epaminondas in "Of Inequality," wherein Montaigne comments on the vast distance separating the Theban "from some men I know—I mean
men capable of common sense" as a *double-entendre* implying that Epaminondas *lacked*
common sense (I, xlii, 250 [189]).
[32]*The Prince,* ch. 17, p. 65.

selfishness must be accepted as an inevitable fact, rather than denounced as sinful (a denunciation that necessarily issues in hypocrisy). Neither Machiavelli nor Montaigne denies the existence of particular individuals of goodness and humanity. (It is worth recalling that Machiavelli was a friend and adviser to Piero Soderini, whose policies he presents in an unfavorable light by virtue of their excessive "goodness": neither in his view nor in Montaigne's is there any necessary incompatibility between admiring a statesman's character and regarding his policies as imprudent.) But both regard it as unwise to base a political policy on the presupposition that such dispositions will generally characterize human behavior.

Bearing this point in mind, let us consider the sequel to Montaigne's account of Epaminondas in III, i, wherein the essayist draws some more general lessons from his account of the Theban hero. Following his inference that there are limits to what "the common interest" should require of people "against the private interest," he observes, "If it is greatness of heart and the effect of rare and singular virtue to despise friendship, private obligations, our word, and kinship, for the common good and obedience to the magistrate, truly it is enough to excuse us from this that it is a greatness that cannot lodge in the greatness of Epaminondas' heart." By contrast, Montaigne professes to "abominate the rabid exhortations of that other uncontrolled soul" (Caesar, as portrayed by Lucan), to the effect that the necessities of war must prevail over all considerations of piety and kinship. And he exhorts his readers to "take away from wicked, bloody, and treacherous natures this pretext of reason. Let us abandon this monstrous and deranged justice and stick to more human imitations. How much time and example can do!" Somewhat curiously, however, he illustrates the last point by citing two ancient examples that demonstrate the capacity of morals to degenerate over time, rendering the commission of fratricide during war an occasion of pride rather than dishonor. Even more curious is the conclusion to the chapter, wherein Montaigne distinguishes the "honor and beauty" of actions from their "utility" and illustrates this distinction by noting that even though marriage is "the most necessary and useful action of human society . . . the council of saints excludes the most venerable occupation of men" from engaging in it, "as we assign to stud those beasts that are of least value" (781 [609–10]).[33]

Given Montaigne's mockery, especially in III, v, of those who contemn the sexual act, as well as his ironic account of Saint Hilary in I, xxxiii, we must doubt that he shares the church's attitude toward the marital state. Our doubt is deepened and broadened when we recall that earlier in III, i, he deprecated the disjunction between utility and honorableness as a popular prejudice; and that elsewhere in the Essays he opposed the standard of

---

[33]The Council of Trent had reaffirmed the requirement of priestly celibacy in 1563.

"beauty" as a criterion for judging human actions. Hence the church's depreciation of marriage despite (or because of) its utility would clearly seem to constitute an erroneous judgment, in Montaigne's view.

That the example in which it culminates—the church's attitude toward marriage—is an ironic one appears to demonstrate that Montaigne's praise of Epaminondas was not grounded on the Theban's having scorned the useful for the sake of the honorable. But how, then, is that praise, along with the exhortation that follows it, to be understood? We may answer this query, I believe, by raising a further question: "Useful to whom?" It may indeed be thought useful to political communities—or at least to their rulers—that the citizenry as a whole should be disposed "to despise friendship, private obligations, our word, and kinship, for the common good and obedience to the magistrate." But it is not at all evident that to set "the common interest" in this sense entirely over the private interest of individual human beings is useful *to those individuals*. Nor, to the extent that such a principle issues in the "rabid exhortations" of Caesar—or of the leaders of the French religious parties—to pursue the cause of war at all costs, can it be said to be "useful" to humanity as a whole. The demand that people, in the name of honor, should subordinate both their interests and their scruples to the commands of "the magistrate" seems illustrative rather of that "special, national justice, constrained to the need of our governments," which Montaigne deprecated as the source of "many vicious actions."

If the foregoing remarks are correct, then the "pretext of reason" of which Montaigne wishes to deprive "wicked, bloody, and treacherous natures" is not the subordination of justice to utility but rather the disregard of people's "private interest[s]" as individuals in the name of the *supposed* common interest of their country.[34] It is precisely this principle, we recall, that guided the conduct of Montaigne's excessively public-spirited father, and that the essayist identified as the cause of his father's unhappiness in "Of Managing One's Will." What Montaigne *père* failed to understand is that the saying "that we are not born for our private selves, but for the public" is in reality a mask behind which selfish motives such as "ambition and avarice take cover" (I, xxxix, 232 [174]). As the result of such precepts, which ultimately derive from the public teachings of philosophers as well as lawgivers, well-intentioned people such as the senior Montaigne become the dupes of "impostors" such as Tiberius, who *profess* to forsake the useful for the honorable. In III, i, Montaigne has cited numerous instances of other rulers who similarly employed the pretext of virtuous repentance as a cover for their immoral actions.

---

[34]Hence, although Nakam errs in underestimating Montaigne's appreciation of the dichotomy between political necessity and conventional morality, she properly states that in III, i, Montaigne "destroys the morality of the pretended general interest" (*Les Essais*, p. 256).

The preceding argument is not meant to deny Montaigne's recognition that the collective well-being of a political community sometimes requires its rulers to violate the ordinary precepts of morality. From this point of view, Timoleon's readiness to commit fratricide in order to liberate his country was a more appropriate attitude for a statesman than Epaminondas' scrupulousness about violating due processes of law for the same end. Yet throughout the *Essays* Montaigne has demonstrated that people are all too prone to find noble or pious excuses for bloodshed and cruelty, when what really motivates them is the "malicious pleasure" that, as he reaffirms near the beginning of III, i, people naturally find "in seeing others suffer" (768 [599]). It should also be noted that in the very chapter of the *Discourses* wherein Machiavelli anticipates Montaigne's account of Epaminondas' failure to secure his country's liberty beyond his lifetime, he points out that Timoleon was no more successful in this regard: "the city remained free so long as [he] lived, but when [he was] dead returned to its ancient tyranny."[35] Given the "Machiavellian" thrust of the argument of III, i, it is unlikely that the fact that Montaigne discusses Timoleon and Epaminondas in the same chapter just as Machiavelli did is coincidental. Rather, the comparison of these examples suggests—just as it did in the *Discourses*—the need to go beyond the policies of both Epaminondas and Timoleon, to effect a more lasting liberation of humanity from the tyranny to which it has thus far been generally subjected.

In order to discover the means by which Montaigne proposes to achieve such a liberation, the reader should recall the contradiction between the essayist's profession of being morally incapable of the kind of dishonesty that political negotiations require and his admission that he has been notably successful as a negotiator. Although we must doubt that Montaigne's manner as a negotiator (or an author) is as frank or naive as he professes, his claims in this regard point toward a more serious theme. They suggest the possibility of a new kind of politics, in which the *need* for perfidy and bloodshed would be greatly reduced. This theme is most directly treated in "Of Managing One's Will" (III, x)—the very essay in which Montaigne describes the miseries his father incurred as the result of taking too literally doctrines obliging the individual to subordinate personal interest to that of one's country.

The Lesson of Montaigne's Mayoralty

The bulk of "Of Managing One's Will" is concerned with the need for people to focus their main attention and concern on "themselves" rather

---

[35]*Discorsi,* I, xvii, 358.

than on "extraneous" concerns—in accordance with the general principles of Montaigne's teaching of self-concern that I examined in Chapter Eleven. Hence the essayist admonishes his readers that "the main responsibility of each of us is his own conduct," and that "he who abandons healthy and gay living of his own to serve others thereby takes, to my taste, a bad and unnatural course" (III, x, 984 [769–70]). But whereas in other chapters Montaigne equates his own self-concern with an almost exclusive focus on his private and bodily needs, the argument of III, x, is noteworthy for its intimation that a proper self-awareness is not incompatible with successful public service. Montaigne demonstrates such a possibility by reference to his accomplishments as mayor of Bordeaux. In contrast to his previous professions of being temperamentally unsuited for public life, he reports having "been able to take part in public office without departing from myself by the width of a fingernail, and to give myself to others without taking myself from myself" (985 [770]). So successful was he in this regard that his two-year term as mayor was "extended by a second election, which happens very rarely" (982 [768]).

Despite the evident success of his administration, Montaigne reports that it was subjected to two sorts of criticism. The first complaint is that Montaigne executed his office "like a man who exerts himself too weakly and with a languishing zeal." Montaigne responds that those who make this criticism "are not at all far from having a case," since "I try to keep my soul and my thoughts in repose"; but that he nonetheless did all while in office that the public good required (998 [781]). The second criticism is that his administration "passed without a mark and without a trace." To this he sarcastically replies, "That's good: they accuse me of inactivity in a time when almost everyone was convicted of doing too much." Montaigne's critics err in equating true statesmanship with ambition, publicity, and constant activity; his policy, by contrast, was to carry out what his public duty "genuinely required," while avoiding those actions "that ambition mixes up with duty and covers with its name," and which "most often fill the eyes and ears, and satisfy men" (999 [781]). Elaborating this defense near the end of the chapter, Montaigne remarks, "I have not at all had that iniquitous and rather common humor of wanting the trouble and sickness of the affairs of this city to exalt and honor my government," and reproaches his critics for not being grateful for "the order, the gentle and mute tranquility" that his administration engendered (1002 [783–4]).

To grasp the significance of what might seem like rather modest self-praise, the reader need only compare this account of Montaigne's mayoralty with the description he provided of the chaotic and disorderly state of France's political affairs as a whole at the time, in the chapter just preceding "Of Managing One's Will." As mayor, Montaigne reports, he had "nothing to do but conserve and endure"; but to "conserve" public

order was just what the French government was then unable to do, according to "Of Vanity" (III, ix, 933, 943 [729, 737]). Yet perhaps the failure of
the country's leaders to achieve a success rivaling Montaigne's was due to
their sharing the attitude of the critics of his administration, according to
which it is the duty of a government to do more than preserve order. Rather
than appreciating that each person's "main responsibility" is "his own
conduct," they saw it as the chief aim of *government* to reform people's
morals and beliefs so as to save their souls. In contrast to Montaigne, who is
"apt to promise a little less than what I can do and what I hope to deliver"
(III, x, 1002 [784]), they promised and aspired to achieve far more than any
human being could deliver. The result was the religious wars.

It will be evident that Montaigne's account of his mayoralty, which he
represents as a model for the management of political affairs, harmonizes
with the lesson of his praise of the cannibals' society in I, xxxi: lowering the
aim of government and reducing the scope of its activity reduces domestic
conflict and political oppression and hence engenders "order" and "tranquility." Let us now consider how that theme may relate to the argument of
"Of the Useful and the Honorable" and the problems that that argument
embodied.

Montaigne's account of his moderate conduct as mayor and its benign
effects surely does not refute the argument made in III, i, that rulers must
sometimes perform acts of treachery for the sake of the public good. Yet
reflection on the reasons for the absence of perfidy among the cannibals
may illuminate how the argument of "Of Managing One's Will" suggests
the possible mitigation of the need for political perfidy. The absence of
dishonesty among the cannibals appears to be due, as noted earlier, to the
limitedness of their thoughts and desires, which in turn prevents them from
perceiving a distinction between their private interests and the common
interest. They do not lie because they harbor no private wishes or aims that
it would be harmful or imprudent to reveal to their fellows—in contrast to
civilized people, whose "private wishes are for the most part born and
nourished at the expense of others" (I, xxii, 106 [77]).

The expansion of selfish desires that has accompanied the development
of the human mind beyond its savage state—an expansion that Montaigne
has no intention of trying to reverse—clearly makes it impossible for a
harmony of interests to exist within a civilized political society comparable
to that of the cannibals' social order. Yet the degree of overt conflict among
the interests of civilized people will vary with the manner in which they
understand their interests and with the substance of their desires. The
public teachings of the classical philosophers, as Montaigne emphasizes in
III, x, aimed at harmonizing the interests of citizens by persuading them, so
far as possible, to identify their individual interests with that of the public,
or to devalue selfish and private goods such as wealth and bodily pleasure in

favor of the goods of virtue and honor. Yet the ultimate consequence of such teachings, Montaigne has indicated, was to encourage such men as Alexander and Guise to oppress their fellows in the name, respectively, of worldly glory or of God. We could come much closer to the goals of civic peace and individual contentment, Montaigne holds, by taking the opposite tack—that is, by encouraging people to pursue private but essentially pacific goods and dispensing with the attempt to regulate such pursuits in the name of virtue. The acceptance of such private-spiritedness enables one to dispense with the need for dishonesty in at least the following sense: human beings no longer need to conceal their natural selfishness behind a mask of public-regardingness. Having dispensed with the pretense of pursuing or attaining transcendent goods, they will, like the Pyrrhonians, have "rid themselves of the need to cover up" (II, xii, 484 [373]). The lesson for rulers is apparent in Montaigne's account of his conduct as mayor: content yourself with preserving order rather than pursuing greatness; regulate your subjects' lives no more than civic order requires; and you will in consequence be esteemed by the people and secure in your position. To the degree that the actions of government are perceived by the citizenry as conducive to the manifest, individual interests of each of them—that is, by providing conditions of security in which each citizen can pursue private welfare and enjoyment—the government, moreover, will have rid itself of the need to justify its authority by recurring to "noble" lies. The redirection of human beings from the pursuit of public goods to that of private ones, or from spiritual to corporeal ones, may also mitigate the need for rulers to employ violence and bloodshed, of the sort Montaigne laments in III, i, to secure their rule; aiming at comfort and security, and perceiving that the government's maintenance in power is conducive to that end, people will have no incentive to contest the right to govern.

The reconstitution of government which Montaigne intends clearly presupposes a reorientation in the psychology of rulers, along the lines I sketched in Chapter Nine: they must learn to value order and tranquility above the pursuit of superhuman glory or greatness. But it appears that a considerable push toward such a change in the orientation of political leaders is to come from the reorientation Montaigne aspires to engender in their subjects' attitude through his book. This intention is most clearly manifest in the chapter "Of Glory," wherein Montaigne not only deprecates the pursuit of glory, by contrast with that of "tranquility," but specifically questions whether it is sensible for people to sacrifice their "real and essential life" in their countries' wars (II, xvi, 612 [476]). The same point is stated in the "Apology," in a passage where the essayist describes war as exemplifying "human absurdity and vanity" and identifies the petty quarrels of rulers as its principal cause; he cites the "greatest" and most powerful emperor, Augustus, as "making a sport and a laughing-stock . . . of so many battles hazarded on both land and sea, the blood and the lives of five hundred thousand men who followed his fortune, and the power and riches of both parts of the world exhausted in the service of his enterprises" (II, xii, 452–3 [348]). That point is further developed at the conclusion of II, xxiii, where Montaigne expresses amazement at the example of "many thousands of foreigners engaging their blood and their lives for money in quarrels in which they have no interest," in "our wars" (666 [519]), and, indirectly, in a discussion of dueling in II, xxvii: "Each man runs enough risk for himself without running it for another, and has enough to do to assure himself in his own virtue for the defense of his life, without committing a thing so dear to the hands of a third party" (674 [525–6]). In Book III Montaigne observes, more forthrightly, that "it properly belongs to kings to quarrel with kings": others should try to avoid enmeshing themselves in their rulers' quarrels (III, i, 770 [602]); and he remarks the spectacle of a soldier "boiling and red with anger" on behalf of a "frivolous cause," despite the fact that he has no "interest" at stake in the battle (III, iv, 816–17 [637]). Finally, in "Of Managing One's Will," to show that people harm themselves by exaggerating their public duties at the expense of their private needs, he invites the reader to consider "how many men risk themselves every day in wars which are no concern to them, and press forward to the dangers of battles, the loss of which will not trouble their next night's sleep" (III, x, 984 [770]). In sum, having intimated the advantages of a posture of "neutrality" in III, i, Montaigne aims to heighten his readers' resistance to participating in or supporting wars that originate in royal ambitions and rivalries.[36] At the same time that he encourages a pacific self-concern on the part of the people, he appeals to rulers to recognize the personal gains from a policy of beneficence and moderation rather than martial valor and vainglory:

> [T]here was never time and place where a surer and greater reward was offered to princes for goodness and justice [than the present]. . . . We see merchants, village justices, artisans keeping up with the nobility in valor and military knowledge. They do honorably in both private and public combats; they fight, they defend cities in our wars. A prince's distinction is smothered amid this crowd. Let him shine with humanity, truthfulness, loyalty, moderation, and especially justice, marks that are rare, unknown, and banished. It is only by the will of the people that he can do his job, and no other qualities can flatter their will as much as these, which are much more useful to them than the others. (II, xvii, 629–30 [490])

This passage from "Of Presumption" immediately precedes the passage I discussed at the outset of this chapter wherein Montaigne, in the spirit of

---

[36]Cf., on Montaigne's critique of militarism, Nakam, *Les Essais*, pp. 117–31.

Machiavelli, suggests the advantages that perfidy may bring to a prince. But I believe that the two passages can be reconciled along the lines I have suggested: a reordering of popular belief, and thereby of the purpose of the political community, so as to favor the open but pacific pursuit of individuals' private interests would reduce the need for and the potential gain from dishonesty or treachery. It is in this way, similarly, that Montaigne's political teaching might ultimately be harmonized with that of Machiavelli, despite the rhetorical differences between them. Without attempting a comprehensive interpretation of Machiavelli's own intention, I have tried to demonstrate that at least the most manifestly distinctive and fundamental elements of the Florentine's teaching—the redefinition of "virtue" in terms of utility and the concomitant lowering of the end of government— are in full agreement with Montaigne's position. Beyond this point, I suggest that the *apparent* differences between Machiavelli's and Montaigne's teachings may result largely from the way the essayist reformulated his predecessor's teaching in a rhetorically more palatable and popularly appealing from (just as Locke was later to do with respect to Hobbes).[37] (This rhetorical difference may reflect a difference in the primary audiences to which they intended to appeal, in that Montaigne aimed to influence a wider "gentlemanly," or vulgar, audience in addition to philosophic "men of understanding." Perhaps also the political chaos of France and the relative security that his noble status gave him provided Montaigne with a freedom to reveal his aim more openly than Machiavelli could: even though the essayist's language is less shocking than Machiavelli's, his antireligious intent is expressed more overtly.)

A concomitant of Machiavelli's redefinition of virtue is a denial that qualities that are traditionally identified as "vices" but that are essential to political success should be regarded as blameworthy. The advice given in the fifteenth chapter of The Prince concerning the need for a prince to "use" so-called vices as well as virtues as necessity dictates is reflected in Montaigne's recommendation that we learn to "use" and "blend . . . goods and evils, which are consubstantial with our life," recognizing that "one element is no less necessary for it than the other" (III, xiii, 1068 [835]). Similarly, Montaigne emphasizes, near the beginning of III, i, that "sickly qualities" such as "ambition, jealousy, envy, vengeance, superstition, despair" are essential to human nature, and consequently to the operation of political society (767–8 [599]). As with Machiavelli, the utilitarian interpretation of morality implies a recognition of the temporal variability of virtue, properly understood, depending on what circumstances require.

[37]Concerning Machiavelli's own rhetorical exaggerations, which also make the difference between his teaching and Montaigne's seem greater than it is, consider the quotation from Virgil in ch. 17 of The Prince, p. 66, in the light of Machiavelli's situation as a "new prince"; Strauss, Thoughts on Machiavelli, pp. 81–2.

Hence, just as Machiavelli emphasizes in chapter 25 of *The Prince* the need for a prince to vary his "nature" in accordance with the "times," Montaigne remarks that "all things have their season, good ones *and all*," and denounces the "unseasonable" and politically harmful rigidity of Cato's moral posture (II, xxviii, 681 [531]; III, ix, 969–70 [758]).[38] In view of the variability of human circumstances, both thinkers endeavor to supplant a fixed notion of "virtue" by a characteristic that Montaigne labels "adaptability." This point merits further consideration.

Political Adaptability

Adaptability as a virtue has at least three related senses or forms in Montaigne's teaching. It connotes, in the first place, a proper ordering of the individual soul in relation to the body. Second, it is a virtue concerned with the individual's relation to others. Third, it is a virtue of the ordering of the political community and its laws as a whole.

I have explained the first of these senses in articulating Montaigne's critique of Stoic morality. While outwardly imitating the Stoic teaching that we should give our souls an attitude "conducive to our repose and preservation," the essayist finds such an attitude to consist not in forsaking concern with external goods but rather in focusing the soul's attention on corporeal as opposed to spiritual goods. In this way the essentially malleable soul can be "adapted" to the relatively fixed needs of the body. This same reorientation of the soul's attitude regarding spiritual and corporeal goods is also the foundation of "adaptability" in the second sense, the harmonizing of people's relations with one another. In "Of the Education of Children" Montaigne renders lip service to the traditional notion that a young man's body should be "toughened"—as his own (he claims) is not—to the endurance of hardship, but he actually develops the distinctive principle that the youth's *soul* should be toughened to accommodate an infinite variety of customs and ways of life, including ways that are commonly thought to be morally opprobrious. "Provided his appetite and will can be kept in check, let a young man boldly be made fit for all nations and companies, even for dissoluteness and excess, if need be"; in this way he may learn to emulate "the wonderful nature of Alcibiades, who could change so easily to suit such different fashions" as "luxury and pomp" in Persia, "austerity and frugality" in Sparta (I, xxvi, 152, 166 [113, 123–4]). There is, Montaigne implies, no greater intrinsic value to temperance than to indulgence, no

---

[38]Cf. also II, xxxiv, 714 [557], concerning the value Caesar attributed to the "manage[ment] of time" and the ability "to seize occasions at the right point"; and III, v, 843 [659], regarding the importance of "opportuneness" in love.

more reason to accustom the youth to the former than to the latter. In later chapters, as we have seen, he actually undermines the case for temperance; while in the concluding essay, as noted in Chapter Eleven, he elaborates the case for adaptability regarding sensual indulgence—that is, the overcoming of moral objections to such indulgence. Resuming his advice to youth in that chapter, he remarks:

> There is no way of life so stupid and feeble as that which is conducted by rules and discipline. . . . [A young man] will even plunge often into excess, if he will take my advice; otherwise the slightest dissipation will ruin him, and he will become awkward and disagreeable in company. The most unsuitable quality for a gentleman is overfastidiousness and bondage to a certain particular way, and it is particular if it is not pliable and supple. (III, xiii, 1061 [830])

Much of the essayist's account of his way of life in "Of Experience," which he represents as a guide to "bodily health," is metaphorical; just as his ostensible advice on dealing with the kidney stone ("your dissipation will do you more good than harm"—1073 [839]) must be interpreted in a broader sense, so his professed taste in "meats" has a deeper political meaning: "Only toughness generally angers me (towards every other quality I am as nonchalant and tolerant as any man I have known)" (1081 [845]). It is, in sum, Montaigne's hedonism, coupled with what might be called a nonjudgmental attitude toward other people's idiosyncratic habits and enjoyments, that enables him to live in harmony with his fellows; the only limit of tolerance is that it cannot be extended to "toughness," that is, toward intolerance.

Montaigne's praise of Alcibiades is significant in another respect as well. The fact that the Athenian general was able to adapt so readily to the ways of various countries—even assisting the Spartans, during his exile, in their war against his native city—suggests that he shared the "cosmopolitan" attitude of Montaigne, who remarks in the last chapter, in contrast to Socrates' example, that if French laws "threatened even my fingertip, I should instantly go and find others, wherever this might be" (III, xiii, 1049 [821]). This remark occurs in the context of a critique of the injustice of French laws, which includes an explicit comparison of Alcibiades' attitude toward legal justice with that of Montaigne himself, and is followed by the passage that expresses Montaigne's preference for being guided "by the general law of the world," known through sensation (1047–50 [819–21]). Taken as a whole, these remarks point toward a conception of adaptability in a third sense: a reformation of the political community itself, designed to harmonize it with human nature in such a way as to overcome the tension between natural and conventional justice.

In order to comprehend this third aspect of adaptability, it will be necessary to bring together scattered passages from several chapters of the

Essays. Let us begin by recalling once more the passage in the "Apology" wherein Montaigne dissents from Socrates' advice that each of us should be guided by the laws of our country, on the ground that he cannot make his judgment so flexible as to conform it to the shifting opinions of the various ruling classes who enact them (II, xii, 562–3 [437]). Montaigne's argument in that context—culminating in his account of the philosophers' "natural," licentious way of life—pointed, I have suggested, to a notion of "natural law" as a standard to which positive laws should be made to conform: the standard, espoused most openly in III, xiii, based on corporeal pleasure and pain. What remains to be clarified is the relation of Montaigne's conception of natural law to the fact of the variety of particular ruling classes to which he called attention in the "Apology." What is the relation, in other words, between Montaigne as founder-lawgiver and the actual governments of particular regimes?

In this context it is useful to recall Montaigne's remark in "Of Custom" concerning the belief shared by "nations brought up to liberty and to ruling themselves" and by "those who are accustomed to monarchy" that the regime that is opposed to their own is "monstrous and contrary to nature," and his observation that even those who succeed in ridding themselves of "the importunity of one master" immediately "supplant him with another, with similar difficulties, because they cannot make up their minds to hate mastery" (I, xxiii, 114–15 [83–4]). In an earlier chapter Montaigne indicates that the desires for liberty and mastery are not simply opposed to each other: "We are so eager to get out from under command under some pretext, *and to usurp mastery;* each man aspires so naturally *to liberty and authority,* that to a superior no useful quality [*utilité*] should be so dear in those who serve him as their natural [*naïfve*] and simple obedience" (I, xvii, 73 [51]).[39] We have seen ample evidence elsewhere that Montaigne's obedience to the laws, however scrupulous it may be, is far from being the product of a naive or simple subservience to rulers. Of greater interest for our present inquiry, however, is a passage in Book III wherein the essayist describes himself as also being free from the desire for "mastery" which he has linked with people's natural love of liberty, and offers a hint as to how his attitude might be developed into a general policy:

> I am disgusted with mastery, both active and passive. Otanes, one of the seven who had a right to aspire to the kingship of Persia, took a course that I would gladly have taken: he abandoned to his competitors his chance of attaining it either by election or by lot, provided that he and his family could live in that

---

[39]Cf. Hobbes's linkage of the natural desire for liberty with that for dominion over others, which must be overcome for the sake of the security of all: *Leviathan,* ch. 17 (first sentence); William Mathie, "Justice and the Question of Regimes in Ancient and Modern Political Philosophy: Aristotle and Hobbes," *Canadian Journal of Political Science* 9 (1976): 460–61.

empire free of all subjection and mastery save that of the ancient laws, and have every freedom that was not prejudicial to these; balking at either commanding or being commanded. (III, vii, 896 [700])

In the relatively brief chapter from which this passage is taken, titled "Of the Disadvantage of Greatness," Montaigne does not elaborate the relevance of Otanes' course to the problem that the chapter discusses—the disadvantages of monarchy as a form of government, and the "natural envy and contention" between monarchs and their subjects. But let us turn, finally, to Montaigne's account, at the conclusion of "Of Physiognomy," of how his "face and . . . frankness" preserved him from harm on two occasions when he was captured by parties of soldiers during the civil wars. At the end of his account of the second incident Montaigne explains how the soldiers' leader

> repeated to me . . . several times that I owed my deliverance to my face and the freedom and firmness of my speech, which made me undeserving of such a misadventure; and he asked me *for assurance of similar treatment*. It is possible that the divine goodness willed to make use of this vain *instrument for my preservation*. (III, xii, 1040 [814])

It is not entirely clear from the text what the "vain instrument" to which Montaigne is referring is. But reading this passage in conjunction with the account of Otanes, I suggest that the agreement Montaigne reached with his captor, by which the latter freed him in return for a promise of "similar treatment" should their situations be reversed, constitutes a prototype of the social contract subsequently described by Hobbes and Locke as the true foundation of political order: an agreement by which human beings, in return for giving up their claims to "mastery" over one another, are assured of their "preservation." Of critical importance to such a tacit contract, if all citizens are to be persuaded to accept it, is that the government is limited in its purpose to securing the one goal that all rational individuals, *regardless of their particular moral or religious beliefs,* can be presumed to desire: their individual preservation—which entails the preservation of their property and of their freedom to live as they like, so long as they do not infringe on the like liberty and security of their fellow citizens.[40] It is just such a

---

[40]See *Leviathan*, ch. 17; Harvey C. Mansfield, Jr., "Impartial Representation," in Robert A. Goldwin, ed., *Representation and Misrepresentation* (Chicago, 1968), pp. 98–106. Cf. also *Essais*, I, xxviii, 191 [142]: "In the associations that bind us only by one end we need only look out for the imperfections that particularly concern that end. The religion of my doctor and my lawyer cannot matter. . . . And I scarcely inquire of a lackey whether he is chaste; I try to find out whether he is diligent. And I am not so much afraid of a gambling muleteer as of a weak one, or of a profane cook as of an ignorant one. I do not meddle with telling the world what it should do." At the conclusion of this argument, Montaigne remarks that his principle of judging people only with regard to those aspects of their character that relate to the purpose of his association with them applies "similarly in other matters."

conception of "limited government"—as instanced by his praise of the cannibals' society, of the philosophers' "natural" way of life, and of Caesar's methods of governing his army—that Montaigne has sought to advance in the *Essays*. His critique of the arbitrariness and conventionality of moral and religious beliefs has been intended to undermine his readers' disposition to attach objective validity to such beliefs, and their consequent inclination to demand that government conform to them. In this respect Montaigne's skeptical epistemological teaching anticipates both the form and the purpose of Hobbes's reduction of moral and political speech to the passions that underlie them.[41] His dissection of the characters of Cato and Alexander similarly anticipates Hobbes's attack on "vainglory." And his denunciation of the pride and "unseasonable" humors that lead human beings to contemn their fellows and to claim exemption from "the common laws" of the human condition prefigures, as I have argued, the "bourgeois" morality enunciated by Hobbes, which is intended to turn people into docile citizens of a state that guarantees their equal rights. Montaigne is, in short, one of the earliest philosophic advocates of the modern liberal regime. It is the genius of this historically novel form of government that it endeavors to resolve the problem of "mastery" by abolishing mastery: liberal or "representative" government, according to its professed aspiration, is a government that does not rule people, in the sense of imposing on them a particular way of life or moral and religious code. In this way positive law is freed from the arbitrariness and injustice that characterize the "undulating" opinions of particular ruling classes, whether peoples or princes. Instead, the laws of each country are derived from universal principles of natural right, which respect the primacy of our instinctive desire to preserve ourselves, to enjoy harmless pleasures, and to avoid pain.

Since the claim I am making here on Montaigne's behalf is not one that to my knowledge has been recognized by other modern scholars, I must postpone a more specific elucidation of how this claim relates to the theme of "adaptability" in order to cite a few more passages from the *Essays* which buttress my interpretation. By remarking, in III, xiii, that he would instantly leave France if its laws threatened him in the slightest way, Montaigne appears to agree with Hobbes that the extent of a citizen's obligation to obey the government is conditional on the government's capacity and disposition to protect the citizen; our natural right of self-preservation is logically prior to any political obligations we may incur.[42] Along these same lines, in "Of Vanity" the essayist laments the fact that the security he

[41]See Harvey C. Mansfield, Jr., "Hobbes and the Science of Indirect Government," *American Political Science Review* 65 (1971): 99–102; Robert P. Kraynak, "Hobbes's *Behemoth* and the Argument for Absolutism," *American Political Science Review* 76 (1982): 837–47.

[42]"The Obligation of Subjects to the Soveraign, is understood to last as long, and no longer, than the power lasteth, by which he is able to protect them. . . . The end of Obedience is Protection" (*Leviathan*, ch. 21, p. 272; see also pp. 268–70).

has thus far enjoyed during the civil wars is contingent on "the alterations and vicissitudes of fortune around me":

> I escape; but it displeases me that this is more by fortune, and even by my prudence, than through justice; and it displeases me to be outside the protection of the laws and under another safeguard than theirs. As things are, I live more than half by others' favor, which is a harsh obligation. *I do not want to owe my safety* either *to the goodness and benignity of the great*, who approve of my law-abidingness and liberty, or to the easygoing ways [*moeurs*] of my predecessors and myself. *For what if I were different?* If my conduct and the frankness of my dealings obligate my neighbors or my kinsmen, it is a cruelty that they can acquit themselves by letting me live, and that they can say: "We grant him liberty to continue the divine service in the chapel of his house, all the churches around having been emptied and ruined by us; and we grant him *the use of his property, and his life,* since he shelters our wives and cattle in time of need". . . . Now I hold that we should live *by right and authority, not by reward or grace.* How many gallant men have chosen rather to lose their lives than to owe them! *I flee from submitting myself to any sort of obligation,* but especially any that binds me by a debt of honor. I find nothing so expensive as that which is given me and for which my will remains mortgaged by the claim of gratitude, and *I more willingly accept services that are for sale.* Rightly so, I think: for the latter I give only my money, for the others I give myself. (III, ix, 943–4 [738])

This remarkable passage embodies in a concise form an almost comprehensive catalogue of the fundamental tenets of classical political liberalism: the right of the individual to a security that derives from the laws, rather than one that depends on the beneficence of a ruling class; the inviolability of such a right regardless of whether the individual chooses to adopt a way of life that differs from others'; the rights to freedom of worship and the protection of one's property; the avoidance of obligations that constrain one's freedom; and even the preference that particular relations among human beings be governed by the cash nexus, which limits and formalizes them, rather than by ancestral or religious obligations. Almost every element of the liberal program that is omitted from this passage, moreover, is contained in the pages that immediately follow it: the principle that individuals should guide themselves, in matters beyond those that the law legitimately regulates, by their own consciences; the moral superiority of praiseworthy acts that "have something of the splendor of freedom" about them to those that result from legal constraint; the need for people to learn to be self-sufficient rather than to depend on "foreign aid"; the pleasure of diversity; people's natural freedom, and the superiority of their ties to humanity, on the one hand, and to friends they have freely chosen, on the other, to the arbitrary ties of common citizenship; the greater knowability of the evils to be avoided in life than of the objective good, if there is any, to be sought in it (944–51 [738–44]).

One major element of the liberal program which is barely hinted at in "Of Vanity" is developed more openly in a few key passages in other chapters: the advantages of economic freedom, as a means of encouraging people to engage for reasons of self-interest in pursuits that ultimately benefit the public, while—even more important—diverting them from less pacific modes of pursuing gain. In "Of Custom" Montaigne contrasts the barbarous French legal system with Isocrates' "ingenious" recommendation that the king make his subjects' trades and negotiations "free, gratuitous, and lucrative, and their disputes and quarrels onerous, by loading these with heavy taxes" (I, xxiii, 116 [85]): the law should rechannel human energies from quarrelsomeness to constructive economic activity. In "Of Freedom of Conscience" Montaigne praises Julian for having "made many good laws, and [having] cut out a large part of the subsidies and taxes that his predecessors had levied" (II, xix, 652 [507]). He forthrightly opposes sumptuary laws, as previously noted, in the chapter bearing that title. And in "Of Coaches" he elaborates Machiavelli's critique of royal "liberality": since such liberality can be exercised only "at the expense of others" who are taxed to pay for the king's largesse, it discourages private industriousness, while the beneficiaries of "excessive" liberality become more strident in their demands; rather than being grateful for what they received, people "love only the future liberality."[43] If princes truly wish to be liberal, they should focus their expenditures neither on personal displays nor on gifts to private individuals but on "useful, just, and durable" public works (III, vi, 879–82 [687–90]). Indeed, "princes give me much" if only "they take nothing from me" (III, ix, 945 [739]).

Montaigne's most important statement regarding economic liberty is an entire chapter (I, xxii) titled "One Man's Profit Is Another Man's Harm," which happens to be the shortest chapter in the Essays.[44] The theme and most of the content of I, xxii, are supplied by an anecdote borrowed from Seneca, leading Villey to judge that this chapter is "without originality."[45] But Montaigne has subtly modified Seneca's version of the story to draw a new lesson from it. According to the anecdote as Montaigne recounts it, "Demades the Athenian condemned a man of his city whose trade was to sell things necessary for burials, on the ground that he demanded too much profit, and that this profit could not come to him without the death of many

---

[43]Cf. The Prince, ch. 16. The similarity of Montaigne's treatment of liberality to Machiavelli's, even in the use of parallel examples to illustrate his point, is noted by Nicolaï, "Le Machiavélisme de Montaigne," BSAM, 3d ser., no. 7 (1958): 3–8. See also, on this subject, the letter of remonstrance of August 31, 1583, addressed by Montaigne (as mayor) and the jurats of Bordeaux to Henry III, protesting the exemption of "the richest and most opulent families" from paying taxes, with the result that the full burden of such taxes must be borne "by the least and poorest group of the inhabitants of the cities" (Oeuvres, p. 1374 [1069]).

[44]It is also one of only three chapters that Montaigne never revised after the first edition (the others are I, xxxiii, and II, xiv).

[45]Villey, Les Sources, 1:343.

people" (I, xxii, 105 [76]). Seneca had actually reported that Demades condemned the burial-supply man for having "prayed for great gain, which he could not achieve without the death of many people."[46] In Seneca's version, in other words, it was because the "great gain" for which the man hoped could be achieved only as the result of a high mortality rate that Demades denounced him. By substituting the conjunction "and" for Seneca's "which" [quod], Montaigne breaks up Demades' charge into two parts: the burial-supply man was wrong both to seek too much profit *and* to depend for this profit on others' death. In the sequel Montaigne concurs in Seneca's judgment that Demades' condemnation was unreasonable, but he leaves it ambiguous which element of the newly bifurcated charge he is objecting to: the rather ridiculous complaint that a man engaged in the funeral trade derived benefit from others' misfortunes or the charge that he sought too great a profit from his trade. Moreover, the essayist's response to Demades' charge embodies a significant modification and radicalization of Seneca's argument. Montaigne omits the initial, most moderate aspect of Seneca's defense of the burial-supply man's wish: that he might have been hoping to make great profits by buying his supplies cheaply rather than by selling in greater volume. And whereas Seneca went on to defend the man by remarking that Demades' criticism would entail the condemnation of "a great part of mankind, for who does not derive gain from another's disadvantage?" Montaigne asserts categorically that "*no* profit is made except at the expense of others, and by [Demades'] reckoning you would have to condemn *every* sort of gain." He proceeds to illustrate this point, as Seneca did, by pointing out how the practitioners of various respectable trades derive their livelihood from the vices or misfortunes of others; but here again there are significant modifications. Seneca remarked that "the vendor of delicacies is enriched by the corruption of youth," while Montaigne holds that "the merchant"—*any* merchant—"does good business only by the dissoluteness of youth." Boldly, Montaigne adds to Seneca's list of trades that of the clergy, whose "honor and function . . . is derived from our death and our vices." And after concurring with Seneca by remarking that "our private wishes are for the most part born and nourished at the expense of others," Montaigne proceeds not to lament this fact but to justify it as the product of the "general policy" of nature, according to which "the birth, nourishment, and growth of each thing is the alteration and corruption of another" (I, xxii, 105–6 [76–7]). This conclusion constitutes a capsule statement of the principle underlying Adam Smith's economics as well as Bernard Mandeville's notorious portrait of the general human condition, according to which the public good is "naturally" built up out of people's

[46]Seneca, *Of Benefits*, VI, xxxviii, 1. Other quotations from Seneca's account of this incident which follow in the text will be found farther on in the same chapter of *Of Benefits*.

private selfishness or "vice."[47] By bifurcating Demades' charge in the manner I have described and proceeding to refute that charge by an argument that would apply equally against both its elements, Montaigne has endeavored to justify not only the general practice of making gains at others' expense but also the specific course of pursuing as great a profit as possible. Montaigne's omission of the initial part of Seneca's defense of the burial-supply man—the fact that he might have been hoping simply to buy his goods more cheaply—appears similarly to reflect the essayist's desire forthrightly to defend the practice of charging what the traffic will bear as a means of maximizing one's profits.[48] The rhetorical beauty of his argument in I, xxii, consists in the way he surreptitiously leads the reader from an easily won acknowledgement of the legitimacy of the burial-supply trade to this more novel and controversial economic doctrine.

We might already have inferred Montaigne's agreement with the Smithean teaching that the common good is better secured when people are allowed freely to pursue their individual self-interest than when the laws attempt to regulate their conduct so as to compel its conformity to justice from his eulogy of the cannibals' society, held together with "so little artifice and human solder." Even more noteworthy in this regard is the following passage from "Of Vanity," the significance of which has been noted by Sanders:[49]

> In sum, I see from our example that human society holds and is knit together at any cost whatever. Whatever position you set men in, they pile up and arrange themselves by moving and crowding together, just as ill-matched bodies, put in a bag without order, find of themselves a way to unite and fall into place together, often better than they could have been arranged by art. King Philip collected the most wicked and incorrigible men he could find, and settled them all in a city he had built for them, which bore their name [Poneropolis]. I judge that *from their very vices* they set up a political system among themselves and *a commodious and just society.* . . . Necessity reconciles men and brings them together. This accidental link afterwards takes the form of laws; for there have been some as savage as any human opinion can produce which have nonetheless maintained their body with as much health and length of life as those of Plato and Aristotle could do. (III, ix, 933–4 [730])

---

[47]Sayce, *Essays,* p. 254, notes the kinship of Montaigne's defense of the political necessity of vices with the teaching of Mandeville as well as Machiavelli.

[48]Cf. also I, xiv, 65 [45]: "It is not easy to establish limits" to the desire for wealth; "they are difficult to find in the things we consider good," with Machiavelli's justification of human acquisitiveness in *The Prince,* ch. 3, pp. 14–15. As noted previously, Montaigne's remedy for the excessive concern with wealth in I, xiv, is not to teach moderation but "to put a check on frugality" (p. 65). Cf. III, xii, 1015 [794]: "In nothing does man know how to stop at the limit of his need: of pleasure, riches, power . . . his greed is incapable of moderation."

[49]Sanders, "Montaigne et les idées politiques de Machiavel," *BSAM,* 5th ser., nos. 18–19 (1976): 95–6.

This passage immediately precedes one that I cited in Chapter Five wherein Montaigne decries "all those artificially simulated descriptions of a government" as "ridiculous and unfit to put into practice" (934 [730]). As I have sought to demonstrate, the true implication of the latter remark is not that Montaigne opposes all efforts at political improvement but that he agrees with Machiavelli's critique of the "imaginary republics" constructed by the ancient philosophers as irrelevant to the practical task of such reformation—precisely because they presuppose the inculcation of a high degree of moral virtue. Efforts at political reformation, to be genuinely useful, must make use of people's vices, as King Philip's city did, by channeling selfish inclination in a politically salutary direction.[50] Far from accepting the existing political order as legitimate, Montaigne, in this very context, denounces the "monstrous . . . inhumanity" of the mores of his time (934 [730]). But his remedy is signified by his lament at the excess of French laws at the beginning of "Of Experience," and by his citation of Tacitus' remark that "as formerly we suffered from crimes, so now we suffer from laws" (III, xiii, 1042 [815]).[51] The greatest crimes, especially in Montaigne's time, are those to which laws and governments have given sanction in the name of spiritual salvation; the remedy is to limit the scope of law to the punishment of acts that directly violate the security or liberty of individuals, while inculcating a morality that encourages people to pursue a pacific and "useful" form of self-interest.

To limit the role of government in this way is, as I have noted, to transform its function from "ruling" people to serving as an "instrument" for their "preservation," in the sense in which these terms are used near the conclusion of "Of Physiognomy" (hence just before the remarks quoted above from the beginning of "Of Experience"). It is in this light, I believe, that we may understand a seemingly insignificant passage in "Of Custom" on which I have not previously commented. Near the middle of the long list of "foreign" customs in that chapter, drawn largely from López de Gómara's reports about the New World, along with such ancient sources as Herodotus, mention is made of one specifically political custom for which, so far as I know, no source has been found: "They vary the form of government according to what affairs require: depose the king when it seems good, and substitute elders to assume the government of the state, and also sometimes leave it in the hands of the people" (I, xxiii, 112 [81]). Whether this anecdote derives from some thus far undiscovered source, or whether, as I suspect, it is one that Montaigne fabricated, I suggest that— unlike most of the customs in the list, which are often either trivial, re-

---

[50]Cf. II, i, 319 [242]: "the strangeness of our condition makes it happen that we are often driven to do good by vice itself."

[51]Recall also Montaigne's transformation of Epicurus' saying at p. 467 [359] of the "Apology," cited in n. 1 to Chapter Three, above.

pellent, or downright barbarous—this custom is one that he seriously approves, and that accords with his overall political intention.

In order to appreciate the significance of the novel political custom Montaigne has described, it is necessary to recall the importance that the *politeia* or regime had in classical political philosophy. In the most thorough treatment of this topic, in Book III of the *Politics*, Aristotle explains that the *politeia* is not simply an arrangement of the chief offices of a city (as is specified, for instance, in the American Constitution). Rather, the principles prescribing the structure of offices and eligibility for holding them determine which class of people is to rule, and consequently the particular end and way of life that the citizenry will be guided to pursue.[52] The range of individual freedom, or the strictness of the legally enforced moral code; the degree to which the pursuit and accumulation of wealth are encouraged or allowed; the disposition toward military aggrandizement and expansion or isolation and self-sufficiency; respect for the ancestral religion or openness to new beliefs; openness or hostility toward foreigners; the structure of the family; the policy regarding slavery—all these issues and more will be determined by the nature of a city's *politeia*. For this reason, it is most unlikely that there could be a system for the peaceable and orderly transition *among* forms of government such as Montaigne has described—so long as government retains the unlimited scope of authority that Aristotle attributes to it, and that most premodern governments either possessed or aspired to achieve. Far too much would be at stake in a change of regime for it to be acceptable to partisans of the existing order. Hence the typical means by which the regimes of ancient cities changed were those described and decried in *The Federalist*: violent revolutions or usurpations, culminating in extremes of tyranny (individual, oligarchic, or democratic), which in turn stimulated counterrevolutions.[53] Nor were the regimes of Montaigne's own time any more open to peaceful, fundamental constitutional change on a regular basis: imagine the response of the French king had it been proposed that the monarchy periodically be supplanted by an oligarchic or democratic regime whenever circumstances were deemed to make such a change desirable!

The significance of the custom of peacefully changing regimes which Montaigne describes is accentuated by the fact that it is mentioned in the same chapter wherein the author alludes to the opposing biases of "nations brought up to liberty" and to monarchy, remarking the failure of the latter ever to liberate themselves from "mastery," but also implying that the subjects of each regime are blinded to the possible advantages of the alternative one. By contrast, the inhabitants of the (probably imaginary)

[52]*Politics*, III.6–9.
[53]*Federalist*, no. 9 (first para.).

382 | The Political Philosophy of Montaigne

country Montaigne has described have the best of both worlds, enjoying the respective benefits of monarchy, aristocracy, and democracy, depending on which regime is appropriate under the prevailing circumstances.

I do not believe Montaigne intended the custom he described to be adopted literally in the form he indicates. (Among other difficulties, the custom would presumably require a supragovernmental authority to determine when the regime should be changed, but how would that authority be constituted? The result is infinite regress.) It points, however, to the sense in which Montaigne's proposed reformation of government, by delimiting the scope of governmental authority, gives political institutions an adaptability they have never before possessed. It does so by fixing the end of government, *independently* of the particular regime that exists, in such a way that that end, together with the fundamental principles of the positive law, no longer varies with the opinions of particular ruling classes. By specifying that the true end of all governments is to protect life, liberty, and property—without endeavoring to inculcate moral perfection or holiness—Montaigne depreciates the choice among regimes from a question of ends to one of means. What is at issue, in determining the form of government a country should possess, is simply which form, under existing circumstances, is most likely to advance the agreed-upon end that derives from the principles of natural justice—principles founded in our prepolitical and premoral nature. When the choice among political forms is understood in this way, government can be allowed to "evolve" peacefully in accordance with the needs of the times (much less being at stake in such an evolution than in changes among regimes in the classical sense). And in a broader sense, government is now eminently well "adapted" to human nature, inasmuch as it no longer entails the imposition of particular principles of morality or religion on human beings, but serves as an instrument for satisfying their most fundamental and universal instincts.

Once again there is an obvious link between Montaigne's political teaching and that of Machiavelli. The bifurcated character of Machiavelli's political teaching—seemingly friendly to monarchical rule in *The Prince* and favorable rather to republicanism in the *Discourses on Livy*—appears to reflect the Florentine's own relative indifference to the choice among regimes, by comparison with his emphasis on a new understanding of the *purpose* of government, and what Carnes Lord terms "a wholly new relationship between princes or political authority generally and the people"—a purpose and relationship that are almost equally attainable under a principality or a republic.[54] Looking forward in time, we observe a parallel

[54]Lord, "On Machiavelli's *Mandragola*," *Journal of Politics* 41 (1979): 827. On the relationship of *The Prince* to the modern argument for democracy, see Bloom, "Commerce and 'Culture,'" p. 11. Cf. also the opening sentence of ch. 1 of *The Prince*, which implies the future possibility of a novel regime that will be neither a republic nor a principality, or else both.

between the teachings of both Machiavelli and Montaigne in this regard and Hobbes's explicit treatment of the choice among regimes as entailing merely the determination of the most efficient means to an agreed-upon end.[55] It was the acceptance of this perspective that enabled the American founders to look with equanimity on the choice between monarchical and republican government, with the delegates to the Constitutional Convention agreeing to opt for the latter owing to its conformity with the people's spirit and inclination, despite the belief of some that the former was in principle superior.[56]

Of the greatest relevance and interest for the understanding of modern liberal politics is a further implication of Montaigne's suggestion regarding the desirability of peacefully alternating regimes as circumstances require: the possibility of combining the advantages of various forms of government in a single regime. The "mixed regime," in which democratic and oligarchic elements are blended so as to moderate the extremes of partisanship, had been a central theme of classical political philosophy.[57] That regime was recognized by its philosophic proponents, however, to be difficult to establish and maintain in practice, owing to its susceptibility to being torn apart by the tension between oligarchic and democratic views of justice.[58] What is distinctive about the modern mixed regime, as originally conceived by Machiavelli and elaborated by such thinkers as Locke and Montesquieu, is that it rests on a single, agreed-upon conception of the political goal, derived from "nature," and blends the aristocratic, popular, and monarchical or tyrannical "humors" only as means of securing that goal. Machiavelli indicates the nature of the blending that is to take place in the new regime by admonishing the prince, on the one hand, to take his bearings by the needs of the common people, since they, rather than the nobles, constitute his firmest potential base of support; and by emphasizing to republics, on the other hand, their need to have people of tyrannical humors as effective "executors" of the laws—while these potential tyrants are kept in check by the rivalry of other ambitious individuals.[59] Locke's system similarly embodies a tension between the "republican" principle of formal legislative supremacy and a broad executive "prerogative" that may be used in viola-

---

[55]*Leviathan*, chs. 19, 21. Cf. Mathie, "Justice and the Question of Regimes," p. 460, regarding Hobbes's refusal to treat "the rival claims of the partisans to rule . . . as posing a problem of justice," as Aristotle had done, owing to Hobbes's revised understanding of the purpose of government; Mansfield, "Hobbes and the Science of Indirect Government," pp. 98–103.
[56]See Max Farrand, ed., *The Records of the Federal Convention of 1787*, rev. ed., 4 vols. (New Haven, 1937), 1:288–9, 398–9; 2:192.
[57]See Plato, *Laws*, 693d–e, 756a; Aristotle, *Politics*, III.11–13, IV.8–9, 11; Polybius, *Histories*, VI.3, 7, 11–18.
[58]Aristotle, *Politics*, 1296a21–b2.
[59]*The Prince*, ch. 9; *Discorsi*, I, vii–viii; I, xviii, 182–3; I, xxxiv; III, xxii. Cf. n. 29 to Chapter Eleven, above.

tion of the laws when it serves manifestly to benefit the people, as well as a Machiavellian reliance on the rivalry of ambitious, "quarrelsome and contentious" individuals, competing for popular favor, as a means of preserving the people's liberties.[60] And similar principles underlie the structure of the American regime—notably through the separation of powers, "checks and balances," the multiplicity of factions and sects, and the construction of a powerful executive, as described in *The Federalist*.[61]

Although the *Essays* does not provide a full-blown theory of the mixed regime comparable to those of Machiavelli or Locke, a number of passages appear to contain hints of such a theory. The emphasis, near the beginning of "Of Experience," on the desirability of having laws that are few and general, and at the same time on the diversity of human situations, such that they can never be encompassed by "fixed and immutable laws," suggests the need to distinguish legislative functions from executive and judicial ones, with the laws allowing great freedom to the people who carry out the latter functions to judge and act as they deem circumstances require.[62] Indeed, Montaigne suggests the possibility of having "the wisest men" settle all disputes "according to circumstances and at sight, without being bound to precedents, past or future. For every foot its own shoe" (III, xiii, 1043 [816]). At the same time he acknowledges the necessity of "executive" functions in a harsher sense, notably in his remark near the beginning of III, i, concerning the existence "in every government" of "necessary offices [that are] not only abject but vicious," but that are made "excusable" by their necessity (768 [600]). Montaigne uses the term *execution* ambiguously, as Machiavelli did:[63] at one point, he encourages princes to undertake "lofty executions" such as Scipio's expedition to Africa; elsewhere, he describes the assassination of Francis of Guise as a "lofty execution" (I, xxiv, 128 [94–5]; II, xxix, 689 [538]). Many of the brief, puzzling chapters of the *Essays* which ostensibly concern problems of military tactics or other odd topics may embody metaphorical discussions of political problems understood from a Machiavellian point of view (just as Machiavelli himself often enunciates his project under the guise of "military" advice). In the chapter "Against Do-Nothingness," for example, Montaigne describes the situation

---

[60]See Locke, *Second Treatise*, chs. 13–14, 19; Harvey C. Mansfield, Jr., *Taming the Prince: The Ambivalence of Modern Executive Power* (New York, 1989), pp. 186–92, 200–204, 210–11; idem, "The Right of Revolution," in *The Spirit of Liberalism* (Cambridge, Mass., 1978), pp. 79–81; Nathan Tarcov, "Locke's *Second Treatise* and 'The Best Fence against Rebellion,'" *Review of Politics* 43 (1981): 213–14.

[61]See esp. nos. 10, 51, and 72.

[62]"I do not much like the opinion of that man [Justinian?] who thought by a multitude of laws to bridle the authority of judges, cutting up their meat for them: he did not realize that there is as much freedom and latitude in the interpretation of laws as in their creation" (III, xiii, 1042 [815]). Recall the discussion in "Of Custom" (I, xxiii, 121–2 [89–90]) of the need for governments sometimes to act in violation of the laws; see also the conclusion of I, xvii (p. 74 [51]), recommending that rulers give their ambassadors and agents "a freer commission," deferring to the claims of specialized knowledge.

[63]See, e.g., *Discorsi*, III, iii, 387; Mansfield, *Taming the Prince*, pp. 102–3, 130, 144.

of "Muley Moloch, King of Fez," who, "for lack of a little life and because he had no one to substitute for himself" in the leadership of his country's affairs, "had to seek a bloody and hazardous victory when he had another one pure and clean in his hands" (II, xxi, 660 [514–15]). Moloch's situation reminds us of that of Cesare Borgia, who was prevented by his father's death and his own illness from achieving the success that his father's labors and his own "virtue" had earned him.⁶⁴ It also reminds us of Epaminondas' inability to establish the liberty of Thebes beyond his death. In the next chapter Montaigne seems to hint, metaphorically, at a solution for this problem: he discusses the use of institutional means for conveying information (relays of men or horses; messenger birds) as a way of avoiding dependence on the virtue of a single person such as Caesar (II, xxii, 661–2 [515–16]). Applied to politics, this discussion suggests the possibility of an institutional substitute for virtue which would render a nation's prosperity independent of the chance occurrence of political leaders of outstanding merit—a notion that was also suggested by Montaigne's intimation of the superiority of craft (or art) to valor in such chapters as I, v–vi. The two chapters that follow embody respectively a quasi-Machiavellian discussion of the need to "purge" the "surfeit of humors" from which a nation may suffer by such means as "deflect[ing]" political passions into foreign wars (the chapter is appropriately titled "Of Evil Means Employed to a Good End") and an indirect consideration of whether there are any fixed limits to the territory that a single empire can encompass. The conclusion suggests that all such limits can be overcome, given the right institutional arrangements (specifically, a sort of federalism) (II, xxiii, 663–4 [517–18]; II, xxiv, 667 [520]).

Of central importance to the modern mixed regime is the use of various "humors" or passions to check opposing ones, in lieu of the effort to subordinate passion to virtue. We have already seen evidence of Montaigne's favoring such a policy, as instanced by his reported "diversion" of a prince from vengeance to ambition, and by his espousal of sexual and alcoholic indulgence as alternatives to tyrannical ambition and spiritual frenzy. Several other remarks suggestive of this policy may be cited. In III, xiii, he holds that "there is jealousy and envy among our pleasures; they clash and interfere with one another" (1086 [849]). In III, x, he remarks that "avarice has no greater impediment than itself" (985 [771])⁶⁵ and appeals to his readers, "since we will not do so out of conscience, at least

---

⁶⁴*The Prince*, ch. 7, p. 32. Cf. also ibid., ch. 11, p. 46, and ch. 25, p. 101, regarding the effect of the "brevity" of various popes' lives on their political enterprises; Descartes, *Discours de la méthode*, in *Oeuvres et lettres*, pt. I, p. 127; pt. VI, p. 169.

⁶⁵Cf. *The Federalist*, no. 72, p. 489, on the manner in which the Constitution gives a president self-interested motives for good behavior: "His avarice might be a guard upon his avarice." See also, on the general principle of employing passion to counteract passion, as espoused by the early advocates of modern capitalism, Albert O. Hirschman, *The Passions and the Interests* (Princeton, N.J., 1977), pp. 20–31.

out of ambition let us reject ambition" (1001 [783]). Such advice appears to reflect the conception of human nature and of the means of influencing people's conduct which underlies Machiavelli's institutional prescriptions.

Republicanism and Indirect Government

I have argued that Montaigne's political teaching, in harmony with that of such thinkers as Machiavelli and Hobbes, reduces the significance of the choice among forms of government by establishing a uniform end for all regimes. This finding is not inconsistent with the evidence I cited in Chapter Five which suggests that the essayist's teaching is more favorable, in principle, to republicanism than to monarchy. It should be emphasized, in the first place, that the "liberal" conception of the purpose of government that Montaigne espouses stands directly opposed to the claim that any individual or social class possesses a natural or God-given superiority that would entitle them to rule others, or would justify governments in treating their subjects unequally. As I noted in Chapter Six, Montaigne emphasizes the contrast between the natural and political hierarchies, and highlights the natural "parity" of kings and commoners. Aside from his specific criticism of monarchs' claims to superiority, in a multitude of passages Montaigne notes the arbitrariness of political hierarchy and argues that relations of "mastery" inevitably give rise to injustice. Having remarked in I, xxvi, that "the chief places are commonly seized by the least capable men" (154–5 [114]), he similarly observes in III, viii, that "dignities [and] offices are necessarily given more by fortune than by merit," and that "the most powerful in cities" are "ordinarily . . . the least able"; hence, contrary to "common fashion," he is "more distrustful of ability when I see it accompanied by greatness of fortune and public esteem" (911, 913 [712, 714]). In III, v, he criticizes the practice of assigning offices on the basis of birth rather than ability and experience (828 [646–7]). This criticism mirrors and elaborates the criticism of hereditary monarchy that he attributed to one of the New World natives at the end of "Of Cannibals."

Several other passages in III, v, dealing with relations between the sexes have a bearing on the more general political issue as well. Montaigne remarks that "women are not at all wrong when they reject the rules of life that have been introduced into the world, inasmuch as it is the men who have made these without them. There is naturally strife and wrangling between them and us" (832 [649]). Similarly, he charges that the conventional rules governing erotic matters reflect such an "iniquitous appraisal of vices," which has been made "according to [the] interest" of the male sex rather than "according to nature," that comparable vices "assume . . . many unequal shapes" (839 [655]). And he holds that men "are in almost all things unjust judges of [women's] actions, as they are of ours" (863 [675]). The more general political principles underlying these remarks are enunciated in "Of the Disadvantage of Greatness," where Montaigne remarks that "superiority and inferiority, ruling and subjection, are forced into a natural envy and contention" (III, vii, 896 [701]); and in "Of Vanity," where he asserts that "the disparity of conditions" among differently situated individuals "easily produces contempt or envy" (III, ix, 960 [750]).

Considered as a whole, these remarks suggest that, whether the government of a country is monarchical or popular, its laws should treat all individuals as equals rather than enforce the superiority of one class (or sex) over another, and that offices should be assigned as far as possible on the basis of merit. Montaigne's defense of women's objection to rules that have been imposed on them without their participation suggests the more general principle that the foundation of legitimate government, as in the Declaration of Independence, lies in the people's consent (recall Montaigne's readiness to leave a country where the laws threaten him in the slightest way), owing to the natural equality and freedom of all individuals.

In principle, Montaigne's argument leaves open the possibility (as does the Declaration) that people's equal rights might be secured by a properly constituted—that is, limited—monarchy. But the discussion of monarchy in "Of the Disadvantage of Greatness" suggests that it is inherently most difficult for a king to treat his subjects justly, given the difference of rank and power that separates him from the populace. Montaigne holds that it is "the toughest and most difficult occupation in the world . . . to exercise a king's role worthily," since "it is difficult to impose limits [mesure] on a power so immoderate." He appears to soften this charge by professing to "excuse more of [kings'] faults than people commonly do, in consideration of the horrible weight of their duty," and by remarking that "even for men of a less excellent nature, it is a singular incitement to virtue to be lodged in a place where you can do no good that is not put in the record and account." But he practically cancels out the last point by remarking that a king's ability "is principally addressed to the populace, an inexact judge, easy to dupe, easy to satisfy" (III, vii, 896 [700]). And the conclusion of the chapter elaborates how a king's monopoly of power compels the people to "authorize" his "defects and vices" rather than encouraging him to act with genuine beneficence (898 [702]).[66]

---

[66]The chapter in which these observations occur is the central one of Book III. The central chapter of Book I alludes to "La Boétie's" antimonarchical treatise *Voluntary Servitude*, and the central chapter of Book II is "Of Freedom of Conscience." In conformity with the painter's technique he described in I, xxviii, Montaigne (as Daniel Martin has noted) thus put freedom at the center of his book, surrounded by references to enslavement (Martin, "Le Chapitre III–7, 'De l'incommodité de la grandeur,' des *Essais*, ou, Montaigne contre les Médicis" [unpublished paper], pp. 19–23).

The chief counterweight to this critique of monarchy appears to be Montaigne's denunciation of rhetoric in "Of the Vanity of Words" (I, li). His criticism of eloquence as "a tool invented to manipulate and agitate a crowd and a disorderly populace" (I, li, 293 [222] constitutes, as the Pléiade editors point out, a sixteenth-century "commonplace."[67] Montaigne associates the use of rhetoric with states that are both "free" and "sick," adding:

> From that it seems that governments which rely on a monarch have less need of it than others; for the stupidity and facility that are found in the common people, and which make them subject to be manipulated and led by the ears to the sweet sound of this harmony without weighing things and coming to know their truth by the force of reason—this facility, I say, is not found so easily in a single man; it is easier to protect him by good education and advice from the influence of that poison. (293 [222])

According to this passage, it "seems" that monarchy is rendered superior to popular rule by the relative invulnerability of kings to the seductive power of rhetoric. However, that argument disregards the susceptibility of kings to individual flattery, which Montaigne acknowledges at several points (I, iii, 18–20 [9]; II, xvi, 602 [468–9]; III, xiii, 1055 [826]). Precisely because of the "commonplace" character of Montaigne's argument in I, li, we have reason to doubt that it represents his authentic view. And the reader must be particularly sensitive to the irony of a denunciation of rhetoric expressed by one of its supreme practitioners!

In view of the evidence brought forward here, as well as in Chapters Five and Six, it appears that Montaigne regards monarchical government as inherently inferior to a properly constituted republic. But since the problem of choice among regimes is, for Montaigne, subordinate to that of fixing the *end* of government, and since monarchies as well as republics might be so organized, as Machiavelli had indicated, that the rivalry of the ambitious would benefit the people at large, we need not suppose that Montaigne had in view any imminent obliteration of the French monarchy. (During the civil wars his political actions evidently aimed to uphold the monarchy as a means of restoring national peace and unity.) Whatever the disadvantages of monarchy as compared to republics, they are almost dwarfed by the need of both sorts of regime for the "good education and advice" Montaigne proffers with a view to rationalizing the opinions on which they rest, and consequently to overcoming the tendency of all governments toward injustice, instability, and oppression.

It should be emphasized that Montaigne's praise of republicanism and his espousal of the cause of "the people" do not rest on any naive faith in the people's inherent goodness or capacity for self-government. As we have

---

[67]Montaigne, *Oeuvres*, p. 1517 (n. 4 to p. 293).

seen, in I, iii, he denounces the "inhuman injustice" of the Athenian *demos;* and in I, xxiv, he alludes to the need to quell popular disturbances by the exercise of a "gracious severity." Nor, in criticizing the claim of monarchs to a natural superiority over their subjects, does Montaigne—any more than Hobbes—deny the importance of the fundamental natural inequality that exists between "men of understanding"—that is, philosophers—and the multitude.[68] As we saw in examining "Of the Inequality among Us," Montaigne's critique of inegalitarian arguments is premised on the fact that natural inequalities in wisdom are least visible to the people at large (as Aristotle had noted)[69] and hence are without *direct* political relevance. But his new teaching concerning the purpose of government, combined with his critique of the conventional inequalities that have characterized political societies, is intended to bridge the gap between the wise and the vulgar in such a way as to make the latter the instrument by which the former indirectly govern humanity. It is the breadth of this political aspiration that most sharply distinguishes Montaigne's teaching from that of the classical philosophers. As he remarks in "Of Pedantry," the ancient sages, "seeing the citadel of political government seized by incapable men," had largely chosen to withdraw from public life (I, xxv, 134 [99]). This secession by the genuinely wise allowed their title to be usurped by useless pedants. The manifest incapacity of the putatively "learned," combined with the defective education that the French nobility receive, has engendered in the latter a "hatred of books" and contempt for knowledge (I, xxv, 132 [97]; I, xxvi, 175 [130]). Such contempt attests to the "stupidity" of those who feel it (II, xii, 415 [319]). But in order to overcome what is wrongly thought to be "the natural incompatibility . . . between the vulgar and people of rare and excellent judgment and knowledge," Montaigne has had to alter the "education" of his readers, emphasizing the pleasant as well as useful character of philosophy (I, xxv, 132 [97]); I, xxvi, 158–61 [117–19]). By making the philosopher the champion of popular enjoyments rather than moral severity, and by emphasizing the conduciveness of a properly constituted science of "medicine" to the people's bodily health, broadly understood, Montaigne aspires to make the public aware of the congruence of needs between themselves and the wise, so that the latter will no longer be "left in extreme need" (I, xxxv, 220 [165]).[70] Unlike the reputedly learned people of his

[68]Cf. *Leviathan,* ch. 15, p. 211, where Hobbes, tacitly conceding that his previous demonstration of natural equality may not have been conclusive, holds considerations of civic peace to dictate that people be publicly *regarded* as equals, even if they are naturally unequal; Joseph Cropsey, "Hobbes and the Transition to Modernity," in Cropsey, ed., *Ancients and Moderns,* p. 226.

[69]*Politics,* 1254b31–1255a1, 1332b16–27.

[70]Note that the title of the chapter in which Montaigne discusses this problem—"Of a Defect in Our Administrations"—is the only chapter title in the *Essays* that embodies an explicit criticism of the existing political order. *The* key defect of that order is its failure to give

time, Montaigne is not content to endure a "base and necessitous fortune" (I, xxv, 135 [99]).[71]

It is noteworthy in this connection that in III, i—the chapter wherein Montaigne professes to have performed "public occupations" in a "private" manner—he discusses Timoleon and Epaminondas, both of whom, as noted previously, were cited in the seventeenth chapter of Machiavelli's *Discourses* as liberators of their countries who were unable to perpetuate their countries' freedom beyond their lifetimes. Timoleon is represented in the *Discourses* as someone who preferred to live a "private" life but was nonetheless not "deprived" of public office, owing to the people's wish that he govern them. Despite or because of Timoleon's fratricide, Machiavelli describes him (along with Aratus the Sicyonian, another morally dubious liberator) as a "good" prince in whose "mirror"—rather than the traditional, morally edifying mirrors of princes—other rulers may find reflected the road to "security and contentment."[72] Machiavelli's account of these "good princes" is shown by Harvey Mansfield, Jr., to signify the possibility of "indirect government," by means of which "the philosopher, as masterconspirator directing but not executing his designs, can intervene in politics from a safe distance," "substantially or altogether hidden from public view," and therefore without forsaking the benefits for the sake of which previous philosophers chose a "private" life.[73]

To judge from several remarks in the *Essays*, Montaigne shares his Florentine predecessor's project of seeking to govern indirectly. By frequently alluding to the shortness of the lifetime remaining to him,[74] Montaigne reminds us of Muley Moloch, the brevity of whose life posed an obstacle to the execution of his designs, but who endeavored nonetheless to carry his influence "forward into death," and beyond it (II, xxi, 661 [515]). Like Timoleon, Montaigne prefers to live privately, despite his capacity for "public occupations" and an admitted desire for glory that is connected to his "compassion" for the common people (III, xiii, 1079 [844]). His "Machiavellian" solution to these difficulties is to carry out his public design in a

---

people of wisdom their proper place and support. The congruence of their needs with that of the multitude is indicated in Montaigne's account of his own disposition to ally himself with the latter, whom he seemingly (but not unambiguously) identifies as "the class of men who need our aid" (III, xiii, 1079 [844]). Cf. also III, viii, 910–11 [711–12], where Montaigne implies that only people of philosophic capacity are truly qualified to rule; and Descartes's suggestion that others provide financial support to one capable of discovering the things that are "greatest and most useful to the public" (*Discours de la méthode*, VI, in *Oeuvres et lettres*, p. 176).

[71]Cf. the Epistle Dedicatory of *The Prince*, with Bloom, "Commerce and 'Culture,'" pp. 9–10, 13.

[72]*Discorsi*, III, v, 389–90.

[73]Mansfield, *Machiavelli's New Modes and Orders*, p. 317; see also idem, "Hobbes and the Science of Indirect Government."

[74]See, e.g., "Au lecteur"; I, xx, 83 [58]; I, lxvii; III, ix, 924 [722]; cf. Friedrich, *Montaigne*, p. 247.

private and long-term manner—that is, in his capacity as author rather than as a public official, and while overtly disclaiming any such public intention. Behind the new regime in which "mastery" has been abolished, so that no one strictly "rules" anyone else, stands Montaigne as well as Machiavelli, governing indirectly through the influence of his thought. The abolition of political rule requires an indirect, philosophic rule in the form of popular "enlightenment" or ideology.

Montaigne's intention is not only to secure his own future influence but to make a place for other wise individuals in the formulation of law and the operation of government. It is relevant to recall here his denunciation of the irrationality and injustice of French laws in "Of Custom." The obstacle to the reformation of those laws, and to the more general adaptation of law to changing circumstances which Montaigne represented as desirable at the conclusion of the chapter, lay not only in the ignorance of rulers but, more important, in the general belief that all such changes are dangerous because they threaten people's reverence for law. Montaigne's proposed transformation of the purpose of law so as to make it directly conducive to the security and freedom that each human being naturally seeks would replace irrational habituation and prejudice by calculations of self-interest as the ground for lawful conduct. Such a replacement would in turn overcome the objection to changing the law based on the fear of undermining respect for it. This replacement therefore opens the way for a thoroughgoing *rationalization* of law, and for allowing its executors a greater freedom of interpretation and adaptation. Hence Montaigne's suggestion (probably an exaggeration) near the beginning of III, xiii, that the wisest people might settle disputes on a case-by-case basis, without being bound by precedents (1043 [816]); and his recommendation in I, xvii, that kings allow their expert subordinates to exercise a wide range of discretion.

Understood in this way, Montaigne's jurisprudential intention accords with that of Hobbes, who denounces judges' reliance on precedents, regardless of their irrationality, and who teaches that whenever possible civil laws should be interpreted in light of the laws of nature, which he identifies with "equity."[75] Like Montaigne, Hobbes conjoins equity with equality; that is, the equality of individual rights.[76] In Montaigne's words, "equality is the principal part of equity"; he denounces positive laws instituted by people who, "in their hatred of equality, are lacking in equity" (I, xx, 92 [66]; III,

---

[75] *Leviathan*, ch. 26; *A Dialogue between a Philosopher and a Student of the Common Laws of England*, ed. Joseph Cropsey (Chicago, 1971), pp. 61, 96–7; cf. William Mathie, "Justice and Equity: An Inquiry into the Meaning and Role of Equity in the Hobbesian Account of Justice and Politics," in Craig Walton and Paul Johnson, eds., *Hobbes's 'Science of Natural Justice'* (Dordrecht, 1987), pp. 257–76; Nakam, *Les Essais*, pp. 139–49.

[76] *Leviathan*, ch. 24, p. 297; ch. 26, pp. 314–15; Mathie, "Justice and the Question of Regimes," pp. 460–61; idem, "Justice and Equity."

xiii, 1049 [821]).[77] As we have observed, this linkage of justice with equality, for Montaigne as well as for Hobbes, derives from the recognition of the security of the individual, rather than the perfection of the soul, as the primary object of governmental concern.

Equality, Liberty, and Liberalism

In view of Montaigne's near equation of justice with equality, the question arises how far his egalitarianism extends to the economic arena. As I noted in Chapter Six, such interpreters as Sayce and Keohane have cited passages in "Of Cannibals" which condemn the arbitrary economic as well as political inequalities that characterize European societies, Sayce even finding these remarks expressive of "socialism or communism"; but these interpreters deny that the passages reflect any practical intention on Montaigne's part, given his obvious antipathy to violent revolutions as well as his more general supposed conservatism. Sayce is surely correct in denying that Montaigne intended to institute a collectivist system, but I suggest that this stance is due precisely to the "liberal" rather than "conservative" character of his teaching. Given his complaint that the laws regulate people's lives too much and his wish to enlarge and secure the private sphere against governmental intervention, Montaigne could scarcely have favored changes aimed at increasing rulers' control over economic life. To the contrary, as we have seen, he praises freedom of commerce and opposes sumptuary laws and the attempt to limit economic gain. But it hardly follows that his intention in these matters was conservative. By advocating a liberation of economic life from narrow political control, Montaigne was encouraging an *opening up* of opportunities for individual industry and gain which would ultimately undermine the aristocratic class structure of his time. In opposition to the aristocratic attitude—exemplified, at the extreme, by the Indian caste system (III, v, 828–9 [647])—Montaigne applauds "Plato's precept that children should be placed not according to the faculties of their father, but according to the faculties of their soul" (I, xxvi, 162 [120]). Yet he criticizes Plato for "giv[ing] much authority" in his *Republic* to uncertain judgments of children's natural capacities based on "the actions of their childhood" (I, xxvi, 148 [109]).[78] In place of a hierarchical class system that fixes each person's status, Montaigne advocates a society in which human beings are free to choose their own trade and status

---

[77]Cf. also I, xiv, 58 [39]: the "natural" "jurisdiction" of our bodily parts with regard to pleasure and pain "cannot fail to be just, being equal and common." Montaigne's attachment to the principle of equality is emphasized by Nakam, *Les Essais*, ch. 2 and pp. 219–22.

[78]The reference is apparently to the power of the city's rulers in the *Republic* to assign children to a particular class on the basis of the supposedly manifest quality of their souls (415a–c).

is determined largely by individual achievement: a system of legal equality of opportunity. This is one reason for his stress on "adaptability" in education: one never knows what position in such a society a child will grow up to occupy; hence the soul should be equipped with "different levels," so as to "be well off wherever its fortune should take it" (III, iii, 799 [623]).[79]

From a philosophic point of view, the very institution of private property is an arbitrary convention; in a purely "rational" society, goods would be held in common and distributed among individuals according to their need and/or desert—as is done among the guardian class in Plato's *Republic*, in Marx's equally imaginary "communist society," and among the unspecified people to whom Montaigne attributes such a practice in "Of Custom" (I, xxiii, 110–11 [80–81]). But as Aristotle indicates in his criticism of Socrates' (probably ironic) proposals in the *Republic*, such a system is unworkable, at least among civilized people, on account of the strength of people's natural self-love and attachment to what is their own.[80] Even while acknowledging the conventionality of economic distinctions, Montaigne stresses that our natural selfishness is considerably less susceptible of being moderated than Aristotle himself had taught. He also alludes to the impossibility of a ruler's having the kind of insight into people's souls that would enable him to determine their proper deserts (III, viii, 911 [712]). It is for these reasons that he favors a solution to the economic problem that is "natural," not in the sense of awarding individuals what reason determines them to deserve, but in enlisting their natural, selfish energies in the improvement of their lot, and allowing their ultimate economic and social position to be determined by the outcome of their efforts rather than by legal prescription. (This is by no means to presuppose, however, that he would oppose public charity for the poor.)

There is, then, no inconsistency in Montaigne's thought—any more than in Locke's—between his teaching that human beings are naturally equal and his critique of conventional inequalities, on the one hand, and his advocacy of an economic system in which people might earn unequal rewards in accordance with their labor and foresight, on the other. The system of liberal capitalism, for which Montaigne was one of the earliest philosophic spokesmen, has been enormously beneficial to the poorer classes of society, not only by widening their opportunities for advancement but also by raising their living standards: as Milton and Rose Friedman have stressed, the fruits of the economic progress that that system has generated have made even more of a difference to the poor than to the rich, who in earlier times had servants to provide much of what machines now do for everyone.[81]

---

[79]Cf. Rousseau, *Emile*, I, pp. 41–2.

[80]*Politics*, 1263a9–20, 1263a38–b3.

[81]Milton Friedman and Rose Friedman, *Free to Choose* (New York, 1980), pp. 137–9. See also F. A. Hayek, ed., *Capitalism and the Historians* (Chicago, 1954).

Ultimately of even greater importance than the economic consequences of the liberal commercial system, however, are its political ones. In "Of Sumptuary Laws" Montaigne alluded to the political function of the economic regulations he opposes: to maintain a system of fixed class distinctions, so as to make the conventional superiority of the upper classes appear natural, and hence to instill an attitude of reverence and subservience among the lower orders. Despite his prudent disclaimers in that chapter, we have seen ample evidence that Montaigne's intention is to *undermine* the belief in a natural political hierarchy and to encourage people to judge the legitimacy of government in terms of its conduciveness to the security of their equal rights. Although Montaigne would surely have abhorred the violence and terror of the French Revolution, it was not without reason that the leaders of that enterprise drew inspiration from the *Essays*. With even greater justice might the American founders, fully cognizant of their debt to Locke and Montesquieu, have looked back to Montaigne as well, as one who formulated the key principles that those thinkers were to elaborate.[82]

Montaigne and the Delimitation of Politics

I have portrayed Montaigne as an intermediary between the founder of modern political philosophy, Niccolò Machiavelli, and the philosophers of the seventeenth and eighteenth centuries, such as Hobbes, Locke, and Montesquieu, who built on Machiavelli's foundation in such a way as to establish the modern liberal regime. In setting forth an interpretation of Montaigne's teaching with regard to political institutions, I have had to bring together scattered remarks from a variety of chapters, since the *Essays* admittedly does not contain a sustained, thematic treatment of political processes (foundings, accusations, and the like) such as is found in Machiavelli's writings; or of legal principles and governmental institutions (for example, the separation of powers), as is offered by subsequent political philosophers. But I hope to have demonstrated that, despite the relatively scant and diffuse character of his remarks on political subjects in the narrow sense, Montaigne merits being regarded as a political philosopher of considerable importance. The most critical element of the modern political project as Machiavelli formulated it was, as I have stressed, a lowering or narrowing of the end of government, a concomitant acceptance of people's selfish and earthly inclinations, and an endeavor to provide greater satisfaction for them, in place of the classical and Christian endeavor to

[82]Cf. Strowski's discussion of the connection between Montaigne's thought and the American spirit (*Montaigne*, pp. 337–42); also Tocqueville's citation of Montaigne to illustrate the characteristically American understanding of virtue as the product of "self-interest rightly understood" (*Democracy in America*, II.ii.8, p. 498).

moderate and subordinate them. With regard to this issue, Montaigne's discussion is actually more explicit than Machiavelli's. In focusing his book on moral and psychological rather than institutional themes, Montaigne undertook a project that in a sense was ancillary to Machiavelli's, but he thereby advanced that project toward its practical culmination. As Clifford Orwin notes, it was as a result of the "tinkering" with Machiavelli's teaching by subsequent philosophers that the Florentine's political doctrine engendered liberalism as we know it.[83] Montaigne may well have been the first of these tinkerers, and the one who originally worked out the modifications of Machiavelli's doctrine that gave rise to modern liberalism: the replacement of war by commerce and technology as the means of satisfying people's newly liberated acquisitive desires, and the deprecation of glory-seeking by comparison with the more "rational" pursuit of safety, comfort, and earthly pleasure.

Perhaps it was Montaigne's desire to deprecate the love of glory and to divert people from the ambition for ruling that explains the relative paucity of his remarks about political institutions. As I have endeavored to demonstrate, his thought is fully concordant with the principles underlying the distinctive institutions of the modern liberal regime, the intention of which is to prevent the "ruling" of some people by others. But as a philosophic propagandist for the liberal way of life, Montaigne appears to have focused his rhetoric on deprecating the significance of public or political concerns as such, by comparison with private, pacific, and bodily goods. His teaching therefore serves to complement rather than contradict Machiavelli's teaching about political institutions and the subsequent elaboration of that teaching by political philosophers of the seventeenth and eighteenth centuries. As Montaigne's account of his mayoralty signifies, politics is henceforth to be understood in a subordinate or instrumental sense, providing an environment of security in which people may freely pursue private and pacific goals, rather than as an arena of grand and glorious undertakings.

In contrast to the classical conception of politics as the "architectonic" sphere of human activity, Montaigne's teaching foreshadows the modern disposition to supplant "politics" with "administration." But that teaching reflects a political ambition on the essayist's part which surpasses that of his ancient philosophic predecessors. Although the most explicit account Montaigne provides of his political activity concerns his relatively modest or "unambitious" (if notably successful) doings as mayor of Bordeaux, the writing of the Essays reflects and embodies his greater ambition. In undertaking to "regulate" the belief of his readers, Montaigne aspires to become a kind of super-ruler of generations of human beings, extending into the

---

[83]"Machiavelli's Unchristian Charity," pp. 1226–7; cf. Strauss, What Is Political Philosophy?, pp 47–8.

indefinite (if not infinite) future, thereby achieving a glory rivaling or surpassing that of the greatest founder-lawgivers, both religious and secular, of the past. Paradoxically, however, his public teaching requires him to obscure the motives that underlie his enterprise. That is, he consistently disparages and seeks to "divert" people from the love of glory that—along with "natural compassion"—has impelled him to undertake this enterprise.[84] Despite Montaigne's emphasis on self-knowledge, his public teaching may be seen as both source and prototype of what one scholar has termed "the self-forgetting of the modern idealist," who in speaking for "the people's" cause must obfuscate his own role in that cause.[85] Just as Montaigne's aspiration to obliterate the tension between philosophy and political society causes him to downplay the distinctiveness of the motive that underlies the philosopher's enterprise, the love of truth (as distinguished from pursuit of the "practical" fruits of knowledge), his political project requires him to depreciate the motives of political people. His intended remolding of human nature is indeed Promethean in scope, as the Propertius quotation at the end of III, iv, suggests, since it appears to entail uprooting the very desires for mastery and self-transcendence from people's souls.

[84]Cf. Montaigne's remarks about the tenacity with which even those who deprecate the concern with glory nonetheless pursue it: I, xli, 248–9 [187]; II, xvi, 603 [469]. We may, however, interpret the "glory" Montaigne seeks primarily in terms of his own awareness of his achievement (see II, xvii, 616 [480] for the use of *gloire* in this sense) rather than in the usual sense of being remembered by others (cf. II, viii, 383 [293]; Descartes, *Discours de la méthode*, VI, in *Oeuvres et lettres*, p. 177).

[85]Harvey C. Mansfield, Jr., "Thomas Jefferson," in Morton J. Frisch and Richard G. Stevens, eds., *American Political Thought*, 1st ed. (New York, 1971), p. 50.

Index of Chapters Discussed

Index of Sources

This index locates the page on which bibliographic information for each source cited is given. Titles are listed only when more than one work by an author has been cited.

Index of Names and Subjects